GLOBAL ISSUES

2018 Edition

GLOBAL ISSUES

SELECTIONS FROM *CQ RESEARCHER*

2018 EDITION

$SAGE | CQPRESS

FOR INFORMATION:

CQ Press

An Imprint of SAGE Publications, Inc.

2455 Teller Road

Thousand Oaks, California 91320

E-mail: order@sagepub.com

SAGE Publications Ltd.

1 Oliver's Yard

55 City Road

London EC1Y 1SP

United Kingdom

SAGE Publications India Pvt. Ltd.

B 1/I 1 Mohan Cooperative Industrial Area

Mathura Road, New Delhi 110 044

India

SAGE Publications Asia-Pacific Pte. Ltd.

3 Church Street

#10-04 Samsung Hub

Singapore 049483

Acquisitions Editor: Scott Greenan
Editorial Assistant: Sarah Christensen
Production Editor: Jane Martinez
Copy Editor: Terri Lee Paulsen
Typesetter: C&M Digitals (P) Ltd.
Proofreader: Laura Webb
Cover Designer: Dally Verghese
Marketing Manager: Erica DeLuca

Printed in the United States of America

ISBN: 978-1-5063-9701-6

This book is printed on acid-free paper.

18 19 20 21 22 10 9 8 7 6 5 4 3 2 1

Contents

Annotated Contents

CONFLICT, SECURITY, AND TERRORISM
North Korea Showdown

Tension is running high between the United States and North Korea, a family-run communist dictatorship with a record of horrific human rights abuses. One of the world's most militaristic nations, the "Hermit Kingdom" is testing increasingly powerful nuclear bombs, seeking to develop ballistic missiles capable of reaching the United States and threatening U.S. ally South Korea with a massive arsenal of artillery and other weapons. After years of attempts by U.S. presidents to rein in North Korea's nuclear ambitions through negotiations and ever-more-stringent economic sanctions, the Trump administration is vowing to eliminate the North Korean military threat. President Trump warns of the possibility of a "major, major conflict" with North Korea, and administration officials say they are considering all options. Neighboring China and Japan fear a full-scale regional war, and South Korea's new government — fearing that tens of thousands of its citizens could die in a war with the North — wants a more conciliatory approach in dealing with Pyongyang.

Military Readiness

A series of Navy and Air Force accidents this year — reflecting strains on the armed forces from the nearly two-decade fight against terrorism in Afghanistan and elsewhere — is raising pressing questions about whether the Pentagon can handle current conflicts and is ready for the next major confrontation. The United States is by far the world's most formidable military power, but some defense experts say the country needs more troops, planes and ships to confront the growing array of challenges posed by China, Russia, North Korea and Iran. Others say that warnings of a readiness crisis are overblown but that the Pentagon needs to be smarter with the resources it has. Most analysts agree the military must improve training for conventional warfare while modernizing its technology as rivals hone their ability to fight in space and cyberspace. The Trump administration, meanwhile, has ordered the Pentagon to review the nation's nuclear arsenal, which the Obama administration had begun to upgrade in its final years in office. The Pentagon also is reviewing space defenses, as U.S. satellites become more susceptible to attack.

Cyberwarfare Threat

The next major conflict between world powers may not begin at sea or along a disputed border, but in cyberspace. In the past decade, hackers have targeted voting systems in the United States, electrical grids in Ukraine, uranium enrichment facilities in Iran and hospitals, universities and major corporations around the world. The attacks have focused new attention on whether the United States is acting quickly enough to protect computer networks serving critical infrastructure, from military bases to power plants. Cybersecurity experts say companies holding sensitive data are particularly vulnerable to digital attacks, such as the recent hack of the Equifax credit reporting agency that potentially affects 145.5 million U.S. consumers. The United Nations is working to develop international rules for cyberwarfare, but the effort faces major hurdles, including deciding how even to define a cyberweapon. Allegations that Russia used social media to disrupt last year's presidential election are another focus of concern as the United States prepares for the 2018 congressional elections.

China and the South China Sea

China has been increasingly aggressive in the strategically vital South China Sea, establishing naval and air bases — and installing weapons — on islands it is constructing atop environmentally sensitive reefs. Tensions in the vast region, heavily patrolled by the U.S. Navy, have risen sharply in recent months. Surrounding nations, including the Philippines, a major U.S. ally, want access to the sea's wealth of natural resources — primarily oil, natural gas and fisheries — and its busy commercial shipping lanes. Responding to China, former President Barack Obama sought to shift more U.S. military resources to the region, but critics say his "pivot" was inadequate. Secretary of State and former Exxon Mobil CEO Rex Tillerson told Congress the United States should forcefully confront China in the South China Sea and possibly deny it access to the islands it has built. Meanwhile, the Philippines' mercurial president has voiced hostility toward the United States and a desire for closer relations with China, injecting further uncertainty into the region.

U.S.-Iran Relations

Under a 2015 agreement with the United States and five other world powers, Iran promised to dismantle its military nuclear facilities and refrain from building a nuclear weapon for at least a decade. In exchange, the United States and other countries lifted stiff economic sanctions placed on Iran because of its nuclear activities. The agreement has raised speculation that Iran might someday join China, Vietnam and Cuba — non-democracies and former U.S. enemies — in cooperating on trade and diplomacy. Indeed, some believe the deal not only could spur trade between the United States and Iran but also unite them in efforts to stabilize the Middle East. Others say, however, that improvement in U.S.-Iranian relations is far from certain. Iran continues to antagonize the United States in national security–related incidents. As a result, the United States has imposed new sanctions on Iran unrelated to its nuclear activity. Moreover, pro-engagement leaders in both countries face internal resistance against forming a closer relationship.

U.S.-Russia Relations

U.S. intelligence officials have raised new concerns about relations between the United States and Russia. A report released on Jan. 6, 2017, concluded that "an influence campaign" ordered by Russian President Vladimir Putin was designed to damage Hillary Clinton and help elect Donald Trump. The U.S. president, who has had long-standing business ties with Russian investors, has angered leaders in both parties by praising Putin's leadership skills and downplaying U.S. intelligence officials' claims that Russian hackers tried to influence the 2016 election. Trump also has stirred controversy by nominating an oil executive with previous business dealings in Russia to head the State Department. Meanwhile, Putin has aggressively pushed to re-establish the country's geopolitical importance by annexing part of Ukraine, joining Iran in supporting Syrian strongman Bashar al-Assad, and using hackers and fake news to promote populist candidates and discredit democracy in Europe. In response, the United States and European Union have imposed economic sanctions and bolstered NATO defenses in Central Europe.

INTERNATIONAL POLITICAL ECONOMY
Democracies Under Stress

Many democracies in Eastern Europe, the Middle East, Latin America and Southeast Asia are veering toward autocracy, stalling or reversing decades of democratic progress. Leaders have postponed elections, jailed opponents, restricted personal and press freedoms and rewritten constitutions to legalize their actions. Freedoms have eroded in such countries as Russia, Venezuela, Turkey, the Philippines and Poland. In addition, Western democracies are struggling with economic, social and political instability, corruption, immigration and frustrated voters who have turned to populist-nationalist leaders for solutions. Donald Trump, elected president in a wave of populist fervor in the United States, has vowed to stop promoting democracy overseas and to withdraw from some treaties. Meanwhile, Russia seeks to undermine democratic institutions, free elections and liberal Western alliances, and China is wooing developing nations in an effort to show that countries can prosper without the constraints of democracy. Still, some observers are optimistic about democracy's future, saying that new democracies are emerging and others are showing surprising resilience.

European Union's Future

After the 28-nation European Union celebrated its 60th anniversary in March 2017, it is struggling to hang together in the midst of numerous challenges, including sluggish economies, a migration crisis and rising populism. Founded in the ashes of World War II, the EU sought to end ruinous national rivalries and forge an organization in which Europeans would work together to build a prosperous future. The EU's supporters say the Union

has largely fulfilled these goals but that its success has led to an irony: Expansion from the original six member states has opened up new divisions between the wealthier north and the poorer south and between those states favoring a stronger central authority and those wanting power returned to national capitals. Britain's vote to exit the EU — dubbed Brexit — has raised further questions about the Union's viability. For now, many analysts agree, steps toward greater integration appear impossible, although the EU might be able to press ahead with plans for closer cooperation among members' militaries after Britain leaves.

Troubled Brazil

Only a few years ago, Brazil seemed poised to fulfill its potential as a global powerhouse. Almost as big as the continental United States and with a population of nearly 206 million, it boasted the world's eighth-largest economy. Thanks to robust economic growth and spending on social programs, millions had moved out of poverty, and the nation's middle class was growing. But plummeting demand for Brazil's commodity exports and a massive corruption scandal have plunged Brazil into the worst recession in its history. In the summer of 2016, just after Brazil hosted the first-ever Olympic Games in South America, an event meant to showcase its progress to the world, President Dilma Rousseff was impeached on charges of political malfeasance. Scores of other politicians and business officials also have been accused or convicted of wrongdoing. Now, analysts say Brazil must pursue major reforms before it can regain its momentum. Meanwhile, government plans to radically expand hydropower along the Amazon River have sparked resistance from environmentalists and indigenous peoples.

New Space Race

When Neil Armstrong stepped onto the moon in 1969, the United States was widely proclaimed the victor in the space race with the Soviet Union. Today, however, with the U.S. space shuttle program no longer in operation, NASA pays Russia to transport U.S. crews to the International Space Station and the Pentagon depends on Russian rocket engines to launch its military satellites into orbit. In addition, China's space program is growing rapidly, and U.S. officials worry it threatens American space assets, including military satellites. Policymakers also fear that U.S. satellites are at risk from accidental collisions. Meanwhile, NASA is planning for deep-space missions, even as some experts say these missions cost too much and the agency should rely more on private spaceflight companies. Other debates focus on whether the United States should return astronauts to the moon, as President Trump wants NASA to do in the next two years, and whether humans or robots should take the lead in exploring space.

Stolen Antiquities

Reports that the Islamist group ISIS may be funding terrorism by selling looted artifacts from war-torn Iraq and Syria have spurred calls for a new crackdown on the illicit antiquities trade. The United States has banned antiquities imports from Iraq and Syria, and the European Union is considering requiring proof that antiquities entering Europe were legally exported from their home countries, as Germany did last year. Archaeologists favor tougher documentation requirements, but antiquities dealers say such rules are impossible to meet and could destroy the legitimate market. Meanwhile, efforts to have ancient objects returned to their country of origin continue to spark controversy. For years Greece has demanded that Britain relinquish sculptures taken from the Parthenon in the 19th century. In the United States, some archaeologists complain that a 1990 law requiring museums and federal agencies to return skeletal remains of Native Americans to tribes for reburial prevents scientific study of North America's earliest inhabitants.

Reforming the U.N.

Seventy-three years after its founding, the United Nations remains a work in progress. Established in 1945 after a murderous world war, the new international organization set out to achieve peace and prosperity around the globe. Its supporters cite a record of success in many areas: The U.N. helped keep the Cold War from turning hot, its peacekeepers routinely monitor post-conflict zones, and it has promoted economic development, education and better health for hundreds of millions of people. But critics say the U.N. is an ineffectual colossus made up of 193 bickering member nations, overseen by a bloated and inefficient bureaucracy whose operations are plagued by corruption. Reform is needed at both the governing and bureaucratic level, they say, to ensure the organization remains relevant in the new century, and the Security Council — dominated by the United States and four other big powers — needs to expand to include more permanent members representing emerging nations such as India.

RELIGIOUS AND HUMAN RIGHTS
Rethinking Foreign Aid

President Donald Trump promised to cut aid to countries that "hate us," and in February 2017, a month after being sworn in, he proposed slashing foreign aid by nearly a third. Advocates of a robust aid program point out that foreign military and economic aid represents a mere 1.3 percent of the federal budget and say it is vital in protecting U.S. security interests, spreading democracy and promoting U.S. exports. More than 120 retired military officers wrote to Congress opposing cuts in foreign aid, saying it prevents conflict and helps keep poor countries from breeding terrorism. But critics of U.S. aid policy argue that too much is spent on programs that fail to produce results or winds up funding despotic regimes. With aid programs scattered across two dozen agencies, both critics and advocates of foreign assistance agree the U.S. aid bureaucracy could be more efficient. Some suggest reducing the number of agencies managing aid programs; others want more privatization of U.S. aid efforts.

Anti-Semitism

In the run-up to the presidential election and afterward, the United States has experienced disturbing outbreaks of anti-Semitism, including a spate of incidents on more than 100 college campuses, where white supremacists have been distributing anti-Semitic fliers and openly recruiting adherents. Some human rights and Jewish activists say President Trump has emboldened right-wing hostility toward Jews, but others say such charges are unjustified. Defining anti-Semitism is controversial. Members of Congress and state legislators want to codify a definition that would include opposition to Israel's existence. But pro-Palestinian and civil liberties groups say that would violate free-speech rights. A similar debate is playing out in Europe, where some countries have seen a rise in deadly attacks on Jews in recent years, often by radicalized Muslims, such as the 2015 terrorist attack on a kosher grocery in Paris. Paradoxically, growing anti-Muslim attitudes in countries experiencing an influx of refugees have also spurred more prejudice against Jews — the target of history's longest hatred.

ENVIRONMENTAL ISSUES
Climate Change and National Security

U.S. military officials increasingly view climate change as a "threat multiplier," a factor that can aggravate poverty, political instability and social tensions. That, in turn, could foster terrorism and other forms of global violence while impairing America's military effectiveness. Rising seas, due mainly to Arctic ice melting, already threaten Naval Station Norfolk in Virginia, the world's largest naval base; dozens of other coastal installations also are at risk. Meanwhile, drought in some regions and record rainfall in others have forced millions of people to migrate across borders, adding to tensions in northern Africa, the Middle East and Southeast Asia. Defense Secretary James Mattis said climate change is affecting the stability of areas where U.S. troops are operating. President Trump, who has labeled climate change a "hoax," now says he has an "open mind" on the issue. Some politicians and economists argue that the real danger to U.S. security lies in the erosion of jobs, trade and industrial productivity caused by the costs of unnecessary federal environmental regulations.

Pandemic Threat

Public health officials say the world is overdue for a pandemic that could kill 30 million people within a year. The possible causes include the expanding and mobile global population, mutating viruses that can outfox vaccine makers, the threat of bioterrorism and accelerating climate change that breeds new diseases. Meanwhile, in the wake of recent outbreaks of the Zika virus in Brazil, Ebola in Africa and a new strain of bird flu in China, many experts say the World Health Organization (WHO) and other agencies charged with protecting against dangerous pathogens are under-resourced and underfunded. But some experts are more optimistic, saying the global health community has taken important steps to prevent and respond to pandemics. For example, the United States has invested in crisis preparation, and WHO set up a global surveillance network and pandemic emergency fund, these experts note. But gaps in funding and leadership remain, and many warn that vaccines exist for just a fraction of the 300 known infectious viruses.

Preface

In this pivotal era of international policymaking, scholars, students, practitioners and journalists seek answers to such critical questions as: Is representative government in retreat worldwide? Can the U.S. stop Chinese expansion in the South China Sea? Can Brazil overcome corruption, inequality and recession? Students must first understand the facts and contexts of these and other global issues if they are to analyze and articulate well-reasoned positions.

The 2018 edition of *Global Issues* provides comprehensive and unbiased coverage of today's most pressing global problems. This edition is a compilation of 16 recent reports from *CQ Researcher*, a weekly policy brief that unpacks difficult concepts and provides balanced coverage of competing perspectives. Each article analyzes past, present and possible political maneuvering, is designed to promote in-depth discussion and further research and helps readers formulate their own positions on crucial international issues.

This collection is organized into four subject areas that span a range of important international policy concerns: conflict, security, and terrorism; international political economy; religious and human rights; and environmental issues. *Global Issues* is a valuable supplement for courses on world affairs in political science, geography, economics and sociology. Citizens, journalists and business and government leaders also turn to it to become better informed on key issues, actors and policy positions.

CQ RESEARCHER

CQ Researcher was founded in 1923 as *Editorial Research Reports* and was sold primarily to newspapers as a research tool. The magazine was renamed and redesigned in 1991 as *CQ Researcher*. Today, students are its primary audience. While still used by hundreds of journalists and newspapers, many of which reprint portions of the reports, *Researcher's* main subscribers are now high school, college and public libraries. In 2002, *Researcher* won the American Bar Association's coveted Silver Gavel Award for magazine excellence for a series of nine reports on civil liberties and other legal issues.

Researcher writers — all highly experienced journalists — sometimes compare the experience of writing a *Researcher* report to drafting a college term paper. Indeed, there are many similarities. Each report is as long as many term papers — about 11,000 words — and is written by one person without any significant outside help. One of the key differences is that the writers interview leading experts, scholars and government officials for each issue.

Like students, writers begin the creative process by choosing a topic. Working with *Researcher's* editors, the writer identifies a controversial subject that has important public policy implications. After a topic is selected, the writer embarks on one to two weeks of intense research. Newspaper and magazine articles are clipped or downloaded, books are ordered and information is gathered from a wide variety of sources, including interest groups, universities and the government. Once the writers are well informed, they develop a detailed outline and begin the interview process. Each report requires a minimum of ten to fifteen interviews with academics, officials, lobbyists and people working in the field. Only after all interviews are completed does the writing begin.

CHAPTER FORMAT

Each issue of *CQ Researcher*, and therefore each selection in this book, is structured in the same way. A selection begins with an introductory overview, which is briefly explored in greater detail in the rest of the report.

The second section chronicles the most important and current debates in the field. It is structured around a number of key issues questions, such as "Is the West engaged in a new cold war with Russia?" and "Should archaeological artifacts be returned to their country of origin?" This section is the core of each selection. The questions raised are often highly controversial and usually the object of much argument among scholars and practitioners. Hence, the answers provided are never conclusive, but rather detail the range of opinion within the field.

Following those issue questions is the "Background" section, which provides a history of the issue being examined. This retrospective includes important legislative and executive actions and court decisions to inform readers on how current policy evolved.

Next, the "Current Situation" section examines important contemporary policy issues, legislation under consideration and action being taken. Each selection ends with an "Outlook" section that gives a sense of what new regulations, court rulings and possible policy initiatives might be put into place in the next five to ten years.

Each report contains features that augment the main text: sidebars that examine issues related to the topic, a pro/con debate by two outside experts, a chronology of key dates and events and an annotated bibliography that details the major sources used by the writer.

ACKNOWLEDGMENTS

We wish to thank many people for helping to make this collection a reality. Thomas J. Billitteri, managing editor of *CQ Researcher*, gave us his enthusiastic support and cooperation as we developed this edition. He and his talented editors and writers have amassed a first-class collection of *Researcher* articles, and we are fortunate to have access to this rich cache. We also thankfully acknowledge the advice and feedback from current readers and are gratified by their satisfaction with the book.

Some readers may be learning about *CQ Researcher* for the first time. We expect that many readers will want regular access to this excellent weekly research tool. For subscription information or a no-obligation free trial of *Researcher*, please contact CQ Press at www.cqpress.com or toll-free at 1-866-4CQ-PRESS (1-866-427-7737).

We hope that you will be pleased by the 2018 edition of *Global Issues*. We welcome your feedback and suggestions for future editions. Please direct comments to Scott Greenan, Senior Acquisitions Editor for International Affairs, Public Administration, and Public Policy, CQ Press, an imprint of SAGE, 2600 Virginia Avenue, NW, Suite 600, Washington, DC 20037; or send e-mail to *Scott.Greenan@sagepub.com*.

—*The Editors of CQ Press*

Contributors

David Hosansky is a freelance writer in the Denver area. He previously was a senior writer at *CQ Weekly* and the *Florida Times-Union* in Jacksonville, where he was twice nominated for a Pulitzer Prize. His previous *CQ Researcher* reports include "Mass Transit" and "Preventing Hazing."

Christina L. Lyons, a freelance journalist in the Washington, D.C., area, writes primarily about U.S. government and politics. She is a contributing author for CQ Press reference books, including *CQ's Guide to Congress*, and was a contributing editor for Bloomberg BNA's *International Trade Daily*. A former editor for Congressional Quarterly, she also was co-author of CQ's *Politics in America 2010*. Lyons began her career as a newspaper reporter in Maryland and then covered environment and health care policy on Capitol Hill. She has a master's degree in political science from American University.

Patrick Marshall, a freelance policy and technology writer in Seattle, is a technology columnist for *The Seattle Times* and *Government Computer News*. He has a bachelor's degree in anthropology from the University of California, Santa Cruz, and a master's degree in international studies from the Fletcher School of Law and Diplomacy at Tufts University.

Chuck McCutcheon is an assistant managing editor of *CQ Researcher*. He has been a reporter and editor for *Congressional Quarterly* and Newhouse News Service and is co-author of the 2012 and 2014 editions of *The Almanac of American Politics* and *Dog Whistles, Walk-Backs and Washington Handshakes: Decoding the Jargon, Slang and Bluster of American Political Speech*. He also has written books on climate change and nuclear waste.

Suzanne Sataline is a freelance writer and former national correspondent for *The Wall Street Journal*, where she covered religion, politics and health care. She also has worked for *The Boston Globe, The New York Daily News* and *The South China Morning Post* in Hong Kong. She was a Nieman fellow at Harvard University. Her writing has been published by *The New York Times, The New Yorker, The Economist, The Guardian, The Washington Post, Popular Science* and *National Geographic*.

Corine Hegland is a freelance journalist based in Scotland, where she writes about foreign affairs and natural resources. She previously worked for *National Journal* in Washington, D.C., and was a policy analyst for the U.S. Department of Transportation. She has won several awards, including the Society of Professional Journalists' Sigma Delta Chi Award for Public Service in Magazine Journalism and the James Aronson Award for Social Justice Journalism.

Christina Hoag is a freelance journalist in Los Angeles. She previously worked for *The Miami Herald* and The Associated Press and was a correspondent in Latin America. She is the co-author of *Peace in the Hood: Working with Gang Members to End the Violence*.

Sarah Glazer is a London-based freelancer who contributes regularly to *CQ Researcher*. Her articles on health, education and social-policy issues also have appeared in *The New York Times* and *The Washington Post*. Her recent *CQ Researcher* reports include "Privacy and the Internet" and "Decriminalizing Prostitution." She graduated from the University of Chicago with a B.A. in American history.

Reed Karaim, a freelance writer in Tucson, Ariz., has written for *The Washington Post, U.S. News & World Report, Smithsonian, American Scholar, USA Weekend* and other publications. He is the author of the novel *If Men Were Angels*, which was selected for the Barnes & Noble Discover Great New Writers series. He is also the winner of the Robin Goldstein Award for Outstanding Regional Reporting and other journalism honors. Karaim is a graduate of North Dakota State University in Fargo.

Bill Wanlund is a freelance writer in the Washington, D.C., area. He is a former Foreign Service officer, with service in Europe, Asia, Africa and South America. He holds a journalism degree from The George Washington University and has written for *CQ Researcher* on abortion, intelligence reform and the marijuana industry.

Bara Vaida is a Washington-based freelancer with more than 25 years' experience as a journalist, covering primarily health care policy issues. She has worked for Agence France-Presse, Bloomberg News, *National Journal* and *Kaiser Health News*. She also has published articles in, among others, *Cancer Today, Stateline, WebMD* and *Washingtonian* magazines.

Global Issues,
2018 Edition

1

North Korea Showdown

David Hosansky

North Korean leader Kim Jong Un, who was about 27 years old when he succeeded his father in 2011, has accelerated the nation's military buildup. In addition to nuclear arms, North Korea is believed to have vast stockpiles of chemical and biological weapons. The Trump administration has urged China, North Korea's main trading partner, to use its economic leverage to help persuade Kim to abandon his nuclear program.

From *CQ Researcher,*
May 19, 2017

When President Obama met with President-elect Donald Trump in the Oval Office after the 2016 election, Obama reportedly warned his successor that North Korea was the nation's most serious foreign policy challenge.

Indeed, Trump had scarcely been sworn in on Jan. 20 when long-simmering tension between the United States and North Korea, a nuclear power with increasingly sophisticated capabilities, threatened to escalate into armed conflict.

Within days, reports surfaced that North Korea had restarted a reactor used to make plutonium for nuclear bombs. In March, after the United States and Japan demonstrated new technology to shoot down incoming ballistic missiles, North Korea test-fired missiles in the Sea of Japan that reached within 200 miles of Japan.

In turn, the United States, South Korea and Japan dispatched high-tech missile defense ships to the region and engaged in large-scale military drills — only to have North Korea conduct additional missile tests. These included, on May 13, an intermediate-range missile that flew more than 430 miles and reached an estimated altitude of more than 1,245 miles, drawing sharp international condemnation and potentially putting U.S. military bases in Guam within range of North Korea's growing arsenal.[1]

With Japan holding evacuation drills to prepare for a North Korean missile attack and U.S. leaders floating the prospect of a pre-emptive military strike, Washington and Pyongyang, North Korea's capital, found themselves agreeing on one thing: the Korean Peninsula potentially faced a catastrophic war.

North Korea Worries Its Neighbors

As one of the world's nine nuclear-armed nations, North Korea poses a major threat to regional U.S. allies, South Korea and Japan, and to the United States itself if it develops long-range ballistic missiles capable of reaching the West Coast. The "Hermit Kingdom's" nuclear ambitions also worry its neighbors to the north and west, Russia and China. North Korea's latest launch test put a missile near the Russian coast. Meanwhile, China fears an onslaught of refugees if war breaks out in the region.

North Korea and Its Environs

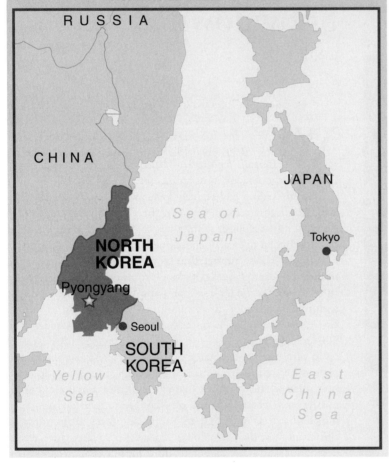

"[W]e could end up having a major, major conflict with North Korea," Trump said on April 28. "We'd love to solve things diplomatically, but it's very difficult."[2] But every warning by White House officials, including repeated declarations by Secretary of State Rex Tillerson and others that "all options are on the table," only served to stiffen North Korea's resolve.

Assailing the United States for "becoming more vicious and aggressive" under Trump, North Korea's vice foreign minister, Han Song-ryol, said, "We will go to war if they choose."[3] A North Korea army spokesman added, "Nothing will be more foolish if the United States thinks it can deal with us the way it treated Iraq and Libya, miserable victims of its aggression."[4]

Long known as the "Hermit Kingdom," North Korea is the world's most isolated and secretive country, ruled since the end of World War II by a family dynasty with Stalinist roots that tightly controls information and brutally stamps out dissent. A 2014 U.N. report said the country's human rights abuses were the worst in the world.[5] Thousands of defectors flee every year, including a small but growing number of more-affluent North Koreans, leading some analysts to wonder if the regime of leader Kim Jong Un is becoming unstable. But Kim has shown remarkable resilience.

U.S.-North Korea animosity dates to 1953, when the Korean War ended with an uneasy armistice and North and South Korea divided by a narrow, 2.5–mile-wide demilitarized zone (DMZ) along the 38th parallel. Washington has never recognized the Democratic People's Republic of Korea — the name North Korea prefers — and Pyongyang repeatedly has launched provocative attacks on South Korea, including a 2010 bombardment of the island of Yeonpyeong that left four South Koreans dead.

The stakes have risen dramatically over the past decade. North Korea has tested five nuclear bombs since

2006 and reportedly is within a few years of developing intercontinental ballistic missiles (ICBMs) capable of reaching America's West Coast — a development U.S. policy makers view as intolerable.[6]

"This is a slow-motion Cuban missile crisis," says Robert Litwak, director of International Security Studies at the Wilson Center, a think tank in Washington chartered by Congress to study global issues. "North Korea is on the verge of a strategic breakout, and their development of multistage ballistic missiles would be a game-changer."

The United States and U.N. Security Council have tried for years to persuade Pyongyang to dismantle its nuclear program, imposing increasingly strict economic sanctions and sharply condemning its nuclear bomb and missile tests. Trump and his foreign policy team have vowed a break from past administration policies, including Obama's "strategic patience" approach of slowly pressuring Pyongyang until it agrees to come to the negotiating table. But it is unclear what course the new administration will take, and foreign policy and military experts warn the crisis will be difficult to resolve.

Kim, who succeeded his father in 2011, has accelerated the nation's push toward greater military capabilities. North Korea has tested three nuclear bombs since the younger Kim took power, including its most powerful yet: an estimated 10–kiloton explosion in 2016, two-thirds the explosive force of the 15–kiloton bomb the United States dropped on Hiroshima during World War II.[7]

North Korea's missiles also are increasingly sophisticated, as shown by a successful February test of its new solid-fuel, intermediate-range missile, the KN-15, which is difficult to detect because it can be fired from a mobile launcher.[8]

In addition, North Korea is believed to have vast stockpiles of chemical and biological weapons. Pyongyang allegedly used a banned chemical agent to kill Kim's estranged half-brother at an airport in Malaysia in February, possibly signaling its willingness to use chemical weapons if provoked.[9]

North Korea also has long-range artillery massed along the DMZ that could destroy much of the South Korean capital of Seoul, one of the world's largest metropolitan areas, and an international center of commerce.[10] For its part, South Korea has a formidable armada of tanks, armored fighting vehicles, fighter jets and attack helicopters.[11]

And this spring the United States, which has more than 60,000 troops stationed in South Korea and nearby Japan, began deploying a powerful antimissile system — the Terminal High Altitude Area Defense, or THAAD — in South Korea, despite strong objections from neighboring China, which views the system as a threat to its own military operations.[12]

Washington also is believed to be using cyber and electronic attacks to sabotage North Korea's test missile launches, under a program initiated by President Obama in 2013. Although it is difficult to assess the effectiveness of the strategy, several recent North Korean missiles have blown up almost immediately upon launch.[13]

North Korea itself also has exhibited considerable cyber-prowess. It was blamed for a massive 2014 hack of Sony Pictures Entertainment after the company produced a movie, "The Interview," about a fictional assassination plot against Kim Jong Un. Although Pyongyang denied it was behind the hacking, President Obama in 2015 ordered additional sanctions against North Korea. Cyber-security firms also found evidence potentially linking North Korea with ransomware attacks in mid-May that crippled computer systems worldwide.[14]

With all sides poised for major retaliation if attacked, policy experts say the situation is highly combustible.

"I'm fairly worried," says Jeffrey Lewis, director of the East Asia Nonproliferation Program at the Middlebury Institute for International Studies in Monterey, Calif. "Every party in this conflict sees their forces as defensive. That's the good news. The bad news is that everybody sees everyone else's forces as offensive. In a crisis, that could be an excuse to strike first."

Roiling the waters, South Korea's newly elected president, Moon Jae-in, has embraced a more reconciliatory approach to Pyongyang than the previous government, which could put it at odds with the Trump administration. China, which shares an 880–mile-long border with North Korea and fears a wave of North Korean refugees if war breaks out, wants Washington to set aside its threats and engage in talks with Pyongyang.

"We must stay committed to the path of dialogue and negotiation," said China's foreign minister Wang Yi. "The use of force does not solve differences and will only lead to bigger disasters."[15]

Still to be determined, however, is the role China will play in bringing Pyongyang to the negotiating table. The

North Korea at a Glance

North Korea is barely larger than Virginia and has a population one-twelfth that of the United States.

> **Area:** 46,540 square miles, slightly larger than Virginia
>
> **Geography:** Borders China, South Korea and Russia
>
> **Natural resources:** Include coal, lead, tungsten, zinc, graphite, magnesite, iron ore, copper, gold
>
> **Population:** 25.1 million (est., July 2016)
>
> **Life expectancy:** 70.4 years
>
> **Religions:** Traditionally Buddhist and Confucianist, some Christian and syncretic Chondogyo (Religion of the Heavenly Way)
>
> **Government:** Communist; ruled by Kim Jong Un since 2011
>
> **GDP per capita:** $1,013 (est., 2015)
>
> **Labor force:** 14 million; agriculture, 37 percent; industry services, 63 percent
>
> **Unemployment rate:** 25.6 percent (est., 2013)
>
> **Industries:** Military products, machine building, electric power, chemicals, mining, metallurgy, textiles, agriculture
>
> **Exports:** $4.2 billion (est., 2015); minerals, metallurgical products, manufactured goods, textiles, agricultural and fishery products
>
> **Imports:** $4.8 billion (est., 2015); petroleum, coking coal, machinery and equipment, textiles, grain

Sources: "Country Comparison: GDP — Per Capita (PPP)," and "East & Southeast Asia: Korea, North," *The World Factbook*, Central Intelligence Agency, Jan. 12, 2017, http://tinyurl.com/2yckfx and http://tinyurl.com/5sajkr; "North Korea GDP," Trading Economics, 2017, http://tinyurl.com/k5gjulg; "North Korea per capita GDP rises above $1,000, think tank says," United Press International, Sept. 29, 2016, http://tinyurl.com/m8j7say

Trump administration has urged China, North Korea's main trading partner, to use its economic leverage to help persuade Kim to abandon his nuclear program. Beijing has been reluctant to clash with Pyongyang but has supported U.N. sanctions and agreed to suspend coal imports from North Korea, a major source of cash for the "Hermit Kingdom."

Nor is it clear that China could sway North Korea even if it turned up the economic pressure. When a Chinese-run media outlet called on Pyongyang to end nuclear tests, North Korean state media harshly criticized China for "a string of absurd and reckless remarks" and warned of unspecified "grave" consequences.[16]

Amid the international cross-currents and tensions, long-time observers sees no easy solution. "It's an extraordinary problem for which there's no good answer," says Doug Bandow, a senior fellow at the Cato Institute think tank in Washington who has written widely on North Korea.

As officials on both sides of the Pacific seek to de-escalate the situation, here are key questions they are debating:

Is there a viable nonmilitary strategy to get North Korea to drop its nuclear weapons program?

When fragments from a North Korean rocket fell into the Yellow Sea last year, international weapons experts who examined them made an interesting discovery: Many of the key components came from China. This and other findings led the United Nations earlier this year to conclude that years of international sanctions have failed to cut off materials and technologies needed by North Korea to keep developing nuclear weapons.

"That case demonstrates the continuing critical importance of high-end, foreign-sourced components" for North Korea's military programs, stated a U.N. report. "The Democratic People's Republic of Korea continues to trade in arms and related materiel, exploiting markets and procurement services in Asia, Africa and the Middle East."[17]

In fact, despite military pressure, global sanctions and on-and-off negotiations, North Korea has continued — and even accelerated — its march toward increasingly powerful nuclear bombs and missiles.

Exasperated, top White House officials say it's time to change strategies.

"[T]he political and diplomatic efforts of the past 20 years to bring North Korea to the point of denuclearization have failed," Secretary of State Rex Tillerson said in March, less than two months after assuming his position. "In the face of this ever-escalating threat, it is clear that a different approach is required."[18]

Policy experts, however, are divided over what, if anything, can stop North Korea from developing an even more potent arsenal.

The two decades of efforts Tillerson referenced began with a 1994 agreement between the United States and North Korea in which Pyongyang agreed to freeze and eventually dismantle its nuclear weapons program in return for U.S. aid and two U.S.-supplied light-water nuclear reactors that could not be used to create weapons. The deal fell apart in 2002, with each side blaming the other for failing to adhere to its terms.

After North Korea tested its first atomic bomb in 2006, President George W. Bush's administration attempted unsuccessfully to negotiate a new deal. The Obama administration then embarked on its strategic-patience policy, refraining from engaging with North Korea until it ceased its provocative behavior while relying on sanctions to help bring it to the negotiating table.

Meanwhile the United Nations, growing alarmed over North Korea's tests of nuclear bombs and missiles, passed a series of increasingly stringent sanctions between 2006 and 2016. These initially targeted certain military goods and luxury supplies and then were expanded to encourage member states to inspect ships suspected of smuggling military goods to North Korea. The U.N. also restricted money transfers and, last year, banned the export of gold and rare earth metals, which are needed to make high-tech electronics and hybrid car batteries, and capped exports of coal and iron.

Some experts say the ever-tougher sanctions, coupled with stepped-up enforcement and China's cooperation, eventually will make a difference. They cite the example of Iran, which agreed to negotiations over halting its nuclear weapons program after years of crippling sanctions.

"Iran sanctions worked," says Anthony Ruggiero, a senior fellow at the Foundation for Defense of Democracies, a think tank in Washington that focuses on fighting terrorism and promoting democracy. "There's a template there." In addition, he says, even though North Korea is not as integrated into the world economy as Iran was, "there are areas where they can be squeezed."

North Korea Raises Nuclear Stakes

Nuclear bombs tested by North Korea have been increasingly powerful, with the latest, in September 2016, generally estimated at 10 kilotons, although some analysts believe it may have been up to 30 kilotons. By comparison, the atomic bomb the United States dropped on Hiroshima, Japan, during World War II was 15 kilotons. North Korea also has tested several ballistic missiles, the most recent of which flew more than 430 miles and demonstrated Pyongyang's increasing military capability.

North Korean Nuclear Bomb Tests, 2006-2016

1 kiloton
October 2006

2-6 kilotons
May 2009

6-9 kilotons
February 2013

6-9 kilotons
January 2016

More than
10 kilotons
September 2016

Source: "A Decade of North Korean Nuclear Tests," Center for Strategic and International Studies, Oct. 17, 2016, http://tinyurl.com/lajcgf2; "North Korea and the History of Underground Nuclear Testing," Atomic Heritage Foundation, Sept. 10, 2016, http://tinyurl.com/k5rhpcl

Ruggiero and other foreign policy experts say the United States should consider so-called "secondary sanctions," or directly targeting companies, including those based in China, that are selling banned goods to North Korea. Such sanctions could, in theory, choke off the flow of goods and money to North Korea.

"We need to do a much better job of, first, devoting sufficient resources to finding out where North Korea's money laundering is going through, and second, we have to have the political will to sanction, to designate, to freeze the assets of companies and banks in third countries, including China, that are helping North Korea violate the sanctions," said Joshua Stanton, a Washington-based attorney and former U.S. Army judge advocate in South Korea who has advised the House Foreign Affairs Committee on North Korean sanctions.[19]

Other foreign policy experts, however, warn that tougher sanctions could further isolate Pyongyang, leaving it more entrenched than ever. In addition, Beijing might not take kindly to the United States

Daily life for the average citizen is extremely difficult in North Korea, one of the world's poorest nations. But in the capital, Pyongyang, above, more-affluent residents enjoy well-stocked stores, cellphones and other modern luxuries. The economy appears to be in somewhat better shape since Kim Jong Un eased government restrictions on commercial activities. And a booming black market is boosting the importation of consumer goods, largely from China.

trying to impose financial penalties against some of its companies.

"That's a really indiscriminate set of tools, and it's not clear that the consequences of imposing those kinds of sanctions are well understood," says Toby Dalton, co-director of the nuclear policy program at the Carnegie Endowment for International Peace. "It may make it much harder to get China on our side."

As an alternative, Dalton suggests the United States consider opening talks with North Korea without preconditions. It is worth exploring whether Pyongyang would agree to freeze its nuclear program in exchange for concessions such as sanctions relief and a reduction in U.S.-South Korea military exercises, he says. Even if that is not a satisfactory, long-term solution, it could at least reduce tensions and open the door for ongoing negotiations, he says.

"We think we're being tough by refusing to negotiate, but we need to negotiate to try to get a freeze on their nuclear program," agrees Lewis of the Middlebury Institute for International Studies. "Talking can keep things at a slow boil so you're not getting major provocations. Generally speaking, I think you have to find a way to get tensions down until whatever is going to happen

in North Korea happens — the regime collapses or they moderate some policies."

Other foreign policy experts, however, doubt that negotiations would do any good. Proponents of such a policy "have provided no rationale for why yet another attempt at negotiations would be any more successful than previous failures," said Bruce Klinger, a North Korea expert with the conservative Heritage Foundation think tank in Washington. Instead, he told a subcommittee of the House Committee on Foreign Affairs in March, sanctions will have an effect — if policymakers give them enough time.[20]

"It is a policy of a slow python constriction," he said, "rather than a rapid cobra strike."[21]

Is military action against North Korea a realistic option?

Battling Islamic State fighters in Afghanistan, the United States this year for the first time deployed its most powerful non-nuclear weapon, known as the "mother of all bombs," on a cave complex where the fighters were hiding. The unusually aggressive tactic left foreign policy experts wondering if the Trump administration was sending a message to North Korea.

If Pyongyang refuses to change course, the United States should consider a pre-emptive military attack on North Korea as a last-ditch option to keep it from developing missiles that could drop nuclear bombs on U.S. cities, some congressional leaders have said. "[There are] no good choices left, but if there's a war today, it's over there," said Sen. Lindsey Graham, R-S.C., a member of the Armed Services Committee. "In the future, if there's a war and they get a missile, it comes here."[22]

Many foreign policy and military experts, however, warn that even a limited attack on North Korea could trigger a full-scale war with almost unimaginable casualties, especially for two of America's closest allies: South Korea and Japan. North Korea has one of the world's largest armies, a formidable array of artillery and chemical and biological weapons in addition to its nuclear bombs — and appears determined to defend itself by any means possible.

"That's a very serious business," says Nicholas Eberstadt, an expert in international security in the Korean Peninsula and Asia at the American Enterprise Institute (AEI), a conservative think tank in Washington. "I would hope that people thinking about a military option would have given a great deal of thought to the risks."

The risks begin with metropolitan Seoul, home to about 25 million people. North Korea has amassed hundreds of long-range artillery pieces near the demilitarized zone that can unleash a catastrophic assault. "They essentially have the equivalent of a nuclear option pointed at Seoul in the form of artillery," says the Wilson Center's Litwak. South Korea, whose army of 655,000 is about half the size of North Korea's, has a modern air force and navy as well as thousands of artillery pieces, but Pyongyang is not within artillery range of the DMZ like Seoul is.[23]

Other risks include the more than 130,000 Americans who live in South Korea and about 28,000 U.S. troops who are stationed there.[24] "If we had 20,000 troops incinerated, I'm pretty sure we would consider that a war," says Jim Walsh, a senior research associate at the Massachusetts Institute of Technology's Security Studies Program.

North Korean missiles also pose a "grave threat" to Japan, says Japanese Prime Minister Shinzo Abe, who has warned that Pyongyang could strike Japan with missiles loaded with sarin, a highly toxic chemical weapon.[25]

While U.S. leaders hope a pre-emptive strike could disable North Korea, military experts say that is unlikely. North Korea is believed to have many hundreds of missiles, some kept in underground bunkers that would be hard to detect and destroy, as well as 10,000 artillery shells in caves and other hiding places that can reach Seoul within minutes.[26]

But Pyongyang's weapons of mass destruction represent its greatest threat. North Korea has an estimated 2,500 tons of chemical weapons, including the deadly VX nerve agent allegedly used to kill Kim's estranged half-brother in Malaysia in February. It also is believed to have biological weapons that could spread deadly diseases such as smallpox. And military experts are deeply uncertain whether a U.S. preemptive strike could wipe out North Korea's approximately 20 nuclear bombs.[27]

North Korea's Economy Dwarfed by South's

The North Korean economy was about 1 percent of South Korea's in 2015. North Korea's GDP — the total market value of its goods and services — in 2015 was $16.1 billion, equal to about half the economic output of Vermont, the lowest of any U.S. state. South Korea's GDP in 2015 was nearly $1.4 trillion.

GDPs of South Korea and North Korea, 2005-2015

Sources: "GDP (current US$)," World Bank, http://tinyurl.com/k9d6hff; "North Korea GDP," Trading Economics, 2017, http://tinyurl.com/k5gjulg; "Vermont," Bureau of Economic Analysis, March 28, 2017, http://tinyurl.com/l9u9koe

"Every U.S. administration, as they have looked at this problem, has said that all options are available. But that's not really true," said Carl Baker, a retired Air Force officer with extensive experience in South Korea who is now director of programs at the Pacific Forum of the Center for Strategic and International Studies. "We really don't have a military option."[28]

U.S. politicians have also floated the idea of targeted attacks on North Korea's leaders. Ohio Gov. John Kasich, a Republican presidential candidate in 2016, recently suggested that the United States could "eradicate" the leadership of North Korea. "The North Korean top leadership has to go," he said. "And, you know, I think that is not beyond our capability to achieve that."[29]

Korean experts, however, say that even if such a strike succeeded, it might unleash chaos, with the country potentially splintering into violent factions squaring off with chemical weapons while U.S. and Chinese forces maneuver to take control.

"It's really astonishing to me that people don't think of the consequences of doing that in any serious way," says Joel Wit, co-founder and senior fellow of the U.S.-Korea Institute at the Paul H. Nitze School of Advanced International Studies at Johns Hopkins University. "We

South Korean activists in Seoul burn images of North Korea's leader Kim Jong Un on Sept. 10, 2016, to protest a North Korean nuclear test. On May 13, 2017, Pyongyang tested an intermediate-range missile that flew more than 430 miles, drawing international condemnation. South Korea's new government — fearing a war with the North — wants to adopt a more conciliatory approach in dealing with Pyongyang.

would have such a security nightmare that people might yearn for the good old days of a nuclear North Korea with a central government."

Is North Korea at risk of collapse?

In 2013, Kim Jong Un turned his guns on his own family. He arranged for two trusted deputies of his uncle, Jang Song-thaek, to be executed in a particularly gruesome way — with antiaircraft guns. He then ordered that his uncle, widely viewed as the nation's second most powerful official and a voice for reform, be executed in the same way.[30]

Since assuming power at the end of 2011, Kim has moved ruthlessly against potential rivals, executing more than 300 people, including senior government, military and ruling Korean Workers' Party officials, according to a 2016 report by a South Korean think tank, the Institute for National Security Strategy.[31]

U.S. policy makers question whether Kim is tightening his grip on power or if the executions indicate that he is struggling to control growing dissent. "There are people who would say he has consolidated his power with these purges and that may be true, but I can't help but wonder if this stuff also undermines his regime," says the AEI's Eberstadt.

Others cite the gradually rising number of mostly low-level North Korean officials and more affluent residents who are defecting every year. The most senior defector in years — North Korea's former deputy ambassador to the United Kingdom, who defected last summer with his family — said dissent is spreading in North Korea. "Kim Jong Un's days are numbered," the defector, Thae Yong Ho, said earlier this year. "Control over the residents has been collapsing due to information seeping in."[32]

Long-time Korean observers, however, cautioned against assuming the regime will fall any time soon. The Kim family has demonstrated enormous staying power since taking control of the country. They survived war with South Korea and the United States in the early 1950s, a famine in the 1990s that killed up to 2.5 million people and the transition to power of Kim Jong Un, who was only about 27 years old at the time, following the sudden death of his father.

The demise of the regime "has always been more of a hope than a realistic policy outcome," says Carnegie's Dalton. "They have survived all manner of calamities, crises, disasters, tricky political transitions. If you were looking for signs of decay, you would look for loss of government control in border regions and more high-level defections that might indicate stress in the system. But I don't see it."

Korean experts say the younger Kim relies on a few trusted aides and a network of security services, often pitted against each other, to reduce threats to the leader. Anyone suspected of disloyalty faces death or years of confinement in extremely harsh prison camps.

A devastating 2014 report by a special U.N. investigative commission documented human rights abuses in North Korea, which the panel said exceeded those of any other contemporary dictatorship. "The gravity, scale and nature of these violations reveal a State that does not have any parallel in the contemporary world," concluded the report. Drawing on public testimony and private interviews with hundreds of victims and witnesses, the report accused the government of retaining its hold on power through such tactics as murder, enslavement, torture, sexual violence and prolonged starvation. It estimated that 80,000–120,000 political prisoners were held in four large political prison camps.[33]

"The key to the political system is the vast political and security apparatus that strategically uses surveillance, coercion, fear and punishment to preclude the expression of any dissent," the report stated. "Public executions and enforced disappearance to political prison camps serve as the ultimate means to terrorize the population into submission."[34]

Daily life is extremely difficult even for average residents. With its GDP per capita ranked 180th out of 193 countries by the United Nations, North Korea is among the world's poorest nations. About half its population is believed to live in "extreme poverty," and 84 percent had "borderline" or "poor" levels of food consumption in 2013, according to the U.N.[35] But the more affluent living in Pyongyang in recent years have enjoyed well-stocked stores, cellphones and other luxuries of modern life.

The combination of brutal repression and extreme poverty might seem a source of substantial discontent among the population. But North Korean experts warn against such a conclusion.

"It's not like you're living in Western Europe and your standard of living has dramatically nosedived," says Wit of Johns Hopkins University. "It's more like you're living in a developing country where you're not used to a very high standard of living, but you can improve your lot.

"There's a lot of nationalism," he adds. "These are not people who grew up in a democracy. It's not as though North Koreans are saying to themselves, 'I wish I lived in the United States.' It's a very different reality there."

In recent years, some central controls have been relaxed, and North Koreans appear to have more economic opportunities. The result has been a slow increase in the buying and selling of goods and services, sometimes under the official aegis of the state and sometimes unofficially tolerated by authorities, who had cracked down more vigorously on the black market under the regime of Kim's father, Kim Jong-Il.

"My perception is at least in Pyongyang things are better than they were 10 years ago," says MIT's Walsh. "The government has clearly recognized that they need to evolve their economy if they are to survive."

That slow marketization, along with an increased awareness of the outside world through cellphone contacts and more access to South Korean media, could nudge the country on a different path, experts say. But it may take time.

"That trend could be five years, it could be 50 years," Walsh says, "before it amounts to something."

BACKGROUND
Early Era

Although North Korea and South Korea emerged as separate nations comparatively recently, the Korean Peninsula has a long history of division and reunification while contending with external threats. From 56 B.C. until 926, the land was divided into three kingdoms, unified under the Silla dynasty and then divided again into three kingdoms.

The peninsula was reunified under the Koryo dynasty, established by a general named Wang Kon, and was first named "Korea." The Koryo royal rulers, who reigned from the 10th to 14th centuries, introduced a civil service, codified a legal system and allowed Buddhism to spread through the peninsula. After the Mongols invaded in 1231, the Koryo family eventually was replaced by the Choson dynasty, started by Gen. Yi Song-gye, in 1391.[36]

The Choson leaders, who would govern Korea as an independent nation for nearly 500 years, depended on China for military protection and borrowed liberally from Chinese society, adopting Confucianism as the official religion. However, after repeated invasions by the Japanese, the Manchu (who ruled China) and others, Korea gradually closed its doors to foreigners in the 18th century, becoming known as the "Hermit Kingdom." Its isolation ended in the mid-19th century, after European and American traders and missionaries moved into the region.

But Koreans remained highly suspicious of Western motives. When the armed merchant vessel *U.S.S. General Sherman* sailed up the Taedon River to Pyongyang in 1866 and became stranded on a sandbar, Koreans attacked it and killed the crew.[37]

Korea remained independent through the late 19th century, but in 1910 Japan annexed the peninsula after victories in both the Sino-Japanese (1894–1895) and Russo-Japanese (1904–1905) wars and claimed Korea as part of its growing empire.

Colonial Period

Under Japan's colonial rule, which lasted until 1945, Korea became more industrialized and began to build a modern infrastructure. But the Japanese repeatedly and savagely crushed resistance. After unsuccessful attempts to overthrow the Japanese, the Western-educated politician,

CHRONOLOGY

1940s–1950s *Korean Peninsula is divided into North and South, followed by war and a tense standoff.*

1945 Korea splits as World War II ends, with the Soviet-backed communist regime ruling the North and a U.S.-backed regime controlling the South in Cold War maneuvering.

1948 As Soviet and U.S. troops begin to withdraw, longtime communist guerrilla fighter Kim Il Sung takes control of the North.

1950 North Korean troops invade the South; U.S. and U.N. troops rapidly enter the war to help the South, and then China enters on the side of the North.

1953 After massive loss of life, armistice divides peninsula at 38th Parallel.

1960s–1980s *Aided by China and Russia, North undergoes industrial growth and escalates provocations against the South.*

1965 North's nuclear weapons program begins as the Soviets help build its first nuclear reactor, at Yongbyon.

1968 North seizes U.S. spy ship *U.S.S. Pueblo*, releases crew a year later.

1983 Amid mounting North Korean provocations, Pyongyang tries unsuccessfully to assassinate South Korean president.

1984 North test-fires first SCUD missile.

1985 North agrees to 1968 Nuclear Nonproliferation Treaty.

1990s *North faces famine and a transfer of political leadership from Kim Il Sung to his son but continues military buildup.*

1991 North and South begin ministerial talks in Pyongyang. . . . U.S. withdraws nuclear weapons from South.

1994 Kim Jong Il takes control after the death of his father, Kim Il Sung. . . . U.S. and North Korea sign

Agreed Framework, with Pyongyang promising to freeze nuclear weapons program in exchange for aid.

1995 Three-year famine leaves up to 2.5 million dead.

1998 North test-fires long-range *Taepodong-1* missile over Japan.

2000s–Present *North develops increasingly powerful nuclear arsenal.*

2002 President George W. Bush calls North Korea part of an "axis of evil." . . . U.S. accuses North of starting uranium-enrichment program.

2003 North withdraws from Nuclear Nonproliferation Treaty. . . . Six-party talks begin among U.S., North Korea, China, Japan, Russia and South Korea.

2006 North conducts its first underground nuclear bomb test; U.N. Security Council imposes sanctions.

2007 North agrees to disable its nuclear facilities for economic aid.

2009 North cuts diplomatic ties with South, carries out second underground nuclear test.

2010 North shells South Korean island of Yeonpyeong months after it reportedly sank a South Korean warship, killing 46 sailors.

2011 Kim Jong Un succeeds his father, Kim Jong Il, as North Korea's leader.

2014 U.N. report details massive North Korean human rights violations.

2016 North Korea tests 10–kiloton nuclear bomb, its most powerful to date.

2017 Kim Jong Un's estranged half-brother is killed with a chemical agent in Malaysia; suspicion quickly turns to Pyongyang (Feb. 13). . . . North Korea test-fires four missiles into the Sea of Japan, penetrating Japan's 200–mile economic exclusion zone (March 6). . . . President Trump warns of the potential for "major, major conflict" with North Korea; (April 28). Moon Jae-in wins South Korean presidency, pledges to reach out to North in potential split with Washington.

Syngman Rhee, established a provisional Korean government in Shanghai in 1919.

Meanwhile, a communist-led guerrilla movement soldiered on against the Japanese until 1940, when some of its leaders, including Kim Il Sung, fled to the Soviet Union to avoid capture by the Japanese. Kim became a major in the Soviet Army and did not return to Korea until 1945.

During World War II, the United States, Britain and China agreed at a 1943 conference in Cairo that Korea would return to its independent status after the war. But after the war the peninsula became caught up in a struggle between the United States and the Soviet Union.

The Soviets, who occupied northern Korea and adjoining areas of Manchuria in China, viewed the peninsula as an important buffer zone to protect against attacks from the east. The United States, in turn, viewed it as a bulwark against communist expansion. In August 1945, the United States decided unilaterally to divide Korea at the 38th parallel into Soviet and U.S. zones. Within a month, 25,000 American soldiers occupied South Korea while Soviet forces took over the north, accompanied by Kim Il Sung and other Korean communist leaders. Koreans protested both occupying forces as a continuation of colonialism.

Joint American and Soviet discussions over the future of Korea made little progress, and the country was permanently divided in 1948. The Republic of Korea was established in the South, with Rhee elected as the first president. The Democratic People's Republic of Korea was established in the North, headed by resistance fighter Kim, who became premier.

Kim nationalized industry and became very popular, while the new leaders in the South were seen as "puppets" of their occupiers. Kim's brand of communism was not a carbon copy of the Soviet model. Rather, he developed a highly nationalistic ideology known as juche, which stressed self-reliance, independence and resistance to foreign influence.

War and Aftermath

After years of border skirmishes, Kim Il Sung — with support from the Soviet Union and the new communist government of China — invaded South Korea on June 25, 1950, quickly taking control of the South except for a small southeastern corner near the port of Pusan. The United States and other allies immediately came to the aid of South Korea.

Before ending in a virtual stalemate, the three-year Korean War produced a massive loss of life: 800,000 Koreans, 115,000 Chinese and 37,000 Americans. An armistice was signed on July 27, 1953, officially splitting the peninsula at the 38th parallel and suspending hostilities, but not technically ending the war.[38]

An uneasy truce prevailed between the two countries throughout the 1950s and '60s. The North, ruled by the autocratic Kim, again became a closed society. A huge personality cult helped lift the "Dear Leader," as Kim was called, to almost godlike status among his people. The communist Korean Workers' Party, the leading political entity in the North, ran the centralized government, the military and the economy.

After the Korean War, Moscow and Beijing helped rebuild the war-torn North, and its industrialized economy surged ahead of the South's. Eventually, however, bolstered by the United States and others, the South developed export-oriented industries and became a growing economic power, surpassing the North in the 1970s. Today it has the world's 15th-largest economy and is home to such industrial giants as Samsung and Hyundai.[39]

By the 1990s, North Korea's sputtering economy and international isolation left it vulnerable to grave crises. Kim Il Sung died of a heart attack in 1994 and was succeeded by his son, Kim Jong Il. After the collapse of the Soviet Union in 1991, the economy went into steep decline because of reduced trade and the loss of subsidized Soviet oil. Economic mismanagement, coupled with widespread floods in 1995 led to a three-year famine that left an estimated 600,000 to 2.5 million dead.[40] As the younger Kim consolidated his hold on power, he announced small market-oriented measures, such as bonuses to high-performing workers.

Rising Provocations

Even as the North and South created contrasting economic systems in the years after the Korean War, they built up massive armed forces. The United States established military bases after the armistice was signed and stationed some of its nuclear arsenal in the South. The North responded by focusing increasingly on strengthening its military, while provoking the leaders of South Korea and the United States.

Personality Cult Makes Kim a God

"All-encompassing indoctrination" begins in early childhood.

North Korea is one of the world's poorest nations, with nearly half its population living in extreme poverty. But that hasn't stopped the ruling regime from erecting massive, 70–foot statues of its leader, Kim Jong Un, in provincial capitals across the country. Residents also can gaze upon miniature statues of Kim's predecessors — his father Kim Jong Il and grandfather Kim Il Sung — at the Pyongyang Folk Park, a theme park that features tiny versions of North Korean landmarks.

From the time the Kim family took power following World War II, the state has attributed godlike powers to them. Now the government is extending this cult of personality to Kim Jong Un, who was just in his late 20s when he took over in 2011 upon his father's death.

From early childhood, North Koreans are bombarded with images of the ruling family. The state requires that portraits of the leaders be cleaned daily with a special cloth and look out at residents in every home, office, classroom and other public spaces, including train cars. Starting in kindergarten, teachers and officials regularly instruct children about the greatness of their leaders.

"The milk would arrive [in kindergarten] and we would go up one by one to fill our cups," a North Korean woman told *The Washington Post*. "The teachers would say: 'Do you know where the milk came from? It came from the Dear Leader. Because of his love and consideration, we are drinking milk today.'" [1]

Governments, especially those run by dictators, regularly try to instill a sense of respect or even awe toward their rulers. But the Kim dynasty takes this veneration to a different level, using a nonstop barrage of propaganda about the nation's leaders as a way of cementing their grip on power.

"It's clear they have very good control of the country, and part of it is because of this cult of personality which permeates the whole system from when you're in kindergarten to when you're in university," says Joel Wit, a senior fellow at the U.S.-Korea Institute at the Paul H. Nitze School of Advanced International Studies at Johns Hopkins University in Washington.

In addition to the ubiquitous images, Pyongyang cultivates quasi-mystical worship of the Kims. The nation's calendar calculates time from 1912, when Kim Il Sung is said to have descended to Earth from heaven. More than two decades after his death in 1994, he remains the "eternal president" under the North Korean constitution. His son, Kim Jong Il, who ruled from 1994 to 2011, was also said to have extraordinary abilities, such as walking at just three weeks, talking at eight weeks and writing 1,500 books while studying at Kim Il Sung University. [2]

Even as this cult of personality continues to extol the virtues of North Korea's first two rulers, it is now also turning to Kim Jong Un. He is said to have demonstrated pistol marksmanship at age 3. As a youth, he supposedly mastered seven languages, discovered new geographical features and became a scholar of famous generals in world history. [3]

In 1964, Pyongyang took its first steps toward developing nuclear weapons by setting up a nuclear-energy research complex at Yongbyon, where the Soviets had built the North's first nuclear reactor.

In 1968, tensions with the United States flared after the North captured the *USS Pueblo*, an electronic spy ship that was cruising in international waters off the coast of North Korea gathering intelligence. After 11 months of negotiations, Pyongyang agreed to release the 82 crew members — who had been starved and tortured — in exchange for an admission of guilt and

an apology, both of which Washington retracted once the crew were safe. The *Pueblo* remains a "hostage" in North Korea, and the loss of its sensitive surveillance equipment to a communist country during the Cold War is considered one of the greatest intelligence debacles in U.S. history.[41]

Despite ongoing tensions, Koreans on both sides of the border hoped for reconciliation. Many families and friends were separated by the DMZ. But border skirmishes and provocations periodically dashed such dreams.

A 2014 United Nations report on human rights violations in North Korea said the propaganda serves as a powerful tool for the government, building up support for the leaders while directing hatred toward other countries, including the United States, South Korea and Japan.

"The State operates an all-encompassing indoctrination machine that takes root from childhood to propagate an official personality cult and to manufacture absolute obedience to the Supreme Leader (Suryong), effectively to the exclusion of any thought independent of official ideology and State propaganda," the report said. [4]

The money spent on advancing this personality cult, the report added, comes at the expense of "providing food to the starving general population." [5]

But some Korean experts say the propaganda is becoming less persuasive. Increasing numbers of North Koreans are able to get alternative views from the outside world because of the growing availability of cellphones, homemade radios and the internet, although access is limited.

Doug Bandow, a senior fellow at the Cato Institute, a Washington think tank, and author of *Tripwire: Korea and U.S. Foreign Policy in a Changed World*, says this technology may make it harder to maintain the cult of personality.

"It's increasingly less effective," he says. "It's so much easier now to be aware that you're being lied to."

— David Hosansky

AFP/Getty Images/Pedro Ugarte

Kim Jong Un and other North Korean officials attend the unveiling of giant statues of Kim's father, Kim Jong Il, right, and grandfather, Kim Il Sung, left, on April 13, 2012. The state attributes godlike powers to the Kim family.

[1] Anna Fifield, "North Korea begins brainwashing children in cult of the Kims as early as kindergarten," *The Washington Post*, Jan. 16, 2015, https://tinyurl.com/nx2wzwk.

[2] Robert Kiener, "North Korean Menace," *CQ Researcher*, July 5, 2011, pp. 315–340.

[3] Christopher Richardson, "North Korea's Kim dynasty: the making of personality cult," *The Guardian*, Feb. 16, 2015, https://tinyurl.com/ldt4tt2.

[4] "Report of the Commission of Inquiry on Human Rights in the Democratic People's Republic of Korea," U.N. Human Rights Council, Feb. 7, 2014, https://tinyurl.com/lbwc8du.

[5] Ibid.

In 1971 negotiations offered hope for reunifying the two nations, and an agreement on ground rules for unification was reached in 1972. But many of the talks were scuttled by provocative actions by the North, such as alleged assassination attempts on South Korean leaders in 1968 and 1974, a bombing that killed 17 South Korean officials in 1983 and the North's continued efforts to develop nuclear weapons. [42]

Nevertheless, in 2000 both nations signed the North-South Declaration, promising to seek peaceful reunification. Over the following decade, the two countries held a series of talks aimed at normalizing relations. The South pursued a so-called Sunshine Policy, which aimed to project diplomatic "warmth" toward the North. But the countries failed to achieve significant breakthroughs. The North's numerous provocations — including an artillery attack on the South Korean island of Yeonpyeong and an apparent torpedo attack on a South Korean warship, both in 2010 — eradicated any chance for reconciliation.

The death of Kim Jong Il in 2011 briefly stirred speculation that the regime might struggle to maintain its

Defectors Risk Death to Escape

"How could our country lie so completely to us?"

Thae Yong Ho grew weary of lying to his sons about the greatness of their country. Posted in London as North Korea's deputy ambassador to the United Kingdom, he kept fending off questions from his oldest son, a high school student who wanted to study computer science at a London university, about why North Korea was so different. Why did their native country not permit access to the internet or allow residents to watch foreign films?

"As a father, it was hard for me to tell lies, and it started a debate within the family," Thae said at a Jan. 25 press conference in Seoul, South Korea. "This North Korean system is a really inhuman system. It even abuses the love between parents and their children."[1]

Finally, last summer, Thae defected with his wife and two sons. He made headlines because he was the highest-ranking defector in years. But several thousand North Koreans reportedly flee the country annually.[2]

For North Koreans, the decision to leave is fraught with peril. The most straightforward route is north across the Yalu River into China, but North Korean ruler Kim Jong Un has increased security along the border in recent years. Those who are caught face imprisonment or even execution.

And those who make it into China can face difficulties, such as human trafficking or being arrested by police and sent back to North Korea.

Defectors also must deal with guilt when the regime punishes relatives left behind. Park Sang-hak fled North Korea in 1999 after discovering his family would be punished because his father, who was working in Japan, had decided against coming back. Park bribed a border guard

to cross the Yalu into China with his mother, brother and sister. But the regime exacted retribution after he escaped: His fiancée was beaten so badly she was left unrecognizable; two uncles were tortured to death; and his teenage cousins lost their jobs and had to beg in the streets.[3]

Nowadays, relatives and a black market are helping a small but growing number of more-affluent North Koreans, especially those with family members already living abroad, to find their way to South Korea or other nations.

"There have been shifts in the composition of defectors," says Scott Snyder, a senior fellow for Korea studies and director of the program on U.S.-Korea policy at the Council on Foreign Relations, a think tank in Washington. "It used to be a lot more people living in the border areas who were marginalized individuals." But today, he says, most defectors are elites who rely on family connections and brokers. "Money is paid, arrangements are made," Snyder says. "People are almost pulled out by their relatives and the growing influence of cash."

Although the numbers don't indicate "true internal instability," Snyder says, the defections are nevertheless important "because they open up greater understanding and information for people on the outside about the parts of the regime that really matter."

Thae, who has both spoken privately with South Korean officials and gone public with media interviews, has painted a grim picture of the Kim government. "When Kim Jong Un first came to power I was hopeful that he would make reasonable and rational decisions to save North Korea from poverty," he said. "But I soon fell into despair watching him purging officials for no proper reason."[4]

hold on power. Kim Jong Un reportedly was his father's favorite, but he was young (about 27 years old, but his exact birth date is unknown). He had been named a four-star general the previous year despite having no military experience and was touted by the state-run media for his alleged high-tech savvy. But outside observers wondered if such a young and inexperienced man would be able to establish his authority, especially in a Confucian society that revered age.

A South Korean journalist said at the time: "The chances of a smooth succession by Kim Jong Un are less than 10 percent" because of his few supporters.[43]

But the younger Kim was named supreme leader after his father's funeral and assumed his father's posts as leader of the Korean Workers' Party and the highest position in the military.

At the same time, he relentlessly purged potential rivals. After his reform-minded uncle, Jang, was spectacularly executed in 2013, along with his family, a

Despite the difficulties of life in North Korea, defectors have had mixed experiences abroad.

Seoul is home to an estimated 28,000 defectors, most of whom are women, possibly because women have more freedom of movement and can defect more easily than men without being immediately detected.[5]

Among the best known is Hyeonseo Lee, who wrote a bestselling book about her experiences, *The Girl with Seven Names*. While she grew up in a comparatively wealthy family, Lee was traumatized by such experiences as seeing an execution when she was 7. Eventually, after secretly watching Chinese television as a teenager, she crossed an icy river into China. After narrowly avoiding servitude in a brothel and surviving a police interrogation by pretending to be Chinese, she made her way to South Korea and then daringly snuck back into North Korea to guide her mother and brother to China.

These experiences haunt her, Lee said, and she sometimes cries. "When I meet people, I forget the pain," she said in an interview last year. "I want to keep positive and show that North Koreans can be positive people. But when I am on my own, I think about the past and it gives me more trauma."[6]

Some defectors seek to liberate those still in North Korea. Defector Park now uses homemade balloons to send millions of leaflets across the border criticizing the Kim government, along with declarations of human rights and booklets about South Korea. He believes such information is the best way to undermine Pyongyang.

"All defectors," he said, "ask the same question: How could our country lie so completely to us?"[7]

— *David Hosansky*

Getty Images/NurPhoto/Seung-il Ryu

When former North Korean deputy ambassador to Great Britain Thae Yong Ho defected with his wife and two sons last summer, he was the highest-ranking North Korean defector in years. Several thousand North Koreans reportedly flee the country annually.

[1] Anna Fifield, "Ex-diplomat: 'I've known that there was no future for North Korea for a long time,'" *The Washington Post*, Jan. 25, 2017, https://tinyurl.com/lem3pvb.

[2] Anna Fifield, "Just about the only way to escape North Korea is if a relative has already escaped," *The Washington Post*, March 31, 2016, https://tinyurl.com/kftz6ta; and Kim Tae-woo, "Number of elite North Korean defectors on the rise," *The Diplomat*, Aug. 19, 2016, https://tinyurl.com/ka3nkjw.

[3] Ian Birrell, "'How could our country lie so completely?': meet the North Korean defectors," *The Guardian*, Aug. 27, 2016, https://tinyurl.com/hh7fmbe.

[4] Mark Hanrahan, "North Korea defector says elite turning their backs on Kim Jong Un," NBC News, Jan. 25, 2017, https://tinyurl.com/gubftg2.

[5] Birrell, op. cit., and Shinui Kim, "Why are the majority of North Korean defectors female?" NK News, July 31, 2013, https://tinyurl.com/kfcf4fe.

[6] Birrell, ibid.

[7] Ibid.

deputy security minister, O Sang-hon, who was accused of conspiring with Jang, reportedly was executed with a flame thrower.[44] Kim also continued his father's military policies and continued to push for his grandfather's dream of developing nuclear weapons.

Nuclear Arsenal

North Korea's interest in nuclear weapons can be traced back to the Korean War, when Kim Il Sung discovered that U.S. Army Gen. Douglas MacArthur had asked to use nuclear weapons against the North. Declassified documents show that during the Korean War Kim asked both Russia and China for help in developing a nuclear arsenal.[45] But the North's nuclear program made its biggest gains after the government obtained centrifuges and nuclear secrets from Pakistani nuclear scientist A. Q. Khan in the 1990s.[46]

The North first tested a ballistic missile in 1984, using Soviet Scud missile technology. Although the North joined the Nuclear Nonproliferation Treaty

(NPT) in 1985, international inspections to determine whether the North was abiding by the treaty did not begin until 1992. In 1994, following nearly 18 months of bilateral negotiations, the United States and North Korea signed the so-called Agreed Framework, in which the North Korea agreed to abide by the NPT and both sides agreed to remove barriers to full economic and diplomatic relations.[47]

For halting its nuclear program the North would receive oil and nuclear reactors to generate electric power. At the time, Western intelligence agencies believed the North had enough plutonium for one or two bombs.[48] In 1999, North Korea agreed to suspend missile testing, and the United States eased trade sanctions it had imposed in 1988, for the bombing of a South Korean jetliner in 1987, which killed all 115 passengers.[49]

In 2002 U.S. negotiators accused the North of running a clandestine uranium-enrichment program. The Bush administration immediately stopped oil shipments to the North and persuaded other nations to follow suit. North Korea responded by expelling international monitors and restarting its nuclear reactor and reprocessing plant.[50]

In 2003, North Korea withdrew from the NPT, prompting creation of six-party talks — negotiations among the United States, Japan, China, Russia, and North and South Korea that aimed to push the North to eliminate or reduce its nuclear arsenal. In return, the North sought, among other things, a guarantee of its security, the right to use nuclear energy for peaceful purposes, the normalization of diplomatic relations and the lifting of trade sanctions. The United States and Japan wanted verifiable, irreversible disarmament, while China and Russia wanted a more gradual disarmament process, in which the North is rewarded with some form of aid.

Negotiations broke down, however, and in October 2006 North Korea tested its first nuclear device, becoming the world's eighth atomic power and drawing strong international condemnation. Simultaneously, North Korea was building a rocket delivery system. In April 2009, it failed in an attempt to launch the long-range *Taepodong-2* rocket, designed to travel more than 3,000 miles.

After a second nuclear test in 2009, the U.N. Security Council unanimously tightened sanctions on North Korea and encouraged member nations to inspect airplanes and vessels suspected of transporting weapons and other military materiel to North Korea. Besides

developing nuclear weapons, Pyongyang also was accused of exporting nuclear and ballistic technology to other states, including Syria and Iran.[51]

Despite the protests and sanctions, North Korea's nuclear weapons program has expanded. In 2012, the Obama administration agreed to provide North Korea with food aid and nutritional supplements for children in return for Pyongyang imposing a moratorium on long-range missile launches and activity at the nation's main nuclear facility. But less than a year later, North Korea conducted its third nuclear test — the first under Kim Jong Un. North Korea's National Defense Commission said the tests and launches will build to an "upcoming all-out action" against the United States, "the sworn enemy of the Korean people."[52]

In 2015, North Korea claimed to have a hydrogen bomb and to have successfully miniaturized nuclear warheads to fit on ballistic missiles. Although U.S. officials expressed skepticism about both claims, no one questioned North Korea's growing nuclear capabilities.

Then last Sept. 9, about a month before the U.S. presidential election, North Korea detonated the nuclear warhead estimated to have the explosive power of 10 kilotons or possibly more — its most powerful to date.[53]

CURRENT SITUATION
Trump Policies

In its first months in office, the Trump administration has made vague, sometimes conflicting statements about North Korea. The underlying message, though, is clear: the United States will not stand by while Pyongyang develops increasingly advanced nuclear weapons that could eventually target the United States.

"We can't allow it to happen," Trump said in an interview in late April. "We cannot let what's been going on for a long period of years to continue."[54]

But the administration's own approach has yet to come into focus. Officials have suggested that tighter sanctions, coordination with China, talks with North Korea and, if necessary, military action might resolve the crisis.

"All options for responding to future provocation must remain on the table," Secretary of State Tillerson told the UN. Security Council on April 29. "Diplomatic and financial levers of power will be backed up by a

Should the U.S. tighten penalties on companies dealing with North Korea?

YES

Sue Mi Terry
Managing Director, Korea,
Bower Group Asia

Excerpted from testimony before the House Committee on Foreign Affairs, on Feb. 7, 2017, http://tinyurl.com/m7skg3v.

Contrary to what many believe, the U.S. has not yet used every option available at our disposal to ratchet up pressure against the Kim regime. As a near-term solution, there's much more we can still do on sanctions, on human rights, on getting information into the North, as well as on deterrence, defense and on diplomacy. . . .

The first step to raise the cost for North Korea is through stricter sanctions, by adding even more individuals and entities to the sanctions list and by seeking better enforcement of sanctions, including secondary sanctions.

Until February 2016 . . . U.S. sanctions against North Korea were a mere shadow of the sanctions applied to Iran, Syria or Burma, and even narrower than those applicable to countries like Belarus and Zimbabwe. Thankfully, with the bipartisan support of this committee, the North Korea Sanctions and Policy Enhancement Act of 2016 was passed and signed into law, and today we finally have stronger sanctions in place.

A month after its passage, in March, the United Nations Security Council also unanimously passed a resolution, U.N. Security Council (UNSC) Resolution 2270, imposing new sanctions on the Kim regime, including mining exports.

In June, triggered by the requirements of the Sanctions Act, the Obama administration finally designated North Korea as a primary money laundering concern, and in July, the Treasury Department sanctioned Kim Jong Un and 10 other senior North Korean individuals and five organizations for human rights violations.

In late November, the U.N. Security Council also got around to another round of sanctions, adopting UNSC Resolution 2321, which further caps North Korea's coal exports, its chief source of hard currency.

But for sanctions to work, [they] will need to be pursued over the course of several years as we did with Iran, and most importantly, they need to be enforced. Here, the chief problem has been that Beijing is still reluctant to follow through in fully and aggressively implementing the U.N. sanctions. . . .

Secondary sanctions must be placed on Chinese banks that help North Korea launder its money and Chinese entities that trade with North Korea or are involved with North Korea's procurement activities. . . . Even if the U.S. has to endure some ire from Beijing for enforcing secondary sanctions, this is exactly what Washington should do.

NO

Doug Bandow
Senior Fellow, Cato Institute; Author, Tripwire:
Korea and U.S. Foreign Policy in a Changed World

Written for *CQ Researcher*, May 2017

No one outside of Pyongyang wants the Democratic People's Republic of Korea (DPRK) to have nuclear weapons. But there is no obvious way to stop North Korea's program, and enhancing sanctions likely won't work.

Despite the claim that the DPRK's leader Kim Jong Un is irrational, he, along with his grandfather and father, behaved rationally in developing nuclear weapons. Otherwise, no one would pay attention to the small, impoverished state. Nukes also offer North Korea national prestige and a tool for extortion. Most important, nuclear weapons are the only sure deterrent to U.S. military action. Washington is allied with the South, routinely deploys threatening naval and air forces near the North and imposes regime change in nations whenever the whim strikes American policymakers.

If diplomacy ever was going to dissuade the North from building nukes, that time has passed. Military action would be a wild gamble and likely would trigger the Second Korean War with catastrophic consequences.

Unfortunately, tougher economic penalties likely will be ineffective without China's cooperation. Winning that assistance requires more than offering unspecified trade concessions. The United States must address Beijing's political and security concerns about a failed DPRK and a reunited, U.S.-allied Korea.

Washington could impose secondary sanctions, penalizing Chinese enterprises dealing with the North. But that would likely generate resistance from China, a rising nationalistic power. Economic penalties also would disrupt Washington's relationship with Beijing in several important areas. North Korea also might well refuse to comply even if the United States imposed more sanctions. The Kim dynasty refused to change policy even during the mass starvation of the 1990s — and survived.

It would be better if the United States took a multifaceted approach toward the DPRK. Washington should coordinate with Japan and South Korea, engage the North, develop a comprehensive offer for Pyongyang, forge a deal with China to win the latter's support and only then press sanctions with Beijing's support if the North refuses to negotiate. Finally, to reduce North Korea's insecurity, Washington should back away from the two Koreas' military struggle. Washington should withdraw its forces from the South because Seoul can defend itself from conventional attack.

There is no simple answer for eliminating Pyongyang's nuclear program, and focusing on more sanctions is unlikely to work.

Kim Jong Nam, the estranged half-brother of North Korean ruler Kim Jong Un, was poisoned on Feb.13 with VX nerve agent at Kuala Lumpur International Airport. VX is among the banned chemical weapons North Korea is suspected of stockpiling. Kim Jong Nam, who had questioned his family's right to hereditary rule, had worried for years that his half-brother might try to kill him. Pyongyang has denied any involvement in his death.

willingness to counteract North Korean aggression with military action if necessary."[55]

Tillerson called for better enforcement of existing sanctions and new international sanctions, such as halting a guest-worker program under which Pyongyang gets hard currency from other countries in exchange for cheap labor.

Underscoring U.S. determination on the issue, Tillerson visited the DMZ in March. A month later, the Trump administration sent Vice President Mike Pence to the border "so they can see our resolve in my face," as he said. The administration also dispatched an aircraft carrier, the *Carl Vinson*, to the Sea of Japan in April to stage drills with the South Korean navy.[56] Also in April, the administration summoned all 100 members of the U.S. Senate to the White House for an emergency briefing on the situation, although officials reportedly said little new.[57] A similar briefing was provided on Capitol Hill for members of the House.

Although Trump's actions on North Korea so far have not differed notably from those of past presidents, the administration's rhetoric has been sharper and more dramatic than that of his predecessors. The "theatrics of the Trump administration can be very useful in sending a message to Pyongyang," said Mark Dubowitz, CEO of the Foundation for Defense of Democracies, a nonpartisan foreign policy think tank in Washington that favors stronger sanctions on North Korea. "So much of this is about psychology."[58]

Other experts, however, worry about administration missteps. For example, the White House for days said the *Carl Vinson* was headed toward the Sea of Japan when, in fact, it was moving in the other direction (it eventually changed course).[59] Trump also angered South Koreans when he said Korea "used to be a part of China" (technically it wasn't) and called on Seoul to pay for the THAAD antimissile system, which was not Seoul's understanding of who was paying for it.[60] Recently, Trump also surprised both U.S. officials and allies by praising Kim Jong Un as a "pretty smart cookie" and saying he would be "honored" to meet with Kim "under the right circumstances."[61]

The abrupt shifts in rhetoric can make the already tense situation more dangerous, Korea experts warn. "When they take position A one day and position B the next, that is inherently destabilizing," says MIT's Walsh. "The chances of misinterpretation are larger than they've been in the past."

If Washington expects to intimidate Kim, there is no sign it is succeeding. During the new president's first 100 days in office, North Korea conducted nine missile tests — although not all were successful — and repeatedly threatened overwhelming retaliation to any U.S. military strikes. The *Rodong Sinmun*, official newspaper of the ruling Korean Workers' Party, warned of a "supermighty preemptive strike" that would reduce American military forces "to ashes."[62]

Subsequently, North Korea accused U.S. and South Korean intelligence agencies in early May of plotting to assassinate Kim Jong Un with biochemical agents and warned it could counterattack. South Korea's National Intelligence Service dismissed the accusation.[63]

In recent months, North Korea has further raised tensions by detaining two American professors working at the Pyongyang University of Science and Technology, bringing the total of detained U.S. citizens to four. The State Department had little comment on the most recent detention, except to say it was "aware of reports" that an American had been detained and was working with the Swedish embassy in Pyongyang.[64]

Further clouding the situation, South Korea on May 9 elected a new president, human rights lawyer Moon

Jaein, who favors a more conciliatory approach with North Korea, emphasizing dialogue instead of sanctions and pressure. He contended that South Korea must "embrace the North Korean people to achieve peaceful reunification one day."[65] This position puts him at odds with the United States and could greatly complicate Trump administration efforts to pressure Pyongyang.

Some experts say the growing tensions may provide the catalyst for China to take a harder line with Kim. Although Beijing has been reluctant to pressure him in the past, alarms are rising in Beijing over the prospect of war. "China may finally be persuaded to put pressure on North Korea," says the Wilson Center's Litwak.

Other foreign policy experts, however, warn that even if Beijing wanted to pressure North Korea — which remains uncertain — it may not have as much influence as the Trump administration hopes.

"Those who focus on China suggest that Chinese leaders can snap their fingers and North Korea would come to heel," says Cato's Bandow. "That almost certainly is not the case. North Korea doesn't want to be subject to anyone."

Fratricide

On Feb. 13, the estranged half-brother of North Korea's ruler Kim Jong Un was waiting to catch a flight at Kuala Lumpur International Airport to his home in Macau when two young women walked up to him and touched something to his face. Within moments, he was struggling to breathe. He died on his way to the hospital.

Authorities rapidly determined that the 45–year-old was killed by VX nerve agent, a banned chemical weapon that North Korea is suspected of stockpiling. Suspicion immediately turned to the North Korean government, even though Pyongyang denied any involvement.

South Korea's acting president Hwang Kyo-ahn said the killing "starkly demonstrated the North Korean regime's recklessness and cruelty as well as the fact that it will do anything, everything, in order to maintain its power."[66]

Kim Jong Nam had questioned his family's right to heredity rule, and he had worried for years that his half-brother might try to kill him. But he had little interest in politics and was living in Macau, an autonomous administrative district of China, under Beijing's protection, including sometimes a round-the-clock security detail.

Foreign policy analysts question why Pyongyang would go to such lengths to kill Kim Jong Nam, and to do so with a banned chemical agent in a public place. Some observers speculate that a key motive may have been self-preservation. If the United States or other countries wanted to assassinate Kim Jong Un, then eliminating his half-brother would make it harder to find a successor.

"It shouldn't be surprising that, if people are talking about decapitation, the logical counter is to decapitate the prospective successors," says MIT's Walsh. "The prospects of the half-brother really being a leader were limited, but China was protecting him because they wanted an option."

Indeed, Beijing officials were reportedly shocked by the effrontery of the murder. "China's inner circle of government is highly nervous about this," said Wang Weimin, a professor at the School of International Relations and Public Affairs at Fudan University in Shanghai. The assassination, he argued, makes China "more aware of how unpredictable and cruel the current North Korean regime is."[67]

Kim also may have been demonstrating that his arsenal extends beyond nuclear weapons. North Korea, which is not a party to the Chemical Weapons Convention — a 1997 treaty that prohibits the use, development, production and stockpiling of chemical weapons — has produced chemical weapons since the 1980s and is believed to have biological weapons.[68]

In a war, experts say, Pyongyang could use aircraft, missiles, artillery or even grenades to attack South Korea and possibly Japan with chemical and biological weapons.

And deploying VX nerve agent — which forces a victim's muscles to clench uncontrollably, preventing breathing — in a crowded airport may have been intended to send a message about Pyongyang's willingness to expose large populations to lethal chemicals.

"This may have been a timely reminder to adversaries that North Korea has more than one way to strike back," Walsh says.

OUTLOOK
Signs of Prosperity

John Delury, an assistant professor of international studies at Yonsei University in Seoul, says that when he used to travel to North Korea he could easily keep track of how many cars he saw. But when he went in 2013, there were too many cars to count, as well as a surprising number of people with cellphones.

"The crude economic indicators that we get are of steady growth," said Delury. "You can see the emergence of a public-consumer culture."[69]

Delury and other Korea specialists say the North Korean economy, while still lagging far behind most countries, seems to be in somewhat better shape since Kim Jong Un eased government restrictions on commercial activities. A booming black market is boosting the importation of consumer goods, largely from China. Residents, especially in Pyongyang, have more access to South Korean soap operas through cellphones, flash drives and other technologies, many made in China.

Some observers of North Korea say the greater affluence and access to information may lead to an increased openness and perhaps an eventual softening in government policies. "There are more cellphones, more North Koreans doing business," says MIT's Walsh. "North Koreans are more aware, and you might make an argument that opening up is a first step toward a resolution."

Like Delury, other recent visitors to Pyongyang have been surprised at signs of prosperity despite years of sanctions. Journalist Jean Lee, who opened up an Associated Press bureau in Pyongyang five years ago and then returned to the country this year as a global fellow with the Wilson Center, said nearly everyone in the city had smartphones and plenty of shopping options.

It's "just amazing the kinds of products that they have on the shelves," she said. "I saw so many varieties of potato chips, varieties of canned goods, what would be their equivalent of Spam, for example, but all kinds of things — computers, tablets, PCs — all kinds of things that you might not expect to see in a country that is still very poor."[70]

An increasing number of goods appear to be made locally, reportedly driven by government policies designed to make the country more self-sufficient and to diminish the potential impact of sanctions. "Around 2013, Kim Jong Un started talking about the need for import substitution," said Andray Abrahamian, associate director of research at the Choson Exchange, a Singapore-based group that trains North Koreans in business skills. "There was clearly recognition that too many products were being imported from China."[71]

If sanctions and negotiations don't work, some foreign policy experts wonder if Washington could play for time, in the hopes that North Korea — like the Soviet Union and Maoist China decades ago — will becomes less of a military threat as it moves toward a more market-oriented system.

Some say the consensus in Washington is that the United States must stop North Korea from developing intercontinental missiles, even if that means covert actions to topple the Kim government or a military strike. "Otherwise, we're staring down the barrel of an ICBM," said Sen. Bob Corker, R-Tenn., chairman of the Senate Foreign Relations Committee.[72]

But some long-time Korean observers say the calculus may not be so clear-cut. "We lived through the Cold War with Soviet missiles aimed at every American city," Walsh says. "It wasn't pretty, but we got through it."

NOTES

1. Choe Sang-Hun, "North Korea launches a missile, its first after an election in the South," *The New York Times*, May 13, 2017, http://tinyurl.com/kc2bvg3.

2. Stephen J. Adler, Steve Holland and Jeff Mason, "Exclusive: Trump says 'major, major' conflict with North Korea possible, but seeks diplomacy," Reuters, April 28, 2017, http://tinyurl.com/mmtw3sn.

3. Gerry Mullany, Chris Buckley and David E. Sanger, "China warns of 'storm clouds gathering' in U.S.-North Korea standoff," *The New York Times*, April 14, 2017, http://tinyurl.com/lbqbf8j.

4. Ibid.

5. "Report of the Commission of Inquiry on Human Rights in the Democratic People's Republic of Korea," U.N. Commission of Inquiry on Human Rights in the Democratic People's Republic of Korea, U.N. Office of the High Commissioner for Human Rights, Feb. 17, 2014, http://tinyurl.com/nxl2d3e.

6. Peter Grier, Jack Detsch and Francine Kiefer, "U.S. missile defense: Getting to 'ready' on North Korea threat," *The Christian Science Monitor*, May 3, 2017, http://tinyurl.com/ms7z6kq.

7. Katie Hunt, K. J. Kwon and Jason Hanna, "North Korea claims successful test of nuclear warhead," CNN, Sept. 10, 2016, http://tinyurl.com/gpnc89e.

8. Elizabeth McLaughlin and Luis Martinez, "A look at every North Korean missile test this year," ABC News, April 28, 2017, http://tinyurl.com/ny2aydd.

9. Russell Goldman, "DNA confirms assassination victim was half-brother of Kim Jong-un, Malaysia says," *The New York Times*, March 15, 2017, http://tinyurl.com/l7nk34h.

10. "South Korea," *The World Fact Book*, https://www.cia.gov/library/publications/the-world-factbook/geos/ks.html.

11. See Niall McCarthy, "How North and South Korea's armed forces compare (infographic)," *Forbes*, April 11, 2017, http://tinyurl.com/lwmm5xp.

12. Troop estimates are summarized in Greg Price, "U.S. military presence in Asia: troops stationed in Japan, South Korea and beyond," *Newsweek*, April 26, 2017, http://tinyurl.com/mt7ygf5. China's objections to the THAAD antimissile system are covered in "China presses South Korea on Thaad missile system," BBC News, May 11, 2017, http://tinyurl.com/muorzqc.

13. Choe Sang-Hun, David E. Sanger and William J. Broad, "North Korean missile launch fails, and a show of strength fizzles," *The New York Times*, April 15, 2017, http://tinyurl.com/mrnyxas.

14. Zeke J. Miller, "U.S. sanctions North Korea over Sony hack," *Time*, Jan. 2, 2015, http://tinyurl.com/lgae9h8. Melanie Eversley, "Ransomware hack linked to North Korea, researchers say," *USA Today*, May 15, 2017, http://tinyurl.com/lgmtr75.

15. Robert Delaney, "Tillerson calls for all countries to downgrade ties with North Korea to pressure country," *South China Morning Post*, April 28, 2017, http://tinyurl.com/jvzprbs.

16. "North Korea threat: Pyongyang directly criticizes China in rare move," Fox News, May 4, 2017, http://tinyurl.com/lee9c9g.

17. "Report of the Panel of Experts established pursuant to resolution 1874 (2009)," U.N. Security Council, Feb. 27, 2017, http://tinyurl.com/kaurzbb.

18. Anna Fifield and Anne Gearan, "Tillerson says diplomacy with North Korea has 'failed'; Pyongyang warns of war," *The Washington Post*, March 16, 2017, http://tinyurl.com/kd63h7t.

19. Jenny Lee, "Sanctions against North Korea: How strong should they be?" Voice of America, Feb. 9, 2017, http://tinyurl.com/mqao2kn.

20. Testimony by Bruce Klingner, "Sisyphean diplomacy: The dangers of premature negotiations with North Korea," House Subcommittee on Asia and the Pacific, Committee on Foreign Affairs, March 21, 2017, http://tinyurl.com/mte2evf.

21. Ibid.

22. Ellen Mitchell, "Graham: There are 'no good choices left' with North Korea," *The Hill*, April 25, 2017, http://tinyurl.com/l5d46yd.

23. McCarthy, op. cit.

24. Kim Chul-soo, "Number of U.S. citizens living in South Korea rises 30 percent in 10 years," *The Korea Times*, July 2, 2015; and Ryan Browne, "Top general: Cheaper to keep troops in South Korea than U.S.," CNN, April 21, 2016, http://tinyurl.com/lo6wo4g.

25. Yoko Wakatsuki and James Griffiths, "North Korea may be able to arm missiles with sarin, Japan PM says," CNN, April 13, 2017, http://tinyurl.com/maxqjwz.

26. John M. Donnelly, "Analysis: U.S. Military Options in North Korea — From Bad to Worse," *Roll Call*, April 25, 2017, http://tinyurl.com/lj2mfa6.

27. Ibid.

28. Anna Fifield, "Twenty-five million reasons the U.S. hasn't struck North Korea," *The Washington Post*, April 21, 2017, http://tinyurl.com/maxmqmp.

29. Philip Rucker, "Kasich: Trump should 'eradicate' North Korean leadership," *The Washington Post*, April 28, 2017, http://tinyurl.com/k5j5cv3.

30. Choe Sang-Hun, "In hail of bullets and fire, North Korea killed official who wanted reform," *The New York Times*, March 12, 2016, http://tinyurl.com/kykaxok.

31. K. J. Kwon and Ben Westcott, "Kim Jong Un has executed over 300 people since coming to power," CNN, Dec. 29, 2016, http://tinyurl.com/lazvyc2.

32. Mark Hanrahan, "North Korean defector says elite turning their backs on Kim Jong Un," NBC News, Jan. 27, 2017, http://tinyurl.com/gubftg2.

33. "Report of the Commission of Inquiry on Human Rights in the Democratic People's Republic of Korea," op. cit.

34. Ibid. See the press release accompanying the report, which is at http://tinyurl.com/peobg3f.

35. Joshua Stanton and Sung-Yoon Lee, "Pyongyang's Hunger Games," *The New York Times*, March 7, 2014, http://tinyurl.com/lmkckq6; and Katie McKenna, "North Korea, South Korea: Economic Snapshot," Fox Business, April 28, 2017, http://tinyurl.com/n4j2zfe.

36. For background, see Robert Kiener, "North Korean Menace," *CQ Researcher*, July 5, 2011, pp. 315–340.

37. Kim Young-Sik, "The Early US-Korea Relations," Association for Asian Research, July 25, 2003, http://tinyurl.com/ms8czat.

38. Mary H. Cooper, "North Korean Crisis," *CQ Researcher*, April 11, 2003, pp. 321–344, http://tinyurl.com/d5wyr7.

39. See "Republic of Korea," World Bank, April 14, 2017, http://tinyurl.com/nuj33xk.

40. Stanton and Lee, op. cit.

41. Ray Locker, "Book reveals new details of N. Korea capture of Pueblo," *USA Today*, Jan. 1, 2014, http://tinyurl.com/mfw6ln8.

42. William Chapman, "North Korean leader's son blamed for Rangoon bombing," *The Washington Post*, Dec. 3, 1983, http://tinyurl.com/lslwjt9.

43. "Kim Jong-Un's chances of success 'less than 10 percent,'" *Chosunilbo*, Oct. 16, 2010, http://tinyurl.com/kwczsc5.

44. Terrence McCoy, "North Korean official reportedly executed with a flamethrower," *The Washington Post*, April 8, 2014, http://tinyurl.com/n6j5knv.

45. Brian Knowlton and David E. Sanger, "N. Korea's first nuclear test draws condemnation," *The New York Times*, Oct. 9, 2006, http://tinyurl.com/lkz2kb3.

46. David E. Sanger, "North Koreans unveil new plant for nuclear use," *The New York Times*, Nov. 21, 2010, http://tinyurl.com/mbb7rhx.

47. Kelsey Davenport, "The US-North Korean Agreed Framework at a Glance," The Arms Control Association, Aug. 17, 2004, http://tinyurl.com/zcqnwo4.

48. Mary Beth Nikitin, "North Korea's Nuclear Weapons: Technical Issues," Congressional Research Service, Jan. 20, 2011, http://tinyurl.com/ke6lfg3.

49. Rupert Wingfield-Hayes, "The North Korean spy who blew up a plane," BBC News, April 22, 2013, http://tinyurl.com/k4svfbz.

50. Simon Jeffery, "Expelled UN inspectors leave N. Korea," *The Guardian*, Dec. 31, 2002, http://tinyurl.com/loc2gmu.

51. Louis Charbonneau, "North Korea, Iran trade missile technology: U.N.," Reuters, May 15, 2011, http://tinyurl.com/lhzg887.

52. "North Korea nuclear timeline fast facts," CNN, April 6, 2017, http://tinyurl.com/z75fcsz.

53. Katie Hunt, K. J. Kwon, and Jason Hanna, "North Korea claims successful test of nuclear warhead," CNN, Sept. 10, 2016, http://tinyurl.com/gpnc89e.

54. Susan Jones, "Trump: North Korean leader 'a pretty smart cookie,'" CBS News, May 1, 2017, http://tinyurl.com/msf4y9g.

55. Margaret Besheer, "Tillerson urges UN Security Council to take action before N. Korea does," Voice of America, April 29, 2017, http://tinyurl.com/kcz5cxs.

56. Michael Crowley, "North Korea defies Trump," *Politico*, April 28, 2017, http://tinyurl.com/kx2yybs.

57. Audie Cornish, "The White House briefs the Senate on North Korea," NPR, April 26, 2017, http://tinyurl.com/mwh2hzj.

58. Crowley, op. cit.

59. Mark Landler and Eric Schmitt, "Aircraft carrier wasn't sailing to deter North Korea, as U.S. suggested," *The New York Times*, April 18, 2017, http://tinyurl.com/kkenv4v.

60. Michelle Ye Hee Lee, "Trump's claim that Korea 'actually used to be a part of China,'" *The Washington Post*, April 19, 2017, http://tinyurl.com/mos6zvu. Also see Choe Sang-Hun, "Trump rattles South Korea by saying it should pay for antimissile system,"

The New York Times, April 28, 2017, http://tinyurl .com/m9s8xws.

61. Ashley Parker and Anne Gearan, "President Trump says he would be 'honored' to meet with North Korean dictator," *The Washington Post*, May 1, 2017, http://tinyurl.com/nxb8p3p.

62. Doug Stanglin, "North Korea threatens 'super-mighty' strike on U.S.," *USA Today*, April 20, 2017, http://tinyurl.com/kndfrxt.

63. Choe Sang-Hun, "North Korea accuses South and U.S. of plotting to kill Kim Jong-un," *The New York Times*, May 5, 2017, http://tinyurl.com/ n5cxqdg.

64. Taehoon Lee, "North Korea detains fourth US citizen," CNN, May 8, 2017, http://tinyurl.com/ m4x2lrj.

65. Choe Sang-Hun, "South Korea elects Moon Jae-in, who backs talks with North, as president," *The New York Times*, May 9, 2017, http://tinyurl.com/ lw7l86x.

66. Choe Sang-Hun and Richard C. Paddock, "Kim Jong-nam killing was 'terrorist act' by North Korea, South says," *The New York Times*, Feb. 20, 2017, http://tinyurl.com/ke4wp2u.

67. Simon Denyer, "In China, a sense of betrayal after the assassination of Kim Jong Nam," *The Washington Post*, Feb. 17, 2017, http://tinyurl .com/mdc3e9m.

68. Hyung-Jin Kim and Kim Tong-Hyung, "North Korea's chemical weapons," *Real Clear Defense*, Feb. 25, 2017, http://tinyurl.com/jr7oxrf.

69. Mark Bowden, "Understanding Kim Jong Un, the world's most enigmatic and unpredictable dictator," *Vanity Fair*, Feb. 12, 2015, http://tinyurl.com/ q4qczez.

70. "In North Korea's capital, more abundance than expected in everyday life," NPR, May 5, 2017, http://tinyurl.com/lryqn6n.

71. Sue-Lin Wang and James Pearson, "Made in North Korea: As tougher sanctions loom, more local goods in stores," Reuters, May 8, 2017, http://tinyurl .com/k96ghk7.

72. Fifield and Gearan, op. cit.

BIBLIOGRAPHY
Selected Sources
Books

Demick, Barbara, *Nothing to Envy: Ordinary Lives in North Korea*, Spiegel & Grau, 2009.
A journalist formerly based in South Korea examines the lives of six "ordinary" North Koreans, based on their reports after defecting to the South.

Lankov, Andrei, *The Real North Korea: Life and Politics in the Failed Stalinist Utopia*, Oxford University Press, 2014.
A native of the Soviet Union who has studied North Korea since visiting as an exchange student in the 1980s looks at how its leaders have sustained the regime with limited resources and amid international hostility.

Lee, Hyeonseo, *The Girl with Seven Names: A North Korean Defector's Story*, William Collins, 2015.
This international bestseller tells of Lee's escape from North Korea at age 17, her subsequent struggles in China and her daring trip back to North Korea to bring her mother and brother to South Korea.

Oberdorfer, Don, and Robert Carlin, *The Two Koreas: A Contemporary History*, Basic Books, 2013.
Two Korea experts examine the ongoing conflicts between South and North and show how the once unified nations might achieve reconciliation.

Articles

Birrell, Ian, " 'How could our country lie so completely to us?': meet the North Korean defectors," *The Guardian*, Aug. 27, 2016, http://tinyurl.com/hh7 fmbe.
The author interviews defectors in South Korea to learn about their life in the North, their escapes and their struggles to adapt to new lives.

Bowden, Mark, "Understanding Kim Jong Un, the world's most enigmatic and unpredictable dictator," *Vanity Fair*, Feb. 12, 2015, http://tinyurl.com/ q4qczez.
Journalist Bowden, author of *Black Hawk Down*, portrays the North Korean leader as clever, ruthless, impetuous and very much in charge.

Crowley, Michael, "North Korea defies Trump," *Politico*, April 28, 2017, http://tinyurl.com/kx2yybs.
A senior correspondent analyzes Pyongyang's responses to the Trump administration's declarations and how President Trump's policies may ultimately resemble those of the previous administration.

Donnelly, John M., "Analysis: U.S. Military Options in North Korea — From Bad to Worse," *Roll Call*, April 25, 2017, http://tinyurl.com/lj2mfa6.
This in-depth look at North Korea's military capabilities underscores the challenges the United States would face in a preemptive strike.

Hunt, Katie, K.J. Kwon and Jason Hanna, "North Korea claims successful test of nuclear warhead," CNN, Sept. 10, 2016, http://tinyurl.com/gpnc89e.
The authors cover North Korea's fifth and most powerful nuclear bomb test and provide context on Pyongyang's nuclear program.

Lee, Jenny, "Sanctions Against North Korea: How Strong Should They Be?" Voice of America, Feb. 9, 2017, http://tinyurl.com/mqao2kn.
Several Korean experts analyze how sanctions can be toughened or better enforced to get Pyongyang to stop its nuclear program.

Snyder, Scott, "How North Korea evades UN sanctions through international 'front' companies," *Forbes*, March 3, 2017, http://tinyurl.com/mxjxs7j.
An expert at the Council on Foreign Relations examines North Korean strategies to evade international sanctions.

Reports and Studies

"Report of the Commission of Inquiry on Human Rights in the Democratic People's Republic of Korea," U.N. Commission of Inquiry on Human Rights in the Democratic People's Republic of Korea, Office of the U.N. High Commissioner for Human Rights, Feb. 17, 2014, http://tinyurl.com/nxl2d3e.
A special U.N. commission says North Korea uses murder, torture, starvation, sexual violence and other tactics to maintain political control.

Chanlett-Avery, Emma, Ian E. Rinehart and Mary Beth D. Nikitin, "North Korea: U.S. Relations, Nuclear Diplomacy, and Internal Situation," Congressional Research Service, Jan. 15, 2016, http://tinyurl.com/k7938np.
Congress' bipartisan research arm discusses Pyongyang's nuclear program, economy and human rights record, as well as past U.S. negotiations and the role of China.

Klingner, Bruce, "Sisyphean Diplomacy: The Dangers of Premature Negotiations with North Korea," Heritage Foundation, March 21, 2017, http://tinyurl.com/mte2evf.
A former CIA analyst and now a senior fellow at the conservative think tank examines the crisis with North Korea and says rather than trying to restart failed negotiations the United States should try using tougher sanctions to pressure Pyongyang.

For More Information

Carnegie Endowment for International Peace, 1779 Massachusetts Ave., N.W., Washington, DC 20036–2103; 202–483–7600; www.carnegieendownment.org. Global network of policy research centers that favors exploring negotiations with North Korea.

The Committee for Human Rights in North Korea, 1001 Connecticut Ave., N.W., Suite 435, Washington, DC 20036; 202–499–7970; www.hrnk.org. Seeks to raise world awareness about conditions in North Korea, including human rights abuses.

The Council on Foreign Relations, 58 E. 68th St., New York, NY 10065; 212–434–9400; www.cfr.org. Think tank that specializes in U.S. foreign policy and international affairs, including U.S. relations with North Korea.

Foundation for Defense of Democracies, PO Box 33249, Washington, DC 20033; 202–207–0190; www.defend democracy.org. Nonpartisan institute focusing on foreign policy and national security that favors imposing stronger sanctions on North Korea.

James Martin Center for Nonproliferation Studies, 460 Pierce St., Monterey, CA 93940; 831–647–4154; www .nonproliferation.org. Affiliated with Middlebury College;

conducts policy-oriented research and trains East Asia scholars and government officials.

U.S.-Korea Institute, Paul H. Nitze School of Advanced International Studies, 1740 Massachusetts Ave., N.W., Washington, DC 20036; 202–663–5600; www.sais-jhu .edu. Researches the Korean Peninsula and maintains a website, 38 North, that offers analysis of North Korean issues.

2

Military Readiness

Christina L. Lyons

Army Chief of Staff Gen. Mark Milley testified at a congressional hearing last year that he had "grave concerns" about the Army's ability to fight a major power such as China or Russia. Marine Gen. Joe Dunford, chairman of the Joint Chiefs of Staff, expressed similar concerns, saying that while the military has focused on terrorism, its adversaries "have developed . . . approaches specifically designed to limit our ability to project power."

Getty Images/Alex Wong

From *CQ Researcher,* November 3, 2017

This year has not been kind to the U.S. Navy. In January, a guided missile cruiser ran aground in Tokyo Bay. In May, another cruiser collided with a South Korean fishing vessel off the Korean Peninsula, injuring several sailors.

Then, the unthinkable. On June 17, a guided missile destroyer, the *USS Fitzgerald*, collided with a container ship off Japan, killing seven sailors. Two months later, on Aug. 21, an oil tanker struck another destroyer, the *USS John S. McCain*, a little before dawn off the coast of Singapore. The collision flooded machinery, communications equipment and sleeping quarters. Ten sailors died.[1]

"This is a very, very dire circumstance for our Navy," says Lyle Goldstein, an associate professor at the China maritime Studies Institute at the Naval War College in Newport, R.I., referring to the *Fitzgerald* and *McCain* collisions. "It speaks to the possibility that there is some kind of crisis in the force."

Vessels patrolling the Western Pacific are crucial to defending against a possible ballistic missile launch from North Korea, but recent testimony before two House subcommittees cited major gaps in training and maintenance on those ships.[2]

The Navy confirmed that assessment in two reports released on Nov. 1. "The collisions were avoidable," Adm. John Richardson, the chief of naval operations, said in summarizing the reports, which detailed a litany of crew and navigation errors.[3]

Overall, the Navy is struggling to cope with constant deployments, fewer ships and sleep-deprived crews, defense analysts say. In the Army, some brigades are exhausted after fighting for

Middle East Led in Military Spending as Share of GDP

Four Middle Eastern nations — Oman, Saudi Arabia, Israel and Jordan — in 2016 were among the global leaders in defense spending as a percentage of gross domestic product (GDP). Oman was first at 13.7 percent. The United States, ranked 18th, spent 3.3 percent of its GDP on its military, behind sixth-ranked Russia at 5.4 percent. In overall spending, however, the United States spends far more on defense than any other nation.

Military Spending as Share of GDP, 2016

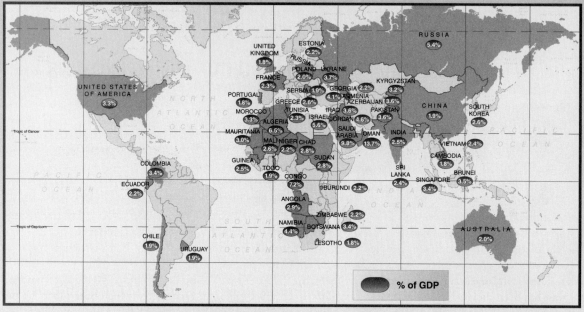

Source: Max Roser and Mohamed Nagdy, "Military Spending," Our World in Data, 2016, https://tinyurl.com/hjm5ewa

16 years in Afghanistan and 14 years in Iraq. In July, in five separate incidents, Air Force F-16 jet fighters crashed, killing three airmen.[4]

Such problems have raised new concerns about U.S. military readiness amid rising tensions with Russia, China, North Korea and Iran, as well as continuing pressure to contain terrorism in the Middle East, Africa and elsewhere.

Nuclear weapons are also raising alarms. Nuclear war seemed a remote possibility a few years ago, but North Korea's progress developing nuclear weapons has renewed fears that the U.S. nuclear arsenal needs updating. Moreover, U.S. forces also face the prospect of fighting wars in cyberspace and outer space.[5]

The United States remains far and away the world's most formidable military power, spending more on defense than the next eight countries combined. However, the many challenges facing the Army, Navy, Marine Corps and Air Force — including peacekeeping missions and terrorism — have prompted worries about whether the Pentagon has the troops, budget, training and equipment it needs. Defense spending has increased about 70 percent since the Sept. 11, 2001, terrorist attacks on the United States but dropped 16 percent between fiscal 2010 and fiscal 2016.[6]

Army Chief of Staff Gen. Mark Milley told a House Armed Services Committee hearing last year that he had "grave concerns" about whether his forces were prepared to fight a major power such as China or Russia.[7]

Other military leaders say the high priority given to fighting terrorism has hurt the armed forces' readiness for a conventional war. "While we are primarily focused on the threat of violent extremism, our adversaries and our potential adversaries have developed . . . approaches specifically designed to limit our ability to project power," Marine Gen. Joe Dunford, chairman of the Joint Chiefs of Staff, told the committee in June.[8]

Traditionally, U.S. officials and scholars often have defined military readiness as the ability to fight two major wars in different parts of the world at the same time. After the Cold War, some defined it as "two-and-a-half" wars, or two wars sequentially rather than simultaneously. Today, many experts disagree on the definition.

"Readiness is a term that's thrown around a lot lately," says Susanna Blume, a former deputy chief of staff for programs and plans at the Defense Department and now a defense strategy fellow at the Center for a New American Security, a Washington think tank focused on national security issues. "It means a lot of different things to a lot of different people."

In the strictest sense, readiness refers to the ability of each military unit "to execute anticipated tasks for which that unit has been designed," says Michael O'Hanlon, a senior fellow at the Brookings Institution think tank in Washington. He says fears that the U.S. military is facing a readiness "crisis" focus on the most immediate challenges, distracting from the need to modernize and innovate to prepare for future threats.

In Washington, discussions of military preparedness focus heavily on troop strength and budgets. The Pentagon's current budget of about $586 billion pays for more than 1.3 million active-duty troops, including 450,000 deployed overseas. The largest numbers are in Afghanistan (about 11,000) and Kuwait (about 15,000).

U.S. military assets include:

- About 274 Navy ships, submarines and aircraft carriers.
- About 5,400 manned and unmanned aircraft, including 1,303 fighter jets.
- More than 2,800 tanks.

- About 1,650 nuclear warheads deployed on ballistic missiles and bombers, and about 180 tactical nuclear weapons at bases in Germany, Belgium, the Netherlands, Italy and Turkey.[9]

Some defense analysts say the U.S. military needs to be bigger to deal with growing global demands. Other experts say long-term investments in training and modernizing equipment and technology are more important than increasing troop strength. Some helicopters and other equipment used by the Army are decades out of date.

Getting equipment to troops quickly also aids military readiness, but years-long delays, waste and fraud have hampered the Defense Department's procurement process, according to studies. The Government Accountability Office (GAO) reported in 2009 that only 20 percent of the largest Defense Department programs had been completed on deadline and within budget.[10]

Such delays are not always the Pentagon's fault, some defense analysts say. They note that many defense projects are highly complex and receive lengthy vetting by members of Congress, who compete to place — and preserve — those projects in their districts as a way to boost employment.

President Trump has proposed giving the Pentagon $639.1 billion in fiscal 2018 (which began Oct. 1), but GOP defense hawks on Capitol Hill say that is not enough. That amount includes $64.6 billion for "contingency" war-related operations such as the current missions in Iraq and Afghanistan.[11]

Trump's proposal is about $59 billion — or 10 percent — more than the $580.3 billion the Pentagon received in fiscal 2016. It also is about $52 billion over budget caps that Congress imposed in 2011 to rein in federal spending as part of a process of automatic spending cuts known as sequestration. Many Republicans say the caps have forced Pentagon officials to make damaging cuts to defense programs.[12]

"How the budget was shaped over the years . . . has had an effect on our readiness," says James Jeffrey, a former U.S. ambassador to Turkey and Iraq. He says budget tightening, combined with a continued focus on "region building" in Iraq and Afghanistan, limited military officials' ability to plan and acquire upgraded combat fighting vehicles, jets, helicopters and other equipment.

Trump Seeks Increase in Military Spending

President Trump has proposed giving the Defense Department about $639 billion in fiscal 2018, a 10 percent increase from fiscal 2016. Among the three major branches, the Air Force would receive the largest amount — $183 billion (left). Operations and maintenance for all branches would get about $272 billion (right).

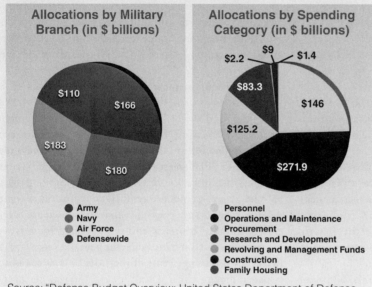

Allocations by Military Branch (in $ billions)

$110
$166
$183
$180

- Army
- Navy
- Air Force
- Defensewide

Allocations by Spending Category (in $ billions)

$2.2 $9 $1.4
$83.3 $146
$125.2
$271.9

- Personnel
- Operations and Maintenance
- Procurement
- Research and Development
- Revolving and Management Funds
- Construction
- Family Housing

Source: "Defense Budget Overview: United States Department of Defense Fiscal Year 2018 Budget Request," Office of the Under Secretary of Defense (Comptroller), May 2017, p. A-4, https://tinyurl.com/y8p3wzbu

Pentagon officials are especially irritated by Congress' practice of funding government operations, including defense programs, through stopgap spending bills called continuing resolutions (CR).

David Norquist, the Pentagon's comptroller and chief financial officer, said in September that officials have had to postpone training and hiring and forgo ship maintenance as a result of uncertainty over funding.[13]

The U.S. military also responds to humanitarian crises, including the recent hurricanes that devastated Puerto Rico. Responding to such emergencies is expected to become more challenging as climate change contributes to more natural disasters, potentially sparking international conflicts over fresh water, food and other resources.[14]

Defense spending in recent years peaked in fiscal 2010 at $691 billion, and Trump's proposal would not bring it up to that level. Some of the country's potential adversaries, meanwhile, have stepped up their military outlays and activities.[15]

China's defense spending increased 26 percent between 2013 and 2016. In addition, since 2014, China has built 3,200 acres of military bases on artificial islands in the South China Sea that U.S. officials say are part of Beijing's plan to dominate Asia.[16]

Russia's military also has become increasingly aggressive, raising alarms among NATO countries in Europe that the United States is pledged to protect under Article 5 of the organization's charter. In September, Russia conducted its largest military exercise in recent history in an area that included the Arctic, the Far East, the Black Sea and Russia's border with Ukraine. The exercise involved tens of thousands of troops, along with warships, submarines, fighter jets, helicopters, tanks, artillery, anti-ship missiles, intercontinental ballistic missiles and swarms of drones.[17]

Another U.S. foe, Iran, says it has increased domestic weapons production 69 percent in the last three years. In January, it conducted its 10th ballistic missile test in two years, raising concerns that it had violated a 2015 agreement with the United States and other world powers to limit its nuclear program in exchange for relief from economic sanctions. According to military reports, 36 U.S. military bases overseas are within range of Iran's missiles.[18]

Joint Chiefs Chairman Dunford last year identified Russia, China, Iran and North Korea, along with Islamic extremism, as the country's top military threats.[19]

But none of those countries matches the United States in military might, analysts say. China, for example, is at low manpower levels, and troops have not faced sustained combat since the Vietnam War and are weak on training, coordination and logistics, according to the Congressional Research Service (CRS), the research arm of Congress.[20]

As the debate about U.S. military readiness continues, here are some of the questions that policymakers and defense experts are asking:

Is the U.S. military too small?

President Trump announced in January that he wanted to oversee "a great rebuilding" of the U.S. military, detailing plans for 540,000 Army troops, 350 Navy ships and a modernized nuclear arsenal.

Pentagon officials and congressional Republicans praised the proposal, although they said it could take years to rebuild the military to something close to Cold War levels, when the Army had more than 750,000 active-duty troops.

That number decreased to about 480,000 during the 1990s, rose after the 2001 terrorist attacks and dropped again beginning in 2011. The Army had 475,000 troops on active duty in fiscal 2016.[21]

As troop numbers have declined, however, their quality has improved, said Steven Kosiak, an adjunct senior fellow at the Center for a New American Security. Higher spending on military health care and veterans' benefits has attracted more high-quality recruits as measured by "education, aptitude and level of experience," he said.[22]

But demands on U.S. soldiers are increasing, which means troop strength also should increase, some defense experts say.

Since the end of the Cold War, "the range of potential conflicts we have to be ready for has grown exponentially," says Todd Harrison, director of defense budget analysis at the Center for Strategic and International Studies, a Washington think tank that researches national security and other issues.

In addition to conducting counterterrorism operations, today's soldiers must be ready to fight "old-fashioned" conventional wars in places such as North Korea, while also preparing for a potential cyberwar, says James F. Cunningham, a former senior research associate at the American Enterprise Institute, a conservative think tank in Washington.

Yet keeping a full brigade trained and ready is difficult when troops constantly rotate out for home leave or are lost through attrition, Cunningham says. "What we have right now is not sufficient," he says.

Dan Goure, senior vice president of the Lexington Institute, a conservative think tank in Virginia focused on national security and other issues, said today's military "is too small, with too few technological advantages and facing too many threats."

"There is now a very real possibility that in a future conflict . . . U.S. forces could suffer such high casualties that regardless of the outcome, this country will lack the capabilities needed to deal with any other major contingency," Goure said.[23]

The National Commission on the Future of the Army, created by Congress in 2015 to determine how many active-duty and reserve troops the Army needed, concluded that 980,000 — a slightly smaller number than is currently deployed — would be just enough to meet near-term obligations "with an acceptable level of national risk."

Commission members also noted that budget cuts had forced Army officials to make "many significant trade-offs," including canceling combat training rotations, laying off civilians and deploying regular Army units in lieu of reserve units. By fiscal 2015, budget reductions also had cut the number of active-duty Army air personnel to its lowest level since 1947.[24]

More recently, the Air Force has struggled to compete with commercial airlines for pilots, Lt. Gen. Gina Grosso, deputy chief of staff for manpower, personnel and services for the Air Force, said in March. The branch ended fiscal 2016 short 1,555 pilots, including 1,211 fighter pilots.[25]

Harrison describes the armed forces' current resources as "constrained," and O'Hanlon at the Brookings Institution says the size of the military is "barely sufficient" and should be increased slightly. He also believes the Pentagon needs to set clearer priorities.

Joseph J. Collins, director of the Center for Complex Operations at the National Defense University in Washington, D.C., agrees, saying clearer priorities are even more important than expanding troop strength. "Are we going to face the most intense threats or the most probable?" asks Collins, who served as deputy assistant secretary of Defense for stability operations during the Obama administration.

Goldstein at the Naval War College also cites Pentagon priorities as a problem area, saying Special Forces and military pilots are used so often for expensive counterterrorism operations that they are not getting enough training time for other types of combat.

An F-35 Joint Strike Fighter jet is readied for a training mission at Hill Air Force Base in Ogden, Utah, on March 15, 2017. Problems with the F-35 reflect the Pentagon's difficulty in accurately estimating the cost of new weapons systems and making sure they are delivered on time and within budget. The F-35 program is nearly a decade behind schedule and is expected to cost about $406 billion for 2,456 planes, more than double its original price tag.

In the Navy, commanders have "extended deployments; increased operational tempos; and shortened, eliminated, or deferred training and maintenance," according to a 2015 GAO report.[26]

In January, Milley, the Army chief of staff, said spending more money modernizing equipment and technology is more important for military readiness than increasing the size of the armed forces.[27]

Harrison agrees. "A larger military and a larger budget will not necessarily make us strong or safer," he said. "The competition is much more about technology and how well you can deploy the technology."[28]

Does the procurement process undermine readiness?

The F-35 Joint Strike Fighter was designed to do virtually anything the Pentagon desired, serving the Air Force, Marine Corps and Navy and replacing the aging F-18 Hornet and Super Hornet. But the program, which began in 2001, has been plagued with delays and technical problems.[29]

The first four Lockheed Martin-built jets, which cost a combined $400 million, could not launch air-to-air missiles because their wings were too weak. They also lacked a functioning gun and would suddenly roll when flying below the speed of sound.[30]

The F-35 program is now nearly a decade behind schedule and is expected to cost about $406.5 billion for 2,456 planes, more than double its original price tag. It is just one example of the Pentagon's spotty record of accurately estimating the cost of new weapons systems and making sure they are delivered on time and within budget. Other examples include Gerald R. Ford-class supercarriers, Zumwalt-class destroyers and littoral combat ships, which are light frigates designed to transport Special Forces on anti-terrorism missions.[31]

The Defense Department "pays more than anticipated, can buy less than expected, and, in some cases, delivers less capability to the warfighter," the GAO reported in February. And a 2014 report from the Congressional Research Service cited criticisms by defense analysts that Pentagon cost overruns and schedule delays "have a debilitating effect on the nation's military and threaten America's technological advantage and military capabilities." The CRS report also noted the Defense Department's efforts to reform its acquisition process "have failed to rein in cost and schedule growth."[32]

Such criticisms, however, overlook the fact that defense projects are highly complex and require thorough vetting by Congress, some defense experts say. "Is it fair to question, how long did it take Boeing to build the 787?" asks Alan Estevez, who once handled acquisition duties at the Defense Department and is now an executive at defense contractor Deloitte Consulting.

In addition, the Center for a New American Security's Blume says military projects involve "all kinds of security considerations" that typically are not a factor in non-military projects.

Since 1959, 17 Defense secretaries have pledged to fix the Pentagon's procurement process, but none succeeded, Harvard Business School professor J. Ronald Fox said in 2010.[33]

Part of the problem is that the Defense Department does a poor job monitoring the production line from beginning to end, says Laura Junor, director for research and strategic studies at the National Defense University in Washington. Managing readiness for war involves ensuring certain equipment is ready and can be sustained throughout the forces, she says. But the department will focus only on preparing equipment for units immediately deploying — not those that aren't scheduled to deploy.

The Marine Corps' F/A-18C Squadron, for example, will look ready when it deploys on Navy aircraft carriers before the end of the year, Junor says, "but that belies the fact that the Navy depots cannot produce enough working F/A-18s . . . to keep [squadrons] as trained as they should be."

Other examples of supply problems include a satellite communications system designed by Lockheed Martin for the Navy, says Brian Weeden, a former Air Force officer and a technical adviser at the Secure World Foundation in Colorado, which advocates for the peaceful use of outer space. The satellites are in orbit but could be outdated by the time the computers they will link with are installed on ships, submarines and tanks, he says.

"Part of it is timeline," Weeden says. "There is a year or two of debating warfare requirements, then a couple years to debate a contract, then build it, then to get it out takes another decade. . . . In that decade, technology hasn't stood still, and today's threat hasn't stood still."

Scharre at the Center for a New American Security says 20-to-30-year procurement cycles impede the Defense Department's ability to purchase "fast-developing technology," particularly computer technology.

Congress is another source of delays, partly because lawmakers are reluctant to abandon projects that produce jobs in their districts. Members of Congress from Missouri, for instance, have long pushed for funding Super Hornet fighter jets, largely made at a Boeing facility in St. Louis.[34]

"There seems to be some sort of push to make sure suppliers come from as many states in the union as possible," says Collins at National Defense University. "So once we get big-ticket items on the plate we can't get rid of them."

Blume, the defense strategy fellow, notes that the defense procurement process can move quickly when it has to. In May 2007, for example, then-Defense Secretary Robert Gates put a high priority on acquiring

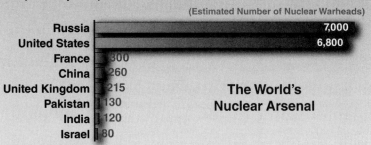

Russia and U.S. Hold Largest Nuclear Arsenals

The estimated 14,905 operational nuclear warheads around the world are held by only eight countries. Russia has the most, with 7,000, followed closely by the United States. The numbers include retired warheads that are still intact. North Korea has produced fissile material for 10 to 20 nuclear warheads but is not thought to have stockpiled any weapons.

(Estimated Number of Nuclear Warheads)

	The World's Nuclear Arsenal
Russia	7,000
United States	6,800
France	300
China	260
United Kingdom	215
Pakistan	130
India	120
Israel	80

Source: Martin Armstrong, "The Countries Holding the World's Nuclear Arsenal," Statista, Feb. 28, 2017, https://tinyurl.com/y87xc6rj

Mine Resistant, Ambush Protected (MRAP) vehicles to replace Humvees to better protect U.S. troops in Iraq and Afghanistan from roadside bombs. Congress immediately authorized $4 billion, and troops in Iraq were training on the new vehicles by November. Six months later, 3,000 MRAPs were in service in Iraq, and deaths from improvised explosive devices were dropping.[35]

"That's a bit of a success story, in that we were able to move quickly and adapt the process to move materials to the field faster," Blume says.

Is the military adequately modernizing its technology?

Navy officials are investigating whether foreign cyberattacks caused the recent collisions involving the *USS John S. McCain* and the *USS Fitzgerald* in the western Pacific. Technology experts consider that unlikely, but North Korea, China, and Russia have been known to jam navigation systems.[36]

All three countries also have demonstrated they are willing to hack into private-sector computers in the United States and elsewhere to gain a military or political advantage.[37]

In 2015, former Joint Chiefs of Staff Chairman Martin Dempsey said the United States does not have an edge in cyberwarfare, calling it instead a "level playing field."[38]

The Army's 1st Stryker Brigade Combat Team participates in jungle warfare training at Schofield Barracks in Honolulu on March 1, 2017. The Pentagon's current budget pays for more than 1.3 million active-duty troops, including 450,000 deployed overseas. Some analysts say the U.S. military is too small to deal with growing global demands, but others say long-term investments in training and modern equipment are more important than increasing troop strength.

In March, Air Force Lt. Gen. William J. Bender, chief information officer at the Air Force secretary's office, said the military hopes to make more rapid advances in information technology and data analysis by teaming up with academics and experts in the private sector.[39]

Pentagon officials have been slow to modernize other military technology as well, Rep. Mike Rogers, R-Ala., then-chairman of the House Armed Services Subcommittee on Strategic Forces, said last year. He pointed to the military's continued use of Vietnam-era Huey helicopters to protect intercontinental missile launch facilities around Air Force bases in the northern Great Plains, leaving the nuclear missiles potentially vulnerable to terrorist attack. Congress and the Pentagon delayed a program to replace the helicopters and redirected funds to counterterrorism fights.[40]

Other Army equipment, including some vehicles, was designed in the 1970s and purchased in the 1980s and needs to be replaced, says Jeffrey, the former ambassador to Turkey and Iraq, now a fellow at the Washington Institute for Near East Policy, a foreign policy think tank in Washington.

Meanwhile, Iran, North Korea, China and Russia are developing advanced weapons to challenge U.S. military dominance, including "anti-access area denial" systems that prevent enemy troops from deploying in a particular area and reduce their movement if they make it inside. Such weapons include anti-ship cruise missiles (ASCMs), short- and medium-range ballistic missiles and cruise missiles.[41]

"There's a real concern about the readiness of the Navy, Marine Corps and the Air Force to take on these systems," Jeffrey says.

China and Russia have surpassed the United States in developing anti-ship cruise missiles, according to Goldstein of the Naval War College. "If you put our best ASCM against China's, ours loses hands down," he says. "It's slower, it does not go as far, it doesn't have the kill maneuvers." Russia has an even better ASCM, he says.

"It's like going into a fistfight with someone who has a knife or a gun," Goldstein says.

Artificial intelligence (AI) represents another area where China is investing heavily to deny the United States and other adversaries an advantage. Officials in Beijing said in July they plan to spend billions of dollars to make China a world leader in AI by 2025 through collaboration among military, industry and research groups.[42]

However, in most areas of military technology, including fighter jets, China lags behind the United States, according to Scharre at the Center for a New American Security and other defense experts.

Apart from land-based and submarine-launched missiles, "no Chinese capabilities come close to surpassing those of the U.S.," said Thomas Christensen, director of the China and the World Program at Princeton University. He said that includes cyber capabilities.[43]

Weeden at the Secure World Foundation says China is only just now rolling out technology such as GPS intelligence satellites, which troops use to communicate and to spy on enemy forces. The United States put such satellites into orbit decades ago.

"The perception is they are moving very, very fast," Weeden says of the Chinese. "But that does not mean they're passing us. . . . They've got a long ways to go."

Pentagon officials are working to make sure the United States stays ahead in drone warfare. In October 2016, they dropped more than 100 micro-drones over China Lake, Calif., in the world's largest test of how such devices communicate with each other as part of a swarm, and how they would perform in a military attack.[44]

The Army also used advanced electronic warfare technology to disable "enemy" tanks during a simulation at the Army National Training Center at Fort Irwin, Calif., earlier this year. The exercise used technology to jam the tanks' communications and hack into their computers, forcing the troops inside to stop and get out.[45]

Scharre, author of *Army of None: Autonomous Weapons and the Future of War*, scheduled for release next year, says the Pentagon is working to develop intelligent machines, including unmanned vehicles that will detect enemy threats and make decisions on how to respond. The military also is equipping some aircraft with automatic ground collision avoidance systems that take over control of a plane about to crash.[46]

Scharre says defense officials need to move faster to take advantage of innovation in the private sector, but that has not always gone well. Some companies, including Silicon Valley software startup Palantir, say the Defense Department improperly favors its largest clients when awarding lucrative contracts. In June last year, Palantir sued Pentagon officials, alleging they barred the company from receiving a $206 million contract. In April, federal officials asked an appeals court to overturn an earlier ruling saying the Army unlawfully refused to consider Palantir's bid.[47]

The Center for a New American Security's Blume acknowledges that military officials have room to improve in making it easier for startups to win government contracts. "There's a lot of red tape, lots of steps, lots of hurdles," she says.

BACKGROUND

Early Problems

English colonists in North America relied on part-time militias, their own martial prowess and occasional help from Britain's army and navy for protection against Indians and French and Spanish forces. When disputes with Parliament and King George III over taxation led to war in April 1775, the colonists lacked the troops, guns, cannons, ships and other military matériel needed for sustained combat operations.

In June 1775, the Continental Congress authorized formation of a full-time army to be commanded by George Washington of Virginia. Congress, however, lacked taxing powers and relied on the newly declared 13 states for troops and supplies.

Washington struggled to keep the Continental Army in the field over the next eight years, ultimately fighting a defensive war.[48]

In 1783, the Treaty of Paris ended the war and assured the United States its independence. But wartime memories of ill-clad soldiers freezing at Valley Forge and going into battle short of ammunition contributed to the belief that the fledgling United States needed a stronger central government with taxing powers. In 1787, the Founders crafted the U.S. Constitution, giving Congress the power to "raise and support Armies." At the time, the Army had about 800 men, including officers.[49] In subsequent decades, the United States repeatedly found itself unprepared for war. When war came — with Britain in 1812, the Mexican-American War in 1846 and the Civil War — the government scrambled to build a large professional fighting force.[50]

During the Civil War, the industrialized North had a larger population and greater economic resources than the agricultural South and was able to field a large and well-equipped military. But the South's military leadership proved superior, and Union forces suffered defeat after defeat through 1863 before eventually turning the tide. In late 1864, the Confederacy was running short of troops, guns, ammunition and other supplies, and its armies surrendered in 1865.

After the war, the U.S. decommissioned most of its army and navy, keeping small numbers of troops in the West to fight the Indian wars. As the U.S. economy expanded in the late 19th century, the nation moved closer to taking a prominent military role globally.

When the Spanish-American War started in April 1898 in Cuba, the U.S. government again mobilized men faster than it could equip them. Less than one-fifth of the nearly 275,000 men mobilized saw combat before the war ended in August. Many who did see action carried obsolete rifles and sweltered in winter uniforms in the Caribbean heat. And they lacked sufficient "wagons, harnesses, tents, camp equipment, and medical supplies," according to military historian James A. Huston.[51]

Nevertheless, by the end of the war, the United States had become a world power.

Wartime Expansion

President Theodore Roosevelt continued to build a navy to challenge those of Great Britain, France and Russia, and particularly to manage increasing tensions with Japan, which dreamed of a Pacific empire after defeating Russia in 1903.[52]

Between 1907 and 1909, Roosevelt sent 16 battleships and accompanying vessels, called the "Great White Fleet," on a 14-month voyage around the world to display U.S. naval power. The fleet, carrying 14,000 sailors and Marines, stopped at 20 ports on six continents.[53]

By then, U.S. shipbuilders could produce 15,000-ton battleships armed with eight-inch guns, and the airplane industry was about to emerge.[54] When the United States declared war on Germany in 1917 during World War I, the Army had fewer than 122,000 enlisted men and 6,000 officers, and one-third of those officers had less than a year of service. The National Guard had about 175,000 officers and enlisted men, less than 40 percent of its authorized strength.

President Woodrow Wilson signed the Selective Service Act on May 18, 1917, which eventually increased the Army to 500,000 troops. But because of the time needed to train, arm and deploy troops across the Atlantic, only one Army division made it to the war's front lines before 1918.[55]

Equipment and munitions production sputtered initially before picking up and overwhelming railroads. Supplies filled East Coast warehouses because the military did not have enough ships to ferry cargo across the Atlantic. The first squadron of U.S. planes did not fly over the Western front in France until August 1918, just three months before the war ended.[56]

Similar problems hampered the U.S. military as it entered World War II. Between November 1939 and June 1940, U.S. active-duty manpower increased by a third and continued to grow rapidly in the months before the country entered the war in December 1941, said Richard K. Betts, a professor of war and peace studies at Columbia University in New York.

Historian Huston said, however, that men "trained with sticks for guns when they might better have remained in shops and factories for another year or two to help produce the weapons and equipment they would need."[57]

On Dec. 7, 1941, after Japanese planes attacked the U.S. naval base at Pearl Harbor, President Franklin D. Roosevelt declared war against Japan, and, days later, against Germany. Within a week of Pearl Harbor, the United States mobilized 130,000 troops in the Philippines, including Filipino troops, to defend the islands against a Japanese invasion.[58]

Half of the U.S. fighter pilots dispatched to protect Clark Field in the Philippines the next day aborted their missions when engine oil shot over their planes' windscreens. Many B-17 bombers did not have tail guns and armor, and crews lacked gunnery training. By Christmas, only a half-dozen U.S. heavy bombers were still in commission in the southwest Pacific.[59]

But as the United States shifted to a wartime footing and began to churn out planes, tanks and other supplies, the nation's economic and military might turned the tide against the Axis powers. Meanwhile, U.S. scientists developed an atomic weapon, which they tested in July 1945 after Germany's defeat. President Harry S. Truman, hoping to avoid the massive casualties that would result if Allied forces invaded Japan, in August ordered two atomic bombs dropped on Hiroshima and Nagasaki. The bombs destroyed both cities, killing tens of thousands of Japanese, and Japan quickly surrendered.[60]

More than 1.2 million officers and nearly 10.8 million enlisted men were on active duty in the U.S. armed forces at the end of the war. Within a year, two-thirds of the officers and three-fourths of the enlisted men had returned to civilian life.[61]

By 1947, military spending had dropped to $10 billion from $83 billion in 1945. In 1949, as tensions with the Soviet Union rose and the Cold War got underway, Truman committed the United States to joining a new Western defense alliance, the North Atlantic Treaty Organization (NATO).[62]

Constant Readiness

After the Japanese surrender, the Soviet Union and the United States temporarily divided responsibility for Korea along the 38th parallel. The United States maintained a small force nearby in Japan and assumed communist forces would remain north of the dividing line.[63]

Instead, North Korea invaded South Korea on June 25, 1950. President Truman provided U.S. air support for South Korea, but it was insufficient. With backing from

CHRONOLOGY

1900s–1940s *U.S. defense spending and troop strength fluctuate.*

1907 President Theodore Roosevelt sends "Great White Fleet" of U.S. battleships around the world on a 14-month display of naval power.

1917 U.S. enters World War I. . . . President Woodrow Wilson signs the Selective Service Act requiring eligible men to sign up for military duty.

1941 Japanese planes bomb the U.S. naval base at Pearl Harbor. . . . U.S. enters World War II with a large number of troops but insufficient equipment. . . . Sen. Harry Truman, D-Mo., launches investigation into waste and fraud in defense contracts related to war production.

1945 At war's end, military spending is $85 billion and troop strength estimated at 12 million. . . . U.S. drops atomic bombs on Japan, ending World War II.

1947 Cold War with the Soviet Union begins as U.S. works to contain communism. . . . Annual military spending is $10 billion and the number of troops is estimated at 1.5 million.

1949 U.S. joins North Atlantic Treaty Organization, pledging to defend Allies against Soviet aggression.

1950s–1980s *U.S. military fights communist threat.*

1950 Communist North Korea invades South Korea, triggering Korean War.

1953 President Dwight D. Eisenhower emphasizes importance of nuclear firepower over troop size, reduces Army.

1961 President John F. Kennedy boosts defense budget, expands size of armed forces.

1965 U.S. forces in South Vietnam are ill-prepared for guerrilla combat and suffer severe losses against Viet Cong. . . . In January 1973, U.S. and North Vietnam sign peace agreement; U.S. troops pull out in April.

1980 U.S. military helicopters crash in failed mission to rescue hostages in Iran, prompting concerns about military readiness.

1981 President Ronald Reagan pursues largest peacetime buildup of military in U.S. history.

1989 Berlin Wall falls, signaling end of Cold War and making U.S. military readiness less urgent.

1990s–Present *Military spending fluctuates.*

1991 U.S. troops liberate Kuwait after Iraqi invasion, boosting confidence in U.S. military readiness.

1993 Clinton administration cuts military personnel; troop strength falls about 19 percent over next eight years.

Sept. 11, 2001 Islamist terrorists crash hijacked planes into World Trade Center and Pentagon. . . . Invasion of Afghanistan begins longest war in U.S. history. . . . Defense spending increases under George W. Bush administration.

2007 Bush submits largest defense budget since Reagan era.

2011 Defense Secretary Robert Gates warns that congressionally mandated caps on defense spending will lead to "hollow force."

2014 U.S. Navy increases patrols in South China Sea after China builds military bases on artificial islands there.

2015 U.S. officials identify cyberattacks and climate change as urgent national security threats.

2016 Defense Department conducts world's largest drone swarm test over China Lake, Calif.

2017 President Trump orders review of nuclear arsenal, proposes 10 percent boost in defense budget. . . . North Korean leader Kim Jong Un and Trump exchange nuclear threats. . . . Navy's readiness questioned after collisions and other accidents. . . . Russia conducts its largest modern military exercise along its western border. . . . Iran conducts ballistic missile tests, potentially violating international agreement aimed at curbing Tehran's nuclear weapons program.

Military Girds for War in Space

U.S. satellites are "highly vulnerable to attack."

With China and Russia rapidly developing the ability to fight in space, the U.S. military's challenges are extending into the cosmos, defense experts say.

The capabilities of the two rivals likely include jamming satellite communications or potentially using a so-called kinetic weapon to destroy satellites, National Intelligence Director Daniel Coats said in May. The Russian military is possibly building an "aircraft-launched missile capable of destroying satellites in low-Earth orbit," he added.[1]

The U.S. military and national security establishment are debating the seriousness of the threats and the steps the Pentagon should take to counter them. The United States is "still a long way ahead" in space defense, although "the Chinese are coming up very fast," says Lyle Goldstein, an associate professor in China maritime studies at the Naval War College in Newport, R.I.

National Security Adviser H.R. McMaster in early October announced he had begun a review that, among other things, aims to deter and defeat adversaries in space and partner with commercial companies to develop space technologies.[2]

The Air Force, meanwhile, plans to appoint a general to act as a "space czar" for that military branch, which has primary oversight of the Pentagon's space activities and is readying other changes designed to protect satellites and spacecraft from cyberattack and enemy missiles.[3]

The Senate blocked a proposal to create a military branch focused on space, which passed the House in July as part of a defense spending bill. Military leaders and the White House opposed a Space Corps as premature and potentially wasteful of resources because it would duplicate much of what the Air Force is already doing.[4]

The U.S. military for decades has used satellites to monitor hostile nations and help direct conventional forces. But Russia and China, defense experts say, are advancing their space capabilities to destroy those satellites, cripple U.S. military operations worldwide and weaken the nation's defenses.

The Center for Strategic and International Studies, a Washington think tank focused on national security issues, on Oct. 3 released a study warning of the potential for a space war that is "more diverse, disruptive, disordered and dangerous" than the space race initiated in 1957 when the Soviet Union launched the first satellite, *Sputnik 1.*[5]

A space war is possible in the near future, and the United States must boost its defense capabilities, says Brian Weeden, a former Air Force officer and a technical adviser for the Secure World Foundation, a Washington nonprofit focused on preventing the militarization of space.

Nearly 1,500 military and civilian satellites orbit the Earth; the United States has 593, while China operates 192 and Russia 135. North Korea in February put its second satellite into orbit.[6]

The U.S. military relies on satellite communications to operate drone aircraft and precision-guided munitions as well as to conduct battlefield reconnaissance. "There is no [sector] of national security that doesn't involve space," Weeden says. "The U.S. is highly dependent on its space systems, and they are highly vulnerable to attack."

Russia tested what national security officials believe was an anti-satellite weapon in December, although it did not hit a target. In May 2014, China launched a rocket which its military said later was to research the magnetic field surrounding the Earth known as the magnetosphere. Weeden found evidence the rocket was designed to launch a "kinetic kill vehicle" that could destroy enemy satellites in high orbits.[7]

Dean Cheng, a senior research fellow at the conservative Heritage Foundation think tank in Washington, said,

the United Nations, the United States committed ground troops and regained the initiative under U.S. Gen. Douglas MacArthur until China intervened in the conflict in late 1950. The war then degenerated into a stalemate that lasted until 1953, when the combatants agreed to an armistice.[64]

After 1950, the United States emphasized a strong defense to contain the communist threat overseas. Over the next three years, the defense budget tripled, and large numbers of troops were deployed to Europe. By then, the Soviets had developed an atomic weapon, and a nuclear arms race began. Readiness had become, in U.S. military

"Chinese military writings emphasize the importance of establishing space dominance . . . as the key to winning future wars."[8]

Even while developing their own anti-satellite systems, Russia and China since 2008 have urged the United Nations to adopt a treaty that would ban the use of weapons in space. The United States opposes the treaty, Weeden says, because "it doesn't address any of the problems" about a space war, such as barring lasers or other ground-based anti-satellite weapons.

Meanwhile, the military continues to rely heavily on satellites, with several programs underway to provide more-secure communications for military operations. But some of the programs have been delayed or have exceeded budget estimates, leading to concerns about harm to military readiness.

For instance, the Advanced Extremely High Frequency satellite program, designed to provide more-secure communications for the military, launched its satellite three and a half years late, in 2010, and the program's cost exceeded original estimates by at least 118 percent, according to the Government Accountability Office (GAO). Likewise, the Wideband Global SATCOM, a system to provide communication services for the military and its allies, more than tripled in cost from the original estimate of $1.3 billion to $4.3 billion and became operational nine years late.[9]

Rep. Mike Rogers, R-Ala., chairman of the House Armed Services Subcommittee on Strategic Forces, along with ranking member Jim Cooper, D-Tenn., raised an alarm about the problems. "The current system is wasting billions of dollars and failing to deliver capability to the warfighter. Our adversaries have already reorganized their space programs and are reaping the benefits."[10]

— *Christina L. Lyons*

A ground-based interceptor rocket is launched from Vandenberg Air Force Base in California on May 30, 2017. The rocket successfully intercepted and destroyed a target missile in space.

Getty Images/Los Angeles Times/Al Seib

[3] Marcus Weisgerber, "The US Air Force Is Reorganizing to Fight in Space," *Defense One*, April 4, 2017, http://tinyurl.com/ya4n2qth.

[4] Rebecca Khelel, "Top general opposes Space Corps plans," *The Hill*, July 18, 2017, http://tinyurl.com/y7yhw48q.

[5] Todd Harrison, "Escalation and Deterrence in the Second Space Age," Center for Strategic and International Studies, Oct. 3, 2017, http://tinyurl.com/yas9pmxh.

[6] "UCS Satellite Database," Union of Concerned Scientists, http://tinyurl.com/y89xdhu2; Tim Fernholz, "China's secret anti-satellite weapons should be on everyone's radar," *Quartz*, March 19, 2014, http://tinyurl.com/y8epbo6n; and "Controversial Rocket Launch: North Korea successfully places Satellite into Orbit," Spaceflight 101. com, Feb. 7, 2016, http://tinyurl.com/z2jsjvx.

[7] Jim Sciutto, Barbara Starr and Ryan Browne, "Sources: Russia tests anti-satellite weapon," CNN, Dec. 21, 2016, http://tinyurl.com/jn3swxu; Fernholz, op. cit.

[8] Patrick Marshall, "New Space Race," *CQ Researcher*, Aug. 4, 2017, p. 664.

[9] Cristina Chaplain, "Space Acquisitions," statement before Subcommittee on Strategic Forces, Armed Services Committee, May 17, 2017, pp. 2–6, http://tinyurl.com/y8r538ee.

[10] "Rogers/Cooper Weigh In On GPS OCX & FAB-T Programs," press release, Committee on Armed Services, July 31, 2017, http://tinyurl.com/y7v97dcx.

[1] Daniel Coats, "Worldwide Threat Assessment of the U.S. Intelligence Community," statement before Senate Select Committee on Intelligence, May 11, 2017, p. 9, http://tinyurl.com/y7b9mpar.

[2] Colin Clark, "SecAF Wilson Touts 'Offense' Space Weapons; McMaster Details 'Framework,'" *Breaking Defense*, Oct. 6, 2017, http:// tinyurl.com/yc62qubo.

and political circles, an "unquestioned virtue," Columbia University's Betts said. In 1953, President Dwight D. Eisenhower substituted nuclear firepower for force size and reduced Army troop strength over the next eight years.[65]

In 1961, tensions with the Soviets rose over the status of Berlin and the botched Bay of Pigs operation, in which a CIA-backed paramilitary group unsuccessfully invaded Cuba. President John F. Kennedy announced in July he would boost military readiness by requesting an immediate $3.2 billion, increasing the number of Army troops from 875,000 to 1 million, and the Navy and Air Force by 29,000 and 63,000, respectively. Caches of

U.S. Is Modernizing Its Nuclear Arsenal

But experts wonder how President Trump will change Obama-era plan.

With North Korea conducting nuclear tests and Russia rebuilding its military, U.S. efforts to modernize its nuclear arsenal — begun during Barack Obama's presidency — are taking on renewed urgency.

In January, President Trump signed an executive memorandum ordering the Defense Department to undertake a congressionally mandated review of U.S. nuclear capabilities. It is expected to be completed by the end of the year.[1] After the last review, in 2010, Obama authorized a plan, estimated to cost at least $1 trillion over the next decade, to maintain and modernize the nation's nuclear warheads as well as the planes, missiles and submarines that deliver them.[2]

The U.S. nuclear stockpile totals about 6,800 weapons, down from 31,000 in the 1960s. Some 1,650 are deployed on ground-based intercontinental ballistic missiles (ICBMs), submarine-based missiles and bombers. About 2,800 are retired and awaiting dismantlement, and 2,200 are in reserve and not deployed. Another 150 tactical nuclear weapons, designed to strike targets on the battlefield, are at bases in Belgium, Germany, Italy, the Netherlands and Turkey.[3]

But several experts and officials say the U.S. arsenal is old and its reliability unknown since no nuclear tests have occurred since 1992. "We are fast approaching the point where [failing to modernize aging nuclear weaponry] will put at risk our . . . nuclear deterrent," retired Adm. Cecil Haney, who from 2013 to 2016 was commander of the U.S. Strategic Command that oversees the military's nuclear forces, said in January 2016.[4]

In August, the Air Force awarded contracts to Boeing and Northrop Grumman to continue developing the next generation of land-based Minuteman ICBMs. The companies have three years to develop a model, after which the Air Force will choose one company to build the missiles.[5] The Air Force is spending another $1.8 billion on the initial development of a new nuclear-armed cruise missile that would be fired from existing bombers.[6]

But Trump's intentions on the nuclear arsenal are unclear. At a July meeting of national security leaders, Trump reportedly said the United States should enlarge its arsenal nearly tenfold — a statement he has denied making.[7] When the Pentagon completes its review, Trump could ask the Defense Department to move forward in a number of new directions, says Richard Weitz, director and senior fellow at the Center for Political-Military Analysis at the Hudson Institute, a conservative Washington think tank.

The most controversial step would be to call for developing a new nuclear warhead, which critics fear could lead to a new arms race or increase the chances of the weapon being used. Because current nuclear warheads date to the Cold War, new warheads would be safer and more secure, Weitz says, "and provide better protection from cyber and other threats."

"Another potentially controversial decision [the president] might make is to resume testing of nuclear warheads to make sure they work," a move Congress has rejected before, Weitz says. Testing last occurred on Sept. 23, 1992, in Nevada, according to the Arms Control Association, a pro-disarmament group in Washington.[8]

The association has opposed modernization efforts, warning that it will only accelerate the arms race because Russia and China would feel compelled to respond. Russia has about 7,000 nuclear warheads and China has about 270.[9]

Barry Blechman, co-founder of the Stimson Center, a Washington think tank, said conventional military forces are adequate for most threats and that a modernized, and possibly larger, arsenal is unnecessary to deter a nuclear attack on the United States.[10]

Congressional Republicans in 2015 began pushing for modernization in response to reports that Russia was

equipment were stockpiled, including new armored personnel carriers, troop-carrying helicopters, M79 grenade launchers and claymore mines.[66] Kennedy got the Soviet Union to back down in 1962 after Moscow tried to install nuclear missiles in Cuba.

Meanwhile, trouble was brewing in Vietnam, which had been divided along the 17th parallel after the First Indochina War between the French and Viet Minh ended in 1954. Kennedy dispatched military advisers to assist South Vietnam in its fight against the communist-backed North.

rebuilding its capabilities. The State Department has accused Russia of violating the 1987 Intermediate-Range Nuclear Forces Treaty that bans ground-launched nuclear cruise missiles with a range of 310 to 3,410 miles.[11]

North Korea on July 4 launched its first ICBM possibly capable of reaching the United States. On Sept. 3, the country tested a nuclear weapon seven times the size of the two nuclear bombs dropped on Japan in World War II.[12] "They [North Koreans] are advancing rapidly. . . . We don't have a lot of time," Secretary of State Rex Tillerson said on CBS' "Face the Nation" on Sept. 17 in reference to U.S. modernization efforts.[13]

The U.S. military has about 40 long-range missile interceptors, mostly in Alaska and California, designed to shoot down an incoming missile in space and destroy it using kinetic energy — the force of energy created by the motion of the interceptor, Weitz says. But Weitz says the military lacks the ability to shoot down multiple missiles arriving simultaneously.

In May, the military reported it successfully tested an upgraded interceptor missile, which downed a mock intercontinental ballistic missile over the Pacific Ocean.[14]

However, Weitz says the interceptor's reliability remains in doubt. "We're going to have to get the effectiveness of our existing interceptors higher," he says. "And we need to consider having more interceptors, and we need to develop the next-generation systems."

— *Christina L. Lyons*

[1] Jeremy Herb, "Trump order sets military buildup in motion," *Politico*, Jan. 27, 2017, http://tinyurl.com/jxplbkn.

[2] Jon B. Wolfsthal, Jeffrey Lewis and Marc Quint, "The Trillion Dollar Nuclear Triad," James Martin Center for Nonproliferation Studies, January 2014, http://tinyurl.com/y8tylsow; John Wagner and Philip Rucker, "Trump warns N. Korea: U.S. nuclear arsenal is 'more powerful than ever before,'" *The Washington Post*, Aug. 9, 2017, http://tinyurl.com/y8g7v4zr. For background, see William Wanlund, "Modernizing the Nuclear Arsenal," *CQ Researcher*, July 29, 2016, pp. 625–648.

[3] "The dangers of our aging nuclear arsenal," *The Week*, Jan. 17, 2015, http://tinyurl.com/oj8z3dh; Hans M. Kristensen and Robert S. Norris,

"Status of World Nuclear Forces," Federation of American Scientists, 2017, https://tinyurl.com/junbna7; Kingston Reif, "U.S. Nuclear Modernization Program," Arms Control Association, August 2017, http://tinyurl.com/7z7yulu; and Robert S. Norris and Hans M. Kristensen, "U.S. tactical nuclear weapons in Europe, 2011," *Bulletin of the Atomic Scientists*, 2011, http://tinyurl.com/ycuvccqk.

[4] "U.S. Nuclear Weapons Capability," 2017 Index of U.S. Military Strength, http://tinyurl.com/yc85a66w; Adm. Cecil Haney, Remarks, Center for Security and International Studies, Jan. 22, 2016, http://tinyurl.com/y9vla2eo.

[5] Aaron Gregg, "Pentagon narrows competition for next big U.S. nuclear missile deterrent," *The Washington Post*, Aug. 22, 2017, http://tinyurl.com/ybkx8xmz.

[6] David E. Sanger and William J. Broad, "Trump Forges Ahead on Costly Nuclear Overhaul," *The New York Times*, Aug. 27, 2017, http://tinyurl.com/ybc6ywqn; Kyle Mizokami, "America Is Building a New, Stealthy Nuclear Cruise Missile," *Popular Mechanics*, Aug. 24, 2017, http://tinyurl.com/y6v8xa8g.

[7] Aaron Blake, "Trump's loose talk on nuclear weapons suddenly becomes very real," *The Washington Post*, Oct. 11, 2017, http://tinyurl.com/y86lqoj7; President Trump, Twitter post, Oct. 11, 2017, http://tinyurl.com/y9w9ohf5.

[8] "23 September 1992 — Last U.S. Nuclear Test," Preparatory Commission for the Comprehensive Nuclear-Test-Ban Treaty Organization, undated, http://tinyurl.com/yclnbajf.

[9] Kristensen and Norris, op. cit.

[10] Wanlund, op. cit.; Barry Blechman, "A Trillion-Dollar Nuclear Weapon Modernization Is Unnecessary," *The New York Times*, Oct. 26, 2016, http://tinyurl.com/yal6ypxg.

[11] Zachary Keck, "Russia Threatens to Build More Nuclear Weapons," *The National Interest*, May 18, 2015, http://tinyurl.com/yb25asrs; Harvey Day, "Putin says Russia has 'caught up with US missile capabilities' and will respond if America quits Cold War arms treaty," *Daily Mail*, Oct. 19, 2017, http://tinyurl.com/y7zhkpj5.

[12] Choe Sang-Hun, "U.S. Confirms North Korea Fired Intercontinental Ballistic Missile," *The New York Times*, July 4, 2017, http://tinyurl.com/y9jz7s9l; Geoff Brumfiel, "Here Are The Facts About North Korea's Nuclear Test," NPR, Sept. 3, 2017, http://tinyurl.com/yaqgv3k5.

[13] The "Face the Nation" episode can be viewed at http://tinyurl.com/y7qkfgk7.

[14] Barbara Starr and Ryan Browne, "US successfully 'intercepts and destroys' target in missile test," CNN, May 31, 2017, http://tinyurl.com/y7pn6ew4.

By 1965, the United States was sending large numbers of ground troops to Vietnam, but they were ill-prepared for guerrilla combat and found themselves in a protracted war.

They also struggled with equipment problems. The automatic M14 rifle was heavy, difficult to aim and unreliable and was outperformed by the Soviet-made AK47 used by Viet Cong soldiers.[67] The M16 rifle became the focus of public controversy in 1967 when Rep. James J. Howard, D-N.J., read a letter to colleagues written by a Marine who said almost all

South Korea test fires its Hyunmu-2 ballistic missile on Sept. 4, 2017, in response to a nuclear test by North Korea the day before (top). South Korean tanks take part in an exercise on Sept. 6, 2017, near the demilitarized zone (DMZ) separating North and South Korea. The U.S. military has some 23,500 personnel at 83 sites in South Korea, and more than 300 tanks and armored vehicles. Its assets in nearby Japan include dozens of ships and submarines as well as helicopters, tactical fighter jets and surveillance planes. In September, over strong objections from China, the United States finished installing an anti-missile system in South Korea.

the war led to violent clashes in cities and on college campuses, and thousands of U.S. military personnel deserted their posts. The White House, under President Lyndon B. Johnson and then President Richard M. Nixon, repeatedly asserted the war was nearly over, while committing an increasing number of troops to the effort. In January 1973, the United States and North Vietnam concluded a peace agreement; American troops were pulled out in April 1973. By July, Congress eliminated the unpopular draft. Fighting between North and South Vietnam continued until April 30, 1975, when North Vietnamese forces captured Saigon. Ultimately, some 59,000 U.S. troops died in the war.[69]

Defense budgets declined steadily for the next seven years. Army Chief of Staff Edward C. Meyer said in 1980 that the cuts had produced a "hollow Army" and that it would cost more than $40 billion beyond planned expenditures over the next five years to rebuild the force to meet a Soviet threat in Europe and cope with dangers in the Persian Gulf, Korea and Latin America.[70]

By September 1981, the Army reported recruitment was up and readiness was improving. In 1982, President Ronald Reagan proposed increased Air Force manpower and more fighter planes, bombers and new strategic weapons. Congress went along.[71]

Reagan in 1983 undertook the Strategic Defense Initiative, dubbed "Star Wars" by its critics, to develop orbital countermeasures against Soviet intercontinental ballistic missiles. By the end of Reagan's first term, some Americans complained defense spending was nearly 50 percent higher than in 1980 without any evidence readiness had improved.[72]

Americans killed in the battle for Hill 881 had died because their M16s had jammed.[68]

By November 1967, nearly U.S. 500,000 troops were in Vietnam, and 15,058 had been killed and 109,527 wounded. Public protests in the United States against

As the military upgraded its technology, Pentagon officials and military field commanders told Congress in March 1987 that U.S. troops were unprepared for sustained combat. They said funding for new weapons had not left money for ammunition, spare parts or adequate medical care for soldiers wounded in battle.[73]

Fears of the Soviet Union subsided after the Berlin Wall dividing communist-controlled East Germany from democratic West Germany fell on Nov. 10, 1989. Two years later the Soviet Union collapsed, breaking into 15 separate countries. The Cold War was over.[74]

Fluctuating Spending

After Iraq invaded neighboring Kuwait in August 1990, the United States sent a half-million troops with advanced weaponry to the region. In January 1991, U.S. forces unleashed their massive firepower in Operation Desert Storm, defeating Iraq in a matter of weeks while suffering negligible casualties.[75]

The operation left the Pentagon and the public satisfied with U.S. military readiness, and the Clinton administration and Congress looked to use the money saved from the postwar "peace dividend" to pay for tax cuts and other domestic needs.[76]

In 1993, President Bill Clinton proposed reducing U.S. troops by 108,000 (from 1.7 million), retiring 28 Navy warships and cutting the number of Air Force fighter wings from 28 to 24. He recommended spending $88 billion less on defense over the next four years than his predecessor had recommended.

Defense Secretary Les Aspen said the military would maintain forces capable of "fighting and winning two major regional conflicts that occur nearly simultaneously." He added, "We are not going to withdraw from our involvement around the world."[77]

But Sen. John McCain, R-Ariz., said in November 1993 that U.S. forces were "going hollow." Russia, Ukraine and Kazakhstan, he warned, possessed nuclear weapons and Iran, North Korea and Iraq were seeking to develop them.[78]

During a Senate defense appropriations hearing, Army Chief of Staff Gordon R. Sullivan defended the force reductions, which had allowed the military to focus more on modernization. "The information age is upon us, and [we] must take full advantage of the maturation of information processing technology," he said.[79]

Defense budgets continued to drop through the 1990s, and debates over readiness continued as the military repeatedly deployed overseas — for a military intervention in Haiti in 1994, military operations in Bosnia and Kosovo from 1995 to 1998, maintenance of no-fly zones in Iraq beginning in 1993 and humanitarian operations.[80]

On Sept. 11, 2001, the Islamist terrorist group al Qaeda coordinated attacks involving four hijacked passenger airliners. Two crashed into the World Trade Center in New York City, one hit the Pentagon in Virginia and one crashed into a field near Shanksville, Pa. Most Americans said they supported defense spending increases to invade Afghanistan (where al Qaeda was based) in 2001 and Iraq in 2003.

President George W. Bush in March 2003 announced the launch of Operation Iraqi Freedom against the regime of Saddam Hussein, which allegedly had developed nuclear and biological weapons (reports that were later discredited) and had ties to al Qaeda. Bush warned troops would be facing enemies "with no regard for the conventions of war or rules of morality," suggesting a different type of combat than the U.S. armed forces had faced in previous wars. More than 100,000 U.S. troops had been deployed for the attack.[81]

The 21–day invasion sent Saddam and his leaders into hiding, and coalition forces successfully occupied Baghdad, the site of Iraq government. Estimates on the number of civilian casualties in the initial invasion ranged from 3,200 to 7,500, while about 138 U.S. troops were killed between March 20 and May 1.[82]

The U.S. withdrew many troops, but battles continued during the occupation of Baghdad as sectarian violence spread after U.S. forces captured Saddam in December 2003. In 2004, U.S. troops complained about insufficient and aging equipment. Secretary of Defense Donald Rumsfeld said, "You go to war with the Army you have, not the Army you might want or wish to have at a later time."[83]

In 2007, Bush ordered a "surge" that sent 20,000 more soldiers to Iraq, and Congress authorized another $42.3 billion in war funding.[84]

Between fiscal 2001 and fiscal 2008, defense spending increased by more than 60 percent. In 2007, Bush submitted a defense request of $481.4 billion, the highest amount since the Reagan era.[85]

But funding for overseas military operations declined 70 percent from fiscal 2008 to fiscal 2015 as the wars in Iraq and Afghanistan appeared to wind down. The

High-stepping Korean People's Army troops in Pyongyang on April 15, 2017, help mark the 105th anniversary of the birth of the late North Korean leader Kim Il Sung. North Korea has been conducting nuclear tests, and its leader, Kim Jong Un, and President Trump have been exchanging nuclear threats. North Korea's state-run media said on Oct. 19 that the United States will face an "unimaginable" military strike, an apparent response to joint U.S.- South Korean military exercises just off the Korean Peninsula.

sharpest decline — from $671 billion to $619 billion — was in 2013, due to President Barack Obama's decision to withdraw troops from those countries and because of automatic funding cuts under sequestration.[86]

In February 2013, Pentagon leaders said the United States might soon have a "hollowed-out" force if it did not increase funding. Defense Secretary Leon Panetta said the "budget uncertainty could prompt the most significant military readiness crisis in more than a decade."[87]

However, Obama told troops that "the time of deploying large ground forces with big military footprints to engage in nation-building overseas" was coming to an end.[88]

In late 2016, news reports revealed the Pentagon had not disclosed a 2015 study by the Defense Business Board, detailing how it could save $125 billion in wasteful spending over five years at the Pentagon.[89]

CURRENT SITUATION
Military Strategy

Tensions between the United States and North Korea continue to rise as North Korean leader Kim Jong Un and President Trump exchange nuclear threats. In part,

to avoid increasing those tensions, Trump probably will not visit the demilitarized zone (DMZ) between North and South Korea when he travels to Asia in November, a White House official said on Oct. 23. Visiting the DMZ has been standard practice for most U.S. commanders-in-chief since Ronald Reagan's presidency.[90]

North Korea's state-run media said on Oct. 19 the United States will face an "unimaginable" military strike from the communist country at an unexpected time, an apparent response to joint U.S.-South Korean military exercises just off the Korean Peninsula.

Three days later, Trump said the U.S. military is "prepared for anything" if war breaks out with North Korea.[91]

The United States has nearly 40,000 personnel at 112 bases in Japan and 23,500 at 83 sites in South Korea. U.S. military assets in the region include more than 300 tanks and armored vehicles stationed in South Korea; helicopters; tactical fighter jets and surveillance planes; dozens of ships and submarines in Japan, including the *USS Ronald Reagan*, a nuclear-powered aircraft supercarrier. In Guam, more than 3,800 personnel are stationed at Anderson Air Force Base, headquarters for B-52 bombers and fighter jets.[92]

Adm. Harry Harris, who heads U.S. forces in the Pacific, said in August it would be "foolhardy" for foreign adversaries to take this year's Navy accidents as a sign the United States is unprepared to defend itself in the region.

"The U.S. Navy is large, we have a lot of capacity, and we will bring that capacity forward if we need to," Harris said.[93]

Following the collision involving the *McCain*, Richardson, the chief of naval operations, ordered an investigation that he said would "examine the process by which we train and certify our forces . . . to make sure that we're doing everything we can to make them ready for operations and war fighting." Two reports issued by the Navy on Nov. 1 blamed a string of crew, training and navigation errors for the deadly collisions involving the *McCain* and the *USS Fitzgerald*.[94]

In September, over strong objections from China, the United States finished installing an anti-missile system in South Korea known as THAAD (for terminal high altitude area defense). South Korea's new liberal president, Moon Jae-in, initially said he would not allow the final four THAAD launchers to deploy, but he reversed course after North Korea tested an ICBM on July 28.[95]

Also in September, the U.S. and Japanese militaries conducted a joint air exercise over the East China Sea that included two Japanese F-15 fighter jets and two U.S. B1–B bombers.[96]

Recent polling finds mixed opinions on whether the United States should take military action against North Korea in response to Pyongyang's progress toward developing a nuclear missile that could hit this country.

In a CNN poll released in August, 50 percent supported military action. But a CBS News poll found just 29 percent support action, with 60 percent of respondents saying the North Korean threat can be contained in other ways. Gallup says its polls show that support for military action has increased between 2003 and this year — from 47 percent to 58 percent.[97]

At the same time, the Pentagon is working to suppress talk of military readiness failures. Defense Secretary James Mattis, for example, has told defense officials to classify all readiness information. This year's National Military Strategy, typically released to the public and scheduled to be updated by 2018, also will be classified.[98]

Trump was similarly tight-lipped when he announced in August that he would send more troops to Afghanistan but did not specify how many or say what results he expects.[99]

Meanwhile, the Pentagon continues to deal with accidents. In June, the Air Force experienced several accidents in one week that destroyed two F-16 Fighting Falcon fighters and a giant unmanned surveillance drone.[100]

The mishaps have raised questions about pilot training and aircraft maintenance, with top brass blaming tight budgets and an aging fleet.

In August, the Marine Corps ordered all its roughly 1,000 aircraft grounded for 24 hours after two crashes that killed 19 service members. And in September, an explosion at Fort Bragg, N.C., during demolition training killed one soldier and injured seven.[101]

Cunningham, the former American Enterprise Institute research associate, says the Army's 2nd Armored Brigade Combat Team of the 1st Infantry Division struggled to fill positions and find qualified personnel as it prepared to deploy to Germany in September.

Under a new "sustained readiness model" of training, the brigade's leaders retrained their 4,000 troops to handle conventional, combined-arms battles such as those the United States might experience in a war with North

Chinese troops fire a howitzer during exercises at a training base in China's Gansu province on Sept. 24, 2017. The country's defense spending increased 26 percent between 2013 and 2016. Since 2014, China has been constructing artificial islands in the South China Sea and installing military bases there that U.S. officials say are part of Beijing's plan to dominate Asia.

Korea. That marked a break with training that for years focused on counterterrorism.

"It's a product of the concern about being ready to fight for anything," Cunningham says, but added that the brigade had to train with old equipment. "Struggling with a lack of available spare parts and maintenance time, the brigade . . . faces significant equipment readiness shortfalls," the institute concluded in its first report, released in May.[102]

Procurement Fixes

In Washington, the Defense Department is proceeding with congressionally mandated changes to its Office of Acquisition, Technology and Logistics in hopes of streamlining the procurement process.

The plan would divide the undersecretary of acquisitions position into two — an undersecretary for research and engineering and an undersecretary for acquisition and sustainment. The research position would focus on improving innovation and getting new technology to troops on time, the Pentagon's report to Congress said.[103]

Is the U.S. military in a readiness crisis?

YES

Thomas Donnelly
Co-director, Marilyn Ware Center for Security Studies, American Enterprise Institute

Written for *CQ Researcher*, November 2017

To describe the problems in manpower, training and equipment faced by the military as a "crisis," as a kind of institutional heart attack, is to misunderstand the maladies plaguing the armed forces. What makes headlines — particularly events like this year's two collisions at sea that claimed the lives of 17 sailors — is more symptom than disease, the result of a larger wasting sickness that has been developing for decades.

The principal cause of this decline is poor nutrition: Since the end of the Cold War, the Pentagon has lost — even when the wartime costs of Iraq and Afghanistan are included — in excess of $7 trillion in investment. Meanwhile, the ever-hectic pace of military operations exacerbates the effects of a calorie-deprived defense diet. Service leaders have made "do more with less" their mantra, but it is not a prescription for long-term health.

What does diminished readiness mean in practice? Consider the Army's 2nd Brigade, 1st Infantry Division. This past month, the "Dagger Brigade" of the "Big Red One" deployed from Fort Riley, Kan., to Germany and Poland as part of the European Reassurance Initiative, the centerpiece of the U.S. effort to bolster deterrence of an increasingly aggressive Russia. The initiative was designed in President Barack Obama's second term and has been carried forward by the Trump administration, and Congress has supported it with billions of dollars.

Despite being an apparently favored child, the Dagger Brigade lacks about one-fifth of its intended personnel. It treats its equipment — particularly its aging M-1 Abrams tanks — with exquisite tenderness, emphasizing stationary gunnery over field maneuver. The result is reduced training opportunity. Not only is the unit's manpower barely adequate but constant turnover — especially of midgrade noncommissioned officers who serve as crew chiefs and in first-line leadership roles — is crippling to unit cohesion.

Indeed, it is difficult to overemphasize how personnel shortages and mismatches contribute to the military's readiness shortfalls. Even more than curtailed modernization or reduced operations and maintenance funding, it is manpower cutbacks that have most sapped the services' strength. When the Navy lacks sufficient numbers of qualified surface warfare officers, accidents at sea are all but inevitable.

Thus, the remedy for the disease isn't a surgical intervention or a miracle medicine — least of all through annual supplements to starvation-level budgets — but rather a long-term program of nourishment, rehabilitation and restoration.

NO

Michael O'Hanlon
Senior Fellow in Foreign Policy, Brookings Institution

Written for *CQ Researcher*, November 2017

As we begin yet another fiscal year with a stopgap funding measure known as a "continuing resolution" rather than a proper annual budget, Pentagon leaders are understandably frustrated. Such arrangements prevent the Department of Defense from entering multiyear contracts that can save money, interfere with innovation and disrupt training and hiring by leaving planners unsure of what the future holds.

However, these budgetary shenanigans, combined with recent high-profile accidents like last summer's *USS Fitzgerald* and *USS McCain* tragedies, have led numerous officials to wrongly declare a military-readiness crisis. That exaggerates the problem and creates unrealistic expectations of what might be needed, or realistically available, to address it. Pentagon officials need to think of what they can do to mitigate readiness problems by better managing the forces at hand. Numerous options are available:

- The Navy can lighten its busy schedule, allowing sailors more time to train and technicians more time to maintain ships and aircraft, by modifying its operations abroad. Rather than having 100 ships out of a fleet of less than 300 at sea at a time, it can scale back by 10 to 25 percent. It can allow some gaps in forward presence rather than slavishly insisting on maintaining continuous operations in both the Persian Gulf and Pacific fleets. It also can use "crew swaps" more often, keeping surface combatants deployed abroad for one to two years at a time and rotating crews to them by airplane.
- The Air Force can alleviate strain on the Navy's aircraft carriers by stationing more combat aircraft in the Persian Gulf region.
- The Army can permanently base one brigade of combat forces in Korea and another in Poland, rather than maintaining its presence in these countries with unit rotations.
- The Marines can scale back the permanent presence of forces on Okinawa (where they number some 15,000, most on temporary deployment), if Japan would provide more space in ports for prepositioning amphibious U.S. Navy ships. That could allow Marines to fly quickly from California and marry with pre-stationed equipment in a crisis.

Today's military is indeed under strain. But the American armed forces are far from unready, and where they have problems, the defense establishment has many options besides waiting for a big influx of additional dollars.

Pentagon officials say they are turning more to industry for help in developing new technology and speeding production. The Pentagon is exploring strategies "that promise to accelerate development of military products in line with the accelerated evolution of threats," Adam Jay Harrison, a national security research fellow at New York University, said in August.[104]

Debates about military readiness and defense spending, meanwhile, continue among congressional lawmakers and administration officials.

In July, the House passed a bill that would authorize about $696 billion for defense spending in fiscal 2018, including $621.5 billion for core operations and $75 billion in war funding. The Senate approved a version in October that would authorize $700 billion, including $640 billion for core operations. Both bills would exceed spending caps set by the 2011 Budget Control Act, which limits Pentagon spending to $549 billion each year.[105]

Republicans and some Democrats continue to blame the automatic spending cuts required under sequestration for damaging military readiness. However, a proposal by Sen. Tom Cotton, R-Ark., to repeal sequestration failed in the Senate in September.[106]

Meanwhile, the House defeated a proposal by Rep. Scott Perry, R-Pa., that would have barred defense officials from addressing climate change. "We would be remiss in our efforts to protect our national security to not fully account for the risk climate change poses to our bases, our readiness and to the fulfillment of our armed forces' mission," said Rep. Elise Stefanik, R-N.Y., who voted against the proposal.[107]

The Pentagon continues to push to close what it says are uneeded military bases. In 2016, it told Congress that if the Defense Department shuttered 22 percent of its bases, the military could use the $2 billion annual savings on "readiness, modernization and other more pressing national security requirements." But the House and Senate rejected base closing proposals this year. Lawmakers with bases in their districts worry that closing them would damage local economies.[108]

OUTLOOK
Evolving Threats

Assessing U.S. military readiness will be as complex in five years as it is now, says Junor at the National Defense University, "but what I hope is that our ability to monitor and manage it will increase." She says data analysis now allows military leaders to see patterns in production lines that could help make Pentagon procurement more efficient.

Scharre at the Center for a New American Security says the United States is the world's only real global military power. "It can go anywhere it wants to . . . and project a significant amount of military capacity," he says.

But U.S. military leaders still face a constantly evolving array of threats.

Cyberwarfare, for example, "affects everything — the control of weapons, the communications between forces, the speed with which things can be done, the way in which one's support systems can be screwed up," says Betts of Columbia University.

Patrolling the seas will remain crucial to military preparedness, according to retired Navy Adm. James Stavridis, dean of the Fletcher School of Law and Diplomacy at Tufts University. "We are not seriously challenged today, but if we neglect fleet size and military spending, the day will come when we cannot take for granted the sea lanes of communication to and from our continent," he said. "This is the basic building block of our [naval] strategy."

Stavridis said the United States will continue to cope with the Chinese military's construction of artificial islands in the South China Sea and will need a long-term maritime plan for dealing with North Korea.[109]

The fight to contain terrorism shows no signs of ending, even though American-backed forces have ousted the Islamic State jihadist group from its base of operations in Raqqa, Syria.[110]

U.S. officials also must reconsider their commitments in Europe, the Middle East and South and East Asia, and develop strategies to tackle climate change, according to Jeremi Suri, a history professor at the University of Texas, Austin, and Benjamin Valentino, an associate professor of government at Dartmouth College.[111]

One key to military readiness is a better system at the Pentagon for setting priorities to make sure troops and other military assets are not stretched too thin, according to Goldstein at the Naval War College.

"A lot of people have been telling us we're the greatest. Maybe this holds for 10 more years," Goldstein says. "If you go in all directions, you can't do everything well . . . you have to choose, you have to make priorities. Yet we refuse. We say we'll do everything."

The Center for a New American Security's Blume warns that if the Pentagon insists on preparing for everything, it will bankrupt the nation. "The appetite for more security is bottomless," she says.

NOTES

1. "US Navy ship and oil tanker collide near Singapore," BBC, Aug. 21, 2017, https://tinyurl.com/ybwfhhqp; Richard C. Paddock, "Remains of 10 Sailors Who Died in Navy Collision Are Found," *The New York Times*, Aug. 27, 2017, https://tinyurl.com/yd27rxdh; Julia Jacobo, Luis Martinez and Emily Shapiro, "USS McCain the 4th Navy warship to crash in Asia this year," ABC News, https://tinyurl.com/ya3ovx74.

2. Eric P. Schmitt, "Navy Ships Kept at Sea Despite Training and Maintenance Needs, Admiral Says," *The New York Times*, Sept. 7, 2017, https://tinyurl.com/ychs4sxm; Mike Fabey, "North Korean missiles are testing a stressed U.S. defense net," *SpaceNews*, Aug. 31, 2017, http://tinyurl.com/y9cna9e2.

3. Eric P. Schmitt, "Navy Collisions That Killed 17 Sailors Were 'Avoidable,' Official Inquiry Reports," *The New York Times*, Nov. 1, 2017, http://tinyurl.com/ydb2o8hs.

4. Dave Philipps and Eric P. Schmitt, "Fatigue and Training Gaps Spell Disaster at Sea, Sailors Warn," *The New York Times*, Aug.27, 2017, https://tinyurl.com/ybxcw6d5; Kevin Sieff, "In Afghanistan, redeployed U.S. soldiers still coping with demons of post-traumatic stress," *The Washington Post*, Aug. 18, 2013, https://tinyurl.com/ya9ps3me; and Dave Ruppe, "Five Air Force F-16s Crashed in July," ABC News, Aug. 7, 2017, https://tinyurl.com/y8cx2dpj.

5. Daniel Goure, "The Measure of a Superpower: A Two Major Regional Contingency Military for the 21st Century," Heritage Foundation, Jan. 25, 2013, https://tinyurl.com/y9d7pzfo; Paul Szoldra, "How the US military is beating hackers at their own game," *Business Insider*, May 24, 2016, https://tinyurl.com/h8brocx; and Jim Sciutto, "US military

prepares for the next frontier: Space war," CNN, Nov. 29, 2016, https://tinyurl.com/jzq3rhp.

6. Tom O'Connor, "What Russia's Military Looks Like Compared to the U.S.," *Newsweek*, April 7, 2017, https://tinyurl.com/ybwg32uh; Lauren Carroll, "Obama: US spends more on military than next 8 nations combined," *PolitiFact*, Jan. 13, 2016, http://tinyurl.com/hnmnyrk; and "Defense Budget Overview," Office of the Under Secretary of Defense (Comptroller), May 2017, https://tinyurl.com/y8p3wzbu.

7. "U.S. military leaders voice concern about readiness of forces," Reuters, March 16, 2016, https://tinyurl.com/y8szlza8.

8. Jim Garamone, "Dunford Urges Congress to Protect U.S. Competitive Advantage," *U.S. Department of Defense News*, June 12, 2017, http://tinyurl.com/y7qfqaha.

9. Daniel Brown and Skye Gould, "The U.S. has 1.3 million troops stationed around the world — here are the major hotspots," *Business Insider*, Aug. 31, 2017, http://tinyurl.com/ybnnlxr6; W.J. Hennigan, "U.S. has more troops in Afghanistan than previously disclosed, Pentagon reveals," *Los Angeles Times*, Aug. 30, 2017, https://tinyurl.com/yaexank2; "U.S. Navy," 2017 Index of Military Strength, Heritage Foundation, https://tinyurl.com/yazxgs43; "U.S. Air Force," 2017 Index of Military Strength, Heritage Foundation, https://tinyurl.com/y7wam7fz; K.K. Rebecca Lai et al., "Is America's Military Big Enough?" *The New York Times*, March 22, 2017, https://tinyurl.com/ktkc8pt; Kingston Reif, "U.S. Nuclear Modernization Programs," Arms Control Association, August 2017, https://tinyurl.com/7z7yulu; and Julian Borger, "New push to remove tactical nuclear weapons from Europe," *The Guardian*, Feb. 3, 2012, https://tinyurl.com/ycfzkz2q.

10. Steven Brill, "Donald Trump, Palantir, And The Crazy Battle To Clean Up A Multibillion-Dollar Military Procurement Swamp," *Fortune*, https://tinyurl.com/lths7lk.

11. Ryan Browne and Jeremy Herb, "Congressional Republicans see Trump's defense budget hike as

insufficient," CNN, May 23, 2017, https://tinyurl .com/yd3bgah9; Todd Harrison, "The Enduring Dilemma of Overseas Contingency Operations Funding," Defense360, Jan. 11, 2017, https:// tinyurl.com/y8votwpq.

12. "Defense Budget Overview," op. cit.; Annie Lowrey, "Why Sequestration Is Poised to Kill Trump's Budget," *The Atlantic*, March 16, 2017, https:// tinyurl.com/kgzlam4; and Kristina Wong, "Committee chairmen urge Republicans to reverse defense cuts," *The Hill*, March 10, 2015, https:// tinyurl.com/ydz8u8bn.

13. Vivienne Machi, "Lawmakers, Pentagon Officials Warn of 'Corrosive' Effects of Continuing Resolution (UPDATED)," *National Defense Magazine*, Sept. 7, 2017, https://tinyurl.com/ yc2wsa3o.

14. "National Security Implications of Climate-Related Risks and a Changing Climate," Department of Defense, July 23, 2015, http://tinyurl.com/p5qlyz9. For background, see William Wanlund, "Climate Change and National Security," *CQ Researcher*, Sept. 22, 2017, pp. 773–796.

15. "Defense Budget Overview," op. cit.

16. James Stavridis, *Sea Power: The History and Geopolitics of the World's Oceans* (2017), pp. 36–37; Eleanor Ross, "How and Why China is Building Islands in the South China Sea," *Newsweek*, March 29, 2017, http://tinyurl.com/y9qxh49e.

17. Eric P. Schmitt, "Vast Exercise Demonstrated Russia's Growing Military Prowess," *The New York Times*, Oct. 1, 2017, http://tinyurl.com/y9566e7w.

18. Michael Rubin, "Iran: Domestic Weapons Production up 69 Percent," American Enterprise Institute, March 13, 2017, https://tinyurl.com/ y9bdvt5d; "Iran: US Presence in Bahrain in the Crosshairs?" Foreign Military Studies Office Operational Environment Watch, U.S. Army, March 2017, p. 6, http://tinyurl.com/y85vkyzs; "Iran Tests Ballistic Missile and Rejects 'Threats,'" Reuters, *The New York Times*, Sept. 23, 2017, http://tinyurl.com/y7jtloud.

19. Colin Clark, "CJCS Dunford Calls For Strategic Shifts; 'At Peace Or At War Is Insufficient,'" *Breaking Defense*, Sept. 21, 2016, https://tinyurl .com/ycob9ku5.

20. Ian E. Rinehart, "The Chinese Military: Overview and Issues for Congress," summary page, Congressional Research Service, March 24, 2016, http://tinyurl.com/ju29zdc.

21. Jeremy Herb, "Trump order sets military buildup in motion," *Politico*, Jan. 27, 2017, http://tinyurl.com/ jxplbkn; Lawrence Kapp et al., "How Big Should the Army Be? Considerations for Congress," Congressional Research Service, Sept. 2, 2016, p. 2, http://tinyurl.com/yc3me67f.

22. Steven Kosiak, "Is the U.S. Military Getting Smaller and Older? And How Much Should We Care?" Center for a New American Security, March 14, 2017, p. 6, http://tinyurl.com/hby9fga.

23. Dan Goure, "Essay: Is the U.S. Military Too Small?" CBS, Nov. 23, 2016, http://tinyurl.com/yczu2wb6.

24. "Report to the President and the Congress of the United States," National Commission on the Future of the Army, Jan. 28, 2016, pp. 2–3, https://tinyurl .com/ychps9lv.

25. Statement of Lt. Gen. Gina M. Grosso before the Subcommittee on Personnel, Committee on Armed Services, U.S. House of Representatives, March 29, 2017, http://tinyurl.com/y97639mn.

26. "Navy Force Structure: Sustainable Plan and Comprehensive Assessment Needed to Mitigate Long-Term Risks to Ships Assigned to Overseas Homeports," Government Accountability Office, May 2015, https://tinyurl.com/yd95vfjj.

27. Scott Maucione, "Milley joins ranks pleading for readiness over capacity," Federal News Radio, Jan. 12, 2017, http://tinyurl.com/ybhbch38.

28. Todd Harrison, "Trump's Bigger Military Won't Necessarily Make the US Stronger or Safer," *Defense One*, March 16, 2017, http://tinyurl.com/ydbo3r7q.

29. Michael Hughes, "What went wrong with the F-35, Lockheed Martin's Joint Strike Fighter?" *The Conversation*, June 13, 2017, http://tinyurl.com/ ybzn6uqt.

30. Carl Prine, "U.S. defense secretary orders review of F-35 Joint Strike Fighter program," *The San Diego*

Union-Tribune, Jan. 27, 2017, http://tinyurl.com/y864uwjc.

31. Hughes, op. cit.; Kyle Mizokami, "The Cost of the F-35 Is Going Up Again," *Popular Mechanics*, July 17, 2017, http://tinyurl.com/ydc4kha3/; Doug Cameron and Andrew Tangel, "Donald Trump Presses Fight Over F-35 Jet Costs," *The Wall Street Journal*, Dec. 12, 2017, http://tinyurl.com/y7ss7x72; and Carl Prine, "Pentagon brass seek culture change, innovations in buying weapons," *The San Diego Union-Tribune,* Feb. 22, 2017, http://tinyurl.com/y9kjkvwc.

32. "High-Risk Series: Progress on Many High-Risk Areas, While Substantial Efforts Needed on Others," Government Accountability Office, February 2017, p. 269, https://tinyurl.com/y83krljd; Moshe Schwartz, "Defense Acquisitions: How DOD Acquires Weapon Systems and Recent Efforts to Reform the Process," Congressional Research Service, May 23, 2014, https://tinyurl.com/ybnzyaa6.

33. J. Ronald Fox, *Defense Acquisition Reform, 1960–2009: An Elusive Goal* (2010), http://tinyurl.com/ycecz2ky.

34. Roxana Tiron, "Congress throws Boeing a lifeline for Super Hornet," Bloomberg News, *St. Louis Post-Dispatch*, Jan. 22, 2014, http://tinyurl.com/y8mr7ors.

35. Adam K. Raymond, "How The Humvee Failed On The Battlefield And Sparked A Culture War Back Home," *Task and Purpose*, March, 18, 2017, http://tinyurl.com/ybenrn85.

36. Elizabeth Weise, "Could hackers be behind the U.S. Navy collisions" *USA Today*, Aug. 23, 2017, http://tinyurl.com/yakvufmf.

37. Jeevan Vasagar and Geoff Dyer, "Chinese hackers targeted US aircraft carrier," *Financial Times*, Oct. 21, 2016, https://tinyurl.com/yantc4ej; John Markoff, "Before the Gunfire, Cyberattacks," *The New York Times*, Aug. 12, 2008, https://tinyurl.com/yblvebvo; David E. Sanger and Charlie Savage, "U.S. Says Russia Directed Hacks to Influence Elections," *The New York Times*, Oct. 7, 2016, https://tinyurl.com/y9d297mh; Victor Luckerson, "Everything We Know About the Massive Sony Hack," *Time*, Dec. 4, 2014, https://tinyurl.com/lvy3j5m.

38. Paul D. Shinkman, "America Is Losing the Cyber War," *U.S. News & World Report*, Sept. 29, 2016, http://tinyurl.com/yda3te7j.

39. "Lt. Gen. William J. Bender: Breaking Barriers: The Air Force and the Future of Cyberpower," speech at Carnegie Council for Ethics in International Affairs, March 9, 2017, https://tinyurl.com/ycs9zfuv.

40. John M. Donnelly, "Exclusive: Aging Helicopters Could Make U.S. Nukes Vulnerable to Terrorists," *CQ Roll Call*, Feb. 29, 2016, http://tinyurl.com/yayjzx9m.

41. Luis Simon, "Demystifying the A2/AD Buzz," *War on the Rocks*, Jan. 4, 2017, https://tinyurl.com/ydg9xs49.

42. Rahul Chadha, "China is looking to invest billions of dollars into artificial intelligence," *Business Insider*, July 29, 2017, http://tinyurl.com/y8y5enbh.

43. Thomas J. Christensen, "China's Military Might: First the Good News," Bloomberg View, June 4, 2015, http://tinyurl.com/yctch3x6.

44. Benjamin Powers, "How Intelligent Drones Are Shaping the Future of Warfare," *Rolling Stone*, March 14, 2017, http://tinyurl.com/grglrkg.

45. Katherine Owens, "Army electronic warfare technology attacks and causes shift in tank," *Defense Systems*, June 5, 2017, http://tinyurl.com/yc23kzea; Jared Keller, "The Army Can Now Stop Enemy Tanks In Their Tracks Without Firing A Shot," *Task & Purpose*, June 8, 2017, http://tinyurl.com/y9xaw54j.

46. David Cenciotti, "Watch an F-16's Automatic Ground Collision Avoidance System save an unconscious pilot from certain death," *Business Insider*, Sept. 14, 2016, https://tinyurl.com/ya9wywha.

47. Patrick Tucker, "The War Over soon-to-be-Outdated Army Intelligence Systems," *Defense One*, July 5, 2016, http://tinyurl.com/y8pfnzou; Daniel Wilson, "Army Says It Didn't Wrongly Reject Palantir For $206M Deal," *Law360*, April 14, 2017, http://tinyurl.com/y7aouz9d; and Jacqueline Klimas and Bryan Bender, "Palantir goes from

Pentagon outsider to Mattis' inner circle," *Politico*, June 11, 2017, http://tinyurl.com/y84hm4z6.

48. E. Wayne Carp, *To Starve the Army at Pleasure: Continental Army Administration and American Political Culture, 1775–1783* (1984), pp. 55–56, http://tinyurl.com/y7yx8lfr.

49. NCC Staff, "On this day: Congress officially creates the U.S. Army," *Constitution Daily*, National Constitution Center, http://tinyurl.com/ycdfm97y.

50. Richard K. Betts, *Military Readiness* (1995), pp. 5–6.

51. James A. Huston, The Sinews of War: Army Logistics 1775–1953, U.S. Army, Office of the Chief of Military History, p. 277, http://tinyurl.com/y9p3b8g7.

52. Stavridis, op. cit., p. 28; Graham Watson, "The United States Navy: Its Rise to Global Parity, 1900–1922, Naval-History.Net, http://tinyurl.com/yal7dsyv.

53. "Great White Fleet," Theodore Roosevelt Center at Dickinson State University, undated, http://tinyurl.com/nrvgo7a; McKinley, op. cit.

54. Mackubin Thomas Owens, "How the U.S. Army Came of Age," *National Review*, May 8, 2017, http://tinyurl.com/y9qs9kjw; "Must Exert All Our Power: To Bring a 'Government That Is Running Amuck to Terms," *The New York Times*, April 3, 1917, http://tinyurl.com/ycodxj65; Stavridis, op. cit., p. 75.

55. "Full text of 'The Queenstown patrol, 1917: the diary of commander Joseph Knefler Taussig, U.S Navy,'" Historical Monograph Series, Naval War College, https://tinyurl.com/ybhb8py6.

56. Betts, op. cit., pp. 7–8.

57. Ibid., p. 8; Huston, op. cit., p. 657.

58. Thomas M. Meagher, *Financing Armed Conflict, Volume 2* (2017), p. 195, https://tinyurl.com/yb9z-7brs.

59. Betts, op. cit., p. 12.

60. John A. Garrity, *A Short History of the American Nation* (1971), p. 442; This Day in History: Atomic bomb dropped on Hiroshima," The History Channel, undated, http://tinyurl.com/kmftwv7.

61. U.S. Department of Defense, "Selected Manpower Statistics: Fiscal Year 1988," as quoted in "Downsizing America's Armed Forces," *CQ Researcher*, June 8, 1990.

62. Robert Higgs, "Policy Analysis: U.S. Military Spending in the Cold War Era: Opportunity Costs, Foreign Crises, and Domestic Constraints," Cato Institute, 1988, p. 2, http://tinyurl.com/y8oafjs7; "Defense spending and troop levels after major U.S. wars," *PolitiFact*, https://tinyurl.com/yclarn5d.

63. T.R. Fehrenbach, *This Kind of War: The Classic Korean War History* (1963), p. 27.

64. Betts, op. cit., pp. 15–16.

65. Ibid., p. 18; Chester J. Pach Jr., "Dwight D. Eisenhower: Foreign Affairs," Miller Center, University of Virginia, http://tinyurl.com/yaaamecy.

66. Donald A. Carter, "The U.S. Military Response to the 1960–62 Berlin Crisis," U.S. Army Center of Military History, 2011, p. 2, http://tinyurl.com/yb5grsqu; Charles E. Heller and William A. Stofft, *America's First Battles: 1776–1965* (1986), pp. 300–302.

67. Heller and Stofft, op. cit., pp. 300–305; Hanson W. Baldwin, "Shortage of Arms and Men Plagues Army and Reserve," *The New York Times*, July 21, 1965, http://tinyurl.com/yavvdju9.

68. "This Day in History: Congressman claims M-16 is defective," History Channel, undated, http://tinyurl.com/28y29rn.

69. "Vietnam War," History.com, 2009, http://tinyurl.com/pgmw6nq; Alex Dixon, "July marks 40th anniversary of all-volunteer Army," Army News Service, July 2, 2013, http://tinyurl.com/k9unoz3

70. Richard Halloran, "$40 Billion is Urged to Modernize Army," *The New York Times*, Nov. 30, 1980, http://tinyurl.com/ycezz3ex.

71. Betts, op. cit., p. 21; Richard Halloran, "Army Reporting Key Gains in Recruiting and Readiness," *The New York Times*, Sept. 7, 1981, http://tinyurl.com/y88cq8po; Bernard Weinraub, "Congress is in doubt over cost and need in Air Force Buildup," *The New York Times*, April 8, 1982, http://tinyurl.com/yarl97x5.

72. Philip M. Boffey, " 'Star Wars' and Mankind: Unforeseeable Directions," *The New York Times*, March 8, 1985, http://tinyurl.com/yagylbqq; Betts, op. cit., p. 21.

73. Richard Halloran, "Despite Arms Buildup, Experts Say U.S. Is Not Ready For War," *The New York Times*, March 24, 1987, http://tinyurl.com/ya9eyyqz.

74. Laurence Dodds, "Berlin Wall: How the Wall came down, as it happened 25 years ago," *The Telegraph*, Nov. 9, 2014, http://tinyurl.com/pjju9g3.

75. Betts, op. cit., p. 22.

76. "Downsizing America's armed forces," *CQ Researcher*, 1990.

77. Les Aspen, "Report on the Bottom-Up Review," Department of Defense, October 1993, pp. iii, 2, http://tinyurl.com/ycmf5r8m.

78. "Going Hollow: The Warnings of Our Chiefs of Staff," press release, Office of U.S. Sen. John McCain, Nov. 17, 1993, http://tinyurl.com/yae5aorl.

79. "Full text of 'Department of Defense appropriations for 1995: hearings before a subcommittee of the Committee on Appropriations, House of Representatives, One Hundred Third Congress, second session,' " Feb. 24, 1994, p. 168, http://tinyurl.com/y7y4yoaw.

80. "Paying for Military Readiness and Upkeep: Trends in Operations and Maintenance Spending," Congressional Budget Office, September 1997, http://tinyurl.com/yday65sg.

81. President's Radio Address, "President Discusses Beginning of Operation Iraqi Freedom," The White House, March 22, 2003, http://tinyurl.com/y8dxdng6; "U.S. has 100,000 troops in Kuwait," CNN, Feb. 18, 2003, http://tinyurl.com/y7pnc47y.

82. Jonathan Steele, "Body counts," *The Guardian*, May 27, 2003, http://tinyurl.com/ycon7h2q; Reuters staff, "Timeline: invasion, surge, withdrawal; U.S. forces in Iraq," Reuters, Dec. 18, 2011, http://tinyurl.com/yacsz95t.

83. Eric P. Schmitt, "Iraq-Bound Troops Confront Rumsfeld Over Lack of Armor," *The New York Times*, Dec. 8, 2004, http://tinyurl.com/y7ocvwbq.

84. Thomas Donnelly, "The Readiness Vortex," *Strategika*, May 2016, p. 3, http://tinyurl.com/yclsmfa3; Josh White and Ann Scott Tyson, "Increase in War Funding Sought," *The Washington Post*, Sept. 27, 2007, http://tinyurl.com/yamcal9r.

85. Anthony H. Cordesman, "The Changing Challenges of US Defense Spending: An Update," Center for Strategic and International Studies, Sept. 24, 2007, http://tinyurl.com/y8wgab7r; Ann Scott Tyson, "Bush's Defense Budget Biggest Since Reagan Era," *The Washington Post*, Feb. 6, 2007, http://tinyurl.com/2q3t63.

86. Dinah Walker, "Trends in U.S. Military Spending," Maurice R. Greenberg Center for Geo Economic Studies, Council on Foreign Relations, July 15, 2014, p. 1, http://tinyurl.com/y8rvel46; Louis Jacobson and Amy Sherman, "PolitiFact Sheet: Military spending under Obama and Congress," *PolitiFact*, Dec. 14, 2015, http://tinyurl.com/qercoka.

87. Jared Serbu, "By year's end, troops will be unable to respond to crises, Pentagon says," Federal News Radio, Feb. 4, 2013, http://tinyurl.com/y8yl5m8e; Russell Rumbaugh, "Defining Readiness: Background for Congress," Congressional Research Service, June 14, 2017, p. 1, http://tinyurl.com/y8k4yahj.

88. President Barack Obama, "Remarks by the President," Joint Base McGuire-Dix-Lakehurst, N.J., Dec. 15, 2014, http://tinyurl.com/y97nwbxt.

89. Craig Whitlock and Bob Woodward, "Pentagon buries evidence of $125 billion in bureaucratic waste," *The Washington Post*, Dec. 5, 2016, http://tinyurl.com/y8lfcb39.

90. David Nakamura, "Trump likely won't visit Korean demilitarized zone during Asia trip, White House says," *The Washington Post*, Oct. 23, 2017, https://tinyurl.com/ybtj7kyo.

91. Choe Sang-Hun and Austin Ramzy, "South Korea and U.S. Begin Drills as North Warns of Rising Tensions," *The New York Times*, Aug. 21, 2017, http://tinyurl.com/y8wlnfrh; "North Korea warns U.S. of 'unimaginable strike,' " CBS News, Oct. 19, 2017, http://tinyurl.com/ybu9wvm8; and Joshua Nevett, "Donald Trump warns North Korea US is

'totally prepared' for WAR in shock interview," *Daily Star*, Oct. 22, 2017, http://tinyurl.com/yan75tt8.

92. Oliver Holmes, "What is the US military's presence near North Korea?" *The Guardian*, Aug. 9, 2017, https://tinyurl.com/y7pmd9d6.

93. Tom O'Connor, "U.S. Military Commander Warns Enemies Not To Test Forces After USS John McCain Crash," *Newsweek*, Aug. 22, 2017, https://tinyurl.com/y85zyfck.

94. John Kirby, "US Navy plans operational pause following warship collisions," CNN, Aug. 21, 2017, https://tinyurl.com/ybhpe6cq; Schmitt, op. cit., Nov. 1, 2017.

95. Seema Mody, "China lashes out as South Korea puts an American anti-missile system in place," CNBC, March 17, 2017, http://tinyurl.com/y72t9e5d; Bridget Martin, "Moon Jae-In's THAAD Conundrum: South Korea's "candlelight president" faces strong citizen opposition on missile defense," *The Asia Pacific Journal*, Sept. 15, 2017, https://tinyurl.com/yafjl8rb.

96. The Associated Press, "North Korea calls Trump's threat a 'load of nonsense,'" *Politico*, Aug. 9, 2017, http://tinyurl.com/y8muoa3ej; David E. Sanger and Choe Sang-Hun, "North Korean Nuclear Test Draws U.S. Warning of 'Massive Military Response," *The New York Times*, Sept. 2, 2017, http://tinyurl.com/ybo27bcc; and Jesse Byrnes, "US, Japan conduct air exercises over East China Sea," *The Hill*, Sept. 9, 2017, http://tinyurl.com/y89qb4lw.

97. Scott Clement and Emily Guskin, "Polls show mixed support for military action against North Korea, but suggest it could rise," *The Washington Post*, Aug. 10, 2017, http://tinyurl.com/y76r4w3w; Lydia Saad, "More Back U.S. Military Action vs. North Korea Than in 2003," Gallup News, Sept. 15, 2017, http://tinyurl.com/ybvpnneg.

98. Maggie Ybarra, "How the U.S. Military Is Trying to Mask Its Readiness Crisis," *The National Interest*, May 18, 2017, http://tinyurl.com/yavxvxta; Colin Clark, "CJCS Dunford Calls For Strategic Shifts; 'At Peace Or At War Is Insufficient," *Breaking Defense*, Sept. 21, 2016, http://tinyurl.com/y8k6m94a.

99. Julie Hirschfeld Davis and Mark Landler, "Trump Outlines New Afghanistan War Strategy With Few Details," *The New York Times*, Aug. 21, 2017, http://tinyurl.com/y74lorj9.

100. Kyle Mizokami, "The U.S. Air Force Just Had an Awful Week," *Popular Mechanics*, June 26, 2017, http://tinyurl.com/yaldw9ga.

101. Ryan Browne, "Military aircraft accidents costing lives, billions of dollars," CNN, June 20, 2016, http://tinyurl.com/y9y9lbgc; "Marine Corps orders all of its aircraft grounded following deadly crashes," Fox News, Aug. 11, 2017, http://tinyurl.com/yb5ozv6x; and Thomas Gibbons-Neff, "One Special Forces soldier killed, seven injured during demolition training," *The Washington Post*, Sept. 14, 2017, http://tinyurl.com/ycpdfm9f.

102. James M. Cunningham and Thomas Donnelly, "Army Readiness Assessment, Vol. 1," American Enterprise Institute, May 2017, http://tinyurl.com/yawpwwft; Stephanie Casanova, " 'Atlantic Resolve': Dagger Brigade cases colors ahead of deployment," *The Mercury*, Sept. 6, 2017, http://tinyurl.com/yaxmhuez.

103. "Document: Pentagon Plan to Split Research and Development from Acquisition," *USNI News*, Aug. 2, 2017, http://tinyurl.com/y9bno3ct.

104. Sydney J. Freedberg Jr., "Army Chief Milley Turns To Industry For Network Overhaul," *Breaking Defense*, July 21, 2017, http://tinyurl.com/y8ysev4p; Adam Jay Harrison, "The Pentagon's Pivot: How Lead Users Are Transforming Defense Product Development," *Defense Horizons*, August 2017, https://tinyurl.com/yahgrp97.

105. Sheryl Gay Stolberg, "Senate Passes $700 Billion Pentagon Bill, More Money Than Trump Sought," *The New York Times*, Sept. 18, 2017, http://tinyurl.com/y9oqnwp4.

106. Joe Gould, "GOP senator blasts 'cowardly' Democrats over scuttled sequestration repeal," *Army Times*, Sept. 18, 2017, http://tinyurl.com/y9zw57mz.

107. Mark Hand, "46 Republicans buck party to help Democrats take down anti-climate action amendment," *Think Progress*, July 14, 2017, http://tinyurl.com/yc8bynvp.

108. Rebecca Kheel, "Defense experts call on Congress to allow military base closures," *The Hill*, June 19, 2017, https://tinyurl.com/y89ncf39; "Department of Defense Infrastructure Capacity," Department of Defense, March 2016, http://tinyurl.com/y9thwv7z; and Jeff Daniels, "Base closings 'hot potato' issue again as Pentagon insists new round could save tens of billions," CNBC, July 14, 2017, http://tinyurl.com/ycwpcwxu.

109. Stavridis, op. cit., p. 331.

110. Anne Barnard and Hwaida Saad, "Raqqa, ISIS 'Capital,' Is Captured, U.S.-Backed Forces Say," *The New York Times*, Oct. 17, 2017, https://tinyurl.com/y7hchp9o.

111. Suri and Valentino, op. cit.

BIBLIOGRAPHY

Selected Sources

Books

O'Hanlon, Michael E., *The $650 Billion Bargain: The Case for Modest Growth in America's Defense Budget,* Brookings Institution Press, 2016.
A senior fellow at a centrist Washington think tank argues a slight increase in defense spending could improve the readiness of the U.S. military.

Stavridis, James, *Sea Power: The History and Geopolitics of the World's Oceans,* Penguin Press, 2017.
A retired admiral and former supreme allied commander for global operations at NATO looks at global naval history and the U.S. military's readiness to handle future conflicts at sea.

Suri, Jeremi, and Benjamin Valentino, eds., *Sustainable Security: Rethinking American National Security Strategy,* Oxford University Press, 2016.
Sixteen scholars show how U.S. military institutions and strategies have not changed since the Cold War, and say defense officials need to better prepare for an expanding range of conflicts.

Articles

Brill, Steven, "Donald Trump, Palantir, and the crazy battle to clean up a multibillion-dollar military procurement swamp," *Fortune*, March 27, 2017, http://tinyurl.com/lths7lk.
A Silicon Valley software startup says the Army blocked it from acquiring a lucrative contract for technology that the company says would save soldiers' lives.

Diamond, Christopher, "Report: U.S. military's shrinking size and growing equipment age reflect DOD priorities," *Military Times*, March 15, 2017, http://tinyurl.com/y9lyt6gl.
Despite consistent defense spending increases, the size of the military has been shrinking in recent decades while its equipment has been aging, according to a Center for a New American Security report.

Philipps, Dave, and Eric Schmitt, "Fatigue and Training Gaps Spell Disaster at Sea, Sailors Warn," *The New York Times*, Aug. 27, 2017, http://tinyurl.com/ybxcw6d5.
Current and former Navy ship commanders describe exhausting schedules and maintenance shortfalls that they said could have contributed to two deadly collisions recently between U.S. destroyers and cargo ships.

Powers, Benjamin, "How Intelligent Drones Are Shaping the Future of Warfare," *Rolling Stone*, March 14, 2017, http://tinyurl.com/grglrkg.
Military scholars discuss the expanded use of drones and autonomous weapons systems as part of an effort to modernize the military, and explore related legal questions.

Tirpak, John A., "Combat Forces in Peril," *Air Force Magazine*, July 2017, http://tinyurl.com/y9pnln37.
A former Air Combat Command chief for the Air Force describes the effects of budgetary constraints on readiness and capability, and offers solutions.

Reports and Studies

"U.S. Military Power: What is the status of America's military power?" 2016 Index of U.S. Military Strength, Heritage Foundation, https://tinyurl.com/ojog8sz.
A conservative Washington think tank assesses the size, equipment and capability of the U.S. military and concludes it could not fight two major conflicts at once.

Kosiak, Steven, "Is the U.S. Military Getting Smaller and Older? And How Much Should We Care?" Center for a New American Security, March 14, 2017, https://tinyurl.com/hby9fga.

An adjunct senior fellow at a Washington think tank says the United States still has the world's most formidable military, despite policy decisions that have led to fewer service personnel.

O'Rourke, Ronald, "Navy Force Structure and Shipbuilding Plans: Background and Issues for Congress," Congressional Research Service, Sept. 22, 2017, http://tinyurl.com/y8na4x9p.
The research arm of Congress outlines projected costs and other issues as lawmakers weigh President Trump's proposal to expand the Navy's fleet to 355 ships.

Audio and Video

Bender, William J., "Breaking Barriers: The Air Force and the Future of Cyberpower," Carnegie Council for Ethics in International Affairs, March 9, 2017, http://tinyurl.com/ycs9zfuv.

The chief information officer for the secretary of the Air Force describes efforts to keep up with changes in digital technology and cybersecurity.

Eaglen, MacKenzie, "Space Corps: A new military branch?" American Enterprise Institute, Aug. 4, 2017, http://tinyurl.com/yadazyfc.
A resident fellow at a conservative Washington think tank discusses a House bill that would create a new military service to handle possible conflicts in space.

O'Hanlon, Michael E., "A discussion with Rep. Mac Thornberry on military readiness, modernization, and innovation," Brookings Institution, May 22, 2017, http://tinyurl.com/kkxpflq.
A senior fellow at a centrist Washington think tank talks with the chairman of the House Armed Services Committee about military readiness and other defense-related issues.

For More Information

Center for a New American Security, 1152 15th St., N.W., Suite 950, Washington, DC 20005; 202-456-9400; www.cnas.org. Think tank that researches warfare issues and the status and future of the U.S. military.

Center for Strategic and International Studies, 1616 Rhode Island Ave., N.W., Washington, DC 20036; 202-775-3242; www.csis.org. Think tank that studies the U.S. military and defense issues; affiliated with Georgetown University.

Hudson Institute, 1201 Pennsylvania Ave., N.W., Suite 400, Washington, DC 20004; 202-974-2400; www.hudson.org. Think tank that studies the U.S. military.

National Defense University Institute for National Strategic Studies, Fort Lesley J. McNair, 300 5th Ave., S.W., Washington, DC 20319-5066; 202-685-4700;

www.ndu.edu. Researches military readiness and the federal procurement process.

Secure World Foundation, 1779 Massachusetts Ave., N.W., Suite 720, Washington, DC 20036; 202-568-6212. Advocates for the peaceful use of space; researches the status and security of U.S. and foreign orbiting satellites.

Union of Concerned Scientists, 2 Brattle Square, Cambridge, MA 02138-3780; 617-547-5552; www.ucsusa.org. Supports arms control, maintains a database of U.S. and foreign orbiting satellites and tracks development of anti-satellite weapons.

U.S. Naval War College, 686 Cushing Road, Newport, RI 02841-1207; 401-841-1310; usnwc.edu. Studies the U.S. Navy and naval defense programs in China and Russia.

3

Cyberwarfare Threat

Patrick Marshall

President Trump has proposed several actions to bolster the country's cyber capabilities, including giving increased independence to the U.S. Cyber Command and ordering strengthened cybersecurity for federal networks and critical infrastructure. "The elevation of United States Cyber Command demonstrates our increased resolve against cyberspace threats and will help reassure our allies and partners and deter our adversaries," Trump said.

From *CQ Researcher,*
October 6, 2017

O n June 27, technicians at the defunct Chernobyl nuclear power plant in Ukraine noticed that the computers monitoring lingering radiation at the plant, destroyed in 1986 by a massive reactor explosion, had stopped working. The same day, ATMs shut down in Ukraine's capital city, Kiev. More than 4,000 miles away in the United States, workers at pharmaceutical giant Merck and Co. found themselves unable to make important vaccines.[1]

The disruptions had a common source — a computer virus that began in Ukraine and spread around the world, crippling more than 12,000 networks and devices in 65 countries. The cyberattack initially appeared to be ransomware, which encrypts digital data and demands payment for decrypting it. But researchers affiliated with NATO said the attack was primarily a "declaration of power" designed to destroy information, not extract ransom.[2]

They also said the attack likely was launched by a government or with backing from a government, raising the possibility that it could be considered an act of war. Ukraine has blamed Russia, but the Kremlin has denied involvement.[3]

Cybersecurity experts point to such attacks as evidence that future wars likely won't begin on land, at sea or in the air but instead in cyberspace.[4]

The rise of digital weapons as a major geopolitical threat raises new concerns about whether the United States should act more aggressively to protect itself from cyberweapons that could change election tallies, shut down power grids or disable key military infrastructure. The United States has powerful digital weapons

Most See Russian Hacking as Election Threat

A majority of Americans believe Russian hacking in the 2016 presidential election means Russia poses a threat to future U.S. elections, though fewer than half view the threat as major.

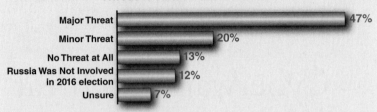

Percentage of Americans Who View Russian Hacking as a Threat to Future U.S. Elections

- Major Threat — 47%
- Minor Threat — 20%
- No Threat at All — 13%
- Russia Was Not Involved in 2016 election — 12%
- Unsure — 7%

Sources: Laura Santhanam, "New poll: 54% of Americans think Trump's dealings with Russia were unethical or illegal," PBS News Hour, July 6, 2017, https://tinyurl.com/y9wu4vto

"Cyber-enabled information warfare is an existential threat to society as we know it," says Lin. "It is people trying to advance the idea that there is no such thing as truth — that truth doesn't matter. There is no shared basis for understanding anymore. Is that a threat to society? You bet it is."

The cyberattack that started in Ukraine in June was just one of a number of such incidents in recent years:

- In May, a ransomware attack disabled hundreds of thousands of computers in more than 150 countries, disrupting operations at hospitals, universities, manufacturers and government agencies. The attack apparently used information stolen from the supersecret U.S. National Security Agency (NSA). FBI officials have noted that such attacks can disrupt the manufacture of electrical components, computer chips and other products important to national security.[6]

- In December, a cyberattack cut about 20 percent of Kiev's electricity supply. Ukraine blamed Russia, saying the Kremlin has waged a "cyber war" against Ukraine since Russia annexed Crimea in 2014 and fighting broke out between Ukrainian forces and pro-Russian separatists in eastern Ukraine. "You can't really find a space in Ukraine where there hasn't been an attack," said Kenneth Geers, a NATO ambassador who focuses on cybersecurity.[7]

- In the United States last year, "Russian government cyber actors," tried to hack into voting systems in 21 states ahead of the presidential election, according to Department of Homeland Security officials. Officials say Russia also used social media, including Twitter accounts and $100,000 in Facebook ads, to distribute propaganda aimed at widening political divisions in the United States as part of a larger campaign to promote Donald Trump's presidential candidacy. And intelligence officials say hackers linked to Russia stole emails from the Democratic National Committee (DNC)

that some cybersecurity experts say will deter attacks by other countries. U.S. intelligence officials, however, say cyberattacks pose more of a threat to the country than terrorism.

"In 2013, 'cyber' bumped 'terrorism' out of the top spot on our list of national threats," then-Director of National Intelligence James Clapper said last year. "And cyber has led our report every year since then."[5]

Protecting computer networks also is important at companies that make weapons systems or other products and services important to national security. But those companies oppose proposals to make their computers more secure through government regulation. Some cite prior bad experiences working with the government on cybersecurity. Others cite a desire to avoid red tape.

Recent cyberattacks have also inspired calls for international agreements to limit the militarization of cyberspace, but critics of the idea say limiting the use of cyberweapons is virtually impossible because computer code cannot be monitored the same way conventional weapons are.

Some cyberattacks target democratic institutions, mounting "influence campaigns" that exploit social media to spread fabricated information disguised as news, says Herbert Lin, a senior research scholar for cyber policy and security at the Hoover Institution, a conservative think tank at Stanford University.

and others that they later released in hopes of damaging the candidacy of Trump's opponent, Hillary Clinton.[8]

- In 2014, hackers broke into computers at Sony Pictures, stealing unreleased movies and making them publicly available. U.S. officials blamed North Korea, saying Pyongyang was retaliating for a Sony comedy, "The Interview," that depicted the assassination of the country's leader, Kim Jong-un. A year earlier, South Korean media reported that Kim had called cyberattacks a "magic weapon."[9]
- In 2014, hackers broke into the computer network for South Korea's nuclear power plants, stealing what government officials said was "non-critical" data. And in April 2016, computers at a nuclear power plant in Germany were found to be infected with viruses.[10]
- A 2015 report by Chatham House, a think tank in London, said cybersecurity risks at nuclear power plants are increasing as the plants "become increasingly reliant on digital systems and make increasing use of commercial 'off-the-shelf' software."[11]
- Western military officials said recently that Russia has been hacking into the personal smartphones used by NATO soldiers to gain operational information, assess troop strength and intimidate the soldiers. Some officials worried that compromised cellphones could be used to create confusion and slow NATO's response to Russian military action in a crisis.[12]

Intelligence officials warn that the stakes in cyberwarfare are high.

"The breadth of cyberthreats posed to U.S. national and economic security has become increasingly diverse, sophisticated and serious, leading to physical, security, economic, and psychological consequences," Clapper, then-Undersecretary of Defense for Intelligence Marcel Lettre and Navy Admiral Michael Rogers, director of the NSA, said in a rare joint statement to Congress in January."[13]

Cyberthreats are as varied as the devices connected to computer networks, and cybersecurity experts say the most important weapons systems in the U.S. military's arsenal could be at risk. In 2010, for example, after President Barack Obama ordered his administration to

find out if there were security flaws in the systems that manage U.S. nuclear missiles, investigators found deficiencies that could have allowed hackers to shut down the missiles' flight guidance systems.[14]

In June, captains of commercial ships in the Black Sea reported that their GPS navigation systems were incorrect by about 20 miles. Navigation experts later concluded the systems were being "spoofed," or fed false signals, and some experts attributed the incidents to Russian hackers.[15]

Federal computer networks were accessed by hackers or infected with malware — software intended to damage or disable computer networks — about 30,000 times between Oct. 1, 2015 and Sept. 30, 2016, the Government Accountability Office (GAO), the investigative arm of Congress, reported in June. The agency also said the vulnerability of Defense Department computer networks "has grown significantly."[16]

On Sept. 20, the Securities and Exchange Commission, an independent federal agency that regulates Wall Street, revealed that hackers exploited a software vulnerability last year to breach agency computers. And in February 2016, a hacker released online the names and contact information of 29,000 Department of Homeland Security and FBI employees.[17]

Computers at other federal agencies also have been targeted by cyberweapons. A 2016 GAO survey of 24 federal agencies found that 18 with "high-impact" computer systems — those containing information that, if lost, could cause "catastrophic harm" — identified cyberattacks by foreign nations "as the most serious and most frequently occurring threat to the security of their systems."[18] Such attacks may seek to gather information on weapons systems, political strategies or economic plans.

Concerns over private companies' digital security focuses on those serving critical sectors such as banking, utilities and government contracting. Potential threats include ransomware that can shut down computer networks or destroy their data, and computer viruses that can shut down power grids.

"The private sector has been really slow to adopt basic cyber hygiene practices," says Ryan Maness, an assistant professor in the Defense Analysis Department at the Naval Postgraduate School in Monterey, Calif. Fifty-seven percent of companies surveyed by the insurance industry said they were targeted in a cyberattack in the past year, and 42 percent reported at least two attacks.[19]

Such findings have prompted demands for federal regulations to improve cybersecurity in the private sector. "There is clearly a bigger role for government," says Peter W. Singer, a strategist and senior fellow at the left-of-center New America think tank in Washington. Government requirements, he says, would ensure that private companies achieve "more than just aspirational goals" in protecting their networks.

President Trump has issued a strong call for building up the country's cyber capabilities. On Aug. 18, he said he would make the U.S. Cyber Command, the Pentagon's offensive cyberwar unit, a "Unified Combatant Command," a plan originally proposed by the Obama administration. The move will not be final until the Senate confirms someone to run the Cyber Command, which is currently headed by Rogers at the NSA.

Trump's decision will give Cyber Command the same status as organizations that oversee military operations in the Middle East, Europe and the Pacific. Cyber Command is currently under the U.S. Strategic Command, one of the military's nine unified commands.[20]

"The elevation of United States Cyber Command demonstrates our increased resolve against cyberspace threats and will help reassure our allies and partners and deter our adversaries," Trump said in a statement.[21]

Some of Trump's other actions on cybersecurity have been more ambiguous. He has, for example, repeatedly questioned reports by his own intelligence agencies that Russia used cyberweapons to influence the presidential election.[22] And former FBI Director James Comey, whom Trump fired in May, testified in June that Trump showed no interest in preventing future election interference by Russia.[23]

Cyberattacks Target Industrial Computers

Vietnam had the highest percentage of industrial control system computers hit by cyberattacks during the first half of 2017, according to a survey of the computers the cybersecurity company Kaspersky Lab has been hired to protect.

Top 10 Countries by Percentage of Industrial Computers Attacked

Vietnam	71%
Algeria	67.1%
Morocco	65.4%
Indonesia	58.7%
China	57.1%
India	56%
Iran	55.3%
Saudi Arabia	51.8%
Egypt	51.6%
Peru	50.8%

Source: "Threat Landscape for Industrial Automation Systems in H1 2017," Kaspersky Lab, Sept. 28, 2017, https://tinyurl.com/y9hgwq83

As experts and policymakers consider the threat of cyberattacks, here are some of the questions they are asking:

Does cyberwarfare pose an existential threat to the United States?

Sen. John McCain, R-Ariz., chairman of the Senate Armed Services Committee, warned in May that "glaring gaps in our national cyber policy, strategy and organization undermine our ability to defend the homeland and deter those seeking to undermine our national security in cyberspace."[24]

Intelligence officials have made similar comments. In their joint statement to Congress in January, Clapper, Lettre and Rogers warned that more than 30 nations are developing offensive cyberattack capabilities and that "the proliferation of cyber capabilities coupled with new warfighting technologies" will increase the incidence of cyberattacks.

What's more, they said, a cyberattack targeting the private sector or U.S. infrastructure could escalate quickly and involve not just national security and military officials but corporations, "blurring the distinction between state and nonstate action. Protecting critical infrastructure, such as crucial energy, financial, manufacturing, transportation, communication, and health systems, will become an increasingly complex national security challenge," they said.[25]

Hackers linked to Russia already have created a cyberweapon that can bring down power grids. The malware, called "CrashOverride," was used in the December cyberattack that shut down one-fifth of the electric power in Kiev.[26]

Kaspersky Lab, a global cybersecurity company in Moscow that makes anti-virus software and defends computers against digital attacks, said that during the first six months of 2017, it blocked attempted attacks on 37.6 percent of customers' computers operating machinery at plants providing water, power, gas and other critical services.[27]

Kaspersky itself is controversial. On Sept. 14, the Trump administration ordered federal agencies to remove the company's products from their networks based on concerns that the firm has close ties to the Kremlin and that using its software could jeopardize national security. The company has rejected those assertions.[28]

Singer says that while a cyberattack targeting infrastructure could paralyze the U.S. military and economy, "for it to be a Pearl Harbor equivalent as opposed to a 9/11 shock" would require an enemy to follow it up with an invasion using conventional arms.

Such a scenario unfolded in 2008 when computer networks in Georgia were hit with cyberattacks weeks before Russia invaded the country by land, air and sea. Cyberwarfare experts say the incident marked the first time a known cyberattack was followed by a war using conventional arms. Georgia blamed Russia for the cyberattacks, but Russian officials denied responsibility.[29]

Maness at the Naval Postgraduate School said it is unlikely Russia would target the U.S. power grid the same way it did in Ukraine in December. "I think they would think twice about that because of our own power," he says. "There are these kind of red lines not to be crossed, at least among the major powers."

However, some countries — North Korea, for example — are less likely to be intimidated by U.S. cyberweapons. "North Korea knows it can target the information architecture that developed economies rely on without fearing any direct, symmetrical response," Brian R. Moore, then a resident fellow at the Center for Strategic and International Studies, a bipartisan Washington think tank, and Jonathan R. Corrado, an Asia analyst at McLarty Associates, an international strategic advisory firm in Washington, wrote in June. "The isolated nation already suffers regular blackouts, nearly nonexistent internet access, and a disconnected, cash-based financial system. It thus stands to lose much less in cyberwarfare, increasing the regime's appetite for online conflicts."[30]

Michael Sulmeyer, director of the Cyber Security Project at Harvard University's Belfer Center for Science and International Affairs, says U.S. policy on cyberwar should not rely on deterrence — the belief that other countries are so afraid of the United States' arsenal of cyberweapons that they would never target U.S. military or national security networks in a cyberattack. Instead, he says, "we need to focus much more on making ourselves harder to hack."

Jason Healey, a senior research scholar at Columbia University's School of International and Public Affairs, warned Congress in March that "there is actually very little evidence of adversaries being deterred by an opponent's fearsome cyber capabilities. But there are many examples, especially between the United States and Iran, where capabilities and operations have led to escalation."

An example of such escalation occurred in 2012, when a group backed by Iran disabled websites at U.S. financial institutions. That cyberattack was viewed as retaliation for a 2010 attack by the "Stuxnet" computer virus — thought to have been developed by the United States and Israel — that damaged Iranian centrifuges used to enrich uranium.[31]

Other cybersecurity experts say deterrence is still important even if it is not the sole answer to cyberthreats. "When we try to deter crime with locks on our doors or signs in the window that say, 'Protected by alarms,' or by police cruisers that go by, it doesn't stop all crime, but without it you would have a lot more," says Joseph Nye, a former assistant secretary of Defense for international security affairs. "That's true with cyber actors as well."

John Arquilla, who teaches defense analysis at the Naval Postgraduate School, said cyberattacks by themselves are not an effective strategy in war. "Think about aerial bombing," he said. "Societies have been standing up to it for the better part of a century, and almost all such campaigns have failed . . . If highly destructive bombing hasn't been able to break the human will, disruptive computer pinging surely won't."[32]

Should the U.S. government regulate private-sector cybersecurity?

Private companies own and operate more than 90 percent of U.S. cyberspace infrastructure and would be "the first line of defense" in a cyberwar, according to the Defense Department's 2015 cyberstrategy report.[33]

However, federal officials have largely avoided issuing regulations to make private-sector computer networks

Demonstrators at the 2016 Democratic National Convention in Philadelphia on July 25, 2016, protest the hacking of Democratic National Committee emails. U.S. intelligence officials say hackers linked to Russia stole the emails and later released them in hopes of damaging the election chances of Democratic presidential candidate Hillary Clinton.

more secure. Exceptions include a 1996 law that imposes requirements on the handling of health care data and a 1999 law that does the same for financial data.

Instead, the government has encouraged private companies to voluntarily improve their cybersecurity practices. "The majority of intrusions can be stopped through relatively basic cybersecurity investments that companies can and must make themselves," the Defense Department's 2015 report states.[34]

Since then, however, private companies and organizations have been hit with major hacking and malware attacks.

- Equifax, the credit reporting agency, said in September that hackers had taken advantage of a flaw in its software to steal personal information on up to 145.5 million people, including names, Social Security numbers and birth dates. The source of the hack is still unknown. Equifax knew two months before its network was hacked that a patch was available to fix the software flaw, but the company did not install it, according to the industry group that discovered the flaw.[35]
- Last year's hack at the SEC targeted the agency's system for storing documents filed by publicly traded companies. SEC Chairman Jay Clayton

issued a statement saying the breach "may have provided the basis for illicit gain through trading." He also said the agency acted quickly to patch the software vulnerability that the hackers exploited.[36]
- In June 2016, a cybersecurity firm hired by the Democratic National Committee said DNC computers had been hacked by groups linked to Russian intelligence. A blogger called Guccifer 2.0 responded by saying he alone was behind the hack and claimed to have passed along thousands of files to WikiLeaks.[37]
- On Oct. 3, Verizon Communications said a previously disclosed digital attack on Yahoo that took place in 2013 affected all 3 billion of Yahoo's user accounts, making it the biggest known breach of a company's computer network. Verizon acquired Yahoo earlier this year. In September 2016, before the acquisition, Yahoo disclosed a separate attack in 2014 in which "state-sponsored" hackers stole personal data on more than 500 million of the internet company's users.[38]

In March, U.S. law enforcement authorities charged two Russian intelligence officers with running the 2014 operation. Federal prosecutors said the Russian government used the stolen data to spy on White House and military officials, bank executives, Russian government officials and others. Investigators believe the attackers behind the 2013 attack were also Russian and possibly linked to the Russian government.[39]

Last year, the Commission on Enhancing National Cybersecurity, created by President Obama to tighten cybersecurity in government, business and society, called for the "public and private sectors to collaborate on cybersecurity activities."[40]

Singer of New America and other cybersecurity experts say that's not enough. The proposed "code of conduct" that federal officials have proposed to improve private-sector cybersecurity has "less power than a code of conduct at a country club," Singer says. "What we have right now is a series of aspirational standards but not enough to backstop them."

Arquilla at the Naval Postgraduate School says the government should regulate how private companies protect their computer networks the same way it regulates how they protect workers from on-the-job injuries. "The government is involved in so many areas of physical safety, it takes just a small leap to understand that the government should also have a role in cybersecurity," he says.

Lin of the Hoover Institution, who served on Obama's cybersecurity commission, disagrees. He says the commission was "very, very wary of explicit regulation" of the private sector, although it never ruled out the possibility. "The market has failed to provide the U.S. with the cybersecurity that it needs," says Lin. "But there are many steps to be tried before imposing regulations." He specifically suggests voluntary programs to help companies improve cybersecurity, as well as holding companies liable for damages resulting from improper security practices.

Not surprisingly, companies generally oppose government regulation of their computer networks. Ann M. Beauchesne, vice president of national security and emergency preparedness at the U.S. Chamber of Commerce, said private companies should spend their money protecting their computer networks "instead of dedicating those resources to dealing with red tape."[41]

Many companies say their experience with federal agencies has taught them to distrust government "cooperation" with the private sector. That's especially true of tech companies that have been pressured by the NSA to equip their products with "backdoors" — hidden openings in encrypted software that allow investigators to monitor data for activity that might threaten national security. Critics of the practice say it is an invasion of privacy and undermines public confidence that encrypted data is secure.[42]

Companies and consumer groups also have criticized the NSA's practice of collecting vulnerabilities in commercial software that the agency might someday want to use to access users' data — without telling companies about those vulnerabilities so they can be fixed. "If the government does not disclose to software companies the vulnerabilities that it obtains, then both public and private systems will be put at risk," according to the Electronic Privacy Information Center, a public-interest research group in Washington.[43]

Insurance companies also play a role in cybersecurity by setting minimum standards that private companies must meet to qualify for coverage against network

Acting Assistant Attorney General for National Security Mary McCord announces the filing on March 15, 2017, of criminal charges in the 2014 theft of personal data on more than 500 million Yahoo users. Federal prosecutors charged two Russian intelligence officers with running the operation and said the Russian government used the hacked data to spy on White House and military officials, bank executives, Russian officials and others.

breaches. But half of companies in the United States are not insured against hacking, and 27 percent of executives at those companies say they have no plans to buy such insurance.[44]

Singer says Congress could help lessen the risk by developing standards and requiring federal agencies to share cyberattack data with insurers. "One of the challenges for the cybersecurity insurance industry is that things are defined in and interpreted in different ways in different locales," Singer says.

He also says companies should hold software and hardware vendors accountable — through litigation — for losses stemming from vulnerabilities in their products.

Sulmeyer, at Harvard's Cyber Security Project, agrees, saying software and hardware makers have never been held accountable for data security during the 30 years they have been doing business.

Microsoft security architect Roger A. Grimes, however, says that is the wrong approach. "All software has bugs and all software has security flaws," he wrote recently. Such potentially huge liability would scare off potential investors in software and hardware firms, he said, and "you'd end up with fewer corporations, fewer jobs, and less innovation."[45]

Should the international community pursue agreements governing cyberwarfare?

In February, Microsoft President Brad Smith noted an alarming increase in cyberattacks around the world and called for a "Digital Geneva Convention" — an international treaty that would establish rules for what targets and retaliatory actions would be considered legitimate in a cyberwar. "The time has arrived," Smith wrote, "to call on the world's governments to implement international rules to protect the civilian use of the internet."[46]

Smith said such a convention should ban countries from launching cyberattacks against tech companies, the private sector or critical infrastructure. "Even in a world of growing nationalism, when it comes to cybersecurity the global tech sector needs to operate as a neutral Digital Switzerland," Smith wrote. "We will assist and protect customers everywhere. We will not aid in attacking customers anywhere. We need to retain the world's trust."[47]

Lin at the Hoover Institution applauds Smith's proposal. "It adds a private-sector voice to this and it's a good thing to have that in the debate," he says. "I'm afraid that in the merits of it, I think that it's going to be really, really hard to do, and actually probably impossible. But that doesn't mean it shouldn't be discussed."

James Carlini, a cybersecurity consultant in Illinois, agrees the chances for an effective cyberwarfare treaty are slim. "Cyber weapons are not part of the Geneva Convention, and the way they are used now, I highly doubt there will ever be a consensus to sign away their latest capabilities," he wrote in August. "To think everyone is going to come to a consensus to limit them or restrict them to only certain areas is ludicrous."[48]

Even advocates for a treaty agree that cyberwar can't be managed like conventional warfare or nuclear weapons.

"You can't outlaw a cyberweapon because you don't know what is a weapon," says Nye, the former Defense official. "It depends on the intention of the user. So you really can't prohibit cyberweapons in a verifiable way."

Arquilla of the Naval Postgraduate School agrees. "Information technology is all dual use, so you can't keep the ability to engage in cyber warfare out of people's hands," he says.

Existing international laws apply to cyberspace, but it's unclear which cyber activities would qualify as military attacks or use of force. "There is a gray area since a cyberattack can cause disruption without causing destruction or casualties," James Lewis, a senior vice president at the Center for Strategic and International Studies think tank, told Congress in 2015.[49]

Michael N. Schmitt, an international law professor at the Naval War College in Rhode Island, says countries "are seemingly hesitant to state where the legal lines in the sand are" regarding cyberwarfare. "It hurts deterrence," he says. "It encourages states to exploit gray areas. We should be really nervous, because as we develop these capabilities we don't know the rules of the game."

Congress is also apparently nervous about the legal status of cyberwarfare. It approved legislation last year that requires the Trump administration to spell out within a year which cyberspace activities would qualify as acts of war against the United States.[50]

Schmitt says reaching consensus won't be easy. "When does a remotely conducted cyberoperation into a country violate that country's sovereignty?" he says. "The lawyers are all over the map on that."

His own view, he says, is that any action that damages a country's cyber infrastructure — including government computer networks and private-sector networks — is a violation of sovereignty. Schmitt says that the hackers who stole and released Democratic National Committee emails, for example, violated international law because they "manipulated our election process." Cyber espionage cases such as the hack that stole data from the SEC, however, are not barred under international law, he said.[51]

Nye says the lack of legal clarity makes it harder to prevent attacks. "One of the things that I worry about is, how do you deter states from creeping up to this threshold," he says.

Because the United States has targeted other countries with aggressive cyberattacks — the 2010 Stuxnet virus that damaged Iranian centrifuges is just one example — some cybersecurity experts say U.S. officials have little credibility to demand that other countries stop such attacks.

Kalev Leetaru, a senior fellow at George Washington University's Center for Cyber and Homeland Security, said it was "somewhat hypocritical" for U.S. officials to file criminal charges against the two Russian intelligence officers who allegedly masterminded the 2014 breach at Yahoo. The charges outline "precisely the same activities the U.S. government itself engages in every day," Leetaru wrote in *Forbes*.[52]

The United Nations has worked to develop cyberwarfare rules through its Group of Governmental Experts on Information Security (GGE), first convened in 2004. The group's latest round of talks stalled without producing consensus, but Nye says he expects some countries to work together on agreements like the one Obama and Chinese President Xi Jinping reached in 2015.

In that deal, China agreed not to conduct commercial cyberespionage to avoid U.S. sanctions against Chinese companies accused of stealing trade secrets.[53] But Clapper noted last year that "China continues to have success in cyber espionage against the U.S. government, our allies, and U.S. companies."[54]

Before the 2015 deal was signed, a spokesman for China's defense ministry accused U.S. officials of conducting their own cyber spying operations. U.S. criticism of cyber espionage by China, he said, was a case of "a thief yelling 'Stop, thief!'"[55]

Paul Rosenzweig, a former Homeland Security deputy assistant secretary for policy who lectures on law at George Washington University, says international adoption of standard practices on cyberattacks is more feasible than a treaty like the one proposed by Microsoft's Smith. He notes that countries already have begun to agree not to target other countries' electricity grids. In 2015, for example, countries participating in that year's round of GGE talks pledged not to target other countries' critical infrastructure in peacetime. "It is not a mandate, but it seems moderately effective," Rosenzweig says.

BACKGROUND
Pre-Internet Attacks

In 1986, Clifford Stoll, a computer analyst at Lawrence Berkeley National Laboratory in California, discovered while investigating a 75-cent accounting anomaly that the lab's network and other high-security government networks had been hacked. Eventually, Stoll tracked the intrusion to a group of West German spies working for the KGB, the Soviet Union's main security agency.[56] The incident — known as the "The Cuckoo's Egg," after the title of Stoll's 1989 book — was the first publicly documented cyberattack by another country on U.S. government computers.

Two years later, on Nov. 3, 1988, about 8,800 computers connected to ARPANET, the forerunner of the internet, were hit by the world's first computer worm and slowed to a crawl or crashed. Robert Morris, a Cornell University graduate student, had released the worm not to cause damage, he said, but to gauge ARPANET's reach. Still, he was convicted under the Computer Fraud and Abuse Act and sentenced to three years of probation.[57]

"Before Morris unleashed his worm, the internet was like a small town where people thought little of leaving their doors unlocked," technology journalist Timothy B. Lee wrote about the incident. "Internet security was seen as a mostly theoretical problem, and software vendors treated security flaws as a low priority. The Morris Worm destroyed that complacency."[58]

In response to the Morris Worm, the Defense Advanced Research Projects Agency (DARPA), a research arm of the Defense Department, contracted with Carnegie Mellon University to create the Computer Emergency Response Team (CERT), a research center focused on software flaws and internet security.[59]

Cyberattacks on the Rise

Increasing use of the internet by government, academia and the private sector prompted the United States and Russia to meet in secret in Moscow in 1996 to talk about a cyberspace disarmament agreement. U.S. officials were focused primarily on protecting data and infrastructure, but the Russians wanted any treaty to cover what they called 'information terrorism,' which referred to "any use of the internet that might threaten domestic stability," wrote Adam Segal, director of the Program on Digital and Cyberspace Policy at the Council on Foreign Relations think tank.[60]

In 1997, U.S. defense officials launched an internal exercise dubbed "Eligible Receiver" in response to evidence that military networks were being probed by unknown sources. NSA hackers were assigned to break into Defense Department networks using only publicly available computer hardware and software to test the networks' security. The NSA hackers were able to take control of Pentagon computers as well as power grids and 911 systems in nine major U.S. cities.[61]

"What Eligible Receiver really demonstrated was the real lack of consciousness about cyber warfare," said John Hamre, deputy secretary of Defense at the time. "The

Getty Images/Sean Gallup

A cyberattack this year on the defunct nuclear plant in Chernobyl, Ukraine, disabled the computers monitoring radiation left over from a massive 1986 explosion at the plant. Ukraine has blamed Russia, but the Kremlin has denied involvement. Cybersecurity experts say such attacks suggest that future wars likely will begin in cyberspace, not at sea, on land or in the air.

first three days of Eligible Receiver, nobody believed we were under cyberattack."[62]

The March 1998 discovery of a two-year pattern of intrusions on government computer networks — later dubbed "Moonlight Maze" — confirmed the security gaps uncovered by Eligible Receiver. Intelligence officials are still investigating the intrusions, which originated in Russia and compromised tens of thousands of files — including maps of military installations and military hardware designs.[63]

Weaknesses in U.S. military and civilian computer networks prompted President Bill Clinton in 1998 to issue the first national cybersecurity strategy. His directive said that "non-traditional attacks on our infrastructure and information systems may be capable of significantly harming both our military power and our economy" and ordered federal agencies to secure their networks within five years.[64]

In 2001, a city network administrator in Mountain View, Calif., noticed suspicious attempts to access the city's website and called the FBI. Analysts at the bureau found that the probes — which sought information about utilities and emergency systems — had originated in the Middle East and South Asia. That information acquired new significance when U.S. intelligence

officials discovered that computers seized from al Qaeda operatives after the 9/11 attacks showed evidence that the terrorist group had engaged in widespread surveillance of U.S. infrastructure.[65]

Two years later, the Bush administration ordered the Homeland Security Department to establish a National Cyber Security Division to develop new technologies, tools and techniques to defend against cyberattacks. Also in 2003, Homeland Security officials issued the National Strategy to Secure Cyberspace, a roadmap for federal agencies and private companies to voluntarily cooperate on cyber security.[66]

The 2007 "surge" in U.S. forces fighting in Iraq marked the first time that defense and intelligence agencies tested cyberwar theories on the battlefield.[67] As part of those tests, U.S. agents sent fake text messages to insurgents in Iraq to entice them to specific locations, where they were then targeted by U.S. troops or drone-fired missiles.[68]

The first known cyberattack targeting an entire country took place in April that same year, when Russian hackers defaced Estonian government websites, posted fake documents and shut down email accounts. The attack was in retaliation for Estonia's decision to remove a statue of a Soviet soldier commemorating World War II.[69]

A year later, Russia launched a more serious cyberattack against Georgia in preparation for a conventional military assault, knocking out commercial banking and media outlets.[70]

In early 2009, almost immediately after winning election, Obama called for a thorough review of federal measures to defend U.S. cyberspace. In June, his administration announced the creation of the U.S. Cyber Command within the Defense Department to defend department networks.[71]

China began to attract attention from U.S. cybersecurity officials in 2010, after Google said Chinese hackers stole intellectual property from the company and broke into the email accounts of human-rights activists.[72] The attack — dubbed Operation Aurora — also targeted dozens of other companies.[73]

As federal agencies worked to strengthen their cyberdefenses, defense officials prepared offensive cyberweapons.

In 2010, a cyberweapon called Stuxnet was accidentally discovered to have migrated from an Iranian nuclear facility to computer networks around the world. The

CHRONOLOGY

1980s *Pre-internet attacks focus on hacking into networks.*

1986 An analyst discovers that the computer network at Lawrence Berkeley National Laboratory in California and other high-security government networks have been hacked by West German spies who sold the information to the Soviet Union.

1988 Thousands of computers in the United States are hit with the first computer worm, called the "Morris Worm," alerting federal agencies to the dangers posed by software and network vulnerability.

1990s–2000s *Internet use expands and cyberattacks increase.*

1997 The Defense Department's "Eligible Receiver" exercise lets the National Security Agency (NSA) hack into department networks to test for vulnerabilities. The NSA team finds it can take control of Pentagon computers and civilian power grids.

1998 U.S. officials discover a pattern of computer intrusions — later dubbed "Moonlight Maze" — that had originated in Russia and had compromised maps of military installations and other sensitive files. . . . President Bill Clinton issues the first national cybersecurity strategy, which directs the federal government to secure its computer networks within five years.

2002 Following the 9/11 terrorist attacks on the United States, Congress increases penalties for several computer crimes, requires federal agencies to better protect their networks and provides $900 million to research cybersecurity improvements.

2003 George W. Bush administration releases the National Strategy to Secure Cyberspace, setting priorities for agencies with responsibility for cybersecurity. . . . Bush makes the Homeland Security Department responsible for protecting the country's non-military cyberspace infrastructure.

2007 Estonia accuses Russia of attacking its government computers.

2008 President George W. Bush calls for a Comprehensive National Cybersecurity Initiative to establish cybersecurity requirements for government agencies. . . . Russian agents hack into Georgian government websites before launching a conventional military attack.

2009 North Korea is suspected in cyberattacks on U.S. and South Korean government, media and financial computer systems.

2010–Present *Governments go on the cyber offensive.*

2010 Google says its servers were hacked, apparently from China, and Secretary of State Hillary Clinton warns the United States will retaliate after such attacks. . . . The Stuxnet cyberweapon, used to destroy centrifuges at an Iranian nuclear facility and attributed to the United States and Israel, is publicly identified.

2012 Iran launches a cyberattack on the Saudi Arabian national oil company. . . . Researchers identify a digital worm called "Flame" that deleted information from computers in Iran, Sudan and the Middle East.

2013 U.S. discloses that hackers, later determined to be Chinese, stole data on the F-35 fighter aircraft. . . . President Obama issues an executive order making it easier for companies and government agencies to share cyberthreat information.

2014 The FBI says North Korea was behind a cyberattack that released confidential data from Sony Pictures. The attack followed North Korean outrage over a Sony comedy film, "The Interview," about a plot to assassinate the country's leader, Kim Jong-un.

2015 Cybersecurity Information Sharing Act allows government agencies and the private sector to share data about cyberattacks and cyberthreats, including data on private citizens.

2016 Intelligence officials say Russia hacked and released Democratic National Committee emails to influence the U.S. presidential election. . . . In December, Russian hackers disable part of Ukraine's power grid.

2017 A computer virus originating in Ukraine disrupts computer networks around the world. . . . Facebook says it sold $100,000 in ads to Russian operatives hoping to influence the 2016 presidential election.

Digital Attacks Spur Calls for Cyberalliance

Some experts want NATO to take offensive in cyberspace.

With 4.7 billion people expected to be online by 2025, cyber officials are expressing growing fears about digital security and urging countries to work together to protect cyberspace.[1]

The question is how best to foster such international collaboration.

The United States already participates in cyberdefense exercises with NATO, a U.S.-European military alliance that says it must defend itself in cyberspace "as effectively as it does in the air, on land and at sea." Under Article 5 of its charter, NATO would treat a cyberattack against one of its members as an attack against all members, according to the alliance's secretary general, Jens Stoltenberg.[2]

NATO has not made clear, however, what type of cyberattack would trigger Article 5, or how it would decide on a proportional response.[3] One challenge is that it is often difficult to say for sure whether a particular cyberattack was launched by a government agency or a private group.[4]

The alliance's policy on cyberwarfare — as in conventional warfare — is to act only in self-defense, which some cybersecurity experts believe is misguided. "Can any military force credibly claim to have advanced capabilities if it does not include offensive cyber operations in its arsenal?" James Lewis, a senior vice president at the Center for Strategic and International Studies, a bipartisan think tank in Washington, wrote in 2015.[5]

A NATO spokesperson said in July the alliance warded off 500 cyberattacks each month in 2016.

"Foreign governments, criminals and terrorists can all be the source of cyberattacks, and attribution can be difficult," Oana Lungescu said. "But of course, nations have the largest resources in the cyber field, and they are responsible for the majority of targeted attacks against NATO networks."[6]

One such attack occurred in June, when computers at government offices, financial firms, utilities and industries around the world were wiped clean in a digital attack that a NATO-affiliated research firm said was likely caused by a "state actor" or by someone with state backing. Researcher Tomáš Minárik at NATO's Cooperative Cyber Defense Centre of Excellence said the attack "could count as a violation of sovereignty" that would justify countermeasures by the targeted countries. Ukraine, where the attack started, has blamed Russia. The Kremlin has denied involvement.[7]

Former NATO Supreme Commander Philip M. Breedlove argued in May that NATO should develop offensive cyberweapons, specifically to deter Russia from launching digital attacks. "We in NATO have incredible cyber capability," he said. "But we in NATO do not have an incredible cyber policy. In fact, our policy is quite limiting. It really does not allow us to consider offensive operatives as an alliance in cyber."[8]

The United Nations also is working to come up with international standards for responding to hostile acts in cyberspace. In June, the U.N.'s fifth Group of Governmental

virus, thought to have been created by the NSA and Israel, was designed to undermine Iran's nuclear weapons program by causing centrifuges that enrich uranium to spin out of control.[74]

One participant in the operation said the aim was not to cause immediate, extensive damage but to make the Iranians think their engineers were incompetent. "The idea was to string it out as long as possible," the person said. "If you had wholesale destruction right away, then they generally can figure out what happened, and it doesn't look like incompetence."[75]

Two years later, researchers identified "Flame," a digital worm that had deleted information from computers in Iran, Sudan and the Middle East. The worm consisted of different modules, including one called "Shredder" that instructed breached computers to remove all traces of the infection. Other modules stole documents, recorded keystrokes and screenshots or lifted data and audio from smartphones or other Bluetooth devices near the targeted computer.[76]

Flame may have been first used in 2004. In 2012, it was considered possibly the most complex piece of

Experts on Information Security (GGE) disbanded, reportedly over disagreements about whether its final report should deal with the use of countermeasures after a cyberattack. (The first GGE group formed in 2004 to examine potential cyberthreats and possible cooperative measures to address them.)[9]

Advocates for cyberdefense cooperation viewed the disbanding as a major setback, saying it leaves the future of international cooperation on cyberspace up in the air.[10] Paul Rosenzweig, a former Department of Homeland Security deputy assistant secretary and a law lecturer at George Washington University, said the GGE's deadlock shows how difficult it will be for countries to agree even on basic standards of behavior in cyberspace.

Some experts say the only way to counter cyberchallenges from Russia, China, North Korea and other authoritarian governments is to form a "cyberalliance" of democratic countries, separate from NATO.

"The alliance will need a common perception that it matters to each of us and each nation to defend the democratic civil societies against the economic losses and political intrusions" of China and other authoritarian countries, Chris C. Demchak, who teaches cybersecurity at the U.S. Naval War College, said in May. She said such an alliance would consist of up to 40 countries containing 900 million people who would have "the economic market weight and the technological talent pool to face China as a peer."[11]

U.S. defense officials have not advocated for a formal cyberalliance, according to Masao Doi, acting deputy chief of public affairs at the U.S. Cyber Command. But, he added, "cooperation and partnership are vital to the success of U.S. Cyber Command's missions."

— *Patrick Marshall*

[1] David Burt et al., "Cyberspace 2025: Today's Decisions, Tomorrow's Terrain," Microsoft, June 2014, https://tinyurl.com/y9ql3vrq.

[2] Roland Oliphant and Cara McGoogan, "Nato warns cyber attacks 'could trigger Article 5' as world reels from Ukraine hack," *The Telegraph*, June 28, 2017, https://tinyurl.com/y9qdxbaq.

[3] "NATO Cyber Defence," NATO fact sheet, April 2017, https://tinyurl.com/y7cnlkee; Oliphant and McGoogan, ibid.

[4] "Massive cyber attack could trigger NATO response: Stoltenberg," Reuters, June 15, 2016, https://tinyurl.com/ydaycggb.

[5] James A. Lewis, "The Role Of Offensive Cyber Operations In NATO's Collective Defence," The Tallinn Papers, NATO Cooperative Cyber Defence Centre of Excellence Tallinn Estonia, 2015, https://tinyurl.com/y7zbby5q.

[6] Ryan Browne, "NATO: We ward off 500 cyberattacks each month," CNN, July 18, 2017, https://tinyurl.com/y83sa5yo.

[7] Luke Graham, "NATO think-tank says a 'state actor' was behind the massive ransomware attack and could trigger military response," CNBC, June 30, 2017, https://tinyurl.com/y73vhbph; Thomas Fox Brewster, "NotPetya Ransomware Hackers 'Took Down Ukraine Power Grid,'" *Forbes*, July 3, 2017, https://tinyurl.com/ya4bscfv.

[8] Patrick Tucker, "Former NATO Commander: Alliance Needs to Take Cyber Fight to Russia's Door," *Defense One*, July 6, 2017, https://tinyurl.com/y8dld49.

[9] "Developments in the Field of Information and Telecommunications in the Context of International Security," fact sheet, United Nations Office for Disarmament Affairs, April 2017, https://tinyurl.com/yaeaplo7; Elaine Korzak, "UN GGE on Cybersecurity: The End of an Era?" *The Diplomat*, July 31, 2017, https://tinyurl.com/ybpa5kpf.

[10] Ibid., Korzak.

[11] "Key Trends across a Maturing Cyberspace affecting U.S. and China Future Influences in a Rising deeply Cybered, Conflictual, and Post-Western World," testimony of Chris C. Demchak before the U.S. China Economic and Security Review Commission, May 4, 2017, https://tinyurl.com/ya6hud5u.

malware ever discovered. Some analysts suspect it was created by the United States and Israel. It also was the first identified virus that used Bluetooth wireless technology to send and receive commands and data.[77]

Government Action

On Nov. 17, 2010, Dean Turner, director of the Global Intelligence Network at Symantec, a private security firm, called Stuxnet "a wake-up call to critical infrastructure systems around the world."

"This is the first publicly known threat to target industrial control systems and grants hackers vital control of critical infrastructures such as power plants, dams and chemical facilities," Turner told a Senate committee.[78]

In retaliation for Stuxnet, an activist group backed by Iran launched about 200 "denial of service" attacks aimed at disabling websites at nearly 50 U.S. financial institutions.[79]

Iran also was reportedly behind a 2012 cyberattack on Saudi Aramco, the Saudi Arabian national oil company and the world's largest oil exporter, using a

Cyberthreats a Growing Concern for 2018 Elections

Bots and trolls are "an existential threat to U.S. democracy."

Securing the nation's voting systems has taken on new urgency ahead of next year's midterm congressional elections, as evidence mounts that Russia used hacking and bogus social media accounts to interfere in last year's presidential race.

But many election officials say they still feel vulnerable to cyberthreats, and security officials are scrambling to find solutions.

In July, officials from the Homeland Security Department, FBI and the Election Assistance Commission — the only federal agency that works exclusively to make sure voting systems are secure — met with state election officials to explain the department's plan to protect voting systems. The plan focuses on sharing information with election officials regarding potential threats, analyzing risks to individual voting systems and ensuring election officials have the tools to support cybersecurity.[1]

On Sept. 22, the Homeland Security Department contacted election officials in 21 states and told them hackers linked to the Russian government attempted to hack their voting systems last year. State election officials and congressional lawmakers earlier had expressed frustration with the department's unwillingness to share information on which states were targeted.

"We heard feedback from the secretaries of state that this was an important piece of information," said Bob Kolasky, acting deputy undersecretary for DHS's National Protection and Programs Directorate. "We agreed that this information would help election officials make security decisions."

He said Homeland Security officials recognized the need for states to strengthen their voting systems now "rather than a few weeks before" the 2018 elections. Department officials left it to individual states to decide whether to publicly reveal they had been targeted.[2]

Even with the new information on which states were targeted, many states say they do not have enough money to secure their voting systems. Of 33 states surveyed by the news organization *Politico*, officials in at least 10 said they had asked state lawmakers this year for more money for election cybersecurity. But officials in only six states said they either received the money or expected to get it.[3]

Officials in 21 states said the federal government should provide money to help states strengthen election security or replace voting machines.

Not all states agree. "The last thing we need to do is create more government bureaucracy and throw federal money at a problem when the states can devise a solution," Georgia Secretary of State Brian Kemp said.[4]

Russia's hacking attempts last year apparently did not affect voting tallies.[5] "What this boils down to is that someone tried the door knob and it was locked," said Reid Magney, a spokesman for the Wisconsin Elections Commission.

Even so, Congress has been trying to find ways to prevent election interference. In January, Rep. Eliot Engel, D-N.Y., introduced legislation that would freeze the assets of foreigners who meddle in U.S. elections and deny them entry visas. In July, six Democratic House members led by Rep. Jim Langevin of Rhode Island announced they had formed a task force that aims to give members of Congress and cybersecurity experts a forum to discuss threats to voting systems. So far, however, no Republicans have joined the group.[6]

Hacking of voting systems is just one source of concern. Some cybersecurity experts say "influence campaigns," conducted through social media to disrupt democratic institutions and processes, are even more dangerous.[7]

Such campaigns, including the one Russia is accused of pursuing last year, may pose "an existential threat to U.S. democracy," says Peter W. Singer, a strategist and senior fellow at New America, a left-leaning think tank in Washington.

Intelligence officials say influence campaigns played a key role in Russia's attempts to interfere in last year's election through the use of "state-funded media, third-party intermediaries, and paid social media users or 'trolls.' "[8]

Special counsel Robert Mueller, the former FBI director investigating Russia's activities before the election, is looking at whether $100,000 of Facebook ads bought by a Russian "troll farm" may have influenced voters. On Sept. 21, Facebook said it would turn over more than 3,000 of the ads to congressional panels probing Russia's election meddling.[9]

The same Russian operatives linked to the Facebook ads also used Twitter accounts, the company told congressional investigators in September. The investigators are probing how Russia used both social media platforms as part of an effort to influence the results of the election by spreading misleading propaganda.[10]

Even before the ad sale, Russian agents had posed as Americans on social media to encourage people to visit sites containing false or derogatory stories about Democratic presidential nominee Hillary Clinton, according to *The New York Times*.[11]

Election-related cyberthreats tend to divide members of Congress along party lines. In early February, Republicans on the House Administration Committee voted to shut down the Election Assistance Commission (EAC). The full House has not taken up the measure.

"If we're looking at reducing the size of government, this is a perfect example of something that can be eliminated," committee Chairman Gregg Harper, R-Miss., said after the vote. He said the EAC has outlived its usefulness and that the Federal Election Commission should take over its functions.[12]

Two experts on election security — Dan S. Wallach, a computer science professor at Rice University, and political consultant Justin Talbot-Zorn — disagree. They wrote in February that the vote to eliminate EAC funding reflects "a radical disconnect between a handful of influential House Republicans and nearly everyone else."[13]

— *Patrick Marshall*

[1] Erica Orden and Byron Tau, "GOP Seeks to Close Federal Election Agency," *The Wall Street Journal*, July 17, 2017, https://tinyurl.com/ya4vc3dm; Tim Starks, "DHS accelerates work to protect 2018 elections under 'critical infrastructure' tag," *Politico*, July 11, 2017, https://tinyurl.com/y6udbaho.

[2] Sari Horwitz, Ellen Nakashima and Matea Gold, "DHS tells states about Russian hacking during 2016 election," *The Washington Post*, Sept. 22, 2017, https://tinyurl.com/ycnmxy3z.

[3] Cory Bennett et al., "Cash-strapped states brace for Russian hacking fight," *Politico*, Sept. 3, 2017, https://tinyurl.com/ybttxsom.

[4] Ibid.

[5] Tal Kopan, "DHS officials: 21 states potentially targeted by Russia hackers pre-election," CNN, July 18, 2017, https://tinyurl.com/y7bfyn33.

[6] "H.R.530 — Secure Our Democracy Act," Congress.gov, Feb. 8, 2017, https://tinyurl.com/yc7mmuzw; Rachael Kalinyak, "Task force focused on securing election systems crystallizes," *Federal Times*, July 27, 2017, https://tinyurl.com/yajamdlg.

[7] Massimo Calabresi, "Inside Russia's Social Media War on America," *Time*, May 18, 2017, https://tinyurl.com/lctxsar.

[8] "Assessing Russian Activities and Intentions in Recent US Elections," Office of the Director of National Intelligence, Jan. 6, 2017, https://tinyurl.com/hye8jnl.

[9] Dylan Byers, "Facebook handed Russia-linked ads over to Mueller under search warrant," CNN, Sept. 17, 2017, https://tinyurl.com/ydyd7zl6; Scott Shane and Mike Isaac, "Facebook to Turn Over Russian-Linked Ads to Congress," *The New York Times*, Sept. 21, 2017, https://tinyurl.com/y9vjagpy.

[10] Elizabeth Dwoskin, Adam Entous and Karoun Demirjian "Twitter finds hundreds of accounts tied to Russian operatives," *The Washington Post*, Sept. 28, 2017, https://tinyurl.com/y7bkjzhj.

[11] Scott Shane, "The Fake Americans Russia Created to Influence the Election," *The New York Times*, Sept. 7, 2017, https://tinyurl.com/ybf6rfw5.

[12] "As Trump fears fraud, GOP eliminates election commission," The Associated Press, Feb. 7, 2017, https://tinyurl.com/ybnzn2ek; "Harper: Time to Eliminate Obsolete Election Assistance Commission & Presidential Election Campaign Fund," press release, Rep. Gregg Harper, Feb. 8, 2017, https://tinyurl.com/y8k47kkx.

[13] Dan S. Wallach and Justin Talbot Zorn, "Want Secure Elections? Then Maybe Don't Cut Security Funding," *Wired*, Feb. 14, 2017, https://tinyurl.com/y7jc545r.

virus called Shamoon. The attack wiped data from 30,000 computers.

"The Shamoon attack in Saudi Arabia seriously spooked the U.S. government," the Council on Foreign Relations' Segal wrote. Later that year, Defense Secretary Leon Panetta warned of a potential "cyber Pearl Harbor" in which hackers would derail passenger trains or trains loaded with lethal chemicals.[80]

U.S. cybersecurity officials were further shaken by the disclosure in June 2013 that hackers had stolen technical and design data for the F-35, America's next-generation fighter aircraft.[81] China was eventually identified as the culprit. "The Chinese might never have to fight the jet if it didn't get off the ground," Shane Harris wrote in his 2014 book @War: The Rise of the Military-Internet Complex.[82]

U.S. officials, however, were making progress themselves on offensive cyber capabilities. By 2013, the NSA had implanted malware in an estimated 85,000 computer systems in 89 countries to allow them to access those networks should they need to in the future.[83] That same year, the NSA's Remote Operations Center received authorization to spend $651.7 million breaking into computer systems around the world — twice the amount the entire intelligence community spent that year defending classified U.S. military networks from attack.[84]

The Obama administration also was focused on securing critical infrastructure. On Feb. 12, 2013, Obama signed an executive order telling federal agencies to start sharing more cyberthreat information with private companies and directing the Homeland Security Department to identify infrastructure elements "where a cybersecurity incident could reasonably result in catastrophic regional or national effects."[85]

The hacking attack targeting Sony Pictures took place a year later when hackers operating under the name "Guardians of Peace" made five unreleased Sony films publicly available.[86]

In 2015, Congress passed the Cybersecurity Information Sharing Act, which allows federal agencies and private companies to share data about cyberattacks and threats, including data on private citizens.

Civil liberties groups say the law threatens individual privacy rights. "It was billed as a cybersecurity bill but it seemed more like a surveillance bill," says Neema Singh Giuliani, legislative counsel with the American Civil Liberties Union (ACLU).

Cybersecurity experts also say the 2015 law is already out of date. They say computer attackers around the world have grown so sophisticated — often with state sponsorship — that the concept of allowing companies and the government to share cyber information seems antique.[87]

In December 2016, nearly 250,000 people in Ukraine lost electricity as the result of a suspected Russian cyberattack that came just six months before the June attack that began in Ukraine and spread around the world. The December attack was linked to the war in eastern Ukraine, where Russian-backed separatists are fighting Ukrainian government forces.[88]

Russia's multipronged campaign to influence the 2016 presidential election has continued to generate headlines since U.S. officials said last October they were confident the Kremlin was behind the hacking and release of Democratic National Committee emails.

"Such activity is not new to Moscow — the Russians have used similar tactics and techniques across Europe and Eurasia, for example, to influence public opinion there," the Department of Homeland Security and Office of the Director of National Intelligence said in a joint statement last year.[89]

In September, Facebook said it would turn over more than 3,000 Russia-linked ads to congressional committees investigating the Kremlin's influence operation prior to the election. Facebook also has given information on the ads to Robert Mueller, the special counsel investigating Russia's activities linked to the election.[90]

Also in September, Department of Homeland Security officials contacted election officials in 21 states and told them Russia had tried to hack into their voting systems before the 2016 presidential election.[91]

CURRENT SITUATION
Trump Administration

On May 11, President Trump issued an executive order aimed at strengthening cybersecurity for federal networks and critical infrastructure. The order identifies three priorities: protecting federal networks, updating antiquated systems, and directing all department and agency heads to work together "so that we view our federal [internet technology] as one enterprise network," said Tom Bossert, Trump's homeland security adviser.[92]

The order also specifically makes agency heads responsible for cybersecurity at their departments, a job that Lin at the Hoover Institution says typically fell to chief information officers or chief security officers. Lin also says requiring interagency cooperation is important because "what happens at the Department of Treasury matters to the Department of Agriculture."

Trump's executive order was in addition to his decision to make U.S. Cyber Command — the Department of Defense's offensive cyber force — its own unified military command.[93]

New America's Singer, who supports the move, says "the battleground and the organization have become more operational since Cyber Command was formed, and this is a natural evolution."

Even as the Cyber Command assumes a higher-profile role, Congress is looking to exercise tighter oversight over cyber operations. In July, the House approved legislation that would require Defense officials to notify Congress within 48 hours of any "sensitive military cyber operation" undertaken by the United States. The measure is part of the 2018 National Defense Authorization Act, which has passed the House and is pending before the Senate. It would apply to both offensive and defensive operations, but exempts covert actions.[94]

NSA Under Scrutiny

NSA officials have made it a practice to identify "zero-day" vulnerabilities in software used by private companies. The term refers to major coding flaws that hackers could exploit and that the companies do not know exist.

The NSA collects such flaws in case it might someday want to use them to launch a cyberattack or extract information from a computer network. But the agency has opted not to tell companies about those vulnerabilities, drawing criticism from companies and consumer groups.[95]

The risks linked to that policy came to light in August 2016, when Cisco and Fortinet, which make networking equipment, alerted their customers that a hacking group called Shadow Brokers had made certain data available for sale on the Web. The data included hacking software that could be used to target networking appliances made by Cisco, Fortinet and other companies.

A billboard promotes the Sony Pictures comedy "The Interview," in Venice, Calif., on Dec. 19, 2014. Earlier that year, hackers broke into Sony computers, stealing unreleased movies and making them publicly available. U.S. officials said North Korea launched the attack in retaliation for the film, which depicts a plot to assassinate the country's leader, Kim Jong-un.

Getty Images/Christopher Polk

Shadow Brokers said they had stolen the data from a group linked to the NSA, and analysts concluded that the data consisted of zero-day vulnerabilities the agency had collected without telling the companies.[96]

The incident took place two years after the Obama administration, in a break with the policy in effect during the George W. Bush administration, directed the NSA to reveal any vulnerabilities it discovered in companies' software, but made an exception for vulnerabilities that could serve "a clear national security or law enforcement need."[97] One former government official said that by 2014 the NSA had stored more than 2,000 zero-day vulnerabilities for potential use against Chinese systems alone.[98]

Security flaws in software and hardware have spawned an entire industry, with private companies finding the holes and then turning them into hacking weapons — known as "zero-day exploits" — that they sell to the NSA and other agencies and companies.

"This gray market is not precisely illegal, but it operates on the fringes of the Internet," Harris wrote in his 2014 book.[99] He said zero-day exploits in software go for $50,000 to $100,000, while exploits based on flaws in computer hardware can earn their creators millions of dollars.[100]

Giuliani at the ACLU says the NSA's handling of zero-day vulnerabilities needs to be more transparent. "It

Should the government regulate private-sector cybersecurity?

YES

John Arquilla
Professor and Chair of Defense Analysis,
U.S. Naval Postgraduate School

Written for *CQ Researcher,* October 2017

In 2003, President George W. Bush issued his "National Strategy to Secure Cyberspace," an attempt to guide — but not to regulate — efforts to protect commercial, infrastructural and personal information systems. Congress soon allocated about $5 billion in support of such efforts, and the public and private resources expended trying to improve cybersecurity have dwarfed that amount since — to little effect.

The list of costly hacks and massive data breaches has only lengthened over time, as major retail firms, leading social media sites and even some of the most sensitive, classified government databases have been penetrated. Add hundreds of billions of dollars' worth of intellectual property raided by hackers each year, and the cyber-cataclysm underway can no longer be denied or ignored.

The fault lies in the choice initially made by Bush — and reaffirmed since — to make government's role informational rather than regulatory. By doing so, government has granted the commercial sector the "freedom to innovate," as the Information Technology Association of America put it. And privacy concerns about government intrusiveness also have been kept at politically acceptable levels. The result: precious little innovation in cybersecurity has come from the business sector, and privacy has been shredded — not by Big Brother, but by a host of Little Brother hacking cliques.

Clearly, this is a case of what economists call "market failure." Consumers continue to purchase insecure products in ever-increasing quantities, so there has been no invisible hand to drive producers toward better cybersecurity. Given that the paths to improvement have been perceptible for some time — cloud computing, block chains and the ubiquitous use of strong encryption — government is now well positioned to require producers to employ such means, and to use its bully pulpit to nudge consumers to make informed purchases.

For the past two decades, government steered by the guardrails when it came to cybersecurity. First it lurched toward reliance on market mechanisms that have failed; then it went in the other direction with the misguided effort to obtain "backdoors" into commercial products that would allow government surveillance of anyone, at any time. The more sensible path is simply to regulate the adoption of the best cybersecurity technologies and practices.

The issue is not one of Right or Left. It has always been a matter of distinguishing right from wrong. If we fail, ruin lies ahead.

NO

Herbert Lin
Senior Research Scholar for Cyber Policy and
Security, Hoover Institution

Written for *CQ Researcher,* October 2017

Regulation should be a tool of last resort that directs private firms to take actions for enhancing the nation's cybersecurity that they would not otherwise take.

Market failure in cybersecurity is apparent in two ways. First, individual entities do not do all they should to provide for their own cybersecurity needs. Providing these entities with the information they need to take cybersecurity-enhancing actions in their own self-interest may be a partial solution to this kind of market failure, and providing information is obviously not a regulatory activity.

Second, even if these individual entities did all that could reasonably be expected, the national cybersecurity posture would still be inadequate because of the interdependencies between private and government entities. This aspect of market failure is much harder to address because it is not in any entity's self-interest to do for the nation more than it needs to do for itself. Here, regulation should be considered only when the risks to public safety and security are material and other approaches fail.

As an example of a nonregulatory approach, the NIST Cybersecurity Framework was designed to provide a systematic and voluntary way for private firms to assess their cybersecurity risks and take corrective action commensurate with them. Broader use of that framework would improve the nation's cybersecurity.

A more controversial — but still nonregulatory — approach would be to subject private vendors of IT products and services to tort liability for security lapses and inadequacies. Vendors say such liability would stifle innovation. But today's market environment has few incentives to attend to security while innovating. Tort liability — with appropriate carve-outs and limits — would help to redress that balance.

In any event, the liability question is likely to be moot with the advent of the Internet of Things (IOT). A robust liability regime already exists for "things"; the manufacturer of a faulty toaster that burns down your house is liable for damages. Adding an IOT dimension to the toaster will not change that; it is inconceivable that the manufacturer will be able to escape liability by denying the toaster's IOT parts caused the fire.

We have not yet exhausted the potential of such measures to improve the nation's cybersecurity posture. If and when we do, regulation may need to be considered as the only way to improve the nation's cybersecurity.

should be written in the law instead of being subject to change every time there's a change of political leadership," she says.

Such transparency was a top priority for Democratic and Republican lawmakers in Congress who introduced legislation on May 17 spelling out criteria for how the NSA and other agencies decide whether to tell companies about software and hardware vulnerabilities the agency has discovered.[101]

"Hoarding technological vulnerabilities to develop offensive weapons comes with significant risks to our own economy and national security," Rep. Ted Lieu, D-Calif., said in introducing the bill.[102]

White House officials say the current process is transparent enough. Michael Anton, a spokesman for the National Security Council, described it as "a disciplined, high-level interagency decision-making process for disclosure of known vulnerabilities."[103]

Internet of Things

Internet security has increasingly become a challenge as more and more everyday devices and machines — driverless cars, pacemakers, refrigerators, virtual personal assistants — send and collect data via computer networks, a phenomenon known as "the internet of things." By 2020, an estimated 34 billion devices will be connected to the internet, up from 10 billion in 2015.[104]

"The 'attack surface' in which anybody — a state or a nonstate actor — can do damage will enormously increase," says former Defense official Nye. Many of the billions of devices connected to the internet "are built not for security but for efficiency," he says.

And while internet-connected devices may not be a security hazard in themselves, they often offer hackers an unprotected entry point. "For a cyber-defender, this means that hackers will not only have three times as many targets — they will also have three times as many vectors from which to attack any given target," James Stavridis, a retired Navy admiral and dean of the Fletcher School of Law and Diplomacy at Tufts University, and Dave Weinstein, New Jersey's chief technology officer, wrote last year. "This creates vast new challenges for network security and complicates the already murky legal and technical landscape for attributing who is responsible for an attack."[105]

In August, Sens. Mark R. Warner, D-Va., Cory Gardner, R-Col., Ron Wyden, D-Ore., and Steve Daines, R-Mont., introduced legislation that would require vendors who supply the U.S. government with internet-connected devices to ensure that their software can be patched if vulnerabilities are found, that the devices do not include passwords that can't be changed, and that they are free of security flaws. The bill was referred to the Senate Homeland Security and Governmental Affairs Committee on Aug. 1. It had not signed up additional cosponsors as of Sept. 29.[106]

Nicholas Weaver, a lecturer in computer science at the University of California, Berkeley, said the bill ideally will create standards that all internet-connected devices — not just those used by the government — will follow.[107]

Stavridis and Weinstein say much more needs to be done, such as requiring that internet-connected devices automatically update their security software. "First, we need to require higher levels of security in any device that will be connected to the Web," they wrote. "Second, we need better technology to manage in real time the vulnerability of Internet of Things devices."[108]

The two said consumers need to play a role. "[W]e all have to recognize that we have a broad responsibility to protect the internet as consumers of it. While it's easy to place blame on device manufacturers, in the end, perhaps the more appropriate culprit is the user."[109]

OUTLOOK
Securing State Elections

Russia's meddling in last year's presidential election has focused the attention of state election officials and congressional lawmakers on making sure voting systems are secure in time for next year's elections.

Officials in many states say the federal government should provide money to help states strengthen election security or replace voting machines. "If we want to enhance people's confidence in our elections, Congress absolutely should secure funding for the modernization and securing of voting systems," said Nicole Lagace, communications director for Rhode Island's Department of State.

But officials in other states say they don't need federal help to solve their voting problems, citing a desire to avoid government bureaucracy.[110]

As cyberattacks by other nations, rogue states and criminals increase, cybersecurity experts say private-sector computer networks must be protected, but many say legislation is not the answer.

"Cyber changes so quickly that if we can actually get a bill passed in Congress and signed by the president, it will be outdated by the time it goes into effect," says Maness at the Naval Postgraduate School. "The private sector taking care of its own will probably be the faster and more efficient way."

Some legislators have proposed allowing companies to "hack back" against attackers to deter future attacks. More than one-third of companies said in a survey that they responded in kind to hacking attacks, even though doing so is illegal in the United States.[111]

In 2013, Microsoft and several other major corporations joined forces, with court approval, to disable a large cluster of hijacked computers being used for online crime.[112]

Jeremy Rabkin, a law professor at George Mason University in Fairfax, Va., has argued for letting federal officials approve a list of cybersecurity firms that private companies could hire to retaliate for hacking attacks.[113]

"That's a bit too much of the Wild West for me," says Arquilla of the Naval Postgraduate School. "We don't want to start a whole business of privateering in cyberspace. Things are already close to out of hand."

Other cybersecurity experts say the government needs to force companies, through regulation, to secure their computer networks. "The United States should continue to improve its regulation and oversight of the development and adoption of new software and technologies," political scientists Chad C. Serena and Colin P. Clarke at the RAND Corp. think tank wrote last year. "Networks and many of their components are inherently and increasingly insecure."[114]

Arquilla disagrees with proposals to impose government regulation on private-sector cybersecurity, saying encryption is the key to security in cyberspace. "Creating Maginot Lines around the military information infrastructure is not the answer," he says. "Expect bad guys to get into systems but make sure they can't do much damage once they are in."

He also advocates storing critical data in the cloud, or remote computer servers that are accessed online. That way, he says, the data is scattered among different servers rather than sitting in one location that hackers can target.

"We are married to a paradigm of cybersecurity based on [antivirus software] and firewalls," Arquilla says. "The problem, of course, is that antivirus programs only recognize what they already know, and good hackers just walk right through firewalls. I think we need a paradigm shift."

NOTES

1. Nicole Perlroth, Mark Scott and Sheera Frenkel, "Cyberattack Hits Ukraine Then Spreads Internationally," *The New York Times*, June 27, 2017, https://tinyurl.com/y7kyr2wm; M. Deleon, "NotPetya Ransomware Disrupts Merck Vaccine Production," University of Hawai'i West O'ahu Cyber Security Coordination Center, Aug. 4, 2017, https://tinyurl.com/y8o7674n.

2. Luke Graham, "NATO think-tank says a 'state actor' was behind the massive ransomware attack and could trigger military response," CNBC, July 7, 2017, https://tinyurl.com/y73vhbph.

3. Ibid.; Jack Stubbs, Matthias Williams, "Ukraine scrambles to contain new cyber threat after 'NotPetya' attack," Reuters, July 5, 2017, https://tinyurl.com/ycbzwx8u.

4. Andy Greenberg, "'Crash Override': The Malware That Took Down a Power Grid," *Wired*, June 12, 2017, https://tinyurl.com/y7qdudt9; Lorenzo Franceschi-Bicchierai, "The History of Stuxnet: The World's First True Cyberweapon," *Motherboard*, Aug. 9, 2016, https://tinyurl.com/y7wk224c.

5. Aaron Boyd, "DNI Clapper: Cyber bigger threat than terrorism," *Federal Times*, Feb. 4, 2016, https://tinyurl.com/ycqh5qm3.

6. Ian Sherr, "WannaCry ransomware: Everything you need to know," CNET, May 19, 2017, https://tinyurl.com/mmlznxl; Testimony of Gordon M. Snow before the Senate Judiciary Subcommittee on Crime and Terrorism, April 12, 2011, https://tinyurl.com/y8rky8ey.

7. "Ukraine power cut 'was cyber-attack,'" BBC, Jan. 11, 2017, https://tinyurl.com/ycmo9cu2; Jackie

Wattles and Jill Disis, "Ransomware attack: Who's been hit," *CNN*, May 15, 2017, https://tinyurl.com/y9sgabhk; Andy Greenberg, "How An Entire Nation Became Russia's Test Lab For Cyberwar," *Wired*, June 20, 2017, https://tinyurl.com/y9gx5thj; Natalia Zinets, "Ukraine hit by 6,500 hack attacks, sees Russian 'cyberwar,'" Reuters, Dec. 29, 2016, https://tinyurl.com/ya5onol4.

8. Elizabeth Dwoskin, Adam Entous and Karoun Demirjian, "Twitter finds hundreds of accounts tied to Russian operatives," *The Washington Post*, Sept. 28, 2017, https://tinyurl.com/y7bkjzhj; Adam Entous, Craig Timberg and Elizabeth Dwoskin, "Russian operatives used Facebook ads to exploit America's racial and religious divisions," *The Washington Post*, Sept. 25, 2017, https://tinyurl.com/ybf22uh2; Adam Entous, Ellen Nakashima and Greg Miller, "Secret CIA assessment says Russia was trying to help Trump win White House," *The Washington Post*, Dec. 9, 2016, https://tinyurl.com/yc27tzml; Scott Shane, "The Fake Americans Russia Created to Influence the Election," *The New York Times*, Sept. 7, 2017, https://tinyurl.com/ybqc4ecx.

9. Victor Luckerson, "Everything We Know About the Massive Sony Hack," *Time*, Dec. 4, 2014, https://tinyurl.com/lvy3j5m.

10. Reuters and Libby Plummer, "Nuclear power plants are at risk of Militant Attacks: UN says recent cyber hacks are the 'tip of the iceberg,'" *Daily Mail*, Oct. 10, 2016, https://tinyurl.com/y9lqwsut.

11. David Livingstone, "Cyber Security at Civil Nuclear Facilities: Understanding the Risks," Chatham House, Oct. 5, 2015, https://tinyurl.com/pj5cds3.

12. Thomas Grove, Julian E. Barnes and Drew Hinshaw, "Russia Targets NATO Soldier Smartphones, Western Officials Say," *The Wall Street Journal*, Oct. 4, 2017, https://tinyurl.com/y82qpbcr.

13. James R. Clapper, Marcel Lettre, Michael S. Rogers, "Joint Statement for the Record to the Senate Armed Services Committee: Foreign Cyber Threats to the United States," Jan. 5, 2017, http://tinyurl.com/ycemrq46.

14. Bruce G. Blair, "Why Our Nuclear Weapons Can Be Hacked," *The New York Times*, March 14, 2017, https://tinyurl.com/y9n8bc6a.

15. David Hambling, "Ships fooled in GPS spoofing attack suggest Russian cyberweapon," *New Scientist*, Aug. 10, 2017, https://tinyurl.com/ycuzl3pz; Mark L. Psiaki and Todd E. Humphreys, "Protecting GPS From Spoofers Is Critical to the Future of Navigation," *IEEE Spectrum*, July 29, 2016, https://tinyurl.com/y97z6vmz.

16. "Department of Defense: Actions Needed to Address Five Key Mission Challenges," Government Accountability Office, June 2017, p. 2, https://tinyurl.com/y7jep8rb.

17. Renae Merle, "SEC reveals it was hacked, information may have been used for illegal stock trades," *The Washington Post*, Sept. 20, 2017, https://tinyurl.com/ydarfzaz; Riley Walters, "Cyber Attacks on U.S. Companies in 2016," The Heritage Foundation, Dec. 2, 2016, https://tinyurl.com/ybnf5kv6.

18. "Information Security: Agencies Need to Improve Controls over Selected High-Impact Systems," Government Accountability Office, May 2016, https://tinyurl.com/ya5xycwj.

19. "The Hiscox Cyber Readiness Report 2017," Hiscox Insurance Company, undated, https://tinyurl.com/yc43xxws.

20. Martin Matishak, "Trump elevates U.S. Cyber Command, vows 'increased resolve' against threats," *Politico*, Aug. 18, 2017, https://tinyurl.com/y9b3ene5.

21. Thomas Gibbons-Neff and Ellen Nakashima, "President Trump announces move to elevate Cyber Command," *The Washington Post*, Aug. 18, 2017, https://tinyurl.com/y7cxtj57.

22. Saba Hamedy, "Trump: Russian meddling story an 'excuse' for why Democrats lost," *CNN*, May 12, 2017, https://tinyurl.com/ycyzt9ax.

23. Ken Dilanian, Hallie Jackson, Likhitha Butchireddygari and Gabriela Martinez, "Trump White House Has Taken Little Action To Stop Next Election Hack," NBC News, June 24, 2017, https://tinyurl.com/ybwop5fv.

24. Sean D. Carberry, "I think we need to throw a few stones," Federal Computer Week, May 12, 2017, https://tinyurl.com/yakjtv5t.

25. Clapper, Lettre and Rogers, op. cit.

26. Ellen Nakashima, "Russia has developed a cyber-weapon that can disrupt power grids, according to new research," *The Washington Post*, June 12, 2017, https://tinyurl.com/yb8r6ytt.

27. "Industrial cybersecurity treat landscape in H1 2017: Every third ICS computer under attack was from manufacturing sector," Kaspersky Lab, Sept. 28, 2017, https://tinyurl.com/y9fmc678.

28. Dustin Volz, "Trump bars US government from using Russian cybersecurity firm Kaspersky," Reuters, Sept. 14, 2017, https://tinyurl.com/ybegkrda.

29. John Markoff, "Before the Gunfire, Cyberattacks," *The New York Times*, Aug. 12, 2008, https://tinyurl.com/yblvebvo.

30. Brian R. Moore and Jonathan R. Corrado, "North Korea Proves You Barely Need Computers to Win a Cyberwar," *Foreign Policy*, June 5, 2017, https://tinyurl.com/ybgzlt4c.

31. "Cyber Warfare in the 21st Century: Threats, Challenges, and Opportunities," testimony of Jason Healey before the House Armed Services Committee, March 1, 2017, https://tinyurl.com/yamylzmh; Nicole Perlroth and Quentin Hardy, "Bank Hacking Was the Work of Iranians, Officials Say," *The New York Times*, Jan. 8, 2013, https://tinyurl.com/y9z3qfx8.

32. John Arquilla, "Cyberwar Is Already Upon Us," *Foreign Policy*, Feb. 27, 2012, https://tinyurl.com/ycwlwz6m.

33. "2015 DoD Cyber Strategy," Defense Department, April 2015, p. 5, https://tinyurl.com/ya42y7g7.

34. Ibid.

35. Ron Lieber and Stacy Cowley, "Trying to Stem Fallout From Breach, Equifax Replaces C.E.O.," *The New York Times*, Sept. 26, 2017, https://tinyurl.com/yck7cvtx; Elizabeth Weise and Nathan Bomey,"Equifax had patch 2 months before hack and didn't install it, security group says," *USA Today*, Sept. 14, 2017, https://tinyurl.com/y7t54ywy; Elizabeth Weise and Nathan Bomey, "Equifax breach hit 2.5 million more Americans than first believed," *USA Today*, Oct. 2, 2017, https://tinyurl.com/yaosx287.

36. Brittany De Lea, "SEC breach can jeopardize trillions of dollars of wealth, cybersecurity expert warns," Fox Business, Sept. 21, 2017, https://tinyurl.com/yckyhksd; Jay Clayton, "Statement on Cybersecurity," Securities and Exchange Commission, Sept. 20, 2017, https://tinyurl.com/y7gtcdr7.

37. "2016 Presidential Campaign Hacking Fast Facts," CNN, Aug. 6, 2017, https://tinyurl.com/had4auj.

38. Nicole Perlroth, "All 3 Billion Yahoo Accounts Were Affected by 2013 Attack," *The New York Times*, Oct. 3, 2017, https://tinyurl.com/yd79ymcf; Robert McMillan, "Yahoo Says Information on at Least 500 Million User Accounts Was Stolen," *The Wall Street Journal*, Sept. 22, 2016, https://tinyurl.com/y7fxhacz.

39. Vindu Goel and Eric Lichtblau, "Russian Agents were Behind Yahoo Hack, U.S. Says," *The New York Times*, March 15, 2017, https://tinyurl.com/yawv3sdq; Perlroth, op. cit.

40. "Report on Securing and Growing the Digital Economy," Commission on Enhancing National Cybersecurity, Dec. 1, 2016, p. 7, https://tinyurl.com/y8rl9oh5.

41. Ann M. Beauchesne, "More Regulation Isn't the Answer," *The New York Times*, Oct. 18, 2012, https://tinyurl.com/y7emxwv5.

42. Shane Harris, *@War: The Rise of the Military-Internet Complex* (2014), p. xxi; Tom McCarthy, "NSA director defends plan to maintain 'backdoors' into technology companies," *The Guardian*, Feb. 23, 2015, https://tinyurl.com/ybctd7y6.

43. "Vulnerabilities Equities Process," Electronic Privacy Information Center, undated, https://tinyurl.com/y8qq7b2v.

44. "Why 27% of U.S. Firms Have No Plans to Buy Cyber Insurance," *Insurance Journal*, May 31, 2017, https://tinyurl.com/y7zhzvb9.

45. Roger A. Grimes, "Vendors should not be liable for their security flaws," CSO, July 12, 2012, https://tinyurl.com/y8tyg9wg.

46. Brad Smith, "The need for a Digital Geneva Convention," Microsoft blog, Feb. 14, 2017, https://tinyurl.com/hxg3w8b.

47. Ibid.

48. James Carlini, "Geneva Convention in Cyberwarfare? Don't Count on It," *International Policy Digest*, Aug. 6, 2017, https://tinyurl.com/yd2pqt3d.

49. "Cyber War: Definitions, Deterrence and Foreign Policy," testimony of James A. Lewis before the House Foreign Affairs Committee, Sept. 30, 2015, https://tinyurl.com/ycs97wpu.

50. Morgan Chalfant, "Legislators grapple with cyber war rules," *The Hill*, March 1, 2017, https://tinyurl.com/yanglsyc.

51. Michael N. Schmitt and Liis Vihul, "Respect for Sovereignty in Cyberspace," *Texas Law Review*, Aug. 12, 2017, https://tinyurl.com/y9vcrvmb.

52. Kalev Leetaru, "Is It Hypocritical To Charge Russia For Hacking Yahoo When The US Does The Same Thing?" *Forbes*, March 16, 2017, https://tinyurl.com/y7y4rvpg.

53. Everett Rosenfeld, "US-China agree to not conduct cybertheft of intellectual property," CNBC, Sept. 25, 2015, https://tinyurl.com/y8b77n2l.

54. Franz-Stefan Gady, "Top US Spy Chief: China Still Successful in Cyber Espionage Against US," *The Diplomat*, Feb. 16, 2016, https://tinyurl.com/yctttoz2.

55. Shannon Tiezzi, "China Decries US 'Hypocrisy' on Cyber-Espionage," *The Diplomat*, March 28, 2014, https://tinyurl.com/yalsx9ya.

56. Clifford Stoll, *The Cuckoo's Egg* (1989), p. 3.

57. Timothy B. Lee, "How a grad student trying to build the first botnet brought the Internet to its knees," *The Washington Post*, Nov. 1, 2013, https://tinyurl.com/yb24zlcb.

58. Ibid.

59. "30 years of risky business: A cybersecurity timeline," *Government Computer News*, June 3, 2013, https://tinyurl.com/ycj2pgdo.

60. Adam Segal, *The Hacked World Order: How Nations Fight, Trade, Maneuver, and Manipulate in the Digital Age* (2016), p. 95.

61. Frontline, "The Warnings?" PBS, April 24, 2003, https://tinyurl.com/2oy2g.

62. Ibid.

63. Ibid.

64. "The Clinton Administration's Policy on Critical Infrastructure Protection: Presidential Decision Directive 63," The White House, May 22, 1998, https://tinyurl.com/ybrb9pdf.

65. Frontline, op. cit.

66. "The National Strategy to Secure Cyberspace," Department of Homeland Security, February 2003, https://tinyurl.com/hzplmb3.

67. Harris, op. cit., p. 25.

68. Ibid., Segal, p. 18.

69. Damien McGuinness, "How a cyber attack transformed Estonia," BBC, April 27, 2017, https://tinyurl.com/y7fen2zx; Segal, op. cit., p. 60.

70. Ibid., Segal, p. 67.

71. "U.S. Cyber Command (USCYBERCOM)," U.S. Strategic Command, Sept. 30, 2016, https://tinyurl.com/ycaf244w.

72. Kim Zetter, "Google Hack Attack Was Ultra Sophisticated, New Details Show," *Wired*, Jan. 14, 2010, https://tinyurl.com/y7ykf4kc.

73. Alina Selyukh, "Long Before 'WannaCry' Ransomware, Decades Of Cyber 'Wake-Up Calls,'" NPR, May 16, 2017, https://tinyurl.com/ybe5lcks.

74. Ellen Nakashima and Joby Warrick, "Stuxnet was work of U.S. and Israeli experts, officials say," *The Washington Post*, June 2, 2012, https://tinyurl.com/ybnndqql.

75. Ibid.

76. Segal, op. cit., p. 124.

77. Ellen Nakashima, "Newly identified computer virus, used for spying, is 20 times size of Stuxnet," *The Washington Post*, May 28, 2012, https://tinyurl.com/yaf9fbpq.

78. Testimony of Dean Turner before the Senate Committee on Homeland Security and Governmental Affairs, Symantec, Nov. 17, 2010, https://tinyurl.com/yb3k96xu.

79. Segal, op. cit., p. 5.

80. Ibid., p. 6.

81. Sydney J. Freedberg Jr., "Top Official Admits F-35 Stealth Fighter Secrets Stolen," *Breaking Defense*, June 20, 2013, https://tinyurl.com/m3z9opn.

82. Harris, op. cit., p. xv.

83. Ibid., p. 70.

84. Ibid., p. 74.

85. Ibid., p. 54.

86. Segal, op. cit., p. 51.

87. David E. Sanger and Nicole Perlroth, "Senate Approves a Cybersecurity Bill Long in the Works and Largely Dated," *The New York Times*, Oct. 27, 2015, https://tinyurl.com/y83kldvf.

88. Holly Williams, "Russian hacks into Ukraine power grids a sign of things to come for U.S.?," CBS, Dec. 21, 2016, https://tinyurl.com/y9uhmqw7.

89. Evan Perez and Theodore Schleifer, "US accuses Russia of trying to interfere with 2016 election," CNN, Oct. 18, 2016, https://tinyurl.com/zlurum7.

90. Scott Shane and Mike Isaac, "Facebook to Turn Over Russian-Linked Ads to Congress," *The New York Times*, Sept. 21, 2017, https://tinyurl.com/yb8ttspd.

91. Sari Horwitz, Ellen Nakashima and Matea Gold, "DHS tells states about Russian hacking during 2016 election," *The Washington Post*, Sept. 22, 2017, https://tinyurl.com/ydx9rh3a.

92. David Jackson and Elizabeth Weise, "President Trump signs cybersecurity executive order," *USA Today*, May 11, 2017, https://tinyurl.com/y94xbe27.

93. Gibbons-Neff and Nakashima, op. cit.

94. Richard Lardner, "Defense Bill Calls Climate Change a National Security Threat," *US News and World Report*, July 14, 2017, https://tinyurl.com/y9lc9t3s.

95. Henry Farrell, "Hackers have just dumped a treasure trove of NSA data. Here's what it means," *The Washington Post*, April 15, 2017, https://tinyurl.com/ycofutmb; Andy Greenberg, "The Shadow Brokers Mess Is What Happens When the NSA Hoards Zero-Days," *Wired*, Aug. 17, 2016, https://tinyurl.com/gv8ebm5.

96. Ibid.

97. David E. Sanger, "Obama Lets N.S.A. Exploit Some Internet Flaws, Officials Say," *The New York Times*, April 12, 2014, https://tinyurl.com/ybuj7xeu.

98. Harris, op. cit., p. 96.

99. Ibid., p. 94.

100. Ibid., p. 95.

101. Sean D. Carberry, "What the PATCH Act doesn't do," *Federal Computer Week*, May 26, 2017, https://tinyurl.com/ybhmy4ea.

102. Chris Bing, "Lawmakers introduce bill to shine spotlight on government hacking stockpile," *Cyberscoop*, May 18, 2017, https://tinyurl.com/y7dpeezk.

103. Nicole Perlroth and David E. Sanger, "Hacks Raise Fear Over N.S.A.'s Hold on Cyberweapons," *The New York Times*, June 28, 2017, https://tinyurl.com/ybkt4gwv.

104. "Here's how the Internet of Things will explode by 2020," *Business Insider*, Aug. 31, 2016, https://tinyurl.com/z3q7ow7.

105. James Stavridis and Dave Weinstein, "The Internet of Things Is a Cyberwar Nightmare," *Foreign Policy*, Nov. 3, 2016, https://tinyurl.com/y9pvcdab.

106. Bruce Sterling, "Spime Watch: The Fact Sheet For The Internet Of Things Cybersecurity Improvement Act Of 2017," *Wired*, Aug. 11, 2017, https://tinyurl.com/ycanztel; "S.1691 — Internet of Things (IoT) Cybersecurity Improvement Act of 2017," congress.gov, undated, https://tinyurl.com/ybxxof8l.

107. Nicholas Weaver, "The Internet of Things Cybersecurity Improvement Act: A Good Start on IoT Security," *Lawfare*, Aug. 2, 2017, https://tinyurl.com/ya6exmah.

108. Stavridis and Weinstein, op. cit.

109. Ibid.

110. Cory Bennett et al., "Cash-strapped states brace for Russian hacking fight," *Politico*, Sept. 3, 2017, https://tinyurl.com/ybttxsom.

111. Segal, op. cit., p. 17.

112. Harris, op. cit., p. 118.

113. Josephine Wolff, "When Companies Get Hacked, Should They Be Allowed to Hack Back?" *The Atlantic*, July 14, 2017, https://tinyurl.com/yau2ubeu.

114. Chad C. Serena and Colin P. Clarke, "America's Cyber Security Dilemma — and a Way Out," *Defense One*, Dec. 22, 2016, https://tinyurl.com/zdtnpsv.

BIBLIOGRAPHY

Selected Sources

Books

Harris, Shane, *@War: The Rise of the Military Internet Program*, Mariner Books, 2014.
A senior writer at *The Wall Street Journal* recounts the development of America's cyber weapons and defenses, and explains the close ties between government and the private sector on cybersecurity issues.

Mazanec, Brian M., *The Evolution of Cyber War: International Norms for Emerging-Technology Weapons*, University of Nebraska Press, 2015.
A George Mason University adjunct professor of policy and government examines global norms for cyberwar and recommends that the United States not pursue practices that limit its development of cyberweapons.

Segal, Adam, *The Hacked World Order: How Nations Fight, Trade, Maneuver, and Manipulate in the Digital Age*, PublicAffairs, 2016.
The director of the Digital and Cyberspace Policy Program at the Council on Foreign Relations think tank argues that because it is difficult to pinpoint where digital attacks originate and to measure their impact, international rules of engagement in cyberspace must be reworked.

Articles

Jensen, Benjamin, Brandon Valeriano and Ryan C. Maness, "Cyberwarfare has taken a new turn. Yes, it's time to worry," *The Washington Post*, July 13, 2017, https://tinyurl.com/yd8247wd.
Three cybersecurity professors at military universities, two of whom have previously described cyberthreats as overblown, explain why they are now worried about these threats.

Moore, Brian R., and Jonathan R. Corrado, "North Korea Proves You Barely Need Computers to Win a Cyberwar," *Foreign Policy*, June 5, 2017, https://tinyurl.com/ybgzlt4c.
Two Asia specialists argue that the relative ease of developing cyberweapons gives outsized power to underdeveloped, isolated nations such as North Korea that have few cybertargets to defend.

Riley, Michael, Jordan Robertson and Anita Sharpe, "The Equifax Hack Has the Hallmarks of State-Sponsored Pros," Bloomberg, Sept. 29, 2017, https://tinyurl.com/yakbka44.
The hackers who stole massive amounts of data from the Equifax credit reporting agency showed a level of sophistication that suggests they were sponsored by a foreign government, but investigators are divided on whether China is the most likely culprit.

Serena, Chad C., and Colin P. Clarke, "America's Cyber Security Dilemma — and a Way Out," *Defense One*, Dec. 22, 2016, https://tinyurl.com/zdtnpsv.
Two RAND Corp. analysts say the United States should lead the way in forging international cybersecurity practices and find ways to rapidly determine the source of cyberattacks.

Stavridis, James, and Dave Weinstein, "The Internet of Things Is a Cyberwar Nightmare," *Foreign Policy*, Nov. 3, 2016, https://tinyurl.com/y9pvcdab.
A retired admiral and dean of the Fletcher School of Law and Diplomacy at Tufts University (Stavridis) and New Jersey's chief technology officer (Weinstein) argue that the emerging network of internet-connected devices will lead to unprecedented cybersecurity challenges.

Wolff, Josephine, "When Companies Get Hacked, Should They Be Allowed to Hack Back?" *The Atlantic*, July 14, 2017, https://tinyurl.com/yau2ubeu.
An assistant professor of public policy at the Rochester Institute of Technology says that allowing companies targeted by hackers to respond in kind would make it harder to tell good actors from bad on the internet.

Reports and Studies

"Critical Infrastructure Protection: Sector-Specific Agencies Need to Better Measure Cybersecurity Progress," U.S. Government Accountability Office, November 2015, https://tinyurl.com/yasqdqbt.
The investigative arm of Congress says it found significant cyber-related risks at 11 of 15 federal agencies it audited between June 2014 and November 2015.

"Department of Defense: Actions Needed to Address Five Key Mission Challenges," U.S. Government Accountability Office, June 2017, https://tinyurl.com/y7jep8rb.
The GAO says the vulnerability of Defense Department computer networks has grown "significantly" as the department has become more dependent on the internet.

"The Department of Defense Cyber Strategy," U.S. Department of Defense, April 2015, https://tinyurl.com/ya42y7g7.
The Defense Department's most recent explanation of its strategy for strengthening cyber defenses discusses three primary missions: defending military networks and information, defending the country against cyberattacks and developing offensive cyber capabilities.

Davis, John S. II, et al., "Stateless Attribution: Toward International Accountability in Cyberspace," RAND Corp., 2017, https://tinyurl.com/y9axtesl.
Analysts at the nonpartisan think tank evaluate options for attributing cyberattacks to specific individuals or groups in a "standardized and transparent" way that make the attribution credible to the public.

For More Information

Alliance for Securing Democracy, 1744 R St., N.W., Washington, DC 20009; 202-683-2650; securingdemocracy.gmfus.org. Bipartisan, transatlantic group that works to expose Russia's "ongoing efforts to subvert democracy in the United States and Europe."

American Civil Liberties Union, 125 Broad St., 18th Floor, New York, NY 10004; 212-549-2500; www.aclu.org. Nonprofit organization that defends individual rights and civil liberties guaranteed by the Constitution and U.S. law.

Council on Foreign Relations, 58 East 68th St., New York, NY 10065; 212-434-9400; www.cfr.org. Nonpartisan think tank focused on foreign policy choices facing the United States and other countries.

Cyber Security Division (Department of Homeland Security), 3801 Nebraska Ave., N.W., Washington, DC 20016; 202-282-8000; www.dhs.gov/science-and-technology/cyber-security-division. Formed in 2010 to defend U.S. computer networks against cyberattacks.

Electronic Privacy Information Center, 1718 Connecticut Ave., N.W., Suite 200, Washington, DC 20009; 202-483-1140; www.epic.org. Public interest research center that works to protect individuals' privacy rights and civil liberties in the internet age.

New America, 740 15th St., N.W., Suite 900, Washington, DC 20005; 202-986-2700; www.newamerica.org. Left-of-center think tank focused on technology and public policy.

Office of Cyber and Infrastructure Analysis (Department of Homeland Security), 300 7th St., S.W., Washington, DC 20024; 202-282-8000; www.dhs.gov/office-cyber-infrastructure-analysis. Responsible for providing analysis to help U.S. officials protect critical infrastructure from cyberattacks.

U.S. Naval War College, 686 Cushing Road, Newport, RI 02841-1207; 401-841-1310; www.usnwc.edu. Simulates cyberwar to build analytical, strategic and decision-making skills and prepare military leaders for disaster scenarios.

4

China and the South China Sea

Patrick Marshall

Protesters from Vietnam and the Philippines demonstrate at China's consular office in Manila on Aug. 3, 2016, to demand that China respect their countries' rights to harvest fish and other resources in the South China Sea. Several Asian nations have overlapping claims to islands, reefs and shoals in the vast sea, which also holds large untapped quantities of oil and natural gas.

From *CQ Researcher*,
January 20, 2017

The Spratly Islands have long been celebrated for their exotic marine life, including more than 1,000 species of birds, fish, turtles and sea grasses.

Lately, however, the remote collection of coral reefs and small islands in the South China Sea has become a source of ominous political and military tension.

Since 2013, China has been using sand dredged from the seafloor to turn coral reefs in the Spratlys into seven artificial islands covering more than 3,200 acres, complete with harbors, runways and hangars for military bases.[1] China's intentions are benign, a government spokesman said in 2015: "The construction activities . . . fall within the scope of China's sovereignty, and are lawful, reasonable and justified. They are not targeted at any other country."[2]

But last month the Chinese Defense Ministry conceded that China has placed weapons, including anti-aircraft missiles, on the man-made islands, saying "they are primarily for defense and self-protection, and this is proper and legitimate."[3]

China's neighbors, along with many U.S. foreign policy experts and at least one likely key member of President Trump's administration, disagree.

Secretary of State nominee Rex Tillerson said at his Jan. 12 confirmation hearing that China's activities are "extremely worrisome." "Building islands and then putting military assets on those islands is akin to Russia's taking of Crimea. It's taking of territory that others lay claim to," Tillerson said. "We're going to have to send China a clear signal that first, the island-building stops, and second, your access to those islands is also not going to be allowed."[4]

Asian Nations Clash Over South China Sea

China, the Philippines, Vietnam and other Asian nations have overlapping claims to islands, reefs and shoals in the 1.4 million-square-mile South China Sea. The stakes include the rights to oil, natural gas, fisheries and other natural resources. China is also constructing controversial military outposts in the disputed Spratly Islands in an attempt to tighten its control over the region.

Claims to the South China Sea

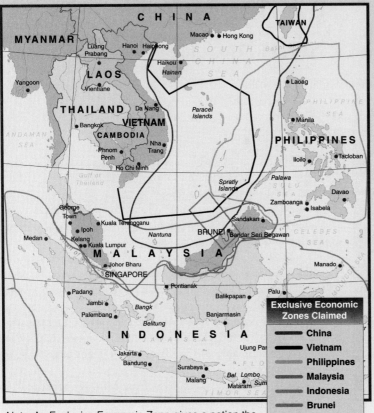

Note: An Exclusive Economic Zone gives a nation the right to drill for oil and gas, fish or pursue other economic activities 200 miles from its shores. In the South China Sea, the zones have resulted in overlapping claims.

Source: Beina Xu, "South China Sea Tensions," Council on Foreign Relations, May 14, 2014, http://tinyurl.com/ckfsb9k

Philippines in the east. M. Taylor Fravel, an associate professor of political science at the Massachusetts Institute of Technology, says the South China Sea is at the heart of "the world's most complicated territorial dispute," one with military, economic and ecological dimensions.

Six countries — China, Brunei, Malaysia, the Philippines, Taiwan and Vietnam — have overlapping claims to waters, islands, and reefs in the South China Sea. China claims four-fifths of the sea — a claim an international tribunal rejected in July. The most hotly contested areas are the Paracel Islands (occupied by China but also claimed by Vietnam and Taiwan); the Spratly Islands (claimed by Brunei, China, Malaysia, the Philippines, Taiwan and Vietnam); and the Scarborough Shoal, a chain of reefs and rocks about 100 miles west of the Philippines claimed by China, Taiwan and the Philippines.

All but Taiwan have signed the United Nations Convention on the Law of the Sea (UNCLOS) under which a country's territory extends 12 nautical miles from its shoreline. In addition, the treaty gives nations the right to drill, fish or pursue other economic activities 200 miles from its shores in an area known as an Exclusive Economic Zone. In the South China Sea, the 200-nautical-mile zones result in multiple overlapping claims, especially because some countries have occupied — and in some cases created — small islands within the Exclusive Economic Zone of other nations.

International tensions over China's buildup are only the latest in a decade-long dispute with Beijing over the strategically important South China Sea, which stretches from Brunei in the south to Taiwan in the north and the

For China, the South China Sea is of huge strategic importance. China's naval expansion and its construction of artificial islands, some analysts say, demonstrate that the Chinese want to control navigation throughout the sea and dominate the region militarily. In early January, for example, China sent its lone aircraft carrier into the Taiwan Strait in what one analyst called a show of force "intended in part to intimidate" Trump and Taiwan.[5]

"They have nationalistic goals," says former Republican Sen. James Talent, a member of the U.S.-China Economic and Security Review Commission, which Congress created to monitor trade between the two countries. The Chinese, he says, see themselves as "rightfully the dominant power in Asia."

Sen. John McCain, R-Ariz., chairman of the Senate Armed Services Committee, put it more harshly in December: "China is militarizing the South China Sea, its leaders continue to lie about that fact, and Beijing is paying little to no price for its behavior."[6]

China has been beefing up its navy in recent years. After launching more ships than any other country in 2013 and 2014, the Chinese navy had more than 300 vessels, including submarines, amphibious ships and missile-armed patrol craft as of 2015, and the trend is expected to continue, according to the U.S. Office of Naval Intelligence.[7]

China's rapid naval expansion makes some policymakers nervous, especially in light of the amount of shipping that moves through the South China Sea.

"The importance of the South China Sea to global commerce and regional stability cannot be overstated, with estimates of more than half the world's merchant fleet tonnage passing through these waters," Colin Willett, deputy assistant secretary of State for multilateral affairs, told Congress last July. "The South China Sea also serves as an important transit route and operational theater for the U.S. and other regional militaries, including those of our allies and partners. It allows us to shift military assets between the Pacific to the Indian Ocean regions."[8]

In addition, control of the region's natural resources — oil and natural gas reserves and rich commercial fishing grounds — is at stake. By some estimates, the South China Sea may contain more oil than any other area of the planet except Saudi Arabia. And according to some estimates, the region has 60 percent of Asia's hydrocarbon resources.[9] The most significant tensions over oil and gas fields have involved China's clashes with Vietnam and the Philippines over their searches for hydrocarbons in fields claimed by China.[10]

Conflicts over fishing rights are also heated. The South China Sea provides 12 percent of the global fish catch, and countries with territorial claims in the region have strongly contested access to fisheries. Competition has led to serious overfishing. Fully half of the fisheries in the South China Sea are either over-exploited or have collapsed, according to experts.[11]

As tensions rose in the past year, critics charged that former President Barack Obama made inadequate attempts to counter growing Chinese influence in the region. Meanwhile, Donald Trump's ascension to the presidency has generated anxiety among many U.S. and Asian experts and policymakers because of his threats to upend alliances and what many see as his unpredictability.

Trump repeatedly has criticized China over trade policy, saying the country unfairly closes its domestic market to imports while flooding the United States with cheap exports. And on Dec. 2, Trump broke decades of diplomatic tradition by taking a congratulatory call from Taiwan's president. Since 1972, despite its close ties to Taiwan, the United States has adhered to a "One China" policy, under which China asserts that Taiwan is a Chinese province and not an independent country.

"I don't know why we have to be bound by a One China policy unless we make a deal with China having to do with other things, including trade," Trump told Fox News on Dec. 11. "We're being hurt very badly by China with [currency] devaluation, with taxing us heavy at the borders when we don't tax them, with building a massive fortress in the middle of the South China Sea, which they shouldn't be doing."[12]

Some argue that China's aggressiveness has actually strengthened the U.S. position in Asia. Citing China's military buildup, retired Adm. Dennis Blair, a former commander of the U.S. Pacific Command and former director of National Intelligence, told Congress last July that other countries were looking to the United States for help in countering an increasingly hard-line China. "China has paid a heavy price for its aggressive activities in the hostility of the other claimant states," he said.[13]

The Obama administration moved to strengthen the U.S. position by undertaking a "pivot" or "rebalance" of American political, economic and military resources toward Asia and away from the Middle East.

The two most important legs of Obama's strategy were a commitment to increase U.S. naval assets in Asia

Asians Back Greater U.S. Military Presence

Asians, with the exception of Malaysians and Pakistanis, generally say more U.S. military resources in the Asia-Pacific region would reduce the chances for conflict with China.

Would more U.S. military resources in the Asia-Pacific area be good or bad for peace in the region?

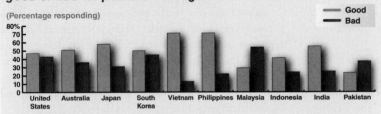

Source: "U.S. Defense Pivot to Asia Welcomed, for the Most Part — But Chinese See U.S. as Trying to Limit China's Power," Pew Research Center, June 22, 2015, http://tinyurl.com/huxa67y

and the negotiation of the Trans-Pacific Partnership (TPP), a trade pact between the United States and 11 Pacific Rim countries finalized in February 2016 but awaiting congressional approval. TPP backers see it as an attempt to strengthen the economies of regional allies, but many think the Republican-controlled Congress is unlikely to ratify the pact after Trump heavily criticized it during the presidential campaign.

As for the other leg of Obama's "pivot" strategy, the United States pledged in 2012 to deploy 60 percent of its naval assets, including warships and submarines, in the Pacific by 2020, up from the current 50 percent.[14]

Despite those efforts, some experts argue the strategy is failing, "primarily for want of power," Talent says. The U.S. Pacific Fleet, which had 192 vessels two decades ago, had 182 as of January 2016.[15]

Congress has failed to fund a larger Navy due to budget constraints, according to Robert D. Kaplan, a senior fellow at the Center for a New American Security, a bipartisan think tank in Washington focused on security policy. "You can have all of the great concepts of an Asia pivot you want," Kaplan says. "It's not going to matter much" without ships.

Further complicating the situation has been last year's election of Rodrigo Duterte as president of the Philippines, historically America's strongest regional ally. Duterte has been a strident critic of U.S. policy and has reached out to China and Russia.

As policymakers assess the future of international relations in the South China Sea, here are some of the questions they are asking:

Is China seeking to dominate the South China Sea?

It's not just China's growing navy that worries some analysts. China also has been expanding its footprint in the South China Sea by occupying contested islands and building artificial islands for use as military bases.

"China has continued to build harbors, communications and surveillance systems, logistical facilities and three military-grade airfields on many of the features it occupies," Abraham M. Denmark, deputy assistant secretary of Defense for East Asia, told Congress in July. "In the past year, China also has deployed radar systems, anti-ship cruise missiles, surface-to-air missiles, and has rotated fighter jets through features it claims in the South China Sea."[16]

China's construction of hangars and underground storage facilities for fuel and water would support extended deployments of aircraft and ships, he said, as would its installation of anti-aircraft weapons.

China's leaders previously promised they would not militarize the South China Sea. During his state visit to the United States in September, in fact, Chinese President Xi Jinping said, "China does not intend to pursue militarization" on the disputed Spratly Islands in the South China Sea.[17]

While some skeptics scoff at those promises, other experts, noting that the weapons systems placed on the Spratly Islands are limited in range, say China is simply positioning itself to defend its territory and trade routes against the United States and others.[18]

"Since around 2010, China's security policy has evolved from a focus on homeland defense to one . . . best characterized as 'peaceful expansion,'" Timothy Heath, a senior international defense research analyst at RAND Corp., a research organization based in California, told the U.S.-China Economic and Security Review Commission last January. Since China's commercial and military interests have expanded geographically, Heath said, its ability to protect those interests also had to expand.[19]

As a result, he said, China has shown a greater willingness to involve itself in mediating disputes in regions far from its own shores.

MIT's Fravel agrees China's military posture is more defensive than aggressive in nature. "I think they want to ensure that they are in a position not to be dominated," he says. "I think they would like to weaken the influence of the United States, but that paradoxically may mean that they are more willing to cooperate with their neighbors on the things that their neighbors value, like investment projects."

Other experts, however, argue that China's intentions are not so benign. China is patiently building toward the day when it can militarily and economically dominate not just the South China Sea but all of Asia, they claim.

President Xi Jinping has "an empire-building intention," says Ming Xia, a professor of political science at the College of Staten Island in New York. "In foreign affairs, China wants to be respected and feared by countries in both the East China Sea and the South China Sea and India. I think the appropriate comparison is to Japan in the 1930s," when the Japanese invaded Manchuria, a region of China, in 1931.

China's need to dominate the region, says former Sen. Talent, is particularly acute because the country's leaders don't have the legitimacy that comes with democratic elections. "They have to be able to show to their people that they have produced success as rulers," he says. "Part of that is quality of life at home and part of that is prestige in Asia. That is what is driving them to assert sovereignty over the seas, including the South China Sea."

Frank Gaffney, president of the Center for Security Policy, a conservative think tank in Washington, agrees that China wants to expand its control. "This is a moment when I think the China dream, as Xi Jinping calls it, is to be realized at the expense of everybody else in that part of the world, and it will return China to what it considers to be its rightful place as the world's preeminent power," says Gaffney, an adviser to Trump.

At the same time, some analysts say China's aggressiveness may reflect tension between its civilian and military leaders.

During a recent fact-finding trip to China, James Clad, senior adviser for Asia at the Center for Naval Analyses, a federally funded research and development organization in Arlington, Va., serving the Navy and other defense agencies, and a former deputy assistant secretary of Defense for Asia, says he got the impression the political leadership "needs to continue to placate the military, with goodies, acquisitions and with rhetoric that approaches hyper-nationalistic sensitivities."

Some analysts say China is only doing what most rising regional powers do. "An increasingly powerful China is likely to try to push the U.S. out of Asia, much the way the U.S. pushed the European powers out of the Western Hemisphere" in the 19th century, writes John J. Mearsheimer, a professor of political science at the University of Chicago. "Why should we expect China to act any differently than the United States did? Are they more principled than we are? Or ethical? Less nationalistic?"[20]

Bonner R. Cohen, a senior fellow at the National Center for Public Policy Research, a conservative think tank in Washington, agrees. "These people are not reckless," he says. "They make their geostrategic moves in a very calculating way.

"If they see opportunities, they will take advantage of those opportunities," he continues. "They have always considered areas immediately adjacent to China — and that includes bodies of water — as being essentially a part of China."

Should America's regional allies pay more for U.S. protection?

In his first major foreign policy speech during the presidential campaign last April, Trump complained that the United States was paying far too much to protect other countries. "We have spent trillions of dollars over time on planes, missiles, ships, equipment — building up our military to provide a strong defense for Europe and Asia," Trump said. "The countries we are defending must pay for the cost of this defense, and if not, the U.S. must be prepared to let these countries defend themselves. We have no choice."[21]

Trump has also suggested that the United States should end its decades-long policy against nuclear proliferation and encourage South Korea and Japan to acquire nuclear weapons with which to defend themselves.[22]

While most analysts and policymakers reject Trump's position on nuclear proliferation, some observers welcomed his call for greater burden-sharing by Asian allies.

Fiery Cross Reef, in the western Spratly Islands, is among the reefs that China has turned into man-made islands housing army and navy bases and airstrips. In an effort to stem China's regional expansion, the United States deployed warships within 12 nautical miles of Fiery Cross Reef in 2015.

"In every case the allies should be shouldering more of their share of the common defense," says Gaffney of the Center for Security Policy, adding that he found Trump's call for allies to pony up "bracing."

Cohen of the National Center for Public Policy Research agrees. "We don't have the resources that we once did. So it is much better for us to encourage other people to look after their own interests," he says. "There are things that they can do for themselves, and if we don't show them how . . . and encourage them to do it themselves, they will simply rely on us to do it."

Cohen says the United States has no territorial claims at stake in the South China Sea so "it is ultimately incumbent upon those countries . . . to do as much as they possibly can for themselves while at the same time leaning on the U.S. Navy as kind of an ultimate plan B."

Others, however, argue that while wealthier allies, most notably Japan, should be prodded to contribute more, the United States shouldn't be just a backup. Elbridge Colby, a senior fellow at the Center for a New American Security, a liberal-leaning Washington think tank, told Congress in September that "because China is so powerful, we do need to take the lead, but actually that leadership role will be more likely to catalyze that burden sharing."[23]

In September, Japanese Defense Minister Tomomi Inada announced that his nation would increase its presence in the South China Sea and would provide more aid to countries in the region, including the Philippines and Vietnam. The moves, he said, "underline my government's resolve to protect our territorial integrity and sovereignty." Inada, however, did not provide details.[24]

Some policy analysts say Trump's push to get allies to pay more will be counterproductive.

"President Trump will need to stop focusing on burden sharing and focus on security relationships," wrote Anthony Cordesman, a national security analyst at the Center for Strategic and International Studies, a nonpartisan Washington think tank. Trump shouldn't ask allies to contribute more than they can afford and should refrain from giving allies and potential foes the impression that the United States is disengaging, Cordesman said.[25]

Although a discussion of burden sharing can be useful, wrote Robert E. Kelly, an associate professor of international relations at Pusan National University in South Korea, "Trump to date has cast the debate in a bean-counting light: How much do allies pay for this or that American capability?"[26]

Rather than getting allies to pay more for protection, Kelly said, the United States should help allies build their own defensive capabilities and coordinate defense efforts with them. "Multilateral operations carry greater international credibility, relieve [the burden] on the U.S. military and signal to opponents that they face a full-bodied international coalition of serious, committed democracies — not just the Americans yet again," he said.

But others warn that calling on Asian allies to build up their own defense capabilities poses its own dangers. "The Chinese would interpret a buildup of allied military, and they say so, as a hostile act," says former Sen. Talent. "So you don't want to do that unless you're certain that the Americans are going to be there backing them up."

Talent also warns of complications in having Japan assume a higher military profile because of the notorious behavior of its soldiers before and during World War II. "For obvious reasons, historical reasons," Talent says, "this needs to be seen in the region as firmly under the umbrella of American leadership."

Oriana Skylar Mastro, an assistant professor of security studies at Georgetown University and a nuclear security fellow at the Council on Foreign Relations, says U.S. alliances in Asia have delivered benefits that are impossible to measure in dollars.

"They allow us access and influence, and access and influence allow us to promote and protect our foreign policy interests," Mastro says. "Outsourcing our national security interests, even to those that we like and trust, is never a good idea."

Is the Trans-Pacific Partnership trade agreement important to maintaining U.S. regional alliances?

One of Trump's most frequent targets on the campaign trail was the Trans-Pacific Partnership (TPP). At a campaign rally last June, he characterized the trade pact as "a continuing rape of our country" because of its potential to harm the middle class.[27]

Congress has yet to approve the TPP. To take effect, six countries that account for 85 percent of the group's economic output must ratify the pact by February 2018. That means both Japan and the United States must ratify the agreement. In December, Japan became the first, and so far only, signatory to do so.[28]

When the TPP was finalized in 2015, it did not include China, which chose not to participate, according to Thomas J. Christensen, a professor of international relations at Princeton University and former deputy assistant secretary of State for East Asian and Pacific affairs. "The U.S. goal in relation to Beijing was not to exclude China from the TPP," he wrote, "but to . . . catalyze China to compete by further opening its own domestic markets and providing protection for intellectual property rights for the first time."[29]

While China has not actively opposed the pact, its "One Belt, One Road" infrastructure project, which is aimed at strengthening China's economic links to countries in Eurasia by building roads and ports, would likely benefit from the TPP's collapse. That is because more

Malaysia Tops Oil and Gas Reserves

Malaysia has the most known oil and natural gas reserves in the South China Sea, according to the latest available estimates. The sea's vast reserves are largely unexplored and may contain more oil than any other region except Saudi Arabia.

Estimated Oil and Gas Reserves in the South China Sea, 2012

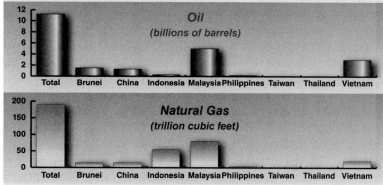

Source: "South China Sea," U.S. Energy Information Administration, Feb. 7, 2013, http://tinyurl.com/znusb9c

countries in Southeast Asia would look to China rather than to Western countries for increased trade and aid.[30]

Trump's adamant opposition to the pact is "clearly going to ruffle feathers" among the TPP's signatories, says Cohen of the National Center for Public Policy Research. Because China is not a party to the TPP, he says, other nations see the pact as having a "not-too-subtle anti-Chinese bent to it." It was, accordingly, viewed positively by American allies in Asia who hoped the creation of a free-trade zone would be a counterweight to an economically powerful China. Nevertheless, Cohen says the new president will likely reject the TPP. "I think the pact is effectively dead," he says.

While the domestic effects of the TPP were debated during the presidential campaign, the foreign policy implications received scant mention, even though the Obama administration pushed the deal as part of its Asian pivot.

"TPP would've anchored the Asian pivot for us," says Kaplan of the Center for a New American Security. "If you have a free-trade zone that you are the head of, you're in a very strong position in Asia." Kaplan says the Trump administration should push a version of TPP through Congress "by calling it something else."

Getty Images/Asahi Shimbun

A Chinese coast guard ship patrols near the Scarborough Shoal in the South China Sea on Dec.13 as a Philippine fisherman watches. The shoal, lying within the Philippines' Exclusive Economic Zone, is claimed by not only the Philippines but also China and Taiwan. In July, the Permanent Court of Arbitration, in The Hague, ruled China was infringing on the Philippines' fishing rights.

Georgetown University's Mastro says the Asian pivot got lost during the presidential campaign as the candidates from both political parties focused on jobs and American competitiveness. "I'm not surprised that people in the Rust Belt weren't thinking about the primacy of the United States in the Asia-Pacific when they voted," she says. "You don't realize how much you need it until you lose it."

Asian countries, according to Mastro, saw the TPP as an indication that the United States was going to be more focused on its strategic interests in the South China Sea. With Trump's election, she says, "a lot of the optimism has been thrown out the window along with TPP. It was a big component of maintaining U.S. leadership in the region."

Publicly, Asian leaders say they hope Trump will reverse course. "I am a strong supporter of developing trade and open regionalism in Asia Pacific," said Malaysian Prime Minister Najib Razak in November. "It is key to benefiting our peoples. I look forward to working with President-elect Trump on our shared goals of strengthening security and ensuring growth that is inclusive, sustainable and fair to all."[31]

Some experts say the Trump administration can accomplish many of the TPP's goals through bilateral trade agreements with friendly countries in the region. "If we're not going to go forward with the TPP, it's important to have a substitute . . . , which could be vigorously pursued through bilateral agreements," says former Sen. Talent.

But other analysts say even if the Trump administration successfully negotiates such agreements, the United States will have lost credibility by not ratifying the pact. TPP's failure "will raise very significant questions about our credibility and about our political will," says Gregory B. Poling, director of the Asia Maritime Transparency Initiative at the Center for Strategic and International Studies. "It will tell Asian states that we are engaged militarily but not necessarily in any other way, whereas China is playing on all fronts. That's damage we're going to have a hard time undoing."

Even if Trump reverses course and the TPP is ratified, America's image has already been damaged, says Mira Rapp-Hooper, a senior fellow with the Asia-Pacific security program at the Center for a New American Security. "It has been deeply concerning to our partners in East Asia broadly to see how trade has been discussed in the U.S. election," she says. "They are keenly aware that this is not just a partisan issue, but that on both the left and the right there was a really strong anti-free trade sentiment in the United States."

BACKGROUND
Colonization and Resistance

Since the early 16th century, European colonization has shaped the countries bordering the South China Sea.

The first sustained Western colonization, driven by commercial and religious motives, began with the Portuguese capture of the city of Malacca on Malaysia's southwestern coast in 1511, a feat that required 1,200 men and more than a dozen warships.[32]

Portugal's occupation of Malacca, where it built a fortress to protect its shipping, was followed by similar occupations elsewhere in Southeast Asia by the Netherlands, England, France and Spain. Eventually, those five powers controlled nearly all of Southeast Asia. Britain came to occupy "Burma, Malaya and Borneo; France controlled Indochina; the Dutch ruled Indonesia; and the United States had replaced Spain as the colonial master of the Philippines," wrote Asia expert Mark J. Valencia, an associate at the Nautilus Institute for Security and Sustainability, a think tank in Berkeley, Calif.[33]

The experiences of the various Asian countries — and, in some cases, even their borders — depended to a large degree upon the colonizing country and on events in Europe.

"The frontiers were drawn so as to avoid disputes among the European powers," wrote Nicholas Tarling, an economist and historian at Australia's University of Auckland. "As a result, especially at the margins, they bore no firm relation to economic, social, cultural, ethnic or even geographical realities."[34]

Changes in borders, governments and policies — from taxation to land ownership — "did not merely, nor even primarily, result from the changes in tensions within Southeast Asia," Tarling said. Instead, events in Europe drove many of the changes.[35]

For example, as a result of the Napoleonic Wars (1803–15), the French gained dominance over the Dutch Republic and its colonies in Southeast Asia. At the same time, the British took possession of Dutch colonies in India, Ceylon and Java.

The European powers were generally more interested in commerce and protection of their shipping lanes than they were about control of land and populations.

"The changing spirit of the times was most closely captured by Britain's establishment of trading centers at Penang (1786), Malacca (1824) and especially Singapore (1819), occasioning the Dutch to establish similar ports within their sphere of influence," said Robert E. Elson, an emeritus professor of history at Griffith University in Queensland, Australia. "This was the beginning of the age of 'free-trade imperialism,' founded on the belief that 'free trade,' commerce unhindered by protection and undiverted by the demands of territorial administration, inevitably meant Britain's economic success as well as greater prosperity for those peoples with which it traded."[36]

China also had significant influence over the region. Like the Europeans, the Chinese were not interested in controlling lands or peoples in Southeast Asia. China was "content with the confession of vassalage" that would ensure profits for the government and protection for Chinese traders, according to Tarling. When they were challenged, China intervened ruthlessly.[37]

Meanwhile, the Chinese dynasties faced increasing domestic difficulties and became increasingly vulnerable to European encroachment. Two conflicts with Great Britain weakened China's last dynasty, the Qing, which ruled from 1644 to 1911.

The first Opium War (1839–42) broke out when China attempted to prevent British traders from selling opium from India in China. "The resulting widespread addiction in China was causing serious social and economic disruption there," wrote Asia historian Kenneth Pletcher. In March 1839, the Chinese government confiscated and destroyed more than 20,000 chests of opium warehoused at Canton by British merchants.

"The antagonism between the two sides increased a few days later when some drunken British sailors killed a Chinese villager," Pletcher said. "The British government, which did not wish its subjects to be tried in the Chinese legal system, refused to turn the accused men over to the Chinese courts."[38]

Hostilities broke out several months later. British forces captured Nanjing in 1842, leading the Chinese government to capitulate. Besides forcing China to pay a large indemnity, the Treaty of Nanjing required China to increase from one to five the number of "treaty ports" where British merchants could trade and to cede the island of Hong Kong to the British.[39]

The Second Opium War erupted in 1857 as China was attempting to put down the Taiping Rebellion (1850–64), a political and religious upheaval that cost an estimated 20 million lives. British forces, joined by French troops, prevailed, resulting in further Chinese concessions, including legalization of the opium trade.

"In the 19th century, as the Qing dynasty became the sick man of East Asia, China lost much of its territory — the southern tributaries of Nepal and Burma to Great Britain; Indochina to France; Taiwan and the tributaries of Korea and Sakhalin to Japan; and Mongolia, Amuria and Ussuria to Russia," wrote the Center for a New American Security's Kaplan.[40]

The growing reach of European colonizers brought resistance from native populations.

Between the mid-19th century and the 1930s, "European governments found themselves engaged in 'pacification' campaigns against traditional states and popular rebellions," said Carl A. Trocki, an Asia historian at Queensland University of Technology.[41]

At the end of the 19th century, a new global power entered the political maelstrom of the South China Sea: the United States. At war with Spain in the Spanish colony of Cuba in 1898, the United States joined forces with Philippine resistance forces to drive the Spanish out of the Philippines.

The rise of nationalist and communist movements in Southeast Asia was encouraged not only by local conditions but, once again, by events in Europe. The onset of World War I in 1914 pitted the colonial powers against each other. The resulting bloodbath demonstrated two things to resistance movements in Southeast Asia.

"The unprecedented scale and carnage of the hostilities served to undermine any pretensions that Western civilization possessed inherent moral superiority, while on a more concrete level, Britain and France, despite emerging as victors, both suffered a serious (and, it would prove, irreversible) erosion of economic and military power," wrote historians Paul Kratoska and Ben Batson of the National University of Singapore.[42]

By 1920, the confluence of domestic conditions and events in Europe enabled nationalist movements to challenge colonial regimes throughout the region.

World War II

These nationalist movements stalled in the 1930s because of a new Asian occupier, Japan, which began invading its neighbors in the lead-up to World War II.

The Japanese empire — in an attempt to secure resources, especially oil and rubber, that were scarce within its territory — expanded into the Asia mainland with its occupations of Korea in 1910 and Manchuria in northeast China in 1931. It also occupied the island of Taiwan from 1895 until World War II ended in 1945.

With the onset of World War II, Japan quickly moved to take control of nearly all the countries in the South China Sea region. Between 1940 and 1942, Japan invaded Hong Kong, Vietnam, Laos, Thailand, the Philippines, Singapore, Cambodia, Malaysia and Burma and occupied all of them until the war's end. Its troops in China and elsewhere were accused of committing war crimes, including mass killings and rapes of civilians.

Although the Japanese occupations had stalled nationalist movements in the region, after Japan's defeat these movements "resurfaced and finally succeeded in throwing off the colonial political yoke," wrote Valencia of the Nautilus Institute for Security and Sustainability.[43]

In China, the end of the war — and the end of fighting against the Japanese — meant a return to internal struggles, primarily between communist forces led by Mao Zedong and nationalist forces led by Chiang Kai-shek. That struggle was settled, at least for mainland China, when Mao triumphed and Chiang and his followers fled in 1949 to Taiwan, which the People's Republic of China still considers its province.

Two years earlier, in the midst of its civil war, China issued a map detailing its South China Sea claims known as the "nine-dash line" — a territory extending hundreds of miles south and east from its southern province of Hainan. China argued that the Paracel and Spratley islands had been integral parts of China for centuries.[44]

The region also became "the cockpit of a contest between Western capitalism and Soviet and Chinese communist ideology," Valencia wrote. "The West, led by the United States, propped up dictators with force to prevent the spread of communism (resulting in the suppression of people's movements in Malaysia and the Philippines) as well as mass humanitarian tragedies in Vietnam and Indonesia."[45]

When French forces withdrew from Vietnam in 1954, the Geneva Accords partitioned the country, with South Vietnam (the Republic of Vietnam) backed by the United States and North Vietnam backed by the Soviet Union and China. Beginning in 1960, American military involvement in Vietnam grew rapidly, especially after the 1964 Gulf of Tonkin incident, in which a U.S. destroyer reportedly clashed with a North Vietnamese fast-attack craft.

With Saigon's fall to North Vietnamese troops in 1974, remaining American forces left Vietnam. China seized the Paracel Islands, which had been occupied by South Vietnam. China and the government of the newly unified Vietnam resolved territorial disputes in the Gulf of Tonkin but not elsewhere in the South China Sea; the two sides are still dueling over the Paracel and Spratley islands.[46] In 1988, Vietnamese and Chinese military forces clashed at Johnson South Reef in the Spratlys, with each country trading accusations of illegally occupying territory in the chain.

The retreat from Vietnam did not mean a U.S. withdrawal from the South China Sea. Since 1979 the United States has carried out a freedom of navigation program, with two goals: preserving freedom of the seas and demonstrating a "non-acquiescence" to coastal states that make "excessive" maritime claims. The centerpiece is regular naval deployments in international waters throughout the region.[47]

CHRONOLOGY

1500–1898 *Outsiders colonize Asia.*

1511 Portuguese warships capture Malacca in Malaysia, marking the beginning of 400 years of European colonization in Southeast Asia.

1839 First Opium War begins after China tries to prevent British traders from importing opium into China; with British victory in 1842, Treaty of Nanjing requires China to increase to five the number of ports open to British traders.

1895 Japan occupies Taiwan.

1898 After the Spanish-American War, the United States colonizes the Philippines.

1914–1945 *Nationalist movements challenge colonial regimes throughout the South China Sea.*

1914 World War I erodes ability of colonial powers to maintain control in Southeast Asia.

1940 With the onset of World War II, Japan — having already occupied Korea in 1910 and Manchuria in 1931 — captures nearly every country in South China Sea region.

1945 Japan surrenders; United States becomes dominant power in western Pacific.

1946–1988 *U.S. Navy dominates the western Pacific.*

1946 French forces battle Vietnamese nationalists backed by China and Russia; French withdraw in 1954 and Vietnam is partitioned.

1947 China publishes map of the South China Sea outlining its claims to nearly all of the sea.

1949 Communist Chinese forces defeat Nationalist Chinese, who flee to Taiwan.

1964 Gulf of Tonkin incident — a reported clash between a U.S. destroyer and North Vietnamese forces — sparks a major increase in U.S. involvement in Vietnam War.

1974 South Vietnam falls to North Vietnam; China seizes the Paracel Islands, which had been claimed by the South Vietnamese government.

1988 Chinese and Vietnamese forces battle at Johnson South Reef in Spratly Islands, claimed by both countries; 64 Vietnamese soldiers reportedly are killed.

2001–Present *Chinese influence in South China Sea grows.*

2001 U.S. reconnaissance aircraft flying near China's Hainan Island collides with a Chinese fighter.

2009 Barack Obama, describing himself as "America's first Pacific president," promises Asian countries "a new era of engagement."

2011 Obama announces a "pivot" to Asia, including a bigger naval presence in the region.

2012 China declares an "air defense identification zone" covering a large maritime area separating China from Japan.

2014 China moves oil exploration gear into the Paracel Islands, renewing tensions with Vietnam. . . . Satellite images show China building an island at Fiery Cross Reef in the Spratlys large enough for an airstrip.

2015 U.S. deploys warships within 12 nautical miles of Chinese-occupied Fiery Cross Reef.

2016 U.S. deploys more ships near Triton Island in the Paracels to reassert its "freedom of navigation" rights (January). . . . International tribunal rules in favor of the Philippines and against Chinese in dispute over ownership of the Spratly Islands (July). . . . Philippine President Rodrigo Duterte visits China and returns with billions of dollars in aid and trade deals after telling the Chinese that "America has lost now" (October). . . . China acknowledges that it has installed weapons on disputed islands in the Spratlys (December). . . . President-elect Donald Trump causes a diplomatic kerfuffle by taking a congratulatory phone call from Taiwanese president; a Chinese warship seizes a U.S. research drone in South China Sea (December).

U.S.-Philippine Relationship Grows Rockier

Mercurial leader "just does not want to work with the United States."

With last year's election of Rodrigo Duterte as Philippine president, the United States' relationship with the Asian island nation — historically America's strongest ally in the South China Sea region — has grown a lot more complicated.

Since taking office in June, Duterte called President Obama a "son of a bitch," threatened to expel U.S. Special Forces from training grounds on the southern Philippine island of Mindanao, announced the end of joint U.S.-Philippine patrols in the South China Sea and suggested he was open to alliances with Russia and China.[1]

The mercurial Duterte visited China in October and came home with billions of dollars in aid after telling the Chinese: "America has lost now. I've realigned myself in your ideological flow. And maybe I will also go to Russia to talk to [President Vladimir] Putin and tell him that there are three of us against the world: China, Philippines and Russia."[2] A few days later, Duterte issued a clarification, saying he did not intend to split from the United States. He said he was calling for a "separation of foreign policy" rather than "a severance of ties."[3]

Then in late October, the Philippine government announced that it had reached an agreement with China on the disputed Scarborough Shoal, an undersea ridge approximately 100 miles west of the Philippines. While details of the agreement were not revealed, a Philippines government spokesman said Chinese ships were no longer blocking Philippine vessels in the area.[4]

Most recently, Duterte, who is scheduled to visit Moscow in April, told Rear Adm. Eduard Mikhailov, head of Russia's Pacific fleet, that he was welcome in the Philippines "anytime you want to dock here for anything, for play, for replenish[ing] supplies or maybe [to be] our ally to protect us."[5]

Some experts have attributed Duterte's antipathy toward the United States to the Obama administration's criticism of Duterte's anti-drug campaign, which the administration said has involved widespread extrajudicial killings and tactics that are "entirely inconsistent with

universal human rights."[6] Others see Duterte's outreach to China as evidence of his long-standing hostility to the United States. Duterte, who previously was mayor of Davao City, is "reflexively anti-American," says Gregory B. Poling, director of the Asia Maritime Transparency Initiative at the Center for Strategic and International Studies, a bipartisan policy research organization in Washington. "He just does not want to work with the United States."

Despite Duterte's anti-American rhetoric, many experts say the United States remains popular in its former colony, which it controlled from 1898 to 1946, when the Philippines gained independence. "The United States is quite popular in the Philippines, and the alliance [between the two countries specifically] is quite popular in the Philippines," says Mira Rapp-Hooper, a senior fellow at the Center for a New American Security, a think tank in Washington. Noting that the United States is a top importer of Philippine goods, such as machinery, Rapp-Hooper says the U.S.-Philippines relationship is broader than just security.

"While Duterte may be deriving some personal satisfaction and perhaps some political points from seeming to push back on a longtime patron, I think his true alignment will ultimately be determined by his interests," she says. "It is pretty clear that his interests are not as black-and-white as his rhetoric would suggest."

The foundation of the nations' security relationship is a 1951 mutual-defense treaty that requires each nation to come to the aid of the other in the event of conflict or a threat to national security. In exchange for providing protection to the Philippines, the United States was allowed to maintain large military facilities in the Philippines, most notably a naval base in Subic Bay and Clark Air Base north of Manila.

In 1991, the Philippine Senate, citing the U.S. military presence as a vestige of colonialism, voted to expel U.S. forces from Subic Bay and Clark Air Base.[7]

In the years just before Duterte's election, the Philippines had been cooperating more with the U.S. military because of rising South China Sea tensions. In 2014 the Philippines approved a 10-year agreement giving U.S. forces greater access to Philippine bases.[8] And last March the two countries signed an agreement providing for a new permanent U.S. military presence at five Philippine air bases under the recently negotiated Enhanced Defense Cooperation Agreement.[9]

After assuming office Duterte benefited from a July ruling by an international tribunal that sided with the Philippines over China in a dispute involving the Spratly Islands.[10]

The tribunal's ruling, rather than increasing tensions between the two nations, seems to have given Duterte an opportunity to move closer to China. Rapp-Hooper calls Duterte's decision not to press Philippine claims to the disputed islands and waters after the ruling a diplomatic turning point.

"Without the ruling, it would be very hard to see this bilateral diplomatic opening between China and the Philippines taking place," she says.

It is unclear how Donald Trump's election will affect U.S.-Philippines relations. Trump and Duterte spoke by phone in early December when, according to Duterte, Trump endorsed Duterte's controversial anti-drug campaign, calling it "the right way" to deal with the problem.[11] The Trump transition team has not confirmed Duterte's account.

"Duterte is wildly popular in the Philippines as someone who is standing up to the rest of the world, and that also means the United States," says Bonner R. Cohen, a senior fellow at the National Center for Public Policy Research. "I fully expect the Trump administration will try to reach out to him. Duterte clearly has no use for Obama, but Obama will be gone."

— *Patrick Marshall*

Getty Images/Pool/Thomas Peter

Chinese President Xi Jinping greets Philippine President Rodrigo Duterte in Beijing, on Oct. 20. Duterte was on a four-day state visit to China aimed at improving relations between the two South China Sea rivals.

[4] Richard C. Paddock, "Chinese Vessels Leave Disputed Fishing Grounds in South China Sea," *The New York Times*, Oct. 28, 2016, http://tinyurl.com/grn94m2.

[5] "Duterte hopes Russia will become Philippines' ally and protector," Reuters, Jan. 6, 2017, http://tinyurl.com/jjqgum3.

[6] Jim Gomez, "Duterte tells Obama 'you can go to hell,' warns of breakup," The Associated Press, Oct. 4, 2016, http://tinyurl.com/hs99v6n.

[7] David E. Sanger, "Philippines Orders U.S. to Leave Strategic Navy Base at Subic Bay," *The New York Times*, Dec. 28, 1991, http://tinyurl.com/z7jpmce.

[8] Mark Landler, "U.S. and Philippines Agree to a 10-Year Pact on the Use of Military Bases," *The New York Times*, April 27, 2014, http://tinyurl.com/hur8vsq.

[9] Andrew Tilghman, "The U.S. military is moving into these 5 bases in the Philippines," *Military Times*, March 21, 2016, http://tinyurl.com/hhmt2so.

[10] Siegfrid Alegado and Ceclia Yap, "Philippines Posts Strongest Economic Growth in Asia at 7.1%," Bloomberg, Nov. 16, 2016, http://tinyurl.com/janttcd.

[11] Felipe Villamordec, "Rodrigo Duterte Says Donald Trump Endorses His Violent Antidrug Campaign," *The New York Times*, Dec. 3, 2016, http://tinyurl.com/zpddqjl.

[1] "President Duterte, the Wild Card in U.S.-Filipino Relations," *The New York Times*, Oct. 4, 2016, http://tinyurl.com/zpzhxoy.

[2] Katie Hunt, Matt Rivers and Catherine E. Shoichet, "In China, Duterte announces split with US: 'America has lost,' " CNN, Oct. 20, 2016, http://tinyurl.com/hrvlp8q.

[3] James Griffiths, Matt Rivers and Pamela Boykoff, "Philippines not really severing ties with US, Duterte says," CNN, Oct. 22, 2016, http://tinyurl.com/hc6g8am.

China Reaching for Superpower Status

But analysts see huge obstacles to its bid for global supremacy.

From China's perspective, it's only a matter of time before it surpasses the United States as the world's premier economic and military power, analysts say. But many say the Asian nation of 1.4 billion people would have to surmount steep economic and military hurdles before it could rival the United States as a global superpower.

"China's leaders believe China represents the future, not just in hard power but also in economy, culture and values," said Mark Valencia, an associate at the Nautilus Institute for Security and Sustainability, a public policy think tank in Berkeley, Calif. "Indeed, China's leaders believe it is China's destiny to regain its prominence, if not preeminence, in the region and perhaps eventually the world."[1]

But Gordon G. Chang, an American author and China specialist, says China's optimism is unwarranted. "The regime that was supposed to own the century may not survive the decade," he said. "The People's Republic of China is now trapped in slow-burning economic and financial crises that are shaking the country."[2]

According to Thomas J. Christensen, former deputy assistant secretary of State for East Asian and Pacific affairs, there is a growing sense among the Chinese that their country is on the rise while the United States is in decline.

"Many in China believe China is significantly stronger and the United States weaker after the [2008] financial crisis," wrote Christensen. That belief, he said, has led to calls within China to become more aggressive in geopolitics. But, he said, "domestic voices calling for a more muscular Chinese foreign policy have created a heated political environment."[3]

Others say China's military leaders already are responding to hawkish voices. "China's military is sending strong signals that it's gearing up to compete with the U.S. as a global superpower, engaging in a multifaceted reform effort to modernize and professionalize its military," said Yvonne Chiu, an assistant professor of politics at the University of Hong Kong.[4]

The government is streamlining China's military, making the army smaller while expanding the navy and air force, analysts say. Chinese aviation technology, according to a recent Pentagon report, is "rapidly" closing the gap with Western air forces. "At the same time," wrote Paul McLeary, Pentagon reporter for *Foreign Policy* magazine, "China's nuclear and missile forces have been reorganized as an independent service and have been bolstered with a new array of weapons that push China's potential reach farther out into the Pacific."[5]

Yet, many experts are not convinced that China's rise as a global superpower is inevitable.

China's days of "heady" economic growth are over, according to Chang. Growth hasn't been in double digits since 2010, he said, and its gross domestic product (GDP) grew 6.9 percent last year, down slightly from 2015. While that's a rate the United States would welcome, Chang said those figures are possibly inflated. "In the middle of last year, a well-known China analyst was privately noting that [analysts] in Beijing were talking 2.2 percent [growth], and there are indications the economy grew at an even slower pace, perhaps 1 percent," Chang wrote.[6]

China's economy has two long-term vulnerabilities, according to Loren B. Thompson, chief operating officer of the Lexington Institute, a national policy think tank in Arlington, Va.: Its pool of low-cost labor is drying up because of China's growing middle class and urbanization, and China is overly dependent on manufacturing exports for growth.

Even if its labor problem could be solved, Thompson said, "the reliance of an export-driven economy on foreign markets makes China's prosperity — per capita

The U.S. Navy's primary base of operations in the Western Pacific after World War II was Subic Bay in the Philippines. In 1991, however, negotiations to remain at Subic and Clark Air Base broke down because, in the account of one reporter, the Philippines viewed the Americans' presence "as a vestige of colonialism and an affront to Philippine sovereignty."[48] The U.S. military left the two bases in 1992.

While China has generally avoided conflict with U.S. forces in the South China Sea, the Chinese government [gross domestic product] is below $10,000 — much more vulnerable than America's."[7] Per capita GDP in the United States — the country's total economic output divided by the population — was $56,116 in 2015.[8]

Others point to fundamental problems in China's military, which lags the U.S. military in hardware. China has 1,230 fighter aircraft to the United States' 2,308. China's navy, with an estimated 714 vessels, is larger than the 415 vessels in the U.S. Navy, but China has only one aircraft carrier to the United States' 19.[9]

China has about 260 nuclear warheads, far fewer than the 7,100 in the U.S. arsenal.[10]

Adding missiles and other hardware isn't the only challenge for the Chinese, some experts say. "The Chinese defense industry management is so corrupt, [it's] like a black hole," says Ming Xia, a professor of political science at the College of Staten Island in New York. "And training is horrible."

Even within Asia, China's ability to project its military power is limited now and for the foreseeable future, says Stephen G. Brooks, an associate professor of government at Dartmouth College. China can project power against the Philippines and other rivals in the South China Sea, says Brooks, "but if the United States says, 'No, we don't want you to project power,' China doesn't have, and won't for a long time have, much ability to get around that."

Regardless of its limitations, China appears intent on asserting itself as a regional power.

And whether China is able to gain dominance in the western Pacific or beyond is not solely up to China, says Frank Gaffney, president of the Center for Security Policy, a conservative think tank in Washington.

"It is a question in part of what they do, obviously, but it's also a question of what we do," he says. "If we persist in the trajectory we have been on [with slowing defense budgets], there is very little doubt in my mind that they will surpass us at some point. In some respects, I think they already have."

— *Patrick Marshall*

Chinese marines train with their Russian counterparts in a drill in the South China Sea on Sept. 19. China's military is sending strong signals that it is gearing up to compete with the U.S. as a global superpower, according to one analyst.

[1] Mark J. Valencia, "The South China Sea and the 'Thucydides Trap,' " in *The South China Sea: A Crucible of Regional Cooperation or Conflict-Making Sovereignty Claims?* (2016), p. 60.

[2] Gordan G. Chang, "A Turbulent China Shakes the World," in *Warning Order: China Prepares for Conflict and Why We Must Do the Same* (2016), p. 40.

[3] Thomas J. Christensen, *The China Challenge: Shaping the Choices of a Rising Power* (2015), p. 260.

[4] Yvonne Chiu, "China's military is gearing up to compete with the U.S.," CNN, March 9, 2016, http://tinyurl.com/zhwq28w.

[5] Paul McLeary, "Pentagon: Chinese Military Modernization Enters 'New Phase,'" *Foreign Policy*, May 13, 2016, http://tinyurl.com/z9fkdhb.

[6] Chang, op. cit., p. 40; 2015 growth rate is from "China GDP Annual Growth Rate," *Trading Economics*, http://tinyurl.com/pzthrrq.

[7] Loren Thompson, "Five Reasons China Won't Be A Big Threat To America's Global Power," *Forbes*, June 6, 2014, http://tinyurl.com/hgtlrru.

[8] "GDP growth (annual%)," the World Bank, http://tinyurl.com/y3vaz2u.

[9] "Global Firepower," GFP, Jan. 21, 2016, http://tinyurl.com/bgsc8df.

[10] "Nuclear Weapons: Who Has What at a Glance," Arms Control Association, October 2016, http://tinyurl.com/6ovpr2v.

passed legislation in 1992 laying claim to four-fifths of the sea.[49] Perhaps emboldened by the expulsion of U.S. forces from the Philippines, China backed up this claim with a series of armed skirmishes with the Vietnamese and Philippine navies in the 1990s.

Only two years after the U.S. departure, wrote Kaplan, "China would move to occupy Philippine-controlled reefs in the Spratlys, and from the mid-1990s forward China would undergo a vast expansion of its air and sea forces, accompanied by a more aggressive posture in the South China Sea."[50]

Part of China's increasingly aggressive posture was shadowing and challenging the presence of other forces, even in international waters and airspace. In early April 2001, a U.S. reconnaissance aircraft flying 70 miles from China's Hainan Island collided with a Chinese fighter that had scrambled to intercept it. The collision killed the Chinese pilot, and the American aircraft was forced to land on Hainan. The Chinese later released the American crew of 24 and returned the damaged aircraft to the United States.[51]

Post 9/11

The Sept. 11, 2001, attacks on the United States by the Qaeda terrorist organization marked a turning point in American foreign policy, with the George W. Bush administration launching invasions of Afghanistan and Iraq.

These wars diverted "the United States away from the rapidly changing strategic landscape of Asia precisely at a time when China [was] making enormous strides in military modernization, commercial conquests, diplomatic inroads, and application of soft power," wrote Kurt Campbell, the assistant secretary of State for East Asian and Pacific Affairs from 2009 to 2013. The Americans' preoccupation with the Middle East greatly benefited China, Campbell said: "Rarely in history has a rising power made such prominent gains in the international system largely as a consequence of the actions and inattentiveness of the dominant power."[52]

In 2009, however, newly elected Obama, describing himself as "America's first Pacific president," promised the countries of Asia "a new era of engagement with the world based on mutual interests and mutual respect."[53]

Two years later, Obama defined his "pivot" to Asia as securing adoption of the Trans-Pacific Partnership and a bigger U.S. naval presence in the region.[54]

China took notice of Obama's plans. It had been debating whether supposedly declining powers like the United States would fall away peacefully or launch preemptive wars against the rising powers, says Georgetown University's Mastro. "That debate came to an end with the rebalancing. The rebalancing was seen as a sign that, no, the United States will not go quietly into the night."

In 2012, in Xi's first year as president, China declared an air defense identification zone that covered an expansive maritime area separating China from Japan. It included a contested group of tiny islands, known as the Senkakus (Japanese) or Diaoyu (Chinese), which have been under Japanese control since 1895.

"China followed up on this action almost immediately with a series of gestures that seemed designed to demonstrate its restored strength to its southern neighbors," wrote Howard W. French, a Columbia University journalism professor who focuses on Asia and whose book on East Asian geopolitics, *Everything Under the Heavens: How the Past Helps Shape China's Push for Global Power*, is scheduled for publication in March. "In Xi's early days in office, the country's first aircraft carrier, the *Liaoning*, which was acquired several years ago from Ukraine and then extensively refurbished, was sent with a full battle group of other warships on a maiden cruise straight into many of the most fiercely disputed areas of the South China Sea."[55]

> ## "We will fly, sail and operate wherever international law permits and whenever our operational needs require."
>
> — *Ashton Carter, then-Defense Secretary*

China then blocked the Philippines from delivering supplies and fresh troops to a Philippine navy ship grounded on the disputed Second Thomas Shoal in March 2014. China also sent a large oil rig in May 2014 to disputed waters near the Paracel Islands.[56]

In October 2015, the U.S. Navy sent ships inside the 12-nautical-mile limit that China claims as territory around its artificial islands in the Spratly archipelago in what author James Bamford described as "a deliberate challenge to Beijing's self-declared sovereignty."[57]

Afterward, then-Defense Secretary Ashton Carter told Congress, "We will fly, sail and operate wherever international law permits and whenever our operational needs require."[58]

CURRENT SITUATION

Rising Tensions

Secretary of State nominee Tillerson's explosive testimony at his confirmation hearing on the South China Sea is setting off alarms throughout the region.

China's *Global Times* newspaper said the United States could be forced to fight a war if it tried to block China from its islands. "China has enough determination and strength to make sure that [Tillerson's] rabble-rousing will not succeed," the paper said.

Carlyle A. Thayer, an emeritus professor of politics at the University of New South Wales in Australia, told *The New York Times*: "Tillerson's proposal would provoke a serious confrontation that could quickly develop into armed conflict."[59]

Other experts expressed confusion about the intentions of the Trump administration, which did not comment on Tillerson's remarks. "Is this a warning? Or will this be a policy option?" said Zhu Feng, executive director of the China Center for Collaborative Studies of the South China Sea at Nanjing University. "If this is a policy option, this will not be able to block China's access to these constructed islands. There is no legal basis."[60]

China faces troubles on other fronts. The Permanent Court of Arbitration at The Hague, Netherlands, in July rejected China's claims to all waters within its "nine-dash" line, saying they were incompatible with the United Nations Convention on the Law of the Sea. The tribunal also said China cannot claim an Exclusive Economic Zone (EEZ) in the Spratlys. Instead, it said Chinese-built islands remain within the EEZ of the Philippines, which had brought the dispute to the arbitration court.[61]

Having sided with the Philippines, the tribunal then ruled that China had violated the Philippines' sovereign rights by interfering with Philippine fishing and petroleum exploration. China refused to take part in the arbitration proceedings and said it would not "accept, recognize or execute" the verdict.[62]

Some observers criticized the tribunal for provoking China. Rather than resolving tensions, *The Economist* warned that "the sweeping condemnation of [China's] activities by the court could raise tensions in the South China Sea further, embolden other

An oil production platform lies off the coast of Brunei in the South China Sea, which by some estimates may contain more oil than any other area of the planet except Saudi Arabia. China's claim to four-fifths of the South China Sea was rejected by the Permanent Court of Arbitration in July.

countries to launch copy-cat court actions and possibly lead China to react strongly."

China's island building in the South China Sea is also drawing criticism for another reason: Environmentalists say it is badly damaging one of the world's most important coral reef systems, which provide habitats and food for hundreds of marine species. China's construction of bases atop delicate reefs, wrote John McManus, a University of Miami marine biologist, "constitutes the most rapid rate of permanent loss of coral reef area in human history."[63]

Troubled TPP

With Trump in the White House, most experts see little hope of Congress ratifying the Trans-Pacific Partnership. According to a transition-team memo obtained by *Politico* in mid-November, Trump plans to pull the United States out of the TPP within his first 100 days in office.[64]

Senate Majority Leader Mitch McConnell, R-Ky., and Minority Leader Chuck Schumer, D-N.Y., told reporters after the election that the pact will likely not receive congressional approval.[65]

Still, a high-profile Republican in Congress and others have suggested TPP could be salvaged. Rep. Kevin Brady, R-Texas, chairman of the House Ways and Means Committee, said on Nov. 15 that Republicans should

Does China's military buildup in the South China Sea threaten U.S. security?

YES   James Clad
Senior Adviser for Asia, CNA Corp.; former Deputy Assistant Secretary of Defense for Asia

Written for *CQ Researcher*, January 2017

China has made rapid changes to marine topography in the South China Sea in the past few years to create mini-islands or to augment existing islets occupied by Chinese personnel. In addition, China has installed airfields, portable air defense systems and military radars. Chinese President Xi Jinping's assurances that this type of activity wouldn't occur have proved worthless.

Unilaterally raising new land features in contested areas doesn't directly threaten American security. Nor does militarizing these features. But the buildup nonetheless threatens U.S. security because it comes accompanied by assertive, often reckless Chinese tactics.

Preoccupied by placating China's security establishment, Xi and his Communist Party allies underappreciate how unfettered freedom of navigation has totemic importance to the American security establishment. The United States insists on unimpeded access to all international waters lying 12 nautical miles beyond sovereign territory. Phrased rather brusquely as "we go anywhere we want," the ability to enter international waters at pleasure mirrors other navies' expectations of access, even China's.

But China claims sovereignty over myriad shoals and sandbars as well as over adjoining seas enclosed by a "nine-dash line," which first appeared in Chinese maps in the 1930s. During the 1970–80s, Beijing preemptively seized shoals and atolls from South and North Vietnamese garrisons alike. The new buildup affects the Philippines most directly: China occupied and then built structures on top of various shoals beginning in the 1990s.

Beyond that, China has refused to abide by an international tribunal's July ruling that said many of the country's actions in the South China Sea, including its construction of artificial islands and its expansive claims to sovereignty over the waters around them, violated the U.N. Convention on the Law of the Sea treaty (UNCLOS) to which China is a signatory.

Much of this resembles the push-and-parry tactics of past decades. But China's dramatically increased maritime and aerial power has changed the calculation. Its navy selectively informs non-Chinese ships that they're "trespassing." Those hailed — naval vessels, petroleum survey ships or fishing vessels — counter that they're in international waters. Ramming and other tactics have ensued.

Much of the undersea and aerial encounters between Chinese and other navies never makes the news. But harassment of foreign naval ships, including U.S. Navy vessels, has increased. The risk of a shooting incident has steadily risen.

NO   Zhu Feng
Executive Director, China Center for Collaborative Studies of South China Sea, Nanjing University

Written for *CQ Researcher*, January 2017

According to media coverage, China is speeding up the militarization of the South China Sea by deploying hundreds of missiles in the reclaimed maritime territories, and this supposedly poses a threat to U.S. security in the region. But few people would find such an idea convincing upon closer examination.

China's military buildup in the reclaimed islands in the Spratlys is quite limited but necessary. All the weapon systems are short-range and defensive in nature. Considering the billions of dollars spent on island reclamation and construction, Beijing is legally justified in building military defenses to protect its huge investment.

Second, it is unlikely these weapons would be used to attack nearby American ships and jet fighters. The reason is that any retaliation would put these islands at risk of being fully destroyed. I don't think that Beijing will risk a huge retaliation by using these island-based light weapons — rifle, guns and short-range missiles.

Third, China's limited weapon systems, along with airstrips in those constructed islands, do not forcefully change the military postures of China and the United States in the western Pacific. China's reclaimed islands, even with military facilities there, are more like "sitting ducks" than islands bases, as China's land-based firepower is too far away to defend them. Even a couple of U.S. destroyers could easily paralyze these islands.

China's activities in the Spratly Islands arise from political, not military, motivations. What's more, it's not China that initiated the reclamation and military buildup. Ironically, it's Vietnam and the Philippines, and they have never terminated their projects in their illegally occupied Spratly assets.

Beijing never disavows its promise of peaceful settlement of any maritime disputes in the South China Sea.

China's island construction and military buildup in the Spratlys might complicate U.S. security strategy in the South China Sea as China emerges as a new competitor in the western Pacific. But China's navy and air force remain far behind those of the United States, and it's unimaginable that China's newly claimed islands, even with a number of short-range missiles, could put the United States in jeopardy.

Beijing should be prudently and transparently handling its military buildup in the Spratlys while seeking to ensure the United States does not overreact. No one in the region seeks an escalation of military tension between the two powers.

defend free trade, including the TPP, in the new Congress. "Republicans are going to continue to support the freedom to trade," Brady told a panel of *The Wall Street Journal* CEO Council. "Don't withdraw, renegotiate. Fix the problems that exist today."[66]

Judging from Trump's appointment of free-trade foe Peter Navarro to lead a new White House office overseeing U.S. trade and industrial policy, Republican free-traders in Congress face an uphill battle.

Navarro, who favors higher tariffs on imports, is a staunch critic of China and other low-cost exporting nations. "Trump will never again sacrifice the U.S. economy on the altar of foreign policy by entering into bad trade deals like the North American Free Trade Agreement, allowing China into the World Trade Organization and passing the proposed TPP," wrote Navarro and a co-author in an article in *Foreign Policy* in November. "These deals only weaken our manufacturing base and ability to defend ourselves and our allies."[67]

Military Rebalance

The other critical component of Obama's pivot to Asia is increasing the U.S. naval presence in the region and the amount of military assistance to allies.

The Pentagon took an initial step in April, when it announced funding for the Maritime Security Initiative (MSI), a five-year, $425 million aid program that seeks to help South China Sea countries improve their ability to monitor activities in their territorial waters and air space.[68]

The Philippines, which remains a U.S. ally despite Duterte's ascension, is receiving the lion's share of the first-year funding, taking in $42 million of the first $50 million. Vietnam, Malaysia, Indonesia and Thailand are getting money to increase maritime security, and Brunei, Singapore and Taiwan for training and headquarter-level integration.

"Countries across the Asia-Pacific are voicing concern with China's land reclamation, which stands out in size and scope, as well as its militarization in the South China Sea," Defense Secretary Carter said last April. "We're standing with these countries. We're helping them build capacity. We're affirming our commitment to their and the region's security with increased posture."[69]

Critics, however, say the Maritime Security Initiative is inadequate. "The problem with MSI is that it's 'budget

dust' in Pentagon-speak," Van Jackson, a former Pentagon official who served in the Obama administration, said. "You can't do much with $425 million."[70]

The Pentagon responded that the MSI is not the only increase directed at the South China Sea.

"From a multitude of exercises across the region, to freedom of navigation operations and presence operations, the Department of Defense continues to fly, sail and operate wherever international law allows so that others can do the same," Assistant Secretary of Defense Denmark told Congress in July, citing carrier operations in the Philippine Sea, exercises conducted with Japan and India and other "enhanced tempo" activities.[71]

But former Sen. Talent says U.S. naval power in the region is inadequate, especially given the logistical advantage the Chinese have in being so close to the theater of operations. "Because it is in their near seas, the Chinese can focus their power very quickly," says Talent. "It takes several weeks for us to steam ships from the West Coast to the region."

Others say U.S. forces are up to the challenge. "Certainly, U.S. assets in the Pacific are sufficient to the task now, and if we follow through on pledges to ship further [naval] assets to the Pacific . . ., they should be up to the challenge of the future," says Poling of the Center for Strategic and International Studies.

Some in Congress urged the Obama White House to increase naval patrols near disputed islands in the South China Sea. The proposed Asia-Pacific Maritime Security Initiative Act of 2016, which did not survive last year's Congress, would have required the administration to report to Congress on its China activities and on U.S. plans for freedom of navigation operations in the region. Additionally, the bill called for delivering more sophisticated military hardware to the Philippines.[72] It is unclear whether similar legislation will be introduced in the current Congress.

A few analysts say the United States may already have too big of a military presence in the region and should work toward sharing power with China rather than trying to contain it.

"As the United States military doubles down in Asia, the chances increase that one side will cross a red line," wrote strategic-intelligence consultant Nicholas Borroz and Southeast Asia analyst Hunter Marston in October. "That does not mean Washington should abandon its allies. But it should avoid creating extensive, untenable defense agreements. Washington should maintain a manageable number of security commitments and take steps toward balancing power with China in the Western Pacific — and it should do so while it has the power to shape that balance in its favor."[73]

OUTLOOK

Trump's Impact

One of the biggest uncertainties regarding the South China Sea, especially in light of secretary of State nominee Tillerson's confirmation hearing testimony, is what Trump will do as president. Trump's transition team had no immediate reaction to Tillerson's comments, but earlier it said the new administration "will take a hawkish view of China, focus on bolstering regional alliances, have a renewed interest in Taiwan, be skeptical of engagement with North Korea and bolster the U.S. Navy's fleet presence in the Pacific."[74]

Some observers hope Trump will take a measured and balanced approach to China and the South China Sea.

"Trump made it abundantly clear during the campaign that he is no friend of open-ended military interventions [and] nation-building exercises such as what we have experienced in Iraq and Afghanistan," says the Public Policy Research Center's Cohen. "At the same time, he has called for restoring U.S. military might and has deplored what he sees as the deteriorated state of the U.S. Navy. In other words, he appears to see a strengthened United States as deterring potential adversaries from engaging in reckless geopolitical behavior."

Cohen adds that Trump's appointments also indicate that he will follow a policy of deterrence grounded on a stronger military. "Having retired General James Mattis as Defense secretary, a man known to friend and foe alike as 'Mad Dog,' only underscores what I see as a 21st-century version of the older, Cold War-era doctrine of deterrence," says Cohen. In the South China Sea, where the United States wants free navigation and secure shipping routes but where it has no direct territorial interests, "what we could see is renewed respect for the United States."

Others point to inconsistencies in Trump's appointments. The selection of Iowa Gov. Terry Branstad, a longtime acquaintance of Chinese President Xi, as U.S. ambassador to China may indicate that Trump's approach to China will be more constructive than his comments on the One China policy indicated.

Of course, the future of the South China Sea depends at least as much on China as it does on the Trump administration. According to many experts, China will continue to expand its influence in the region.

"The fundamental problem is that China is not stable [due to potential challenges to its leadership from the military], so its leaders, for various reasons, are in no position, in no mood, to deal with their counterparts in other capitals on a good-faith basis," wrote Gordon G. Chang, a China specialist and *Forbes* magazine contributor.[75]

The Center for Security Policy's Gaffney agrees, pointing to the growing importance of China's military. "The military there is becoming sort of the key power-broker, and everybody is trying to accommodate them," he says. "It's a worrying thing that the Chinese military is clearly feeling its oats."

According to the Center for a New American Security's Kaplan, the situation in the South China Sea is, indeed, at a "contradictory, unstable inflection point," although he says China's growing influence is not unexpected.

"Nothing we can do will deter China from gradually, inexorably trying to [extend its influence] in the South China Sea, because it is in their demonstrable self-interest to do so," says Kaplan.

His advice for Trump is to resist the temptation for surprises. "Surprises may work from time to time, but, generally, diplomacy requires predictability," he says. "We should establish a predictable relationship with China."

NOTES

1. "China's New Spratly Island Defenses," Asia Maritime Transparency Initiative, Dec. 13, 2016, http://tinyurl.com/jofu276.

2. "Foreign Ministry Spokesperson Lu Kang's Remarks on Issues Relating to China's Construction Activities on the Nansha Islands and Reefs," Ministry of Foreign Affairs of the People's Republic of China, June 16, 2015, http://tinyurl.com/zeer2sw; "Country: China," Asia Maritime Transparency Initiative, http://tinyurl.com/hv3fd8g.

3. Chris Buckley, "China Suggests It Has Placed Weapons on Disputed Spratly Islands in South

China Sea," *The New York Times*, Dec. 15, 2016, http://tinyurl.com/z3ofp2g.

4. Katie Hunt, "Tillerson sets stage for showdown with Beijing over South China Sea," CNN, Jan. 12, 2017, China's New Spratly Island Defenses," http://tinyurl.com/jdzdfru.

5. Michael Forsythe and Chris Buckley, "Taiwan Responds After China Sends Carrier to Taiwan Strait," *The New York Times*, Jan. 10, 2017, http://tinyurl.com/zzjafe9.

6. Buckley, op. cit.

7. Christopher P. Cavas, "China's Navy Makes Strides, Work Remains To Be Done," *Defense News*, May 24, 2015, http://tinyurl.com/ov2mvmq; See also Ronald O'Rourke, "China Naval Modernization: Implications for U.S. Navy Capabilities — Background and Issues for Congress," Congressional Research Service, June 17, 2016, http://tinyurl.com/h83nt3k.

8. Testimony of Colin Willett, deputy assistant secretary of State for multilateral affairs, Bureau of East Asian and Pacific Affairs, U.S. Department of State, before the House Armed Services Committee, Seapower and Projection Forces Subcommittee, and House Foreign Affairs Committee Subcommittee on Asia and the Pacific, July 7, 2016, http://tinyurl.com/hdz7ymp.

9. Robert D. Kaplan, *Asia's Cauldron: The South China Sea and the End of a Stable Pacific* (2015), p. 10; Tim Daiss, "Why the South China Sea has More Oil Than You Think," *Forbes*, May 22, 2016, http://tinyurl.com/z9qokas.

10. Bonnie S. Glaser, "Armed Clash in the South China Sea, Contingency Planning Memorandum No. 14, Council on Foreign Relations, April 2012, http://tinyurl.com/zf4u4ws.

11. Adam Greer, "The South China Sea Is Really a Fishery Dispute," *The Diplomat*, July 20, 2016, http://tinyurl.com/hur9mcz; Trefor Moss, "Five Things About Fishing in the South China Sea," *The Wall Street Journal*, "July 19, 2016, http://tinyurl.com/zrgw334.

12. Caren Bohan and David Brunnstrom, "Trump says U.S. not necessarily bound by 'one China' policy,"

Reuters, Dec. 12, 2016, http://tinyurl.com/zb3b84g.

13. Dennis C. Blair, written testimony before the Senate Foreign Relations Subcommittee on East Asia, the Pacific, and International Cybersecurity Policy, July 13, 2016, http://tinyurl.com/jzzw32b.

14. Demetri Sevastopulo and Ben Bland, "US plans to boost Pacific naval forces," *Financial Times*, June 2, 2012, http://tinyurl.com/hcds9xo.

15. Audrey McAvoy, "U.S. Pacific Fleet shrinks even as China grows more aggressive," *U.S. News & World Report*, Jan. 5, 2016, http://tinyurl.com/zpodvbb.

16. Abraham M. Denmark, testimony before the House Committee on Armed Services Subcommittee on Seapower and Projection Forces and the House Committee on Foreign Affairs Subcommittee on Asia and the Pacific, July 7, 2016, http://tinyurl.com/guq2wn6.

17. Shannon Tiezzi, "China Won't 'Militarize' the South China Sea — But It Will Build Military Facilities There," *The Diplomat*, Oct. 16, 2015, http://tinyurl.com/z3dlaqc.

18. Jeremy Page, Carol E. Lee and Gordon Lubold, "China's President Pledges No Militarization in Disputed Islands," *The Wall Street Journal*, Sept. 25, 2015, http://tinyurl.com/oeayky3; Buckley, op. cit.

19. Timothy Heath, testimony before the U.S.-China Economic and Security Review Commission, Jan. 21, 2016, http://tinyurl.com/hk9c274.

20. Quoted in Kaplan, op. cit., p. 44.

21. "Transcript: Donald Trump's Foreign Policy Speech," *The New York Times*, April 27, 2016, http://tinyurl.com/hdfurda.

22. Stephanie Condon, "Donald Trump: Japan, South Korea might need nuclear weapons," CBS News, March 29, 2016, http://tinyurl.com/jp3qzuk.

23. Elbridge Colby, testimony before the House Foreign Affairs Committee, Sept. 22, 2016, http://tinyurl.com/gtd8oev.

24. Emiko Jozuka, "Japan to join US in South China Sea patrols," CNN Wire, Sept. 16, 2016, http://tinyurl.com/gnk98ed.

25. Anthony H. Cordesman, "Trump Takes Office: The National Security Agenda He Must Address by the End of the Coming Spring," Center for Strategic and International Studies, Nov. 14, 2016, http://tinyurl.com/zzjmplc.

26. Robert E. Kelly, "The Misplaced Burden-Sharing Fight," *The National Interest*, Dec. 4, 2016, http://tinyurl.com/j7twtns.

27. Cristiano Lima, "Trump calls trade deal 'a rape of our country,' " *Politico*, June 28, 2016, http://tinyurl.com/jautjrd.

28. Mitsuru Obe, "Japan Ratifies Trans-Pacific Partnership, Which Trump Has Promised to Leave," *The Wall Street Journal*, Dec. 9, 2016, http://tinyurl.com/hkeuz6u.

29. Thomas J. Christensen, *The China Challenge: Shaping the Choices of a Rising Power* (2015), p. 250.

30. "TPP: What is it and why does it matter?" BBC, Nov. 22, 2016, http://tinyurl.com/psjahsa.

31. "Trump to dump TPP trade deal: World Leaders React," BBC, Nov. 22, 2016, http://tinyurl.com/zbrbxdb.

32. Constanca, "Portuguese Malacca, 1511–1641," Portuguese World Heritage, June 21, 2015, http://tinyurl.com/j72jceu.

33. Mark J. Valencia, "The South China Sea and the 'Thucydides Trap,' " in *The South China Sea: A Crucible of Regional Cooperation or Conflict-Making Sovereignty Claims?* (2016), p. 56.

34. Nicholas Tarling, ed., "The Establishment of the Colonial Regimes," in *The Cambridge History of Southeast Asia*, vol. 2, part 1, (1999), p. 4.

35. Ibid., p. 7.

36. "International Commerce, the State and Society: Economic and Social Change," in *The Cambridge History of Southeast Asia*, vol. 2, part 1 (1999), p. 135.

37. Tarling, op. cit., p. 61.

38. Kenneth Pletcher, "Opium Wars," *Encyclopaedia Britannica*, last updated April 17, 2015, http://tinyurl.com/jxw9hus.

39. Ibid.

40. Kaplan, op. cit., p. 21.

41. "Political Structures in the Nineteenth and Early Twentieth Centuries," in *The Cambridge History of Southeast Asia*, vol. 2, part 1, p. 77, p. 100.

42. Paul Kratoska and Ben Batson, "Nationalism and Modernist Reform," in ibid., p. 249.

43. Valencia, op. cit., p. 60.

44. "Why is the South China Sea contentious?" BBC, July 12, 2016, http://tinyurl.com/m2tfywy.

45. Valencia, op. cit., p. 60.

46. Kaplan, op. cit., p. 171.

47. U.S. Department of Defense, Freedom of Navigation Program Fact Sheet, March 2015, http://tinyurl.com/jvblqfc.

48. David E. Sanger, "Philippines Orders U.S. to Leave Strategic Navy Base at Subic Bay," *The New York Times*, Dec. 28, 1991, http://tinyurl.com/z7jpmce.

49. Mohan Malik, "Historical Fiction: China's South China Sea Claims," *World Affairs Journal*, May/June 2013, http://tinyurl.com/zv94bff.

50. Kaplan, op. cit., p. 126.

51. Rodolfo C. Severino, "Global Issues and National Interests in the South China Sea," in *The South China Sea: A Crucible of Regional Cooperation or Conflict-Making Sovereignty Claims?* (2016), p. 39.

52. Richard Baum et al., "Whither U.S.-China Relations?" NBR Analysis, vol. 16, no. 4, December 2005, p. 25, http://tinyurl.com/j3abrs5.

53. Mike Allen, "America's first Pacific president," *Politico*, Nov. 13, 2009, http://tinyurl.com/hw7l8b7.

54. Kenneth Lieberthal, "The American Pivot to Asia: Why President Obama's turn to the East is easier said than done," *Foreign Policy*, Dec. 21, 2011, http://tinyurl.com/zubnx9c; Elisabeth Bumiller, "Words and Deeds Show Focus of the American Military on Asia," *The New York Times*, Nov. 10, 2012, http://tinyurl.com/j46hnt5.

55. Howard W. French, "What's behind Beijing's drive to control the South China Sea?" *The Guardian*, July 28, 2015, http://tinyurl.com/go8nr8t.

56. Christensen, op. cit., p. 265.

57. James Bamford, "Could American Spooks Provoke War with Beijing?" *Foreign Policy*, Dec. 8, 2015, http://tinyurl.com/z7bz7td.

58. Ibid.

59. Javier C. Hernández, "Chinese State Media Denounce Rex Tillerson's Call to Block Island Access," *The New York Times*, Jan. 13, 2017, http://tinyurl.com/jhb3wxl.

60. Michael Forsythe, "Rex Tillerson's South China Sea Remarks Foreshadow Possible Foreign Policy Crisis," *The New York Times*, Jan. 12, 2017, http://tinyurl.com/hwe5ej2.

61. "The South China Sea Arbitration (The Republic of the Philippines v. the People's Republic of China," press release, The Hague, July 12, 2016, http://tinyurl.com/h7wpv9e.

62 "Why a tribunal has ruled against China on the South China Sea," *The Economist*, July 13, 2016, http://tinyurl.com/jmqgafr.

63. Greg Torode, "'Paving paradise': Scientists alarmed over China island building in disputed sea," Reuters, June 25, 2015, http://tinyurl.com/hfz46bw.

64. Adam Behsudi and Nancy Cook, "Trump will quit TPP in first days," *Politico*, Nov. 10, 2016, http://tinyurl.com/zjnl4zk.

65. Jackie Calmes, "What Is Lost by Burying the Trans-Pacific Partnership?" *The New York Times*, Nov. 11, 2016, http://tinyurl.com/h9a3mcu.

66. Patrick Rucker and Howard Schneider, "Top tax-writing Republican says TPP trade deal not dead in Congress," Reuters, Nov. 15, 2016, http://tinyurl.com/je8efs5.

67. Alexander Gray and Peter Navarro, "Donald Trump's Peace Through Strength Vision for the Asia-Pacific," *Foreign Policy*, Nov. 7, 2016, http://tinyurl.com/hhqj3ps.

68. Megan Eckstein, "The Philippines at Forefront of New Pentagon Maritime Security Initiative," USNI News, April 18, 2016, http://tinyurl.com/hbnmnzl.

69. Ibid.

70. Prashanth Parameswaran, "America's New Maritime Security Initiative for South-east Asia: A look at the Southeast Asia Maritime Security Initiative as it gets underway," *The Diplomat*, April 2, 2016, http://tinyurl.com/j689647.

71. Denmark, op. cit.

72. Dan De Luce, "Lawmakers to White House: Get Tough With Beijing Over South China Sea," *Foreign Policy*, April 27, 2016, http://tinyurl.com/zz3xy9m.

73. Nicholas Borroz and Hunter Marston, "Washington Should Stop Militarizing the Pacific," *The New York Times*, Oct. 9, 2016, http://tinyurl.com/hjabnvo.

74. Forsythe, op. cit.; Josh Rogen, "Trump could make Obama's pivot to Asia a reality," *The Washington Post*, Jan. 8, 2017, http://tinyurl.com/hpnma6w.

75. Gordan G. Chang, "A Turbulent China Shakes the World," in *Warning Order: China Prepares for Conflict and Why We Must Do the Same* (2016), p. 56.

BIBLIOGRAPHY
Selected Sources
Books

Christensen, Thomas J., *The China Challenge: Shaping the Choices of a Rising Power*, **W.W. Norton & Co., 2015.**
A former deputy assistant secretary of State for East Asian and Pacific affairs argues that the United States should focus on deterring Chinese aggression in Asia while encouraging its cooperation in global economic and security efforts.

Fleitz, Fred, ed., *Warning Order: China Prepares for Conflict and Why We Must Do the Same*, **Center for Security Policy Press, 2016.**
A collection of essays urges a strong military response to China's attempts to displace the "post-World War II Pax Americana with a new order" that would make China the pre-eminent global power.

Jenner, C. J., and Tran Truong Thuy, eds., *The South China Sea: A Crucible of Regional Cooperation or Conflict-Making Sovereignty Claims?* **Cambridge University Press, 2016.**
Jenner, a research fellow at Kings College in London, and Thuy, deputy director of the Bien Dong Institute in Vietnam, compile a primer on issues surrounding the ongoing conflicts over the South China Sea.

Kaplan, Robert D., *Asia's Cauldron: The South China Sea and the End of a Stable Pacific*, **Random House, 2014.**

A senior fellow at the Center for a New American Security, a liberal-leaning Washington think tank, writes that a fundamental change in the balance of power in the western Pacific has taken place, and the change is leading to rising tensions, and the potential for major conflict, in the South China Sea region.

Articles

Gray, Alexander, and Peter Navarro, "Donald Trump's Peace Through Strength Vision for the Asia-Pacific," *Foreign Policy*, **Nov. 7, 2016, http://tinyurl.com/ hhqj3ps.**

Gray, a senior adviser to the Trump campaign, and Navarro, tapped as President Trump's chief trade adviser, offer an insiders' view of the new administration's Asia policies. They predict Trump will bring stability to the region.

Lieberthal, Kenneth, "The American Pivot to Asia: Why President Obama's turn to the East is easier said than done," *Foreign Policy*, **Dec. 21, 2011, http:// tinyurl.com/zubnx9c.**

A senior fellow at the centrist Brookings Institution assesses the Obama administration's evolving policies in Asia and concludes that both the United States and China "must keep in mind that they are best served by adopting positions that engender a healthy respect in the other capital concerning capabilities and goals so that neither acts rashly."

Thompson, Loren, "Five Reasons China Won't Be A Big Threat To America's Global Power," *Forbes*, **June 6, 2014, http://tinyurl.com/hgtlrru.**

The head of the Lexington Institute, a conservative think tank focused on national security, spells out the reasons he believes China is incapable of challenging the United States; the two primary ones, he says, are China's over-reliance on exports and its aging population.

Reports and Studies

"Annual Report to Congress: Military and Security Developments Involving the People's Republic of China 2015," Office of the Secretary of Defense, **2015, http://tinyurl.com/j8fkvbv.**

In its annual assessment of China's military power, the Department of Defense concludes that the country is rapidly modernizing its forces, although it still lacks the ability to project significant power far from its own shores.

"Asian Views on America's Role in Asia: The Future of the Rebalance," Asia Foundation, 2016, http:// tinyurl.com/ztqmjx5.

Specialists from Asian countries offer strategic recommendations to the incoming U.S. president regarding foreign policy toward Asia; the report stemmed from a series of meetings held by this nonpartisan international development organization.

"Asia-Pacific Rebalance 2025: Capabilities, Presence, and Partnerships," Center for Strategic and International Studies, January 2016, http://tinyurl .com/gpqktxj.

This report by a bipartisan think tank, commissioned by the Department of Defense, finds that the Obama administration's efforts to rebalance U.S. strategic resources in Asia may be insufficient to protect American interests in the region.

"The PLA Navy: New Capabilities and Missions for the 21st Century," U.S. Office of Naval Intelligence, April 2015, http://tinyurl.com/hvf63on.

This report by the U.S. Navy's intelligence service details China's recent efforts to modernize its navy, and finds that while East Asia remains China's primary focus, it is seeking to build a navy capable of deploying beyond that region.

Rinehart, Ian E., "The Chinese Military: Overview and Issues for Congress," Congressional Research Service, March 24, 2016, http://tinyurl.com/ ju29zdc.

A report by the research arm of Congress examines in detail China's efforts to modernize its military and finds that it is building "a modern and regionally powerful military with a limited but growing capability for conducting operations away from China's immediate periphery."

For More Information

American Enterprise Institute, 1789 Massachusetts Ave., N.W., Washington, DC 20036; 202-862-5800; www.aei .org. Conservative think tank that focuses on an array of public policy issues, with a special emphasis on foreign and defense policy.

Center for Naval Analyses, 3003 Washington Blvd., Arlington, VA 22201; 703-824-2000, www.cna.org. Nonprofit research organization that produces analysis on foreign policy and other issues.

Center for Security Policy, 1901 Pennsylvania Ave., N.W., DC 20006; 202-835-9077; www.centerforsecuritypolicy.org. Public policy research organization focused on national security issues.

Center for Strategic and International Studies, 1800 K St., N.W., Washington, DC 20006; 202-887-0200; www .csis.org. Centrist think tank that offers bipartisan proposals on U.S. security issues.

Greenpeace Southeast Asia, Room 201 JGS Building, #30 Scout Tuazon St., 1103 Quezon City, the Philippines; +63-2-3321807; www.greenpeace.org/seasia/ph/. Branch of the Greenpeace environmental advocacy organization that monitors environmental issues in Southeast Asia, including the South China Sea.

Lexington Institute, 1600 Wilson Blvd., Suite 203, Arlington, VA 22209; 703-522-5828; www.lexington institute.org. Conservative think tank that studies national security issues.

U.S.-China Economic and Security Review Commission, 444 N. Capitol St., N.W., Suite 602, Washington, DC 20001; 202-624-1407; www.uscc.gov. Created by Congress to monitor the national security implications of the bilateral trade and economic relationship between the United States and the People's Republic of China.

U.S. Naval War College, 686 Cushing Road, Newport, RI 02841-1207; 401-841-1310; www.usnwc.edu. Navy's staff college supports research on strategy, maritime and security issues.

5

U.S.-Iran Relations

Chuck McCutcheon

Graffiti on a building in Tehran, Iran's capital, says "Down with the USA." Despite Iran's bellicose attitude toward the U.S. government, 53 percent of Iranians have positive feelings about Americans in general, though nearly 90 percent view the U.S. government negatively.

From *CQ Researcher,*
January 20, 2017

For years, a nuclear reactor complex near Arak, Iran, stirred global fears that World War III could be looming. The Iranian government claimed the complex had a peaceful purpose: conducting research that could benefit hospitals and businesses.[1] Western experts thought differently, however.

Antiaircraft guns and missiles protected the complex, and Iran refused to allow outside inspectors inside. Finally, the world's worries were confirmed: Experts declared in 2014 that the facility was on the verge of being able to produce weapons-grade uranium that could be used to make an atomic bomb.[2]

After years of international pressure, including the imposition of onerous U.S. economic sanctions, Iran has stepped away from its nuclear program in a highly controversial deal with far-reaching global-security implications. Under pressure from the United States, China, France, Russia, the United Kingdom and Germany, Iran said it removed the core of the Arak reactor, pledged to let inspectors visit the site and put other nuclear research on hold for up to 15 years. In return, the other countries lifted many — though not all — economic sanctions against Iran in January 2016, providing some relief to its struggling economy and helping the country's moderate president to win reelection a year later.

The deal does not limit Iran's development of civilian nuclear sites.

"We have a rare chance to pursue a new path — a different, better future that delivers progress for both our peoples and the wider world," then-President Obama said in announcing Iran's reactor removal and the lifting of sanctions.[3] The agreement has raised speculation in political and foreign-policy circles about whether Iran can someday join China, Vietnam and Cuba — formerly staunch U.S. enemies that now cooperate on trade, diplomacy and other matters, even as their political systems remain far from American-style democracy.

But any uptick in relations that could bring a flood of U.S. products to Tehran, unite the two countries in stabilizing the Middle East or yield other large benefits is far from imminent — if it occurs at all. Many U.S. sanctions remain in place. And despite some diplomatic cooperation under Obama, Iran has continued to antagonize the United States in several national security–related incidents in the close of Obama's term and the first year of Donald Trump's.

Trump, along with many other U.S. lawmakers — as well as Prime Minister Benjamin Netanyahu of Israel, a stalwart U.S. ally — remain highly suspicious of Iran, which the State Department says supports terrorists and critics say wants to eradicate Israel. Trump called the nuclear agreement "the worst deal ever," though his secretary of Defense, James Mattis, considers remaining part of it to be in the best interest of U.S. national security.[4] Trump in October 2017 "decertified" the international arrangement, calling on Congress to determine its eventual fate.

The president's remarks came after Iran reportedly launched several ballistic missiles earlier in the year and Congress easily passed a sweeping bill imposing more sanctions on that country as well as on Russia and North Korea.[5] On the other hand, many U.S. allies are reluctant to jettison the deal because they see big trade opportunities with Iran, and diplomats who were involved in negotiating the arrangement said that it had been satisfactorily implemented as of summer 2017.

Tense talk over nuclear weapons has dominated U.S.-Iranian relations for years, to the dismay of some who say it has overshadowed other areas. Obama's predecessor, George W. Bush, in 2002 labeled Iran part of an "axis of evil" (along with Iraq and North Korea) for its alleged pursuit of atomic weapons despite Iran's insistence that its nuclear development was for peaceful purposes only.[6]

"We used to have a wide-ranging and often well-informed debate about Iran," Suzanne Maloney, deputy director of the foreign policy program at the Brookings Institution, a centrist think tank in Washington, said at a 2015 forum before the International Atomic Energy Agency (IAEA) certified Iran's early fulfillment of its nuclear commitments. "Our conversations on Iran have been afflicted with an almost obsessive focus on one question, the nuclear issue."[7]

On foreign policy, Iran shares the United States' opposition to the Islamic State and al-Qaeda terrorist groups. Economically, Iran is enticing to foreign companies. It has a population of 80 million — second only to Egypt among Middle East countries and almost as large as California, Texas and Florida combined.[8]

Iranian President Hassan Rouhani, a moderate, initially took a wait-and-see stance on the nuclear deal, saying that if it was implemented to Iranian leaders' satisfaction, "we can put other topics on the table for discussion" with the United States.[9] But after Trump's election he confined his comments about U.S.-Iran relations largely to the nuclear deal, saying he strongly disagreed with the U.S. president that the deal could ever be reopened for another round of talks.[10]

Rouhani won a second term in 2017, and experts said his reelection hinged on his promises to continue to improve Iran's economy after the easing of sanctions.[11]

But Rouhani, like Obama, is constrained. Rouhani is the civilian leader of an authoritarian theocracy led by Ayatollah Ali Khamenei, who has a lifelong position, final word on Iranian policy and a penchant for using the slogan "Death to America."[12]

Khamenei is the "supreme leader" of Iran's predominantly non-Arab Shiite Muslim population, which is surrounded by Sunni Muslim-dominated Arab countries that — along with Israel — generally have better relations with the United States. Long-standing racial and religious animosity between Iran and its neighbors complicates U.S. diplomacy in the region. America's Arab allies deeply distrust Iran and accuse it of seeking to destabilize the Middle East by backing armed terrorist groups from Lebanon to Iraq.[13] The U.S. State Department has listed Iran as a state sponsor of terrorism since 1984.

In January 2016, Iran pleased supporters of closer relations with the United States by concluding a controversial prisoner swap negotiated separately from the nuclear talks. Under the agreement, Iran released *Washington Post* reporter Jason Rezaian, an Iranian-American, and two other Americans. In return, the

A Neighborhood of Turmoil

About the size of Alaska, Iran sits in one of the world's most unsettled regions. It borders the Persian Gulf and Strait of Hormuz — both militarily strategic and vital for crude-oil transportation. Surrounding Iran are war-torn Iraq and Afghanistan, plus Turkey and Pakistan — both wracked by civil unrest. Saudi Arabia, a key U.S. ally and longtime nemesis of Iran, lies just across the Persian Gulf. Most Iranians are Shiites, creating racial and religious tension with Iran's predominantly Arab and Sunni Muslim neighbors. More than a dozen civilian nuclear facilities operate in Tehran or elsewhere in Iran.

* Being repurposed to produce non-uranium materials

Sources: "The World Factbook, Iran," CIA, http://tinyurl.com/yoex73; "World Development Indicators, Iran, Islamic Rep.," The World Bank, http://tinyurl.com/y3kcemn; "From the Sky," Institute for Science and International Security, http://tinyurl.com/zpu4xbt

Iran at a Glance

Population: 81.8 million (2015)

Ethnicity: 60 percent are Persian. Others include Azeri, Kurd, Lur, Arab, Turkmen.

Area: 636,372 sq. miles

GDP: $396.9 billion (2015)

Per Capita Income: $16,900 (2013)

Life Expectancy: 71 years (2015)

Adult Literacy Rate: 86.8% (2015)

Legislature: Islamic Consultative Assembly, 290 members

Religions: Shia Islam (the national religion) (90-95%); Sunni Muslim (5-10%); others include Zoroastrian, Jewish, Christian and Bahá'í.

Key Trading Partners:
- **Exports** — China (29%), India (11.9%), Turkey (10.4%)
- **Imports** — United Arab Emirates (30.6%), China (25.5%), Algeria (8.3%)

United States legally cleared seven Iranians charged or imprisoned for violating economic sanctions and dismissed legal charges against 14 others outside the United States.[14]

But Iran has refused to release Siamak Namazi, an Iranian-American businessman arrested and subsequently convicted, along with his father, of allegedly collaborating with the United States.[15] Iran also has provoked U.S. anger recently by:

- Displaying renewed hostility toward U.S. ally Saudi Arabia. A January 2016 mob attack on the Saudi embassy in Tehran led the Saudis and several of their allies to cut formal ties with Iran. In November 2017, the Saudi government accused Iran and Hezbollah, which acts as a proxy for Iran in Lebanon, of carrying out an "act of war" with a missile they said was fired at them by Iranian-backed rebels in Yemen.[16]

- Launching non-nuclear ballistic missiles, leading Obama in January 2016 to impose new sanctions — separate from those lifted as part of the nuclear deal — on people and companies involved with Iran's missile program. Further missile launches were what motivated Congress to impose additional sanctions after Trump took office.[17]

Americans, Iranians Eye Each Other Warily

An overwhelming majority of U.S. adults view Iran unfavorably, according to a February Gallup poll. Another poll found nearly 90 percent of Iranian adults view the U.S. government negatively, but 53 percent of Iranians had positive feelings about Americans.

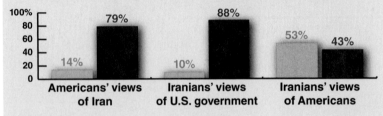

Views of One Another's Governments and People

Sources: Andrew Dugan, "After Nuclear Deal, U.S. Views of Iran Remain Dismal," Gallup Poll, Feb. 17, 2016, http://tinyurl.com/jdaaggy; Ebrahim Gallagher, Nancy Mohseni and Clay Ramsay, "Iranian Attitudes in Advance of the Parliamentary Elections: Economics, Politics, and Foreign Affairs," Center for International and Security Studies, University of Maryland, January 2016, p. 33, http://tinyurl.com/zxrs4kk

that only 14 percent of Americans have a favorable view of Iran, just slightly above the 11 percent average since 1989.[22] A telephone poll of more than 1,000 Iranians found that 53 percent had positive feelings about the American public, but 88 percent felt unfavorably toward the U.S. government.[23]

As politicians, scholars, diplomats and others assess whether U.S.-Iran relations will improve or worsen, here are some questions being debated:

Should the United States seek closer ties with Iran?

The United States severed diplomatic relations with Iran after the 1979 revolution, when supporters of Ayatollah Ruhollah Khomeini — Khamenei's predecessor — stormed the U.S. embassy in Tehran and took 52 Americans hostage for 444 days. Since then, neither country has had an embassy in the other, so contacts are severely restricted.

Advocates of improved ties cite improved U.S. relations with two former adversaries as guides for gradually making up its rift with Iran: Vietnam, where the United States waged a 21-year war in a failed bid to stop the spread of communism in Southeast Asia, and communist Cuba, which has been shut off from U.S. commerce and diplomatic ties until an easing by the Obama administration.[24]

"If the United States and Vietnam could reconcile after America's Vietnam fiasco, and if the U.S. is able to restore relations following some six decades of enmity with Cuba, a similar development with Iran is not to be viewed as insurmountable," says Amin Saikal, a professor of political science at Australian National University and author of the 2015 book *Iran at the Crossroads*.

Democratic presidential candidate and Vermont senator Bernie Sanders, often described as a "socialist independent," said at a January 2016 debate that the United States should not open an embassy in Tehran immediately. "But I think the goal has got to be, as we've done with Cuba, to move in [the direction of] warm relations with a very powerful and important country," he said.[25]

- Hacking computer systems at U.S. banks and other entities. Experts say those attacks have risen since the nuclear agreement was reached. Moreover, Iran "may be preparing" larger cyberattacks, said Martin Libicki, a senior management scientist at the RAND Corp., a think tank specializing in national security.[18]

Although Khamenei accepted Rouhani's request to pursue the nuclear deal, he has said Iran should not negotiate with the United States about anything else.[19] But Middle East experts question how long Khamenei will remain in power.[20]

Iranian lawmakers voted overwhelmingly in August 2017 to boost the country's budget for its ballistic missile program and foreign operations by the hardline Revolutionary Guards, a military group that has been far less inclined than Rouhani to improve relations with the United States. The actions came in retaliation to the sanctions legislation passed by the U.S. Congress over Iran's missile program.[21]

Americans and Iranians harbor deep suspicions about one another. A Gallup poll in February 2016 showed

The National Iranian American Council, a group in Washington that seeks better U.S.-Iran relations, says the United States should follow former Republican President Richard M. Nixon's example of reaching out to communist China on trade. Nixon's move in 1972 lessened three decades of U.S.-Chinese hostility. The two countries restored diplomatic relations in 1979. Two council members called for "a new [U.S.] outlook towards Iran — one in which economics facilitates an evolution of political relations."[26]

Some advocates say closer U.S.-Iran relations would build on diplomatic ties forged by the nuclear deal. For instance, in October 2015 Iran agreed to participate in multination talks aimed at ending the violent, years-long rebellion in Syria against President Bashar al-Assad's government.[27] Then, in January 2016, Iran captured 10 U.S. sailors and accused them of illegally straying into its waters in two small patrol boats. Then-Secretary of State John Kerry, who played a leading role in negotiating the nuclear deal with Iran, worked with his counterpart, Foreign Minister Javad Zarif, with whom he had forged a partnership during the nuclear talks. Iran released the sailors within 16 hours, defusing what Kerry said would have been a major crisis had it occurred a few years earlier.[28]

Kerry and Zarif "have reshaped the relationship between Iran and the U.S. at least on the diplomatic level, and that is something to look at" in building better relations, says Vera Eccarius-Kelly, a professor of political science at Siena College in Loudonville, N.Y. "Now we have staffers at the State Department and Iran Foreign Ministry who know each other. It's not just individuals, but entire structures . . . that have the element of more familiarity and trust."

Some Iranian business leaders embrace an opportunity for closer ties. They say 60 percent of the country's population is under age 35 and is far more interested in improving its standard of living than adhering to the ayatollah's dictates. "This generation is worldly. . . . They have a different range of thinking," said Said Rahmani, the CEO of Iran's first venture-capital fund.[29]

Stephen Kinzer, a senior fellow in international and public affairs at Brown University, said Iran's opposition to the Islamic State and al Qaeda — terrorist movements based on extreme interpretations of Sunni Islam — separates it from other Middle Eastern countries and offers potential for cooperation in trying to stabilize the Middle East.

"Our perception of Iran as a threat to vital American interests is increasingly disconnected from reality," Kinzer said in a January 2016 op-ed column. His 2010 book, *Reset: Iran, Turkey and America's Future*, argued that Iran should join Turkey — another Muslim country struggling to modernize — as a crucial U.S. ally.[30]

But critics of Iran say it remains unreliable and dangerous and should be kept at arm's length. After Sanders' remarks about Iran, his Democratic rival Hillary Clinton responded that the lifting of sanctions and prisoner swap should not cloud U.S. judgment.

"We've had one good day over 36 years, and I think we need more good days before we move more rapidly" toward better relations, she said. Her top foreign policy adviser, Jake Sullivan, later said Iran "seeks the destruction of Israel" and is "flouting international law with its ballistic missile threats."[31]

Republicans have shared Clinton's skepticism. Before the sailors' release in January, Trump — then the GOP frontrunner — called the incident "an indication of where the hell we're going" with Iran.[32] He continued to express his suspicions about Iran after taking office, calling the Iran deal "one-sided" because it enabled Iran to receive money that had previously been frozen in banks from its legal oil sales.[33]

Iran's computer hacking also worries U.S. critics. Administration officials said they detected a surge in cyberattacks by Iran's Revolutionary Guards — an elite branch of the military enforcing internal security — coinciding with the arrest of Namazi, who had advocated closer relations.

Namazi and his father were convicted of "collaborating with an enemy state," the United States, and each was sentenced to 10 years' imprisonment. Iran does not recognize dual citizenship and considers the Namazis to be Iranian citizens, with none of the rights given to people of other nations.[34]

Iran in July 2017 also arrested a Princeton University graduate student, Xiyue Wang, and accused him of spying for the United States. The university said Wang, a naturalized U.S. citizen from China, was doing scholarly research in the country, but Iran's news agency accused him of doing "super-confidential" work for the U.S. State Department and other entities.[35]

Experts say the computer attacks and arrests of Namazi and his father are the Revolutionary Guards' warning against closer ties. "If there's a warming of relations, the reason for existing that unites hard-liners will dissipate and wither away — it's their biggest fear," says Nader Hashemi, director of the Center for Middle Eastern Studies at the University of Denver's Josef Korbel School of International Studies.

Iran's hard-liners have discouraged the smallest appearances of U.S. influence. In November 2015, they shut down an Iranian fast-food store that mimicked Kentucky Fried Chicken; an Iranian news agency contended the knockoff company's red-and-white décor too closely resembled the American flag.[36]

Some experts also suspect Iran may be holding Robert Levinson, a retired FBI agent who vanished in the country in 2007. Iranian leaders have denied knowing anything about his whereabouts, but in January 2016 *The New York Times* reported that an Iranian official had acknowledged in 2011 that Levinson was being used as a bargaining chip in nuclear negotiations at the time.[37] Levinson's family filed a lawsuit in U.S. District Court in March 2017 against Iran over his disappearance.[38]

And the hard-liners would much rather sully the reputation of the United States, some observers say. Iran released images of the captured U.S. sailors kneeling on deck with their hands clasped behind their heads, called by Senate Armed Services Committee Chairman John McCain, R-Ariz., "one of the great propaganda triumphs that the Iranians have ever had."[39]

Despite anti-U.S. attitudes in some Iranian circles, "Moving forward, Iran's leadership is likely to exploit this channel [of closer contacts] with the United States whenever doing so suits its own interests," said Aaron David Miller, a vice president at the Woodrow Wilson Center for International Scholars, a foreign-policy think tank in Washington.[40]

Within Iran, at least one prominent onetime advocate of closer relations now is more skeptical of the idea. Former Iranian diplomat Sadegh Kharrazi was the author of a 2003 memo sent to the State Department proposing a broad dialogue between the two nations, but the Bush administration rejected the offer.[41] Kharrazi in 2015 said, "We need more positive gestures from the Americans" before Iran reciprocates.[42]

Should better U.S.-Iranian relations depend on whether Iran improves its human-rights record?

Human-rights groups consider Iran one of the world's worst countries on the issue. Its execution rate per capita is among the highest of any country, accounting for 55 percent of all recorded executions in 2016. Amnesty International said the overall number of executions dropped by 42 percent between 2015 and 2016, from at least 977 to at least 567.[43]

Amnesty International says the punishment is imposed "either for vaguely worded or overly broad offenses or acts that should not be criminalized at all," such as speaking out against the government.[44] Iranian officials say more than two-thirds of all executions are for drug-related offenses, with some of the country's officials calling for easing the use of capital punishment in those cases.[45] An Iranian female cartoonist who depicted members of Iran's parliament as animals was sentenced in 2015 to more than 12 years in prison.[46] The government also is accused of discriminating against Baha'is, the country's largest non-Muslim religious minority, by imprisoning its followers, restricting their ability to worship and shutting down Baha'i-owned businesses.[47]

The situation has led human-rights activists and others to argue that the United States and other countries should demand improvements as a precondition of conducting more trade or forming ties in other areas. Western countries "should remember that increasing economic, financial and diplomatic integration with Iran will give them greater leverage not only to make lucrative business deals but to speak out strongly against rights abuses," said Faraz Sanei, a researcher for Human Rights Watch's Middle East and North Africa division.[48]

The nuclear talks led to a "de-prioritization" of human rights that must be reversed, said Mark Lagon, president of Freedom House, a U.S.-based human rights and democracy advocacy group. "In dealings with Iran, the United States should address the serious human-rights concerns with at least the same energy as it did in negotiating a nuclear accord," he said.[49]

Rep. Dana Rohrabacher, R-Calif., who chairs a House Foreign Affairs Committee panel on emerging threats, agreed. "History teaches that it is not necessarily wrong to parley with the world's bad actors, but that doesn't mean ignoring the evil nature of those on the other side of the table," he said. "If a regime is based on beating its people into submission, how can we count on its good faith with us?"[50]

But many experts say if the United States uses human rights as a condition of better relations it risks further antagonizing Iran. In addition, they note, Iranian officials are quick to cite what they contend are U.S. human-rights abuses, such as supporting the Saudi government, which tightly restricts women's rights.

"We don't expect the West to impose its assumptions on human rights and human dignity to all societies," said Sadeq Amoli Larijani, chief of Iran's judiciary.[51]

Such assertions show why "it will take generations for the United States to gain some measure of trust with the Iranians" about human rights, says Christopher Dolan, a professor of politics and director of global studies at Pennsylvania's Lebanon Valley College. In the meantime, he and other experts say the United States should let the U.N. continue to assume the lead on monitoring and demanding progress on human rights, given its established mission in that area.

"We should support that U.N. role of holding Iran accountable so it's not a bilateral, tit-for-tat in terms of who's more guilty" on human rights, the University of Denver's Hashemi says.

Can Iranian nuclear activities be accurately monitored?

Backers of the nuclear deal say it addresses all the ways in which Iran could cheat to pursue a bomb. But critics are unpersuaded.

The deal commits Iran to what the Obama administration called "extraordinary and robust monitoring, verification and inspection." Inspectors from the International Atomic Energy Agency (IAEA) — an arm of the U.N. — have authority to verify that Iran has not hidden any weapons-grade materials.

The IAEA in August 2017 issued a report concluding that Iran's supply and enrichment level of uranium fuel were well within the agreement's allowed limits. Iran's supply of heavy water, used in reactors that can produce plutonium, another nuclear-weapons fuel, also was within the limits, the report found.[52]

"The nuclear agreement with Iran is working," said Federica Mogherini, a European Union official who helped negotiate the deal, two months later. "It has

Israeli Prime Minister Benjamin Netanyahu urges U.S. lawmakers not to negotiate the nuclear deal with Iran during an address to Congress made at the invitation of congressional Republicans. The State Department says Iran supports terrorists, and critics of Iran say it wants to eradicate Israel, a stalwart U.S. ally.

ensured that Iran's nuclear program is and will remain exclusively peaceful. . . . The deal is not based on trust. It is based on the most intrusive monitoring regime ever set up in history."[53]

If the IAEA learns of possible suspicious sites, Iran has agreed to allow its inspectors to assess them. The agency will search for sites that could be uranium mines, along with any unexplained international purchases of potential bomb-making materials. It will rely on intelligence gleaned from U.S. and other foreign sources.[54]

"I come away pretty confident" in the U.S. spy network's ability to "observe and monitor what the Iranians are doing," said Director of National Intelligence James Clapper, who oversees the CIA and other intelligence agencies.[55]

If Iran is found to have cheated, the deal calls for re-imposition of international economic sanctions. The deal establishes a formal process in which the IAEA and Iran have up to 24 days to resolve any disputes over inspection.[56] Supporters of the agreement say 24 days are plenty of time: In 2003, they said, it took six months for Iran to grant the U.N. the access it sought to one facility, but testing still uncovered nuclear activity, despite Iran's attempt to cover it up.[57]

"If Iran should decide to start producing weapon-grade highly enriched uranium, it would take about a

Details of Iran's Nuclear Deal

The nuclear deal that Iran struck in January 2015 with the United States and five other world powers limits Iran's uranium enrichment for 15 years. Some limits on Iran's nuclear research and development loosen in about 10 years, but other restrictions will remain for up to 25 years.

Components of Nuclear Deal

Most American trade with Iran remains banned by other long-standing sanctions imposed by the U.S. government, but sales of American commercial aircraft are permitted while luxury Iranian goods such as carpets and caviar, along with nuts, can be imported by the United States.

U.S. sanctions were lifted on foreign companies involved in Iran's automobile or energy sectors that conduct business with most major Iranian banks. American companies in those sectors still cannot do business with Iran without being penalized.

The European Union ended its ban on oil and gas purchases from Iran and a ban on the use of an electronic payments system, enabling Iran to move money among international banks.

The deal requires a future American president to ask Congress within eight years to lift virtually all U.S. sanctions still in place. All remaining U.N. sanctions are to end within 10 years.

Sources: William J. Broad and Sergio Pecanha, "The Iran Nuclear Deal — A Simple Guide," *The New York Times*, Jan. 15, 2015, http://tinyurl.com/njnl4mh; Kenneth Katzman and Paul K. Kerr, "Iran Nuclear Agreement," Congressional Research Service, Jan. 19, 2016, http://tinyurl.com/hwhso9m

year before it could accumulate enough for a first bomb," said deal supporter Frank von Hippel, senior research physicist and professor of public and international affairs emeritus at Princeton University's Program on Science and Global Security.[58]

But some lawmakers, arms-control experts and critics of Iran remain unconvinced that all cheating can be detected. And they predict the country will seek to drag the inspections process past 24 days.

"There is a lot the regime can do [to hide material] in a few hours, let alone days," said Charles Duelfer, who led the Iraq Survey Group that searched for evidence of chemical, biological and nuclear weapons in that country a decade ago. "So this allows room for Iran to maneuver and potentially hide much of what it is doing regarding weapons design or component testing."[59]

Other skeptics say that for all of the attention the agreement pays to places where Iran was known to

have done nuclear work, they are not as certain that inspectors will be able to ferret out work at new secret sites. That includes any that Iran might choose to establish in other nuclear-capable countries, such as North Korea.[60]

"In the previous cases of nuclear proliferation over the past two decades . . . the issue was the use of undeclared material, primarily at undeclared facilities," said a report by Olli Heinonen, a former IAEA deputy director general who is now a senior fellow at Harvard University's Belfer Center for Science and International Affairs.

The inspections process is "unclear and leaves unanswered questions," Heinonen said. Inspectors cannot simply visit any Iranian site unannounced; they must first give the Iranians evidence of suspected wrongdoing. Moreover, Heinonen questions whether the process allows inspectors to protect highly confidential spying sources and methods. And he worries the United States and other monitoring countries may not agree on what constitutes conclusive proof of cheating, such as suspicious work that Iranians contend is for non-nuclear purposes.

"What happens when . . . the evidence provided does not meet the standards of all [U.S. allies]?" Heinonen asked. "In other words, the bar will be set very high to begin with and may not allow for gray areas where intelligence is not foolproof."[61]

The Government Accountability Office (GAO), Congress' investigative arm, said in a February 2016 report that the IAEA will need an extra $10 million each year for the next 15 years to police the nuclear deal. Some members of Congress who opposed the deal said the report raises concerns about the IAEA's ability to do a thorough job.[62]

Even some nuclear deal supporters wonder how the United States will respond if it encounters relatively minor, yet punishable, evidence of possible nuclear activity. The United States could come under pressure from allies not to impose penalizing economic sanctions because doing so could erode future leverage if evidence of even bigger cheating emerges later.

"We can detect and enforce this if we find an egregious violation," says Ross Harrison, a nonresident scholar at the Middle East Institute, a Washington think tank, and a faculty member at Georgetown University's School of Foreign Service. "The bigger issue is, what constitutes a real breach of the deal? If we impose [sanctions], they might cheat even more."

BACKGROUND
Hot and Cold Relations

For much of the 20th century, the United States and Iran were on friendly terms and partners in some areas. But since 1979, relations have been marked by demonization on both sides, with a few less tense periods in between.

"Iran's attitude toward the United States is like someone pining for a former, perhaps abusive, lover," said Banafsheh Keynoush, who served as an interpreter for four Iranian presidents. "It has declared its contempt but also longs again to be a partner."[63]

The tension can be traced to Mohammed Reza Pahlavi, the "shah" or ruler of the country from 1941 to 1979. His father, Reza Khan Pahlavi, a military officer, had become shah in 1921 after launching a coup against the royal family that had ruled the country since 1794.

In 1935 Reza Shah's government began asking other countries to refer to it as Iran, which in Farsi means "land of the Aryans," instead of its traditional name of Persia. Britain and Russia accused him of supporting Nazi Germany and forced him from power during World War II, but those countries permitted his son, Mohammed Reza, to succeed him.[64]

As with other Middle Eastern countries, Iran's vast oil reserves sparked U.S. and British interest in the country. In 1951, nationalist Prime Minister Mohammad Mosaddeq — whom Shah Pahlavi appointed under pressure from members of Iran's parliament — nationalized the oil industry, removing it from British control. The shah tried to dismiss Mosaddeq, but his followers started an uprising, and Pahlavi fled the country in 1953.

The United States and Great Britain were in the midst of a Cold War with the communist Soviet Union,

Iranians vote on Feb. 26 to elect members of Parliament and the Assembly of Experts. Moderates and reform-minded politicians who back the nuclear deal won majorities in both bodies, dealing a blow to hard-liners. But those gains may not have a significant effect on U.S. relations as long as Ayatollah Ali Khamenei, the anti-American supreme leader of Iran's theocracy, remains in power.

and American and British leaders felt that "while Mosaddeq was certainly not a communist, . . . the things he was doing might give the Communist Party of Iran an opportunity to strengthen itself and perhaps eventually take over," said Mark Gasiorowski, a professor of political science at Tulane University and author of a book on the shah.[65]

Pahlavi was restored to power within several days in a CIA-backed coup, leading to Mosaddeq's surrender and imprisonment. U.S. officials hailed it as a triumph. But author Tim Weiner wrote in a history of the spy agency: "A generation of Iranians grew up knowing that the CIA had installed the shah."[66]

Seeking to bring Iran closer to the United States, Pahlavi instituted the "White Revolution," a series of development reforms — such as land redistribution — and moved to liberalize women's rights.[67] The two countries worked together on oil extraction, education and nuclear energy. The United States in 1957 signed a civilian nuclear-cooperation deal that provided Iran with technical assistance.[68]

But the program alienated religious Iranians and the Shiite clergy, who felt such Westernization was antithetical to Islam.[69] And the shah's SAVAK spy service was loathed for torturing dissidents.

In 1964 the autocratic Pahlavi government exiled Ayatollah Khomeini, a religious leader without formal political power who passionately argued that Iran had ceded its sovereignty to the United States.[70] The shah never listened to the public, *Reset* author Kinzer said, imposing his policies "by decree or through acts of Parliament, which he corrupted and used like a toy."[71]

But successive U.S. presidents remained loyal. At a 1977 state dinner in Tehran, Democratic President Jimmy Carter lauded the expanded economic cooperation between the two countries. "Iran, because of the great leadership of the shah, is an island of stability in one of the more troubled areas of the world,"[72] Carter said.

The exiled Khomeini continued to demand a revolution, however, triggering rioting and turmoil in Iran. On Jan. 16, 1979, the shah left Iran to seek medical treatment, and in February Khomeini returned, declaring a new Islamic Republic with himself as supreme leader. The country adopted a new constitution through a referendum.

The biggest rupture between the countries came that November, when a group of Khomeini's followers seized the U.S. Embassy in Tehran and took 52 Americans hostage. Carter cut diplomatic ties in April 1980, two weeks before his administration staged a failed military mission to rescue the hostages.[73]

Carter imposed what became "perhaps the most comprehensive sanctions effort ever marshaled by the international community," according to a Harvard Belfer Center report. The initial executive orders froze Iranian assets in U.S. banks and restricted financial transactions between the countries.

The 28-country European Union (EU) and the U.N. followed suit, imposing separate but related sanctions on Iran. The EU and U.N. joined in threatening harsh fines or other penalties on member countries that sold Iran weapons or any nuclear- or military-related equipment. They also imposed further restrictions on their member countries' banks doing business with Iranian banks and severely limited trade and investment with Iran's energy, telecommunications and transportation industries.[74]

Iran's inability to do business with other countries sharply constricted its economy. A Gallup poll conducted in Iran in 2012 found that 31 percent of Iranians rated their lives poorly enough to be considered "suffering," one of the highest rates of any country in the Middle East or North Africa. The polling company said countries with comparable suffering levels either were at war, such as Afghanistan, or experiencing severe instability, such as Tunisia.[75]

Iran approached the Carter administration in September 1980 about ending the crisis, but an agreement could not be reached. Iranians ended up freeing the hostages within minutes of Republican Ronald Reagan's inauguration as president in January 1981, in what some historians say was intended as a final insult to Carter.[76]

Reagan designated Iran a state sponsor of terrorism in 1984 in response to Iran's funding and training of Hezbollah, a militant Islamist group based in Beirut, Lebanon, which was blamed for a 1983 suicide bombing at a Marine barracks in Beirut that killed 241 U.S. military personnel. During the 1980s, Iran was drawn into a bloody eight-year war with Iraq, after that country's leader, Saddam Hussein, attacked Iran with, among other things, nerve and mustard gas. Iraq's use of those deadly agents led the United States, two decades later, to invade Iraq on the suspicion that it might again deploy such weapons.[77]

During the Iran-Iraq War (1980–1988), the United States tilted its support toward Iraq and became entangled in several incidents as it sought to protect international oil shipments in the Persian Gulf. For example, in 1988 a U.S. warship shot down an Iranian commercial jet that the Pentagon later said had been mistaken for a military plane, killing 290 people aboard. Outraged Iranians labeled the incident a "barbaric massacre."[78]

Nevertheless, the two sides talked secretly about the release of seven U.S. hostages held in Lebanon by Iranian-backed militants. The Reagan administration also secretly sold weapons to Iran — in violation of U.S. and international sanctions — using the profits to fund anti-government "contra" rebels in Nicaragua in what became known as the "Iran-Contra affair."[79] The sale of arms to Iran did little to improve relations between Iran and the United States: When Reagan left office, several Americans remained in captivity in Beirut.

When President George H. W. Bush succeeded Reagan in 1989, he tried to defuse U.S.-Iran tensions. In seeking Iranian help for getting the hostages in Lebanon released, in exchange for easing sanctions, Bush said that "goodwill begets goodwill." But even the presidency of centrist Hashemi Rafsanjani (1989–1997), who advocated closer U.S.-Iranian ties, could not bridge differences because of the ayatollah's grip on power.[80]

CHRONOLOGY

1950s–1980s *U.S. and Iran forge ties; Revolt in Iran forces out shah and sours U.S. relations.*

1951 Prime Minister Mohammed Mosaddeq nationalizes the oil industry, negating Britain's majority interest.

1953 CIA directs coup that ousts Mosaddeq and returns shah to power.

1977 President Jimmy Carter, on visit to Tehran, toasts Shah Mohammed Rezi Pahlavi as a key ally.

1978 Civil unrest against shah's rule erupts, inflamed by Ayatollah Ruhollah Khomeini's taped sermons.

1979 Shah leaves Iran. . . . Khomeini returns and establishes Islamic republic following referendum. . . . Militants storm U.S. embassy and take 52 Americans hostage.

1980 Iraq attacks Iran, triggering eight-year war. . . . U.S. breaks off diplomatic relations and begins imposing economic sanctions on Iran.

1981 Iran frees the hostages on the day Carter leaves office.

1983 Iranian-backed Hezbollah terrorists attack U.S. Embassy and Marine barracks in Lebanon, killing 304.

1984 President Ronald Reagan's administration designates Iran a state sponsor of terrorism.

1986 Reagan admits his administration illegally sold weapons to Iran and funneled profits to "contra" guerrillas in Nicaragua.

1989 Ayatollah Khomeini dies.... Conservative Ayatollah Ali Khamenei replaces Khomeini as supreme leader.

1990s *U.S.-Iran relations deteriorate further.*

1992 Iran restarts nuclear program begun under shah's rule.

1995 U.S. imposes oil and trade embargo because of Iran's alleged efforts to acquire nuclear weapons and its hostility toward Israel.

1997 Reformist cleric Mohammed Khatami elected Iranian president.

2000–2008 *Iran steps up nuclear activities in defiance of United States.*

2001 Iran helps U.S. military during its invasion of Afghanistan.

2002 President George W. Bush calls Iran part of the "axis of evil," along with North Korea and Iraq, for its alleged pursuit of nuclear weapons.

2005 Hardliner Mahmoud Ahmadinejad elected Iranian president, declares United States an international bully.

2006 U.N. Security Council imposes sanctions on Iran's trade in nuclear materials and technology.

2009–Present *Iran reaches nuclear deal with U.S. and other world powers.*

2009 Newly elected President Obama sends negotiator to meet with Iranian counterpart on nuclear issues.

2011 Iran denies International Atomic Energy Agency (IAEA) report warning of its increasing nuclear weapons capabilities.

2013 Moderate Hassan Rouhani is elected Iranian president by pledging to get sanctions lifted and improve the economy. . . . Iran reaches interim nuclear deal with the United States and five other powers.

2015 At the invitation of U.S. House Republican leaders, Israeli Prime Minister Benjamin Netanyahu argues against the deal in address to Congress. . . . Iran and other countries finalize the agreement. . . . Congressional opponents fail to override threatened presidential veto, leaving deal intact. . . . Iran launches ballistic missiles in defiance of international ban.

2016 IAEA certifies Iran has fulfilled initial commitments under the deal, leading to lifting of many sanctions. . . . Iran releases *Washington Post* reporter Jason Rezaian and two other Americans as part of a prisoner swap with the United States. . . . Iran holds 10 U.S. sailors captive for 16 hours after they cross into Iranian waters.

Sanctions Continue to Limit U.S.-Iran Business

Trade supporters hope more American products can be sold to Iran.

The recent easing of economic sanctions against Iran permits U.S. companies to sell it commercial planes and aircraft parts — but hardly anything else.

Backers of closer relations, however, hope that someday American consumer goods ranging from iPhones to Marlboros might legally be exported to the long-standing U.S. enemy.

The nuclear deal among the United States, Iran and five other countries continues to prohibit a variety of U.S. companies from doing business with Iran. While it did lift U.S. sanctions related to Iran's nuclear work, it did not affect other U.S. sanctions, such as those imposed after the 1979 Iran hostage crisis or others implemented after the State Department designated Iran a state sponsor of terrorism in 1984. Under the 1984 sanctions, for instance, U.S. companies cannot export products to Iran that could have both commercial and military purposes, such as computer equipment.[1]

Suzanne Maloney, deputy director of the foreign policy program at the Brookings Institution, a centrist Washington, D.C., think tank, said it could be difficult to ease future sanctions, in part because U.S. policymakers have come to depend on them as a tool to punish the country.

"The sanctions are now a semi-permanent fixture of American policy" towards Iran, Maloney wrote in a 2015 book on Iran's economy.[2]

The recent deal allows American aircraft to be sold to Iran, and it also allows certain Iranian products into the United States: Those include so-called "luxury items" such as carpets and caviar, along with pistachio nuts, one of Iran's biggest exports.[3]

Experts say conservatives in Iran's government who control many industries are wary of the impact of trade with the West. They cite iBridges, a nonprofit international technology consortium that held meetings in Berkeley, Calif., and Berlin to discuss future investment possibilities in Iran. Hardline media in Iran accused the group of seeking a "soft overthrow" of the Iranian government by trying to supplant home-grown companies.[4]

American groups supporting greater U.S.-Iranian engagement, such as the National Iranian American Council in Washington, D.C., say the United States is the biggest loser of all sanctions-enforcing nations, having sacrificed between $134.7 billion and $175.3 billion in potential export revenue to Iran from 1995 to 2012 alone.[5]

However, the Washington-based Iran-American Chamber of Commerce, an association of Iranian-American business executives, is optimistic that Iran's eagerness to improve its economy eventually could pave the way for U.S. investment.

"There is a vast area for expanding the two countries' future trade relations [because] the demands and resources of the two countries are abundant and, in Iran's case, untapped," according to the group.[6]

Supporters of greater engagement say if U.S. sanctions against Iran are ever lifted, attention should be paid to the potential trade benefits. Meanwhile, companies like Apple are watching to see if things are likely to change. Here are some areas in which American companies see potential for U.S.-Iranian trade:

Airplanes: Under the terms of the nuclear agreement, U.S. aircraft firms can sell commercial aircraft to Iran, which needs up to 600 new planes for its aging fleet, and in February the government cleared Boeing Co. to begin selling in Iran.[7]

Even if Boeing doesn't sell Iran any planes, it could still provide parts and maintenance, said Richard Aboulafia, an analyst with the Teal Group aerospace consulting firm in Fairfax, Va.[8] In 2014, Boeing sold manuals, drawings, navigation charts and data to Iran Air, the national airline — its first transaction with the country since 1979. Because the sales were aimed at improving commercial aircraft safety, they were not prohibited under U.S. sanctions.[9]

Oil and gas infrastructure: Iranian officials said they want to invest upward of $100 billion to modernize aging oil pipelines and other parts of the industry.[10]

U.S. companies are best-positioned to provide oil pipeline and drilling technology, according to Amin Saikal, a professor of political science at Australian National University and author of the 2015 book *Iran at the Crossroads.* However, Russia already is working with Iran on the issue and would be a competitor.[11]

Consumer electronics: *The Wall Street Journal* has reported that Apple has approached Iranian distributors about selling iPhones and other products if U.S. sanctions eventually are lifted on consumer products. However, the technology giant has declined to comment.[12]

Currently, Iran's 50 million cellphone users rely on Chinese technology.[13] However, Apple and Dell computer products are smuggled into Iran, where they are resold.[14] China will continue to be a U.S. competitor in consumer electronics: In January, Chinese president Xi Jinping signed 17 agreements with Iran on technological and economic cooperation.[15]

Cars: Iran is the Middle East's biggest automobile market, with 900,000 passenger cars and trucks — mostly Chinese imports — purchased in 2014. But the National Iranian American Council says U.S. manufacturers could sell cars in Iran, where they were once popular and where Chinese cars are seen as low-quality.[16]

Tobacco: Western cigarette brands such as Marlboro were popular during the 1970s in Iran, where the number of smokers reportedly has risen in recent years and a pack of cigarettes costs about 50 cents. The state-owned Iranian Tobacco Company controls just over one-third of the market, and British and Japanese companies share the rest.[17]

— *Chuck McCutcheon*

AFP/Getty Images/STR

Pipelines for oil exports stretch along the shore of the Persian Gulf. Iranian officials have promised to spend as much as $100 billion to upgrade aging pipelines and other infrastructure.

[1] Kenneth Katzman, "Iran Sanctions," Congressional Research Service, Jan. 21, 2016, http://tinyurl.com/hq2vgbe.

[2] Suzanne Maloney, *Iran's Political Economy Since the Revolution* (2015), p. 487.

[3] Steven Mufson, "For U.S. firms, the Iran deal means pistachios, airline parts and carpets," *The Washington Post*, July 14, 2015, http://tinyurl.com/gst8d6h.

[4] Saeed Kamali Dehghan, "From Digikala to Hamijoo: the Iranian startup revolution, phase two," *The Guardian*, May 31, 2015, http://tinyurl.com/pzngcyv; David Ignatius, "Despite the nuclear deal, Iran continues its economic sabotage," *The Washington Post*, Dec. 29, 2015, http://tinyurl.com/h86wbsf.

[5] Jonathan Leslie, Reza Marashi and Trita Parsi, "Losing Billions: The Cost of Sanctions to the U.S. Economy," National Iranian American Council, July 2014, http://tinyurl.com/gsnvaub.

[6] "About Us," United States-Iran Chamber of Commerce, undated, http://tinyurl.com/zgggug5.

[7] Jon Ostrower, "Boeing Secures Iran License," *The Wall Street Journal*, Feb. 19, 2016, http://tinyurl.com/zn4q3lm.

[8] Jackie Northam, "Boeing Can Sell Planes To Iran, But Does Iran Want Them?" NPR, Feb. 7, 2016, http://tinyurl.com/zax8bjj.

[9] "Boeing books first sales to Iran since 1979," Reuters, Oct. 22, 2014, http://tinyurl.com/zhrnrfm.

[10] Najmeh Bozorgmehr, "Iran eyes $100bn of western investment in oil industry," *Financial Times*, July 1, 2015, http://tinyurl.com/h8us5k9.

[11] Andy Tully, "Russia To Help Iran Reboot Oil Industry," OilPrice.com, Jan. 3, 2016, http://tinyurl.com/z9knnrt.

[12] Benoit Faucon, "Apple in Talks to Sell iPhone in Iran," *The Wall Street Journal*, Oct. 29, 2014, http://tinyurl.com/ohl69fq.

[13] "Losing Billions," op. cit.

[14] Garrett Nada, "If sanctions are lifted, here's what trade between Iran and the US could look like," *Quartz*, April 24, 2015, http://tinyurl.com/m4vht25.

[15] Steve Mollman, "Iran plans to boost trade with China by about 1,000% over the next 10 years," *Quartz*, Jan. 24, 2016, http://tinyurl.com/jqdhpb6.

[16] "Losing Billions," op. cit.; Andy Sharman, "Carmakers eye golden Iranian opportunity in wake of nuclear deal," *Financial Times*, July 15, 2015, http://tinyurl.com/j7awtwk; Mathieu Rosemain and Golnar Motevalli, China Carmakers Will Challenge West in Iran When Sanctions Lift," *Bloomberg*, April 15, 2015, http://tinyurl.com/ong249x.

[17] Elizabeth Whitman, "Iran Nuclear Deal: Big Tobacco Sees Opportunity For Cigarette Market Amid Lagging Revenues Elsewhere," *International Business Times*, Oct. 27, 2015, http://tinyurl.com/gtboxjz.

Iran President a 'Loyalist of the System'

Rouhani watching nuclear deal before committing to better U.S. relations.

When it comes to dealing with the United States, Iranian President Hassan Rouhani is no Mahmoud Ahmadinejad, his antagonistic predecessor who accused America of trusting the devil.[1] But he's also no Mikhail Gorbachev, the former Soviet leader who helped end the Cold War and ushered in better U.S.-Russian relations.

Rouhani, elected in 2013, is a sophisticated, Western-educated politician who pushed for last year's nuclear deal with the United States and five other nations. He is vastly different from Ahmadinejad, who was reviled worldwide for his scathing criticisms of the United States and Israel and stout defense of his country's nuclear program.

Many foreign-policy experts say, however, that Rouhani should not be mistaken for Gorbachev, who, upon becoming the Soviet Union's president in 1990, oversaw the dismantling of communism to spur more trade with the United States and other nations. Unlike Gorbachev, they say, Rouhani is a careful political insider unwilling to upend his country's entrenched power structure for the sake of improving its standing in the world.

"Rouhani is a loyalist of the system," says Nader Hashemi, a professor at the University of Denver's Josef Korbel School of International Studies and director of its Center for Middle East Studies. "To the extent he can bring about change within it, he'll try to do so by making speeches and appeals within the corridors of power. But he's not going to rock the system."

Rouhani showed his cautiousness when asked about the prospects for U.S.-Iranian relations after Iran agreed to curtail nuclear work in exchange for the West lifting numerous economic sanctions on Iran. Without providing specifics, he said he first wants to see whether the deal is carried out to his satisfaction, such as ensuring sanctions are not reimposed for what he considers unfair reasons.

"If it is well implemented, it will lay the foundations for lesser tension with the U.S., creating the conditions for a new era," he told an Italian newspaper. "But if the Americans don't meet their nuclear deal commitments, then our relationship will certainly be the same as in the past."[2]

Rouhani, 67, who was born with the last name Feridoun, studied religion and changed his name in his youth to the Persian word for "cleric." He received a Ph.D. in law from Glasgow Caledonian University in Scotland in 1995.[3]

Rouhani became a supporter of Ayatollah Ruhollah Khomeini in the 1970s before the Khomeini-led Islamic Revolution toppled the U.S.-backed shah, whom hard-liners reviled for his use of torture. But Rouhani also became close with Hashemi Rafsanjani, Iran's centrist former president (1989-1997) who advocated repairing ties with the United States.[4]

"Rouhani's pragmatic policy approach on issues such as the nuclear issue and relations with the United States approximate Rafsanjani's views," the Congressional Research Service, which studies issues for Congress, said in an analysis published in January.[5]

Rouhani's long background in government posts has given him credibility with Iranian conservatives loyal to Ayatollah Ali Khamenei, Khomeini's successor and current "supreme leader." In 1986, as deputy speaker in parliament, Rouhani took part in secret talks with U.S. officials as part of what became known during the Ronald Reagan administration as the Iran-Contra "arms-for-hostages" affair. Administration officials defied an arms embargo on Iran and sold it weapons to obtain the release of hostages held in Lebanon by a group with Iranian ties. The money then was funneled to the "contra" guerrillas fighting Nicaragua's left-wing government.[6]

Bush's successor, Democrat Bill Clinton, wanted to prevent either Iraq or Iran from interfering with his broader goal of reaching an Israeli-Palestinian peace agreement. His administration initially imposed tougher bans on trade and investment with Iran.

The 1997 election of moderate Iranian President Mohammad Khatami, who called for eroding the "wall of mistrust" between the two countries, raised hope of better relations.[81] The United States agreed to lift some sanctions and by 2014 was annually exporting to Iran about $180 million in humanitarian goods, such as medical instruments and pharmaceuticals.[82]

"Axis of Evil"

After the November 2000 election of Republican George W. Bush and the Sept. 11, 2001, terrorist

Rouhani drew attention last November when he accused Iran's hardline, anti-Western media of being too closely aligned with the ayatollah-controlled Revolutionary Guards Corps, which enforces internal security.[7] Before the February 2016 parliamentary elections in Iran, Rouhani also rebuked an internal election committee's attempt to limit the number of moderate candidates.[8]

For now, Rouhani is popular in Iran. A recent telephone poll of more than 1,000 Iranians by the University of Maryland with the University of Tehran and Canadian firm IranPoll.com found he had a favorability rating of 82 percent, with 42 percent of those surveyed regarding him "very favorably."[9]

Rouhani has succeeded in cutting Iran's annual inflation rate from about 40 percent to less than 13 percent over the past two years and ending three straight years of economic downturns.[10] But experts say he needs to achieve more economic progress by 2017, when he would be eligible to seek re-election.

If the sanctions-unburdened economy doesn't dramatically improve by then, they agree, impatient voters may be more willing to back a challenger less inclined to work with the United States. At the same time, they say, a new U.S. president might try to undo the nuclear deal and reimpose sanctions.

"Rouhani does not have a lot of time on his hands," says Amin Saikal, a professor of political science at Australian National University and author of the 2015 book *Iran at the Crossroads.* "He will have to move really fast to show evidence of the nuclear agreement not only to the public, but the hard-liners."

— *Chuck McCutcheon*

AFP/Getty Images/Atta Kenare

Moderate President Hassan Rouhani says that if the nuclear deal is implemented to Iranian leaders' satisfaction, "we can put other topics on the table for discussion" with the United States.

[3] Ian Black and Saeed Kamali Dehghan, "Hassan Rouhani, 'ultimate insider' who holds key to a more moderate Iran," *The Guardian*, June 20, 2013, http://tinyurl.com/hfrsrw3.

[4] Robin Wright and Garrett Nada, "Latest on the Race: Rafsanjani Redux?" U.S. Institute of Peace Iran Primer, May 20, 2013, http://tinyurl.com/zgrxpeh.

[5] Kenneth Katzman, "Iran, Gulf Security and U.S. Policy," Congressional Research Service, Jan. 14, 2016, http://tinyurl.com/gw2ca94.

[6] Shane Harris, "When Rouhani Met Ollie North," *Foreign Policy*, Sept. 28, 2013, http://tinyurl.com/jgxqurv.

[7] Thomas Erdbrink, "Iran's President Suggests Link Between Hard-Line Media and Arrests," *The New York Times*, Nov. 8, 2015, http://tinyurl.com/j2mykab.

[8] "Rouhani Enters Iran Election Row Over Barred Candidates," Agence-France Press, Yahoo News, Jan. 21, 2016, http://tinyurl.com/z67a4mz.

[9] Nancy Gallagher, Ebrahim Mohseni and Clay Ramsay, "Iranian Attitudes in Advance of the Parliamentary Elections: Economics, Politics, and Foreign Affairs," University of Maryland Center for International & Security Studies, January 2016, http://tinyurl.com/zowabqs.

[10] Najmeh Bozorgmehr, "Iran desperate for nuclear deal dividend as economy stagnates," *Financial Times*, Sept. 20, 2015, http://tinyurl.com/gnu4zdd.

[1] Dana Hughes and Amy Bingham, "Iran's Ahmadinejad Says America Entrusted Itself to the Devil," ABC News.com, Sept. 12, 2012, http://tinyurl.com/bt8j9dc.

[2] Viviana Mazza and Paolo Valentino, "Rouhani: 'A New Era Between Iran and the World,'" *Corriere della Sera* (Italy), Nov. 12, 2015, http://tinyurl.com/h5qay2o.

attacks by al Qaeda, U.S.-Iranian relations took a far rockier course. Khatami publicly condemned the attacks and sought to help the United States defeat the Taliban in Afghanistan, which was sheltering al-Qaeda leader Osama bin Laden.[83]

But two days after the president's "axis of evil" speech, Bush's national security adviser, Condoleezza Rice, criticized Iran's "direct support of regional and global terrorism" and "its aggressive efforts to acquire weapons of mass destruction," including nuclear weapons.[84]

An exiled opposition group in 2002 revealed the existence of two previously unknown Iranian nuclear sites.[85] The resulting international criticism helped spur Khatami's government to reach agreement with France, Germany and the U.K. to temporarily suspend some aspects of its program and invite inspections of the

Young women chat at a coffee shop in Tehran. Some experts on Iran see bright potential for improved U.S.-Iran relations over the long term, given the greater influence they say Iran's youthful, well-educated population will exercise over the country's politics.

facilities, which Khatami claimed were for non-military work. The United States joined in the negotiations in 2005, but talks sputtered after Iran insisted on resuming uranium enrichment before continuing to try to strike a deal.[86]

Khatami's elected successor, Mahmoud Ahmadinejad, ratcheted up the tension with the United States by labeling it an international bully and offending Israel by proclaiming the Holocaust — in which Nazi Germany exterminated 6 million Jews — a "myth."[87] Many outraged U.S. and Israeli officials said Ahmadinejad had vowed that Israel should be "wiped off the map," but experts say he was incorrectly paraphrasing Khomeini, who consistently has said "the cancerous tumor called Israel must be uprooted from the region."[88]

At a 2007 Democratic presidential debate, Obama — then a U.S. senator from Illinois — said that if elected, he would seek to talk to Iran's leader and those from other hostile countries.[89] Once in office, Obama sent a senior official to meet with Iran's chief nuclear negotiator. But Iran continued to expand its nuclear program and in 2011 refused to make concessions. International negotiations broke off for more than a year.[90]

Meanwhile, the U.N. Security Council in 2010 had imposed even tougher sanctions, including a tightening of the arms embargo and a ban on international travel for those involved in Iran's nuclear program.[91]

The IAEA warned the country had sought to learn how to put a nuclear payload onto an intermediate-range missile capable of reaching Israel, but Iran said the allegations were based on false Israeli and U.S. information. Nevertheless, Ahmadinejad agreed to restart negotiations.[92]

The Obama administration continued a program, begun during the second Bush administration, to use an Israeli-developed computer virus to shut down computer-driven nuclear processing machines.[93]

Nuclear Negotiations

As the number of Iranian families living in poverty reached 40 percent of the population by 2013, Rouhani won election that year by promising to lift Iran's economy.[94]

The same year Rouhani spurned a chance to meet Obama while visiting New York City for a U.N. meeting, but he did speak with his White House counterpart by telephone. The gesture was the highest-level contact between the two countries in decades and was widely interpreted as underscoring Tehran's seriousness about wrapping up nuclear negotiations.[95]

The deal was finalized in July 2015 over the vehement objections of Israel's Netanyahu, whom congressional Republicans had invited earlier to address a joint session of Congress to make his case against negotiating with Iran.[96] The agreement was not a formal treaty requiring U.S. Senate ratification, but negotiators gave Congress the opportunity to consider a "resolution of disapproval." Congressional opponents had enough votes to pass such a measure but not enough to override a threatened presidential veto, leaving the deal intact.[97]

The two sides continued talks even after Rezaian, a dual U.S.-Iranian citizen and *The Post*'s Tehran bureau chief, was abducted in July 2014 and charged with spying. He was tried behind closed doors and sentenced to prison. Obama resisted calls from journalism organizations, human-rights groups and politicians to make the reporter's release a condition of the nuclear deal, saying he did not want to set a precedent or complicate negotiations.[98]

In January 2016, Obama announced he had resolved a separate dispute with Iran dating back to the shah's era, when Iran demanded more than $400 million in payments for U.S. military equipment sold to the shah but never delivered after his overthrow. The Iranians received the money in January, plus $1.3 billion in accumulated interest.

But in response to Iran's 2015 missile tests, Obama imposed new sanctions on a handful of Iranian business officials and some foreign companies accused of shipping crucial technologies to Iran, including missile parts. Because the new sanctions were focused on those individuals and firms — not the government — the penalties were small compared to the nuclear-based sanctions and did not affect most Iranians.[99]

Renewed oil exports, and not the relief from sanctions, were mainly responsible for helping Iran's economy to grow in 2016 and 2017.[100]

CURRENT SITUATION

Iranian Elections

Rouhani easily won re-election as Iran's leader in May 2017 in what was widely regarded as a rejection by the country's younger voters of Iran's hardline politics. He criticized the hard-liners' favorite in the race, Ebrahim Raisi, a judge who said that the nuclear agreement had weakened the country.

Hard-liners behind Iran's national television and radio aggressively sought to promote Raisi, leading Rouhani to criticize them in a pre-election speech: "The era when [the national] TV and radio could dominate the people's mind is over."[101]

Rouhani also had harsh words for the United States, however. Upon being sworn in for another term in August, he criticized the U.S. government for being "addicted to the illegal and futile policy of sanctions and humiliation." He also said in reference to Trump, "We do not wish to engage with political novices."[102]

Other reform-minded politicians prevailed in the election. They took all 21 seats on Tehran's municipal council for the first time since such votes were held in 1999.[103] Brookings' Maloney said many Iranians viewed Trump as "a dark shadow," but also with "some amusement," and that she did not consider the U.S. president a significant factor in influencing their votes.

"The Trump presidency has not yet made itself felt on the lives or livelihoods of individual Iranians, so I think they're going to vote on the same kind of pocketbook issues that most people do around the world," she said shortly before votes were cast.[104]

Imposing Sanctions

In imposing new sanctions on Iran in 2017, Congress saw a bipartisan opportunity to respond to Iranian missile launches that had made the country's Middle East neighbors anxious via a familiar international tool of seeking diplomatic leverage.

Trade directly between the countries has been minimal. In 2015, the last full year before the nuclear deal was put in place, the United States sold $281 million in goods to Iran and imported $10 million worth of Iranian products. The next year imports from Iran rose to $86 million, but U.S. exports remained low at just $172 million.[105]

But the U.S. airline industry has sought to benefit from building planes to help Iran's badly aging and depleted airline sector, which sanctions have significantly affected. Boeing Co. reached an agreement to sell 80 new planes to Iran Air and another 30 to Iranian carrier Aseman for a total of about $20 billion.[106]

The House of Representatives passed legislation in December 2017 that would make it more difficult for Iran to purchase commercial aircraft from firms doing business in the United States. Experts said Iran would regard the bill's passage as a violation of the nuclear deal.[107]

If the nuclear deal ends, the Congressional Research Service said the United States could consider a variety of far-reaching sanctions either by itself or with other nations. Those sanctions, it said, include sanctioning all non-humanitarian trade, putting in place a comprehensive ban on energy-related transactions, and setting limits on travel and cultural exchanges.[108]

Nuclear Deal Certification

After months of internal debate within the Trump administration, Trump in October 2017 announced a "decertification" of the nuclear deal. But his decision did not amount to an outright immediate killing of the pact.

Trump called for Congress to make a decision on the deal, a move that essentially gave lawmakers on Capitol Hill three options:

- Take no action and impose no new sanctions, which would maintain the existing deal;
- re-impose lifted economic sanctions that would in effect kill the agreement; or

AT ISSUE

Should the United States seek closer ties with Iran?

YES
Trita Parsi
Founder and President, National Iranian American Council

Written for *CQ Researcher*, March 2016

The idea of improving relations with Iran has spread panic among both U.S. and Iranian hard-liners. The latter fear that improved U.S.-Iran relations will open a window for Washington to regain influence in Iran and bring about its "cultural subversion." The former fear that a U.S.-Iran thaw will cause the United States to betray its security commitments to historical allies in the Middle East — and jeopardize military contracts worth billions of dollars.

Clearly, a wide gulf separates U.S. and Iranian interests, particularly if viewed from a narrow and immediate security perspective. But it is a profound mistake to reduce Iran to its current regime and discount Iran's vibrant society. That perspective led to the West consistently being surprised by Iranian presidential elections.

If we study Iran's society, however, we will quickly notice that it holds one of the region's most modern, well-educated and liberally oriented populations. In fact, Iranian society tends to share far more values with Western liberal democracies than do the societies of most of America's Middle Eastern allies.

Consider: Among 15- to 24-years-olds in Iran, literacy rates are near universal for men and women. Primary school enrollment is at 99.9 percent. Most Iranians (69 percent) live in cities and have adopted both an urban lifestyle and the values that come with it. Astonishingly, women represent one-third of Iran's doctors, 60 percent of its civil servants, 60 percent of its university students and 80 percent of its teachers. Compare that to Saudi Arabia — American's chief Arab ally — where the question of whether women should drive continues to be debated.

Moreover, according to economist Djavad Salehi-Isfahani of Virginia Tech, 60 percent of Iran's population is middle class. If Iran grows a moderate 5 percent a year for 10 years as a result of the nuclear deal, its middle class will constitute 85 percent of the population by 2025. A country with such a large middle class is more likely to pursue moderate, status-quo policies, both internally and externally, than promote radicalism. Clearly, engagement with Iran would benefit Iran's moderate society.

Granted that the U.S. interest in the region is stability and not domination, then the long-run compatibility of U.S. and Iranian interests are clear. But to gain a friend in the long run, America must look beyond Iran's current regime in the short run.

NO
Sen. Dan Sullivan, R-Alaska
Member, Senate Armed Services Committee

Written for *CQ Researcher*, March 2016

When President Obama and Secretary of State John Kerry were selling the Iranian nuclear deal to Americans, implicit in their appeal was that it would mark the beginning of a more transparent and cooperative Iran, as it shed its pariah-state identity and re-entered the community of nations. However, since its signing, we have seen no evidence of this hoped-for transformation, only an escalation of provocations by an emboldened regime.

Since the deal was negotiated, Iran has captured U.S. sailors in the Persian Gulf and used their detention for propaganda, conducted ballistic missile tests in violation of U.N. Security Council resolutions, launched rockets near a U.S. aircraft carrier and used innocent Americans as bargaining chips for the release and clemency of Iranian criminals. The regime continues to hold rallies where leaders chant "death to America." It also refuses to renounce its sponsorship of terrorism by continuing to finance groups such as Hezbollah, whose long history of activities includes the 1983 bombing of a U.S. Marine barracks in Beirut and the dispatch of troops and weapons to fight Americans in the Iraq War.

This is a regime with the blood of thousands of American soldiers on its hands, for which it refuses to take responsibility.

Might Iran change in the future? We hope so. Data suggest that Iranian youths are as open to change as any similar Middle Eastern demographic. More than 60 percent of Iran's population is under 30. The possibility that a future U.S. administration could strike an understanding with a more democratic and peaceful Iran — if its politics moderate — shouldn't be discounted, but it is not likely to occur with the current Iranian president, nor in the next decade. Indeed, the regime most recently barred thousands of pro-reform candidates from running in the February elections — seen as the largest suppression of human rights in Iran since 2009.

The Islamic Republic's revolutionary identity is tied to advancing an agenda that seeks the destabilization of the Middle East and complete hegemony in the region. Even so-called political moderates are more pragmatists than reformists. This presents a challenge. There is no incentive for political change because the nuclear deal, which should have been a reward for good behavior, was offered before such good behavior transpired.

The regime, as it is, is no friend of the United States, our policies or our people, and until reformation replaces radicalism, we should remain vigilant.

- call for new negotiations between the countries to add fresh elements to the deal that Trump said would place more pressure on Iran.[109]

Some experts supporting the nuclear deal said the president's action would lead to the deal's eventual collapse. But others pointed out that if Congress did nothing, the status quo would prevail. "If Congress can't do anything, then essentially this agreement perpetuates," said Sarah Kreps, a Cornell University professor of government who studies international security matters.[110]

Some influential Republicans in Congress called for staying with the agreement. "As flawed as the deal is, I believe we must now enforce the hell out of it," Rep. Ed Royce (R-Calif.), chairman of the House International Relations Committee, said in October.[111]

OUTLOOK
Uncertain Relations

Closer diplomatic relations between the United States and Iran appear highly unlikely in the short term.

In fact, tensions could "increase dangerously in the near future," given the differences that have emerged over the nuclear deal, said Alireza Nader, a senior international/defense researcher for RAND.

But Nader said that the nations do share a common interest in defeating the Islamic State terror group. "America cannot change Iran, and Iran cannot defeat America in the Middle East," Nader said. "The U.S. and the Islamic Republic don't have to maintain formal diplomatic relations or be partners, but there are issues that affect both, including the Islamic State."[112]

Other experts consider closer relations possible over the longer term, given the greater influence they say Iran's youthful, well-educated population will exercise over the country's politics.

"It's a young, dynamic, incredibly well-positioned society for the future," Brookings' Maloney said. "If I were to place a bet on the long-term democratic opportunities in the region, Iran is it, by a long shot."[113]

Many experts agree that the future of U.S.-Iran relations depends on partly how long Khamenei is in control.

"As long as the supreme leader remains in power, I don't think Iran and America will normalize relations," said Karim Sadjadpour, a senior associate for the Middle East

program at the Carnegie Endowment for International Peace, a Washington think tank.[114]

RAND Corp. researchers said Khamenei's departure "will mark a fundamental change" in how Iran deals with the world, since a successor could be more willing to engage the United States.[115] However, other experts said the hardline faction who is fiercely loyal to him will ensure his replacement commits to protecting its interests.[116] The Middle East Institute's Harrison says while it's difficult to predict what will happen in the region, it could remain highly unstable, which could compel a closer U.S.-Iran partnership on fighting terrorism.

"Given the challenges Iran and all the major players [in the Middle East] are going to have in the next 10 years, I would expect a more pragmatic relationship to evolve" between Iran and the United States, he says. But he expects that on some "deeply ideological" issues such as human rights, "We are going to cross swords."

The recent University of Maryland poll conducted with the University of Tehran and IranPoll.com found a split among Iranians about the future of relations between the two countries. Thirty-eight percent said relations would improve in the next three years, while 36 percent predicted they would stay the same. Just over one-fifth speculated that relations would worsen.[117]

Because of the persistent ideological constraints between Iran and the United States, Trita Parsi, the National Iranian American Council's founder and president, is pragmatic about how much can be achieved over the short term.

"I don't think they're going to be best friends anytime soon," Parsi said. "But I think they can stop being worst enemies."[118]

NOTES

1. "Iran Fact File: Arak Heavy Water Reactor," U.S. Institute of Peace, April 28, 2014, http://tinyurl.com/zo9vt5y.

2. William J. Broad, "Plutonium Is Unsung Concession in Iran Nuclear Deal," *The New York Times*, Sept. 7, 2015, http://tinyurl.com/gmpqt9m.

3. "Statement by the President on Iran," White House Office of the Press Secretary, Jan. 17, 2016, http://tinyurl.com/j5p9y2o.

4. Carol Morello and Julie Vitkovskaya, "5 Reasons that Trump Hates the Iran Deal," *The Washington Post,* Oct. 13, 2017, http://tinyurl.com/y6vje4hc.

5. Kathryn Watson, "Senate Passes Sanctions Bill Targeting Russia, Iran and North Korea," CBSNews.com, July 27, 2017, http://tinyurl.com/y99gzjfh.

6. "How Iran Entered the 'Axis,'" PBS Frontline, undated, http://tinyurl.com/zbfehph.

7. Remarks of Suzanne Maloney at Brookings Institution forum on Iran, Oct. 15, 2015.

8. "Florida Passes New York to Become the Nation's Third Most Populous State, Census Bureau Reports," news release, U.S. Census Bureau, Dec. 23, 2014, http://tinyurl.com/mj2slhp.

9. "Transcript: Hassan Rouhani's Full NPR Interview," NPR, Sept. 28, 2015, http://tinyurl.com/jhmtclt.

10. "Iran Nuclear Deal Cannot Be Renegotiated: Rouhani," Reuters, Sept. 21, 2017, http://tinyurl.com/y75btuc9.

11. Thomas Erdbrink, "Rouhani Wins Re-election in Iran by a Wide Margin," *The New York Times,* May 20, 2017, http://tinyurl.com/ljjraq5.

12. For background, see Roland Flammini, "Rising Tension Over Iran," *CQ Global Researcher,* Feb. 7, 2012; Peter Katel, "U.S. Policy on Iran," *CQ Researcher,* Nov. 16, 2007.

13. "Country Reports on Terrorism 2014," U.S. Department of State, http://tinyurl.com/plvrsfz.

14. Carol Morello, Karen DeYoung, William Branigin and Joby Warrick, "Plane Leaves Iran with Post Reporter, Other Americans in Swap," *The Washington Post,* Jan. 17, 2016, http://tinyurl.com/h2mkdvc.

15. Jessica Schulberg, "Siamak Namazi's Friends Thought He'd Be Freed From Iranian Prison, But The Media Had It Wrong," *Huffington Post,* Jan. 19, 2016, http://tinyurl.com/hm7gyxm; Rick Gladstone, "Iran Upholds Convictions of Iranian-American Father and Son," *The New York Times,* Aug. 28, 2017, http://tinyurl.com/y75akc4l.

16. Thomas Erdbrink, "Iran's Supreme Leader Condemns Mob Attack on Saudi Embassy," *The New York Times,* Jan. 20, 2016, http://tinyurl.com/hjmbeao; Karen DeYoung and Anne Gearan, "U.S. Warns Saudis, Iran of Threats to Stability in Lebanon," *The Washington Post,* Nov. 10, 2017, http://tinyurl.com/ybx273mq.

17. Gregory Korte, "U.S. Sanctions Iran's Ballistic Missile Program," *USA Today,* Jan. 17, 2016, http://tinyurl.com/zwxctqx.

18. Martin C. Libicki, "Iran: A Rising Cyber Power?" RAND.org blog, Dec. 16, 2015, http://tinyurl.com/je95d4l.

19. "Khamenei Says Iran Will Not Negotiate with U.S. Beyond Nuclear Talks," Reuters, Sept. 9, 2015, http://tinyurl.com/jp83n6y.

20. Teresa Welch, "Supreme Leader's Poor Health Injects Instability Into Iranian Politics," *U.S. News,* March 10, 2015, http://tinyurl.com/mj4jqtv.

21. Thomas Erdbrink, "Iranian Parliament, Facing U.S. Sanctions, Votes to Raise Military Spending," *The New York Times,* Aug. 13, 2017, http://tinyurl.com/yab3bwmm.

22. Andrew Dugan, "After Nuclear Deal, U.S. Views of Iran Remain Dismal," Gallup.com, Feb. 17, 2016, http://tinyurl.com/jdaaggy.

23. Nancy Gallagher, Ebrahim Mohseni and Clay Ramsay, "Iranian Attitudes in Advance of the Parliamentary Elections: Economics, Politics, and Foreign Affairs," University of Maryland Center for International & Security Studies, February 2016, http://tinyurl.com/zowabqs.

24. For background see Peter Katel, "Restoring Ties With Cuba," *CQ Researcher,* June 12, 2015.

25. "Transcript of the Democratic Presidential Debate," *The New York Times,* Jan. 17, 2016, http://tinyurl.com/h8espoy.

26. Tyler Cullis and Amir Handjani, "US Should Forge Economic Ties With Iran," *The Hill,* Oct. 8, 2015, http://tinyurl.com/gsqhmgo.

27. Thomas Erdbrink, Sewell Chan and David E. Sanger, "After a U.S. Shift, Iran Has a Seat at Talks in War on Syria," *The New York Times,* Oct. 28, 2015, http://tinyurl.com/ntjqaq4.

28. Karen DeYoung, "Intense Diplomacy Between Secretary of State Kerry and His Iranian Counterpart

to Secure Sailors' Release," *The Washington Post,* Jan. 13, 2015, http://tinyurl.com/gsakfm6.

29. Robin Wright, "Tehran's Promise," *The New Yorker,* July 27, 2015, http://tinyurl.com/omnvsdk.

30. Stephen Kinzer, "Is Iran Really So Evil?" *Politico Magazine,* Jan. 17, 2016, http://tinyurl.com/z9o7r9n. For background on Turkey, see Brian Beary, "Unrest in Turkey," *CQ Researcher,* Jan. 29, 2016.

31. Leigh Ann Caldwell, "Clinton Expands Her Attacks Against Sanders Over Foreign Policy," NBCNews.com, Jan. 21, 2016, http://tinyurl.com/hcredzg.

32. Barbara Starr et. al., "10 U.S. Sailors in Iranian Custody," CNN.com, Jan. 12, 2016, http://tinyurl.com/zpwdkqv.

33. Morello and Vitkovskaya, op. cit.

34. Gladstone, op. cit.

35. Rick Gladstone, "Iran Sentences U.S. Graduate Student to 10 Years on Spying Charges," *The New York Times,* July 16, 2017, http://tinyurl.com/yaptbvys; Jay Solomon, "U.S. Detects Flurry of Iranian Hacking," *The Wall Street Journal,* Nov. 4, 2015, http://tinyurl.com/nkwwmae; Yeganeh Torbati and Bozorgmehr Sharafedin, "Iranian-American Businessman Detained in Iran Denied Access to Lawyer," *Business Insider,* Feb. 21, 2016, http://tinyurl.com/zpouqce; Haleh Esfandiari, "Iran Arrests 80-Year-Old Father of Dual-Citizen Already in Custody," *The Wall Street Journal,* Feb. 24, 2016, http://tinyurl.com/guph95f.

36. Tim Craig, "In Islamic Countries, Kentucky Fried Chicken Isn't Always 'Finger-Lickin' Good,'" *The Washington Post,* Nov. 4, 2015, http://tinyurl.com/jto3mc8.

37. Dugald McConnell and Brian Todd, "Despite Iran Prisoner Swap, Robert Levinson's Family Still Seeks Answers," CNN.com, Jan. 16, 2016, http://tinyurl.com/z3x8hgn; Barry Meier, "Clues Emerge on Robert Levinson, C.I.A. Consultant Who Vanished in Iran," *The New York Times,* Jan. 22, 2016, http://tinyurl.com/j5ypj5b.

38. Euan McKirdy, "Family of Missing Former FBI Agent Sues Iran for Kidnapping and Torture,"

CNN.com, March 22, 2017, http://tinyurl.com/yab5gwn6.

39. Sarah Mimms, "The GOP's Iran Frustration," *National Journal,* Jan. 20, 2016, http://tinyurl.com/zh8lagr.

40. Aaron David Miller, "America's Awkward Iran Dance," CNN.com, Feb. 2, 2016, http://tinyurl.com/je75hxn.

41. Glenn Kessler, "In 2003, U.S. Spurned Iran's Offer of Dialogue," *The Washington Post,* June 17, 2003, http://tinyurl.com/rt9lb.

42. Karl Vick, "Is Iran Finally Ready for Change?" *Time,* Nov. 5, 2015, http://tinyurl.com/h7fyhry.

43. Amnesty International, "Death Sentences and Executions 2016," Apr. 11, 2017, http://tinyurl.com/mqrfxh4, p. 4.

44. Ivan Sascha Sheehan, "An Opportunity to Focus on Human Rights in Iran," Al Jazeera English, Sept. 28, 2015, http://tinyurl.com/zcdyrfv; "Iran's 'Staggering' Execution Spree: Nearly 700 Put to Death in Just Over Six Months," Amnesty International, July 23, 2015, http://tinyurl.com/j69pnnc.

45. Frud Bezhan, "Iranian Deputies Push to Abolish Execution for Drug-Related Offenses," Radio Free Europe/Radio Liberty, July 23, 2017, http://tinyurl.com/yd3quc3g.

46. Michael Cavna, "Iranian Artist, Sentenced to 12 Years for Cartoon, Wins CRNI's Courage Award," *The Washington Post,* Aug. 14, 2015, http://tinyurl.com/zwqqjry.

47. "Situation of Baha'is in Iran," Baha'i International Community, Feb. 5, 2016, http://tinyurl.com/ztjn78d.

48. Faraz Sanei, "Dispatches: Time to Prioritize Human Rights With Tehran," Human Rights Watch, July 14, 2015, http://tinyurl.com/jsl6acl.

49. "U.S. Interests in Human Rights: Leveraging Prudent Policy Tools," testimony, Mark P. Lagon before the Senate Foreign Relations Committee, July 16, 2015, http://tinyurl.com/zxwcuoy.

50. Dana Rohrabacher, "Obama and Iran's Human Rights Record," *The Washington Times,* Oct. 28, 2015, http://tinyurl.com/jv2lhed.

51. "Judiciary Chief: US Human Rights Allegations Against Iran 'Ridiculous,'" FARS News Agency, Dec. 14, 2015, http://tinyurl.com/h844wqq.

52. David E. Sanger and Rick Gladstone, "Contradicting Trump, U.N. Monitor Says Iran Complies With Nuclear Deal," *The New York Times,* Aug. 31, 2017, http://tinyurl.com/y9yy4ed5.

53. Federica Mogherini, "EU Foreign Policy Chief: Renegotiation of the Iran Deal Is Not an Option," *The Washington Post,* Nov. 7, 2017, http://tinyurl.com/yb7v6rh4.

54. "Member States," International Atomic Energy Agency, undated, http://tinyurl.com/z4eeu6v; "The Historic Deal That Will Prevent Iran From Acquiring a Nuclear Weapon," White House Briefing Room, undated, http://tinyurl.com/qbotkze.

55. Jamie Crawford, "U.S. Spy Chief: We Can Catch Iran If It Cheats on Nuclear Deal," CNN.com, Sept. 9, 2015, http://tinyurl.com/jkwov7g.

56. Glenn Kessler, "Schumer's Claims About '24 Days Before You Can Inspect' in Iran," *The Washington Post,* Aug. 17, 2015, http://tinyurl.com/gmpuhlz.

57. John Kerry and Ernest Moniz, "John Kerry and Ernest Moniz: The Case for a Nuclear Deal With Iran," *The Washington Post,* July 22, 2015, http://tinyurl.com/ohmro78.

58. John Mecklin, "The Experts Assess the Iran Agreement of 2015," Bulletin of the Atomic Scientists, July 14, 2015, http://tinyurl.com/h7oauys.

59. "The Iranian Inspections Mirage," *The Wall Street Journal,* July 22, 2015, http://tinyurl.com/zne7r6m.

60. Bill Gertz, "Verifying Iran Nuclear Deal Not Possible, Experts Say," *Washington Free Beacon,* Apr. 6, 2015, http://tinyurl.com/h727f23. For background on North Korea, see Robert Kiener, "North Korean Menace," *CQ Global Researcher,* July 5, 2011.

61. Olli Heinonen, "Strengthening the Verification and Implementation of the Joint Comprehensive Plan of Action," Foundation for the Defense of Democracies, Nov. 25, 2015, http://tinyurl.com/hqfcewy.

62. Julian Pecquet, "Will IAEA Be Able to Verify Iran's Nuclear Program?" Al-Monitor.com, Feb. 23, 2016, http://tinyurl.com/jx3w4ut.

63. Banafsheh Keynoush, "The Secret Side of Iran-US Relations Since the 1979 Revolution," *The Guardian,* July 10, 2015, http://tinyurl.com/owq3bna.

64. Kenneth Katzman, "Iran, Gulf Security and U.S. Policy," Congressional Research Service, Jan. 14, 2016, http://tinyurl.com/gw2ca94; Ehsan Yarshater, "When 'Persia' Became 'Iran,'" Iran Chamber Society, http://tinyurl.com/87srszs.

65. "U.S. Comes Clean About the Coup In Iran," CNN transcript, Apr. 19, 2000, http://tinyurl.com/gp8yksj.

66. Tim Weiner, *Legacy of Ashes: The History of the CIA* (2007), p. 105.

67. "Mohammed Reza Shah Pahlavi," Encyclopaedia Brittanica, undated, http://tinyurl.com/z2x6wsv.

68. Ishaan Tharoor, "The Key Moments in the Long History of U.S.-Iran Tensions," *The Washington Post,* April 2, 2015, http://tinyurl.com/zq7h24b.

69. "Mohammed Reza Shah Pahlavi," op. cit.

70. Katzman, op. cit.

71. Stephen Kinzer, Reset: Iran, Turkey and America's Future (2010), p. 113.

72. President Jimmy Carter, "Tehran, Iran Toasts of the President and the Shah at a State Dinner, Dec. 31, 1977," University of California–Santa Barbara American Presidency Project, http://tinyurl.com/jb38ttz.

73. Katzman, op. cit.

74. Gary Samore, ed., "Sanctions Against Iran: A Guide to Targets, Terms and Timetables," Harvard University Belfer Center for Science and International Affairs, June 2015, http://tinyurl.com/jaxf68r; Zachary Laub, "International Sanctions With Iran," Council on Foreign Relations, July 15, 2015, http://tinyurl.com/hllembb.

75. Mohamed Younis, "Iranians Feel Bite of Sanctions, Blame U.S., Not Own Leaders," Gallup.com, Feb. 7, 2013, http://tinyurl.com/cqj7v4o.

76. Louis Jacobson, "Mitt Romney Says the Iranians Released Hostages in 1981 Because They Feared Ronald Reagan's Approach to Foreign Policy," *PolitiFact,* March 7, 2012, http://tinyurl.com/893j9ao.

77. "Chemical Warfare, 1983–88," BBC News, undated, http://tinyurl.com/pgz5ozs.

78. Katzman, op. cit.; George C. Wilson, "Navy Missile Downs Iranian Jetliner," *The Washington Post,* July 4, 1988, http://tinyurl.com/baooj.

79. "General Article: The Iran-Contra Affair," PBS.org, undated, http://tinyurl.com/3djty9z.

80. Maureen Dowd, "Iran Is Reported Ready for a Deal to Recover Assets," *The New York Times,* Aug. 9, 1989, http://tinyurl.com/j8w4ngf.

81. Tharoor, op. cit.

82. Garrett Nada, "If Sanctions Are Lifted, Here's What Trade Between Iran and US Could Look Like," Quartz, Apr. 24, 2015, http://tinyurl.com/z5l63kc.

83. Amin Saikal, *Iran at the Crossroads* (2015), p. 62.

84. "How Iran Entered the Axis," op. cit.

85. Tharoor, op. cit.

86. Kenneth Katzman and Paul K. Kerr, "Iran Nuclear Agreement," Congressional Research Service, Jan. 19, 2016, http://tinyurl.com/hwhso9m; Molly Moore, "Iran Restarts Uranium Program," *The Washington Post,* Feb. 15, 2006, http://tinyurl.com/co3eyc.

87. Karl Vick, "Iran's President Calls Holocaust 'Myth' in Latest Assault on Jews," *The Washington Post,* Dec. 15, 2005, http://tinyurl.com/ckvug.

88. Glenn Kessler, "Did Ahmadinejad Really Say Israel Should be 'Wiped Off the Map'?" *The Washington Post,* Oct. 5, 2011, http://tinyurl.com/ht49sak.

89. "Fact Check: Would Obama Meet 'Unconditionally' With Iran?" CNN.com, Sept. 25, 2008, http://tinyurl.com/zwtda96.

90. "Iran Nuclear Agreement – a Timeline," CBS News, July 14, 2015, http://tinyurl.com/jmr8ra4.

91. Katzman, op. cit.

92. Ibid.

93. David E. Sanger, "Obama Order Sped Up Wave of Cyberattacks Against Iran," *The New York Times,* June 1, 2012, http://tinyurl.com/d264zk4.

94. Beheshteh Farshneshani, "In Iran, Sanctions Hurt the Wrong People," *The New York Times,* Jan. 22, 2014, http://tinyurl.com/hal6uan.

95. Jeff Mason and Louis Charbonneau, "Obama, Iran's Rouhani Hold Historic Phone Call," Reuters, Sept. 13, 2013, http://tinyurl.com/zpsokq8.

96. "5 Things to Know About Netanyahu's Speech to Congress," CBS News, March 3, 2015, http://tinyurl.com/gstfbyh.

97. Jordain Carney, "Senate Dems Stonewall Iran Resolution, Handing Victory to Obama," *The Hill,* Sept. 17, 2015, http://tinyurl.com/owxghqm.

98. Gregg Zoroya, "Timeline: From Jason Rezaian's Arrest to Release in Iran," *USA Today,* Jan. 16, 2016, http://tinyurl.com/hklevth.

99. David E. Sanger, Rick Gladstone and Thomas Erdbrink, "3 Freed Americans Leave Iraq; U.S. Places New Sanctions," *The New York Times,* Jan. 17, 2016, http://tinyurl.com/jt68l7r.

100. Trita Parsi, "The Coming Crisis With Iran," *The New York Times,* Apr. 20, 2017, http://tinyurl.com/lvs3gry.

101. Shahir Shahidsaless, "Rouhani vs. Raisi. Iran's Knockout Election," *Newsweek,* May 18, 2017, http://tinyurl.com/yaw3eh6l.

102. Saeed Kamali Dehghan, "Hassan Rouhani Takes Oath for Second Term With Swipe at Trump," *The Guardian* (U.K.), Aug. 6, 2017, http://tinyurl.com/y7nn6bcd.

103. Amir Vahdat and Jon Gambrell, "Iran Reformists Sweep Tehran Municipal Council Election," The Associated Press, May 22, 2017, http://tinyurl.com/ycg2nfnc.

104. Jesselyn Cook, "What Iran's Election Could Mean for the Nuclear Deal and U.S. Relations," *Huffington Post,* May 17, 2017, http://tinyurl.com/y9ctsgva.

105. Kenneth Katzman, "Iran Sanctions," Congressional Research Service RS20871, Oct. 17, 2017, http://tinyurl.com/y9qdjuoe, p. 63.

106. Jason Gewirtz, "If Trump Scraps the Iran Nuclear Deal, the First Loser May be Boeing," CNBC.com, Oct. 2, 2017, http://tinyurl.com/y9dx85nl.

107. Bryant Harris, "Congress Moves Bill Jeopardizing Iran Nuclear Deal," Al-Monitor, Nov. 14, 2017, http://tinyurl.com/y998zwp2; Joel Gehrke, "House Passes Bill Requiring More Transparency on

US Aircraft Sales to Iran," *Washington Examiner*, Dec. 14, 2017, https://tinyurl.com/y979hthf.

108. Katzman, op. cit.

109. Jessica Durando, "Iran Nuclear Deal and Trump: What Does Decertification Mean and Other Questions, Answered," *USA Today*, Oct. 13, 2017, http://tinyurl.com/yacazju4.

110. Zack Beauchamp, 'What Trump's Decision to "Decertify" the Iran Nuclear Deal Actually Does," Vox.com, Oct. 13, 2017, http://tinyurl.com/y8t9v4g6.

111. Rebecca Kheel, "House Foreign Affairs Chairman: US Should Stay in Iran Deal, but 'Enforce the Hell' Out of It," *The Hill*, Oct. 11, 2017, http://tinyurl.com/y6uctuk8.

112. Alireza Nader, "Sticking With the Complicated U.S.-Iran Relationship," The Cypher Brief, March 2, 2017, http://tinyurl.com/y9sscufd.

113. Suzanne Maloney and Fred Dews, "Suzanne Maloney Talks U.S.-Iran relations, the Iran Nuclear Deal, and the Future of Iran," Brookings Institution, Sept. 11, 2015, http://tinyurl.com/hokw789.

114. Isaac Chotiner, "'Iran Is the Arsonist and the Fire Brigade,'" Slate.com, Jan. 6, 2016, http://tinyurl.com/jghn89p.

115. Alireza Nader, David E. Thaler and S. R. Bohandy, "The Next Supreme Leader: Succession in the Islamic Republic of Iran," RAND Corp., 2011, http://tinyurl.com/hpkmqqd.

116. Sanam Vakil and Hossein Rassam, "Iran's Next Supreme Leader," Foreign Affairs, May/June 2017, http://tinyurl.com/yd8z3evg.

117. Gallagher, Mohseni and Ramsey, op. cit.

118. "Arena: What Is the Future of U.S.-Iran relations?" "Upfront," Al-Jazeera, Sept. 19, 2015, http://tinyurl.com/ovy296w.

BIBLIOGRAPHY
Selected Sources
Books

Berman, Ilan, *Iran's Deadly Ambition: The Islamic Republic's Quest for Global Power*, **Encounter Books, 2015.**

A vice president at a foreign-policy think tank details what he says are conflicts between Iran's ambitions and those of Israel and the United States.

Edwards, Brian T., *After the American Century: The Ends of U.S. Culture in the Middle East*, **Columbia University Press, 2015.**

A Northwestern University professor of Middle Eastern studies examines how Iran and neighboring countries have interpreted American popular culture through comic books, social networking sites and other means.

Maloney, Suzanne, *Iran's Political Economy Since the Revolution*, **Cambridge University Press, 2015.**

The deputy director of the Brookings Institution's foreign policy program explores the changing nature of Iran's economy and future foreign investment.

Saikal, Amin, *Iran at the Crossroads*, **Polity, 2015.**

An Australian National University professor of political science and author of several books on the Middle East contends closer U.S.-Iranian ties would benefit both countries as well as the region.

Secor, Laura, *Children of Paradise: The Struggle for the Soul of Iran*, **Riverhead Books, 2016.**

A journalist who frequently writes about Iran chronicles the efforts of several people pressing for greater Iranian engagement with the United States and the West.

Articles

"The Iranian Inspections Mirage," *The Wall Street Journal*, **July 22, 2015, http://tinyurl.com/zne7r6m.**

The newspaper's conservative editorial page argues that Iran's nuclear program cannot be adequately inspected.

Kinzer, Stephen, "Is Iran Really So Evil?" *Politico Magazine*, **Jan. 17, 2016, http://tinyurl.com/z9o7r9n.**

The author of several books on Iran and the Middle East contends the threat Iran poses to the United States is greatly overstated.

Libicki, Martin C., "Iran: A Rising Cyber Power?" RAND.org, Dec. 16, 2015, http://tinyurl.com/je95d4l.**

A researcher for a think tank specializing in national security assesses recent Iranian cyberattacks.

Miller, Aaron David, "America's awkward Iran dance," CNN.com, Feb. 2, 2016, http://tinyurl.com/j3s72us.**

A former Middle East negotiator who is now at the Woodrow Wilson International Center for Scholars think tank examines why improved U.S-Iran relations could be difficult.

Nada, Garrett, "If sanctions are lifted, here's what trade between Iran and the US could look like," *Quartz*, April 24, 2015, http://tinyurl.com/m4vht25.
A writer for a business website provides an overview of areas most likely to benefit from future U.S.-Iranian trade.

Tharoor, Ishaan, "The key moments in the long history of U.S.-Iran tensions," *The Washington Post*, April 2, 2015, http://tinyurl.com/gkokj2g.
A journalist looks at the events that have formed the basis for hostile relations between the United States and Iran since 1979.

Wright, Robin, "Tehran's Promise," *The New Yorker*, July 27, 2015, http://tinyurl.com/omnvsdk.
A journalist specializing in the Middle East visits Iran and interviews residents who want improved relations with the United States.

Reports and studies

Gallagher, Nancy, Ebrahim Mohseni and Clay Ramsay, "Iranian Attitudes in Advance of the Parliamentary Elections: Economics, Politics, and Foreign Affairs,"

University of Maryland Center for International & Security Studies, February 2016, http://tinyurl.com/zowabqs.
American and Iranian universities, together with a Canadian firm, present the results from a poll of more than 1,000 Iranians on the United States, President Hassan Rouhani and the February parliamentary elections.

Heinonen, Olli, "Strengthening the Verification and Implementation of the Joint Comprehensive Plan of Action," Foundation for the Defense of Democracies, Nov. 25, 2015, http://tinyurl.com/j7kekhk.
A former International Atomic Energy Agency official critiques the implementation of the nuclear deal.

Katzman, Kenneth, "Iran, Gulf Security and U.S. Policy," Congressional Research Service, Jan. 14, 2016, http://tinyurl.com/gw2ca94.
An analyst for the agency researching background issues for Congress provides an overview of Iran's politics.

Samore, Gary, ed., "Sanctions Against Iran: A Guide to Targets, Terms and Timetables," Harvard University Belfer Center for Science and International Affairs, June 2015, http://tinyurl.com/jrr3vrf.
The university's scientific and foreign policy research group provides an overview of economic sanctions.

For More Information

Belfer Center for Science and International Affairs, Harvard University, 79 John F. Kennedy St., Cambridge, MA 02138; 617-495-1400; http://belfercenter.ksg.harvard.edu. Conducts research on international security issues and sanctions.

Brookings Institution, 1775 Massachusetts Ave., N.W., Washington, DC 20036; 202-797-6000; www.brookings.edu. Centrist think tank that studies U.S.-Iran relations.

Foundation for Defense of Democracies, P.O. Box 33249, Washington, DC 20033; 202-207-0190; www.defenddemocracy.org. Conservative think tank focusing on national security and foreign policy.

International Atomic Energy Agency, P.O. Box 100, A-1400 Vienna, Austria; 431-2600-0; www.iaea.org. UN agency charged with overseeing international nuclear research and development.

National Iranian American Council, 1411 K St., N.W., Suite 250, Washington, DC 20005; 202-386-6325; www.niacouncil.org. Nonprofit advocating for improved U.S.-Iran relations.

U.S. Department of State, 2201 C St., N.W., Washington, DC 20520; 202-647-4000; www.state.gov. Oversees diplomatic relations between Iran and the United States.

6

U.S.-Russia Relations

Suzanne Sataline

Getty Images/TASS/Mikhail Klimentyev

Russian President Vladimir Putin awards the Order of Friendship to then-Exxon Mobil Chairman Rex W. Tillerson, President Trump's pick for secretary of State, in St. Petersburg on June 21, 2013. Some prominent Republicans worry that Tillerson's previous dealings with the Russian oil industry and warm relations with Putin might, Sen. John McCain, R-Ariz., said, "color his approach to . . . Putin and the Russian threat."

From *CQ Researcher,*
January 13, 2017

For a president with major issues to handle across the globe, Donald J. Trump spent his first year in office repeatedly trying to tamp down news of one country: Russia.

In January 2017, the nation's top intelligence leaders told him that agencies with links to the Kremlin had tampered with the election. In May, Trump fired FBI director James B. Comey, the top person leading an investigation into whether the president's advisers worked with Russia to drive the election's outcome.[1] The next month, Michael Flynn, who served as Trump's national security adviser, resigned soon after reports said he misled officials about his communications with Russian Ambassador Sergey Kislyak.[2] Attorney General Jeff Sessions later recused himself from involvement — after news reports disclosed he had met with a Russian ambassador.

Then in October 2017 a special counsel investigating Russian interference brought criminal charges against the president's former campaign manager and a business partner, indicted on charges related to their business activities in Ukraine.[3] The day the indictment was made public, the special counsel's office disclosed that a former foreign-policy adviser for the Trump campaign had become a cooperating witness, as he admitted that he lied to federal investigators about his dealings with Russian nationals and their associates.[4] Weeks later, a U.S. Senate judiciary investigation disclosed that Jared Kushner, the president's son-in-law, shared emails with the Trump campaign team concerning leaked materials and a proposed secret overture from Russia — material he failed to reveal with investigators.[5] Senators

Tensions Rise Among Russia's Neighbors

A quarter-century after the Soviet Union collapsed, Russian President Vladimir Putin is aggressively pushing to re-establish his nation's geopolitical importance. He has strengthened Russia's military, annexed Crimea, supported separatists in Ukraine and joined Iran in supporting Syrian strongman Bashar al-Assad. Putin's actions have heightened fears among Russia's neighbors, especially former Soviet states in the Baltics, and exacerbated tensions between Russia and the United States and its European allies.

* Crimea was annexed by Russia in 2014 but the action was not recognized by the United Nations. Abkhazia and South Ossetia are Russian-controlled separatist states in Georgia.

Hillary Rodham Clinton sought to become America's first female commander-in-chief.

On the campaign trail, Trump praised Putin and his leadership. Since assuming office, Trump tried to deflect accusations that his campaign knew about Russia's alleged meddling, even saying several times that it was "fake news" and that the investigators should instead investigate Clinton.[7] After former President Barack Obama learned about Russian interference in the U.S. election, he expelled 35 Russian diplomats suspected of being intelligence operatives and he sanction Moscow's intelligence services.[8]

In November, after the two presidents met during an international economic conference in Vietnam, Trump told reporters that he asked Russian President Vladimir Putin about the accusations and was assured by his Russian counterpart that Russia did not interfere in the 2016 balloting.[9]

"He said he absolutely did not meddle in our election," Trump said after the two men had informal talks. "I really believe that when he tells me that, he means it. I think he's very insulted, if you want to know the truth." The disclosure rattled former FBI Director James B. Clapper, who said in a statement, "the president was given clear and indisputable evidence that Russia interfered in the election. The fact that he would take Putin at his word over the intelligence community is unconscionable."[10]

There are several simultaneous investigations into Russian interference, as well as disclosures by social media companies such as Facebook that ads created by firms related to Russians were bought to cast doubt on Clinton's suitability and honesty.[11] Relations between the two countries — the world's biggest nuclear powers — are more strained than at any time since the Cold War's end. A quarter-century after the Soviet Union collapsed in 1991, Russia has morphed again into an authoritarian state, with

Richard M. Burr, Republican of North Carolina, and Mark Warner, Democrat of Virginia, agreed with U.S. spy agencies that said President Putin directed a campaign of hacking and propaganda to disrupt the 2016 presidential election.[6]

Trump's maiden year was consumed with investigations into the stunning disclosure by federal intelligence agencies that Russian concerns with ties to the Kremlin engaged in a broad campaign of propaganda, disinformation and hacking to tilt the balloting toward Trump. America's former Cold War enemy did this by sowing doubt and discord as former Secretary of State

Putin aggressively pushing to re-establish his nation's geopolitical importance. He has strengthened Russia's military, annexed Crimea, joined with Iran to support the regime of Syrian strongman Bashar al-Assad, and used hackers and fake news to boost right-wing populists and sow discord in Western democracies. The West has responded by imposing tough economic sanctions on Russia and increasing NATO defenses in central Europe and the Baltic states.

Putin's goal is to dismantle the post–Cold War, NATO-European Union order in Europe, argues Fiona Hill, director of the Center on the United States and Europe at the Brookings Institution think tank in Washington. "Putin wants to turn the clock back 70 years to the old 'Yalta agreement' of 1945," Hill wrote in 2015, referring to the agreement among the United States, Great Britain and the Soviet Union giving the Soviets control of Eastern Europe after World War II. Putin wants "a new division of spheres of influence" corresponding "with the historic boundaries of the Russian Empire and the USSR," Hill said.[12]

A former KGB agent, Putin solidified control over Russian politics and society by using Soviet control tactics — propaganda and repression. He has created a vast state information machine, with state-owned TV stations and digital sites that spin events to burnish the image of Putin and his government, as they criticize Western democracies.[13] His state security services have investigated, imprisoned and been implicated in the killings of critics and potential challengers.[14]

Putin also has overseen the largest Russian arms buildup since the Soviet Union's demise. Russia has retained its nuclear warheads and is amassing next-generation weapons, including tanks, helicopters, planes and submarines.[15] Internationally, according to the Finnish Institute of International Affairs, a research institute in Helsinki, Putin has sought to reinforce Russia's image as a powerful global actor, raising concerns in the West that his military "poses a serious threat to its neighbors, the whole of Europe and global peace."[16]

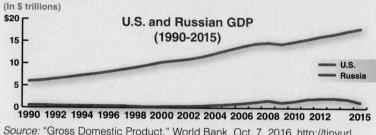

U.S. Economy Dwarfs Russia's

Russia's gross domestic product (GDP), a measure of a nation's total economic activity, fell sharply in 2015 to $1.3 trillion because of falling oil prices, while U.S. GDP rose to $18 trillion. The Russian economy, which relies heavily on sales of oil, gas and weapons, has struggled since the demise of the Soviet Union in 1991.

Source: "Gross Domestic Product," World Bank, Oct. 7, 2016, http://tinyurl.com/jbdsyla

In 2014, Russia supported anti-government rebels in the former Soviet state of Ukraine. After Putin's protégé, Ukrainian President Viktor Yanukovich, was forced from office, Russia invaded and annexed Ukraine's southern province of Crimea, claiming it was an "integral part of Russia" stolen from the country 60 years earlier.[17] The move proved popular at home: Many Russians consider the Black Sea peninsula, which Catherine the Great annexed in 1783, part of the motherland.[18]

But the annexation was widely condemned elsewhere. The United States, the European Union and Australia froze the assets of Russians implicated in the invasion and imposed travel bans and other sanctions on them.[19] NATO, a Western military alliance with 28 member countries, said it would reinforce its forces in Eastern Europe, prompting Russian threats to retaliate if the United States placed missiles near its borders, such as along Romania or Poland.[20]

Putin then challenged U.S. methods for combating Islamic terrorism in Syria, a longtime Russian ally. Addressing the United Nations in September 2015, he called for "a genuinely broad international coalition" to fight the Islamic State (ISIS) and soon began airstrikes in Syria.[21] Putin's critics said he was seeking to build support at home, where Western sanctions had battered the Russian economy.[22] The Syrian campaign brought international anger, however, after it became clear the Russian airstrikes were targeting anti-Assad rebels rather than

ISIS, while also destroying humanitarian convoys and civilian hospitals.[23]

Putin has felt threatened by NATO's expansion — former Soviet-controlled Bulgaria, Estonia, Latvia, Lithuania, Romania, Slovakia and Slovenia joined the alliance in 2004 — and has sought to establish a firm line the West should not cross.

"The Ukraine crisis is not just about Eastern Europe; it is also about the world order," said Dmitri Trenin, director of the Carnegie Endowment Moscow Center, the Russian affiliate of the Washington-based international-affairs research organization. "The Kremlin is seeking Washington's recognition of what it regards as its core national security interest: keeping Ukraine as a buffer zone between Russia and the West, particularly NATO."[24]

Some Western leaders fear that at a volatile time in the Middle East, a new cold war had erupted, one potentially more dangerous and volatile than the last as there are more countries with nuclear weaponry than just the United States and Soviet Union. The heightened tensions pose a particular challenge for the Trump administration.

Trump has frequently praised Putin's leadership and said better relations with Moscow would benefit the United States. "Wouldn't it be nice if we actually got along, as an example, with Russia?" he said during the campaign, in more than one iteration. "I'm all for it."[25]

Trump has not said what those warmer relations might look like.

Some foreign-policy experts worry that those investments could persuade Trump to help Putin, perhaps by lifting the sanctions, which have harmed Russia's economy and damaged the business interests of Russian oligarchs.[26] Besides the damage from the sanctions, Russia's centralized, oil-dependent economy has been hamstrung by slumping oil prices and outdated manufacturing in a country steeped in corruption.[27]

Since the United States joined other countries in imposing the sanctions, it won't be easy for Trump to cancel them unilaterally, some experts say. Given the Russian economy's weaknesses, several analysts say, the only way Putin would retain his popularity at home in the face of continued sanctions would be to project Russia's power abroad.[28]

With Trump in office, here are some questions that lawmakers, academics and foreign policy experts are debating:

Is the West engaged in a new cold war with Russia?

Some scholars believe the United States and Russia have entered a new cold war similar to the tense communism-versus-capitalism political and nuclear standoff that defined the period between the end of World War II and the Soviet Union's collapse in 1991.

Today, key flash points between Washington and Moscow include Syria, where Russia's military has intervened to save the Assad regime opposed by the United States, and Ukraine, which has lost two swaths of territory to Russia despite Western protests.

Robert Legvold, a professor emeritus of political science at Columbia University, views tensions between the two nations as a new cold war. "Russia and the West are now adversaries," he wrote. But unlike during the 1980s, the last decade of the post–Cold War period, "when each party viewed the other as neither friend nor foe," the crisis in Ukraine has created a new, less ambiguous relationship, he said.[29]

This deteriorating relationship is reflected in the language used by the two sides, he said, with Putin faulting Washington's "rule of the gun" and Alexander Vershbow, former deputy secretary-general of NATO, saying Russia should now be considered "more of an adversary than a partner."[30]

Just as worries about European stability initially defined the central tension of the original Cold War, in which Moscow and Washington presided over rival alliances, uncertainty over security in Central and Eastern Europe drives the newest crisis. For instance, Russia's annexation of Crimea and invasion of eastern Ukraine triggered fears of similar Russian action in Poland and the Baltic states, which Moscow controlled for more than 40 years after World War II.

Rising tensions between Russia and the Baltics prompted NATO to undertake its biggest military buildup since the Cold War. The alliance, announced in October 2016 that it was stationing 4,000 troops on the border between Russia and the Baltic states and in November 2016, the Western alliance put 300,000 troops on high alert.[31]

"We have seen a more assertive Russia implementing a substantial military build-up over many years — tripling defense spending since 2000, in real terms;

developing new military capabilities; exercising their forces and using military force against neighbors." NATO Secretary-General Jens Stoltenberg told *The Times* of London.[32] Claiming Russia had used propaganda among NATO allies in Europe, he added, "That is exactly the reason why NATO is responding . . . with the biggest reinforcement of our collective defense since the end of the Cold War."[33] A 2016 RAND Corp. report had warned earlier in the year that Russia, with its heavier weaponry and larger ground forces, could overrun the Baltics within 60 hours.[34]

The United States and Russia also took opposing sides in the conflict in Syria. Washington urged Syrian President Assad to step down, while Russia backed his regime with air and artillery strikes. Putin has vehemently opposed U.S. efforts to restructure the Syrian government, Legvold says, and has refused to join an international effort to allow such a change. Russia has had long-standing ties with Syria, which allowed the Soviet Union to build a resupply station at Tartus, which remains Russia's sole naval base in the Mediterranean region.[35] The two nations still disagree about how best to manage the war-torn country; in November 2017, as Trump pleaded for a last-minute deal, Russia vetoed a U.N. resolution that would have extended the length of an investigative team that blamed Syrian President Bashar al-Assad's forces for a chemical weapons attack that killed more than 80 people.[36]

In dealing with both Syria and Ukraine, U.S.-Russian tensions peaked at levels similar to those in the original Cold War, said Stephen F. Cohen, a professor emeritus of Russian studies at New York University and Princeton. "We're approaching a Cuban Missile Crisis nuclear confrontation with Russia, both along Russia's borders and possibly over Syria," he said in July 2017, referring to the 1962 standoff between the United States and the USSR over the Soviet placement of nuclear-armed missiles 90 miles from the U.S. mainland.[37] Even if the outcome is a nonmilitary move to isolate Russia, the consequences will be dire, he said.

"Moscow will not bow but will turn, politically and economically, to the East, as it has done before, above all to fuller alliance with China," Cohen wrote in *The Nation*.[38] As a result, "the United States will risk losing an essential partner in vital areas of its own national security, from Iran, Syria and Afghanistan to threats of a new arms race, nuclear proliferation and more terrorism. And — no small matter — prospects for a resumption of Russia's democratization will be terminated for at least a generation."[39]

Cohen argued that the seeds of the current conflict were sown after the Soviet Union collapsed, years before Putin came to power, by NATO's eastward expansion.[40] If the West continues to reject Putin's argument that Russia's perceived boundaries must be respected, "then war is possible, if not now, eventually," Cohen continued.[41]

However, Thomas Graham, a former senior director for Russia at the National Security Council now managing director at Kissinger Associates, an international consulting group, says the new cold war rubric is inaccurate because the motivations for the old rivalry no longer exist. "Every time a serious problem emerges in U.S.-Russian relations, someone reaches for the Cold War trope. It is time to put it to rest," says Graham, a former special assistant on Russia during the George W. Bush administration. "The Cold War rivalry resulted from a set of circumstances — ideological and geopolitical — that no longer exist today. What is taking place between Russia and the United States is a not-so-unusual rivalry between great powers."

Mark Kramer, program director for Russian and Eurasian studies at Harvard University's Davis Center, also dismisses a cold war framework. "There's a difference between having acrimonious relations and having a new cold war," he says. "The Cold War was a very bleak period."

Putin's instincts are authoritarian, but post-Soviet Russia is far weaker than the Soviet Union was and does not command global superpower reach, Kramer says. For instance, the Russian army is only about one-fifth the size of the Soviet army, and Russia does not have the Soviet Union's Marxist ideological appeal, because communism has been discredited, he says. Analysts say Putin's political ideology is a mixture of Russian ultra-nationalism, Orthodox Christian fundamentalism and a rejection of liberal Western democracy.[42]

Thus, Kramer concludes, Russia is not the mighty adversary it once was. "It's not even the United States' most powerful rival. I would put China there," Kramer says, adding that while Russia is the larger nuclear rival, "China is the main rival of the United States looking over the next 20 to 30 years."

Should the United States try to forge a working relationship with Russian President Vladimir Putin?

The United States and Russia disagree on numerous issues: Ukraine, Syria, NATO's reach and authority, U.S. activities in the Middle East and the role of democracy and civil liberties in Russia. Yet, the two share some common goals: ending the war in Syria, albeit with differing outcomes; keeping North Korea from launching a nuclear attack; controlling the spread of nuclear weapons; stopping the spread of Islamic terrorism; solving environmental problems; and halting human trafficking and the trade in illegal arms.[43]

Scholars, government officials and even the U.S. presidential candidates have debated if the United States should build a working partnership with Russia to tackle more international issues. "I think he respects me," candidate Trump said in July 2016. "I think it would be great to get along with him."[44]

The debate unfolds in Washington amid questions about how best to punish suspected Russian interference in the presidential election.

Columbia's Legvold says that if Russia and the United States continue to view each other as adversaries, it could warp both countries' foreign policies, damage important components of international politics and divert attention and resources from major security issues. "In general, it's a deteriorating situation, because of the unknown crises — the potential crisis around Ukraine, or because of . . . arms racing or militarization of the Central European front," he says.

And with Russia patrolling near the Baltics with ships and aircraft, if NATO takes a step Russia sees as aggressive, "you get a situation that's heating up," Legvold says. The best way to ratchet down the tension, he says, is for the two sides to talk to each other, at the highest levels, and without preconditions.[45] The Russians are most concerned that "their national interests are respected and not directly assaulted" in the former Soviet countries.

The two nations have a common enemy in ISIS, Legvold points out.

Graham of Kissinger Associates says that nuclear nonproliferation is another topic that has historically been "a good place to start" discussions with the Russians, since "we are the two critical countries dealing with that." But

such cooperation has deteriorated due to tensions created by the expansion of NATO and Russia's annexation of Crimea in 2014.[46]

Graham wrote in a National Interest forum that the United States needs a holistic approach to dealing with Russia on foreign policy. "The Syrian conflict, whether we like it or not, is connected to Ukraine and the larger crisis in Europe. What we do with or to Russia in Europe will have consequences for what Russia does in Asia, particularly with China, and therefore for our interests in East Asia."[47]

In Ukraine, Graham added, the United States should consider easing sanctions in return for concrete steps that would make Ukraine "less of a geopolitical battleground" between the two countries.

Some U.S. hardliners doubt that establishing a Moscow–Washington partnership is possible. Russia "is undermining the principles of European order and is seeking to rally countries against U.S. leadership," Graham said at a debate just before the election. "We cannot ignore these challenges."[48]

Rather, he continued, "in an interconnected world we need to engage Russia [but] keep in mind the proper balance between cooperation and competition."[49] Graham would like for Trump to ramp up sanctions and provide weapons to Ukraine, but he realizes that is unlikely. He also says the new administration needs to reassure its NATO allies that the United States will defend and support the "sovereignty and territorial integrity of Russia's neighbors who seek to join NATO or the European Union."[50] Four more former Soviet-sphere countries have asked to join the alliance: Bosnia and Herzegovina, Georgia, Montenegro and the former Yugoslav Republic of Macedonia.[51]

Citing Russia's annexation of Crimea, Alina Polyakova, deputy director of the Dinu Patriciu Eurasia Center at the Atlantic Council, a research center in Washington, D.C., said, "This is a pattern. A pattern of complete disregard for international law, which Russia signs and then willingly breaks, a pattern of no respect for sovereignty of independent states, and, of course, a brutal disregard for basic human rights. This pattern clearly shows us that Russia is not a trustworthy partner."[52]

Speaking at the McCain Institute debate, Polyakova warned, "Many administrations, both Republican and Democratic, have tried to engage with Russia, and they have failed." She urged the next American president not to "fall" for Russia's claims of a fresh start.[53]

Can Putin maintain his power in Russia?

Putin was an unlikely person to lead the post-Soviet nation. A former KGB colonel, he served as deputy mayor of St. Petersburg and became a Kremlin aide before President Boris Yeltsin named him first prime minister and then acting president in 1999.

Constitutionally barred from serving more than two consecutive terms, Putin stepped aside after his second presidential term ended in 2008 to serve as prime minister under handpicked successor Dmitri Medvedev. Then Putin was re-elected president in the summer of 2012.[54]

Putin has faced daunting challenges in his current term, including plummeting oil and gas prices, international condemnation of Russia's air war against Assad's opponents in Syria, and pressures from NATO and Western sanctions after Russia invade Ukraine.

Under the Russian constitution, Putin can serve until 2024 — a total of 12 years if he is re-elected in 2018, bringing to 24 the number of years he will have led Russia either as president or prime minister. Many Russia observers think he will likely serve that full tenure.

Although Russia faces economic struggles, Clifford Gaddy, a senior fellow with the Brookings Institution, says he does not see any domestic political threats to Putin because "they are nonexistent in Russia," because most dissenters have fled to the West. "And the idea that there'd be a palace coup, an internal revolt? I see no evidence for that. I'm convinced he has full control of security," Gaddy says. "So yeah, he'll be in power."

Harvard's Kramer says Putin does not appear to be grooming a successor. In the meantime, he remains popular, although some signs indicate his domestic support

Americans Sharply Divided Over Putin

Only 8 percent of voters who supported Democratic presidential candidate Hillary Clinton viewed Russian President Vladimir Putin favorably, compared to 35 percent of supporters of Republican winner Donald Trump.

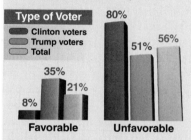

U.S. Voters' Views of Vladimir Putin, 2016

Source: Kathy Frankovic, "Americans and Trump part ways over Russia," YouGov, Dec. 14, 2016, http://tinyurl.com/jtw6fnb

is flagging. For instance, 55 percent of Russians told the Levada Center, a Moscow research group, in October that the country is headed in the right direction, but that was down 6 percentage points from a year earlier.[55]

Putin's earlier high popularity numbers were attributed to perceptions about the economy's robust health. During his first two terms, Russians lauded him for their rising standard of living. But in 2011, after Putin announced he would again seek the presidency, Russians balked. In massive demonstrations and rallies, citizens demanded democratic change. Their hopes soared in 2012 after Putin returned to the presidency and the government enacted stiff fines on demonstrators while some opposition leaders were charged with a variety of offenses, seemingly to neuter their power.[56] One of the most prominent, former Deputy Prime Minister Boris Nemtsov, was shot to death near the Kremlin.[57] Five Chechen men are being tried in the killing, but Nemtsov's family believes there is little evidence tying these individuals to the crime.[58]

After the United States and the European Union sanctioned Russia in 2014 for its Ukraine invasion, most Russians supported Putin for defying the West and seizing territory they considered part of Russia. They believed Putin was "protecting them from external threats and has made Russia into a great power again," said Donald Jensen, a resident fellow at the Center for Transatlantic Relations in the Nitze School of International Studies at Johns Hopkins University.[59]

But some evidence indicates Putin's support may be shallower and more volatile than the numbers indicate. Many poll respondents who said they supported Putin may have feared repercussions if they criticized him, Jensen said.[60] Serious challengers to Putin's power have been sentenced, imprisoned or end up dead, experts say.[61]

Yet an opposition movement survives. Lawyer Alexei Nalvany, a leader of the anti-Putin protests in 2012 and whose nonprofit exposes government corruption, says he plans to oppose Putin in the March 2018 election.[62] The opposition figure has faced jail three times this year and vows to run in the election, even though the government's electoral office says he's ineligible to run because of a corruption charge.[63] Other candidates who have announced their run include Ksenia Sobchak, a TV anchor and opposition figure.

Russia's oligarchs — insiders and friends who managed to buy state-owned enterprises, often at deeply discounted prices, after the USSR dissolved — are no doubt furious that Western sanctions and lower oil prices have dented their wealth. "These critics do not want Putin's personal ambitions to destroy their fortunes, but believe that if they openly opposed him they would be crushed," Jensen said. Putin is vulnerable, he said, and a single event could tip into social unrest, buoy a new opponent and split the elite.[64]

Signs have emerged that Putin may be, once again, eliminating disloyal figures. In November 2016, the nation's economic development minister, Aleksei Ulyukayev, was detained on charges of soliciting a $2 million bribe, which some saw as punishment for contradicting Putin's wishes over a merger of two state-owned energy companies.[65]

To the McCain Institute's Kramer, the arrest is "a sign the element of predictability is starting to erode." Future leaders, he says, likely will come from the state security sphere: Defense Minister Sergei Shoigu; Alexander Bortnikov, director of the Federal Security Service, one of the KGB successor agencies; Nikolai Patrushev, secretary of the security council; and the longtime aide, Igor Sechin, CEO of the state-owned oil giant Rosneft.

Even so, Kramer says he assumes Putin will survive in office. "If change comes it will be through a coup or a forced resignation," he says, adding, however, that such a scenario is unlikely.

"He's become a hostage of his own system, through corruption and self-enrichment. He cannot afford to leave," says Kramer. Some Kremlin watchers have estimated that the president is worth $200 billion.[66]

"He's the only one who can preserve the system and protect himself." If he stepped down, "either he'll be killed, or investigated and arrested, thrown in jail [or have his] money taken away," Kramer says.

BACKGROUND
USSR Emerges

Strikes and protests surged in the early years of the 20th century as Russian workers pushed against a hobbled monarchy that used martial law and prison camps to maintain control. The 1914 decision by Czar Nicholas II (reigned 1894–1917) to enter World War I on the side of France and the United Kingdom against Germany and Austro-Hungary triggered economic and political chaos.[67]

By 1917 a popular uprising forced Nicholas to abdicate. A provisional government was created, but it was toppled later that year by the Bolshevik Party and its leader, Vladimir Lenin. In service of their ideological goal to create a workers' state, the Bolsheviks established a "dictatorship of the proletariat," as defined by German philosopher and socialist revolutionary Karl Marx. Lenin withdrew Russia from the war and initiated broad social and cultural changes under a centralized government that other governments treated as a rogue state.

In 1922, the Bolsheviks organized their nation into the Union of the Soviet Socialist Republics (USSR). When Lenin died two years later, a Georgia-born communist revolutionary Josef Stalin succeeded him. Stalin began a crash industrialization program, forcing farmers into collectives and drawing factory workers from the countryside.

To forestall potential rivals, Stalin ordered a series of purges in the 1930s that began with party officials and eventually included artists, clerics, government officials and army generals.[68] Millions of people were rounded up and shot or exiled to prison camps, or gulags, in the far north and east.[69]

The purges hampered Soviet readiness for the next war against the Germans, which began with a powerful German invasion in June 1941. Nevertheless, despite suffering extreme privation and losses of life, the Soviets repelled the Germans and helped the United States and Great Britain win World War II.

But the victory in what Russians still call their "Great Patriotic War" came at a great cost: An estimated 26 million Soviet soldiers and civilians were killed, leaving the country shattered, with a large population of widows, orphans and maimed veterans.[70]

Cold War

The Soviets' sacrifices were rewarded. Before the war even ended, Stalin had persuaded Allies meeting in 1945 in Yalta (in Crimea) to ratify his seizure of the Baltic nations of Estonia, Latvia and Lithuania, and the return of most of the vast territory Russia had lost in World War I. He orchestrated takeovers of Central and Eastern Europe and pushed those nations, including what became East Germany, into an economic union. British Prime Minister Winston Churchill in 1946 said an "iron curtain" had descended across the continent.[71]

In little more than three decades, the Soviet state had achieved world-power stature. But Stalin's brutal methods — mass detentions and executions and reliance on slave labor — and his expansionist policies repulsed Western leaders.[72] The resultant Cold War locked the Soviet Union and the West in an intense geopolitical battle, usually with the capitalist West trying to stem communism's spread. In 1949, the United States, Canada and several Western European countries created the North Atlantic Treaty Organization (NATO), a military alliance to protect against Soviet expansion.[73] In response, the Soviet Union and seven Eastern European countries in 1955 formed the Warsaw Pact, a military alliance to counter NATO.[74]

In the next decades, the Soviets pushed their security zone beyond Eastern Europe to encompass North Korea, Central Asia and the Middle East. The United States tried to influence nations in Latin America, Western Europe, Southeast Asia and Japan.[75] But the political standoff sometimes erupted into armed conflicts.

Among the tensest Cold War moments was a 1948–1949 Soviet blockade of West Berlin designed to force Western powers to withdraw from the city. The United States responded by airlifting supplies into Berlin. In a dangerous nuclear standoff in 1962, the United States vowed to blockade Cuba if the Soviets did not remove nuclear missiles placed there secretly and threatened to use nuclear weapons against the Soviets if they used them against the United States.

Proxy Cold War conflicts ignited in Korea, Vietnam, Central America, southern Africa, the Middle East and Afghanistan, sometimes with the Soviet Union aided by communist-led China.[76] In the 1960s and 1970s, the Soviets tried to use left-wing terrorist groups to destabilize Italy and Germany and break up NATO.[77]

James Clapper, director of National Intelligence, center, tells a Senate Armed Services Committee hearing on Jan. 5 that election-year hacking by Russia could not have occurred without approval at the "highest levels" of the Russian government. Clapper is flanked by Adm. Michael Rogers, director of the National Security Agency, right, and Marcel Lettre II, under-secretary of Defense for intelligence.

Getty Images/Bloomberg/Andrew Harrer

After Stalin died in 1953, his successor, Nikita Khrushchev, denounced his predecessor's repression and violence and sought to reform the economy. He began releasing millions of citizens from labor camps. Residents of some Eastern bloc states began to agitate for change: Poles struck against the government in 1953, and Hungarians demanded greater sovereignty three years later.[78] Khrushchev sent tanks to quell an anti-communist uprising in Budapest in 1956. In 1961 the communist government of the German Democratic Republic raised a concrete barricade known as the Berlin Wall to seal off that city's eastern, communist-controlled sector.

In 1968 Leonid Brezhnev, who ousted Khrushchev in 1964, deployed troops to Czechoslovakia to suppress a movement seeking democracy and personal freedoms.

In the 1970s, high oil prices helped prop up the Soviet economy, even as consumer goods, priced artificially low, constrained how much money state-owned factories made.[79]

The USSR devoted a large portion of its budget to maintaining military parity with the United States. Moscow's 1979 decision to intervene militarily in Afghanistan to support a shaky communist regime enmeshed the Soviets in a losing, decade-long war. Soviet troubles deepened in 1980 when a Polish trade union, Solidarity, staged mass strikes.

CHRONOLOGY

1917–1991 *Soviet Union rises and falls.*

1917 A socialist revolution in Russia overthrows the Romanov dynasty and brings Vladimir Lenin's Bolsheviks to power.

1922 Union of Soviet Socialist Republics (USSR) is formed as a multi-ethnic, atheistic state and embarks on a massive plan to build a modern industrial nation.

1928 Soviet leader Josef Stalin launches the first of several five-year plans, pushing the USSR from its agrarian past to an industrial economy. He will cement control through massive surveillance, arrests and murder.

1945 USSR helps Allies win World War II. Concerns about Stalin's quest to control Eastern Europe lead to the Cold War, a global rivalry between the United States and USSR.

1955 Eight communist countries in Central and Eastern Europe sign the Warsaw Pact military alliance with USSR.

1989 After Communist Party leader Mikhail Gorbachev promotes openness in the Soviet state, anti-communist activism flares in the Soviet bloc. The Berlin Wall separating East and West Germany falls.

1991 The USSR is dissolved; 15 republics emerge. Russia joins the North Atlantic Cooperation Council (1991) and the Partnership for Peace program (1994).

1990s–Present *After turmoil, Russian economy stabilizes. Putin accused of trying to influence U.S. presidential election.*

1992 Russian lawmakers privatize state-owned enterprises in effort to rapidly transform from communism to capitalism.

1999 Russian President Boris Yeltsin names Prime Minister Vladimir Putin as acting president; Putin, a former KGB agent, quickly begins consolidating his power.

2003 Rose revolution in Georgia and Orange revolution the next year in Ukraine demand democratic reforms. Worried Russian officials clamp down on civic freedoms.

2004 European Union (EU) and the North Atlantic Treaty Organization (NATO) expand to Russia's western border.

2008 Dmitri Medvedev wins presidency and appoints Putin as prime minister. . . . Russia's demand that Georgia end its bid to join NATO ends with Russia occupying Georgian territory.

2011 Activists assert that Russia's legislative election was marred by fraud. Massive protests erupt, but die out after government crackdown.

2012 Russia joins World Trade Organization. . . . Putin easily wins a new term as president.

2013 EU-Russia relations weaken after the Union announces plans for free-trade pacts with several former Soviet republics, including Ukraine. EU-Ukraine deal falls apart amid accusations of Russian intimidation (November).

2014 More than 100 people are killed in Ukrainian protests over the rejected EU deal, forcing President Viktor Yanukovych to resign. . . . Russia annexes Crimea; U.S. and NATO impose economic sanctions on Russia.

2015 Putin sends tanks, artillery and planes to Syria to defend President Bashar al-Assad, triggering international outrage.

2016 A secret CIA report in October says hackers connected with the Russian government stole information from the Democratic National Committee and leaked embarrassing details about presidential candidate Hillary Clinton in an effort to help businessman Donald Trump win the election. Trump dismisses the allegations. President Obama demands full report on the hacking, expels 35 Russian diplomats and sanctions Moscow's intelligence services.

2017 Intelligence officials release unclassified portion of report on Russian election-year hacking. . . . President-elect Trump is briefed on evidence of hacking and later says he believes the Russians were involved. Trump vows Russia will "have much greater respect" for the U.S. under his leadership.

USSR Collapses

After coming to power in 1985, Soviet President Mikhail Gorbachev began to overhaul his country's relations with the West. The nation signed major disarmament treaties with U.S. President Ronald Reagan.

The pace of change accelerated in 1986 after a nuclear reactor exploded in Chernobyl, Ukraine, ultimately causing thousands of deaths. The Soviet government waited days to disclose the disaster, likely increasing injuries and the body count. Buffeted by intense criticism over this decision, Gorbachev realized the government needed to reform quickly if it was to survive.[80]

He instituted policies of *glasnost* (openness) and *perestroika* (restructuring), which relaxed some controls on the economy and permitted greater freedoms. He spoke of "common human values," but the Soviet economy still stagnated.[81] Gorbachev began to suggest that citizens of Warsaw Pact countries should be free to select their own governments.[82]

In mostly free elections in June 1989 Poland chose a non-communist government — the first since World War II ended. The Baltic states began agitating for independence, and East Germany's Communist Party boss was ousted. When a new East German government said citizens could cross into the West, residents massed at the Berlin Wall and were allowed to walk through, ending their imprisonment. The sledge hammers used to destroy the hated barrier sounded the death knell of the Cold War.

Other Eastern-bloc countries soon joined Poland in determining their governments. Lithuania's declaration of independence from the Soviet Union in March 1990 signified the start of the union's demise, which accelerated in 1991 after a hardline coup failed and Ukrainians overwhelmingly voted for independence. On New Year's Eve of that year, all 15 Soviet republics officially became independent countries.

Putin and New Tensions

As the Soviet Union crumbled, so did the Russian economy. Industry nearly collapsed, inflation soared and the nation had to import grain. Boris Yeltsin's presidency (1991–1999) was rocked by accusations of corruption after the government sold off state-owned oil, gas, minerals, banks and communications entities to a handful of cronies who became very wealthy.

Ethnic tensions that the Soviet Union had kept in check ignited throughout the region. Russian troops brutally suppressed secessionist uprisings — twice — in Chechnya, a republic in the Caucasus. In the mid-1990s, Ukraine agreed to rid itself of nuclear weapons in return for U.S. and Russian guarantees of its territorial integrity.

Putin, whom Yeltsin tapped as his successor, became president in 2000. Rising oil prices boosted the country's GDP and gave Putin a strong mandate. But he was less friendly to the West than Yeltsin had been. Although Putin supported the initial U.S. response to the Sept. 11 terrorist attacks, he opposed the U.S.-led Iraq War in 2003, the NATO-sponsored secession of Kosovo from Serbia in 2008 and the U.S. plan to install a missile defense system in Eastern Europe in the mid-2000s.

As Eastern European countries sought to join NATO, Putin considered the alliance a provocative intrusion on Russia's sphere of interest.[83] He was especially angered in 2004 when former Soviet republics Estonia, Latvia and Lithuania joined the alliance. The Russian government also blamed the CIA and American officials for encouraging anti-Russian revolts that fed the so-called 2003 Rose Revolution in Georgia and the 2004 Orange Revolution in Ukraine.

Putin's handpicked successor Medvedev was elected in 2008, with Putin serving as his prime minister. Eight months later Obama won the U.S. presidency and vowed to "reset" U.S.-Russian relations.

Medvedev made clear Russia's goal would be to limit U.S. power. "The world should be multipolar," he said. "We cannot accept a world order in which all decisions are taken by one country, even such a serious and authoritative country as the United States of America. This kind of world is unstable and fraught with conflict." He added: "Russia, just like other countries in the world, has regions where it has its privileged interests."[84]

The two nations cooperated on combating militant Islamic fighters in Afghanistan. During the Arab Spring uprisings in 2011, Russia did not veto a U.N. Security Council move to deploy a NATO military mission in Libya, where Libyan leader Moammar Gadhafi was toppled that year. And the United States backed Russia's bid to join the World Trade Organization, allowing greater access to global markets.

Facts and Free Expression Become Russian Casualties

"Putin has seized upon information as a key weapon."

On the eighth floor of a nondescript building in southwest Moscow, the successor agency to the KGB employs what researchers call the world's most intrusive listening tool. Referred to by its Russian acronym SORM, the machine scours emails and internet searches and scoops up data from Skype and social media networks used in Russia, according to Russian investigative journalists Andrei Soldatov and Irina Borogan.[1]

SORM is the tip of an iceberg, a central component in a vast Russian effort to weaponize information as an instrument of state policy. The effort peers both inward and outward — monitoring and controlling information created by and about Russian citizens in order to prevent challenges to Russian President Vladimir Putin and to burnish his image and advance his geopolitical goals by spreading disinformation.[2]

"Since Putin's return to the presidency [in 2012], the government has successfully pushed for legislative changes to establish stronger state control over all kinds of civic expression and introduced disproportionately harsh sanctions for violating such restrictions," says a report by PEN America, a free speech advocacy group based in New York. "Putin has seized upon information as a key weapon in his fight to promote Russia's resurgence in the world."[3]

A major part of the domestic program is what Soldatov and Borogan call "the Red Web," an effort — patterned on China's "Great Firewall" censorship machine — to sift and control all the online information accessed by Russian citizens.[4] Russia's compliant parliament enacted a series of laws that enable the information collection. One, a 2014 law requiring websites that store data on citizens to use only Russian servers, was used in 2016 to block citizens from accessing the social networking site LinkedIn.[5]

Another, enacted in 2016, gave the Kremlin broad tools to monitor cyberspace, including a provision requiring communication companies to retain users' cellphone, text and internet records for at least six months and to make that information accessible to Russian security services. The government also gained the right to demand the keys to encrypted electronic traffic. The so-called "Yarovaya law" of 2016 was needed to fight terrorism, the government said.[6]

But human rights groups called it an attack on fundamental rights and freedoms and said it was really aimed at limiting internet use by the opposition.[7]

Russia's disinformation campaign has two goals. One is to feed fake news and false information to the Russian public in an effort to deflect attention from internal problems. The program also aims to make the government's foreign policy efforts seem necessary by sowing confusion and falsehoods, a program that the West has used as well, according to a study by journalists Michael Weiss and Peter Pomerantsev. "The aim of this new propaganda is not to convince or persuade, but to keep the viewer hooked and distracted, passive and paranoid, rather than agitated to action," they wrote.[8]

The government-run RT channel (formerly Russia Today) broadcasts conspiracy theories — such as claims that the 9/11 attack was a hoax or intimations that there's a "hidden hand" behind the Syrian conflict. RT and Voice of Russia also republished dubious stories that Syrian rebels engaged in sarin attacks in Damascus.[9] The Kremlin employs an army of "trolls" who inundate Western media companies' comment sections and Twitter feeds with provocative comments, tying up newsroom staff who must clear out the specious comments, according to Weiss and Pomerantsev.[10]

The disinformation program also promotes foreign politicians sympathetic to Putin, such as French ultranationalist leader Marine Le Pen, whose party sought a $28 million loan from Russia last year 2016.[11] In 2014, the far right leader had received a loan of 11 million euros from a bank with Russian ties.[12]

The program also strives to undermine foreign leaders whose views are antithetical to the Russian president. After the U.S. presidential election, CIA and FBI officials announced that Russian hackers had broken into

Democratic Party servers and stolen information embarrassing to the party, with the aim of helping Donald Trump win the presidency. Russia denied involvement, and Trump said he doubted the truth of the intelligence.[13]

Putin's drive to control the news media began early in his presidency. In 2000, once-independent TV networks criticized him and the government after an explosion sank the nuclear-powered submarine Kursk.[14] A year later a state gas company took over one network.[15] By 2004, when more than 300 school children being held captive by terrorists were killed during a raid by special forces, Russian TV stations cut away from the event and broadcast movies and TV shows.[16]

After that, Putin "realized that people would not revolt for freedom of the press and would support some quelling of journalism," says Vasily Gatov, a visiting fellow at the University of Southern California's Annenberg Center on Communication Leadership and Policy and a former journalist for Russian and Western media companies. "He started to believe that journalists by definition are traitors of the state," Gatov says. In time, the Russian press code dictating what cannot be covered grew from a few paragraphs to several pages, he says.

In addition, Federal Law No. 398, which Putin signed in 2013, allowed prosecutors to order a state carrier to block websites that call for mass riots, "extremist" activities and participation in illegal assemblies. In early 2014, Roskomnadzor, Russia's communications regulatory agency, blocked more than 85 websites for "extremist content."[17]

During the 2013-14 revolution in Ukraine and Russia's annexation of Crimea in 2014, the Kremlin disseminated fake and misleading news via the state-owned news organizations RT and Sputnik, Gatov says. After Russia invaded Georgia in 2008 the mission of RT — started in 2005 to burnish Russia's image abroad — had changed to one of disseminating disinformation. While RT covered some news accurately, Gatov says, it also has broadcast conspiracy theories, including stories that the United States started the Ebola crisis.[18]

Russian TV and internet sites also have asserted that the conflict in eastern Ukraine was a popular uprising against local rule and that Russia had to intervene to protect the rebels.[19] Western governments say forces that opposed the new government in Kiev were aided and directed by Russia, and in some cases were disguised Russian soldiers.[20]

— Suzanne Sataline

[1] Andrei Soldatov and Irina Borogan, "The Red Web: The Struggle Between Russia's Digital Dictators and the New Online Revolutionaries," PublicAffairs, 2015, http://tinyurl.com/gudemdr.

[2] Peter Pomerantsev and Michael Weiss, "The Menace of Unreality: How the Kremlin Weaponizes Information, Culture and Money," The Interpreter, Institute of Modern Russia, November 2014, http://tinyurl.com/khfg2rp.

[3] "Discourse in Danger: Attacks on Free Expression in Putin's Russia," PEN America, Jan. 25, 2016, http://tinyurl.com/jx8qj8n.

[4] Andrei Soldatov and Irina Borogan, "Putin brings China's Great Firewall to Russia in cybersecurity pact," *The Guardian*, Nov. 29, 2016, http://tinyurl.com/js3pd69.

[5] Maria Tsvetkova and Andrew Osborn, "Russia starts blocking LinkedIn website after court ruling," Reuters, Nov. 17, 2016, http://tinyurl.com/j58r9nx.

[6] Ksenia Koroleva, "Yarovaya" Law — New Data Retention Obligations for Telecom Providers and Arrangers in Russia," Latham & Watkins LLP, July 29, 2016, http://tinyurl.com/hz64bkr.

[7] Ivan Nechepurenko, "Russia Moves to Tighten Counterterror Law; Rights Activists See Threat to Freedoms," *The New York Times*, June 24, 2016, http://tinyurl.com/hvrv9xw.

[8] Pomerantsev and Weiss, op. cit.

[9] Ibid.

[10] Ibid.

[11] Ivo Oliveira, "National Front Seeks Russian cash for election fight," *Politico*, Feb. 19, 2016, http://tinyurl.com/h3uozkn.

[12] Ibid.

[13] Adam Entous and Ellen Nakashima, "FBI in agreement with CIA that Russia aimed to help Trump win White House," *The Washington Post*, Dec. 16, 2016, http://tinyurl.com/gl7k53v.

[14] Robert Service, *A History of Modern Russia* (2009), p. 549.

[15] "Gazprom completes NTV takeover," Committee to Protect Journalists, April 3, 2001, http://tinyurl.com/hnubfta.

[16] Arkady Ostrovsky, The Invention of Russia: *The Journey from Gorbachev's Freedom to Putin's War* (2015), pp. 295-296.

[17] Jennifer Dunham, Bret Nelson and Elen Aghekyan, "Freedom of the Press 2015: Russia," Freedom House, 2015, http://tinyurl.com/gu2v67b.

[18] Ibid.

[19] Ostrovsky, op. cit.

[20] Vincent L. Morelli, "Ukraine: Current Issues and U.S. Policy," Congressional Research Service, Jan. 3, 2017, http://tinyurl.com/gr879w4.

Russian Economy Hit by Sanctions, Falling Oil Prices

"It's a highly industrial economy that . . . has to be retooled top to bottom."

At a cement plant in Pikalevo, Russia, 150 miles east of St. Petersburg, employee Nina Suslova learned firsthand about the Russian economy's weaknesses. Her job was to be split among three people, cutting her work hours to just a few each day, with a corresponding reduction in wages, but keeping everyone employed.

"We need to eat. We need to pay our bills. We can only think about surviving now, not about the future," Suslova said.[1]

Once the Texas of Europe, Russia has seen its oil boom go bust. As one of the world's top three oil producers (along with the United States and Saudi Arabia), Russia was battered during the global recession and is slowly emerging from a contraction that lasted about two years. Oil and gas prices began sliding in recent years because of greater competition with alternative energy sources and a global glut, which lowered the country's growth rate.

Sanctions imposed by Western nations after Russia invaded Ukraine in 2014 worsened Russia's problems. As real incomes have fallen, two decades of achievements brought about by the resource-rich economy could be erased, according to some economists.[2] In 2015, Russian GDP shrank by close to 4 percent.[3] The World Bank predicted last spring that the nation's poverty rate would increase in 2016 to 14.2 percent of the population, "undoing nearly a decade's worth of gains."[4]

The economic contraction has highlighted an underlying problem with the Russian economy: Decisions made during the Soviet era — including an overdependence on natural resources, heavy state control of the economy, widespread corruption and an inability to innovate — are hampering the nation, say economists, including Robert Orttung, assistant director of the Institute for European, Russian and Eurasian Studies at George Washington University.

In addition, despite Russia having a well-educated citizenry, small business — which fosters innovation — represents a tinier share of the economy than in Western Europe and the United States, Orttung says.

"The main reason the Russian economy is collapsing is because of its overall structure — its dependence on oil and natural gas and a lack of innovative technologies," Orttung says. "Russia doesn't really export anything besides energy and weapons. You have incredible amounts of innovation in Russia, but it doesn't turn it into product. There's not an economic system that can take advantage of all that talent and commercially use it."

Economist Clifford Gaddy of the Brookings Institution in Washington says Russian President Vladimir Putin has no viable plan to solve the economy's ills. Gaddy expects Putin to continue to rely on megaprojects and spend tens of trillions of rubles to update the defense industry and factories in Russia's bleak eastern regions. But Putin has no clear recognition of what should be done to fix the economy, Gaddy says.

"It's a highly industrial economy that's completely wrong and has to be retooled top to bottom," Gaddy says.

Russian scientists and engineers invented the laser, incandescent bulbs and hydraulic fracking, and its people are renowned in physics and mathematics. Yet the new Russian economy has failed to benefit from scientific breakthroughs.[5] The nation churns out a great deal of heavy machinery and military equipment as in Soviet times, but it struggles to make telecommunications and consumer electronics and appliances that the public wants to buy.[6]

Tensions flared, though, when Georgia and Ukraine sought to join NATO, which the United States supported but Russia firmly opposed.[85] The Russia-Georgia war that erupted in 2008 ended with Russia tightening its control over Georgia's two secessionist regions, Abkhazia and South Ossetia.[86]

When he was reelected president in May 2012, Putin faced mounting political problems. At home, near-monthly civic protests grew larger. Initially concerned with accusations of voting fraud in the 2011 legislative elections, protesters eventually turned on Putin and government corruption. In 2012, Putin's party passed a law

Barry Ickes, chairman of the economics department at Pennsylvania State University, likens Russia's economy to a cockroach, primitive and inelegant in many respects but possessing a remarkable ability to survive in the most adverse and varying conditions. The country will continue to lose its most talented people, he says, if it does not improve education and allow those people to thrive.

"They were way ahead in the Soviet period, in the sciences," he says. "Many of the universities have not modernized much in the region. . . . They lose a lot of their people."

Rosstat, the Russian state statistics agency, reported that 350,000 people left Russia in 2015, the most in decades.[7] Lauren Goodrich, a senior Eurasia analyst at research firm Stratfor says the brain drain could hurt the country's competitiveness. "Russia already has a problem funding research and development," she said. "If the people who work in them are also leaving, progress will stagnate across the board," she says.

In recent years, Russian and international investors have moved their money to places considered safer for investments, said Sergei Guriev, a professor of economics at Sciences Po, an international research university in Paris. Since 2011, four to eight percent of Russian GDP has been lost annually in capital outflow. That's a large amount, he said, considering that total capital investment in Russia makes up 20 percent of GDP.[8]

The government faces three choices: imposing steep budget cuts, asking the West to lift sanctions or instituting structural reforms, said Guriev, who fled Russia in 2013. Changes in such areas as ease of starting a business and adopting a floating exchange rate have improved the climate, he said, but state-owned companies and politically connected businesses continue to benefit from the status quo.[9]

Long-lasting growth, he said, can come through the protection of property rights, a stronger rule of law, more competition, an end to corruption and integration into the global economy.[10]

— *Suzanne Sataline*

Russian coal miners head home after work in the Kemerovo region. The nation's faltering economy worsened after Russia invaded Ukraine in 2014, prompting Western nations to impose economic sanctions. Many experts say Russia's industrial economy must be radically retooled.

[1] Andrew Higgins, "Putin Took Credit for the Boom. Now There's a Bust," *The New York Times*, May 2, 2016, http://tinyurl.com/zkmf2vh.

[2] "Russian Federation Overview," World Bank, 2015, http://tinyurl.com/blgs8zg; "Russia Economic Report," The World Bank, Nov. 9, 2016, http://tinyurl.com/hcxwq2e.

[3] Sergei Guriev, "Russia's Constrained Economy," *Foreign Affairs*, May/June 2016, http://tinyurl.com/hrptzb8.

[4] Higgins, op. cit.

[5] "Milk Without the Cow," *The Economist*, Oct. 22, 2016, http://tinyurl.com/z2alld6; Pavel Koshkin, "How Russia can overcome its innovation challenges," Russia Direct, Nov. 11, 2015, http://tinyurl.com/ztm762j.

[6] "Russia: sales of technical consumer goods decreased by 14.4% in 2015 compared to 2014," Household Appliances Parts and Components, March 11, 2016, http://tinyurl.com/zfmm5sp.

[7] Deidre McPhillips, "Russia's 'Slow Bleeding' Brain Drain," *U.S. News & World Report*, Oct. 6, 2016, http://tinyurl.com/hg7y7my.

[8] Guriev, op. cit.

[9] Ibid.

[10] Ibid.

imposing heavy fines on people who joined unapproved demonstrations.[87] Russian law enforcement also raided the homes of several leading activists, chilling the growing democracy movement.[88]

Russia then annexed Crimea from Ukraine in 2014 and stoked separatist forces in eastern Ukraine.[89]

President Yanukovych was overthrown in a popular revolt that February after renouncing a pledge to sign an agreement with the European Union (EU).

Some analysts have said the crisis was triggered by the EU's ultimatum for the divided country to choose between the West and Russia.[90] Others say Yanukovych faced heavy pressure from Moscow — including threats and gas cuts — to renounce the EU deal.[91]

After Putin annexed Crimea, the United States, the EU and Australia in July 2014 imposed travel and financial sanctions on Russia and later strengthened them.[92]

CURRENT SITUATION
Confirmation Controversies

Energy executive Rex W. Tillerson was confirmed by the U.S. Senate, despite his seemingly close ties with Putin and his Exxon dealings.

Before he was confirmed, his nomination attracted several Republican senators who expressed doubts about Tillerson's business connections with Russia, led by Sens. McCain, Marco Rubio of Florida, and Lindsey Graham of South Carolina.[93] They have questioned how Tillerson could represent the United States' best interests when the company he led made a $500 billion Arctic oil drilling deal — presided over by Putin — with the state-owned Rosneft.[94] That agreement has been on ice since the West imposed sanctions on Russia in 2014, raising questions about whether Tillerson, who has publicly opposed sanctions, might push for lifting them in order to revive the Arctic deal.[95]

"If [someone doesn't] believe sanctions are appropriate, given what Putin has been doing all over the world, including in our backyard, then I don't think they have the judgment to be secretary of state," Graham said. "Because if you don't go after Russia, you're inviting the other bad actors on the planet to come after you."[96]

Tillerson criticized the Russian government in the past for not ensuring a strong legal system, but as Putin established his power over Russia's elite, the oil executive toned down such comments.[97] "This was a man who was deeply skeptical of Russia, and a person who [appeared] unwilling to commit his firm's famous reputation . . . to the risks of dealing in an anarchic environment," said Bernard Sucher, a former Russia director of Merrill Lynch. But with the Arctic deal, "Tillerson had done a 180 on what I understood his views to be."[98]

In early January Tillerson said that he would sell and restructure his assets, and he resigned from organizations that might pose a conflict of interest, such as the American Petroleum Institute trade group. "I am committed to the highest standards of ethical conduct," Tillerson wrote in a letter to the State Department's ethics lawyer. "If confirmed as secretary of State, I will not participate personally and substantially in any particular matter in which I know I have a financial interest directly and predictably affected by the matter."[99]

Others worried that Tillerson's world experience did not include international diplomacy. "Can he step out of the Exxon Mobil persona and then pursue a whole bunch of interests with interlocutors who don't share our interests?" asked Steven Pifer, a retired foreign service officer who served as U.S. ambassador to Ukraine.[100]

Russian Hacking

After the intelligence community revealed that it had "high confidence" that Russian hackers interfered in the U.S. presidential election to help elect Trump — and the president-elect's doubts about those allegations — U.S. officials began to reveal various ways in which hacking and information were used to sway the November 2016 election.[101] Investigators and Congressional officials said it was clear that Russian trolls and automated bots promoted messages for Trump, as social media sowed discord by stoking disagreement around lightening rod topics such as immigration and Islamophobia.[102]

On Jan. 5, McCain convened the Senate Armed Services Committee, which he chairs, in the first of several hearings on cybersecurity, particularly any foreign efforts to influence U.S. elections, which he equated to "an act of war."[103] At the hearing, lawmakers on both sides of the aisle expressed concern about Trump's criticism of U.S. intelligence community's claims. And Director of National Intelligence James R. Clapper Jr. reiterated his contention that Russia was behind the election-year hacking and that it could not have occurred without approval at the "highest levels" of the Russian government. The hacking was part of an aggressive, multifaceted "information war" being waged by Russia, which includes hacking, disinformation and dissemination of fake news — all designed to, among other things, "drive wedges between us and Western Europe," Clapper said.[104]

Clapper suggested reviving the U.S. Information Agency (USIA) — which existed from 1953 until 1999 to disseminate information abroad about America. Having a "USIA on steroids," he said, would enable the United States to "fight this information war a lot more aggressively than . . . we're doing right now."[105]

Trump was briefed the next day by intelligence officials on the Russian hacking, and appeared to concede that the Russians might have been among those responsible for the election hacking.[106]

During the election, the anti-government secrecy site, WikiLeaks, published reams of stolen emails from the Democratic National Committee and Democratic nominee Hillary Clinton's campaign manager. The move, according to people who viewed a secret intelligence brief, was designed to strengthen Trump's candidacy and sink Clinton's.[107]

During the year, three separate investigations into Russian meddling took shape. One is an FBI probe. The scope was expected to encompass cyberattacks that targeted the Democratic party in 2016 and dissemination of stolen emails from the Democratic National Committee and Clinton campaign chairman John Podesta.[108] The bureau also is delving into the nature of "any links between individuals associated with the Trump campaign and the Russian government, and whether there was any coordination between the campaign and Russia's efforts."[109]

Both the House and Senate intelligence committees launched their own inquiries. In October, Senators Richard M. Burr, Republican of North Carolina, and Mark Warner, Democrat of Virginia, endorsed the findings of U.S. spy agencies that said President Putin directed a campaign of hacking and propaganda to disrupt the 2016 presidential election.[110]

During the campaigns, Russian agents disseminated inflammatory posts that reached 126 million users on Facebook, published more than 131,000 messages on Twitter and uploaded over 1,000 videos to Google's YouTube service, according to Congressional investigators.[111]

Analysts say Moscow also has used false news to create doubt about liberal parties and to support right-wing candidates in Europe. In one incident, a false claim that Islamic migrants in Berlin raped a Russian-German girl was shared repeatedly, an attempt, analysts said, to embarrass German Chancellor Angela Merkel, who welcomed hundreds of thousands of refugees to her country.[112] In November, researchers disclosed that more than 150,000 Russian-language Twitter accounts posted tens of thousands of messages in English that prodded British voters to quit the European Union days before last year's referendum on the issue.[113]

To be sure, fake news during the presidential election originated in many countries, including the United States, often by writers seeking to make money from online ads. After the election, Obama decried the spread of falsehoods posing as news stories, and Facebook said it was considering ways to stop the trend.[114]

But Graham, of Kissinger Associates, says the public should not put too much stock in the power of Putin or Russia to use state media companies to influence the West. "Fake news is a general problem, not a problem created by the Russians," he says. "As we move into a digital age . . . plenty of people are making up news."

International Tensions

Concerns about President Trump's comments praising Putin worried many hawks in Congress and in the foreign-policy and intelligence communities, some of whom view Putin's aggressive moves in Syria and Eastern Europe as dangerous to international peace and cooperation.

With the war in eastern Ukraine stuck in a frozen, no-end conflict, the International Criminal Court said in November 2016 that it was investigating the killings of more than 9,500 people in the region since February 2014, the disappearance of more than 400 people and more than 800 crimes.[115] Russia immediately announced it would withdraw from the organization, saying it no longer met the criteria of being "a truly independent, authoritative international tribunal."[116]

Putin's invasion of Ukraine was wildly popular with the Russian public, says James Collins, U.S. ambassador to the Russian federation from 1997 to 2001. "He is seen as the stalwart defender of what Russia is against assaults by the global Americanizer," Collins says.

Some Ukrainian officials feared that the new American president would build closer ties to Putin at Kiev's expense. "Donald Trump's election is a strong signal that Ukraine should be ready to carry out reforms and resist Russian aggression without U.S. and Western support," said Alyona Getmanchuk, director of the Institute of World Policy, a nongovernmental think tank in Kiev.[117]

International resentment lingers about Russia's intervention in Syria, where anti-Assad rebels suffered grave losses against the Assad regime, thanks in part to Russian air support. In early January Russia announced it was reducing its military forces in Syria, under the terms of a

Should the Trump administration engage with Russia?

YES

Jack F. Matlock Jr.
U.S. Ambassador to the Soviet Union, 1987–1991

Excerpted from "Advice to President Trump on U.S.-Russia Policy," an online symposium commissioned by The National Interest and Carnegie Corporation of New York

The most important foreign policy task President-elect Donald Trump will face . . . will be to restore cooperation with Russia to reduce the danger to the world posed by nuclear weapons. The only truly existential threat to the United States today is that of nuclear war.

President Ronald Reagan and [Soviet] General Secretary Mikhail Gorbachev recognized this danger in their 1985 Geneva Summit when they agreed that "a nuclear war cannot be won and must never be fought," and concluded therefore that there could be no war between the United States and the Soviet Union. Their agreement on this point underlay the subsequent mutual steps that ended the arms race and, in remarkably short time, the Cold War itself. By the end of 1991, Europe was whole and free and at peace.

Over the past two decades, American and Russian leaders have allowed the truism recognized by Reagan and Gorbachev to slip from their attention. The recent presidents of both countries, through a series of misconceived actions and emotional reactions, have created an atmosphere of hostility and confrontation that damages both countries and militates against cooperation even when their interests are in harmony. That has brought us to the brink of another senseless nuclear arms race along with the danger that militarized competition over territory could escalate into actual war. . . .

Restoring cooperation with Russia on nuclear issues will be possible only if we overcome the confrontational mentality that pervades much interaction between the United States and Russia today. In fact, the most fundamental interests of both countries are not in conflict: whether it be avoiding a nuclear arms race, combating terrorism, coping with the effects of global warming, building mutually beneficial economic ties or managing the many problems stemming from failed states, cooperation between the United States and Russia — along with the European Union, China and India — is essential.

The Obama administration attempted a "reset" that had some important positive results, notably the New START treaty, but eventually failed following the developing civil war in Syria and, above all, the shock of the Maidan revolution and its aftermath in Ukraine. President Trump's challenge will be to work with [Russian] President [Vladimir] Putin to transcend differences over these issues so that both countries, along with the European Union, can concentrate on dealing with the global challenges that face us all.

NO

Mark Kramer
Program Director, Russian and Eurasian Studies, Harvard University

Written for CQ Researcher, January 2017

Donald Trump will have many tasks facing him when he takes office on Jan. 20. One thing he must decide promptly is how to counter the Russian government's use of cyberwarfare against the United States and other Western countries. Instead of responding to U.S. intelligence reports about this matter with childish petulance, Trump should take the issue seriously and decide how he can best protect U.S. national interests against Russian encroachments.

But instead of doing this, Trump seems determined to establish a friendly relationship with the authoritarian government of Vladimir Putin, no matter what the cost to U.S. interests and values. Putin has demonstrated his antipathy toward the United States and his willingness to challenge U.S. interests. Yet Trump throughout the presidential campaign expressed fondness for Putin and a desire to have a friendly relationship with him. Trump did this even as he made clear that he had no particular desire to maintain good relations with long-standing U.S. allies. Trump's sense of priorities is so skewed that one wonders what could be behind it.

Most likely what is motivating Trump is a shared desire with Putin to upend the international order that U.S. leaders helped create after World War II. That international order, resting on a global free trade regime and U.S. security commitments to key allies, has immensely benefited U.S. interests and security. Trump and Putin share the goal of reconfiguring this international order, even though they do so for opposite reasons.

Putin has long been seeking to undermine U.S. preeminence in the world, and he is going all-out to see the U.S.-led international order overturned.

Trump, by contrast, mistakenly believes that the U.S.-led international order is detrimental to American interests. This position is baffling, but it is characteristic of Trump. It is leading him to endorse positions that will be hugely damaging to the United States and greatly beneficial to Russia and other tyrannical regimes such as China.

Instead of providing succor to hostile authoritarian states, Trump should be giving top priority to solidifying ties with U.S. allies and reassuring them that he has no intention of abandoning them. He should be going to Ottawa and London and Berlin and Tokyo and Canberra. But I fear his priorities are so warped that he instead will be going to Moscow soon after taking office.

ceasefire brokered between opposition groups and the Syrian government.[118]

In Europe, Russia has considered how to respond to a plan to station a multinational force in Eastern Europe, which some U.S. analysts say could provoke Moscow.[119] Putin warned that he might target NATO sites if he sees them as a threat to Russia. "We are forced to take countermeasures — that is, to aim our missile systems at those facilities which we think pose a threat to us," Putin told American filmmaker Oliver Stone in an interview.[120]

Putin's government has been trying to counter U.S. and European political and economic decisions that he sees as weakening Russian interests. In particular, he has been unhappy with Western entreaties to former Eastern bloc countries to trade primarily with the West, as well as decisions to base NATO forces close to the Russian border. "The Russians were always concerned that they were seen by the West as inferior," says William Courtney, the former U.S. ambassador to Russia. "The notion that the West was double-dealing against the Russian empire, they [the Soviets] played up on that."

The West should realize that Putin has not backed Assad just to oppose the United States, says Paul Saunders, the executive director of the Center for National Interest and a former state department official. About 2,000 Russian-speaking people are fighting for ISIS in Syria, and Putin does not want them returning to Russia. If the Assad government fell, "a lot of those people might flood back to Russia," he says.

Putin also has been upset over U.S. democracy-building efforts in Russia's backyard, says Saunders, such as support for the so-called color revolutions in Georgia in 2003, in Ukraine in 2004 and Kyrgyzstan in 2005. "In most cases, these protests led to a government being ousted," Saunders points out.

Putin's international interventions have been designed not just to garner support at home, but to make the global community realize that Russia is no longer the weak, defeated nation that emerged from the 1990s, many experts say. Putin said as much after annexing Crimea, when he said the world needed to take his country's global concerns seriously.[121]

Russia now faces defiance from many Western governments for its actions in Syria and for creating what could become a frozen conflict in Ukraine. "They're stuck in a simmering war in Ukraine," says Courtney, the former ambassador to Russia who now serves as executive director of the RAND Business Leaders Forum. And Crimea, he says is "an economic burden."

OUTLOOK
Economic and Political Challenges

As President Putin tries to buff Russia's global image and demand international respect, some domestic challenges could tarnish his leadership, experts say.

Putin faces some domestic dissent. Activist Navalny has vowed to run against Putin in 2018, although the government says he is barred from doing so. Shortly after he led the 2012 anti-Putin demonstrations, Navalny was charged and convicted of embezzling timber from a state-owned company — a verdict many say was politically motivated due to his support for the protests. Although that verdict recently was overturned, another conviction — which many expect — could make him ineligible for office.[122]

"No one has the potential to challenge Putin," Harvard's Kramer says. "Perhaps Putin, at some point, seven to eight years from now, will designate a successor, but that's long in the future."

Meanwhile, Russia's ossified economy limps along, but some economists and political observers do not expect Putin to restructure the economy, because the political and social costs would be too great. "For Mr. Putin to modernize the economy, he has to change the system, and if does, his popularity is in jeopardy," says former ambassador to Russia Collins.

If Putin were to address corruption, for instance, he would alienate his powerful, wealthy supporters, analysts say. And closing down inefficient production centers would cause huge job losses, potentially sparking labor unrest, says Gaddy of Brookings. Russia already saw several walkouts in 2015, when some teachers and factory workers complained they had gone months without pay.[123] A major strike "might be the end of everything in Russia," he says. "He's doing everything to preserve those jobs, as bad as the products may be, they have to continue."

The quickest way for Putin to gain economic relief would be to pull out of Ukraine, which has been a costly drain on the Russian economy, says Courtney of the RAND Corp.

While it's not clear what tactics Putin might try, Gaddy says, "Putin is going to be testing Trump" to see what actions might provoke him. And it is "very naïve," he says, to think that Trump is "Putin's man."

Sen. Tom Cotton, R-Ark., made a similar point during the McCain hearings on the Russian hacking. "Donald Trump has proposed to increase our defense budget, to accelerate nuclear modernization, to accelerate ballistic missile defenses and to expand and accelerate oil and gas production, which would obviously harm Russia's economy," Cotton said.[124]

Russia, some analysts argue, does not aspire to emulate the West or match its strength. Rather, Putin seeks a weaker, more fractured NATO and America, so Russia can claim superiority.[125] To do that, Putin aims to undermine Western institutions while "solving" crises the West cannot, such as in Syria, writes Molly K. McKew, once an adviser to Mikheil Saakashvili, the former president of Georgia.[126]

Jeffrey Gedmin, a senior fellow at the Atlantic Council's Future Europe Initiative, said Putin is working to divide Europe into two spheres of influence and to weaken and fragment the European Union, "rendering NATO, our key alliance, obsolete," while working with Iran to push the United States out of the Middle East. "If that is the world that emerges in three, or five or 10 years," he said, "does that help American security? I say no."[127]

The West's best move might be to disrupt the Kremlin's plans by exposing the tactics and wealth of Putin and his cronies, said Stephen Sestanovich, a professor in the international diplomatic practice at Columbia University. That would create instability in Moscow and show that the West will not back down when it comes to the Kremlin, he said.[128]

NOTES

1. Michael D. Shear and Matt Apuzzo, "F.B.I. Director James Comey Is Fired by Trump," *The New York Times,* May 9, 2017, https://www.nytimes.com/2017/05/09/us/politics/james-comey-fired-fbi.html.

2. Michael Colins, "Who's Who: Key Players in the Investigation Into Russian Interference in the 2016 Election," Oct. 30, 2017, https://www.usatoday.com/story/news/politics/onpolitics/2017/10/30/whos-who-key-players-investigation-into-russian-interference-2016-election/813596001/.

3. Matt Ford and Adam Serwer, "Robert Mueller Is Just Getting Started," *The Atlantic,* Oct. 30, 2017, https://www.theatlantic.com/politics/archive/2017/10/robert-mueller-indictments-russia/544409/.

4. Ibid.

5. Karoun Demirjian, "Senate Judiciary Panel: Kushner Had Contacts About WikiLeaks, Russian Overtures He Did Not Disclose," *The Washington Post,* Nov. 16, 2017, https://www.washingtonpost.com/powerpost/senate-judiciary-panel-kushner-had-contacts-about-wikileaks-russian-overtures-he-did-not-disclose/2017/11/16/402586b4-cb05-11e7-8321-481fd63f174d_story.html?utm_term=.d11004d420eb.

6. "Russian Hacking and Influence in the U.S. Election," no date, https://www.nytimes.com/news-event/russian-election-hacking.

7. Rachel Roberts, "Donald Trump Attacks Hillary Clinton and 'Fake News' Amid Probe Into Russian-Bought Facebook Ads," *The Independent,* Oct. 21, 2017, http://www.independent.co.uk/news/world/americas/us-politics/donald-trump-facebook-hillary-clinton-russian-propaganda-claims-fake-news-troll-factory-a8013306.html.

8. David E. Sanger, "Obama Strikes Back at Russia for Election Hacking," *The New York Times,* Dec. 29, 2016, http://tinyurl.com/z3zh3ue; Neil MacFarquhar, "Vladimir Putin Won't Expel U.S. Diplomats as Russian Foreign Minister Urged," *The New York Times,* Dec. 30, 2016, http://tinyurl.com/hl755mq.

9. Karen DeYoung, Ashley Parker and David Nakamura, "Trump Says Putin Sincere in Denial of Russian Meddling," *The Washington Post,* Nov. 11, 2017, https://www.washingtonpost.com/world/national-security/trump-insists-putin-means-it-in-denying-election-meddling-critics-say-thats-unconscionable/2017/11/11/af0b7c9e-c71a-11e7-afe9-4f60b5a6c4a0_story.html?utm_term=.482e29fe0e4e.

10. DeYoung, Parker and Nakamura, op. cit.

11. Nicholas Fandos, Cecilia Kang and Mike Isaac, "House Intelligence Committee Releases Incendiary Russian Social Media Ads," *The New York Times,* Nov. 1, 2017, https://www.nytimes.com/2017/11/01/us/politics/russia-technology-facebook.html.

12. Fiona Hill, "This Is What Putin Really Wants," Brookings, Feb. 24, 2015, http://tinyurl.com/zt3hxs8.

13. "The fog of wars," *The Economist,* Oct. 22, 2016, http://tinyurl.com/zteevls.

14. Peter Baker, "Russian Dissident Opens New Chapter in His Anti-Putin Movement," *The New York Times,* Oct. 2, 2014, http://tinyurl.com/jq44h6r. Also see Alexis Flynn, "Putin 'Probably' Approved Litvinenko Poisoning, U.K. Inquiry Says," *The Wall Street Journal,* Jan. 21, 2016, http://tinyurl.com/hspuaj6.

15. Nikolas K. Gvosdev, "The Bear Awakens: Russia's Military is Back," The National Interest, Nov. 12, 2014. http://tinyurl.com/paqkunz.

16. "European Security: Russia's Actions and Possible Responses," The Finnish Institute of International Affairs, Oct. 5, 2016, http://tinyurl.com/h2b7fa9.

17. Hill, op. cit.

18. Carolyn Harris, "When Catherine the Great Invaded the Crimea and Put the Rest of the World on Edge," Smithsonian.com, March 4, 2014, http://tinyurl.com/zqfaart.

19. Steve Holland and Jeff Mason, "Obama Warns on Crimea, Orders Sanctions Over Russian Moves in Ukraine," Reuters, March 6, 2014, http://tinyurl.com/glm9jlr.

20. Stephen Cohen, "'We Are Not Beginning a New Cold War, We Are Well Into It,'" Democracy Now! April 17, 2014, http://tinyurl.com/jhksyb7. Also see Denis Dyomkin, "Putin Says Romania, Poland May Now Be in Russia's Cross-hairs," Reuters, May 27, 2016, http://tinyurl.com/j9623l7.

21. Somini Sengupta and Neil MacFarquhar, "Vladimir Putin of Russia Calls for Coalition to Fight ISIS," *The New York Times,* Sept. 27, 2015, http://tinyurl.com/oy4kttu.

22. Neil MacFarquhar, "On Syria, Putin Is Catering to an Audience at Home," *The New York Times,* Sept. 26, 2015, http://tinyurl.com/hn7esyd.

23. Jonathan Marcus, "Syria War: How Moscow's Bombing Campaign Has Paid Off for Putin," BBC News, Sept. 30, 2016, http://tinyurl.com/zl8b5og; Adam Entous, et al., "U.S. Believes Russia Bombed Syrian Aid Convoy," *The Wall Street Journal,* Sept. 20, 2016, http://tinyurl.com/jq4fa3u; Ellen Francis and Tom Perry, "Warplanes Knock Out Aleppo Hospitals as Russian-backed Assault Intensifies," Reuters, Sept. 29, 2016, http://tinyurl.com/zclown9.

24. Dmitri Trenin, "From Cooperation to Competition — Russia and the West," Carnegie Endowment for International Peace," Jan. 21, 2015, http://tinyurl.com/zclgwbp.

25. Jeremy Diamond, "Timeline: Donald Trump's Praise for Vladimir Putin," CNN, July 29, 2016, http://tinyurl.com/jsrw3p5. Also see "What Donald Trump Said About Russian Hacking and Hillary Clinton's Emails," *The New York Times,* July 27, 2016, http://tinyurl.com/jcn9lbk.

26. Peter Feaver and Eric Lorber, "Understanding the Limits of Sanctions," Lawfare, July 26, 2015, http://tinyurl.com/gp83jck.

27. Anna Andrianova, "Russian Economy Edges Near End of Recession as Contraction Eases," Bloomberg, July 28, 2016, http://tinyurl.com/zogwkbe.

28. MacFarquhar, "On Syria . . . ," op. cit.

29. Robert Legvold, "Managing the New Cold War," Foreign Affairs, July/August 2014, http://tinyurl.com/o9sscg9.

30. Ibid.

31. Gabriel Samuels, "NATO Puts 300,000 Ground Troops on 'High Alert' as Tensions With Russia Mount," *The Independent,* Nov. 7, 2016, http://tinyurl.com/jfv5rk6.

32. Ibid.

33. Ibid.

34. See David A. Shlapak and Michael W. Johnson, "Reinforcing Deterrence on NATO's Eastern Flank: Wargaming the Defense of the Baltics," RAND Corp., 2016, http://tinyurl.com/zl95hm7.

35. "Why Russia Is an Ally of Assad," *The Economist,* Sept. 30, 2015, http://tinyurl.com/nm2qxyv.

36. Kambiz Foroohar, "Russia Vetoes U.S. Plan to Extend UN Syria Chemical Probe," Bloomberg, Nov. 16, 2017, https://www.bloomberg.com/news/articles/2017-11-16/trump-weighs-in-urging-un-to-extend-syria-chemical-weapons-panel.

37. Tim Hains, "Trump Wants to Stop the New Cold War, but the American Media Just Doesn't Understand," RealClear Politics, July 30, 2016, http://tinyurl.com/hk8qkg8.

38. Stephen F. Cohen, "Why Cold War Again?" *The Nation,* April 2, 2014, http://tinyurl.com/jdwr3ds.

39. Ibid.

40. Ibid.

41. Stephen F. Cohen, "Cold War Again: Who's Responsible?" *The Nation,* April 1, 2014, http://tinyurl.com/hu6bl99.

42. Timothy Snyder, "How a Russian Fascist Is Meddling in America's Election," *The New York Times,* Sept. 20, 2016, http://tinyurl.com/jmf7dde. Also see Masha Gessen, "Russia Is Remaking Itself as the Leader of the Anti-Western World," *The Washington Post,* March 30, 2014.

43. Bryony Jones and Nic Robertson, "Syria Talks: What Russia and the U.S. Agree and Disagree on," CNN, Sept. 8, 2016, http://tinyurl.com/jue8u3v. Also see Brad Plumer, "A Short Timeline of Deteriorating U.S.-Russia Relations," *The Washington Post,* Aug. 8, 2013, http://tinyurl.com/huf6e2j.

44. Diamond, op. cit.

45. Ibid.

46. Robert Einhorn, "Prospects for U.S.-Russian Nonproliferation Cooperation," Brookings Institution, Feb. 26, 2016, http://tinyurl.com/jz8sxo6.

47. Thomas E. Graham, "Three Steps to Set the Tone on Russia: The Next U.S. Administration Must See Russia in a Global Context," National Interest, Dec. 12, 2016, http://tinyurl.com/gut7jzg.

48. "After the U.S. Election: Time to Re-Engage Russia?" McCain Institute, October, 2016, http://tinyurl.com/hn9egh7.

49. Ibid.

50. Ibid.

51. "Enlargement," North Atlantic Treaty Organization, Dec. 2, 2015, http://tinyurl.com/j4h8kel.

52. "After the U.S. Election: Time to Re-Engage Russia?" op. cit.

53. Ibid.

54. Ben Judah, "The Ruthlessness of Vladimir Putin," *New Statesman,* Oct. 7, 2015, http://tinyurl.com/j6bco8n.

55. "Approval Ratings," Levada Center, Dec. 2, 2016, http://tinyurl.com/zks9q8q.

56. Donald N. Jensen, "The Myth of Putin's 89%," Institute of Modern Russia, June 25, 2015, http://tinyurl.com/jyhuxjh.

57. Andrew Kramer, "Fear Envelops Russia After Killing of Putin Critic Boris Nemtsov," *The New York Times,* Feb. 28, 2015, http://tinyurl.com/p5pqfk2.

58. Carter Stoddard, "Boris Nemtsov Murder Trial Begins in Moscow," Politico, Oct. 3, 2016, http://tinyurl.com/zrno4of.

59. Jensen, op. cit.

60. Ibid.

61. "Boris Nemtsov Murder Trial Begins at Moscow Military Court," BBC News, Oct. 3, 2016, http://tinyurl.com/gshk89p. Also see Jeremy Wilson, "Here's a List of Putin Critics Who've Ended Up Dead," Business Insider, March 11, 2016, http://tinyurl.com/znjzn8q.

62. Ivan Nechepurenko, "Aleksei Navalny, Putin Critic, Says He'll Run for President of Russia," *The New York Times,* Dec. 13, 2016, http://tinyurl.com/hqyjjd8.

63. Emmet Livingstone, "Russian Electoral Body: Navalny Can't Run for President in 2018," Politico, June 24, 2017, https://www.politico.eu/article/russian-electoral-body-navalny-cant-run-for-president-in-2018/.

64. Jensen, op. cit.

65. Neil MacFarquhar, "In a Late-Night Move, Russia Arrests a Top Economic Official in a Bribery Case,"

The New York Times, Nov. 15, 2016, http://tinyurl.com/haxebhm.

66. Adam Taylor, "Is Vladimir Putin Hiding a $200 Billion Fortune?" *The Washington Post,* Feb. 20, 2015, http://tinyurl.com/jmgktwt.

67. Robert Service, *A History of Modern Russia,* Third Edition (2009), p. 25.

68. Alexander N. Yakovlev, *A Century of Violence* (2002), p. 21.

69. Ibid., pp. 234–235.

70. Mark Harrison, "Counting Soviet Deaths in the Great Patriotic War: Comment," Europe-Asia Studies, Vol. 55, 2003, pp. 939–944, http://tinyurl.com/gu9sdfo.

71. Anne Applebaum, *Iron Curtain: The Crushing of Eastern Europe* (2012), pp. 192–193.

72. Service, op. cit., p. 294.

73. "North Atlantic Treaty Organization (NATO), 1949," Department of State, Office of the Historian, accessed on Dec. 21, 2016, http://tinyurl.com/h2oqj3a.

74. "The Warsaw Treaty Organization, 1955," Department of State, Office of the Historian, accessed on Dec. 21, 2016, http://tinyurl.com/jpbbq83.

75. "Cold War," The Eleanor Roosevelt Papers Project, accessed Dec. 21, 2016, http://tinyurl.com/zdlhjtz.

76. Mark Kramer, "Five Myths About the Cold War," *The Washington Post,* March 13, 2014, http://tinyurl.com/jastj6o.

77. Nick Lockwood, "How the Soviet Union Transformed Terrorism," *The Atlantic,* Dec. 23, 2001, http://tinyurl.com/7ndpmwa.

78. Service, op. cit., pp. 342–343.

79. Ibid., p. 410.

80. Ibid., p. 446.

81. Ibid., pp. 454–455.

82. Ibid., p. 483.

83. Mark Mazzetti and Eric Lichtblau, "CIA Judgment on Russia Built on Swell of Evidence," *The New York Times,* Dec. 11, 2016, http://tinyurl.com/hnx7sza.

84. "Medvedev on Russia's Interests," *The Economist,* Sept. 1, 2008, http://tinyurl.com/zfgwgy5.

85. Adam Taylor, "That Time Ukraine Tried to Join NATO – and NATO Said No," *The Washington Post,* Sept. 4, 2014, http://tinyurl.com/hxxjwpa.

86. For background, see Brian Beary, "Separatist Movements," *CQ Global Researcher,* April 1, 2008, pp. 85–114.

87. David M. Herszenhorn, "New Russian Law Assesses Heavy Fines on Protesters," *The New York Times,* June 8, 2012, http://tinyurl.com/6vgzwvr.

88. Ellen Barry, "Raids Target Putin's Critics Before Protest," *The New York Times,* June 11, 2012, http://tinyurl.com/74vd3xk.

89. Yasmeen Serhan, "The Separatists' Cease-Fire in Ukraine," *The Atlantic,* Sept. 13, 2016, http://tinyurl.com/jbs5jab.

90. Cohen, op. cit.

91. Will Englund and Kathy Lally, "Ukraine, Under Pressure From Russia, Puts Brakes on E.U. Deal," *The Washington Post,* Nov. 21, 2013, http://tinyurl.com/gt65gvw.

92. James Kanter, "E.U. to Extend Sanctions Against Russia, but Divisions Show," *The New York Times,* Dec. 18, 2015, http://tinyurl.com/j4xwzeg.

93. Ibid.

94. Kristina Peterson et al., "Exxon CEO Rex Tillerson Faces Senate Dissent as Potential State Pick," *The Wall Street Journal,* Dec. 13, 2016, http://tinyurl.com/jg42orb. Also see Nataliya Vasilyeva, "Exxon Mobil Will Look for Oil in Russian Arctic and Black Sea," The Associated Press, April 18, 2012, http://tinyurl.com/z4jxgdy.

95. Andrew E. Kramer and Clifford Krauss, "Rex Tillerson's Company, Exxon, Has Billions at Stake Over Sanctions on Russia," *The New York Times,* Dec. 12, 2016, http://tinyurl.com/gqarcxc.

96. "Stephen Collinson, "GOP on Brink of New Cold War Over Whether to Work With Russia," CNN, Dec. 16, 2016, http://tinyurl.com/jln682o.

97. Neil MacFarquhar and Andrew E. Kramer, "How Rex Tillerson Changed His Tune on Russia and Came to Court Its Rulers," *The New York Times,* Dec. 20, 2016.

98. Justin Scheck et al., "Global Deals That Made Exxon's CEO Now Pose Big Test," *The Wall Street Journal,* Dec. 13, 2016, http://tinyurl.com/gvpgw3c. Also see MacFarquhar and Kramer, ibid.

99. Gearan, op. cit.

100. Scheck, et al., ibid.

101. David E. Sanger and Scott Shane, "Russian Hackers Acted to Aid Trump in Election, U.S. Says," *The New York Times,* Dec. 9, 2016, http://tinyurl.com/h2bem5w.

102. Tom McCarthy, "How Russia Used Social Media to Divide Americans," *The Observer,* Oct. 14, 2017, https://www.theguardian.com/us-news/2017/oct/14/russia-us-politics-social-media-facebook.

103. Matt Flegenheimer and Scott Shane, "Russia Looms Large as Senate Committee Is Set to Discuss Hacking," *The New York Times,* Jan. 5, 2017, http://tinyurl.com/hyvg3r8.

104. "Watch: Full Senate Hearing on Russian Hacking and US Cybersecurity," PRI's The World, Jan. 5, 2017, http://tinyurl.com/z93avn9.

105. Yasmin Tadjdeh, "Clapper: United States Must Beef Up Information Warfare Capabilities," National Defense, Jan. 5, 2017, http://tinyurl.com/jdpgfzt.

106. Michael D. Shearjan, "After Security Meeting, Trump Admits Possibility of Russian Hacking," *The New York Times,* Jan. 6, 2017, http://tinyurl.com/hhrko4q.

107. Adam Entous, et al., "Secret CIA Assessment Says Russia Was Trying to Help Trump Win White House," *The Washington Post,* Dec. 9, 2016, http://tinyurl.com/h9mxpr3.

108. Matt Ford, "What Exactly Is the 'Russia Investigation'?" *The Atlantic,* May 10, 2017, https://www.theatlantic.com/politics/archive/2017/05/what-is-the-russia-investigation/526278/.

109. Ibid.

110. "Russian Hacking and Influence in the U.S. Election," *The New York Times,* undated, https://www.nytimes.com/news-event/russian-election-hacking.

111. Mike Isaac and Daisuke Wakabayashi, "Russian Influence Reached 126 Million Through Facebook Alone," *The New York Times,* Oct. 30, 2017, https://www.nytimes.com/2017/10/30/technology/facebook-google-russia.html.

112. Nadine Schmidt and Tim Hume, "Berlin Teen Admits Fabricating Migrant Gang-Rape Story, Official Says," CNN, Feb. 1, 2016, http://tinyurl.com/hcpjesk.

113. David D. Kirkpatrick, "Signs of Russian Meddling in Brexit Referendum," *The New York Times,* Nov. 15, 2017, https://www.nytimes.com/2017/11/15/world/europe/russia-brexit-twitter-facebook.html.

114. Mike Isaac, "Facebook Considering Ways to Combat Fake News, Mark Zuckerberg Says," *The New York Times,* Nov. 19, 2016, http://tinyurl.com/j35j5tb.

115. "Report on Preliminary Examination Activities," The Office of the Prosecutor, International Criminal Court, Nov. 14, 2016, http://tinyurl.com/jsbwvfj.

116. Sheena McKenzie, "Russia Quits International Criminal Court, Philippines May Follow," CNN, Nov. 17, 2016, http://tinyurl.com/hvfgvdx.

117. David Stern, "Donald Trump's Win Shakes Ukraine," *Politico,* Nov. 9, 2016, http://tinyurl.com/zx3mmzk.

118. "Russia Says Has Begun Reducing Forces in Syria," Reuters, Jan. 6, 2017, http://tinyurl.com/jrgl9du.

119. Nathan Hodge, "Russia's Buildup in Kaliningrad to Test Donald Trump on NATO," *The Wall Street Journal,* Dec. 9, 2016, http://tinyurl.com/h9tqm5r.

120. David Filipov, "Putin Says Russia Planning 'Countermeasures' to NATO Expansion," *The Wall Street Journal,* Nov. 21, 2016, http://tinyurl.com/z2hn7vp.

121. Steven Lee Myers and Ellen Barry, "Putin Reclaims Crimea for Russia and Bitterly Denounces the

West," *The New York Times,* March 18, 2014, http://tinyurl.com/hxrxmqb.

122. Ivan Nechepurenko, "Aleksei Navalny, Putin Critic, Says He'll Run for President of Russia," *The New York Times,* Dec. 13, 2016, http://tinyurl.com/hqyjjd8. Also see Ellen Barry, "Rousing Russia With a Phrase," *The New York Times,* Dec. 2, 2011, http://tinyurl.com/jl4sp6w.

123. Andrew E. Kramer, "Unpaid Russian Workers Unite in Protest Against Putin," *The New York Times,* April 21, 2015, http://tinyurl.com/mwtfbje.

124. Ellen Nakashima, Karoun Demirjian and Philip Rucker, "Top U.S. Intelligence Official: Russia Meddled in Election by Hacking, Spreading of Propaganda," *The Washington Post,* Jan. 5, 2017, http://tinyurl.com/jd4gg5u.

125. Molly K. McKew, "Putin's Real Long Game," *Politico,* Jan. 1, 2017, http://tinyurl.com/zh7rpx9.

126. Ibid.

127. "US-Russia Relations in the Trump Era," *America Abroad,* Dec. 14, 2016, http://tinyurl.com/j6exbqr.

128. Stephen Sestanovich, "Why Exposing Putin's Wealth Would Be Obama's Best Revenge," *The Wall Street Journal,* Dec. 23, 2016, http://tinyurl.com/h4j87d3.

BIBLIOGRAPHY

Selected Sources

Books

Hill, Fiona, and Clifford G. Gaddy, *Mr. Putin: Operative in the Kremlin*, Brookings, 2013.
Two senior fellows at the Brookings Institution think tank assess Russian President Vladimir Putin's leadership.

Hosking, Geoffrey, *Russian History: A Very Short Introduction*, Oxford University Press, 2012.
An emeritus professor of Russian history at University College London provides a succinct history of Russia, from its medieval origins to contemporary events.

Judah, Ben, *Fragile Empire: How Russia Fell In and Out of Love with Vladimir Putin*, Yale University Press, 2013.

An associate fellow at the European Council on Foreign Relations sketches a revealing portrait of the Russian leader.

Myers, Steven Lee, *The New Tsar: The Rise and Reign of Vladimir Putin*, Knopf, 2015.
A longtime *New York Times* foreign correspondent argues that the Russian president is a flawed individual swinging between crises rather than an example of an historic Russian leader.

Ostrovsky, Arkady, *The Invention of Russia: The Journey from Gorbachev's Freedom to Putin's War*, Atlantic Books, 2015.
A correspondent for *The Economist* describes how Putin solidified his control, in part, by restricting the mass media.

Pomerantsev, Peter, *Nothing Is True and Everything Is Possible: The Surreal Heart of the New Russia*, Public Affairs, 2015.
A Ukrainian-born media consultant heads to the new Russia and witnesses the creation of an empire empowered by propaganda.

Service, Robert, *A History of Modern Russia, Third Edition*, Harvard University Press, 2009.
A British historian traces Russia's seismic shifts from Nicholas II through Vladimir Putin.

Stent, Angela E., *The Limits of Partnership: US-Russian Relations in the Twenty-First Century*, Princeton University Press, 2014.
The director of the Center for Eurasian, Russian and East European Studies at Georgetown University describes U.S.- Russian relations since the collapse of the Soviet Union.

Articles

Cohen, Stephen F., "Cold War Again: Who's Responsible?" *The Nation*, April 1, 2014, http://tinyurl.com/hu6bl99.
The Russian studies scholar observes how degraded relations between the United States and Russia shaped a new cold war.

Graham, Thomas E., "The Sources of Russian Conduct," *National Interest*, Aug. 24, 2016, http://tinyurl.com/jajp7up.

A Russian scholar and former White House adviser offers strategic advice as to how to deal with a military-minded Russian leader.

Jensen, Donald N., "The Myth of Putin's 89%,"
Institute of Modern Russia, June 25, 2015, http://
tinyurl.com/jyhuxjh.
A resident fellow at the Center for Transatlantic Relations in the Nitze School of International Studies at Johns Hopkins University analyzes what the Russian leader's high popularity statistics might mean.

Plumer, Brad, "A short timeline of deteriorating U.S.-Russia relations," *The Washington Post*, **Aug. 8, 2013,**
http://tinyurl.com/huf6e2j.
The newspaper provides a snapshot of the grudges and missed connections between two of the world's great rivals.

Roth, Kenneth, "What Trump Should Do in Syria,"
New York Review of Books, **Dec. 22, 2016, http://**
tinyurl.com/hbn8n9c.
The executive director of Human Rights Watch, a non-governmental organization dedicated to ensuring civil rights, analyzes the great powers and how they could end the Syrian civil war.

Reports and Studies

"Inside the bear," *The Economist*, **Oct. 22, 2016,**
http://tinyurl.com/zlvsaa5.
In a special section, the British publication traces the economic stagnation and political dysfunction that threatens Putin's hold on his people.

Pomerantsev, Peter, and Michael Weiss, "The Menace of Unreality: How the Kremlin Weaponizes Information, Culture and Money," The Interpreter, Institute of Modern Russia, November 2014, http://
tinyurl.com/khfg2rp.
Journalists assess how state-sponsored hacking and disinformation create scandal and sow doubts about politics.

Rumer, Eugene, "Russia and the Security of Europe,"
Carnegie Endowment for International Peace, June 30, 2016, http://tinyurl.com/jsfh2mw.
The director of Carnegie's Russia and Eurasia Program suggests a Western strategy in the wake of Russia's annexation of Crimea, which he argues was the latest step in Moscow's rejection of the post-Cold War Euro-Atlantic security order.

For More Information

American Enterprise Institute, 1150 17th St., N.W., Washington, DC 20036; 202-862-5800; www.aei.org. Think tank that studies a wide range of policy issues.

Brookings Institution, 1775 Massachusetts Ave., N.W., Washington, DC 20036; 202-797-6000; www.brookings .edu. Think tank that conducts research on domestic and international issues.

Carnegie Endowment for International Peace, 1779 Massachusetts Ave., N.W., Washington, DC 20036; 202-483-7600; www.ceip.org. International-affairs research organization with an affiliate in Moscow.

Center for Strategic and International Studies, 1800 K St., N.W., Suite 400, Washington, DC 20006; 202-887-0200; www.csis.org. Nonpartisan think tank.

Council on Foreign Relations, The Harold Pratt House, 58 East 68th St., New York, NY 10065; 212-434-9400;

www.cfr.org. Nonpartisan membership organization that conducts research, sponsors discussions and publishes the journal *Foreign Affairs*.

Eurasia Foundation, 1350 Connecticut Ave., N.W., Suite 1000, Washington, DC 20036; 202-234-7370; www .eurasia.org. Funds programs seeking to build democratic and free-market institutions in Russia and other former Soviet republics.

German Marshall Fund of the United States, 1744 R St., N.W., Washington, DC 20009; 202-683-2650; www.gmfus .org. Foundation that promotes trans-Atlantic relations; has several Russia-specialist scholars.

Rand Corp., 1776 Main St., Santa Monica, CA 90401; 310-393-0411; www.rand.org. Think tank that studies domestic and international issues.

7

Democracies Under Stress

Suzanne Sataline

AFP/Getty Images/Rolando Schemidt

President Nicolás Maduro of Venezuela, Latin America's oldest democracy, has been accused of dragging the oil-rich nation into dictatorship by delaying elections, jailing opposition activists and other actions. Experts blame the decline in democracy in Venezuela and elsewhere in part on resentment over rising immigration and public fury over social changes and economic hardships.

From *CQ Researcher,*
October 20, 2017

One day last May, after a government council in Venezuela announced it would redraft the constitution and delay elections, the bluish mist of tear gas drifted over the streets of Caracas, the capital. A line of young protesters — their t-shirts pulled up over their noses as makeshift gas masks — rushed toward riot police.

Shots rang out. Tear gas canisters exploded over the protesters' heads. Some demonstrators threw Molotov cocktails; others hid behind wooden shields. Engineering student Andres Muñoz said he was in the streets because the police were using force.

"I know that my main duty is to prepare myself for a better future, and that is precisely why I am protesting," said Muñoz, a pseudonym he assumed to protect against reprisals. "This is as much a part of my future as my studies."[1]

Latin America's oldest democracy, with more than 30 million people, has devolved into chaos, with the opposition accusing Venezuelan President Nicolás Maduro of dragging the oil-rich nation into a dictatorship by delaying elections, jailing opposition activists and pressuring lawmakers to overhaul the constitution. Scholars say the country's troubles started decades earlier, when a power-hungry populist leader mismanaged the state-run oil industry and suppressed citizens' rights.

Like Venezuela, many of the world's representative democracies in recent decades have veered toward autocracy, stalling 30 years of democratic growth. Leaders in some countries in Eastern Europe, the Mediterranean, Latin America and Southeast Asia have postponed elections, jailed opposition activists, restricted human

Status of Democracy in 2017

This year, a quarter of the world's 195 countries were listed as not free by Freedom House, a democracy advocacy group. The number of free countries has remained relatively stable since 2000 because as some countries slipped in the rankings — such as when Venezuela fell from partly free to not free this year — others, such as Brazil, Croatia and Tunisia, became more democratic.

A Snapshot of Global Democracy, 2017

Designation	No. of Countries
Free	87
Partly Free	59
Not Free	49

★ Largest decline in last decade
☆ Countries in transition

Countries with Largest Decline in Freedom in the Past Decade

Country	Population (in millions)	Key leader(s)	Key Issues/Prognosis
Azerbaijan	9.9*	President Ilham Aliyev	Constitutional amendments extending the presidential term were passed in allegedly rigged voting.
Central African Republic	5.6	President Faustin-Archange Touadéra	The government is struggling to recover from conflict in 2013 that killed thousands and displaced millions.
Ethiopia	105.3	President Mulatu Teshome	Security forces have responded violently to peaceful protests.
Hungary	9.8*	President János Áder, Prime Minister Viktor Orbán	Orbán has accumulated unprecedented power while praising authoritarian countries such as China and Russia.

rights and press freedoms and rewritten constitutions to legalize their actions.

"There has been a dramatic shift in global power and behavior, whereby the most important authoritarian countries in the world — first China and Russia, second, Iran and a few others — are more powerful and, in particular, more assertive," says Larry Diamond, a professor of political science and sociology at Stanford University. "Democracy has lost some of its luster, enabling autocrats or elected leaders with authoritarian ambitions to delve into a narrative that says: 'Democracy doesn't work.'" Without forceful checks on authoritarian power, he adds, autocrats will "perceive little or no cost to ruling as nastily as they want."

Countries with Largest Decline in Freedom in the Past Decade (Cont.)

Country	Population (in millions)	Key leader(s)	Key Issues/Prognosis
Russia	142*	President Vladimir Putin	Putin has curtailed media freedoms, ended regional elections and harassed political opponents.
Turkey	80.8*	President Recep Tayyip Erdoğan	Government crackdown after failed 2016 coup has led to mass arrests and firings of thousands of perceived enemies.
Ukraine	44*	President Petro Poroshenko	The government has struggled to maintain democratic gains and independence from Russia.
Venezuela	31.3*	President Nicolás Maduro	Maduro has delayed elections and pushed to rewrite the constitution to eliminate the opposition-led legislature.

Top Countries in Democratic Transition in 2017

Country	Population (in millions)	Key leader(s)	Key Issues/Prognosis
Denmark	5.6	Prime Minister Lars Løkke Rasmussen	Parliament is considering restricting immigrant rights.
Ecuador	16.3	President Lenín Moreno	The vice president was recently jailed following a bribery investigation, and Moreno has accused his predecessor, Rafael Correa, of spying on him with hidden cameras.
Iraq	39.2	Prime Minister Haider al-Abadi	The government faces challenges from ISIS and tensions between Sunni and Shiite Muslims.
Kyrgyzstan	5.8	President Almazbek Atambayev	Atambayev's term is expiring, but he may try to become prime minister, a position strengthened in a December 2016 referendum. Sooronbai Jeenbekov, a protégé of Atambayev, was elected on Oct. 15 by a surprisingly large margin.
Philippines	104.2	President Rodrigo Duterte	Extrajudicial killings in Duterte's anti-drug crackdown have taken thousands of lives.
South Africa	54. 8	President Jacob Zuma	Rival parties may clash as a new leader is chosen for the African National Congress.
Tanzania	53.9	President John Magufuli	Magufuli faces discontent from semi-autonomous Zanzibar. Threats, attacks and arrests target journalists frequently.
Zimbabwe	13.8	President Robert Mugabe	Politicians are jockeying for position in the struggle to succeed 93-year-old strongman Mugabe.

* July 2017 estimate by the CIA *World Factbook*

Sources: Elen Aghekyan et al., "Populists and Autocrats: The Dual Threat to Global Democracy," Freedom House, 2017, https://tinyurl.com/jkyw8ta; *The World Factbook*, Central Intelligence Agency, https://tinyurl.com/n27azxz; "Hungary profile — Leaders," BBC News, June 14, 2017, www.bbc.com/news/world-europe-17382823; Roger Southall, "How ANC presidential elections trump South Africa's constitution," University of the Witwatersrand, Johannesburg, June 2, 2017, https://tinyurl.com/y9kogat3; "Tanzania country profile," BBC News, Sept. 21, 2017, https://tinyurl.com/y8u89c39.

Experts cite many reasons for the democratic retreat, including a globalized, increasingly competitive economy that has spurred some politicians to cater to populist fury over social changes and economic hardships. Citizens in democracies also are disheartened when elected officials are guilty of mismanagement and corruption. And, finally, some Western governments have shrunk their long-standing democracy-promotion programs.

Political scientists define a democracy as a political system that lets people or their representatives govern themselves using laws, rather than the authority of a single leader, monarch, party or military dictatorship. Healthy democracies generally have independent judiciaries, protect citizens' civil rights and hold fair elections.[2]

Between 1975 and 2006, the number of democracies grew, as dozens of Latin American and African autocracies and military dictatorships — and then former Soviet satellite states — adopted competitive, multiparty elections, independent judiciaries and civilian rule. By the mid-2000s, many of those fledgling democracies had begun to crumble.[3]

Then, starting in late 2010, a wave of protests spread across the Middle East, with citizens demanding democratic change, only to see their campaigns for broader rights devolve into civil wars or even more repression. In Egypt, for instance, authoritarian President Hosni Mubarak stepped down in 2011 after months of massive anti-government demonstrations, only to have his popularly elected successor, Mohamed Morsi, ousted by the military in 2013.[4]

Signs of faltering democratic institutions can be seen in a variety of countries or regions, including:

- Russia, where President Vladimir Putin has allowed officials to investigate rivals, prevented opponents from running for office and overseen constitutional revisions that will have enabled him to serve, if re-elected in 2018, as either president or prime minister for a total of 24 years.[5]
- Hungary and Poland, where citizen fury grew over rapid social and economic changes wrought by globalization and the European Union's (EU) open-borders policies. That led many citizens to embrace populist leaders' proposals to limit immigrant and refugee rights. Once in power, those leaders have begun to dismantle democratic institutions.[6]
- The Philippines, where citizens and courts until recently have largely lauded President Rodrigo Duterte's vigilante campaign against drug abuse, which triggered thousands of extrajudicial killings of alleged drug sellers and users — a campaign President Trump has praised as an "unbelievable job."[7]
- Turkey, where a failed coup in 2016 prompted President Recep Tayyip Erdogan to jail tens of thousands of journalists, teachers and government employees he says opposed him.[8]
- Southeast Asia, where human-rights abuses and crackdowns on freedom are on the rise, notably in Myanmar. The military there has carried out what the United Nations has called ethnic cleansing, which has included rapes, beatings and killings of

minority Rohingyans after a militant group attacked police stations. The violence prompted about 500,000 members of the Muslim group to flee Buddhist-dominated Myanmar for neighboring Bangladesh.[9]
- The United States, where voters frustrated with what they call the Washington elite elected populist Republican Trump in 2016. As president he has repeatedly denigrated or attacked democratic institutions such as the press, judiciary, intelligence community and Congress.
- Various countries, such as China, Russia, Egypt and Cambodia, where authoritarian governments have blocked local nongovernmental organizations (NGOs) from providing funds to promote democracy.[10]

"The single biggest factor" causing the decline in democracy, says Diamond, "is that the United States and Europe — the advanced industrial democracies — have pulled away from making the promotion and defense of democracy a high priority."

While some political scientists and pro-democracy groups have criticized Trump for not supporting U.S. democracy-building activities, others point out that the pullback from democracy promotion started under the Obama administration, which rejected the fervid nation-building that the George W. Bush administration began after the Sept. 11, 2001, terrorist attacks on the United States.

Some experts say it may seem paradoxical, but the rise of Islamist terrorism has pushed Western countries to reject democracy promotion. The West needs the cooperation of certain autocratic regimes to fight terrorism. "The stomach for democracy promotion has lessened in the last 10 years," says political scientist Brian Klaas, a fellow in comparative politics at the London School of Economics and the author of the 2017 book *The Despot's Accomplice: How the West is Aiding and Abetting the Decline of Democracy.*

As officials in emerging democracies — such as Brazil, Indonesia, South Africa and Turkey — gained power, they often acted as cold realists instead of becoming powerful advocates for representative government, as Western policymakers and political scientists had assumed they would, according to Joshua Kurlantzick, a

Southeast Asia fellow at the Council on Foreign Relations think tank in Washington.[11]

Some political scientists are more optimistic about the state of democracy around the world. "While pluralism is no longer on the rise, democracy has survived in a range of countries with highly unfavorable conditions for fostering democracy," writes Lucan Ahmad Way, a professor of political science at the University of Toronto, pointing to Benin, the Dominican Republic, El Salvador, Ghana, Mongolia and Romania. In fact, he argues, the last decade could be viewed "as a period of democratic resilience."

Some democracy experts warn that a number of leaders are attracted to what they call the "authoritarian capitalist" model followed by China, which has achieved rapid economic growth since the 1980s without being hampered by free elections and independent courts. In contrast, many Western democracies have struggled to recover from the 2007-09 recession and are torn by factions and fighting, as their citizens reel from strains caused by globalization and the digital revolution.

"Today, China — and to a lesser extent other successful authoritarian capitalists — offer a viable alternative to the leading democracies," wrote Kurlantzick. "In the wake of the global economic crisis and the dissatisfaction with democracy in many developing nations, leaders in Asia, Africa and Latin America are studying the Chinese model far more closely — a model that, eventually, will help undermine democracy in their countries." Such authoritarian capitalists "pose the most serious challenge to democratic capitalism since the rise of communism and fascism in the 1920s and early 1930s," he said.[12]

Democracies have crumbled in places where elected governments have not delivered basic public services and where corrupt judiciaries or police forces have shown bias, according to Diamond. Disillusioned citizens can become receptive to "anti-system" messages by populists promising quick fixes who then try to dismantle democratic structures once in power. When Poland joined the EU in 2004, experts hailed it as a post-communist triumph. Eleven years later, Poland's populist and nationalist right-wing Law and Justice Party won the presidency and a parliamentary majority, and soon sought to control the courts.[13]

Worldwide, several social and economic trends are stressing democracies, says Diamond, and democratic

President Trump welcomes Egyptian President Abdel Fattah al-Sisi to the White House on April 3, 2017. Some political scientists say that by making al-Sisi and other autocratic leaders among his first invitees to the White House, Trump has sent a strong signal to global leaders that the United States is no longer concerned about protecting democracy or human rights.

Getty Images/Mark Wilson

institutions — such as the courts or a free press — have weakened in many developing and post-communist countries where conditions needed to sustain democracy are relatively weak.

In Europe, the EU's open-borders policy for goods and people has allowed many Middle Eastern refugees and African migrants to enter, just as Islamist extremists carried out terror attacks in France, England and elsewhere. Populists fanned the resultant fear of those new arrivals into a seething antagonism toward immigrants and the liberal governments and interest groups that support them. That anger, in turn, made many middle- and lower-income citizens receptive to restrictions on immigrants' rights; in Hungary, the government decided in February to restrict new arrivals to government camps until their legal status is resolved.

Intelligence agencies say Russia has helped some of those anti-immigrant, populist candidates with money, propaganda and so-called disinformation campaigns that aimed to sow confusion during elections in Western democracies such as the United States, France and Germany.

As political scientists, policymakers and government officials evaluate the democratic landscape worldwide, here are some of the questions they are asking:

Is China's authoritarian capitalism a viable alternative to democracy?

Political theorist Daniel A. Bell, a philosophy professor at Tsinghua University in Beijing, touched off a controversy in 2015 when he said, "I disagree with the view that there's only one morally legitimate way of selecting leaders: one person, one vote."[14]

In his book published that year, *The China Model: Political Meritocracy and the Limits of Democracy*, Bell said China's government, far from being an opaque tyranny, offered a "meritocratic" alternative to liberal, multiparty democracy. China chooses leaders based on experience and friendships, without the need for elections, confirmations, public hearings and U.S.-style popular approval. China's model, he said, has worked in a country with a population triple that of the United States.[15]

However, critics say China's so-called meritocracy is riddled with cronyism, and its economy — reliant on government spending and borrowing — could falter as economic growth slows and workers demand higher wages.

China's "authoritarian capitalism" began in the late 1970s when former Premier Deng Xiaoping introduced "socialism with Chinese characteristics." His policies sought to open China to some aspects of capitalism and international trade while retaining the central government's control on individual rights. While economists have credited Deng's policies with making China the world's fastest-growing economy and raising the standard of living for hundreds of millions of citizens, others have criticized the communist government for blocking open elections, imprisoning critics, censoring the press and the internet and barring criticism of the government and its human rights record.[16]

Nevertheless, some political observers have questioned whether the China model proves that prosperity is possible without democracy. China's ability to complete major infrastructure projects, such as a nationwide high-speed rail network, without public hearings or debate showed a country could build wealth and a modern state without bickering legislatures, intrusive judiciaries and a probing, free media.[17]

Moreover, the West has reeled from the recession while China's system appeared to weather it well, although Chinese finances are not transparent. When Western governments were scrambling to save failing banks, China was investing billions worldwide — largely through government-financed construction projects, according to the Council on Foreign Relations' Kurlantzick. Under Beijing's form of capitalism, he wrote, the government controls certain industries, favors certain corporations and influences banks to finance certain firms. When Beijing wants closer ties with, say, Thailand or South Africa, it pressures its state-linked banks to lend money to Chinese companies working abroad, he explained.

However, many economists say China's economy rests on a shaky foundation that relies heavily on construction fueled by state bank loans and has produced gargantuan debt.[18] Other experts say China's political system works well only in theory.

"There is massive factionalism, factional struggle, clientelism, patronage and corruption," wrote Timothy Garton Ash, an Oxford University historian and an expert on authoritarianism. Without free discussion, China allows no consensus or negotiation, perpetuating a system that is, in fact, not meritocratic, he argued.[19] President Xi, who came to power in 2012, has spent much of his first term investigating and even imprisoning party leaders accused of committing theft and amassing fortunes.

"It's actually going to be very difficult for this system to manage the extremely complex challenges it's facing as economic growth slows down, the supply of cheap labor is exhausted, and society becomes increasingly mature and educated, with higher aspirations," Ash wrote.[20]

"They already are in a slowdown," says sociology professor Ho-Fung Hung at Johns Hopkins University, and signs point to growing unemployment. "Unemployment and discontent are the number-one thing they worry about." Political reforms, however, are "the last thing they think of," he says.

Andrew J. Nathan, a Columbia University political scientist, argued that liberal democracy is superior to China's authoritarian model not because of elections but because democracy's independent legislatures and courts hold leaders accountable. "The selection of leaders is very important, but what makes democracy better than authoritarianism is the checking of leaders by the freedom of others," he said. Such limits on power do not exist in China. Rather, "China views democracy promotion, human-rights diplomacy, humanitarian interventions, and the rise of international criminal law . . . as efforts by the Western powers to weaken rivals."[21]

In a notable example, when the U.N. Security Council debated a resolution in 2014 to refer the Syrian civil war and crimes documented there to the International Criminal Court, China joined Russia to veto the move. A nation's internal affairs, Chinese officials argued, are not concerns of other countries.[22]

Should the United States promote democracy abroad?

The State Department says its mission is "to shape and sustain a peaceful, prosperous, just and democratic world and foster conditions for stability and progress."[23] Democracy promotion has been a key U.S. foreign policy goal since the end of World War II, when the United States helped to rebuild former foes Germany and Japan, turning them into powerful democratic allies.

Other U.S. agencies, including the U.S. Agency for International Development, the Millennium Challenge Corp. and the Middle East Partnership Initiative, also strive to promote democracy.[24]

After the Sept. 11, 2001, terrorist attacks, President George W. Bush vowed to create allies in the Middle East by turning autocratic governments into democracies, especially in Iraq and Afghanistan. Those efforts, which continued during Barack Obama's presidency, look to be in peril.

President Trump has proposed an "America first" policy in which the United States focuses on its own goals and does not embroil itself in civil affairs abroad or conduct engage in so-called nation-building. When Trump announced plans to send more troops to Afghanistan, he pointedly rejected the efforts of the Bush administration, saying, "We are not nation-building again. We are killing terrorists."[25]

To carry out Trump's agenda, Secretary of State Rex Tillerson considered deleting any mention of promoting

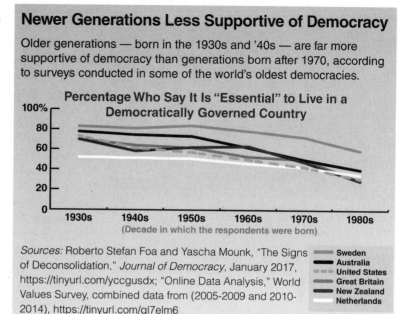

Newer Generations Less Supportive of Democracy

Older generations — born in the 1930s and '40s — are far more supportive of democracy than generations born after 1970, according to surveys conducted in some of the world's oldest democracies.

Percentage Who Say It Is "Essential" to Live in a Democratically Governed Country

Sources: Roberto Stefan Foa and Yascha Mounk, "The Signs of Deconsolidation," *Journal of Democracy*, January 2017, https://tinyurl.com/yccgusdx; "Online Data Analysis," World Values Survey, combined data from (2005-2009 and 2010-2014), https://tinyurl.com/gl7elm6

- Sweden
- Australia
- United States
- Great Britain
- New Zealand
- Netherlands

democracy from the State Department's mission statement.[26] He also proposed slashing spending for programs that promote democratic governance to $1.6 billion in 2018 — down from $2.3 billion in 2016. The proposal "reflects the president's 'America First' agenda that prioritizes the well-being of Americans, bolsters U.S. national security, secures our borders and advances U.S. economic interests," Tillerson said.[27]

Some political scientists say Trump's actions and his decision to welcome several autocratic leaders — Philippine strongman Duterte, Turkey's Erdogan and Egyptian leader Abdel Fattah al-Sisi — as some of his first visitors to the White House sent a strong signal to global leaders that the United States is no longer concerned about protecting democracy or human rights.

Yet, Trump's supporters point out that he has softened his isolationist tendencies with regard to Venezuela. On Aug. 25, the president imposed sanctions on anyone sending funds that fuel President Maduro's dictatorship.[28] In a Sept. 19 address to the United Nations, Trump urged world leaders to help restore "democracy and political freedoms" in Venezuela, adding, "We are prepared to take further action if the government . . . persists on its path to impose authoritarian rule on the Venezuelan people."[29]

Nanette Castillo grieves beside her son Aldrin, an alleged drug user killed by unidentified assailants, in Manila, Philippines, on Oct. 3, 2017. President Trump has told Philippine President Rodrigo Duterte he is doing an "unbelievable job" with his anti-drug campaign, which has resulted in thousands of extrajudicial killings of alleged drug sellers and users.

Other political scientists say U.S. skittishness about democracy promotion began in the Obama administration, after what critics called the post-9/11 debacles in Iraq and Afghanistan. Political scientist Klaas said half-hearted attempts to build a democracy in Iraq fed long-standing Muslim rivalries — which had been suppressed by dictator Saddam Hussein — that exploded into a civil war.[30] Such unintended consequences, he said, contributed to a sense in the West that "there are so many fires around the world, maybe we shouldn't make another one."

Reuel Marc Gerecht, a senior fellow at the Foundation for Defense of Democracies, a conservative Washington think tank, said, "Barack Obama came into office mistrusting American hegemony, which had led us into Afghanistan and Iraq." Obama believed in "diplomacy untethered from the use of force," he continued, and tried to persuade Syrian President Bashar al-Assad to leave office and to smooth over relations with Russia's Putin. But U.S. foes saw his outreach as weakness, Gerecht said.[31]

The Obama administration slashed U.S. spending to promote democratic institutions and human rights, from $3.5 billion to $1.9 billion annually between 2010 and 2015, before increasing it to $2.3 billion in 2016, according to Pippa Norris, director of the Electoral Integrity Project, a program at Harvard University and the University of Sydney that assesses elections worldwide. Because the United States has led the spread of democracy and human rights over the years, she said, "any abandonment of this work sends damaging diplomatic signals about America's priorities."[32]

While promoting democracy has enjoyed bipartisan support, some current members of Congress question the effectiveness and appropriateness of past democracy efforts.

"Creating reasonably effective democracies took centuries in the West, and it was often a highly contentious — even violent — process," wrote Stephen M. Walt, a professor of international relations at Harvard University. "To believe the U.S. military could export democracy quickly and cheaply required a degree of hubris that is still breathtaking to recall."[33]

Bruce Fein, a constitutional attorney and conservative activist, wrote that democratically elected leaders "can be every bit as tyrannical and aggressive towards the United States as unelected dictators," citing the election of Islamist extremist leaders of Hamas in the West Bank or the Muslim Brotherhood in Egypt. If a country is "insufficiently mature, literate and homogeneous," democracy degenerates into "majoritarian, sectarian or tribal tyrannies," he continued.[34]

Klaas counters that when America abandons democracy promotion it leaves a vacuum in unstable states that Moscow and Beijing can fill. "It's a global foreign policy battle, and the West's losses are China's and Russia's gains," he said.[35]

Do the internet and social media strengthen and foster democracy?

The internet's power to spread democracy has been undeniable.

Before the wave of popular revolts known as the Arab Spring shook the Middle East in 2010-11, activists, writers and citizens used digital media to help Tunisians, Egyptians, Libyans, Yemenis, Bahrainis, Syrians and others mobilize for political change. Digital media melded journalism, citizen reporting, activism and entertainment, wrote Jeff Ghannam, a journalist and lawyer with the Center for International Media Assistance, a U.S.-government funded nonprofit that promotes independent media abroad. When Syria barred international news organizations from covering the civil war there, media companies used images and videos sent through social media from citizen journalists. Private, upstart channels offered alternatives to state TV.[36]

"To be sure, these were not Facebook or Twitter revolutions, however much cyberutopians would like them to be," Ghannam wrote. "However, the internet's potential as a tool that can help the process of democratization is undeniable."

In Russia, opposition leader Alexei Navalny's Progress Party has aired investigative reports on YouTube for more than a year documenting the wealth of allies of former President Dmitri Medvedev and Putin.[37] Last spring, after a video accused Medvedev of using friends' charities to hide riches, including mansions and yachts, he apparently accumulated while in office, tens of thousands of citizens demonstrated nationwide.[38]

In China, social media has allowed citizens to air opinions and grievances, despite that nation's heavy censorship. After the July death of Nobel Peace Prize recipient Liu Xioabo — whom the authorities refused to release despite his advanced-stage cancer — citizens flocked online to pay tribute. Censors quickly scrubbed the comments from social media forums. In 2015, millions of residents downloaded a damning documentary about pollution until censors blocked it.[39]

It is unclear, some academics say, whether such online actions drive long-term commitment to reform. While social media enables organizers to quickly pull off large protests, such actions do not necessarily build permanent opposition movements, according to Zeynep Tufekci, an associate professor of sociology at the University of North Carolina, Chapel Hill, and Christopher Wilson, co-founder of The Engine Room, a Web-based democracy-promotion activist group. Previous large demonstrations, such as the 1963 civil rights March on Washington, required months of preparation that helped to strengthen the movement, they wrote, and helped organizers build future campaigns, such as voter-registration drives in the South.[40]

Several recent social movements have struggled to achieve much beyond large protests. In 2011, Occupy Wall Street activists staged demonstrations in hundreds of cities in more than 80 countries, protesting the role large banks and financial firms played in causing the 2007-08 recession, but few things changed, despite the large crowds. Likewise, protests in Istanbul in 2013 and Hong Kong in 2014 — both of which sought greater political freedoms — did not produce much if any concrete change.[41]

Protests should be only a first, potential step, wrote Tufekci and Wilson, because without follow-up, such as building coalitions, officials will not see such movements as threats.

More ominously, according to Ghannam, the internet can be used by authoritarian governments. The online world operates in the open and is easily viewed by the government and police, he said. China and Russia have detained activists, sometimes in secret, based on what they have written online.[42]

Social media also enables authoritarian governments to undermine democracy, such as efforts by the Russian government to sway the 2016 U.S. election, says Diamond. Governments also can pelt social media with propaganda, fake news and negative publicity that can shape voters' opinions. Some governments are using propaganda, fake news and disinformation "as offensive tools against democracy," says Marc F. Plattner, founding co-editor of the *Journal of Democracy*.

"On the whole, the internet is a plus for freedom, but we're only now starting to grapple with the negative impact," says Arch Puddington, a distinguished fellow for democracy studies at Freedom House, a nonprofit in New York that publishes an annual survey on the status of freedom around the world. "I would expect 10 years from now we are going to see many societies with laws and policies in place that will make the internet less free-wheeling than it is. And some will be enacted by democracies."

Courtney Radsch, advocacy director for the Committee to Protect Journalists, worries that as countries move to ban hate speech, they may end up suppressing free speech. "Governments are calling on private companies to remove content and accounts," she says. "Of course they are going to remove more content than they should." Governments provide little if any guidance on this, she adds.

In April, the German cabinet passed a bill to combat disinformation and hate speech on social media. It requires media companies to remove hate speech 24 hours after they receive a complaint and to block any other content deemed offensive within seven days.

Jewish groups hailed the law. "Jews are exposed to anti-Semitic hatred in social networks on a daily basis," said the Central Council of Jews, a federation of German Jewish organizations. "This law is the logical consequence to effectively limit hate speech." Facebook and free speech activists said the law could smother all kinds of speech. "This law as it stands now will not improve efforts to tackle this important societal problem," Facebook said in a statement.[43]

"Technology moves so fast," says Plattner. "There's a kind of arms race between the people who want to create greater freedom and people who want to create greater oppression."

BACKGROUND
Greek and Christian Roots

Democracy dates to the citizen states and philosophers of ancient Greece. In Athens in the sixth century B.C., as citizens chafed under rule by the elite, philosophers argued that wider citizen participation would best secure the public's loyalty and ensure stability.[44]

The Roman Empire experimented with popular governance, but eventually supplanted it with imperial power. As it did so, a countervailing force emerged that challenged slavery and pagan beliefs — a new religion called Christianity. The influential Christian theologian Augustine argued that community bonds created a moral force for self-governance.

However, after Germanic tribes overran the empire's western flank in the fifth century A.D., the notion of citizen power nearly vanished for several centuries.[45]

In 1215, under pressure from rebel barons, King John in England reluctantly accepted the Magna Carta, which established the notion that a king was subject to laws and that his power could be checked. It also enshrined individual rights, especially the principle of habeas corpus, which allowed a person to challenge his imprisonment in court.[46]

Since its early days, Christianity had promoted the idea that kings were anointed by God. Catholic and Protestant political thinkers began contesting the so-called divine right of kings in the 16th century, and the notion that subjects' could question authority spread during the Protestant Reformation. Opponents of Roman Catholicism challenged religious hierarchy and backed the right of ordinary people to make decisions in their churches and, ultimately, in government.[47]

The concept of democratic rule re-emerged in 17th-century England amid civil wars, as King James — and later his son, Charles I — clashed with Parliament over taxes, religion and other issues. Religious radicals known as Puritans, who wanted to "purify" Anglicanism, fled to North America starting in the early 1600s, where they established the Massachusetts Bay Colony.[48]

Democracy's First Wave

As the English colonies in North America grew in the 17th and 18th centuries, colonial assemblies gained power and stature. These early democratic institutions levied taxes and regulated colonial life. In the 1760s, when British officials attempted to tighten imperial control and tax the colonists, they ignited a rebellion.[49]

On July 4, 1776, the Continental Congress declared the colonies "free and independent states," stating in the Declaration of Independence that governments derive "their just powers from the consent of the governed" and that "whenever any Form of Government becomes destructive of these ends, it is the Right of the People to alter or to abolish it."[50]

After independence was won, the American states in 1787 established a federal government that shared powers among a president, a congress and a judiciary. The American experiment inspired other nations, including France, where citizens launched a revolution of their own in 1789. It ended with a constitution that established the French Republic and a legislature. Democracy grew in Europe over the next century, especially after the Hapsburg and Hohenzollern empires collapsed.[51]

World War I, and the overthrow of Russia's empire, marked a dire moment for democratic government. The Bolsheviks, the radical wing of a labor party whose members followed the writings of German philosopher Karl Marx, overthrew the monarchy. They created the Soviet Union, the world's first communist state. While supporters talked of the wonders of a worker-led government, the system became a brutal dictatorship that eventually killed tens of millions of citizens through starvation, imprisonment and mass executions.

In the 1920s and '30s, with the brutalities almost unknown beyond Soviet borders, people elsewhere — craving stability and economic opportunity, fearful of

CHRONOLOGY

1900s–1970s *Dictatorships rise and fall; Western democratic alliances are established.*

1917 Russia establishes the world's first government based on communism.

1933 Adolf Hitler seizes power in Germany, setting stage for World War II.

1945 World War II ends; 50 countries form the United Nations.

1947 India wins independence from Britain and later becomes the world's largest democracy.

1948 South Africa establishes apartheid to guarantee white dominance.

1949 Mao Zedong transforms China into a communist state.

1952 European Coal and Steel Community establishes an economic and political alliance that evolves into the European Union in 1993.

1956 Soviet tanks crush pro-democracy uprising in Hungary, killing more than 3,000.

1961 Soviet Union builds the Berlin Wall, separating East Germany from the city's democratic Western half.

1975 Thirty-five nations sign the Helsinki Accords to improve relations between communist countries and the West.

1980s–1990s *Democracy rises in former Soviet-controlled nations.*

1989 Chinese soldiers gun down hundreds of pro-democracy protesters in Beijing's Tiananmen Square. . . . The Berlin Wall falls. . . . Pro-democracy demonstrations erupt in Czechoslovakia, Bulgaria, Hungary and Romania.

1990 Lech Walesa becomes Poland's first democratically elected president, marking the end of Soviet control.

1991 Soviet Union is dissolved. The last president, Mikhail Gorbachev, hands power to Russian Federation President Boris Yeltsin. The country struggles to establish democratic institutions.

1994 Anti-aparteid leader Nelson Mandela is released from prison after 29 years and becomes the first democratically elected president of South Africa.

1998 Venezuelans elect populist Hugo Chávez as president; he installs a socialist government.

2000–Present *Democracies falter in Russia, Venezuela and Eastern Europe.*

2000 Russia elects former KGB agent Vladimir Putin as president. He consolidates control over the media and courts and ends regional elections.

2009 Venezuelan voters end presidential term limits, letting Chávez rule indefinitely.

2010 Hungarian Prime Minister Viktor Orbán and his Fidesz party take power; constitutional changes give him control over courts.

2011 A Tunisian street vendor commits suicide to protest government oppression, sparking the so-called Arab Spring uprisings in Egypt, Yemen, Libya, Bahrain and Syria that unseat authoritarian leaders, yet new ones replace them.

2014 Thai military suspends the country's constitution and ends democratic rule.

2015 Poland's right-wing Law and Justice Party controls parliament and weakens the constitutional court, politicizes the civil service and restricts the media.

2016 After quelling an attempted coup, Turkish President Recep Tayyip Erdogan blames an old opponent and arrests about 45,000 people, including teachers, journalists and government workers.

2017 Newly elected U.S. President Donald Trump attacks the press, judicial system, Congress and intelligence agencies, disparages NATO and compliments Putin and Philippine President Rodrigo Duterte, who directs a murderous anti-drug campaign that kills thousands of suspected drug dealers and users.

Venezuela Sinks into Dictatorship

Critics say President Nicolás Maduro threatens the once-thriving democracy.

In Venezuela, Latin America's oldest democracy and the country with the world's largest proven oil reserves, grocers' shelves are bare, corruption is rampant and democratic institutions are in tatters.[1]

Venezuela's stunning descent in recent years from a wealthy, stable democracy into a nation gripped by chaos and political intrigue has led to concerns that the country of more than 30 million people could fall permanently into dictatorship.

Elections held Oct. 16 threatened to deepen the country's political crisis by strengthening the ruling Socialist United Party, which won at least 17 of 23 governorships, a result some opposition leaders and the U.S. State Department blamed on fraud.[2]

The shift began under the late Venezuelan president Hugo Chávez, an autocrat elected in a wave of populist enthusiasm in the late 1990s, and continues under his successor, Nicolás Maduro, who has tried to dissolve the country's legislature and rewrite the constitution.

Maduro wants "to eliminate not only our democracy but any institution that still survives in Venezuela," opposition leader Julio Borges said recently.[3]

Ongoing mass demonstrations that began in the spring led to the deaths of about 125 people (as of August), and more than 5,051 people had been arbitrarily detained, according to a United Nations report.[4] Military tribunals have prosecuted hundreds of people protesting Maduro's socialist government on charges that could send them to prison for 30 years.

The protesters say Maduro became more authoritarian as the country's economy deteriorated due to collapsing world oil prices and mismanagement of the state-owned oil industry. Falling oil revenues have triggered massive government borrowing, and production of domestic goods has plummeted. Desperation has grown as food and medicine have run low, creating what Human Rights Watch has called a "humanitarian crisis."[5]

The devolution of Venezuela's democracy is an example of how some longtime democracies have faltered in recent years when authoritarian leaders, buoyed by populist movements, have begun dismantling constitutional protections and destroying checks on their power, usually amid massive economic problems.

But Maduro has not dismantled democracy on his own, according to some of his critics. They say Chávez, who died in 2013, had expanded presidential powers and weakened democracy by, among other things, limiting press freedom and the right to protest.[6] "Democracy was on thin ice by the time [Maduro] came to power," says Michael McCarthy, a research fellow at the Center for Latin American and Latino Studies at American University in Washington.

The conditions that led to Chávez's election in 1998 had begun decades earlier. In the 1970s Venezuela was awash in oil money, making it the richest country in Latin America. But after the oil industry was nationalized in 1976, mismanagement of the industry threw the economy into disarray, with inflation and foreign debt rising sharply in the 1980s and '90s.[7]

When world oil prices fell in the 1980s, Venezuela's government imposed austerity measures. Hundreds of people died in anti-government protests.[8] "From that point on, the system was essentially morally bankrupt," McCarthy says.

Chávez was elected in 1998 after promising to clean up government waste, graft and patronage, redistribute the country's oil wealth and boost social program budgets.[9] He spent oil revenue on education, housing, health and food programs — a component of his wildly popular leftist governing philosophy. The share of households in poverty fell from 55 percent in 1995 to 26 percent in 2009. Unemployment fell from 15 percent when Chávez took office to under 8 percent in June 2009.[10]

Chávez also clashed with the national oil company, Petroleos de Venezuela (PDVSA), which he said was controlled by foreigners and hid profits. Production fell after Chávez cut the company's budget for oil well maintenance. In 2002, Chávez fired at least 20,000 striking PDVSA workers and replaced them with political loyalists. Production fell even lower.[11] He also directed the state to take over food producers, fertilizer plants, farmland, banks, manufacturers, gold production, telecommunications and utilities.[12]

Meanwhile, Chávez capitalized on populist anger by making other sweeping changes. He suspended Supreme Court judges who opposed him and packed the court with allies.[13] A constitutional assembly amended the constitution to eliminate the Senate and authorize Chávez to recall legislators.

"The state was gradually eroding the checks and balances," according to Javier Corrales, a political science professor at Amherst College in Massachusetts. "Once you have no way of controlling . . . the executive [by] blocking a spending [bill] or suing him through the courts, the space is completely open for corruption."[14]

When Chavez dies in 2013, Maduro assumed power and was elected as Chavez's successor in a special election. By then, the country was struggling to pay its debts, as world oil prices were tumbling again. His allies have tried to disband the nation's opposition-controlled legislature, first by using the court system. When that failed, Maduro planned to create a new political body, a Constituent Assembly, which would rewrite the country's constitution, grant unlimited power to officials loyal to him and dismantle or reorganize the branches of government viewed as disloyal.[15]

In July, more than 98 percent of Venezuelan voters signaled their disapproval of the Constituent Assembly proposal in a voting exercise, called a popular consultation, organized by opposition parties.[16] Despite the staggering display of public disapproval, the Constituent Assembly was formed after a July 30 vote to elect assembly members. Venezuelans were not given the option to reject the assembly.

Since then the Constituent Assembly has voided the opposition-led legislature and granted itself full authority to write and pass legislation, consolidating control for Maduro's Party.[17]

In July the Trump administration imposed economic sanctions on Venezuela in an effort to block Maduro from altering the nation's constitution, which U.S. officials said could doom Venezuelan democracy.[18] Two months later, Trump attacked Maduro in a speech at the United Nations.

One country leapt to the South American nation's defense — China — an authoritarian communist country.[19]

— *Suzanne Sataline*

[1] Max Fisher and Amanda Taub, "How Does Populism Turn Authoritarian? Venezuela Is a Case in Point," *The New York Times*, April 1, 2017, https://tinyurl.com/mkufv9w; Juan Carlos Garzón and Robert Muggah, "Venezuela's raging homicide epidemic is going unrecorded," *Los Angeles Times*, March 31, 2017, https://tinyurl.com/y73cl7zb; Jessica Dillinger, "The World's Largest Oil Reserves By Country," *World Atlas*, updated April 25, 2017, https://tinyurl.com/hp7f72a.

[2] Fabiola Sanchez and Christine Armario, "Venezuela opposition looks for answers after election loss," The Associated Press, *The Washington Post*, Oct. 16, 2017, https://tinyurl.com/y7ovwtxk.

[3] Mariana Zuñiga and Nick Miroff, "Maduro wants to rewrite Venezuela's constitution. That's rocket fuel on the fire," *The Washington Post*, June 10, 2017, https://tinyurl.com/y86bz96l.

[4] Brian Ellsworth and Stephanie Nebehay, "U.N. decries excessive force in Venezuela's crackdown on protests," Reuters, Aug. 8, 2017, https://tinyurl.com/yb9m8nqc.

[5] Mercy Benzaquen, "How Food in Venezuela Went From Subsidized to Scarce," *The New York Times*, July 16, 2017, https://tinyurl.com/y8nyd98h; "World Report 2017: Venezuela, Events of 2016," Human Rights Watch, https://tinyurl.com/y7gsyrkc.

[6] "Venezuela: Chávez's Authoritarian Legacy, Dramatic Concentration of Power and Open Disregard for Basic Human Rights," Human Rights Watch, March 5, 2013, https://tinyurl.com/y9sfapow.

[7] Javier Corrales, "Venezuela in the 1980s, the 1990s and beyond, Why Citizen-Detached Parties Imperil Economic Governance," *ReVista: The Harvard Review of Latin America*, Harvard University, 1999, https://tinyurl.com/y8n4gdb4; Alejandro Velasco, "Explaining the Venezuelan Crisis," North American Congress on Latin America, Oct. 28, 2016, https://tinyurl.com/y73bldae; Henkel Garcia U, "Inside Venezuela's economic collapse," *The Conversation*, July 10, 2017, https://tinyurl.com/ybkdcj4x.

[8] Simon Romero, "Carlos Andrés Pérez, Former President of Venezuela, Dies at 88," *The New York Times*, Dec. 26, 2010, https://tinyurl.com/y7rz29mq.

[9] Fisher and Taub, op. cit.; Brian A. Nelson, "Hugo Chávez, President of Venezuela," *Encyclopædia Britannica*, undated, https://tinyurl.com/ya9kkemg.

[10] Oscar Guardiola-Rivera, "Hugo Chávez kept his promise to the people of Venezuela," *The Guardian*, March 5, 2013, https://tinyurl.com/ybhzlmsq.

[11] Scott Tong, "How oil-rich Venezuela ended up with a miserable economy," Marketplace.org, April 5, 2016, https://tinyurl.com/y7okfj2o.

[12] Steve Mufson, "Conoco, Exxon Exit Venezuela Oil Deals," *The Washington Post*, June 27, 2007, https://tinyurl.com/ybargmbe; Tamsin Carlisle, "Venezuela seizes 60 firms," *The National*, May 9, 2009, https://tinyurl.com/ybwful4u.

[13] Fisher and Taub, op. cit.

[14] Javier Corrales, "The Authoritarian Resurgence, Autocratic Legalism in Venezuela," *Journal of Democracy*, April 2015, Volume 26, No. 2, https://tinyurl.com/ya77n9my.

[15] Nicholas Casey, "As Venezuela Prepares to Vote, Some Fear an End to Democracy," *The New York Times*, July 29, 2017, https://tinyurl.com/yan8r6lx.

[16] Ana Vanessa Herrero and Ernestor Londoño, "Venezuelans Rebuke Their President by a Staggering Margin," *The New York Times*, July 16, 2017, https://tinyurl.com/ycljcktu.

[17] Nicholas Casey, "Venezuela's New, Powerful Assembly Takes Over Legislature's Duties," *The New York Times*, Aug. 18, 2017, https://tinyurl.com/y9xvnnpx.

[18] Tracey Wilkinson, "Trump administration hits Venezuela with more sanctions, targeting civilian and military officials," *Los Angeles Times*, July 26, 2017, https://tinyurl.com/ya92njc4.

[19] "China offers support for strife-torn Venezuela at United Nations," Reuters, Sept. 20, 2017, https://tinyurl.com/ya7j6k3e.

immigrants and invasions and swayed by powerful propaganda — embraced the idealism of communism, as well as fascism and militarism. Such ideologies soon morphed into autocratic regimes. Fascist Benito Mussolini overthrew a corrupt democracy in Italy. Meanwhile, authoritarianism spread to Poland and the Baltics, whose fledging post-World War I governments collapsed after military coups.[52]

Adolf Hitler, leader of the National Socialist German Workers' (Nazi) Party, called democracy "a monstrosity of filth and fire" in his book *Mein Kampf*.[53] After seizing power in Germany and eliminating most citizen protections, Hitler established the Third Reich and launched invasions in late 1939 that led to World War II. Hitler's conquest of most of Europe obliterated the Continent's democracies, including France's, and eventually killed millions, including 6 million Jews in the Holocaust.

Cold War Competition

With the Allies' victory in World War II in 1945, democracy returned to Europe and Japan. The United States helped rebuild ravaged Western economies through the Marshall Plan, which delivered more than $13 billion (about $132 billion today) in aid to European countries. In Japan, U.S. occupying forces imposed military, political, economic and social reforms. Former foes West Germany and Japan eventually flourished as democracies.[54]

The war also ended Europe's colonial regimes, creating many new democracies in Africa and Asia. In Greece, Spain, Argentina, Brazil and Chile, once-autocratic regimes expanded voting rights and civil freedoms.[55]

Soon after the war's end, 50 countries formed the United Nations, which aimed to prevent future wars and promote democratic governments and human rights, a goal laid out in the Universal Declaration of Human Rights in 1948. At about the same time, several European nations formed an economic and political alliance, the European Coal and Steel Community, which eventually became the European Union (EU).[56]

In 1949 Western democracies formed a military alliance, the North Atlantic Treaty Organization (NATO), to match the Soviet Union's united front.

But democracy had formidable foes. A civil war in China ended in 1949 with the victory of Mao Zedong's communist forces, which proceeded to build a one-party state that essentially turned citizens into spies and informers. Tens of millions died of starvation during the so-called Great Leap Forward, an economic "modernization" effort in 1958-61. Many more died during the Cultural Revolution (1966-76), as the government tried to eliminate "enemies of the revolution."[57]

The Soviet Union, meanwhile, had established impenetrable borders, dubbed the Iron Curtain, between its satellite states in Eastern Europe and democratic Western Europe. Soviet forces tried to block citizens from fleeing the communist-run states in the East to the democratic West; violators were often shot dead. The Berlin Wall that separated East and West Berlin remained in place until citizens tore it down in 1989.[58]

The "Cold War" between nations allied with the United States or the Soviets fanned proxy wars. Civil war erupted in Korea in the early 1950s and Vietnam in the 1960s and '70s. In Africa and Latin America, many former colonial states devolved into military dictatorships, supported by the United States, as they sought to defeat socialist uprisings supported by the Soviet Union or Communist China.[59]

In the late 1980s, the Soviet Union's mounting economic problems — fueled by an inefficient, centrally managed economy — prompted the country to borrow massive amounts of money. Former Soviet leader Mikhail Gorbachev announced new policies of *glasnost* and *perestroika*, or openness and reform. With more freedom to discuss and organize, discontent within the Soviet bloc grew.[60]

On June 12, 1987, in a famous speech in front of West Berlin's Brandenburg Gate, part of the Berlin Wall, U.S. President Ronald Reagan challenged Gorbachev to give his people freedom and "tear down this wall!"[61]

Rather than Reagan's words, the Soviet bloc's faltering economy created the greatest pressure on Gorbachev. As the Soviet Union competed with the United States in expanding its nuclear defenses, it robbed its manufacturing economy of crucial resources.[62] A politically weakened Gorbachev did not interfere when opposition movements arose in satellite states, such as Poland's Solidarity labor movement, which won seats in the Polish legislature in 1989.[63]

After Poland and Hungary gained some freedoms, citizens in East Germany agitated for their government to open the border to the West, sealed since 1961 and manned by armed guards. When the gates opened, suddenly on

Nov. 9, 1989, a tide of people crossed to the West, unmolested by the border guards.[64] Two years later, communist hardliners tried to depose Gorbachev in a coup, but military officers and leaders from the autonomous republics refused to cooperate, and on Dec. 31, 1991, the Soviet Union was dissolved. The new leader, President Boris Yeltsin, steered the Russian Federation toward a rudimentary democracy.[65]

Former Soviet republics — Ukraine, Latvia, Lithuania and others — quickly voted for independence. By 2004, after several peaceful protests — the "color revolutions" — voters in former Soviet bloc countries chose new presidents. Many of the emerging states formed democratic governments to qualify for EU membership in what some called the reunification of Europe.[66]

Democratic Backsliding

In the late 1970s, Democratic President Jimmy Carter sought to make human rights central to foreign policy and linked economic and military aid to countries' human-rights records.[67]

The number of world democracies expanded throughout the 1980s and '90s, especially after the Soviet Union ended.

Republican President George W. Bush aggressively promoted democracy after Islamist terrorists attacked the United States on Sept. 11, 2001, arguing that democracy would help alleviate anti-U.S. sentiment in the Middle East and block further attacks on the West.

Yet, the U.S. democracy-promotion campaign of the 2000s had inconsistencies, just as it had during the Cold War, when the United States sometimes supported military dictators who opposed communism. The Bush administration spent billions of dollars, and lost thousands of lives, trying to establish democratic institutions in Iraq, Afghanistan and other nations, while retaining close ties with repressive regimes such as Saudi Arabia, the birthplace of most of the 9/11 terrorists.[68]

However, Bush's efforts to fight Islamist extremists while building new democratic nations in the Middle East largely failed, says author Klaas. Beginning in December 2010, protests and rallies erupted in several Arab states, largely powered by young people's frustration with their autocratic governments and poor job prospects. In Cairo, huge crowds filled the streets for months, demanding that Egyptian President Mubarak resign.[69]

However, the Arab Spring protests did not usher in vast democratic change, except in Tunisia, where democracy remains a work in progress. Egypt elected the religiously conservative Morsi, who was ousted in 2013 by the military, led by Sisi. Since becoming president, Sisi has imposed even more repressive measures than Mubarak's. In Syria, the military remained loyal to Assad and is used as a tool of sectarian power.[70]

During the presidential campaign and after his election in 2008, Democrat Barack Obama vowed to end U.S. involvement in Iraq and Afghanistan, and promoted a policy of restraint in the region as violence grew.

Meanwhile, Putin, first elected president of Russia in 2000, had instituted many changes to ensure his power. His government took over television stations, curtailed media freedoms, ended regional elections, imposed harsh penalties on protesters and harassed political opponents. Many of Putin's critics were killed or died under suspicious circumstances. In 2014, when Ukrainian protests prodded that country's president to resign, Putin annexed the country's eastern portion, claiming it was historically part of Russia. In response, the West imposed sanctions that, coupled with the collapse of world prices for oil (Russia's major export), severely damaged the Russian economy.[71]

Democracy and human rights faced challenges elsewhere in the West. In Britain, voters backed restrictions on immigrants, as nationalists who opposed the EU's open-border policies blamed new arrivals for taking jobs and dragging down the U.K. economy. In June 2016, British voters stunned the establishment by backing the U.K.'s exit from the European Union.[72]

Five months later the Republican nominee for president, billionaire real estate developer and political neophyte Donald Trump, won an upset victory over Democrat Hillary Clinton. Trump ran a campaign infused with nationalistic slogans that attacked immigrants and refugees, denigrated NATO and vowed to place American interests before those of other nations. In office, he has lambasted Congress and the judiciary, sought to temporarily ban immigrants from certain Muslim-majority nations from entering the United States, and suggested that the press be restricted. His policies prompted many scholars to warn that democracy in America was threatened.

Shortly after his election, the U.S. intelligence community concluded that Russia's intelligence services had meddled in the 2016 presidential election through hacking and planting of "fake news" online that damaged Clinton and favored Trump. In addition, according to the spy agencies, Trump campaign associates communicated with Russians during the election in ways that caused "concern."[73] Senate and House committees opened investigations into the Russian interference.

In May, Trump fired FBI Director James B. Comey, who said later that the president had pressed him to state publicly that Trump was not under investigation. That month, the Justice Department appointed former FBI Director Robert S. Mueller III to investigate possible ties between the Trump campaign and Russian officials.[74]

CURRENT SITUATION

America First

Since taking office, President Trump has insisted that the United States not try to recreate countries "in our own image" or impose democratic policies on others. The administration also proposed cutting aid to developing nations by one-third and diverting the money to national security.[75]

Both the foreign aid and national security communities blasted the plan. Cutting the foreign aid budget would mark "U.S. withdrawal from the world, rather than continued leadership and engagement," says Travis Adkins, senior director for public policy and government relations at InterAction, a Washington alliance of nongovernmental organizations. Sen. Lindsey Graham, a Republican from South Carolina and the chair of the Appropriations Subcommittee on State and Foreign Aid, said cutting aid would damage national security. "Now is not the time for retreat," he said. "Now is the time to double down on diplomacy and development."[76]

The Senate Appropriations Committee approved $51 billion for the State Department, foreign operations and related programs for fiscal 2018 — almost $11 billion above Trump's request.[77]

While disparaging democracy-building, Trump continues to praise authoritarian leaders. Trump said Egyptian strongman al-Sisi was doing a "fantastic job," and during a May trip to the Middle East he promised to sell weapons to the repressive Saudi Arabian monarchy and urged regional leaders to get tougher on Islamist terrorists — without mentioning that the Saudis had been accused of human-rights abuses.[78]

Human-rights activists say extrajudicial killings and other abuses in Egypt spiked after Trump's trip. "The visit has emboldened Arab rulers that whatever violations they commit against their people are going to be accepted by the Trump administration," said Gamal Eid, executive director of the Arab Network for Human Rights Information. In Egypt, he said, Trump's actions gave Sisi "the green light to increase the repression. He's been empowered."[79]

Obama had frozen part of Egypt's annual military aid package for two years after al-Sisi-led troops overthrew Morsi, and Obama never invited al-Sisi to the White House. In mid-August, the Trump administration said it would cut or delay $290 million in military and economic aid to Egypt after the government passed a law restricting NGOs from engaging in pro-democracy political activity. It was later revealed that the aid was frozen in part because Egyptians were buying contraband weapons from North Korea.[80]

Meanwhile, the congressional and FBI investigations into Russian interference in the 2016 presidential election continue. In September, Facebook CEO Mark Zuckerberg notified Congress that his company had discovered that Russian operatives had paid $100,000 for 3,000 ads posted on 470 phony Facebook pages during the presidential election. The ads aimed to create social chaos, religious and racial division and suppress the vote, said those who had viewed them. Similar ads were discovered on Twitter, Facebook and Google.[81]

The Kremlin's goal is "to encourage discord in American society," said Michael A. McFaul, a former U.S. ambassador to Russia and currently director of the Freeman Spogli Institute for International Studies at Stanford University. Putin believes "our society is imperfect, that our democracy is not better than his, so to see us in conflict on big social issues is in the Kremlin's interests."[82]

Embattled Democracies

As the European Union prepares for uncertainty after the upcoming departure of Great Britain, member states also must decide how to handle rising populism and nationalism.

In September, when Angela Merkel earned a fourth term as German chancellor, Alternative for Germany won parliamentary representation, the first time a far-right party earned seats in parliament in more than 60 years.[83]

In Poland, where leaders took a cue from nationalist Hungarian Prime Minister Viktor Orbán, Jarosław Kaczyński, leader of the ruling Law and Justice Party, pushed to appoint loyalists to the constitutional court and public broadcasting station. A law passed in July would allow the government to fire Supreme Court judges, the very people responsible for approving election results. After tens of thousands of protesters demanded that Poland's courts remain free, President Andrzej Duda said he would veto the law.[84]

In Turkey, President Erdogan has tried to silence opposition activists after a military coup failed in 2016. A state of emergency remains, and the government has fired or suspended 130,000 workers and arrested about 45,000, including thousands of lawyers, teachers, doctors, journalists and jurists. Recently, hundreds of officials accused of fomenting the plot were sentenced to life in prison. In the spring, voters narrowly approved constitutional amendments that ended the parliamentary system and granted vast powers to the winner of the 2019 presidential election; observers say Erdogan will likely win that. Erdogan's slide toward autocratic rule led the EU Parliament last November to suspend negotiations over Turkey's 1987 application to join.[85]

In Russia, Putin continues to wield enormous control after 17 years as either president or prime minister. Freedom House rates Russia as "not free" and ranks political rights there among the lowest anywhere. After Russia invaded Ukraine's Crimean region in 2014, Western nations, including the United States, imposed tough economic sanctions that have hampered Russia's economy.[86]

With revenues down, some wages unpaid and poverty rising, opposition leader Navalny's website, which carries investigative pieces detailing what he says are Putin's cronies' corrupt practices, has found a receptive audience. The government has imposed heavy fines on protests deemed illegal and prosecuted Navalny for embezzlement in a case international officials call a sham.[87]

In Southeast Asia, the Philippines' Duterte continues a war on drug users and dealers begun when he took office in June 2016. At least 7,000 Filipinos are dead, most killed without charges or prosecutions. The extrajudicial killings and threats against journalists led Freedom House to reclassify the onetime established democracy as "partly free." Religious and international human-rights groups have condemned the campaign, but Trump has said Duterte is doing an "unbelievable job on the drug problem."[88]

The backsliding on democracy in the former U.S. colony was especially dramatic because the Philippines was known as the "ultimate Third World democracy," with a modern judiciary, free press and speech, a two-party political system with open elections and separation between the church and state, wrote William H. Overholt, a senior fellow at the Asia Center at Harvard University. Moreover, Duterte's predecessor, Benigno Aquino, had set the country on "an upward path of improved growth, democracy and alliance with the United States," he said.[89]

Elsewhere in Southeast Asia, the Rohingya crisis continues to unfold in Myanmar (formerly Burma), once praised as an example of how a former military junta converted to a democratically elected civilian government, led by Nobel Peace Prize-winner Aung San Suu Kyi.[90]

In late August, after Rohingya rebels attacked a local police station, Myanmar's military torched Rohingya villages and shot residents, forcing some 500,000 Rohingyans to flee to neighboring Bangladesh. Although the Muslim Rohingya have lived in predominantly Buddhist Myanmar for centuries, the current government says they are illegal immigrants and has denied them citizenship, largely because of their Bangladeshi heritage. The situation is a "textbook example of ethnic cleansing," according to the U.N. high commissioner for human rights. Although foreign officials have criticized Suu Kyi for not condemning the army, her advisers say she worries it could antagonize the military and prevent her from building a full democracy.[91]

In a bright spot for democracy, opposition parties and civil society groups in Africa have persistently pushed for elections, legal reforms and anticorruption laws. Kenya's Supreme Court on Sept. 1 took the unprecedented step

AT ISSUE

Is democracy in retreat around the world?

YES   Arch Puddington
Distinguished Scholar for Democracy Studies, Freedom House

Written for *CQ Researcher*, October 2017

During the late 20th century, societies everywhere threw off dictatorship and embraced freedom. It was understood that the world's democracies offered peace and prosperity, while authoritarianism brought poverty and oppression.

Today, democracy seems in retreat. Russia and China add layer on layer of repression; new democracies like Poland and Hungary move sharply toward authoritarianism; conditions continue to erode throughout Southeast Asia and the Middle East. Populist parties with nativist streaks are fixtures in Europe, and a populist-nationalist sits in the White House.

Still, things could turn around in the future. Consider these points:

- Both U.S. and European economies are rebounding, with growth rising and unemployment falling. The major democracies remain the world's wealthiest countries.
- The Venezuelan catastrophe has had major ripple effects in the region and beyond, with South American voters rejecting parties associated with the left-wing ideology of former Venezuelan President Hugo Chávez.
- In Europe, centrist forces have maintained government control, even as populist parties have made gains.
- Vladimir Putin's repressive model remains highly unpopular in the Russian neighborhood and beyond. Russian speakers in the Baltics prefer EU democracies to a kleptocratic, prop-aganda-driven, petro-state. Likewise, the people of Georgia and Ukraine are clearly hostile to the Putin dictatorship. The loss of influence in Ukraine is a major setback for Putin.
- Likewise, the people of Taiwan and Hong Kong have made clear their revulsion at Beijing's police-state regimentation.
- Enthusiasm for democracy remains high throughout Africa. Spurred by unhappy experiences with venal leaders-for-life, opposition parties and civil society have persisted in their drive for honest elections, anticorruption laws and legal reforms.
- U.S. democratic institutions — the media, courts and civil society — have resisted President Trump's agenda and limited the administration's ability to challenge constitutional norms.

Despite some serious setbacks, democracy remains the system of choice for the majority. Freedom's formerly smug advocates, having experienced reversals, are now resisting — focusing on populists at home and autocrats abroad. Meanwhile, as insecure strongmen desperately seek new methods of censorship and political control, the appeal of the China model, Bolivarian socialism and Putinism are fading. Dictatorship is not the wave of the future.

NO   Lucan Ahmad Way
Professor of Political Science, University of Toronto

Written for *CQ Researcher*, October 2017

Rarely have things looked so bad for democracy as they do today. The world's most formidable democracy promoter, the European Union, is in disarray and faces possible disintegration. Far right forces have gained unprecedented support in Europe. Russia and China are resurgent. And most important, the United States itself is now led by a president who openly attacks the foundations of democracy. Democracy is backsliding in three countries where pluralism was once well-established: Venezuela, Hungary and (probably) Poland. The most recent report from Freedom House says the world has witnessed "the 11th straight consecutive year of decline in global freedom."

Overall, however, the case for democratic decline is relatively weak.

According to Freedom House, the number of democracies has remained more or less stable since the start of the millennium — fluctuating between 85 and 90. While several countries that Freedom House ranked as "free" in the late 1990s — including Venezuela — lost that ranking in the 2000s, several other countries became democratic during this same period, including Brazil, Croatia, Serbia and Tunisia.

And although the average Freedom House autocracy score has increased over the last decade — from 3.2 in 2005 to 3.4 in 2016 — the shift has been vanishingly small, and the level of autocracy has decreased very slightly since 2000. In addition, the widely used Polity Data Series index of the level of democracy in countries across the globe indicates that the number of democracies (countries with a score of 7 or above) has increased significantly from 67 in 2000 to 84 in 2016.

Thus, while the last decade has almost universally been seen as a time of democratic deterioration, Freedom House's own data suggests that it may be better understood as a period of democratic resilience. Indeed, while pluralism is no longer on the rise, democracy has survived in a range of countries with highly unfavorable conditions for fostering democracy, such as Benin, the Dominican Republic, El Salvador, Ghana, Mongolia and Romania. The question of why and how so many new democracies have survived in the face of far less favorable international environments merits further study. A better understanding of this democratic survival would help democracy advocates prepare for the all-too-likely day when authoritarian resurgence does, in fact, arrive.

of annulling the results of the Aug. 8 re-election of President Uhuru Kenyatta. The court said the election was "neither transparent or verifiable" and ordered a new election, scheduled for Oct. 26.[92]

Conservatives also advanced recently. On Oct. 15, right-wing parties in Austria made solid gains in parliamentary elections after promising a hard line on immigration. The conservative People's Party, led by rising political star Sebastian Kurz, 31, won at least 31.7 percent of the vote, and the far-right Freedom Party won 26 percent. The contest echoed some of the current trends in Europe's 2017 elections, including populist leaders stoking fear of Muslim immigration, disillusion with established politicians and the decline of center-left parties.[93]

Meanwhile, China continues to woo other countries to show that authoritarianism and modernization can co-exist. "For now, China is using the U.S. playbook from the 1970s: 'How to be a superpower — use wads of cash and back dictators,'" said Michael Vatikiotis, the Asia regional director at the Geneva-based Centre for Humanitarian Dialogue. "But it's not clear how long that strategy will last."[94]

Michael Pillsbury, the director of the Center on Chinese Strategy at the Hudson Institute, a conservative think tank in Washington, has argued that if China's economy continues its robust growth — which many economists doubt — and if strict communists maintain control, China could become the dominant world power by mid-century.[95]

But Andrew J. Nathan, a Columbia University political scientist, said many countries would struggle to emulate China. "The Chinese model requires large fiscal resources, technological sophistication, a well-trained and loyal security apparatus, and sufficient political discipline . . . not to take power struggles public," he wrote.[96]

OUTLOOK
Dangerous Populist Age

The rise of nationalist movements and virulent autocracies presents a growing problem for democratic principles, human rights and independent judiciaries. Facing these pressures, many global leaders and nations will pursue their own narrow interests, unrestrained and

Members of Myanmar's Rohingya minority demonstrate in Kuala Lumpur, Malaysia, on Nov. 25, 2016, against persecution of the predominantly Muslim group. In late August, Myanmar's military torched Rohingya villages and shot residents, forcing some 500,000 Rohingyans to flee to neighboring Bangladesh, in what U.N. officials have called a campaign of ethnic cleansing.

Getty Images/Samsul Mohd Said

unconcerned with global peace, freedom, prosperity and health, according to Freedom House.[97]

The coming years will be "suspended between a continued instability and erosion of democracy globally and the possibility of a full-blown reverse wave of democratic breakdowns," says Stanford professor Diamond. "The prospects for democratic transitions don't look very good," he adds. "The best one could realistically hope for is a kind of stabilization around this rather difficult moment — so not much further deterioration."

"The sheen has been taken off the Washington model," says political scientist Klaas. Some African leaders, for instance, admire China for its strong economy and governing efficiency, he says, citing several countries where leaders have tried to stay in power by changing their constitutions, such as the Democratic Republic of the Congo, Rwanda, Burundi, Djibouti, Cameroon, Chad, Uganda, Gabon and Togo.[98]

Yascha Mounk, a lecturer on political theory at Harvard, and Roberto Stefan Foa, a political scientist at the University of Melbourne in Australia, developed a stress test to detect how susceptible democracies are to massive failures. Among other categories, they rate public support for continued democracy, whether citizens support nondemocratic forms of government such as military rule and whether "anti-system parties and movements" are gaining strength by insisting that the government is illegitimate. If support for democracy plummets as the other measures rise, the two professors say, a country is "deconsolidating," a kind of low-grade fever that can lead to a full-blown crisis.[99]

Their theory has drawn criticisms, however. Ronald Inglehart, a political scientist at the University of Michigan, has questioned whether Mounk and Foa's methods truly signal democracy's long-term decline.[100]

Along with Stanford University's Diamond, Mounk and Foa say that if nations intend to stop the slide into authoritarianism, politicians and voters must work to counter anti-democratic forces. "In countries where populists have not yet taken power, radical reforms are needed to counteract the social and economic drivers of democratic deconsolidation," Mounk and Foa write. "Establishment politicians with a real commitment to liberal democracy may be more likely to undertake these reforms — and to disregard the protestations of interest groups that oppose them — when they are afraid that anti-system parties are about to take power. In that sense, the dangerous age of populism may harbor an opportunity for righting the ship of state after all."[101]

In his book *The Despot's Accomplice*, Klaas offers 10 principles for promoting democracy and steering foundering democracies and autocracies to freedom. Two involve thinking long-term and not trying to impose democracy through war.[102]

The world's democracies, he suggested, might also establish a "League of Democracies," a sort of U.N. for free trade in which members would be required to support democratic norms.[103]

Diamond says the United States can support ailing democracies by supporting a foreign policy that is not necessarily interventionist but "calls out regressions from democratic norms and standards."

NOTES

1. Virginia Lopez, "On the Frontline of Venezuela's Punishing Protests," *The Guardian*, May 25, 2017, https://tinyurl.com/yaonchdc.

2. Larry Diamond, *In Search of Democracy* (2015). Also see Larry Diamond and Leonardo Morlino, "The Quality of Democracy: An Overview," *Journal of Democracy*, October 2004, https://tinyurl.com/ycspherk.

3. "Freedom in the World 2017," Freedom House, 2017, https://tinyurl.com/ybvxftur.

4. "Middle East and North Africa," Freedom House, undated, https://tinyurl.com/ktav62d. "Freedom in the World 2017: Egypt," Freedom House, 2017, https://tinyurl.com/yd4uucmw.

5. "Freedom in the World 2017: Russia," Freedom House, 2017, https://tinyurl.com/yd7nsu64.

6. Daniel McLaughlin, "EU rebels Hungary and Poland reaffirm anti-immigrant alliance," *The Irish Times*, Sept. 22, 2017, http://tinyurl.com/y8uvtll3.

7. "Death toll continues to rise in Duterte's war on drugs," Al-Jazeera, Aug. 17, 2017, https://tinyurl.com/y785wbb5. Also see David Sanger and Maggie Haberman, "Trump Praises Duterte for Philippine Drug Crackdown in Call Transcript," *The New York Times*, May 23, 2017, https://tinyurl.com/ydeqvrjd.

8. Kareem Shaheen, "Erdogan to continue crackdown as Turkey marks failed coup," *The Guardian*, July 16, 2017, https://tinyurl.com/y9tbaudp.

9. Vincent Bevins, "It's not just Burma: Human rights are under attack across Southeast Asia, advocates say," *The Washington Post*, Sept. 8, 2017, http://tinyurl.com/y9edl8ht. "Rohingya refugee crisis a 'human rights nightmare,' UN chief tells Security Council," UN News Centre, Sept. 28, 2017, http://tinyurl.com/ybc653fr.

10. Sarah Bush, "Democracy promotion is failing. Here's why," *The Washington Post*, Nov. 9, 2015, https://tinyurl.com/y99j57o6. Prak Chan Thul, "Cambodia accuses U.S. of political interference, calls US democracy 'bloody and brutal,'" Reuters, Aug. 23, 2017, http://tinyurl.com/ycxy28ow.

11. Joshua Kurlantzick, "The great democracy meltdown," *The New Republic*, May 19, 2011, https://tinyurl.com/y7vuqwmr. Also see Joshua Kurlantzick, "Why the 'China Model' Isn't Going Away," *The Atlantic*, March 21, 2013, https://tinyurl.com/y8bfkcdx.

12. Ibid.

13. Diamond, op. cit., pp. 8-9; Amanda Taub, "How Stable are Democracies? 'Warning Signs are Flashing Red,'" *The New York Times*, Nov. 29, 2016, https://tinyurl.com/yardxl9f.

14. Matt Schiavenza, "Could China's System Replace Democracy?" Asia Society, Jan. 19, 2017, https://tinyurl.com/ycxrwgf9.

15. Daniel A. Bell et al., "Is the China Model Better Than Democracy?" *Foreign Policy*, Oct 19, 2015, https://tinyurl.com/ybv3bo9m.

16. Daniel A. Bell, "Chinese Democracy Isn't Inevitable," *The Atlantic*, May 29, 2015, https://tinyurl.com/yc57z49o.

17. Schiavenza, op. cit.

18. Ibid.

19. Bell et al., op. cit.

20. Ibid.

21. Ibid.

22. Ibid.

23. "U.S. Department of State: Agency Financial Report, Fiscal Year 2016," U.S. Department of State, 2016, https://tinyurl.com/y7wntol7.

24. "Advancing Freedom and Democracy," U.S. Department of State, undated, https://www.state.gov/j/drl/rls/afdr/.

25. Krishnadev Calamur, "Trump's Plan for Afghanistan: No Timeline for Exit," *The Atlantic*, Aug. 21, 2017, https://tinyurl.com/y9bju64w.

26. Joshua Muravchik, "What Trump and Tillerson don't get about democracy promotion," *The Washington Post*, Aug. 4, 2017, https://tinyurl.com/ybrn23zr.

27. Pippa Norris, "Trump's Global Democracy Retreat," *The New York Times*, Sept. 7, 2017, http://tinyurl.com/yacwfrwf.

28. Alexandra Ulmer and David Lawder, "Trump slaps sanctions on Venezuela; Maduro sees effort to force default," Reuters, Aug. 25, 2017, https://tinyurl.com/y8upm87b.

29. Kelly Swanson, "Read: Trump's full speech to the UN General Assembly," *Vox*, Sept.19, 2017, https://tinyurl.com/yc9v6d8x.

30. Brian Klaas, *The Despot's Accomplice* (2017), p. 63.

31. Reuel Marc Gerecht, "The World Senses Our Wariness of Power," *The New York Times*, March 11, 2014, https://tinyurl.com/ycz7chve.

32. Norris, op. cit.

33. Stephen M. Walt, "Why Is America So Bad at Promoting Democracy in Other Countries?" *Foreign Policy*, April 25, 2016, https://tinyurl.com/h6ezfbc.

34. Bruce Fein, "Stop U.S. Democracy Promotion Abroad," *The Washington Times*, Dec. 24, 2014, https://tinyurl.com/pft962g.

35. Schiavenza, op. cit.

36. Jeffrey Ghannam, "Digital Media in the Arab World One Year After the Revolutions," Center for International Media Assistance, March 28, 2012, https://tinyurl.com/ydgqy5hy. Also see Zeynep Tufekci and Christopher Wilson, "Social Media and the Decision to Participate in Political Protest: Observations From Tahrir Square," *Journal of Communication*, 2012, pp. 363-379, https://tinyurl.com/ydee7g3c.

37. "Don't Call him, 'Dimon,'" Anti-Corruption Foundation, March 2, 2017, https://tinyurl.com/yd8opnjv.

38. Roland Oliphant, "Why are Russians protesting? The investigation accusing the prime minister of corruption that sparked biggest demonstrations in five years," *The Telegraph*, March 27, 2017, https://tinyurl.com/hfbjtsx; Svetlana Reiter and Andrew Osborn, "Anti-Kremlin protesters fill Russian streets, Putin critic Navalny jailed," Reuters, June 11, 2017, https://tinyurl.com/y9dgpzty.

39. Amy Qin, "Liu Xiaobo's Death Pushes China's Censors Into Overdrive," *The New York Times*, July 17, 2017, https://tinyurl.com/y9mjvzhr. Also see Edward Wong, "China Blocks Web Access to 'Under the Dome' Documentary on Pollution," *The New York Times*, March 6, 2015, https://tinyurl.com/ycwsm4wd.

40. Tufekci and Wilson, op. cit.

41. Isaac Chotiner, "Has Protesting Become Too Easy?" *Slate*, May 8, 2017, https://tinyurl.com/lkdwz4j.

42. "Russia enacts 'draconian' law for bloggers and online media," BBC, Aug. 1, 2014, https://tinyurl.com/kakz67p.

43. Courtney C. Radsch, "Proposed German legislation threatens broad internet censorship," Committee to

Protect Journalists, April 20, 2017, https://tinyurl.com/yame2r5v. Also see "Germany approves plans to fine social media firms up to €50m," *The Guardian*, June 30, 2017, https://tinyurl.com/yb5gm4v6.

44. James T. Kloppenberg, *Toward Democracy: The Struggle for Self-Rule in European and American Thought* (2015), pp. 27-28.

45. Ibid., pp. 38-43.

46. Paul Cartledge, *Democracy: A Life* (2016), Kindle location 4835.

47. Kloppenberg, op. cit.

48. Norman Davies, *The Isles: A History* (1999), pp. 556-561.

49. "The American Revolution — A Documentary History," The Avalon Project, undated, https://tinyurl.com/y9zk7xfa.

50. Daniel Thurer and Thomas Burri, "Self-Determination," *Oxford Public International Law*, undated, https://tinyurl.com/japkzpu. See "Declaration of Independence: A Transcription," National Archives, https://tinyurl.com/h2zqchv.

51. Lyonette Louis-Jacques, "Influence of the U.S. Constitution Abroad," University of Chicago, Sept. 7, 2011, https://tinyurl.com/yce8cka3; Samuel Huntington, *The Third Wave* (1991), p. 17.

52. Huntington, ibid., p. 18.

53. Adolf Hitler, *Mein Kampf* (2017; originally published in 1925), p. 74.

54. "History of the Marshall Plan," George C. Marshall Foundation, undated, https://tinyurl.com/gwfcf9q.

55. Huntington, op. cit.

56. "History of the European Union," European Union, undated, https://tinyurl.com/gnmkpwy.

57. Frank Dikotter, "Mao's Great Leap to Famine," *The New York Times*, Dec. 15, 2010, https://tinyurl.com/36bpas8. Also see Austin Ramzy, "China's Cultural Revolution, Explained," *The New York Times*, May 14, 2016, https://tinyurl.com/y7xng7xq.

58. "Cold War," *Encyclopedia Britannica*, https://tinyurl.com/y8jaecb5.

59. Odd Arne Westad, *The Cold War: A World History* (2017).

60 Stephen Kotkin, *Uncivil Society: 1989 and the Implosion of the Communist Establishment* (2010).

61. Peter Robinson, "Tear Down This Wall," National Archives, Summer 2007, https://tinyurl.com/y783bcrr.

62. Liam Hoare, "Let's Please Stop Crediting Ronald Reagan for the Fall of the Berlin Wall," *The Atlantic*, Sept. 20, 2012, https://tinyurl.com/yauxsfuu.

63. Tony Judt, *Postwar: A History of Europe Since 1945* (2005).

64. Mary Elise Sarotte, *The Collapse: The Accidental Opening of the Berlin Wall* (2014).

65. Robert Service, *A History of Modern Russia*, 3rd ed. (2009), pp. 497-502.

66. "European Neighbourhood Policy and Enlargement Negotiations: From 6 to 28 members," European Commission, undated, https://tinyurl.com/y9dkdupy.

67. "Carter and Human Rights, 1977-1981," Department of State, https://tinyurl.com/l3jzkom.

68. Shiavenza, op. cit.

69. "Ben Hubbard and Rick Gladstone, "Arab Spring Countries Find Peace Is Harder Than Revolution," *The New York Times*, Aug. 14, 2013, https://tinyurl.com/yct5p6v3.

70. Amanda Taub, "The unsexy truth about why the Arab Spring failed," *Vox*, Jan. 27, 2016, https://tinyurl.com/ycmvkss2.

71. "Freedom in the World 2017: Russia," op. cit. Also see Steven Lee Myers and Ellen Barry, "Putin Reclaims Crimea for Russia and Bitterly Denounces the West," *The New York Times*, March 18, 2014, https://tinyurl.com/y9coml5z; Rebecca M. Nelson, "U.S. Sanctions and Russia's Economy," Congressional Research Service, Feb. 17, 2017, https://tinyurl.com/yc3npv7a; and Suzanne Sataline, "U.S.-Russia Relations," *CQ Researcher*, Jan. 13, 2017, pp. 25-48.

72. For background, see Corine Hegland, "European Union's Future," *CQ Researcher*, Dec. 16, 2016, pp. 1037-1060.

73. "Learn More About the Trump-Russia Imbroglio," NPR, https://tinyurl.com/y9klh6mg.

74. Matt Apuzzo and Michael S. Schmidt, "Comey Says Trump Pressured Him to 'Lift the Cloud' of Inquiry," *The New York Times*, June 7, 2017, https://tinyurl.com/y7ka9yhf; Rebecca R. Ruiz and Mark Landler, "Robert Mueller, former F.B.I. Director, Is Named Special Counsel for Russia Investigation," *The New York Times*, May 17, 2017, https://tinyurl.com/lq69yck.

75. "Full Transcript and Video: Trump's Speech on Afghanistan," *The New York Times*, Aug. 21, 2017, https://tinyurl.com/ybf9pn4o. Also see Bryant Harris et al., "The End of Foreign Aid as We Know It," *Foreign Policy*, April 24, 2017, https://tinyurl.com/yb5attfc.

76. For background, see Patrick Marshall, "Rethinking Foreign Aid," *CQ Researcher*, April 14, 2017, pp. 313-336.

77. Robbie Gramer, "Senate Panel Rejects Trump Plan for Cutting Foreign Assistance," *Foreign Policy*, Sept. 7, 2017, https://tinyurl.com/ybsa35qs.

78. Phillip Rucker, "Trump keeps praising international strongmen, alarming human rights advocates," *The Washington Post*, May 2, 2017, https://tinyurl.com/yavgtyj5.

79. Sudarsan Raghavan, "As Trump embraces Egypt's Sissi, abuses rise," *The Washington Post*, Aug. 31, 2017, https://tinyurl.com/y74j6kvo.

80. Ibid.; Joby Warrick, "A North Korean ship was seized off Egypt with a huge cache of weapons destined for a surprising buyer," *The Washington Post*, Oct. 1, 2017, https://tinyurl.com/y6va9v3l.

81. Adam Entous, Craig Timberg and Elizabeth Dwoskin, "Russians exploited social wedges," *The Washington Post*, Sept. 26, 2017, https://tinyurl.com/y838a7pz; Elizabeth Dwoskin, Adam Entous and Craig Timberg, "Google finds links to Russian disinformation in its services," *The Washington Post*, Oct. 10, 2017, https://tinyurl.com/ybtokgjo.

82. Ibid.

83. Anoosh Chakelian, "Rise of the Nationalists: A Guide to Europe's Far-Right Parties," *New Statesman*, March 8, 2017, https://tinyurl.com/z6pgcnb.

84. Anoosh Chakelian, "How Poland's government is weakening democracy," *The Economist*, July 25, 2017, https://tinyurl.com/yd939fpl. Also see Slawomir Sierakowski, "Poland Turns Away from Democracy, Thanks to the U.S.," *The New York Times*, July 24, 2017, https://tinyurl.com/ycr5te35.

85. Patrick Kingsley, "Over 1,000 People Are Detained in Raids in Turkey," *The New York Times*, April 26, 2017, https://tinyurl.com/mx43kex; Kareem Shaheen, "Turkish court hands down 40 life sentences over plot to kill Erdogan," *The Guardian*, Oct. 4, 2017, https://tinyurl.com/y8ppq56g; and Patrick Kingsley, "Erdogan Claims Vast Powers in Turkey After Narrow Victory in Referendum," *The New York Times*, April 16, 2017, https://tinyurl.com/k9nbhgf.

86. "Freedom House 2017: Russia," op. cit. "America's new economic sanctions may hurt Russia's recovery," *The Economist*, Aug. 5, 2017, https://tinyurl.com/y86so3h9.

87. Website of Alexei Navalny, https://navalny.com; Alexandra Sims, "Vladimir Putin signs law allowing Russia to ignore international human rights rulings," *The Independent*, Dec. 15, 2015, https://tinyurl.com/ose44fc.

88. "Philippines: Duterte Threatens Human Rights Community," Human Rights Watch, Aug. 17, 2017, https://tinyurl.com/y8vr2f8k; "Freedom in the World 2017: Philippines," Freedom House, 2017, https://tinyurl.com/ydycf84q. Also see Sanger and Haberman, op. cit.

89. William H. Overholdt, "Duterte, democracy and defense," Brookings Institution, Jan. 31, 2017, https://tinyurl.com/jjddgrc.

90. Aung San Suu Kyi is the state counselor, a position akin to a prime minister; For background, see Robert Kiener, "Myanmar's New Era," *CQ Global Researcher*, July 17, 2012, pp. 329-352.

91. Sarah Wildman," Aung San Suu Kyi's disappointing speech about Myanmar's humanitarian catastrophe," *Vox*, Sept. 19, 2017, https://tinyurl.com/ycamrogx; Niharika Mandhana and James Hookway, "Behind the Silence of Myanmar's Aung San Suu Kyi," *The New York Times*, Oct. 6, 2017, https://tinyurl.com/y9x3cpka.

92. "Kenya's Supreme Court criticises IEBC electoral commission," BBC News, Sept. 20, 2017, https://tinyurl.com/y88cdzh3.

93. Marcus Walker, "Austria's Right-Wing Parties Enjoy Strong Showing in Parliamentary Elections," *The Wall Street Journal*, Oct. 16, 2017, https://tinyurl.com/yac4ajea.

94. Bevins, op. cit.

95. Michael Pillsbury, *The Hundred-Year Marathon: China's Secret Strategy to Replace America as the Global Superpower* (2015), chp. 9. Also see Larry Diamond, Marc F. Plattner and Christopher Walker, eds., *Authoritarianism Goes Global: The Challenge to Democracy* (2016).

96. Andrew J. Nathan, "China's Challenge," in *Authoritarianism Goes Global*, ibid., pp. 23-29.

97. "Freedom in the World 2017: Populists and Autocrats: The Dual Threat to Global Democracy," Freedom House, 2017, https://tinyurl.com/jkyw8ta.

98. Brian Klaas, "Throw the bums out, African edition," *The Washington Post*, July 28, 2017, https://tinyurl.com/ycg9kwbb.

99. Amanda Taub, "How Stable Are Democracies? 'Warning Signs Are Flashing Red,'" op. cit. Also see Roberto Stefan Foa and Yascha Mounk, "The Signs of Deconsolidation," *Journal of Democracy*, January 2017, https://tinyurl.com/y77roe6q.

100. Ronald Inglehart, "The Danger of Deconsolidation: How Much Should We Worry?" *Journal of Democracy*, July 2016, https://tinyurl.com/hghco7a.

101. Foa and Mounk, op. cit.

102. Klaas, *The Despot's Accomplice*, op. cit.

103. Ibid., pp. 152-154.

BIBLIOGRAPHY

Selected Sources

Books

Cartledge, Paul, *Democracy: A Life*, Oxford University Press, 2016.
An authority on ancient Greek culture traces the rudiments of modern democratic society.

Diamond, Larry, *In Search of Democracy*, Routledge, 2016.
One of the world's leading scholars on democracy presents a compendium of articles by him or others evaluating the status and prospects for democracy around the world.

Diamond, Larry, Marc F. Plattner and Christopher Walker, *Authoritarianism Goes Global: The Challenge to Democracy*, Journal of Democracy, 2016.
This collection of journal articles outlines the rise of authoritarianism worldwide.

Klaas, Brian, *The Despot's Accomplice: How the West Is Aiding and Abetting the Decline of Democracy*, Oxford University Press, 2017.
An American political scientist argues that the West has been responsible for the destruction of democracy through careless and narrow-minded foreign policies.

Kloppenberg, James T., *Toward Democracy: The Struggles for Self-Rule in European and American Thought*, Oxford University Press, 2016.
A Harvard historian describes how ideas about self-governing changed over time on both sides of the Atlantic.

Articles

"What's gone wrong with democracy?" *The Economist*, March 1, 2014, https://tinyurl.com/mhsl5pm.
A British business publication reports on democracy's worldwide setbacks.

Filkins, Dexter, "Turkey's Thirty-Year Coup," *The New Yorker*, Oct. 17, 2016, https://tinyurl.com/jq7u9t3.
A veteran reporter explains how a political rivalry between two men helped Turkey tumble from democracy to authoritarianism.

Fisher, Max, and Amanda Taub, "How Venezuela Stumbled to the Brink of Collapse," *The New York Times*, May 14, 2017, https://tinyurl.com/nyuxkrq.
This clear, concise primer describes how Venezuela's oil-rich economy collapsed into bedlam.

Taub, Amanda, "How Stable Are Democracies? 'Warning Signs Are Flashing Red,'" *The New York Times*, Nov. 29, 2016, https://tinyurl.com/y99jqdw3.
A reporter analyzes a government scholar's argument that liberal democracies worldwide may be at risk of decline.

Traub, James, "The Party That Wants to Make Poland Great Again," *The New York Times Magazine,* **Nov. 2, 2016, https://tinyurl.com/ya4899rc.**
A journalist explores how Poland, which resisted Soviet communism, came to embrace authoritarianism.

Reports and Studies

"The Brookings Democracy Dashboard," The Brookings Institution, June 2, 2016, https://tinyurl .com/y8dg4b5m.
A Washington think tank offers data to evaluate political systems and government performance in the United States.

"Democracy Index 2016," The Economist Intelligence Unit, *The Economist,* **accessed on Aug. 29, 2017, https://tinyurl.com/j8tydf2.**
A British business publication ranks countries by their civil liberties and the openness of their electoral processes.

"Freedom in the World 2017: Populists and Autocrats: The Dual Threat to Global Democracy," Freedom House, January 2017, https://tinyurl.com/jkyw8ta.
A nonprofit that annually tracks rights and civil liberties worldwide finds that populist and nationalist forces have grown, as has authoritarianism.

Felter, Claire, and Danielle Renwick, "Venezuela in Crisis," Council on Foreign Relations, Aug. 1, 2017, https://tinyurl.com/y7dhj64d.
A New York think tank provides background on the status of governance in South America's oldest democracy.

Foa, Roberto Stefan, and Yascha Mounk, "The Signs of Deconsolidation," *Journal of Democracy,* **January 2017, http://tinyurl.com/y7voh95z.**
Political scholars argue that young people globally are less invested in democracy than their elders, skeptical of liberal institutions and in search of strong leaders.

Lawson, Marian L., and Susan B. Epstein, "Democracy Promotion: An Objective of U.S. Foreign Assistance," Congressional Research Service, May 31, 2017, https://tinyurl.com/yal89sx3.
Congress' research arm says lawmakers continue to debate the effectiveness and appropriateness of democracy promotion assistance.

Pomerantsev, Peter, and Michael Weiss, "The Menace of Unreality: How the Kremlin Weaponizes Information, Culture and Money," *The Interpreter,* **Institute of Modern Russia, November 2014, http://tinyurl.com/khfg2rp.**
Journalists assess how state-sponsored hacking and disinformation create scandal and sow doubts about democratic politics.

For More Information

Brookings Institution, 1775 Massachusetts Ave., N.W., Washington, DC 20036; 202-797-6000; www.brookings .edu. A think tank that researches domestic and international issues.

Carnegie Endowment for International Peace, 1779 Massachusetts Ave., N.W., Washington, DC 20036; 202-483-7600; www.ceip.org. An international affairs research organization that reports on the health of democracies and the rule of law.

Center on Democracy, Development, and the Rule of Law, Freeman Spogli Institute for International Studies, Encina Hall, 616 Serra St C100, Stanford University, Stanford,

CA 94305-6055; 650-723-4581; https://cddrl.fsi.stanford .edu. A research center that studies how countries can become prosperous and democratic.

Center for Strategic and International Studies, 1800 K St., N.W., Suite 400, Washington, DC 20006; 202-887-0200; www.csis.org. A nonpartisan think tank that evaluates democracy-promotion programs.

Council on Foreign Relations, The Harold Pratt House, 58 East 68th St., New York, NY 10065; 212-434-9400; www.cfr.org. A nonpartisan think tank that studies foreign policy choices facing the U.S. and other countries.

(Continued)

(Continued)

Freedom House, 1850 M St., N.W., 11th floor, Washington, DC 20036; 202-296-5101; https://freedomhouse.org. An independent watchdog group that researches and advocates for democracy, political freedom and human rights.

National Endowment for Democracy, 1101 15th St., N.W., Suite 700, Washington, DC 20005; 202-293-9072; www.ned.org. A foundation financed largely by Congress that funds groups abroad working for democratic goals.

8

European Union's Future

Corine Hegland

Getty Images/Anadolu Agency/Mustafa Yalcin

Paris police intervene after fighting broke out on Nov. 20, 2016 between supporters of the Kurdistan Workers' Party (PKK) and Turks protesting the pro-independence organization. As the European Union approaches its 60th anniversary, numerous crises cloud its future, including an influx of unwanted refugees and immigrants, terrorist attacks and fast-growing populist movements.

From *CQ Researcher,*
December 16, 2017

For a European Union (EU) under siege, nothing comes easily these days. Not even a cruise on the Danube River.

In September 2016, the leaders of 27 EU member nations gathered in Bratislava, Slovakia, to discuss the organization's future after the anticipated departure of the 28th member, the United Kingdom (U.K.), whose citizens voted on June 23 to leave the Union. On the agenda were the economy, migration and terrorism, among other topics.

When lunchtime came, the presidents, chancellors, premiers and other dignitaries boarded a riverboat for a cruise on the Danube, only to discover when it was time to go ashore that the boat could not dock. The river was too low, and they were stuck on board.[1]

Observers wryly noted that the leaders' plight was an apt metaphor for a European Union that is struggling with deep problems ranging from growing political divisions to economic malaise.

Among EU members, "there is a feeling of being stuck, or moving at a very slow pace," says Janis Emmanouilidis, director of studies at the European Policy Centre, an independent think tank in Brussels working for a more unified Europe.

As the European Union — a political and economic entity representing 28 of the continent's 50 nations — marked its 60th anniversary in March 2017, it faced serious questions over whether it is cohesive and nimble enough to grapple with the centrifugal forces threatening to tear it apart.

"Our European Union is, at least in part, in an existential crisis," said Jean-Claude Juncker, president of the EU's executive and

EU Membership Has Nearly Quintupled

The EU has grown from six members in 1957 to 28 nations today and 500 million constituents. It has a single market with free movement of goods, services, capital and people, and 19 of its countries share a common currency. Brussels is the EU's capital, but various EU institutions (below) are scattered throughout Europe.

EU Member Nations and Countries Seeking to Join

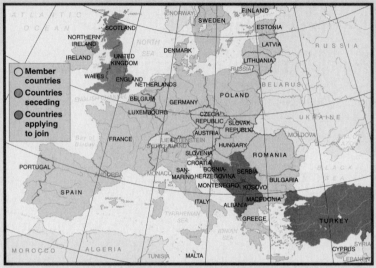

Major EU Institutions

European Council (Brussels) — Made up of member nations' heads of state who meet in summits, usually quarterly. Sets the EU policy agenda by providing strategic and political guidance to various branches, including the European Commission. Elects its own president, who serves for two and a half years.

European Commission (Brussels) — Proposes legislation to implement the European Council's strategic guidance. Each member state appoints one commissioner for a five-year term. Proposed legislation is reviewed by national parliaments; if enough national parliaments object, then the commission must reconsider the proposal before passage.

European Parliament (Brussels; Luxembourg; and Strasbourg, France) — Together with the European Parliament, considers whether to adopt European Commission proposals. Has up to 751 members, elected by EU citizens every five years. Each state has a minimum of six seats and a maximum of 96.

Council of the European Union (Brussels) — Consists of the ministers from EU member nations; helps coordinate agriculture, trade and other policies.

European Court of Justice (Luxembourg) — Responsible for interpreting EU law and ensuring it is implemented uniformly. Consists of one judge from each EU country.

European Central Bank (Frankfurt) — The main bank for the 19 countries that share the euro is charged only with keeping prices stable.

Source: "EU Institutions in Brief," European Union, http://tinyurl.com/hcgrevz

administrative branch, the European Commission, during his 2016 State of the Union address.[2] "It is as if there is almost no intersection between the EU and its national capitals anymore."

The European Union is struggling with numerous immediate crises, including troubled economies, unwanted refugees, terrorist attacks and fast-growing populist movements that have secured some impressive electoral victories. The EU also faces long-term strategic difficulties, including internal political divisions and a newly aggressive Russia that annexed part of the Ukraine in 2014, the year the EU neighbor took steps to join the Union. Its most pressing challenge, however, might be Europeans' rising skepticism of the EU itself.

Only 42 percent of Europeans trust the EU, according to the 2017 European Union survey.[3] A Pew Research Center Survey found that the vast majority of Europeans disapprove of how the Union is handling economic and immigration issues, and just 51 percent of Europeans have a favorable view of the EU.[4]

Europe's sluggish economy is one factor fueling this unhappiness. Although growth has recently ticked up, unemployment in the eurozone — the 19 EU states that use the euro currency — is 8.1 percent; youth unemployment is 18.7 percent, but it tops 35 percent in Greece, Spain and Italy.[5]

Another factor is the refugee crisis, which began in 2015 and triggered a backlash against the EU's open-borders policies and its demands that each member country admit a share of the refugees.[6] More than 1 million refugees, many from war-torn Syria, and other immigrants have made perilous sea journeys from Turkey and Northern Africa to arrive in what they hoped would be the safe haven of Europe.[7]

At the same time, Islamic extremists carried out horrific terrorist attacks in France, Belgium and Germany, killing more than 240 people and further hardening attitudes toward the predominantly Muslim refugees. Although the migration wave slowed throughout most of 2016 and 2017, the EU still hasn't reached agreement on what to do.

Republican Donald Trump's surprise victory in the U.S. presidential election, meanwhile, emboldened populist groups across Europe, many of which oppose the EU. Most of the populist groups haven't achieved power, but in several countries, including the EU's powerhouse of Germany, they have siphoned off enough votes to weaken mainstream, pro-EU parties.[8]

Headquartered in Brussels, the EU was one of the world's first supranational organizations, meaning its power transcends national governments. The original purpose of the Union, whose predecessor organization was founded in the aftermath of World War II, was to prevent war in Europe by drawing nations into what the founding treaty called an "ever-closer union," based on the member nations' evolving mutual interests.[9]

Members maintain their sovereignty, but they also agree to transfer to Brussels authority over some policies, including agriculture, imports and exports, fisheries and the rules governing the functioning of the Union's single market. Many decisions require significant, if not unanimous, support across the EU's diverse member nations.

In the last six decades, the EU and its predecessor organizations have seen their dominion spread from six countries to 28, and from a common market in coal and steel to a shared currency and a single market with free movement of goods, services, capital and people

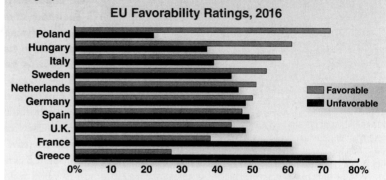

Skepticism of EU Rising

Support for the European Union is dropping among its largest member states, according to the Pew Research Center. Greeks have the most negative view of the EU and the French the second most. Support is highest in two former communist states, Poland and Hungary.

EU Favorability Ratings, 2016

Poland, Hungary, Italy, Sweden, Netherlands, Germany, Spain, U.K., France, Greece

■ Favorable
■ Unfavorable

Source: "Euroskepticism Beyond Brexit," Pew Research Center, June 7, 2016, http://tinyurl.com/j32cpnf

that covers much of the continent. Growth has been especially fast in the 26 years since the Soviet Union's dissolution, with the number of member states doubling as former communist nations from Eastern and Central Europe joined the democracies of the West. The European Union now has 500 million constituents and is governed by seven major institutions with 55,000 civil servants.[10]

A central irony is that Europe's successful integration and expansion — designed to prevent bickering among European nations — has led to some of the region's political divisions. "We set some very ambitious goals, fulfilled them, and now we are facing the aftermath of that ambition," says Pierre Vimont, a former senior French and EU diplomat who is a senior fellow with Carnegie Europe, a division of the Carnegie Endowment for International Peace think tank.

In addition to divisions between wealthier northern states and the poorer southern states, the EU is struggling with a split between mainstream parties that support a stronger central authority in Brussels and populist parties that want power returned to national capitals. The Union's rapid expansion into eastern Europe has

The Polish seaport of Gdynia on the Baltic Sea is a hive of activity for container ships and ferryboats. The EU's single market removes all trade barriers among member states and allows free movement of goods. Support for the European Union among EU members is highest in the former communist states of Hungary and Poland, both of which receive billions of euros from the EU annually for development projects.

also exposed fault lines between the EU's liberal democratic pillars and the illiberal, if not authoritarian, tendencies of some new democracies, particularly Hungary and Poland, which, together with Slovakia and the Czech Republic, are known as the "Visegrad Group."[11]

"When you look at the political climate in the current EU, you get the sense that the community spirit has been seriously weakened" as countries act in their own, rather than the communal interest, says Josef Janning, a senior policy fellow at the European Council on Foreign Relations, a think tank headquartered in London, and the head of its Berlin office. "The political culture is dominated by national interests."

In June 2016, the United Kingdom, one of the EU's largest members, stunned many by voting to leave the Union in a decision popularly known as Brexit. "Obsessed with the idea of instant and total integration, we failed to notice that ordinary people, the citizens of Europe, do not share our Euro-enthusiasm," said Donald Tusk, president of the EU's European Council.[12]

EU leaders face an unpalatable choice, analysts say. They can move aggressively to solve the Union's problems and risk further alienating Europeans who are unhappy with what they see as Brussels' heavy-handed ways, or they can do little and let problems fester.

"Everybody is looking at how to go with what exists already and prevent it from faltering," says Vimont. "If we can make some progress here and there on the different issues, that would be great. But to go further than that . . . and try to go for a more integrated and federal Europe seems out of the question now."

The leaders who met in Bratislava in September 2016 settled for declaring that "the EU is not perfect but it is the best instrument we have for addressing the new challenges we are facing," and they vowed to offer "a vision of an attractive EU [that citizens] can trust and support."[13]

They did offer a few brief specifics, such as deploying the European Border and Coast Guard to protect the Union's external borders and conducting more-comprehensive security checks on travelers. But most of the agenda was deferred for later.

As political leaders, academics and others ponder the EU's future, here are some of the questions they are debating:

Can the European Union survive growing populism?

Trump's win in the U.S. presidential election drew measured responses from many EU leaders, but Europe's populists were jubilant. France's populist leader, Marine Le Pen of the National Front, hailed Trump's election and the U.K.'s Brexit vote as "democratic choices that bury the old order and [provide] stepping stones to building tomorrow's world."[14] Le Pen harnessed discontent with the status quo to finish a once-unthinkable second in the 2017 French presidential elections.[15]

The National Front and its counterpart in the Netherlands, the Dutch Party for Freedom, which is the second largest party in the Dutch House of Representatives, advocate Brexit-style referenda.[16] In other parts of Europe, populist groups tend to be more interested in reforming the EU and ensuring that certain powers, such as control over borders, "are given back to the nation states," says Sarah de Lange, a political science professor at the University of Amsterdam.

Populism is an amorphous term, but it generally means delineating the interests of the "pure people" from those of the "corrupt elite," and it holds that "politics should be an expression of the general will of the people," according to Cas Mudde, an associate professor at the University of Georgia's School of Public and International Affairs. The pure people tend to be whomever agrees with the populists. Such a definition has ramifications for Europe's liberal democracies, wrote Mudde. "Populism is not necessarily anti-democratic, [but] it is essentially illiberal . . . in its disregard for minority rights, pluralism and the rule of law."[17]

President Obama offered a similar assessment while visiting Greece in mid-November 2016, saying that Americans, Europeans and others "have to guard against a rise in a crude sort of nationalism . . . or tribalism" taking root amid populist movements.[18]

In the former communist states of Hungary and Poland, both of which receive billions of euros from the EU each year for development projects and other types of aid, populists have full political control and have proudly donned the "illiberal" badge. Hungarian Prime Minister Viktor Orbán came to power in 2010 and began reducing the independence of the country's judiciary, media and civil-society organizations. "We have to abandon liberal methods and principles of organizing a society," Orbán said in 2014.[19]

The populist Law and Justice Party took office in Poland in 2015 and followed Hungary's path. Its leader, Jaroslaw Kaczyński, has boasted with Orbán about leading a "cultural counter-revolution" in predominantly Christian Europe based on national and religious identities.[20]

Orbán is trying to position himself as Europe's populist leader, according to Péter Krekó, the director of the Political Capital Policy Research and Consulting Institute, a think tank in Hungary. In October 2016, Orbán backed a national referendum calling on Hungary to reject a European Union law requiring member states to accept a quota of refugees.[21]

That controversial referendum — Orbán claimed victory but foes said not enough people voted to make the outcome valid — wasn't just for Orbán's domestic constituents, Krekó says, but for all European electorates with immigration anxieties, including those in France, the Netherlands, Austria and Germany. Orbán "hopes that his time will come and he can be a leader of the populist forces in Europe," he says.

But populists don't need to win power outright to threaten the future of the EU. Their rising strength pushes the mainstream parties further from their pro-EU

consensus, said Charles Grant, director of the Centre for European Reform think tank in London. "The centrist politicians who run nearly every EU member-state are now on the defensive against the populists who oppose them and the EU," he wrote.[22]

The populists are part of governing coalitions in several countries, including Switzerland, Finland, Latvia, Lithuania and Norway, and they challenged centrist parties in EU heavyweights Germany, France, Italy and the Netherlands in 2017 elections. The populists lost badly in France, but they gained seats in Germany and the Netherlands; in Italy, meanwhile, even the mainstream parties have begun campaigning on populist economic themes such as exiting the euro and raising the deficit.[23]

Widespread populism makes it "even more difficult to agree at the European level because the governments are under pressure" to respond to national populists, says the European Policy Centre's Emmanouilidis, citing the euro and migration crises as examples of problems in need of European-level agreements.

The mainstream parties are "still the majority in most European parliaments," says Stefan Lehne, a visiting scholar at Carnegie Europe and a former Austrian and EU diplomat. But in competition with the populist parties, they tend to "take on some of the parties' messages, so they are infected to some extent."

Lehne says populists tend to moderate their stances when they come to power. Finland's populist Finns group, for example, "became much more moderate once they joined the government," he says, as did the left-wing Greek Syriza party. Lehne has advocated that the EU bring populists into the mainstream when they come into power; directly address the issues, such as migration, that motivate populists and become more responsive to citizens.[24]

But de Lange says her research suggests that although populists might moderate their behavior while in power, they return to their base messaging as soon as they leave office.[25] Populism is now a "permanent feature of European politics," she says.

Can the euro survive without stronger centralized fiscal and banking authorities?

In 2015, the presidents of the five main European Union institutions called for currency reform, stating that the euro today is "like a house that was built over decades but only partially finished."

EU Unemployment Remains High

The European Union's jobless rate was 8.3 percent in October — much higher than the U.S. rate of 4.9 percent. The rate was far higher among the EU's southern members: 23.4 percent in Greece, 19.2 percent in Spain and 11.6 percent in Italy. All of these rates are down from a 2013 peak, when EU joblessness reached 10.9 percent following Europe's 2009 financial crisis.

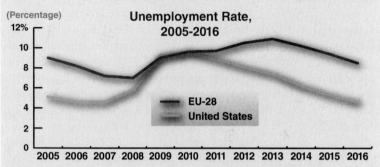

Unemployment Rate, 2005-2016

(Percentage)

— EU-28
— United States

Sources: "Euro area unemployment at 9.8%," EuroStat, Dec. 1, 2016, http://tinyurl.com/j4jmypd; "Labor Force Statistics from the Current Population Survey: Unemployment Rate," Bureau of Labor Statistics, November 2016, http://tinyurl.com/3gss8qd

Although the house's walls and roof were quickly stabilized during the euro crisis that began in 2009, the report said it is now "high time to reinforce its foundations" by completing Europe's economic and monetary union with stronger banking and fiscal powers.[26]

The 2009 crisis started when a new Greek government admitted that its debts were far higher than the previous government had acknowledged.[27] Concern over Greece's ability to meet its obligations soon spilled over to the heavily indebted EU states of Portugal, Ireland and Spain, and then to many European banks, which were holding the sovereign debt of the troubled countries. Several countries needed bailouts from the predominantly northern, wealthier countries, but their creditors, led by Germany, insisted on deeply unpopular austerity programs.

While the United States has mostly overcome the 2007–2009 recession, much of the eurozone only recently emerged into a fragile recovery, with high unemployment and low growth in some countries, particularly in the south. Gross domestic product (GDP) — the value of all the goods and services produced

within a given period — in the eurozone didn't return to 2008 levels until 2015.[28] Greece, in particular, is in desperate straits, with youth unemployment of nearly 50 percent and debts of nearly 310 billion euros (about $332 billion).[29]

"I do not think the eurozone has a bright future," says Steven Woolfe, the European Parliament member for northwest England and, until recently, a spokesman for the populist United Kingdom Independence Party (UKIP). But because the monetary union is a critical part of the "EU elites' dream of a federal, united states of Europe," he says, it will continue to exist, but "to the detriment of many European nations such as Greece."

Euro supporters blame the EU's fiscal structure for the problems, because it offers a currency union without a fiscal or banking union. "The economic and monetary union was half-baked," says Carnegie Europe's Vimont. "We knew it from the beginning; it was a compromise" to begin with the currency and trust that as it gained momentum, countries would take the further fiscal and banking integration steps necessary to complete the Union.

Sharing a currency without a full fiscal and banking union means that eurozone countries have a common interest rate, but each individual country is responsible for its own taxes, borrowing, expenditures and banking.

"If you are all under the same interest rate but doing completely different things with the money at your disposal, the whole thing will fall apart," says Jan Techau, director of the Richard C. Holbrooke Forum, a diplomatic initiative of the American Academy in Berlin.

"The euro can either go toward full political integration," meaning a fiscal union with authority over spending, taxation and debt to complement the existing economic integration, "or we lose the currency," says Techau. Either option represents an "earthquake," he says.

A true fiscal union would allow a grand bargain, European economists say, in which national parliaments would transfer some of their budget powers to the EU. A eurozone authority would set the size of each country's budget, including how much money it can borrow. In return, the authority could issue joint debt instruments such as bonds. Without such a bargain, however, the more affluent northern states are unwilling to sign up for mutual debts that could result in them subsidizing the poorer southern states that the northern states view as fiscally irresponsible.[30]

Although the parameters of a grand bargain are generally understood, how to implement it is not, says the European Council on Foreign Relations' Janning: "It is unclear to me what sort of crisis would be needed to get the actors to take the plans they have out of their drawers and actually discuss them."

Others say the euro can survive without further integration if policymakers simply make better choices. One example, says Charles Grant, director of the Centre for European Reform, a London think tank that advocates for a more effective EU, is to partially forgive Greek debts.[31]

The German-led austerity measures, which require eurozone countries to cut public spending even when their economies are struggling, need to be "softened," Grant said, to avoid "deflation, shrinking economies and growing debt burdens." Greece, Italy and France, among others, must implement structural changes, he said, such as reforming workforce policies, to make their economies competitive. And Germany needs to "rebalance its own economy," Grant continued, by increasing investment and domestic consumption.[32]

Even without full integration, "there is still a very broad commitment to keep the euro alive," says Carnegie Europe's Lehne. He points to the reforms enacted during the debt crisis, including an expansion of European Central Bank powers and an EU-based emergency fund, as evidence that the eurozone can come together to avoid collapse.

Sebastian Dullien, a senior policy fellow at the European Council on Foreign Relations and a professor of international economics at HTW Berlin, a public university in Berlin, says one impediment to stabilizing the euro through centralized authority is the "fear of transfers [of money] from rich countries to poor countries."

"How catastrophic is it to not see the first-best solutions?" asks Dullien. "I don't know." If everything goes smoothly, he says, the problems might dissipate as the system stabilizes and banks begin earning profits again. However, if something big happens sparking a crisis in another eurozone country — such as a populist party doing well enough in the polls to threaten a referendum on leaving the EU — that could spark capital flight from that country's banks, for which "Europe is not very well prepared."

Does migration threaten EU cohesion?

Eighteen-year-old Arij fled war-torn Syria with one baby in her arms and another still in her belly. She and her husband paid traffickers to take them across the Mediterranean Sea to Greece, where they hoped to continue into the relative safety of northern Europe.

But in March 2016, Macedonia — on Greece's northern border — erected a barbed-wire fence, trapping thousands of migrants in an overwhelmed Greece. For the last two months of her pregnancy, Arij told the International Federation of Red Cross and Red Crescent Societies she and her family were stuck in a shelter where "we had to sleep on the stone floor with only one blanket for the whole family. When it rained, we all got soaked."[33]

Arij and her family are just a few of the 61,000 migrants caught in Greece, waiting to find out whether the EU can decide what to do with the refugees and immigrants inside its borders.[34] More than 1 million others — over 660,000 in Germany alone — have asylum applications pending in EU countries.[35] In 2016, to stem the immigration flow, the European Union struck an agreement with Turkey, a non-EU member that borders Syria, in which the EU sends Turkey money to help migrants remain in Turkey.

Following the Turkey agreement, which coincided with the closing of Greece's northern border, the number of incoming migrants decreased from the 2015 peak of 6,000 a day, although more than 1,000 a day were still entering Europe in October 2016.[36] In 2017, the EU and the Italian government struck controversial, multifaceted agreements with a number of Libyan forces, including both the Navy and human traffickers, to prevent migrants in Libya, a significant portal for Northern African migrants, from crossing to Italy.[37] The result was a dramatic drop in the number of arrivals in Italy, but the future of the agreements is uncertain. The UN has condemned the Libyan detention centers as "inhumane,"

Hundreds of refugees and migrants await security checks after crossing from Macedonia into Serbia. Europe's refugee crisis, which began in 2015, triggered a backlash against the EU's open-borders policies and its demand that each member country admit a share of the refugees. More than 1 million refugees, many from war-torn Syria, as well as migrants fleeing poverty, have made perilous sea journeys from Turkey and Northern Africa in hopes of finding safety in Europe.

and video of migrants being sold as slaves in Libya has sparked global outrage.[38]

No matter what Europe does, the "migrations will continue," says Carnegie Europe's Vimont. He says migrants fall into two categories. One group, like Arij, are fleeing violent conflicts and are often entitled to refugee protection under international law. Most are from Syria, Iraq and Afghanistan, and they tend to enter through Greece.

Those in the other group, he says, tend to be from Northern Africa and are usually considered "economic migrants" because they are fleeing poverty rather than war. They tend to enter the EU through Italy and generally are not entitled to refugee protection.[39] In both cases, Vimont says, the root drivers of the exodus will not abate soon. The EU does not yet have a functioning policy for either group of migrants. Economic migrants are supposed to go through the normal immigration process, while refugees fleeing war-torn countries are supposed to apply for asylum in the first EU country they enter. If their application is approved, they need to remain within that country for five years before they can legally move around the EU.[40]

But neither Greece nor Italy can cope with the influx. As a result, many migrants try to cross, undocumented,

through Europe's 26-country, border-free area known as the Schengen Area to reach the northern countries before claiming asylum or finding work. The enormous migration tide has caused a backlash throughout Europe, and at least six states have abrogated the Schengen Area agreement to erect barriers along their borders since 2015.[41]

After recent terrorist attacks in Paris, Brussels and Nice, Europeans "fear that the recent wave of refugees will mean more terrorism and fewer jobs," says Bruce Stokes, director of global economic attitudes at the Pew Research Center. He cites Pew's surveys of 10 EU countries, which found an "overwhelming belief that the EU has mishandled the refugee crisis."[42]

"Every single migrant poses a public security and terror risk," said Hungarian Prime Minister Orbán.[43]

In Germany, Chancellor Angela Merkel tried to get ahead of the crisis in 2015 by offering to process the asylum applications of any refugees who arrived in Germany; the ensuing backlash propelled the anti-immigration political party Alternatives for Germany in regional and national elections.[44]

Germany, France and Brussels have called for a joint response to the refugee crisis, arguing that member states must share the burden now falling on Greece and Italy, but the call has largely landed on deaf ears.[45] The European Union passed a law requiring members to accept a quota of refugees, but countries have not complied, and the EU has been unable to find another solution.

Part of Europe's paralysis on migration, according to Camino Mortera-Martinez, a migration specialist at the Centre for European Reform, is due to the fact that much of the Continent shares a common border within the Schengen Area, but it has no common agreement about who can enter Schengen. Individual countries dictate migration policy with respect to how and whether non-EU residents can settle within their country. "We cannot have a common border unless we have a common migration policy," she says.

Mortera-Martinez says she is confident that an agreement can be found on a migration policy "if the numbers don't go up." But in the worst-case scenario, she says, rising migration can "bring down the EU project altogether. If you continue having high numbers, if you continue showing that you are unable to control them, if populist parties get in, then you are heading for disintegration."

Others say migration is solvable. Countries that decline to accept EU-wide quotas of refugees could instead pay more money into a fund supporting the countries that accept refugees, while migrants who do not qualify for refugee status could be handled through national migration policies, says the Holbrooke Forum's Techau.

"The dirty little secret of the EU is that to forge agreement among 28 [members], you can buy compromises," he says. "I'm confident we can find a solution, [although] not in the next three to four months."

BACKGROUND

Fears of War

The European Union's origins can be traced to the horrors of World War II.

On May 8, 1945, fighting ended in the European theater with the unconditional surrender of German forces. But the victorious Allies — including the United States, United Kingdom and Soviet Union — presided over a continent in ruins. New technologies had enabled destruction on a scale never before seen in human history: Armies had bombed or burned entire cities, and more than 35 million people died.

In Greece, Hungary, Yugoslavia, Estonia, Latvia, Lithuania and Poland, between 5 percent and 15 percent of the populations were killed. Millions were exterminated in the Holocaust, including 6 million Jews.[46]

What's more, the Second World War had begun less than 30 years after the First World War, which had also devastated the Continent. Both conflagrations had grown from nationalist sparks, ignited in Germany and France, to envelop the entire globe. It wasn't at all clear that humanity would survive another such war, especially with the development of the nuclear bomb.

Europe, with American support, wanted to find a way to permanently supersede the national interests that had nearly destroyed the world.

"Europe will not be made all at once, or according to a single plan. It will be built through concrete achievements, which first create a de facto solidarity," Robert Schuman, the French foreign minister, said in proposing the EU's forerunner, the European Coal and Steel Community (ECSC). His 1950 speech is now celebrated as a milestone in the birth of the European Union.[47]

Schuman's proposal called for France and Germany to surrender their coal and steel production to the world's first supranational body, the ECSC. Coal and steel being vital components of war-making, "the solidarity in production thus established will make it plain that any war between France and Germany becomes not merely unthinkable, but materially impossible," said Schuman.[48]

In 1951, the Western democracies of Belgium, Luxembourg, Italy and the Netherlands joined France and West Germany in signing the Treaty of Paris that established the ECSC.[49] But by then, the backdrop was not only the ruins of World War II but also the burgeoning communist empire to the east. After World War II, the Americans, British and Soviets had agreed to divide Europe, with the Soviets claiming a swath of Eastern and Central European border nations as well as eastern Germany.

An "Iron Curtain" fell across the continent, as Winston Churchill famously declared in 1946, dividing democratic Western Europe from communist Eastern and Central Europe.[50] The movement of both people and information was curtailed; Berlin, the capital of Germany, was divided in two with first a barbed wire fence and later a wall.

A few months after Schuman proposed the economic union, the French prime minister, René Pleven, proposed a parallel military union, called the European Defense Community. The intention was to prevent West Germany from waging war again by placing its military under a supranational authority and to present a united military front to the communists, but the French parliament refused to ratify the treaty, and it collapsed.[51]

Instead, in 1955, West Germany joined the fledgling, then-14-member anti-communist North Atlantic Treaty Organization (NATO) with the United States. The Soviet Union responded by pulling the communist nations of Eastern and Central Europe into a defense alliance called the Warsaw Pact.

By 1957, with the Cold War well underway, the six members of the ECSC were ready to deepen their integration by adopting the Treaty of Rome. The treaty, which saw its 60th anniversary celebrations in March 2017, created the European Economic Community and the European common market by committing members

CHRONOLOGY

1940s–1950s *Europe splits into democratic and communist camps after World War II.*

1945 World War II ends, leaving Europe devastated. U.S., U.K. and Soviet Union divide Europe into democratic and communist spheres.

1951 Treaty of Paris establishes the European Coal and Steel Community, the EU's forerunner; France, West Germany, Italy, Luxembourg, Belgium and the Netherlands join.

1957 Treaty of Rome creates the European Economic Community (EEC) with a common market for agriculture, transport, customs and trade policies; France, West Germany, Italy, Luxembourg, Belgium and the Netherlands are signatories.

1970s–1980s *Common Market slips into stagflation, sparking new push for economic integration.*

1973 Britain, Denmark and Ireland join the EEC. . . . Greece joins in 1981.

1985 Schengen Agreement abolishes internal border controls among Belgium, France, Luxembourg, the Netherlands and West Germany; it now covers 22 EU states.

1986 Spain and Portugal join the EEC. . . . All 12 EEC members sign the Single European Act committing members to create a single market by 1992.

1990s Single European Act and the Cold War's end spur further integration.

1990-2000s East and West Germany reunify, bringing the former into the EEC.

1992 Maastricht Treaty, also known as the Treaty on European Union, replaces the EEC with the European Union and establishes the European Economic and Monetary Union, committing members to preparing for the euro currency.

1995 Austria, Finland and Sweden join the EU.

1997 Treaty of Amsterdam strengthens the European Parliament's role and streamlines decision-making.

1999 Euro introduced in 11 countries.

2000s–Present *EU expands as crises worsen.*

2001 Treaty of Nice improves EU procedures in preparation for expansion.

2004 Formerly communist Czech Republic, Estonia, Latvia, Lithuania, Hungary, Poland, Slovakia and Slovenia, plus Malta and Cyprus, join the EU. . . . Draft constitution for Europe signed, but French and Dutch voters reject it, forcing its abandonment.

2007 EU member states sign the Treaty of Lisbon, incorporating most of the draft constitution's changes. . . . Romania and Bulgaria join the EU.

2010 Investors become worried about the most heavily indebted eurozone countries: Greece, Ireland, Portugal and Spain. Greece and Ireland receive bailouts coupled to domestic austerity programs. . . . Populist Viktor Orbán becomes prime minister of Hungary.

2011 Global leaders fear a eurozone-wide debt crisis.

2012 EU enacts emergency measures to grapple with the eurozone debt crisis.

2013 Croatia joins the EU, increasing membership to 28.

2014 Russia annexes Crimean region of Ukraine, an EU neighbor, sparking fears of Russian aggression. Populist parties gain seats in European Parliament elections.

2015 Thousands of migrants enter Europe after dangerous sea crossings to Greece and Italy. Europe struggles to find a united response. . . . Terrorists kill 130 people in Paris.

2016 Terrorist bombings kill 32 in Brussels (March), increasing fears about immigration. . . . Britain votes to leave the EU over concerns about immigration and sovereignty (June). . . . European populists praise election of real estate mogul Donald Trump as U.S. president, hope it will boost their prospects (November). . . . Anti-EU forces help defeat a constitutional referendum in Italy (December).

to removing customs duties on one another's goods and establishing common agricultural, transport, customs and trade policies.[52] The signatories declared that they were "determined to lay the foundations of an ever closer union among the peoples of Europe."[53]

The Common Market, like the rest of Western Europe, boomed for the next 15 years, but by the 1970s it was in trouble. In 1973 the Organization of the Petroleum Exporting Countries retaliated against the United States for its support of Israel by halting oil shipments to the United States and cutting oil production. The world price for oil quadrupled, plunging much of the Western world into stagflation, a perilous combination of high inflation, high unemployment and low growth.

As stagflation settled in, the Common Market grew less common. Although tariff barriers remained nonexistent within the European Economic Community, economic woes led countries to steadily increase non-tariff barriers, such as protective rules and regulations designed to shelter domestic industries from foreign competitors.

The stagnant European Economic Community was losing credibility and suffering from "Eurosclerosis," when "politicians and academics alike lost faith in European institutions," according to EU scholar Andrew Moravcsik, a professor of politics at Princeton University.[54]

By then, the European Community had grown to 12 members. Denmark, Ireland and the U.K. joined on Jan. 1, 1973. Newly democratic Greece joined in 1981, and Spain and Portugal, similarly emerging from dictatorships, began talks but didn't complete the years-long accession process until 1986.

Single European Act

The problems of struggling economies and high unemployment weren't all that different from today, but the European Community of the 1980s responded with a major integration drive.

"It took almost a decade for things to get moving again," says the European Policy Centre's Emmanouilidis. Since the European Community was much looser than it is today, however, the path into deeper integration was easier to see: The community had no single market, single currency, Schengen Zone or political union.

"The agreement among member states was quite strong on the trajectory" toward an ever-closer Europe, but they had "secondary disagreements" about how to get there, says Janning of the European Council on Foreign Relations. In June 1983, German Chancellor Helmut Kohl chaired a summit at which European leaders recommitted themselves to integration and to several dormant proposals for how to achieve it, including plans for a single market and monetary union.[55]

The initial result was the 1986 Single European Act (SEA) in which leaders of the European Community agreed to "transform relations as a whole among the states into a European Union." The act committed 12 member states to creating the single market by removing all barriers to trade by 1992. It included more than 260 proposals to liberalize the market, instituting "an area without internal frontiers in which the free movement of goods, persons, services and capital is ensured" — the so-called four freedoms of the Common Market.[56]

The SEA also expanded the number of market-related policy arenas that would be decided by majority, rather than unanimous, votes, and strengthened the role of the European Parliament, which had been established in 1958 but wasn't directly elected until 1979.[57] The reforms greatly reduced an individual country's veto power.

Some European Community members were ready to establish a truly free-movement zone among their countries. In 1985, Belgium, France, Luxembourg, the Netherlands and West Germany signed an agreement near Schengen, Luxembourg, committing themselves to gradually abolish their internal border controls. The resulting Schengen Zone gradually expanded across 22 EU member countries and four non-EU members and was incorporated into the EU treaties in 1999.[58]

The Europe of 1992 was very different from the Europe of 1950. The Berlin Wall had fallen in 1989, allowing East and West Germany to begin the painful reunification process. The rest of the Iron Curtain fences were demolished during a wave of popular revolutions in 1989. After the collapse of the Soviet Union on Dec. 31, 1991, the former communist countries of Eastern and Central Europe were free to pursue the liberal democratic policies of the more affluent Western Europe.

U.K. Seeks a Smooth Exit From EU

"It's very difficult to see how we get there from here."

If Prime Minister Theresa May was hoping for a warm reception from European Union (EU) leaders over Britain's exit from the political and economic alliance, she was in for a rude awakening.

The European Council, an assembly of EU member states, gave May only five minutes to speak at the end of an hours-long dinner in October 2016. When she finally addressed the council at 1 a.m., her words were met with a chilly silence.[1]

Since the U.K. voted June 23 to leave the 28-member EU — a decision known as "Brexit" — the other members have resolved not to negotiate exit terms until Britain gives formal notice of its intention to quit and agrees on the amount of money it owes the EU — probably between 20 and 60 billion euros ($24–72 billion) to cover existing liabilities.[2]

In March 2017, Britain gave formal notice of its intention by initiating a mechanism in the 2009 Lisbon Treaty called Article 50. Once the provision was triggered, Britain had two years to reach an agreement with the EU on departure terms. Britain seeks a multiyear transition agreement ensuring the two parties have time to negotiate a new, permanent relationship. If it does not reach a departure agreement, Britain will be evicted from the EU, losing its largest trading partner overnight.

Because of the challenges ahead, May said she wants to begin pre-negotiations with the EU. For the same reason, however, EU leaders are determined to avoid early discussions. They believe that as the eviction date draws nearer, their negotiating hand becomes stronger.

Areas of negotiation include how much money Britain owes the EU under prior commitments; how much access, and under what conditions, Britain will have to the Union's single market; and how much freedom of movement EU and U.K. citizens will have.

In campaigning to leave the EU, Brexit supporters wanted to "ensure the U.K.'s future prosperity as a global trading, outward-looking nation and to leave the undemocratic EU institutions," says Steven Woolfe, a member of the European Parliament and former spokesman for migration for the United Kingdom Independence Party (UKIP), which pushed hard for Brexit.

The U.K. has been a member of the European Union and its predecessor, the European Community, for more than 40 years. Nearly half of Britain's exports go to the EU's single market, and the U.K. imports a little more than half of its goods and services from the EU.[3] Brexit's economic impact on the U.K., analysts say, will depend largely on how much access Britain maintains to the single market and what kind of trade deals it can strike outside of it.

If Britain departs both the European Union and the single market, it would essentially become like any other non-EU country, dependent on either a negotiated free-trade agreement or World Trade Organization rules to continue trading with the EU.

But in return, Brexit supporters say, Britain would regain full authority over its laws and borders, would no longer contribute to the EU budget and would be free to strike its own trade agreements with non-EU countries.[4]

The European Community members had risen to the challenge of the Single European Act, passing innumerable laws removing trade barriers and increasing trade. Perhaps more important, the European Community had successfully integrated the emergent democracies of Europe into its liberal democratic order.

"Considered in the sweep of history, what the Community has achieved in some 30 years is remarkable," then-British Foreign Secretary Douglas Hurd said in 1992. "In the aftermath of war it produced reconciliation. It has provided a framework within which a democratic reunited Germany could emerge. . . . The liberal principles of the Treaty of Rome have been the foundation for Western Europe's exceptional prosperity. This foundation will be strengthened by the single market."[59]

"We are leaving to become, once more, a fully sovereign and independent country," May said in October.[5]

Alternatively, Britain could seek a "soft" Brexit by negotiating to retain access to parts of the single market, likely in return for two concessions: The U.K. contributes to the EU budget and continues to allow EU citizens to move freely to the country.

Not wanting to undermine its negotiating position, the British government has declined to identify its priorities, but Brexit leaders say they hope Britain can limit EU immigration while retaining access to the single market. "Our policy is having our cake and eating it," Foreign Secretary Boris Johnson, a leader of the Brexit campaign, said in September 2016.[6]

A soft Brexit would benefit both Britain and the EU, according to economist Jonathan Portes, a research fellow at the National Institute of Economic and Social Research, a London think tank, and previous chief economist at the British Cabinet Office.

Sector-by-sector compromises that "preserved some degree of free movement of workers and a lot of the current trade access and integration make sense" economically, he says. Both immigration and access to the free market support an enormous swath of the British economy, Portes says. Still, he says, "it's very difficult to see how we get there from here."

The U.K. will continue to have close ties with Europe, the EU's Woolfe says. "We will work with them on all diplomatic and political challenges going forward. Brexit was never about isolationism," he says. "It was about being outward looking to the whole world — not just Europe. It is in the interests of both the U.K. and the EU to have an open, tariff-free relationship with each other."

— *Corine Hegland*

AFP/Getty Images/Daniel Leal-Olivas

Opponents of Britain's decision to leave the European Union — dubbed Brexit — demonstrate in London on Dec. 7, 2016 outside the U.K. Supreme Court, which is considering whether Parliament should vote on the issue.

---

[1] Rob Merrick, "EU Leaders Make Theresa May Wait Until 1am to Deliver Five-Minute Brexit Speech, Before Ignoring Her," *The Independent*, Oct. 21, 2016, http://tinyurl.com/hehbqu8.

[2] Alex Barker, "Britain Prepares Case to Cut Brexit Divorce Bill," *Financial Times*, Nov. 17, 2017, https://tinyurl.com/yd4bjp9m

[3] Andrew Walker, "UK and the EU: Trade and Economy," BBC News, May 31, 2016, http://tinyurl.com/hrhtfo6.

[4] Anthony Reuben, "Reality Check: How Much Does the EU Budget Cost the UK?" BBC News, April 5, 2016, http://tinyurl.com/gppqu5u.

[5] "Theresa May's Keynote Speech at Tory Conference in Full," *The Independent*, Oct. 5, 2016, http://tinyurl.com/zstqb56.

[6] Tom Newton Dunn, "We'll Have Our Cake and Eat it," *The Sun*, Sept. 30, 2016, http://tinyurl.com/zz6vojj.

Shortly after Hurd's remarks, he signed the Maastricht Treaty. It built on the success of the SEA to establish the political union of the modern European Union and the European Economic and Monetary Union, which required states to align their economic policies to support targets on inflation, deficits, debt, interest rates and exchange rates in preparation for the new currency in 1999.[60]

The day Maastricht took effect "lacked a certain pomp and circumstance compared with other historic breaks with the past, like the start of Robespierre's revolutionary calendar or Year Zero under Pol Pot," Edward Pilkington drily observed. "But Nov. 1, 1993, may come to be remembered as the dawn of a new era for Europe. Or, then again, it may not."[61]

EU Members Seek Closer Military Cooperation

But a "European army is not . . . going to happen anytime soon."

European Union leaders see at least one positive in the United Kingdom's vote to leave the EU. A key roadblock to improving cooperation among members' militaries will vanish after the U.K. departs.

For years, Britain stymied all defense initiatives within the EU, arguing that any coordination of European militaries risked undermining NATO — a 67-year-old mutual-protection pact between the United States, Canada and most European countries.

But when Britain leaves the EU, its veto departs with it, presenting members with "an opportunity and an incentive to take this [defense] agenda forward," says Nick Witney, former first chief executive of the European Defense Agency, an EU institution supporting the Union's defense efforts. "It's an opportunity in that the British foot is off the brake," adds Witney, now a senior policy fellow with the European Council on Foreign Relations.

Advocates say Europe must improve its military capabilities because of the Russian threat on the east, rising terrorist attacks and doubts about the U.S. commitment to European security under a Donald Trump administration.

Within days of the U.K.'s June 23 "Brexit" referendum to leave the European Union, Federica Mogherini, the EU's high representative for foreign affairs and security policy, called for strengthening the Union's cooperative defense efforts. "Europeans must be better equipped, trained and organized to contribute decisively to . . . collective [defense] efforts," said her office's global strategy document for the EU.[1]

The defense and foreign ministers of EU member states soon agreed on a proposal to strengthen the Union's defense capacity, including facilitating the use of rapid response forces known as "battlegroups," creating a joint military investment fund and allowing interested countries to pursue greater military cooperation without approval from the entire EU.[2]

A standing military force on the continent, with visions of, say, a German general ordering French and Spanish troops into battle, isn't on the horizon, however. "The European army is not something that is going to happen anytime soon," said Mogherini, although "50, 60, a 100 years from now, who knows?"[3]

Closer cooperation is "easy" to talk about, says Jan Techau, director of the Richard C. Holbrooke Forum, a diplomatic initiative of the American Academy in Berlin, and a former German defense official. But "to bring about substantive change that will increase capabilities is a much more difficult task." Although the British were the most outspoken opponents of EU defense integration, he says, many other countries quietly shared the British view.

Europe's primary defense strategy depends on NATO, and most European Union members belong to NATO.

Besides the impending U.K. departure, the EU's enthusiasm for defense initiatives stems from growing threats. In 2014, Russia invaded eastern Ukraine and annexed part of Crimea. Ukraine is interested in EU membership, and Russia fears losing influence over this former Soviet ally on Russia's southwestern border. Russia's aggressiveness in Ukraine, together with its efforts to support populist groups in Europe and stoke extremism on the continent, has rattled Europe's sense of security.[4]

Furthermore, during the 2016 presidential campaign, President Trump cast doubt on his commitment to defend

Maastricht created a European Union of three pillars: the powerful supranational European Communities, consisting of the European Council, Commission and Parliament; and two others significantly less powerful: a common foreign and security policy, and police and judicial cooperation, both of which were largely given over to intragovernmental cooperation.[62]

Maastricht also opened freedom of movement for everybody living within the EU and effectively created a European citizenship. As a result, an entire generation of

Europe. He praised Russian President Vladimir Putin and said he would come to the defense of NATO members that "fulfilled their [financial] obligation to us."[5]

"In the short term, defense will remain fairly high on the EU agenda," says Daniel Keohane, a senior researcher at the Center for Security Studies, a think tank at ETH Zurich. "There's a momentum now, post-Brexit."

European nations spend far less on their militaries than the United States does. Only four European members — the U.K., Greece, Estonia and Poland — meet NATO's requirement of spending at least 2 percent of gross domestic product (GDP) — the value of all goods and services produced by a country — on defense.[6] The median outlay is 1.18 percent of GDP, compared with 3.7 percent for the United States.[7]

Critics say some of the funds European nations allocate to defense are wasted on duplication among member states. EU countries have 37 types of tanks, 12 different tanker aircraft and 19 different combat aircraft, according to the Centre for European Reform, a London-based think tank focused on improving the EU.[8]

Witney is cautiously optimistic that EU members can integrate their militaries. He has been pursuing that goal for 20 years, and while the logic is "unassailable," so too are the opposing political interests of national defense establishments, he says. Nevertheless, some progress might occur, he says, albeit "not in dramatic new initiatives, but in a series of steady steps."

As for Trump, Witney says, "Let's see what he actually does." If Trump's policies reflect his campaign's praise for Putin and tepid support for NATO, he says, then Europe will have more incentive to get serious about coordinated defense.

However, he says, "if Trump's actual policies shape up better than feared, complacency and inertia will filter back in."

— *Corine Hegland*

AFP/Getty Images/Jonathan Nackstrand

Irish troops training near Malmo, Sweden, are part of the EU's Nordic "battlegroup," a rapid-response force that includes troops from Sweden, Finland, Norway, Estonia, and elsewhere.

[2] Jacobo Barigazzi, "EU Backs Greater Military Cooperation," *Politico*, Nov. 14, 2016, http://tinyurl.com/j4koqcu.

[3] Daniel Keohane, "EU Defense, Where Political Opportunity Meets Strategic Necessity," Carnegie Europe, Sept. 15, 2016, http://tinyurl.com/hfxbclr.

[4] Stefan Wagstyl, "Merkel: Russia Has 'Profoundly Disturbed' Eastern Europe," *Financial Times*, July 7, 2016, http://tinyurl.com/j64e86e; Fredrik Wesslau, "Putin's Friends in Europe," European Council on Foreign Relations, Oct. 19, 2016, http://tinyurl.com/jbbrwob.

[5] David E. Sanger and Maggie Haberman, "Transcript: Donald Trump on NATO, Turkey's Coup Attempt and the World," *The New York Times*, July 21, 2016, http://tinyurl.com/jlgh3ep.

[6] "Defence Expenditures of NATO Countries (2009–2016)," NATO, Public Diplomacy Division, July 4, 2016, p. 2, http://tinyurl.com/z55dc8m.

[7] Glenn Kessler, "Trump's Claim That the U.S. Pays the 'Lion's Share' for NATO," *The Washington Post*, March 30, 2016, http://tinyurl.com/gogu458.

[8] Sophia Besch, "Security of Supply in EU Defense: Friends in Need?" Centre for European Reform, Aug. 17, 2016, http://tinyurl.com/jq6mn34.

[1] "Shared Vision, Common Action: A Stronger Europe," European Union Global Strategy, June 2016, p. 19, http://tinyurl.com/gwg5f8n.

Europeans has grown up without borders among most EU countries.[63]

But Europe waited seven years to establish the euro in 1999 and paid a price for the delay, Janning says. The lag was necessary to allow member states to meet the requirements of the Economic and Monetary Union, he says. Many countries needed to bring their budget deficits under control and fulfill complex requirements, including freeing central banks from government control.

Italian Prime Minister Matteo Renzi resigned in early December, 2016 after voters rejected his proposed changes to the nation's constitution. Renzi had sought greater flexibility to deal with Italy's struggling economy by reducing the Senate's powers. Analysts say the vote turned into a referendum on Renzi's — and the EU's — popularity.

At the same time, though, the euro represented a giant step in Europe's integration, and people were fearful of the change. Because of these worries, Janning says, the delay was "necessary, but it was very unfortunate. I think it broke the traditional diffused support that Europe enjoyed."

1999–2007 Expansion

By the late 1990s, the EU had expanded to 15 members with the 1995 addition of Sweden, Austria and Finland, and a flood of applicants, mostly from the former Soviet Union, was hoping to join. In 1998 and 1999, the Czech Republic, Estonia, Hungary, Poland, Slovenia, Latvia, Lithuania, Romania and Slovakia joined Cyprus and Malta in accession talks with the Union, which would take between five and eight years.

The EU applicants needed to meet a set of rules established in 1993 requiring countries to have stable, liberal democracies and "functioning" markets before joining the Union. Once countries met the criteria, they needed to adopt, implement and enforce all EU rules, which are detailed in 35 different policy fields, or chapters, before they can officially become members.[64]

Flush from the success of Maastricht and looking at the ongoing expansion negotiations, European leaders began the ambitious project of forging the European

Union into one coherent unit. They amended the EU's basic structure to simplify decision-making with the treaties of Amsterdam (1999) and Nice (2003), but their major effort consisted of drafting a constitution.[65]

The document, presented in 2003, was intended to replace the proliferating treaties of the European Union, further streamline the Union's decision-making powers and increase its democratic legitimacy. "We will have a clearer, simpler Union which citizens will be able to understand," then-European Commission President Romano Prodi said.[66]

The constitution was signed in 2004, and ratification referenda began in 2005. Spain and Luxembourg approved the constitution, but France and the Netherlands rejected it. Voters had a variety of concerns, including struggling domestic economies and the potential loss of sovereignty to a stronger Brussels.[67]

After a brief period of reflection, EU leaders proposed a new treaty that would simply amend existing treaties along largely the same lines as the defeated constitution. The new agreement, called the Lisbon Treaty, thus could avoid potentially embarrassing referenda.

"The proposals in the original constitutional treaty are practically unchanged," wrote Valéry Giscard d'Estaing, the former French president who had chaired the convention drafting the 2004 constitution proposal.[68]

The Lisbon Treaty was signed in 2007. Irish law required a referendum on the treaty, notwithstanding its status as an amendment, and Irish voters promptly rejected it. After a few small concessions, the Irish approved the treaty in a second referendum, and it took effect in 2009.[69]

In 2013, Croatia joined the EU and became the 28th member. An additional five countries (Albania, Macedonia, Montenegro, Serbia and Turkey) are officially recognized as candidates, while Bosnia-Herzegovina and Kosovo are "potential candidates," which means they've been promised the prospect of joining when they are ready to do so.[70]

CURRENT SITUATION
Latest Rebukes

In March 2017, Britain finally gave formal notice of its intention to depart the EU, or Brexit.[71] The notice triggered a two-year clock for negotiating the terms of its

Is British withdrawal from the European Union inevitable?

YES   Camino Mortera-Martinez
Research Fellow and Brussels
Representative, Centre for European Reform

Written for *CQ Researcher*, December 2016

A complete withdrawal (known as a "hard Brexit") seems highly likely. But the possibility remains of a "soft Brexit" — a less acrimonious divorce that benefits both parties. After all, Switzerland, Norway and Iceland, which are not EU members, are part of the European Union's internal market and Schengen's borderless area.

But a soft Brexit depends on whether the British government and the EU can come to some accommodation on several key issues, including Britain's openness to allowing EU workers into the country.

The problem, as it often is, is politics. The British government insists on having its cake and eating it, too. British Prime Minister Theresa May, who took over in July, shortly after Britons voted in favor of Brexit, is in political trouble: As a former Home secretary, she knows what is at stake for her country (and the EU) if a hard Brexit happens. She also campaigned to remain in the EU, so she now finds herself having to unsay what she said.

May is not delusional. She knows that, whatever deal she may get, it will be less advantageous than the one she has now, unless she bows to unpalatable conditions such as Britain making budgetary contributions to the EU and accepting generous terms for EU migrants. But by acknowledging this, she risks alienating her backbenchers.

As a prime minister whose main task is to take Britain out of the EU, that is a luxury she cannot afford. As a result, May remains vague and contradictory at times. And she sometimes lets her ministers run wild.

The alarming tone of October's Conservative Party conference, where ministers floated ideas, such as requiring companies to declare the number of foreign workers they employ or deporting European doctors en masse, has convinced Brussels that even a soft Brexit is impossible.

Neither Brussels nor London has been very good at talking to each other recently. Brexit is partially the result of this lack of communication. A soft Brexit can still happen, but it would require Brussels to pick up the phone when London is calling.

The British government should also accept that there will be no single market without free movement of people across borders. If it does, it may seek an association agreement similar to that of Norway, which would benefit both parties. For the time being, however, this seems unlikely.

NO   Donald Tusk
President, European Council

Excerpted from Oct. 13, 2016, speech to European Policy Centre

Our task will be to protect the interests of the European Union as a whole and the interests of each of the 27 member states, [and] to stick unconditionally to the treaty rules and fundamental values.

By this I mean the conditions for access to the single market with all four freedoms [the free movement of goods, capital, services and people]. There will be no compromises in this regard.

When it comes to the essence of Brexit, it was largely defined in the U.K. during the referendum campaign. We all remember the promises, which cumulated in the demand to "take back control."

Namely the "liberation" from European jurisdiction, a "no" to the freedom of movement or further contributions to the EU budget. This approach has definitive consequences, both for the position of the U.K. government and for . . . negotiations. Regardless of magic spells, this means a de facto will to radically loosen relations with the EU, something that goes by the name of "hard Brexit."

This scenario will in the first instance be painful for Britons. In fact, the words uttered by one of the leading campaigners for Brexit and proponents of the "cake philosophy" was pure illusion: that one can have the EU cake and eat it too. To all who believe in it, I propose a simple experiment. Buy a cake, eat it and see if it is still there on the plate.

The brutal truth is that Brexit will be a loss for all of us. There will be no cakes on the table. For anyone. There will be only salt and vinegar. If you ask me if there is any alternative to this bad scenario, I would like to tell you that yes, there is. And I think it is useless to speculate about a "soft Brexit" because of all the reasons I've mentioned. These would be purely theoretical speculations. In my opinion, the only real alternative to a hard Brexit is "no Brexit."

Even if today hardly anyone believes in such a possibility. We will conduct the negotiations in good faith, defend the interests of the EU 27, minimise the costs and seek the best possible deal for all. But as I have said before, I am afraid that no such outcome exists that will benefit either side.

Of course, it is and can only be for the United Kingdom to assess the outcome of the negotiations and determine if Brexit is really in its interests.

withdrawal, but Brexit has already changed some of the bloc's internal political dynamics, says Carnegie Europe's Lehne. The U.K. was the "largest and most important country outside the eurozone," he says. With its departure, the other eight non-euro countries (Denmark, Sweden, and newcomers Bulgaria, Croatia, the Czech Republic, Hungary, Poland and Romania) are weaker. As a result, Lehne says, "it is more likely that the eurozone will turn into an inner circle" of the EU, leaving the non-euro countries as a less-integrated second tier.

Britain and Germany, together with some of the other northern countries, have worked together as advocates of free-market policies and for tough budget discipline, while Britain has advocated a more activist EU foreign policy but opposed some European Union integration initiatives.

Many experts say Britain ceased being a major player in the EU well before Brexit. When David Cameron became British prime minister in 2010, his government, beset by populist and euro-skeptic dynamics, largely disassociated itself from EU politics. Brexit "isn't a massive change of power dynamics," says Emmanouilidis of the European Policy Centre. The U.K. "was no longer a strong actor at the European level."

Britain's expected departure increases the leadership pressure on Germany. But Germany is beset by its own internal difficulties. In 2017, a far-right party, Alternatives for Germany, harnessed populist resentment against migrants and the EU to enter parliament for the first time since World War II.[72] The AfD is now the third largest party in the German parliament. Chancellor Angela Merkel's party, the Christian Democratic Union, remains the largest bloc, but with only 30 percent of the seats she struggled to form a governing coalition.

Germany is the most affluent and influential member of the EU. Under Merkel, who is now the EU's longest-serving leader, it has led the EU's response to most recent crises, including those on the euro debt, migration and Russia's annexation of part of the Ukraine.[73] But leadership carries a price: As the most affluent member of the EU, Germany has become the primary creditor of the eurozone, having pledged more than 190 billion euros (about $250 billion) to back loans to troubled eurozone countries.[74] As a result, Germany has been responsible for many of the policies that have aggravated tensions with the highly indebted Greece and other eurozone countries.[75]

Resentment over Germany's debt policies has reduced the willingness of EU members to work with Germany on other crises. The European Council on Foreign Relations found that the migration crisis, for example, was worsened because "Berlin's need for help with the refugee issue was seen as an opportunity to redress the asymmetric power balance between Germany and the rest of the Union."[76]

Britain's expected departure from the EU deprives Germany of another heavyweight leader and its most reliable free-market partner in the EU. Many experts in Berlin and elsewhere worry that Germany will be resented even more as its power grows in the wake of the U.K.'s departure. To head off that potentiality, Germany will need to form other coalitions within the EU, experts say.[77]

Germany's traditional EU partner, France, also held a critical election in 2017. The Franco-German partnership has historically been a driving force for integration within the EU, but in the last 10 to 15 years, France's economy has fallen far behind Germany's, due largely to France's inability to enact labor market reforms. As a result, France's "image and credibility within the EU has been undermined," says Carnegie Europe's Vimont, and now "you have a gap between Germany and France."

The election of Emmanuel Macron in May 2017 reenergized French leadership in the EU. Macron, an unabashed EU supporter, quickly pushed to reform the French labor market and presented an ambitious reform and integration agenda for the EU.[78] Among other initiatives, Macron called for a joint military force, a common eurozone budget, and a tax on financial transactions to pull the EU closer together.[79] "The Europe of today is too weak, too slow, too inefficient, but Europe alone can enable us to take action in the world in the face of the big contemporary challenges," he said.[80] Enacting any type of reform agenda, however, requires leadership from Germany as well as France; it is unclear how much maneuvering room a weakened Merkel will have.

Visegrad Group

Catalyzed by the now-abandoned plan to make all EU countries accept a quota of refugees, the Visegrad countries have emerged as strong opponents of some Brussels-led initiatives. They advocate a clear division between pan-European interests such as the euro and national interests, with a return of more governmental powers to national capitals. Hungary Prime Minister Orbán, in particular, has promised to "stop all ideas, political actions and initiatives which seek to withdraw powers from the nation states."[81]

The European Commission is investigating Poland's censorship of its high court, in which the government has fired judges and prevented the publication of a judgment criticizing the government. But Hungary has effectively used its membership in the European Parliament's largest bloc, the European People's Party, to stymie investigations into its own democratic shortcomings.[82] "The illiberal regime of Orbán remains intact," says the Political Capital Policy Research and Consulting Institute's Krekó. "There have been some threats over freezing funds, but nothing has happened."

Luxembourg's foreign minister has advocated expelling Hungary from the EU, but no one has backed him. The Holbrooke Forum's Techau counsels patience.[83] "A lot of people have freaked over Orbán and Kaczyński, and for good reason," he says. "They are doing things that are very unhelpful to their countries. But they are still very young democracies," having only emerged from communism 25 years ago. "The idea of throwing the Hungarians out of the EU is nuts."

Turkey, a U.S. ally and NATO member, became an official candidate to join the EU in 1999 amid deep concerns over its ability to meet the EU's political, economic and human rights criteria. Talks began in 2005, but they have made little progress.

In 2016, the EU and Turkey agreed to quicken the pace of negotiations as part of a wide-ranging deal to stem the refugee flow from Turkey, but the future of both the deal and its EU candidacy is questionable: The EU has been reluctant to grant the promised visa-free access for 75 million Turks, who are mostly Muslim. In addition, the Turkish government's crackdown on civil liberties following a failed coup in July has heightened Europe's concerns about Turkey's ability to meet the liberal democratic standards required of EU members.

In November 2016, the European Parliament passed a nonbinding resolution calling for suspension of Turkey's accession talks; in response, the Turkish government threatened to break the 2016 refugee deal and allow 3 million refugees to cross its borders into Europe. Both sides still hope something can be worked out. "No one wants to sever ties, because everyone benefits from

[the relationship]," a Turkish official told *The Wall Street Journal*. "We'll talk and reach a consensus."[84]

OUTLOOK
Three Possible Paths

Many experts see one of three possible paths for the European Union. It can muddle along, as it is doing now, albeit at the expense of its credibility; it can disintegrate; or it can separate into a multitiered Europe, in which some countries continue to pursue an ever-close union and others form a looser tier of membership. The Union's future depends on what crises erupt next and how its leaders and electorates respond.

"I have learned to stop thinking that I am able to look into a crystal ball," says the European Policy Centre's Emmanouilidis, explaining that if he went back five or 10 years, he wouldn't have foreseen the current challenges. For the immediate future, he predicts continued muddling through, but beyond that, he says, he just doesn't know. "I think there will be progress, but we don't know how to get from here to there."

Janning, from the European Council on Foreign Relations, began researching possible EU membership tiers in the 1990s, because it was apparent even then that a larger European Union would not be able to continue integrating based on consensus. He points to the establishment of the Schengen Area as a model: Only half of the then-10 members of the EU's predecessor organization wanted to abolish their internal border controls. Instead of allowing the lack of consensus to paralyze the group, the five members signed an agreement among themselves; the other member states joined later.

"Schengen came about because the founding members, minus Italy, said this is enough, we are not waiting for you," says Janning. "To survive, the EU may well need to get back to that sort of approach."

Carnegie Europe's Lehne envisions another outcome. "The most likely scenario is the ever-loosening Union," he says. "It's extremely unlikely to disintegrate altogether, because there is a solid underpinning in economic interests. It would be totally mad to go back to national markets."

But, Lehne says, the EU could become less relevant; he cites the League of Nations, the predecessor to the United Nations that persisted for a decade after it effectively collapsed in the 1930s, and the Holy Roman Empire, which survived for centuries after losing power.

"It is not unlikely that [the EU] will continue but deteriorate, and member states will become less conscientious in applying the legislation, and the whole thing will become a tired mechanism," he says.

"Nobody has an idea about what kind of political horizons we want to talk about and share among all 27 [post-Brexit] member states," says Carnegie Europe's Vimont. "I'm not sure there is any kind of consensus among the 27 member states about where they want to go."

NOTES

1. Alex Barker et al., "EU Leaders Go With the Flow in Bratislava," *Financial Times,* Sept. 16, 2016, http://tinyurl.com/z7a348l.

2. Jean-Claude Juncker, "State of the Union Address 2016: Towards a Better Europe — A Europe That Protects, Empowers and Defends," European Commission, Sept. 14, 2016, http://tinyurl.com/jve5wq8.

3. "Eurobarometer," First Results, European Commission, Spring 2017, p. 14, http://tinyurl.com/y885hm47.

4. Bruce Stokes, "Euroskepticism Beyond Brexit," Pew Research Center, June 7, 2016, http://tinyurl.com/j32cpnf.

5. "Euro Area Unemployment at 8.9%," Eurostat, Oct. 31, 2017, https://tinyurl.com/ych8ysmf.

6. For more information, see Sarah Glazer, "European Migration Crisis," *CQ Researcher,* July 31, 2015, pp. 649–672.

7. Jonathan Clayton and Hereward Holland, "Over One Million Sea Arrivals Reach Europe in 2015," U.N. High Commissioner for Refugees, Dec. 30, 2015, http://tinyurl.com/z3m9g2y.

8. Steven Erlanger, "Germany's Far Right Complicates Life for Merkel, and the E.U.," *The New York Times,* Sept. 25, 2017, https://tinyurl.com/ycp5nmdb.

9. "Treaty Establishing the European Economic Community," EUR-Lex, March 25, 1957, http://tinyurl.com/hk95emg.

10. "EU Administration — staff, languages and location," European Union, http://tinyurl.com/hpr6app.

11. The Visegrad name derives from the castle town of Visegrad in Hungary, where the founding members met in a 1991 summit.

12. Charles Grant, "How Brexit Is Changing the EU," Centre for European Reform, July 2016, http://tinyurl.com/j9cuv7r.

13. "Bratislava Declaration and Roadmap," European Council, Sept. 16, 2016, http://tinyurl.com/jgu5nnj.

14. Henry Samuel, "Marine le Pen 'Can Win' the French Presidency After Trump Victory, Warns Mainstream Right," *The Telegraph,* Nov. 9, 2016, http://tinyurl.com/nkfdnr2. For more on populism, see Chuck McCutcheon, "Populism and Party Politics," *CQ Researcher,* Sept. 9, 2016, pp. 721–744.

15. Michael Birnbaum and Anthony Faiola, "With Le Pen Defeat, Europe's Far-Right Surge Stalls," *The Washington Post,* May 7, 2017, https://tinyurl.com/y9zua9gb.

16. Matthew Bergman, "The Dutch Pushed Back Against Geert Wilders's 'Patriotic Spring.' Here's What You Need to Know," *The Washington Post,* March 16, 2017, https://tinyurl.com/y9bm7aqz.

17. Cas Mudde, "Europe's Populist Surge," Foreign Affairs, Oct. 17, 2016, http://tinyurl.com/gvy8rz2. For more information, see Chuck McCutcheon, "Populism and Party Politics," *CQ Researcher,* Sept. 9, 2016, pp. 721–744.

18. Juliet Eilperin and Greg Jaffe, "Obama Warns Against 'a Crude Sort of Nationalism' Taking root in the U.S.," *The Washington Post,* Nov. 15, 2016, http://tinyurl.com/zh4a5y4.

19. Henry Foy and Neil Buckley, "Orbán and Kaczyński, Vow 'Cultural Counter-Revolution' to Reform EU," *Financial Times,* Sept. 7, 2016, http://tinyurl.com/gvv4pp3; Zoltan Simon, "Orbán Says He Seeks to End Liberal Democracy in Hungary," Bloomberg, July 28, 2014, http://tinyurl.com/gra5vzs.

20. Foy and Buckley, ibid.

21. "Hungary PM Claims EU Migrant Quota Victory," BBC News, Oct. 3, 2016, http://tinyurl.com/zg5t23z.

22. Grant, op. cit.

23. Gavin Jones, "Italy's Election Pits Populists Against Populists," Reuters, Nov. 14, 2017, https://tinyurl.com/yblr2mum.

24. Heather Grabbe and Stefan Lehne, "Can the EU Survive Populism?" Carnegie Europe, June 14, 2016, http://tinyurl.com/zusnjwh.

25. Tjitske Akkerman, Sarah L. de Lange and Matthijs Rooduijn, eds., *Radical Right-Wing Populist Parties in Western Europe: Into the Mainstream?* (2016).

26. Jean-Claude Juncker et al., "The Five Presidents' Report: Completing Europe's Economic and Monetary Union," European Commission, June 2015, p. 4, http://tinyurl.com/gl5ptnm.

27. "Timeline: The Unfolding Eurozone Crisis," BBC News, June 13, 2012, http://tinyurl.com/czmqxmd.

28. Henrik Enderlein et al., "Repair and Prepare: Growth and the Euro After Brexit," Gütersloh, Berlin; Paris: Bertelsmann Stiftung; Jacques Delors Institut – Berlin and Jacques Delors Institute in Paris, 2016, p. 11, http://tinyurl.com/zaaddwr.

29. "Greece's Financial Assistance Program," European Parliament, Directorate-General for Internal Policies, March 2017, http://tinyurl.com/hkbmwl8.

30. Philine Schuseil, "Germany: What About Eurobonds?" Bruegel, May 31, 2012, http://tinyurl.com/z2542mz.

31. Charles Grant, "25 Years On: How the Euro's Architects Erred," Centre for European Reform, Nov. 5, 2015, http://tinyurl.com/jqnbq9l.

32. Ibid.

33. "Surviving War and a Dangerous Journey at 18, While Pregnant With a Second Child," International Federation of Red Cross and Red Crescent Societies, June 20, 2016, http://tinyurl.com/hb6lq7f.

34. "Mixed Migration Flows in the Mediterranean and Beyond," International Organization for Migration, Aug. 2017, p. 12, http://tinyurl.com/ybfmkucp.

35. "Persons Subject of Asylum Applications Pending at the End of the Month," Eurostat, http://tinyurl.com/gp7oclu.

36. "Mixed Migration Flows in the Mediterranean and Beyond," International Organization for Migration, 2016, p. 5, https://tinyurl.com/yczwzk7s.

37. Declan Walsh and Jason Horowitz, "Italy, Going It Alone, Stalls the Flow of Migrants. But at What Cost?" *The New York Times*, Sept. 17, 2017, https://tinyurl.com/ya433t6o.

38. Ibid.; Nellie Peyton, "Sale of Migrants in Libya 'Slave Markets' Sparks Global Outcry," Reuters, Nov. 20, 2017, https://tinyurl.com/yce7qxgs.

39. Walter Mayr, "Refugee Crisis Shifts to North Africa," Spiegel Online, April 27, 2016, http://tinyurl.com/jnll793.

40. "Asylum Seekers, the UK, and Europe," Full Fact, Oct. 25, 2016, http://tinyurl.com/ha64p27.

41. "The Future of Schengen" European Council on Foreign Relations, 2016, http://tinyurl.com/zvle86r.

42. Stokes, op. cit.

43. Cynthia Kroet, "Viktor Orbán: Migrants Are a Poison," *Politico*, July 27, 2016, http://tinyurl.com/javzzxj.

44. Mathew Karnitschnig, "Angela Merkel Stands by Refugee Policy Despite AfD Gains," *Politico*, Sept. 5, 2016, http://tinyurl.com/gplxysc; "Berlin State Poll: Losses for Merkel's CDU Gains for AfD," BBC News, Sept. 19, 2016, http://tinyurl.com/jmnxtpl.

45. Steven Wagstyl, "Merkel and Hollande Call for Equal Spread of Refugees Across EU," *Financial Times*, Aug. 24, 2015, http://tinyurl.com/zrdz82h.

46. Keith Lowe, *Savage Continent: Europe in the Aftermath of World War II* (2012), pp. 16, 19.

47. Robert Shuman, "The Shuman Declaration," European Union, May 9, 1950, http://tinyurl.com/j7osw5k.

48. Ibid.

49. "Treaty Establishing the European Coal and Steel Community, ECSC Treaty," Eur-Lex, http://tinyurl.com/hjz8kpo.

50. "Sinews of Peace," National Churchill Museum, http://tinyurl.com/j7guc8b.

51. "European Defense Community," GlobalSecurity.org, http://tinyurl.com/hoon366.

52. "Treaty Establishing the European Economic Community," Eur-Lex, http://tinyurl.com/hk95emg.

53. Ibid.

54. Andrew Moravcsik, "Negotiating the Single European Act: National Interests and Conventional Statecraft in the European Community," International Organization, Winter 1991, http://tinyurl.com/78uvcln.

55. "Solemn Declaration on European Union," European Council, June 19, 1983, http://tinyurl.com/jv8a7m6.

56. Moravcsik, op. cit.

57. Ibid.

58. "Schengen: Controversial EU Free Movement Deal Explained," BBC News, April 24, 2016, http://tinyurl.com/3p8ol6e.

59. Douglas Hurd, Speech to Cambridge University Conservative Student Association at the Cambridge Union, Feb. 7, 1992, http://tinyurl.com/zqslcp5.

60. "Treaty of Maastricht on the European Union," EUR-Lex, http://tinyurl.com/z8ld7zz.

61. Edward Pilkington, "Silent Birth of the Europerson Era," The Guardian, 1993, http://tinyurl.com/jmalkxb.

62. "Treaty of Maastricht on the European Union," op. cit.

63. Jennifer Rankin, "Freedom of movement: The Wedge That Will Split Britain From Europe," The Guardian, Oct. 6, 2016, http://tinyurl.com/z9x4d4b.

64. European Neighborhood Policy and Enlargement Negotiations, European Commission, Nov. 18, 2016, http://tinyurl.com/q824w57.

65. "A Draft Constitution for Europe," European Union, 2004, http://tinyurl.com/h7hrdmw.

66. "In Quotes: EU Constitution," BBC News, June 20, 2003, http://tinyurl.com/jgpknu2.

67. Craig Whitlock, "France Rejects European Constitution," The Washington Post, May 30, 2005, http://tinyurl.com/jgfxjbn; "Dutch Say Devastating 'No' to EU Constitution," The Guardian, June 2, 2005, http://tinyurl.com/ldja6sy.

68. Valéry Giscard d'Estaing, "The EU Treaty Is the Same as the Constitution," The Independent, Oct. 30, 2007, http://tinyurl.com/jwlrs9e.

69. "Ireland Backs EU's Lisbon Treaty," BBC News, Oct. 3, 2009, http://tinyurl.com/hg6sz99.

70. European Union Countries, European Union, http://tinyurl.com/z9lzdz6.

71. "Article 50: UK Set to Formally Trigger Brexit Process," BBC News, March 29, 2017, https://tinyurl.com/n7x8kf6.

72. Judith Vonberg and Nadine Schmidt, CNN, "Far-Right Party Wins Seats in German Parliament for First Time in Decades," CNN, Sept. 25, 2017, https://tinyurl.com/yaom6pnp.

73. Josef Janning and Almut Möller, "Leading From the Centre: Germany's New Role in Europe," European Council on Foreign Relations, July 2016, http://tinyurl.com/j39pfyv; Gregor Aisch, "How Angela Merkel's Longevity Compares to 3 Decades of European Leadership," The New York Times, Sept. 24, 2017, https://www.nytimes.com/interactive/2017/09/24/world/europe/merkel-germany-election-twelve-years.html.

74. Karin Matussek and Rainer Buergin, "Germany Role in Europe Stability Mechanism Upheld," Bloomberg, March 18, 2014, http://tinyurl.com/z4h44ox.

75. Paul Krugman, "The Austerity Delusion," The Guardian, April 29, 2015, http://tinyurl.com/ln8yldn.

76. Janning and Möller, op. cit.

77. Ibid.

78. Steven Erlanger, "Emmanuel Macron's Lofty Vision for Europe Gets Mixed Reviews," The New York Times, Sept. 28, 2017, https://tinyurl.com/y9ymuvse.

79. Pierre Briançon, "Five Takeaways From Macron's Big Speech on Europe's Future," Politico EU, Sept. 26, 2017, https://tinyurl.com/yaj2s49v.

80. Emmanuel Macron, Sorbonne Speech, Sept. 26, 2017, https://tinyurl.com/y7o7supe.

81. Viktor Orbán's speech at Bálványos Summer Open University and Student Camp, July 23, 2016, http://tinyurl.com/gnw9lmc.

82. Jennifer Rankin, "Poland's Rule of Law Under Systemic Threat, Says EU Executive," *The Guardian,* July 27, 2016, http://tinyurl.com/zswcqtm.

83. Duncan Robinson and Andrew Byrne, "Hungary Should be Ejected From EU, Says Luxembourg," *Financial Times,* Sept. 13, 2016, http://tinyurl.com/hp79bv3.

84. Laurence Norman and Emre Peker, "European Parliament Calls for Suspension of Talks on Turkey Joining the EU," *The Wall Street Journal,* Nov. 24, 2016, http://tinyurl.com/gvfdvzb; Laura Pitel and Arthur Beesley, "Erdogan Threatens to Let 3m Refugees Into Europe," *Financial Times,* Nov. 25, 2016, http://tinyurl.com/joozj8n.

BIBLIOGRAPHY

Selected Sources

Books

Akkerman, Tjitske, Sarah L. de Lange and Matthijs Rooduijn, eds., *Radical Right-Wing Populist Parties in Western Europe: Into the Mainstream?* Routledge, 2016.
An analysis edited by three University of Amsterdam professors includes an overview of European right-wing populism and case studies of nine parties.

Dyson, Kenneth, *States, Debt, and Power: 'Saints' and 'Sinners' in European History and Integration,* Oxford University Press, 2014.
A professor of politics at Cardiff University in the U.K. examines the eurozone crisis in the context of European history.

Kingsley, Patrick, *The New Odyssey: The Story of Europe's Refugee Crisis,* Guardian Faber Publishing, 2016.
A correspondent for Britain's *Guardian* newspaper draws on his reporting from 17 countries on three continents to explain and humanize Europe's migration crisis.

Lowe, Keith, *Savage Continent: Europe in the Aftermath of World War II,* Penguin, 2012.
A British historian portrays the social and political chaos that followed World War II, providing valuable insights into the conditions that fueled the creation of the European Union.

Sandbu, Martin, *Europe's Orphan: The Future of the Euro and the Politics of Debt,* Princeton University Press, 2015.
An economics writer at *Financial Times* argues that the politics of the euro, not its structure, is responsible for the financial crises in countries that use the currency.

Articles

Buckley, Neil, and Henry Foy, "The Visegrad four: Brussels' eastern critics," *Financial Times,* Aug. 29, 2016, http://tinyurl.com/jmwl4ne.
Reporters examine the four former communist states now challenging a Brussels-centered European Union.

Mudde, Cas, "Europe's Populist Surge: A Long Time in the Making," *Foreign Affairs,* November/December 2016, http://tinyurl.com/gvy8rz2.
A professor from the University of Georgia's School of Public and International Affairs takes a historical view of populism's rise in Europe and argues that it is here to stay.

Münchau, Wolfgang, "The high price of Europe's misguided pragmatism," *Financial Times,* July 24, 2016, http://tinyurl.com/j8zgmwk.
The newspaper's associate editor analyzes the costs of the EU's short-term compromises on such issues as the economic and monetary union.

Reports and Studies

"Weekly Report — Europe," U.N. High Commissioner for Refugees, 2016, http://tinyurl.com/qad78zn.
A U.N. agency provides detailed weekly summaries of developments in Europe's migration crisis, including up-to-date information on land and sea arrivals, refugee resettlements and policy developments.

Archick, Kristin, "The European Union: Questions and Answers," Congressional Research Service, Jan. 19, 2016, http://tinyurl.com/7sz6num.

A European affairs specialist for the nonpartisan research arm of Congress explains the EU's structure, governance, policies and relations with the United States.

Emmanouilidis, Janis, and Fabian Zuleeg, "EU@60 — Countering a regressive and illiberal Europe," European Policy Centre, Oct. 13, 2016, http://tinyurl.com/zvlbpgd.
An influential Brussels think tank explores the EU's many interlinked crises and warns that Europe's liberal democracy is in danger.

Enderlein, Henrik, and Enrico Letta, et al., "Repair and Prepare: Growth and the Euro after Brexit," Jacques Delors Institute, Sept. 20, 2016, http://tinyurl.com/hnpwyv6.
Some of the preeminent experts on the euro compile a detailed report on the eurozone crisis and explain its remaining challenges.

Grabbe, Heather, and Stefan Lehne, "Can the EU Survive Populism?" Carnegie Europe, June 14, 2016, http://tinyurl.com/zusnjwh.

Specialists at Carnegie Europe, a branch of the Carnegie Endowment for International Peace think tank, examine rising populism in the EU and offer concrete suggestions on how to address it.

Grant, Charles, "25 Years On: How the Euro's Architects Erred," Centre for European Reform, Nov. 5, 2015, http://tinyurl.com/grvjbcj.
The director of an influential London think tank explains why and how the euro's structural problems developed.

Stokes, Bruce, Richard Wike and Jacob Poushter, "Europeans Face the World Divided," Pew Research Center, June 13, 2016, http://tinyurl.com/hkdzk3c.
In a survey of residents of 10 EU member nations, the Pew Research Center, a centrist think tank, finds that general support for the EU has declined and many disapprove of how the organization has handled the migrant and economic crises. But most believe the EU should be a more active global player.

For More Information

Bruegel, Rue de la Charité 33-1210, Brussels, Belgium; +32 2 227 4210; www.bruegel.org. An influential economics think tank supported by EU member states, corporations and institutions.

Carnegie Europe, Rue du Congrès, 15, 1000 Brussels, Belgium; +32 2 735 56 50; www.carnegieeurope.edu. A research organization that analyzes strategic issues facing the European Union and its member states.

Center on the United States and Europe, Brookings Institution, 1775 Massachusetts Ave., N.W., Washington, DC 20036; 202-797-6000; www.brookings.edu/center/center-on-the-united-states-and-europe/. Branch of the centrist think tank that conducts original research and encourages U.S.-European dialogue on European and trans-Atlantic challenges.

Centre for European Reform, 14 Great College St., Westminster, London, SW1P 3RX, UK; +44 (0) 20 7233 1199; www.cer.org.uk. A pro-EU research group that advocates for a more effective and open Union.

Delegation of the European Union to the United States of America, 2175 K St., N.W., Washington, DC 20037; 202-862-9500; www.euintheus.org. EU's official delegation to the United States, which offers a wealth of accessible information about the EU's structure and policies.

European Council on Foreign Relations, 7th Floor, Kings Building, 16 Smith Square, London SW1P 3HQ, UK; +44 (020) 7227 6860; www.ecfr.eu. The first pan-European think tank with staff and researchers from across Europe.

European Policy Centre, 14-16 Rue du Trône/Troonstraat, B-1000, Brussels, Belgium; +32 (0) 2 231 03 40; www.epc.eu. Think tank promoting European integration.

International Organisation for Migration, 17, Route des Morillons, CH-1211 Geneva 19, Switzerland; +41 22 717 9111; www.iom.int. Intergovernmental organization that works closely with governments and nongovernmental organizations to ensure the orderly management of global migration.

9

Troubled Brazil

Christina Hoag

Marcelo Odebrecht, head of Brazil's Odebrecht Group, a global construction firm, was sentenced to 19 years in prison in March 2016 after his conviction on charges stemming from Operation Car Wash, a sweeping corruption probe. In the last three years, more than 230 politicians and business executives have been implicated in the bribery and kickback probe that also ensnared then-President Dilma Rousseff and Petrobras, the government-owned oil giant.

From *CQ Researcher,*
April 7, 2017

In a country where graft seldom is punished, the sentence billionaire businessman Marcelo Odebrecht received was stunning. As CEO of the Odebrecht Group, he presided over a respected global construction conglomerate that symbolized Brazil's ability to compete with more-developed nations.

But the company's sterling reputation collapsed last March when Odebrecht was sentenced to 19 years in prison for corruption, including overseeing an elaborate kickback system that paid $64 million in bribes to secure lucrative contracts from the state oil company, Petrobras.[1]

The sentence has been one of the most resounding outcomes of the sweeping political corruption probe known as Operation Car Wash, which arose from a routine investigation in 2013 into the laundering of drug profits by a gas station owner and an associate in Brasilia, the nation's capital.[2]

In a bid for leniency, the defendants told prosecutors they were laundering much more than drug proceeds. In fact, they said, they were part of a widespread system of corporate kickbacks paid to lawmakers who had power over government contracts.

Three years later, the scandal has implicated more than 230 politicians and business executives, notably in the construction sector, and courts have imposed more than $10 billion in fines.[3]

The scandal comes just a few years after Brazil won acclaim as a model of economic success and social progress in the developing world. "Emerging markets have to have an example, and Brazil was that example," says Lourdes S. Casanova, academic

A Struggling Goliath

Brazil, the world's sixth-most-populous country, has the largest economy in Latin America and eighth-largest globally. Almost as big as the continental United States, it was seen as an emerging global leader among developing nations in the early 2000s. But a political scandal, a presidential impeachment and the worst recession in its history have set Brazil back in the past four years.

Brazil at a Glance, 2016

Area: 3.2 million square miles

Population: 205,823,665

Labor force: 110.4 million

Unemployment rate: 12.6 percent

GDP: $1.769 trillion, 3.6 percent lower than in 2015

Trade: $190 billion exports (coffee, sugar, beef/poultry, aircraft, textiles); $144 billion imports (oil, autos)

Religions: Catholic (65%); Protestant (22%); Other (5%); None (8%)

Government: Federal republic; president elected to four-year term.

Sources: "The World Factbook," Central Intelligence Agency, http://tinyurl.com/33leeb; "Economic indicators," Banco Central do Brasil, March 15, 2017, http://tinyurl.com/mqv9xpu

in world affairs, analysts say. At the start of 2017, Brazil's gross domestic product (GDP) — a measure of a country's economic output — was 8 percent smaller than in 2014, and 12.6 percent of the workforce — 13 million Brazilians — were unemployed. January's unemployment rate was double that of late 2013.[4]

Now, analysts see Brazil as a cautionary tale for what can go wrong in a developing nation. The crisis is "pretty disastrous," says Peter Hakim, senior fellow and president emeritus of the Inter-American Dialogue, a think tank in Washington that focuses on the Americas. "For a while, Brazil was looking so promising. That's what's so awful about it."

With a population of nearly 206 million occupying a land mass almost as big as the continental United States, Brazil is the world's sixth-most-populous country and eighth-largest economy. It is also the heavyweight in Latin America, with a gross domestic product of $1.7 trillion in 2015, ahead of Mexico's $1.1 trillion. Nicaragua has the region's smallest economy, with a 2015 GDP of $12.7 billion.[5]

Brazil is rich in raw materials, such as iron ore and timber, and in agricultural products, including coffee, sugar and soybeans. Aircraft and textiles are among its manufacturing exports.[6]

"Brazil has huge potential as a great economic powerhouse," says Monica de Bolle, a senior fellow at the Peterson Institute of International Economics, a think tank in Washington. "It's a huge country with a huge domestic market."

Earlier this century, Brazil seemed to be on track to fulfill its oft-discussed potential. During the presidency of leftist Luiz Inácio Lula da Silva from 2003 to 2010,

director of the Emerging Markets Institute at Cornell University in Ithaca, N.Y. "Brazil became a symbol."

But corruption and a punishing recession — the worst in its history — have kept Brazil from fulfilling its potential and prevented it from exercising a greater role the economy boomed, thanks to global demand for the country's commodities.

Lula, who left office with an 80 percent approval rating, instituted welfare programs that lifted 36 million people out of poverty. According to the World Bank, the poverty rate dropped from 22 percent in 2003 to 7 percent in 2009. Officials from developing countries in Africa, the Middle East and Asia flocked to Brazil to learn how to replicate its model. In 2010, Brazil's economy grew 7.5 percent.[7]

The spotlight on Brazil got still brighter. The country was chosen to host the 2014 FIFA World Cup soccer championship and then the 2016 Summer Olympics, a first for South America. Ten times, Brazil has served as a temporary member of the U.N. Security Council — along with Japan, the most of any nation — and has lobbied for a permanent seat to represent emerging economies. (Proposals through the years to enlarge the Security Council have met with resistance from permanent members and others for a variety of reasons.)[8]

But for decades, Brazil has been dogged by income inequality, ranking 16th-worst globally.[9] About 30 percent of Brazilians are functionally illiterate, meaning they can read words and numbers but cannot comprehend sentences. Nevertheless, more than half of Brazil's population qualifies as middle class, and economists have long seen the country as a huge emerging market, comparable to India and Russia.[10]

Corruption, however, has held the economy back. Transparency International, a Swiss organization that monitors corruption around the world, places Brazil above the global average. In a ranking of 176 countries, with 1 as the least corrupt (Denmark), Brazil places 79th, tied with China and India but well above Russia, at 131st. The United States ranks 18th.[11]

Under Operation Car Wash, prosecutors have uncovered a system of kickbacks, the extent of which took even many Brazilians by surprise. "Brazilians always knew corruption existed, but no one ever really understood the

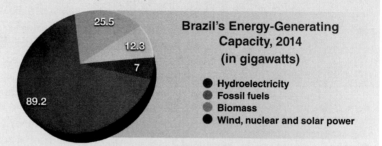

Hydroelectricity Is Main Power Source

Hydroelectricity provided much of Brazil's power in 2014, with fossil fuels a distant second. Despite opposition from environmentalists and other allies of indigenous peoples, the government is pressing ahead with plans to build as many as 100 dams along the Amazon River and its tributaries.

Brazil's Energy-Generating Capacity, 2014 (in gigawatts)

25.5
12.3
7
89.2

● Hydroelectricity
● Fossil fuels
● Biomass
● Wind, nuclear and solar power

Source: "Brazil: Electricity," U.S. Energy Information Administration, U.S. Department of Energy, Dec. 2, 2015, http://tinyurl.com/kkuk7om

magnitude of ties between the state political system and capitalism," says Matthew M. Taylor, an associate professor in the School of International Service at American University in Washington who specializes in Brazil's economy.

Operation Car Wash grew to encompass some of the country's most important companies, including Petrobras, and some of its top politicians. Among them was Lula, who as president survived a 2005 scandal known as the Mensalão, in which his Workers' Party gave legislators cash payments in return for votes.[12]

The scandals helped plunge Brazil into recession. In 2013, when Operation Car Wash was getting underway, the economy started to slow as world demand for commodities dropped. The investigation slowed it even more. "The major drivers of the economy, the housing and construction sectors, were paralyzed," says Mark S. Langevin, director of the Brazil Initiative at George Washington University in Washington. "Executives were blacklisted from doing business with the government. They couldn't finish projects or start new ones. If [Operation Car Wash] hadn't happened, the economy would have slowed, but it wouldn't have sunk to the depths that it did."

The scandal rocked the political establishment. As public anger grew, Lula's handpicked successor, Dilma Rousseff, was impeached in 2016 for borrowing $11 billion from public banks to cover budget gaps, a

A worker separates coffee beans during harvest in Brazil's Minas Gerais state. Brazil is rich in raw materials, such as iron ore and timber, and crops including coffee, sugar and soybeans. Aircraft and textiles are among its leading manufacturing exports. Global demand for its commodities helped the economy boom from 2003 to 2010.

move she said her predecessors had done routinely despite it being illegal. Her removal from office spurred many to claim she was a scapegoat for the country's reversal of fortune.[13]

One consequence of the turmoil has been Brazil's embrace of foreign investment as a means to jumpstart the economy. Last fall, the administration of President Michel Temer, who succeeded Rousseff, loosened regulations on foreign and private investment in several key sectors, including oil, aviation and land ownership.[14]

China, a key trading partner during Brazil's commodity boom, has emerged as the country's top foreign investor. Looking favorably at Brazil's growth prospects and sizable consumer market, China invested $4 billion in the country in 2016, well ahead of the United States, which ranked second with $2.5 billion. Among notable Chinese purchases were three ships from the Brazilian mining company Vale. A Chinese consortium bought the vessels for $269 million. Meanwhile, a Chinese utility acquired a 24 percent stake in an energy company from the ailing Brazilian construction firm Camargo Corrêa.[15]

Analysts hail Brazil's turn to foreign investment but warn that the country is significantly behind others such as Mexico and even tiny Paraguay in adopting more business-friendly laws in areas such as taxes and labor. As an example of Brazil's uncompetitiveness, they point to

provisions for the oil and gas industry stipulating that foreign companies must buy equipment from local Brazilian firms. Those rules are scheduled to be rolled back for oilfield bidding later this year.[16]

But protectionist measures have hurt the country's global competitiveness for decades, says Riordan Roett, director of Latin American studies at Johns Hopkins University in Washington.

Brazil is keen to expand its energy sector. The country is the world's 11th-largest oil producer, producing enough heavy crude to meet its domestic demand.[17] However, due to a lack of refining capacity for the heavy oil, Brazil imports light oil to refine into gasoline and other derivatives for domestic consumption.[18]

The government plans to build a series of hydroelectric dams along the Amazon River and its tributaries to provide cheap power, saying the region's vast waterways are an under-tapped resource.

As Brazil struggles to stabilize its economy and government, here are some of the questions being debated:

Can Brazil eliminate its corruption?

It was supposed to be a pioneering anti-corruption law, but during a marathon congressional session that lasted into the wee hours last November, federal lawmakers rewrote and approved a bill that would significantly dilute the power of prosecutors investigating graft.

Among the changes, the lower house watered down provisions allowing prosecutors to reach more plea deals and seize civil servants' assets in corruption cases. Moreover, instead of making it easier to bring graft cases against legislators, the lower house retained statutes of limitations that ruled out many such cases. The revisions came a week after lawmakers tried to give themselves amnesty, a move they canceled after a public outcry.[19]

The legislators' actions underscore the difficulty of combating corruption in Brazil. Despite the aggressive prosecutions of some of the country's biggest names in business and politics, some experts say Operation Car Wash may not ultimately do much to curb corruption because it is so ingrained in the way transactions are done in Brazil. Others disagree, arguing that Operation Car Wash is holding people of all social strata accountable and showing that the judicial system works.

De Bolle of the Peterson Institute of International Economics says she isn't optimistic that Operation Car

Wash is a game-changer. "I don't see that much of a change in mentality," she says.

Experts see several signs that attitudes aren't changing sufficiently to eliminate corruption.

Although public approval of the investigations is generally high, the resulting economic paralysis has caused many Brazilians to wonder whether Operation Car Wash has been worth the effort. Some feel that graft helped grease the wheels and enabled the system to work. "There's a sense of 'could we put the genie back a bit in the bottle?'" says Hakim of the Inter-American Dialogue.

The length of the investigation, which formally started in 2014, is contributing to the public's growing weariness of fighting corruption, says Taylor of American University. "This has been a roiling crisis for three years now. Brazilians are reaching an exhaustion point," he says.

Perhaps most important, the lawmakers' lack of action to support the prosecutions with anti-corruption laws has led some observers to worry about the political will to root out graft.

If Congress were serious about ending kickbacks, a key first step would be a law protecting whistleblowers, says Langevin of George Washington University. "An anti-corruption campaign is not in place," he says. "Everybody's just running for cover."

Moreover, because the investigations have ensnared politicians, some Brazilians say the prosecutions are politically motivated. For instance, former President Lula has been indicted in five corruption cases, the latest in December for allegedly orchestrating a scheme in which Odebrecht paid $22.1 million in kickbacks to secure eight construction contracts with Petrobras.[20]

According to prosecutors, Lula appointed executives to the board of Petrobras who would go along with the scheme and used the money to fund his leftist Workers' Party and its allies. Still Brazil's most popular politician, Lula has said he will run for president in 2018, but a conviction in any of the cases would bar him from the race.[21]

"The cases against him are really weak," Langevin says. "There's no smoking gun, no evidence. They've really targeted Lula, it looks like, more for political reasons."

Judge Sergio Moro, who is handling most of the Operation Car Wash cases, said last fall that there is "just cause" for Lula's indictments, although he added the extent of the former president's involvement in the graft cases was unclear.[22]

The country's electoral system also needs revamping if corruption is to be eliminated, scholars say. Brazil has a federal system with a bicameral Congress consisting of a Senate and a lower house called the Chamber of Deputies. While the president and senators are elected directly, deputy seats are a hybrid where candidates must win votes for themselves and their party against dozens of candidates. Moreover, Brazil's statewide electoral districts are huge, with some containing as many as 32 million voters. Candidates thus often resort to buying votes by slipping bills equivalent to $14 to $28 inside campaign pamphlets.[23]

That leads to a need for huge campaign chests, often more than parties can acquire through legal donations. Brazil also does not have a strong tradition of individual voters donating to political campaigns. Parties, as a result, rely heavily on corporate funding, although in a bid to wipe out corporate graft, the Supreme Court last year outlawed company donations to parties altogether.[24]

Overall, de Bolle says, Brazil's political system produces a "very cozy relationship between the public and private sector." But others say Operation Car Wash has sent powerful messages that the justice system can punish corrupt officials.

"Brazilians are taking some comfort in that. [Car Wash] is putting some very powerful people behind bars," Taylor says, pointing to former Rio de Janeiro state Gov. Sérgio Cabral and former Chamber of Deputies President Eduardo Cunha. "There's a nervous hope that things will get better."

Some analysts add that while corruption will probably always exist, the well-oiled system of organized kickbacks exposed by Operation Car Wash is likely done.

"The cost-benefit analysis of corruption in Brazil has forever changed because of [Car Wash]," says Brian Winter, vice president for policy at the Council of the Americas, a Washington-based organization that advocates free trade and democracy in the region. "It's not to say corruption will disappear or even be dramatically reduced, but corruption on a massive scale will be ended."

Can Brazil resolve its social problems?

In the 1970s, an economist came up with a term for Brazil's social landscape: "Belíndia," for "Belgium-like bubbles surrounded by destitution worthy of India."[25]

The term remains apt, with slums ringing Brazil's cities in belts of misery.

In Rio de Janeiro, nearly a quarter of the city's population, or about 1.5 million people, live in overcrowded, violence-plagued slums, known as favelas, that dot the city's hillsides.[26] Built without planning, the shantytowns feature jerrybuilt brick houses; most lack running water, trash pickup and sewage lines. Just a few miles away lies one of the world's most famous beaches, Copacabana, lined with luxury apartment towers and trendy boutiques and restaurants.

Social problems resulting from vast income disparities have dogged Brazil for centuries. Ten percent of the population controls 43 percent of the wealth, while the poorest 34 percent owns just over 1 percent, according to 2012 figures. That made Brazil the world's 16th-most inequitable country in 2012, the latest year for which data are available. By comparison, Mexico, Latin America's second-biggest country, ranked 25th, and the United States 43rd, out of 145 countries.[27]

Analysts say the inequity is the result of the government's long-term neglect of the poor in education, small-business development and social services. After courting the poor to get elected, legislators often represent the interests of the middle class and elites since those are the classes that wield the most economic power.

"Congress is organized to benefit 30 million to 50 million Brazilians and manage the rest," says Langevin of George Washington University.

Brazil has had success reducing poverty in recent years. Under Lula's "Brazil without Misery" welfare programs, almost one in four Brazilians, or 50 million people, receive a monthly cash payment averaging $54 a month. (The government-mandated minimum monthly wage in Brazil is about $300.[28]) One program is Bolsa Família (Family Grant), which gives monthly cash stipends in return for families enrolling children in school and taking them for health checkups. The programs are credited with halving Brazil's extreme poverty, those living on less than $1.90 per day, from 9.7 percent of the population in 2003 to 4.3 percent in 2013. "This stipend makes a huge difference in people's lives, and it's relatively cheap for the government," the Peterson Institute's de Bolle says.

But analysts say more needs to be done to create economic opportunity to improve Brazilians' lives without creating a culture of dependency. Just 46 percent of Brazilian adults ages 25 to 64 have completed secondary school.[29] Inadequate public K-12 education is a key area that perpetuates social inequality because impoverished youths lack the skills to attend the best universities or land higher-paying jobs, says Roett of Johns Hopkins University.

Public schools are so shoddy that the middle and upper classes typically send their children to private schools, which better prepare them to enter the country's prestigious public university system, according to experts. The majority of graduates of public schools, who typically have weaker academic skills than their private-school counterparts, cannot get into public universities and often turn to private for-profit colleges.[30]

The government last fall announced a plan to bolster public education, mainly by offering more flexibility to students in their choice of study in a bid to make school more attractive to students and lower the 11.5 percent dropout rate. The government also said it would offer more technical high schools to teach marketable skills. Critics said the plan does not address core issues such as deteriorated school buildings, poor teacher training and methods and overcrowded classrooms.[31]

The poor also suffer from inadequate state-run health care, often waiting months for treatment while those who can afford it go to private doctors. The mosquito-borne Zika virus, which has resulted in some 2,500 babies born over the past year with microencephaly, or undersized heads, and other severe defects, has underscored the health system's inequities. Many of the Zika babies were born to poor mothers in Brazil's impoverished northeast, where the disease was first detected.[32]

Many poor parents are on lengthy waiting lists for treatment and services provided by the public health system. Meanwhile, costs are rising to treat a growing list of Zika-related impairments: breathing problems, trouble swallowing, clubbed feet, seizures, severe muscle weakness that prevents the babies from lifting their heads and behavioral symptoms such as extreme irritability.

The government has given poor families modest disability payments to help them care for affected children and mobilized campaigns to eradicate mosquitoes and raise public awareness about Zika. Meanwhile, researchers continue researching the virus.

Crime, particularly drug trafficking, is another key concern. With high poverty, little economic opportunity and weak security forces, Brazil is becoming a haven for transnational narco-trafficking driven by gangs that have expanded beyond their bases in urban slums, scholars say. "The urban violence of the south has shifted into the northeast and less developed areas," says Taylor of American University.

In January, the government announced a national security plan calling for federal officials to take a bigger role in combating homicides and the narcotics trade.[33] Still, it is unclear what that will entail. "The government hasn't had any serious policy dealing with drug trafficking," says de Bolle.

Steep Recession Grips Brazil

An economic downturn that began in Brazil in 2012 deepened in 2016, with the country's gross domestic product (GDP) — a measure of total economic output — shrinking by 3.6 percent. Economists blame the recession on falling commodity prices, political corruption and deep structural problems, such as an inefficient workforce and inadequate infrastructure.

Brazilian GDP in Current U.S. Dollars, 1986-2016

GDP (in $ trillions)

Sources: "Economic indicators," Banco Central do Brasil, March 15, 2017, http://tinyurl.com/mqv9xpu; "GDP (current US$)," World Bank, http://tinyurl.com/krt9esg

Roett says opportunity in Brazil comes down to how much money a person is born into, as the system offers little chance of upward social mobility. "If you're wealthy in Brazil, you're fine," he says.

Can Brazil be a global economic leader?

In one of Brazil's most dramatic reversals of fortune, the tycoon who just five years ago was ranked the country's richest man with a $35 billion fortune was jailed in February to await trial on charges that he paid $16.5 million in bribes to the former governor of Rio de Janeiro state in exchange for government contracts. After commodity prices tumbled, Eike Batista said his oil and mining conglomerate is now $1 billion in debt.[34]

For many observers, Batista's rise and fall epitomize Brazil's boom-and-bust story. Just when its economy appears to make progress, Brazil slides backward. One problem, economists say, is its overreliance on commodities, whose prices are subject to the whims of global markets. Another is economic mismanagement and corruption.

"Brazil needs to stop being the land of missed opportunities, because that's what it's been time and time again," the Peterson Institute's de Bolle says.

Experts say economic progress hinges on several reforms that will require significant shifts in policy direction, such as moving away from commodity-driven exports to more finished goods and high-tech products that will enable Brazil to compete globally.

Brazil also needs to shore up its dilapidated infrastructure and improve its workforce, as well as streamline taxes and regulations, says Roett of Johns Hopkins. "Brazil is neither a productive nor a competitive economy," he says. He points to basic improvements that could boost Brazil's competitiveness, such as upgrading highways so that trucks traversing bumpy roads don't spill a portion of their crops. Trucks are the main method of transporting goods across the vast country because railways, ports, airports and waterways remain underdeveloped.[35]

The country's public and private sectors underinvest in capital infrastructure, according to a report by the global business consulting firm Accenture. In 2014, Brazil invested 17 percent of GDP in roads, buildings and machinery, compared with 25 percent for other emerging markets. The government is addressing this problem with a $52.2 billion plan to grant contracts to companies to operate highways, ports, airports and railroads.[36]

The workforce also harms Brazil's competitiveness. Brazilian workers are a quarter as productive as those in the United States.[37] "There's never been a commitment to investing in human capital," Roett says. "The workforce is poorly trained."

The Cantagalo shantytown, or favela, rises above Rio de Janeiro, Brazil's capital. About 1.5 million people, nearly a quarter of the city's population, live in the overcrowded, violence-plagued slums that dot Rio's hillsides. The favelas reflect the income disparity and other social problems that have dogged Brazil for centuries.

The country particularly lacks technical skills and managerial expertise, and labor costs have risen steadily because of government-mandated annual increases in the monthly minimum wage. In 2017, the minimum monthly salary rose 6 percent from 2016. Labor productivity, increased only 12 percent from 2005 to 2014 while labor costs doubled.[38]

Labor laws heavily favor employees. Among the mandates, employers are supposed to provide meals and cover transportation costs, pay a month's bonus salary at year-end, give 30 days' dismissal notice and provide 30 days' vacation per 12 months worked. Because of the extensive rights they are granted under labor laws, Brazilians also have a penchant for suing employers, experts say.[39]

The cost of doing business in Brazil hampers entrepreneurs as well. Due to inefficiencies in the public and private sectors, including excessive red tape, high taxes and chronic underinvestment in infrastructure, it takes 84 days to launch a business in Brazil — compared with just four days in South Korea, 29 in India and 32 in China, all competitors of Brazil, according to Accenture. And the average cost of exporting a shipping container from Brazil is $2,323, compared with $1,332 in India, $1,224 in the United States, $823 in China and $670 in South Korea.[40]

Despite these challenges, Brazil has success stories. São Paulo sandal maker Alpargata turned flip-flops into a worldwide fashion item in the 2000s with its Havaianas brand.[41] Embraer, an aircraft manufacturer based in São José dos Campos, is a top global aviation company; Vale, based in Minas Gerais, is a world name in the mining industry; and Petrobras remains a major state-owned oil company despite its setbacks in the corruption scandal, notes Casanova of Cornell University.

Still, for a country its size, Brazil should have more global companies and a stronger private sector, Casanova says. Only seven Brazilian companies are in the Global Fortune 500, while China, whose economy is five times Brazil's, has 95.[42]

The government particularly needs to support small- and medium-sized enterprises so they can grow, Casanova says. The National Bank for Economic Social Development (known by its Portuguese acronym BNDES) typically finances already-large companies and infrastructure projects but should be reoriented to boost smaller companies, especially as recovery from the recession gets underway, she says.

Others agree that Brazil's companies could use help to revive the economy. With labor costs rising annually, credit lacking and consumer demand languishing because of the recession, "the prospects for the private sector really aren't that great at all," says de Bolle of the Peterson Institute of International Economics.

As the economic and political turmoil continues, Brazilian companies are moving to other nations, many to Paraguay, which is striving to become South America's low-cost manufacturing hub. From toy to textile companies, about 80 percent of Paraguay's foreign manufacturers are now Brazilian businesses taking advantage of energy prices that are 60 percent lower and labor costs that are more than 50 percent cheaper than in Brazil.[43]

With unemployment rising, Brazil's Ministry of Industry, Trade and Services says it's trying to keep Brazilian businesses at home. The country has many natural advantages, including its huge population, the absence of internal racial and ethnic strife and good standing with its neighbors, that make it a natural magnet for investors, says Winter of the Council of the Americas. "People ignore Brazil at their own peril," he says.

BACKGROUND

Portuguese Colonization

After Portuguese explorer Vasco da Gama discovered a new route to India by circumnavigating the Cape of Good Hope, the Portuguese crown was eager to capitalize on the trading riches this maritime path promised.

In 1500, the year after da Gama returned from his epic two-year voyage, King Manuel sponsored a fleet of 13 ships and appointed Pedro Alvares Cabral to lead the expedition. The fleet left Lisbon in March 1500, but just weeks later Cabral's lead ship veered off course to the west and ended up on what is now Porto Seguro in Brazil's central-eastern Bahia state.[44]

Much like Christopher Columbus' accidental discovery of the Caribbean islands in 1492, the Portuguese had stumbled on a vast new territory. Cabral's landing party spent the next nine days observing the natives' hunter-gatherer existence and mapping the coast. Cabral christened the terrain Vera Cruz, or True Cross, and dispatched a ship to Portugal to notify the king of the discovery.[45]

The news did not generate much enthusiasm in Lisbon because the territory was thought to be a large island, devoid of riches. Nevertheless, the Portuguese established trading posts along the coast, soon finding a redwood called the brazil tree, valuable as a dye and timber. The land began to be known as "Brazil" as early as 1503, and trading brazil wood for trinkets formed the main economic activity until 1535.[46]

To solidify its claim on the territory, the crown had to colonize it or risk losing it to other European powers. Sugarcane imported from Africa became the cash crop, and a capital was established at Salvador.

Sugar cultivation generated a high demand for labor. Colonists enslaved Indians, whose populations were being decimated by smallpox, influenza and measles brought by the Europeans. Surviving Indians fled inland and were chased by "bandeirantes," flag-bearing colonists charged with capturing Indians. In the process, these colonists explored much of Brazil's interior and sought gold and other riches.

Facing a decimated Indian population and resistance from Jesuit missionaries trying to help the natives, the Portuguese turned to Africa for labor. By 1580, some 2,000 African slaves a year were arriving in Brazil. Their labor helped make Brazil a world sugar power from 1600 to 1650.[47] But competition from sugar plantations in Spanish, English and Dutch colonies in the Americas sent Brazil's industry into decline in the late 17th century.

The discovery of gold in 1695 in today's Minas Gerais state boosted Brazil's fortunes, sparking a gold rush and the first major wave of immigration. Over the next six decades, some 600,000 Portuguese and other Europeans settled Brazil's interior.[48]

In a bid to prop up its own ailing economy, Portugal in the late 18th century reasserted control over its colony, which was growing increasingly wealthy due to tobacco, cattle ranching and gold mining. Brazil's colonial elites, however, bristled at Lisbon's moves, including the creation of monopolistic trading companies and an overhaul of the colony's administrative structure that caused Brazilian laws to favor the mother country.[49]

Brazilian Independence

Ironically, Brazil's independence movement was spurred by the monarchy. In 1807, French emperor Napoleon Bonaparte invaded Spain and Portugal, causing the latter's royal family and 10,000 citizens to flee to Brazil. After settling at Rio, Prince regent Dom João VI, ruling in place of his mentally incompetent mother, Queen Maria I, wasted no time in installing European-style amenities, including a theater, orchestra and newspapers. By 1822, Rio's population had doubled to 150,000.[50]

In 1821, political upheaval in Portugal pushed João VI, who had become king after his mother's death, to return to Lisbon and leave his son Pedro as regent in Brazil. The new Portuguese parliament soon returned Brazil to colonial status. In 1822, an angry Pedro declared Brazil's independence and was crowned Dom Pedro I, emperor of Brazil.[51]

His reign lasted just nine years. After a costly war to prevent the secession of present-day Uruguay and growing political dissension, Pedro abdicated and returned to Portugal, leaving his 5-year-old son, Pedro II, as future emperor. For the next nine years, regents ruled Brazil until Pedro turned 14.[52]

In the following decades, Brazil debated how it was to be governed. Its wealth, meanwhile, was growing from coffee, rubber, and cotton exports, which led to the construction of railroads and other infrastructure. As with sugar, the coffee plantations relied on slave labor. Although British pressure had led Brazil to end the slave

CHRONOLOGY

1500–1888 *Europeans colonize territory that becomes Brazil.*

1500 Portuguese nobleman Pedro Álvares Cabral steers off course during a voyage to India and lands at Porto Seguro. He claims the territory for the king of Portugal.

1700s Discovery of gold spurs large-scale European settlement.

1808 Fleeing Napoleon, Portugal's prince regent, Dom João VI, arrived in Rio de Janeiro, transforming the city with business and culture.

1821 Dom João returns to Lisbon after Napoleon's fall, leaving his son Pedro I as prince regent.

1822 Pedro declares independence from Portugal, forms the Empire of Brazil and rules as emperor for nine years before unrest forces him to abdicate in favor of his 5-year-old son, Pedro II.

1840 Fourteen-year-old Pedro II takes over after nine years of rule by regents.

1888 Brazilian slavery is abolished.

1889–1963 *Power swings between civil and military governments.*

1889 A republic is formed after a military coup backed by landowners upset about the end of slavery.

1930 Military installs Getúlio Vargas as president in a coup. He retains power until 1945.

1945 Another coup ousts Vargas, leading to a period of democratically elected presidents and economic growth.

1960 President Juscelino Kubitschek moves the capital from Rio de Janeiro to a newly made inland city, Brasilia.

1964–1984 *Repressive military dictatorships seize power.*

1964 Brazilian military overthrows President João Goulart after he attempts socialist reforms; five generals rule for the next 20 years.

1968 Guerrilla movement starts, causing the government to suppress dissent through arrests, torture, disappearances and killings over the next decade. Future President Dilma Rousseff, a Marxist guerrilla, is arrested and tortured.

1985–Present *Democracy takes hold amid economic struggles.*

1985 With inflation soaring, the military passes power to Tancredo Neves, a civilian, but he dies days before his inauguration.

1988 Brazil adopts a new constitution.

1990 Fernando Collor de Mello is the first popularly elected president in 30 years.

1992 Collor de Mello, facing impeachment, resigns.

1994 Fernando Henrique Cardoso is elected president and implements an austerity plan to rein in inflation and government spending.

2002 Labor leader Luiz Inácio Lula da Silva, a founding member of the Workers' Party, is elected president. He implements a social program that lifts millions out of poverty and supports big business, sparking economic growth and talk of Brazil rising onto the world stage.

2011 Rousseff, a Lula acolyte, becomes Brazil's first female president.

2014 A probe reveals massive graft between business and politicians; sending the nation's economy into a nosedive.

2015 Rousseff starts second term after narrow re-election victory.

2016 Rio hosts the Olympics Games, a first for South America, as Rousseff is impeached.

2017 Brazil endures its worst recession as interim President Michel Temer tries to jumpstart the economy. . . . Olympic venues deteriorate as nation struggles to find uses for stadiums, athletes' village.

trade in 1831, the government did not enforce the law, and an estimated 712,000 slaves arrived during the 1830s and 1840s. Slavery was finally abolished in 1888 after increasing international pressure.[53]

In the wake of abolition, plus a costly five-year war to repel an invasion by Paraguay, Pedro II lost the support of key allies. In 1889, the military staged a bloodless coup and the royal family fled to Portugal.[54]

Early Republic

The military government promulgated a new constitution in 1891 that declared Brazil a federation of states. Over the next four decades, the country's first presidents hailed from powerful coffee oligarchies as a huge influx of immigrants arrived, largely from Portugal, Italy and Spain, but also from Japan, Syria and Lebanon. Drawn by the coffee industry and opportunity in the new republic, some 2.7 million immigrants arrived in Brazil between 1872 and 1910.[55]

This new urban class challenged the domination of the coffee producers, and political unrest followed. In 1937, with a worldwide depression collapsing coffee prices, the military overthrew the elected government and installed Getúlio Vargas as dictator-president. Vargas, an authoritarian populist, implemented protectionist policies and oversaw the modernization of Brazil. But in 1945, with labor unrest and opposition against the dictatorship growing in favor of an elected president, the military again intervened and ousted Vargas to return the nation to an elected presidency.[56]

In the post-World War II years, inflation eroded wages and caused popular discontent. This created a path for Vargas to return to power by winning the 1951 presidential election. During his term, he nationalized the oil industry, creating the state company Petróleos Brasileiros (Petrobras), but industrial strikes, corruption and a decision to double the minimum wage weakened him politically. In 1954, with a military coup looming, Vargas killed himself.[57]

As fertility rates rose (an average 6.28 children per mother by 1960), the 1950s witnessed rapid population growth and rural migration to industrialized urban centers.[58] Faced with a housing shortage, the migrants built shantytowns on city outskirts. The youthful population also outstripped the capacity of public schools and health care, setting the foundation for a vast gap between haves and have-nots.

In the late 1950s, President Juscelino Kubitschek embarked on an ambitious development plan that included creating a national automobile industry and building roads, electricity plants and a new inland city, Brasília, to serve as the nation's capital. Although the plan lifted the economy, Kubitschek's successors were saddled with the bills for his "Program of Goals." Inflation started climbing in the early 1960s. A bleak economy prompted the military to depose President João Goulart in 1964.[59] Military chiefs also were unhappy with Goulart's leftist measures, such as giving the vote to illiterates, allowing enlisted soldiers to unionize and permitting the expropriation of underused properties.

Unlike its previous takeovers, the military did not immediately relinquish power to civilians. Instead, a succession of five generals ran the country over the next 21 years. By 1969, more than a dozen guerrilla groups — largely Marxists, but also liberation theologists and radical opponents to the dictatorship — had sprung up in opposition. The government responded with repression, including the arrests and torture of dissenters, press censorship and spying. By 1974 it had defeated the armed groups, including the Comandos of National Liberation and the Revolutionary Armed Vanguard.[60]

The economy flourished under authoritarian rule, as foreign investment, notably in the automotive sector, increased and exports diversified beyond coffee. Inflation dropped from 92 percent in 1964 to 28 percent in 1967, and GDP grew an average of 10.9 percent over the next six years. Much of the economic expansion, however, was contingent on foreign loans and imports such as oil, which made up 43 percent of Brazil's imports by 1980.[61]

In the wake of a 1979 oil price increase and a subsequent rise in interest rates globally, Brazil's foreign debt ballooned to $100 billion, from $3 billion in 1964. Inflation hit triple digits, and Brazil plunged into recession in 1981.[62]

Democracy Returns

The mass urbanization of society, which started in the 1950s and resulted in profound social inequality, coupled with dissatisfaction with the military's handling of the economy, led to political movements that pushed for a return to democracy. In 1985, the military handed control of the country to a civilian, Tancredo Neves,

Hydropower Plans
Spark an Amazon Water War

"We see these projects as a disaster."

Brazil's environmental and indigenous-rights activists scored a key victory last summer when the government denied permits for the construction of the $9.4 billion São Luiz do Tapajós dam in the Amazon basin, a joint Brazilian-European project slated to have been the world's sixth-largest hydroelectric dam.[1]

In its decision, Brazil's environmental institute ruled that the consortium had not presented enough evidence about the social and ecological effects of the 8,000-megawatt dam, which would have flooded 145 square miles of Munduruku tribal ancestral land.[2]

The win, however, may not amount to much for dam opponents. The Brazilian government has given no indication it is backing off its strategy of harnessing the Amazon's prodigious water resources to meet the country's energy needs. Brazil's National Energy Plan calls for as many as 100 dams mostly along tributaries throughout the world's largest rainforest.[3]

"Let's not forget that in the developed world almost 70 percent of the hydro potential has already been exploited, whereas here in Brazil, 70 percent of our hydro has not been explored yet," said Luiz Augusto Barroso, president of Empresa Pesquisa de Energética, the government's energy-planning agency. "It makes sense for the country, and it's a resource that benefits society."[4]

Activists argue that the government's plan is shortsighted. Not only do the dams wipe out indigenous tribes' habitats and disrupt one of the planet's most diverse biosystems of fish, animals and plants, but deforestation contributes to climate change when forested areas are flooded. Trees absorb carbon dioxide in the atmosphere while rotting vegetation in the dam reservoirs produces methane. Higher levels of both gases are linked to global warming.

Moreover, construction workers' settlements often turn into towns after projects are completed when some workers stay on. And the presence of towns leads to more logging and ranching, which further reduce forests and cause more environmentally harmful emissions from vehicles, activists say.

"We see these projects as a disaster," says Christian Poirier, program director for Amazon Watch, a nonprofit in Oakland, Calif., that monitors issues affecting the Amazon region. "Even small projects have had irreversible impacts."

The most controversial project to date has been the $18 billion Belo Monte megadam, partially completed on the Xingu River, a major Amazon tributary, and slated to be the world's fourth-largest hydroelectric dam in terms of installed capacity (11,000 megawatts) when fully operational in 2019.[5] Last year, Brazil's environmental agency fined dam developer Norte Energie $10.8 million after 16.2 million tons of fish were killed when a river tributary was diverted to fill the dam's reservoir.[6]

The project also has become a national symbol of corruption. Last year, a Brazilian state senator testified that $12 million skimmed from overpriced Belo Monte construction contracts helped pay for former President Dilma Rousseff's 2010 and 2014 election campaigns.[7] Also last year, an appeals court found a conflict of interest because

elected by the electoral college. But he abruptly died and Vice President José Sarney succeeded him.[63]

Sarney unsuccessfully tried to tame inflation with a new currency, price freezes and a minimum wage indexed to inflation, as well as political reform through a new constitution. In 1989 the first free presidential elections were held in three decades. Fernando Collor de Mello, who hailed from a powerful northeastern family, won on a platform of neoliberal economics and anti-corruption.[64]

Collor de Mello's first initiative was to tackle inflation by freezing savings accounts. He then fired thousands of federal workers, slashed tariffs and privatized state assets, all accomplished mainly via decree. By

Eletrobras, the state energy utility, had awarded the Belo Monte environmental assessment study without competitive bidding to three of Brazil's largest construction companies. The companies, Odebrecht Group, Andrade Gutierrez and Camargo Corrêa, later formed part of a consortium that built the dam.[8]

Researchers see alternatives to hydropower that are less invasive to the environment and cheaper to produce than building dams. "Brazil has a huge capacity for wind and solar. It's underinvested in these areas," says Eve Bratman, an assistant professor of environmental studies at Franklin & Marshall College in Lancaster, Pa., who specializes in the Brazilian Amazon.

Additionally, shoring up the electricity supply grid would increase the power supply, Poirier says. "[Utilities] lose up to 20 percent of energy in transmission lines," he says. "Just fixing old lines would make them more efficient."

Brazil's 2024 energy plan calls for increasing both hydropower and non-hydro renewable energy sources, plus natural gas and nuclear generation. The country, which currently relies on hydroelectricity for 70 percent of its power, has seen power shortages in recent years because of drought.[9]

With the government reeling from a recession, many dam projects are on hold. Another factor slowing the projects is an ongoing corruption investigation called Operation Car Wash that has implicated scores of politicians and key players in the country's construction industry. But activists fear that once the dust settles, the development floodgates will reopen, especially if the government pursues infrastructure projects to reignite the economy. The Tapajós dam, for instance, can be revived with a new permit application, Poirier notes.

"There's good reason for activists to keep fighting," Bratman says.

— Christina Hoag

The Belo Monte dam on the Xingu River, a major Amazon tributary, has been plagued by corruption and environmental problems during its construction. The $18 billion hydroelectric dam will be the world's fourth-largest when completed in 2019.

Getty Images/Bloomberg/Dado Galdieri

[1] John Vidal, "Major Amazon dam opposed by tribes fails to get environmental licence," *The Guardian*, Aug. 5, 2016, http://tinyurl.com/mojxtd4.

[2] Ibid.

[3] Wyre Davis, "Amazon culture clash over Brazil's dams," BBC News, Jan. 10, 2017, http://tinyurl.com/m9djyfw.

[4] Ibid.

[5] Ibid.

[6] Sue Branford, "Fish kills at Amazon's Belo Monte Dam point up builder's failures," *Mongabay*, July 13, 2016, http://tinyurl.com/k24pauk.

[7] "Brazil's Rousseff benefited from Belo Monte dam graft," Reuters, March 11, 2016, http://tinyurl.com/kr3rcqs.

[8] Sarah Bardeen and Brent Millikan, "Belo Monte Operating License Suspended," *International Rivers*, Sept. 6, 2016, http://tinyurl.com/mafgj7m.

[9] "Hydroelectric plants account for more than 70 percent of Brazil's power," *Electric Light & Power*, Aug. 17, 2016, http://tinyurl.com/lfychsh.

1992, his backing had dwindled, and he resigned just hours before a Senate vote to impeach him on corruption charges.[65]

Minister of Finance Fernando Henrique Cardoso, an academic who had turned to politics, was elected president in 1994 on the strength of his economic plan that had started to yield results. During his two terms (1995-2002), Cardoso helped stabilize Brazil's economy and eliminate its chronic hyperinflation (from 2,489 percent in 1993 to 4 percent in 1997) through a series of liberal reforms and privatizations. But the changes did little to alleviate poverty, and by the end of his second term his popularity had plummeted amid the onset of recession.[66] That set the stage for the

Catholics, Evangelical Protestants Battle for Brazilian Souls

"The days when everybody is born and dies in the Catholic Church are long gone."

Brazil has long had the world's largest population of Roman Catholics, but it may not hold that title much longer. Large numbers of Brazilians are turning to evangelical Protestant sects, mainly Pentecostalism, while many others are abandoning organized religion altogether.

"Brazil is on an inexorable march toward no longer being majority Catholic," says R. Andrew Chesnut, a professor of religious studies at Virginia Commonwealth University in Richmond, Va. "The days when everybody is born into the Catholic Church and dies in the Catholic Church are long gone."

According to a survey by São Paulo pollster Datafolha published last December, 50 percent of Brazilians over age 16 identified as Catholic, down from 60 percent in 2014, or about 9 million worshippers. In 1970, 92 percent of Brazilians declared themselves Catholic.[1]

The percentage who said in the Datafolha survey that they followed no religion doubled from 2014 to 2016, from 6 percent to 14 percent.[2] The proportion of Brazilians who identified as evangelical Protestants remained at about 29 percent. Only 1 percent said they were atheists.[3]

Catholicism has been steadily shrinking in Brazil since the late 1960s, when military dictatorships saw Catholic liberation theology, which advocated social justice for the poor, as a threat and sought to repress church teachings, experts say. In addition, Brazil, whose slaves brought their African religions with them in earlier periods, has had a long history of embracing non-Catholic alternatives.

"Brazilians are less afraid of trying new religions. They're very open," says Virginia Garrard-Burnett, director of the Benson Latin American Studies and Collections at the University of Texas, Austin.

While Pentecostalism has become popular in other parts of Latin America, its growth in other nations has not mirrored that in Brazil. Other Protestant sects also have made inroads in Brazil and Latin America, including Mormonism, which has doubled its number of Brazilian congregations since the 1980s and now has 1.3 million adherents.[4]

Brazil's urban poor, with little access to medical care, were the first to turn to Pentecostalism, finding appeal in the movement's emphasis on faith healing. Many Brazilian poor also embraced Pentecostalism's other rituals, including speaking in tongues and exorcism, that had parallels with African-based religions such as candomblé, scholars say.

Moreover, the urban poor felt more affinity with their pastors, many of whom were darker skinned and less educated than Catholic priests, traditionally regarded as part of the elite, who are mostly lighter skinned, Chesnut says.

Pentecostalism has since grown to encompass the middle and upper classes and expanded to rural and suburban areas. Faith leaders have succeeded by conducting marketing surveys to determine people's needs and building programs to address them, establishing media networks to reach more converts and building so-called megachurches.

presidential triumph of labor leader Lula, who had run unsuccessfully for president three times as the Workers' Party candidate.

Under Lula, Brazil's economy boomed. Durable consumer goods manufacturing, construction, financial services and consumer credit, and commerce all grew. Exports of agricultural and mineral products, in concert with global demand led by China, increased as well. The expansion led to lower unemployment and social

inequality and a rise in internal consumer demand. Inflation was halved, from 12.5 percent in 2002 to just under 6 percent in 2010.[67]

A key part of Lula's economic strategy was "state capitalism," in which the government took minority stakes in private companies and projects as an economic stimulus. It also expanded social programs such as the Bolsa Familiar cash aid program that bolstered the poor's living standards.

One such center is the Universal Church of the Kingdom of God's Temple of Solomon in São Paulo, designed to resemble the ancient temple in Jerusalem. It can accommodate 10,000 congregants, says Garrard-Burnett.

"[Evangelical churches] are really a presence in every level of society in a way that few Brazilian institutions are," says Garrard-Burnett, a history and religious studies professor who specializes in Latin American Protestantism.

The Catholic Church has responded to the membership loss by establishing charismatic churches, which, like Pentecostalism, offer faith healing, prophecy, speaking in tongues and popular music during Mass. It also has endorsed personalities such as Marcelo Rossi, a charismatic-church pop-star priest with a Snapchat account who gives concerts and records albums, experts say. Formally known as the Catholic Charismatic Renewal, the movement originated in the 1960s and has become an accepted part of the Catholic Church with Vatican support.

"There was lightning-speed approval of charismatic churches in all the episcopacies," Chesnut says. "They saw it as the best way to compete."

The choice of Pope Francis, an Argentinian, in 2013 to lead the Catholic Church was widely seen as an effort by the Vatican to stem the exodus of Catholics throughout Latin American. But while Francis is extremely popular in Brazil, experts say the hemorrhaging continues. "He's more likely to stanch the flow of secular conversions rather than conversions to the Pentecostals," Garrard-Burnett says.

In societies with widespread poverty, weak social support from government and little opportunity, evangelical Protestant churches can be hard to beat, scholars say. Besides preaching the prosperity gospel, which holds that faith will be rewarded by material wealth, such churches typically offer life resources, such as literacy skills and instruction about how to open a bank account.

Getty Images/Victor Moriyama

Evangelicals participate in the March for Jesus on June 4, 2015, in São Paulo. Once solidly Roman Catholic, Brazil has seen a steady rise of evangelical Protestant sects in recent years.

"They've sort of understood the culture they're working in, Brazilians' history, their worldview, and they've been incredibly successful," Garrard-Burnett says. "The Catholic Church took Brazil for granted for the longest time."

— *Christina Hoag*

[1] "Brazil: Loss of at least 9 million Catholics in two years," Documentation Information Catholiques Internationales, Feb. 2, 2017, http://tinyurl.com/mc7dos5; "The Catholic Church in Brazil and the evangelical offensive," Documentation Information Catholiques Internationales, Sept. 8, 2013, http://tinyurl.com/myhltrq.

[2] Ana Estela de Sousa Pinto, "At Least Nine Million Brazilians Give Up Catholicism, Shows Datafolha Survey," Folha de S. Paulo, Dec. 26, 2016, http://tinyurl.com/jvqmldb.

[3] "Brazil: Loss of at least 9 million Catholics in two years," op. cit.

[4] "Brazil," Church of Jesus Christ of the Latter-day Saints, http://tinyurl.com/ktv3mkz.

Barred from seeking a third consecutive term under Brazil's constitution, Lula in 2011 passed the presidential baton to his handpicked successor, his chief of staff Rousseff, a former Marxist guerrilla who was tortured while imprisoned under the military dictatorship from 1970 to 1973.[68]

Brazil's first female president, Rousseff continued Lula's policies but increased the government's interventionist role in the economy, which was reeling from the global collapse in commodity demand. She narrowly won a second term in 2015 but soon became enmeshed in Operation Car Wash.

Rousseff denied knowledge of the kickbacks, but because she was chairwoman of the Petrobras board from 2003 to 2010, many doubted her credibility. Rousseff's political support suffered as a result.[69] As more corporate executives and politicians were arrested, the economy became paralyzed and the recession deepened.

Brazilian President Dilma Rousseff delivers her farewell address after her impeachment in August 2016. Handpicked by President Luiz Inácio Lula da Silva as his successor, Rousseff was removed from office for illegally borrowing $11 billion from public banks to cover budget gaps. Vice President Michel Temer, who replaced her, is trying to jumpstart the economy by loosening regulations on foreign and private investment in several key economic sectors.

In 2016, just after the Summer Olympic Games were held in Rio de Janeiro, Rousseff was impeached in August for procuring loans from public banks to cover budget deficits, and Vice President Michel Temer assumed the presidency until the 2018 election.

CURRENT SITUATION

Sputtering Economy

Although signs of an anemic recovery are emerging, Brazil's deep recession continues. Analysts say economic activity in both the private and public sectors remains weak amid fears of further fallout from Operation Car Wash.

Moreover, unrelated investigations are exposing graft in other places. In March, prosecutors arrested more than two dozen people, alleging officials at Brazil's two biggest meatpacking companies bribed food sanitation inspectors to approve contaminated meat. Analysts say the scandal could jeopardize Brazil's $12 billion exports of poultry and beef.[70]

The recession is squeezing public coffers, resulting in months-long delays in paying civil servants, including teachers, police officers and firefighters, as well as pensioners. The recession also is contributing to supply shortages in hospitals and affecting other social services.

Many of Brazil's 26 states are in dire fiscal straits due to overspending, high borrowing from federal banks and overly generous tax breaks awarded during the boom years of the early 2000s.[71]

The financial situation in the states of Rio de Janeiro, Minas Gerais and Rio Grande do Sul is especially serious, with the latter declaring "a state of financial calamity" in November. Despite an $850 million federal emergency loan to stave off bankruptcy last summer, Rio de Janeiro state has money only to cover salaries until mid-2017.[72]

Last year, the state declared a fiscal emergency weeks before the Summer Olympics so it could borrow federal funds. Private companies and the city of Rio de Janeiro, which was in a much better financial position than the state, financed much of the Games' $4.56 billion cost. Many of the Olympic buildings, including athletes' housing, a swimming pool, stadium, handball arena and broadcast center, are boarded up despite officials' promises not to leave any "white elephants." Mayor Marcelo Crivella says the city is on an austerity budget.[73]

Brazil's financial crisis has led to a breakdown in public services. In early February, police demanding higher wages and better working conditions in the southeastern state of Espírito Santo found a way to circumvent a law prohibiting strikes by law enforcement: Their families blockaded police stations, preventing them from leaving to patrol streets. Looting, street muggings and other types of crime spiked, with homicides rising from four in January to 143 over the nine days of the police work stoppage.[74] The impasse largely ended when President Temer called in troops to patrol the streets, airlifted the officers out of the stations and consented to considering raising their base monthly pay of $850.[75]

The federal government has little choice but to bail out the states, analysts say. In November, Finance Minister Henrique Meirelles said the federal government would use revenue from the repatriation of Brazilians' undeclared foreign income and holdings to help the bankrupt governments.[76]

The debate now focuses on whether the federal government should impose austerity measures on the states. In late December, Temer vetoed a bailout bill after legislators stripped out cost-cutting mandates, such as salary freezes, increased pension contributions and privatizations, in return for debt relief.[77]

Should Brazil have a permanent U.N. Security Council seat?

YES
Mark S. Langevin
Director, Brazil Initiative, Elliott School of International Affairs, George Washington University

Written for *CQ Researcher*, April 2017

The United Nations Security Council should be expanded, and Brazil should be granted a permanent seat. Brazil was an original member of the first Council of the League of Nations following World War I.

During the establishment of the United Nations, U.S. President Franklin D. Roosevelt pushed for a six-nation U.N. Security Council, including Brazil. Roosevelt's untimely death put Brazilian ambitions on hold.

A permanent Security Council seat remains the holy grail for Brazilian officials, but even temporary membership has played a central role in the formation of the nation's foreign policies. Brazil has served as a frequent rotating member on the Security Council and is well-known in U.N. circles as a constructive voice for moderation and consensus building. Brazil participates in the G-4, along with Germany, India and Japan, to advocate for seats on the Security Council.

Moreover, Brazil's longtime leadership role in the Group of 77 developing nations and its more recent innovative, multilateral engagements with the BRICS nations (an association for five emerging economies) and the IBSA Dialogue Forum (India, Brazil and South Africa) provide a compelling argument that Brazil is one of a handful of member-states that could make the Security Council more representative and effective.

Brazil's notable stature at the United Nations, its demonstrated diplomatic capacity to work with many different member-states to open up lines of dialogue and even forge consensus, and its experience as a rotating member of the council provide ample evidence to make the case that Brazil, along with the other G-4 member-states, should be granted Security Council seats. That would make the institution more representative and better positioned to confront 21st-century collective security challenges.

These impressive credentials, however, are insufficient to move existing council members to agree to expansion. If Brazil wants to realize this national goal, its political leaders must pay more of the costs of collective security and expand the nation's capacity to respond to humanitarian emergencies, such as the Syrian refugee flows.

Brazil must also consider its current political distance from the United States, especially in terms of its General Assembly votes, given the U.S. strategic partnerships with all nations of the G-4 except Brazil. Today, the world needs Brazil's special voice and vote on those multilateral matters at the heart of the struggle for peace and prosperity for all.

NO
Riordan Roett
Director, Latin American Studies Program, Paul H. Nitze School of Advanced International Studies, Johns Hopkins University

Written for *CQ Researcher*, April 2017

Brazil has always aspired to greatness but has failed to achieve it. Brazil is a strong advocate of "soft power," such as peacekeeping and transferring agricultural technology to poor countries in Africa.

But "hard power" is not in the Brazilian elites' DNA. Brazil will never commit troops to geopolitical missions such as those in Iraq or Afghanistan. Respecting sovereignty, and not interfering in the internal affairs of its neighbors, is a paramount belief of the foreign policy elites.

Brazil also faces frequent social and economic internal crises. The elites fail to understand that the world powers have reasonably stable political systems — democratic or authoritarian. The G-7 nations also have advanced educational and health standards. Deep disparities in educational levels prevent Brazil from becoming a competitive or productive economy. Its economy is still based on the export of commodities and minerals.

It has never fully industrialized and produces very little that would be attractive on world markets. Therefore, it is always the victim of swings in international prices for iron ore, coffee, sugar, etc. And it remains a closed economy in terms of world trade. Unproductive firms in Brazil are not allowed to fail.

Brazilians were very disappointed when President Barack Obama visited India and publicly endorsed it for a seat on the U.N. Security Council. He did not do so when he visited Brazil. The foreign policy elites in Brazil don't seem to understand that India is an important geopolitical player in Asia. It has difficult neighbors — Pakistan and China — and it is a nuclear power.

That gives India a global status that is very different from that of Brazil. Brazil is not a nuclear power; it does not have any border disputes with its neighbors; it does not have a terrorist threat or jihadists within its national territory. Geographically, it is far removed from the major theaters of world politics.

Brazilian leaders must understand that given the country's relative isolation in world politics, their main challenge is to address inequality and underdevelopment within their own borders. They must improve the conditions needed to be competitive and productive economically, and they must find a formula to achieve political stability. Then, the country might receive the respect it so desperately wants from the global players in world politics.

A homeless man sleeps outside Maracana Stadium in Rio de Janeiro. Since the iconic soccer venue hosted events at the Summer Olympics and World Cup it has fallen into disrepair along with many other Olympic buildings. Rio de Janeiro state is among several Brazilian states in dire economic straits. Despite an $850 million federal emergency loan to stave off bankruptcy last summer, Rio de Janeiro state has money only to cover salaries until mid-2017.

However, a month later the federal government reached a deal with the Rio de Janeiro state government, allowing it to suspend its debt payments for three years in exchange for budget cuts and tax increases. Meirelles said the plan, if approved by federal and state lawmakers, could be a model for other states, although critics warned that it simply postpones Rio's day of reckoning.[78]

Faint Progress

The International Monetary Fund forecasts that Brazil's economy will turn the corner this year, but just barely, growing 0.5 percent. Rises in commodity prices, including iron ore, soybeans, corn and oil, will help. Commodities make up about half of Brazil's exports.[79]

Although analysts stress the economy has a long way to go, signs of recovery are surfacing. Foreign investment surged to $78.9 billion in 2016, up 6 percent from 2015, as investors anticipate a more favorable investment climate under Temer. The Chinese utility State Grid bought a majority stake in the Brazilian utility CPFL Energia, while Britain's Jaguar Land Rover Automotive opened a $296 million factory in Rio de Janeiro state.

Investors say the country is too big a market to discount. "[Brazil] is a strong economy, and once it shakes off its troubles it will go back to having an economic rally again," said Hanno Kirner, executive director of strategy at Jaguar Land Rover. "It has got resources, it has got a young dynamic population. It has got everything in the long term."[80]

In February, Swiss food multinational Nestlé announced plans to build an $86 million Purina dog food plant in São Paulo state, seeing a huge consumer market for 75 percent of the plant's output and an ideal location to export the remainder to surrounding South American countries.[81]

Over the past year, Brazil's currency, the *real*, has strengthened 20 percent against the U.S. dollar, and the stock market has surged 37 percent, buoyed by Temer's more business-friendly government than Rousseff's. Investors have been encouraged by the willingness of Temer's administration to tackle some necessary but politically unpopular reforms. The 76-year-old constitutional lawyer has said he is not planning to seek another term and thus is not concerned about currying favor with voters by pursuing "fiscal populism." His public approval rating stands at just 15 percent.[82]

He scored a major victory in December when he pushed through Congress a 20-year cap on public spending, the cornerstone of an austerity program to rein in a growing budget deficit.[83]

Next on Temer's agenda are plans to simplify the country's complex tax code, liberalize labor laws that deter hiring, cut pension costs by raising the retirement age for public workers from 54 to 65 and improve the public school system by raising graduation rates to produce a more competitive workforce.[84]

Analysts say getting those reforms through Congress will be an uphill battle. Temer may not be worried about re-election, but legislators are. "I don't know if the government has the legitimacy to do these reforms," says Langevin of George Washington University.

Going forward, the economy also may not get much of a lift from Brazil's sprawling companies, particularly those in construction, that have been significantly weakened by the corruption scandal. The Odebrecht Group has shed nearly 60,000 of its 180,000 employees while its revenues have plummeted 50 percent since the investigation began.[85] "It's been banned from doing government work. It will be a shadow of its former self," Taylor of American University says.

The outlook for Petrobras is a bit more optimistic. The company has a new CEO, Pedro Parente, who has downsized the workforce, revamped its governance and announced the sale of $40 billion in assets over the next decade. Last fall, 11,700 employees agreed to voluntarily leave, and Congress approved allowing foreign companies to take over offshore oil fields.[86]

"Petrobras is a fifth of its size at its peak in 2008-09. It's going to be a very different company," says Taylor.

Corruption Fallout

Brazil's ongoing corruption investigation is turning global as prosecutors in several countries undertake their own probes of the Odebrecht Group's bribery schemes. In February, a Peruvian judge issued an arrest warrant for former President Alejandro Toledo, who is accused of receiving $20 million in bribes from the construction giant for infrastructure contracts, including a highway connecting Peru and Brazil.[87] In Colombia, prosecutors said President Juan Manuel Santos' 2014 campaign may have received a $1 million contribution from a third party linked to Odebrecht, prompting Santos to call for an investigation.[88]

The expanding investigations come on the heels of Odebrecht's agreement in December to pay $3.5 billion in global penalties after the U.S. Department of Justice revealed that the construction multinational had a secret department tasked with funneling bribes totaling $800 million to government officials in 12 countries in Latin America and Africa.[89]

The widening scandal has caused more embarrassment for Brazilians. "Brazil's international prestige has just melted," says Hakim of the Inter-American Dialogue.

Brazil's own investigation is set to expand significantly with the public release of details from a wave of plea bargains reached last year between prosecutors and dozens of Odebrecht executives in which defendants received more lenient sentences in exchange for their testimony. The plea agreements are believed to implicate top politicians in Brazil and other countries, possibly including Temer, who has been mentioned in other plea bargains but never charged. A court could remove him if evidence surfaces of illegal campaign funds that he has long been accused of receiving. Temer has denied any wrongdoing.[90]

"I would say that the new plea agreements could allow the Car Wash operation to double its size in the future," Deltan Dallagnol, the federal prosecutor in charge of the operation, told The Associated Press.

Dallaganol said no end to the investigation is in sight, and he vowed that he and Judge Moro, the other key figure in the investigation, will continue despite significant political pressure from legislators to scale it back or drop it.[91]

In the meantime, the nation waits for further revelations from the plea bargain testimony and the political fallout that will cause, experts say. "People are worrying about the next shoe to drop," says Winter of the Council of the Americas.

Operation Car Wash promises to be front and center for some time because prosecutions will take time, Winter says. "Winding down the investigation will allow some degree of stability to return, but the trials will last years," he says.

The scandals are having a spillover effect on politics. Underscoring public discontent with the political class and system, Brazil's two largest cities inaugurated outsiders as mayors in January: Joao Doria, a São Paulo millionaire businessman, and Crivella, an evangelical Protestant bishop in Rio de Janeiro. Both men had defeated allies of the president, and Doria also defeated the incumbent.[92]

OUTLOOK
More Political Uncertainty

The near-term outlook for Brazil pivots on the October 2018 presidential election, analysts agree. So far, no candidates have emerged as overwhelming front-runners, although Lula, 72, has said he will run as the Workers' Party candidate.

Still, even if he avoids conviction on the five corruption indictments pending against him, he may not have the popular support to win. A December poll by São Paulo pollster Datafolha put Lula as the front-runner with just 25 percent support and Marina Silva, his former environmental minister who would run for her newly created party Sustainability Network (REDE), in second place with 15 percent.[93]

A fragmented race could boost Lula into a second-round runoff between the top two vote-getters, but that may not be enough to net him the presidency, says Taylor of American University. (Brazil's presidential election system calls for a second runoff election between the two top contenders if no candidate wins more than 50 percent.)

That could benefit Silva, an Afro-indigenous former rubber tapper from the Amazon who is supported by a strong evangelical movement. The December poll had Silva beating Lula by 9 points in a runoff.[94]

However, experts note that with such scant support for the two leading contenders, the electoral landscape remains an open field. "No one knows who will be the next president," says Hakim of the Inter-American Dialogue.

Full economic recovery and long-term growth, economists say, will depend on whether the new president has the popular support and political will needed to tackle unpopular but necessary reforms, such as restructuring the generous pension system and the byzantine tax code.

Although the Temer government has started to implement some reforms, such as opening Petrobras to more private investment and streamlining business regulations, there is no guarantee the incoming leader will be of the same mind-set.

"I see a very large chance that a new government may not continue these reforms," de Bolle of the Peterson Institute of International Economics says.

Others, however, say Brazil has no choice but to open up its economy. "By 2020, it'll be a more liberal country in the economy," Langevin says.

Casanova of Cornell University says weaknesses in the private sector pose another problem. "The big private-sector companies are dismantled, and there is no strong private sector," she says. "I don't know how the country is going to recover."

As the political landscape evolves, Brazil's economic fortunes will continue to depend on commodities. If world demand and prices recover, that could spur a revival in government spending on public infrastructure projects and thus help restore economic growth. "If the price of oil goes up, everything will be all right again," Johns Hopkins University's Roett says.

Absent that spark, observers note that recovery of Brazil's private sector may lag for some time, as it was never strong to begin with and has been badly harmed by the recession and the weakening of consumer demand.

Experts agree that for the foreseeable future, Brazil will continue to be an underachieving country whose potential will be much talked about but not fulfilled.

"What has happened over the past four years has been a huge blow to Brazil. I'm pretty pessimistic about what's coming," says Winter of the Council of the Americas. "They'll move out of recession soon, but getting back to reducing poverty and to growth of 3 to 5 percent won't be in the short term. Deep structural issues need to be addressed."

NOTES

1. Blake Schmidt and Sabrina Valle, "Brazil's Marcelo Odebrecht Gets 19 Years in Jail in Carwash," Bloomberg, March 8, 2016, http://tinyurl.com/mo8t4xo.

2. Andrew Jacobs and Paula Moura, "At the Birthplace of a Graft Scandal, Brazil's Crisis Is on Full Display," *The New York Times*, June 10, 2016, http://tinyurl.com/llj4q8c.

3. Brian Winter, "Brazil's Car Wash Probe: Tell Me How This Ends," *Americas Quarterly*, Sept. 28, 2016, http://tinyurl.com/k57fjrz.

4. Merrit Kennedy, "Brazil's Recession The Longest And Deepest In Its History, New Figures Show," NPR, March 7, 2017, http://tinyurl.com/knbgwjm; "Brazil Unemployment Hit Fresh High of 12.6%," *Trading Economics*, undated, http://tinyurl.com/7rzyjnf.

5. "Brazil: People & Society" and "Brazil: Economy," *CIA World Factbook*, http://tinyurl.com/kzfjzg5; "Brazil National Economic Profile," United Nations Economic Commission of Latin America and the Caribbean, http://tinyurl.com/kpsko9h; "Mexico National Economic Profile." United Nations Economic Commission of Latin America and the Caribbean, http://tinyurl.com/n5gnm7f; and "Nicaragua National Economic Profile," United Nations Economic Commission of Latin America and the Caribbean, http://tinyurl.com/lu2p76k.

6. Ibid., "Brazil: Economy."

7. "Brazil's Lula to leave office with record-high popularity," Reuters, Dec. 16, 2010, http://tinyurl.com/lo5qq9w.

8. "Brazil and the United Nations Security Council," Ministry of Foreign Affairs, undated, http://tinyurl.com/m7dkdaq.

9. "Country Comparison, Distribution of Family Income: GINI Index," *CIA World Factbook*, http://tinyurl.com/mn8how.

10. Jessica Brice, Ney Hayashi and David Biller, "Brazil Suffers Slow Growth with Lula China Policy Sowing Doubts," Bloomberg, Sept. 22, 2014, http://tinyurl.com/laex39m.

11. "Corruption Perceptions Index 2016," Transparency International, http://tinyurl.com/z7bmnu8.

12. "Brazil starts jailing those convicted in 'Mensalao' trial," Agence France-Presse, *The Telegraph*, Nov. 16, 2013, http://tinyurl.com/ksahhpq.

13. Fabiola Moura and Jessica Brice, "Brazil Has a School Problem," Bloomberg News, March 2, 2017, http://tinyurl.com/me96mas; Simon Romero, "Dilma Rousseff Is Ousted as Brazil's President in Impeachment Vote," *The New York Times*, Aug. 31, 2016, http://tinyurl.com/ko4joz2.

14. Samy Adghirni, "After Oil Industry Shift, Brazil Seeks to Open Up Defense," Bloomberg, Oct. 25, 2016, http://tinyurl.com/kgmq6wl.

15. Vinicy Chan, "The Gold Medal for Buying Up Brazilian Assets Goes to China, Inc.," Bloomberg, Aug. 18, 2016, http://tinyurl.com/n733fsx.

16. "Brazil to ease local content rules in oil industry," Reuters, Oct. 17, 2016, http://tinyurl.com/m92754u.

17. "Country Comparison Crude Oil Production," *CIA World Factbook*, http://tinyurl.com/kssswhm.

18. Rebeca Duran, "Importation of Oil in Brazil," *The Brazil Business*, Aug. 26, 2013, http://tinyurl.com/meg8o9z.

19. Simon Romero, "As a Distracted Brazil Mourns, Lawmakers Gut a Corruption Bill," *The New York Times*, Nov. 30, 2017, http://tinyurl.com/m23pdsz.

20. Brad Brooks, "Brazil prosecutors hit ex-president Lula with more corruption charges," Reuters, Dec. 15, 2016, http://tinyurl.com/l7x8hyp.

21. "Lula indictment may affect 2018 race," *The Economist*, Sept. 22, 2016, http://tinyurl.com/kovbclo.

22. Mario Sergio Lima, Anna Edgerton and Bruce Douglas, "Lula Faces Trial as Judge Accepts Corruption Charges," Bloomberg, Sept. 20, 2016, http://tinyurl.com/zpwuojn.

23. Ryan Lloyd and Carlos Oliveira, "How Brazil's electoral system led the country into political crisis," *The Washington Post*, May 25, 2016, http://tinyurl.com/kw7shgn.

24. Igor Utsumi, "Funding of Political Parties in Brazil," *The Brazil Business*, Oct. 3, 2014, http://tinyurl.com/k4s7eeo; Anthony Boadle, "Millionaires, evangelicals benefit from Brazil campaign funds ban," Reuters, Sept. 29, 2016, http://tinyurl.com/lxelz32.

25. Alex Cuadros, *Brazillionaires: Wealth, Power, Decadence, and Hope in an American Country* (2016), p. 12.

26. Erik Ortiz, "What is a favela? 5 Things to Know About Rio's So-Called Shantytowns," NBC News, Aug. 4, 2016, http://tinyurl.com/hp3sssz.

27. Jing Xu, "Economic Inequality in Brazil," The Borgen Project, July 28, 2014, http://tinyurl.com/krgj9h3; "Country Comparison: Distribution of Family Income, Gini Index," *CIA World Factbook*, Central Intelligence Agency, http://tinyurl.com/lf7gjwy.

28. Deborah Wetzel, "Bolsa Família: Brazil's Quiet Revolution," World Bank, Nov. 4, 2013, http://tinyurl.com/mopjhv5; Sarah Illingworth, "Bolsa Família: The Program Helping 50M Brazilians Exit Poverty," *The Huffington Post*, June 10, 2015 (updated June 9, 2016), http://tinyurl.com/kvbfbov; and Jay Forte, "Brazil Raises 2017 Monthly Minimum Wage to R\$937," *Rio Times Online*, Dec. 30, 2016, http://tinyurl.com/l7t7puo.

29. "Brazil," Organisation for Economic Co-Operation and Development, http://tinyurl.com/lc2q2de.

30. Fabiola Moura and Jessica Brice, "Brazil Has a School Problem," Bloomberg, March 2, 2017, http://tinyurl.com/k6wod3d.

31. Lise Alves, "Brazilian Government Announces New Education Model," *Rio Times*, Sept 23, 2016, http://tinyurl.com/kbaw8ka.

32. Pam Bellick and Tania Franco, "For Brazil's Zika Families, a Life of Struggles and Scares," *The New York Times*, March 11, 2017, http://tinyurl.com/k32waok. Also see Alan Greenblatt, "Mosquito-Borne Disease," *CQ Researcher*, July 22, 2016, pp. 601–624.

33. "National Security Plan will rationalise prison system," Brazil Office of the Presidency, Jan. 4, 2017, http://tinyurl.com/k5zm8br.

34. "Brazil's former richest man Eike Batista sent to prison," BBC, Jan. 31, 2017, http://tinyurl.com/kb53vho; Anderson Antunes, "Former Billionaire Eike Batista Bemoans His Return to the Middle Class," *Forbes*, Sept. 18, 2014, http://tinyurl.com/nxa34pe.

35. "Brazil: Transportation," U.S. International Trade Administration, Export.gov, Oct. 14, 2016, http://tinyurl.com/km85no9.

36. Athena Peppes and Armen Ovanessoff, "What Business Must Do To Reignite Brazil Productivity Growth," Accenture, 2015, p. 17, http://tinyurl.com/mu2z5p9; Ibid., "Brazil: Transportation."

37. Moura and Brice, op. cit.

38. Forte, op. cit.; Peppes and Ovanessoff, op. cit., p. 18.

39. Cynthia Fujikawa Nes, "Brazilian Employment Law in a Nutshell," *The Brazil Business*, Nov. 20, 2016, http://tinyurl.com/llmftkf.

40. Peppes and Ovanessoff, op. cit., p. 15.

41. Luiza Belloni, "Despite Brazil's Financial Crisis, Havaianas Still Has the World at Its Feet," *The Huffington Post*, Dec. 4, 2015, http://tinyurl.com/me2mqj6.

42. Lourdes Casanova, "Making the Brazil Dream a Reality," *Latin Trade*, undated, http://tinyurl.com/m3a85vx.

43. Bruce Douglas and Matthew Malinowski, "Brazil Worries the 'China of South America' Is Eating Its Lunch," Bloomberg, Jan. 9, 2017, http://tinyurl.com/lbb64yp.

44. Thomas E. Skidmore, *Brazil: Five Centuries of Change* (1999), p. 5.

45. Marshall C. Eakin, *Brazil: The Once and Future Country* (1997), p. 15.

46. Boris Fausto, *A Concise History of Brazil* (1999), pp. 9-11.

47. Skidmore, op. cit., pp. 17, 19.

48. Fausto, op. cit., p. 49.

49. Skidmore op. cit., p. 30.

50. Eakin, op. cit., p. 27; ibid., Skidmore, p. 36.

51. Fausto, op. cit., p. 70; ibid., Eakin, pp. 28-29.

52. José Fonseca, "A Brief History of Brazil," *The New York Times*, undated, http://tinyurl.com/kx35luw.

53. Skidmore, op. cit., pp. 54, 70.

54. Eakin, op. cit., p. 37.

55. Ibid., Eakin, p. 34.

56. Ibid., pp. 43-46.

57. Skidmore, op. cit., pp. 136-138.

58. Ibid., p. 139.

59. Eakin, op. cit., p. 55.

60. Skidmore, op. cit., pp. 165-166.

61. Ibid., pp. 177, 181.

62. Eakin, op. cit., p. 59; Fausto, op. cit., p. 305.

63. Fonseca, op. cit.

64. Fausto, op. cit., p. 315; Skidmore, op. cit., p. 217.

65. Ibid., Fausto, p. 319.

66. Mark S. Langevin and Timothy Stackhouse, "Brazil and Development: Growth, Equity and Sustainability in the 21st Century," Brazil Initiative, George Washington University Elliott School of International Affairs, August 2015, p. 4, http://tinyurl.com/mxo4ppb; Skidmore, op. cit., p. 228.

67. Ibid., Skidmore; "Historic inflation: Brazil," Inflation.eu, undated, http://tinyurl.com/mpg4dkb.

68. Walter Brandimarte and Vivianne Rodrigues, "From Guerrilla to Impeachment: The Dilma Rousseff Story," Bloomberg, Aug. 30, 2016, http://tinyurl.com/jauahf6.

69. Ibid.

70. Brad Haynes and Sergio Spagnuolo, "Brazil police raid BRF and JBS plants in meatpacking probe," Reuters, March 17, 2017, http://tinyurl.com/labmr7d.

71. Alonso Soto and Reese Ewing, "Brazil's federal, state governments reach accord to balance accounts," Reuters, Nov. 22, 2016, http://tinyurl.com/kgjcrd4.

72. Mac Margolis, "In Brazil, State Debt Is a Ticking Time Bomb," Bloomberg, Dec. 2, 2016, http://tinyurl.com/mr697fp.

73. Jonathan Watts, "Rio de Janeiro governor declares financial emergency ahead of Olympics," *The Guardian*, June 17, 2016, http://tinyurl.com/lzdrfxh; "The cost of hosting this year's Olympics in Rio lowest since 2004," *Sports Illustrated*, Aug. 24, 2016, http://tinyurl.com/jk6c6a2; and Anna Jean Kaiser, "Legacy of Rio Olympics Is So Far Series of Unkept Promises," *The New York Times*, Feb. 15, 2017, http://tinyurl.com/lt678fp.

74. Marina Lopes, "Police went on strike in a Brazilian state. The result was near anarchy," *The Washington Post*, March 1, 2017, http://tinyurl.com/knr7ee6.

75. "Brazil army takes over state's security as 100 killed amid police strike," *The Guardian*, Feb. 9, 2017, http://tinyurl.com/za7swg8.

76. Soto and Ewing, op. cit.

77. Rachel Garnarski and Walter Brandimarte, "Brazil's Indebted States Dealt Blow as Temer Vetoes Relief," Bloomberg, Dec. 28, 2016, http://tinyurl.com/kjqecpr.

78. Rachel Garnarski and Samy Adghirni, "Brazil's Government Deal With Rio Won't Solve Its Debt Crisis," Bloomberg. Jan. 31, 2017, http://tinyurl.com/m8ppwvx.

79. Mary Sadler, "Is Brazil's Recovery Back on Track for 2017?" *Market Realist*, Feb. 24, 2017, http://tinyurl.com/n9xgss7.

80. Joe Leahy, "Business bets big on Brazil economic rally," *Financial Times*, Feb. 6, 2017, http://tinyurl.com/ltrpfm4.

81. Fabiola Moura, "Nestle to Open $86 million Brazil Plant to Tap Dog Food Demand," Bloomberg, Feb. 2, 2017, http://tinyurl.com/lrjggpj.

82. Joe Leahy, "Temer stays tough on Brazil economic reforms," *Financial Times*, Feb.2, 2017, http://tinyurl.com/mb5qqab.

83. Anthony Boadle and Marcela Ayres, "Brazil Senate passes spending cap in win for Temer," Reuters, Dec. 13, 2016, http://tinyurl.com/mm5arwp.

84. Leahy, op. cit.

85. Marina Lopes and Nick Miroff, "How a scandal that started in Brazil is now roiling other Latin American countries," *The Washington Post*, Feb. 22, 2017, http://tinyurl.com/l3yadjc.

86. Zainab Calcuttawala, "Brazilian Congress Authorizes Sale of Petrobras 'Pre-Salt' Fields," Oilprice.com, Nov. 29, 2016, http://tinyurl.com/jwacxt9.

87. Andrea Zarate, "Corruption Scandal Ensnares Leaders of Peru and Colombia," *The New York Times*, Feb. 7, 2017, http://tinyurl.com/k7nzcm9.

88. "Colombia's Santos calls for probe of Odebrecht's role in 2014 campaign," Reuters, Feb. 8, 2017, http://tinyurl.com/ldzko87.

89. Alexandra Stevenson and Vinod Sreeharsha, "Secret Unit Helped Brazilian Company Bribe Government Officials," *The New York Times*, Dec. 21, 2016, http://tinyurl.com/mmtu77q; Marina Lopes and Nick Miroff, "How a scandal that started in Brazil is now roiling other Latin American countries," *The Washington Post*, Feb. 22, 2017, http://tinyurl.com/l3yadjc.

90. Peter Prengaman, "Brazil Prosecutor Says Massive Corruption Prosecution Could Double in Size," *Time*, Jan. 26, 2017, http://tinyurl.com/mhoty99.

91. Ibid.

92. Sarah DiLorenzo and Mauricio Saverese, "Fed up with politics, Brazil cities swear in outsider mayors," The Associated Press, Jan. 1, 2017, http://tinyurl.com/l7xx2nq.

93. Flavio Ferreira, "Marina Silva is the leader in all second round scenarios, points Datafolha," Folha de S. Paulo, Dec 12, 2016, http://tinyurl. com/kq3wqy3.

94. Ibid.

BIBLIOGRAPHY
Selected Sources
Books

Alston, Lee J., et al., *Brazil in Transition: Beliefs, Leadership and Institutional Change*, Princeton University Press, 2016.
Academics and other experts analyze Brazil's political and economic history over the last 50 years, examining how the nation evolved into a potential world superpower and what remains to be done to achieve that status.

Barbassa, Juliana, *Dancing with the Devil in the City of God: Rio de Janeiro and the Olympic Dream*, Touchstone, 2015.

A former Associated Press correspondent examines the city of her birth, detailing both its glamour and drawbacks.

Cuadros, Alex, *Brazillionaires: Wealth, Power, Decadence, and Hope in an American Country,* **Spiegel & Grau, 2016.**
A journalist chronicles how Brazil's superrich amassed spectacular wealth through political skullduggery, their soap opera lives and their downfalls amid economic collapse.

Mares, David R. and Harold A. Trinkunas, *Aspirational Power: Brazil on the Long Road to Global Influence,* **Brookings Institution Press, 2016.**
Scholars at a Washington think tank explain why Brazil, despite its size, has never emerged as a global power.

Reid, Michael, *Brazil: The Troubled Rise of a Global Power,* **Yale University Press, 2016.**
The Latin American columnist for *The Economist* explores why Brazil has been overshadowed by other emerging economies such as Russia, China and India, and what the South American nation must do to gain equal status to those nations.

Schneider, Ben Ross, *New Order and Progress: Development and Democracy in Brazil,* **Oxford University Press, 2016.**
A professor in the Massachusetts Institute of Technology's Brazil program explains why Brazil has not achieved its potential despite gains in its economic and political stability since the days of military dictatorship.

Articles

DiLorenzo, Sarah, and Mauricio Savarese, "Fed up with politics, Brazil cities swear in outsider mayors," The Associated Press, Jan. 1, 2017, http://tinyurl.com/l7xx2nq.
Sao Paulo and Rio de Janeiro inaugurated political outsiders as mayors, underscoring the public's frustration with politicians and rampant corruption.

Phillips, Dom, "Once underfed, Brazil's poor have a new problem: obesity," The Washington Post, Nov. 21, 2016, http://tinyurl.com/mvxkkqo.
Brazilians' emergence from poverty has led to new diets of junk and processed food, which in turn has caused a sharp rise in obesity.

Rapoza, Kenneth, "Brazil's Sale of the Century," The Boston Globe, June 5, 2016, http://tinyurl.com/ln2uan2.
Brazil's state oil company, Petrobras, can recoup from corruption scandal setbacks by allowing foreign companies full control over deep-water oil wells.

Stevenson, Alexandra, and Vindo Sreemarsha, "Secret Unit Helped Brazilian Company Bribe Government Officials," The New York Times, Dec. 21, 2016, http://tinyurl.com/lbtpedu.
Latin America's biggest construction company had a division that coordinated and facilitated bribes and kickbacks.

Watts, Jonathan, "Fresh crisis in Brazil as new president faces corruption allegations," The Guardian, Nov. 25, 2016, http://tinyurl.com/mgjr45z.
A former Cabinet colleague of President Michel Temer alleges he used his influence in a construction project, fueling opposition moves for impeachment.

Reports and Studies

Brasil, P., et al., "Zika Virus Infection in Pregnant Women in Rio de Janeiro," The New England Journal of Medicine, Dec. 15, 2016, http://tinyurl.com/gp5fda9.
Medical experts study the effects of the Zika virus on pregnant women and their newborns.

Moro, Sergio, "Handling Systemic Corruption in Brazil," Wilson Center for International Scholars, Dec. 8, 2016, http://tinyurl.com/ktfn3e7.
A Brazilian judge known for his efforts to reform the judicial system discusses the extent of graft and the partly successful efforts to combat it.

Muggah, Robert, "The State of Security and Justice in Brazil: Reviewing the Evidence," Brazil Initiative, George Washington University, March 2015, http://tinyurl.com/kmedcl9.
A specialist in security and development examines the challenges and reforms in Brazil's public safety and justice systems.

Nobre, Carlos A., et al., "Land-use and climate change risks in the Amazon and the need of a novel sustainable development paradigm," National Academy of Sciences, Aug. 11, 2016, http://tinyurl.com/n3p3svu.
Scientists examine deforestation in the Brazilian Amazon over the past 50 years and say a new sustainable development approach is needed.

For More Information

Brazilian-American Chamber of Commerce, 509 Madison Ave., New York, NY 10022; 212-751-4691; www.brazilcham .com. Promotes trade and investment and closer business ties between Brazil and the United States.

The Brazil Initiative, George Washington University, 1957 E St., N.W., Suite 501, Washington, DC 20052; 202-994-4060; www.brazil.elliott.gwu.edu. Promotes understanding of Brazilian culture, development, history and foreign policy.

Brazil-U.S. Business Council, 1615 H St., N.W., Washington, DC 20062; 202-463-5729; www.brazil council.org. Promotes policies for increasing cooperation, bilateral trade and investment between the United States and Brazil.

Council of the Americas, Suite 250, 1615 L St., N.W., Washington, DC 20036; 202-659-8989; www.as-coa.org.

Business think tank focusing on free trade, open markets and democracy in the Americas.

Embassy of Brazil, 3006 Massachusetts Ave., N.W., Washington, DC 20008; 202-238-2700; www.washington .itamaraty.gov.br/en-us. Official diplomatic mission of Brazil in the United States.

Inter-American Dialogue, 1155 15th St., N.W., Suite 800, Washington, DC 20005; 202-822-9002; www.thedialogue .org. Think tank that works to foster better understanding and mutual cooperation in the Americas.

Lemann Center for Brazilian Studies, Columbia University, 420 W. 118th St., 8th Floor IAB, MC 3339, New York, NY 10027; 212-854-4642; www.ilas.columbia. edu/centers-and-programs/brazil-center. Sponsors lectures and visiting scholars on contemporary and historical aspects of Brazil and funds research grants.

10

New Space Race

Patrick Marshall

AFP/Getty Images/STR

China's Hard X-ray Modulation Telescope, known as Insight, is lifted onto a *Long March-4B* rocket at the Jiuquan Satellite Launch Center in the Gobi Desert. The telescope was launched on June 15 to observe black holes, neutron stars and other phenomena. China is now the third major space power, after Russia and the U.S. Since launching its first astronaut into space in 2003, China has landed a rover on the moon, placed its own space lab into orbit and boosted its space spending to an estimated $110 million in 2015. U.S. officials worry that China's rapidly growing space program could threaten American space assets, including military satellites.

From *CQ Researcher,*
August 4, 2017

On July 28, U.S. astronaut Randy Bresnik wedged himself into a seat custom-molded to his body and braced himself to hurtle into the sky at about 17 times the speed of sound on his second trip to the International Space Station. But the retired Marine colonel from Santa Monica, Calif., wasn't aboard a U.S.-made rocket, nor was he lifting off from iconic Cape Canaveral in Florida.

Instead, he and his fellow crew members — a Russian cosmonaut and an astronaut with the European Space Agency — arrived at the space station aboard a Russian-made *Soyuz* spacecraft about six hours after launching from Kazakhstan.[1]

Since 2011, when the U.S. space shuttle program ended, the United States has paid hundreds of millions of dollars to Russia to ferry U.S. astronauts to the space station.[2]

America's dependence on the *Soyuz* is just one of the many ways international activities in space have changed in the 48 years since the United States won the space race with the Soviet Union by landing humans on the moon.

Today, space is a much more crowded, complicated and strategically important arena, not only for the United States but for its adversaries. U.S. officials are working to determine how to protect vital satellites and other space hardware from sabotage and accidental collisions, how much of a role the aerospace industry should play in space exploration and how to prioritize space missions in an era of competing visions and tight budgets.

"Our adversaries have seen what a significant advantage space provides the U.S. and have responded by looking for ways to neutralize or destroy our space capabilities," said Republican

NASA's Budget Fell After Moon Race

The nation's civilian space agency received almost 4.5 percent of the federal budget in 1966 as the United States raced to beat the Soviet Union to the moon. But NASA's share of overall federal spending declined after that and has not topped 1 percent since 1993. Still, the United States led Russia and China on spending on space programs in 2013, the most recent year for which data were available for all three nations. U.S. space-related spending totaled $39.3 billion that year, compared to $6.1 billion in China and $5.3 billion in Russia.

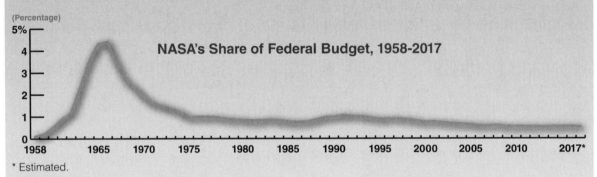

(Percentage)

NASA's Share of Federal Budget, 1958-2017

* Estimated.

Sources: Kimberly Amadeo, "NASA Budget: Current Funding and History," *The Balance*, May 25, 2017, https://tinyurl.com/y95uksdm; "The U.S. Federal Budget," *Inside Gov*, undated, http://tinyurl.com/y7ck77gq; "Nasa budgets: US spending on space travel since 1958 UPDATED," *The Guardian*, 2010, https://tinyurl.com/m72mnb8; and "Which countries spend the most on space exploration?" World Economic Forum, Jan. 11, 2016, https://tinyurl.com/y7fofo73

Rep. Doug Lamborn of Colorado, a member of the House Armed Services Committee's Subcommittee on Emerging Threats and Capabilities. "The U.S. is in the unique position of having the most to gain and most to lose in space."[3]

The flurry of new activity in space has produced "a new space race" involving "a crowd of new actors, from developing countries to small startups," according to Dave Baiocchi and William Welser IV, engineering professors at the Pardee RAND Graduate School in Santa Monica, Calif.

"Unlike in the first space race, the challenge in this one will not be technical," they said. "It will be figuring out how to regulate this welter of new activity."[4]

The United States owes much of its military dominance on the ground to its satellites. It has 576 working satellites in orbit — more than twice as many as any other country — providing communications, weapons guidance, navigation and other services.[5]

"We can attack any target on the planet, anytime, anywhere, in any weather," Gen. John Hyten, commander of the U.S. Air Force Space Command, said recently.[6]

But those satellites are increasingly vulnerable to attack themselves.

Lt. Gen. John W. Raymond, commander of the Joint Functional Component Command for Space, an arm of the U.S. Strategic Command tasked with securing U.S. military satellites, told Congress in 2015 that Russia and China have successfully tested anti-satellite weapons (ASATs).

"We are quickly approaching the point where every satellite and every orbit can be threatened," he said.[7]

The U.S. space programs' dependence on Russia also poses a potential national security concern, experts say. Besides paying Moscow for rides to the International Space Station — the price is now $74.7 million per seat — the United States also relies on Russian-made rockets to launch American military satellites into space.[8]

"Today, Russia holds many of our most precious national security satellites at risk before they ever get off the ground," Republican Sen. John McCain of Arizona, chairman of the Senate Armed Services Committee, said during a hearing in January 2016.[9]

Even apart from national security concerns, "it is embarrassing that the U.S. has not for years had the ability to put a human in orbit and must rely on Russia," James A. Lewis, a senior vice president at the Center for Strategic and International Studies (CSIS), a Washington think tank, told Congress last year.[10]

Further complicating U.S. space strategy is China's rapid rise as the third major space power. China launched its first astronaut into space in 2003. Since then, it has landed a rover on the moon, placed its own space lab into orbit and boosted its space spending to an estimated $110 million in 2015.[11] In January, Wu Yanhua, deputy chief of China's National Space Administration, announced that the country plans to launch its first Mars rover around 2020.[12]

Chinese officials have made clear they plan to rapidly develop offensive capabilities in space. In a 2014 speech at China's air force headquarters, President Xi Jinping told officers "to speed up air and space integration and sharpen their offensive and defensive capabilities." In 2007, the country caused an international furor when it destroyed one of its own satellites to test an anti-satellite missile.[13]

Other countries also pose potential threats to U.S. satellites, according to a recent report by the National Academy of Sciences. India, Iran, South Korea, North Korea and the 22 member states of the European Space Agency are capable of launching their own satellites into orbit, increasing the likelihood of accidental or deliberate collisions. At the end of 2016, there were 1,459 active satellites in orbit.[14]

Meanwhile, the National Aeronautics and Space Administration (NASA), continues to suffer from shifting political winds and frequent funding shortfalls. The space agency typically cannot complete major projects during the four or eight years a president holds office, so those projects are subject to cancellation or redirection by an incoming administration.[15]

In May, NASA announced it would delay the first test flight of its deep-space *Orion* capsule, originally scheduled for November 2018, until 2019 at the earliest, because of budgetary pressures.

President Trump's proposed fiscal 2018 budget would cut funding for another major NASA program designed to move an asteroid into lunar orbit and use it to test technologies critical for a crewed mission to Mars.[16]

Support for U.S. space programs is flagging among the American public and members of Congress, and that concerns some lawmakers. Republican Rep. Lamar Smith of Texas, chairman of the House Science, Space, and Technology Committee, called for boosting budgets for space initiatives at a May 2016 hearing.

"America leads the world in space exploration, but that is a leadership role we cannot take for granted," Smith said. "It has been over 40 years since astronaut Gene Cernan became the last man to walk on the moon. It is time to press forward. It is time to take longer strides."[17]

American aerospace companies hope to take some of those strides. Companies such as SpaceX, Boeing and Blue Origin are playing an increasingly vital role in U.S. space programs, sparking debate about how the government should regulate them.

On June 3, SpaceX, a Hawthorne, Calif., company started by Tesla founder Elon Musk, launched a *Falcon 9* rocket carrying supplies to the space station. The rocket's first stage then returned to the launch site for reuse. It was the 39th launch by SpaceX since 2006. In February, the company announced plans to send two space tourists on a trip around the moon in 2018.[18]

As a privately owned company, SpaceX does not have to report its profits, but documents obtained by *The Wall Street Journal* indicate the company expected to make a profit of $55 million in 2016 on revenues of $1.8 billion from launches. The documents also revealed that the company expects to earn between $15 billion and $20 billion by 2025 delivering internet services using its own satellites.[19]

Eight new space-related companies have opened their doors, on average, each year since 2010, according to a recent Congressional Research Service report. And the commercial launch industry booked $2.6 billion in revenues in 2015, up from about $307 million in 2010 and nothing at all in 2011.[20]

"We are on the verge of surpassing NASA," says Rick Tumlinson, co-founder and chairman of the board of Deep Space Industries, which develops technologies to mine asteroids. "I have predicted that the first human spacecraft to land on Mars is probably going to be a private-sector spacecraft, not NASA."

Landing astronauts on the Red Planet, however, remains one of NASA's top goals. The agency is moving ahead with its Space Launch System designed to carry

Companies Receive Millions to Develop New Space Vehicle with NASA

Since 2010, NASA has given six aerospace companies more than $300 million to help the space agency develop a replacement for the space shuttle.

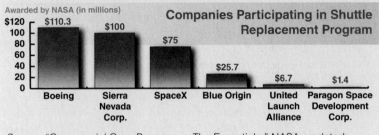

Awarded by NASA (in millions)

Companies Participating in Shuttle Replacement Program

- Boeing: $110.3
- Sierra Nevada Corp.: $100
- SpaceX: $75
- Blue Origin: $25.7
- United Launch Alliance: $6.7
- Paragon Space Development Corp.: $1.4

Source: "Commercial Crew Program — The Essentials," NASA, undated, https://tinyurl.com/ybvr96oj

the *Orion* capsule into Martian orbit with a crew of up to six astronauts.

Some experts wonder whether manned deep-space missions even make sense, given the dangers of space travel, rapid advances in robotics and the fact that robots also are much less expensive to send into space than humans. Another debate focuses on the pros and cons of sending astronauts back to the moon, as Trump wants NASA to do by 2019. The space agency has said that deadline is unrealistic.[21]

As experts and policymakers consider the future of U.S. space programs, here are some of the questions they are asking:

Are U.S. satellites adequately protected?

U.S. military officials are taking steps — somewhat belatedly, some experts say — to protect their satellites.

"The . . . bureaucratic and procurement wheels have begun to move, albeit very slowly," said Elbridge Colby, a senior fellow at the Center for a New American Security, a Washington think tank.[22]

Satellites, including those intended for civilian use, are vulnerable not only to collisions with space debris but also to sabotage by anti-satellite weapons. All three major space powers — the United States, Russia and China — can disable or destroy satellites. The 1967 Outer Space Treaty, signed by those three countries and

about 100 others, prohibits participants from deploying weapons of mass destruction in space. However, it does not address devices that can disable or destroy satellites.[23]

The major space powers already have tested ASATs, including ballistic missiles capable of hitting satellites in low-Earth orbit (about 500 miles from the surface) and those as high as 22,000 miles from Earth, which are in geosynchronous orbit, meaning they remain in the same position relative to a location on Earth. Ground-based lasers also can blind orbiting cameras and damage fragile satellites.[24]

A satellite can also be destroyed by simply maneuvering another satellite into its path. "It's ugly," says Dean Cheng, a senior research fellow at the Heritage Foundation, a conservative think tank in Washington. "It's a kamikaze, and you lose a satellite in the process, but you can collide satellites."

Any satellite equipped with a robotic arm, including those designed to make repairs, also can be used to "rip a solar panel off or pull other sensitive parts apart," Cheng says.

Satellites are just one point of vulnerability for U.S. space programs.

"Space is not just about what is in orbit," Cheng says. "You also have terrestrial facilities, mission control facilities, tracking facilities." Even if the United States could turn its critical satellites into "armored death stars," he says, an enemy could still target ground-based assets to disable control over satellites.

"Space is actually a giant integrated system," Cheng says. "Integrated systems have advantages, but they are also extremely vulnerable."

Colby said the Pentagon is working to make its satellites maneuverable enough to evade attacks and be more resistant to electronic jamming. In addition, it has deployed two satellites to monitor other countries' activities in space.

He called these actions "encouraging," but said it could be years before their benefits are apparent. He also said it is unlikely the United States will ever completely solve the problem of how to protect its satellites.[25]

U.S. satellites are a particularly tempting target, some experts say, because the military depends so heavily on them for intelligence gathering, communications, navigation and weapons guidance. "Foreign military leaders understand the unique advantages that space-based systems provide to the United States," James R. Clapper, then-director of national intelligence, warned in February 2016.[26]

Peter W. Singer, a national security analyst at New America, a nonpartisan, public policy think tank in Washington, agrees. "It is woven into Chinese and Russian plans to try to take away U.S. space capabilities," Singer says. "What is a strength for us they would like to turn into a weakness."

He says the United States depends more on its space assets — including satellites, satellite tracking facilities, rockets, launch vehicles and space stations — than either China or Russia.

Cheng is not sure this country's adversaries will ever depend as much on space as the United States does.

"The only reason they would look like us is if they were going to do expeditionary warfare — warfare on the other side of the globe from where they are," he says. "There is just no evidence that China intends to spend a lot of time operating in the Western Hemisphere or that Russia is going to do more than fly a few bombers to be obnoxious up and down the East or West Coast of the United States. We are not talking about far-flung global capabilities except for the United States."

Many experts say the United States should deploy larger numbers of small satellites, seeking protection in redundancy. "We are still overly dependent on a few large, expensive platforms, which are easy targets for the Russians and the Chinese," says Lewis of CSIS. "We would be much better off moving toward smaller satellites. There is general acceptance of that now, I think, in the space community, but we haven't yet started to do it."

Brian G. Chow, a physicist and adjunct physical scientist at the RAND Corp. think tank in Santa Monica,

Earth Orbit Is Getting Crowded

The global community had 1,381 operational satellites orbiting the planet as of Dec. 31, 2015, a 39 percent increase from 2011. The United States currently has about 576 satellites, more than twice as many as any other country. These satellites provide communications, guidance, navigation and other services.

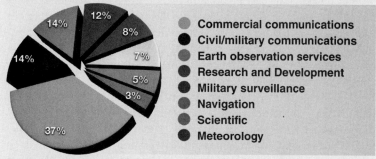

Active Satellites, by Function (as of Dec. 31, 2015)

- Commercial communications
- Civil/military communications
- Earth observation services
- Research and Development
- Military surveillance
- Navigation
- Scientific
- Meteorology

Sources: Peter B. de Selding, "The state of the satellite industry in 5 charts," *SpaceNews,* June 20, 2016, https://tinyurl.com/j5hxmpb; Bill Canis, "Commercial Space Industry Launches a New Phase," Congressional Research Service, Dec. 12, 2016, p. 1, https://tinyurl.com/y7kw5lxa

Calif., says one way for the United States to protect its satellites is for the country to make clear it will destroy any other satellite that displays "stalking" behavior indicating a threat. Only that, he says, "can prevent a space Pearl Harbor."

Should the private sector play a greater role in space exploration?

The United States has long encouraged private contractors to participate in space programs, developing products according to NASA specifications. Increasingly, however, the country is depending on aerospace companies to launch satellites and eventually use their own rockets to send humans into space.

During his presidential campaign, Trump said he wanted to let private companies operate the International Space Station, ferry astronauts to the space station within two years and handle other low-Earth orbit tasks.[27]

SpaceX, which has been carrying supplies to the space station since 2012, is not the only private spaceflight company launching satellites and delivering cargo. On April 22, Orbital ATK, based in Dulles, Va., outside Washington, launched its seventh supply mission to the space station. Another company — Blue Origin in Kent, Wash., owned by Amazon founder Jeff Bezos — said in April it will offer space tourism flights by the end of 2018.[28]

Some analysts and industry leaders say private-sector companies — rather than NASA — also should handle deep-space exploration.

"People in the industry are pretty confident that deep-space programs can be done more efficiently and for a lot less money," says an industry spokesperson who spoke anonymously for fear of compromising his relationship with NASA. He described the agency's deep-space plans as "an incredibly large, expensive program that doesn't have a really clear vision."

Historically, NASA has tightly controlled project designs and contractors' work, which some experts say impedes innovation and cost efficiency. James Muncy, founder of PoliSpace, a consultancy in Alexandria, Va., specializing in space entrepreneurship, says contractors are not motivated to save money.

Those who win a contract to deliver a product to the government "are not rewarded . . . the way the competitive marketplace works — [for] innovation, improvement of quality, reduction of price and delivering new capabilities that don't exist anywhere in the marketplace," Muncy says.

NASA's relationship with private spaceflight companies is changing, largely because of the agency's Commercial Crew Program, a partnership between NASA and the private sector to build a replacement for the space shuttle to transport supplies and eventually crew to the International Space Station. Under the program, NASA's private-sector partners will develop the spacecraft and other equipment themselves, with full ownership of the final product.[29]

That is how NASA should handle all work done by private companies, says space historian and author Robert Zimmerman.

"The government should leave the design work and ownership of the product to the private sector," Zimmerman wrote in a January report that generated heated debate in the space community. "The private companies know best how to build their own products to maximize performance while lowering cost, especially because it is in their own self-interest to do this well, as an unreliable rocket will not attract many customers."[30]

Zimmerman cites NASA's Space Launch System as an example of the agency's inefficiencies. The system "is not tied to any results, their work is vague, it takes forever, and the costs balloon," he says. "That has structurally been the problem with how things have been done at NASA and in the space program now for pretty much a half-century."

Tumlinson of Deep Space Industries says NASA's role should involve supporting basic research and serving as a customer of services delivered by private companies.

Other experts are less impressed by the private sector's accomplishments in space.

"Elon Musk sat in my office in 2002 and told me he'd have 10 launches a year by 2006," says Scott Pace, director of the Space Policy Institute at George Washington University. "I'm still looking at my watch."

Pace also says commercial firms usually are more efficient than government agencies because the private sector "doesn't have the same kind of [bureaucratic] shackles and responsibilities that governments have." Those companies largely operate under strict NASA oversight, but some experts worry their performance will suffer when that oversight is gone or reduced.

Loren Thompson, chief operating officer of the Lexington Institute, a libertarian think tank in Arlington, Va., that advocates for smaller government, said SpaceX, despite offering launches at lower cost than NASA, "isn't the model of market-driven responsiveness that Zimmerman would have you believe."

"On average, its launches are over two years late, and the unlaunched missions it is carrying in its backlog on average are nearly three years late," Thompson wrote. "You can see where that might be a problem for the Air Force if the payload being launched was a high priority such as a missile-warning or spy satellite."[31]

Three of the 86 launches attempted by private companies in 2015 failed, destroying launch vehicles and payloads, according to a Congressional Research Service report.[32] In September 2016, a SpaceX rocket exploded on the launch pad at Cape Canaveral.

Pace says NASA clearly has a role to play in conducting scientific missions in space and in exploring beyond Earth orbit. The agency has landed a man on the moon, sent rovers to Mars and achieved other feats that private companies have yet to match. Pace also says that while such missions eventually may pay off commercially, they probably would not have attracted private-sector investment initially.

"Some people argue that NASA ought to be just a conduit of money and not try to do anything," Pace says. "I believe that's incorrect. That's because there are activities that make no commercial sense."

He wrote in April that the United States does not face a stark choice between government and private efforts in space but should pursue "a mixed strategy, using a variety of tools, to serve national interests. It would be wise to mistrust any purist strategy, that is, one which is all-government or all-private, where taxpayer dollars are needed."[33]

Should the United States establish a moon base?

On June 20, British theoretical physicist Stephen Hawking called for countries to collaborate on constructing a moon colony within 30 years and then to send a manned mission to Mars.

"We are running out of space [on Earth], and the only place we can go to are other worlds," he said via video link to a conference in Trondheim, Norway. "It is time to explore other solar systems. Spreading out may be the only thing that saves us from ourselves. I am convinced that humans need to leave Earth."[34]

President Trump made similar comments when he signed legislation on March 21 giving NASA $19.5 billion for the current fiscal year, $200 million more than the agency received last year. "Almost half a century ago our brave astronauts first planted the American flag on the moon," he said. "That was a big moment in our history. Now this nation is ready to be the first in space once again."[35]

Former President Barack Obama wanted to send a manned mission to Mars, but Trump has prioritized returning astronauts to the moon and perhaps establishing a permanent base there.[36]

Blue Origin's Bezos supports the same plan. In March, he circulated a white paper to NASA leadership indicating his interest in developing a lunar lander and

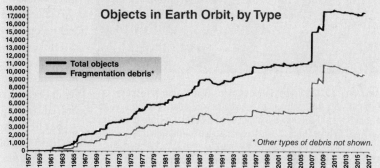

Space Junk Prompts Fear of Collisions

Tens of thousands of man-made objects orbit the Earth, including active and defunct satellites, pieces of spent rockets and fragments created by collisions. Experts warn that these fast-moving pieces of space junk could seriously damage working satellites and other spacecraft, including the International Space Station — and that as more debris accumulates, these risks will grow.

Objects in Earth Orbit, by Type

— Total objects
— Fragmentation debris*

* Other types of debris not shown.

Sources: "STO AVT-262 Lecture series and VKI workshop on Space debris reentry and mitigation," NATO Science and Technology Organization, https://tinyurl.com/yaayjd55; "Space Surveillance," U.S. Space Command, undated, https://tinyurl.com/m5upk3

establishing a base on the moon. "It is time for America to return to the moon — this time to stay," Bezos said. "A permanently inhabited lunar settlement is a difficult and worthy objective. I sense a lot of people are excited about this."[37]

Rep. Bill Posey, R-Fla., has introduced legislation that would direct NASA to build a base on the lunar surface. He and other policymakers say the need is urgent because Russia and China have announced plans to do the same.[38]

Those countries "don't colonize places just for scientific study; they generally militarize their colonizations," Posey, a member of the House Science, Space and Technology Committee, told a reporter in February. "So if we want to remain the leader in space, we obviously need to at least keep pace with the Russians and Chinese."[39]

Some experts see the moon as a potential staging area for missions to Mars and other deep-space destinations.

"Perhaps one of the greatest practical discoveries of our generation is the presence of vast quantities of water on the moon, verified by NASA in 2009," Robert Richards, CEO of Moon Express, a Mountain View, Calif., company that plans to mine lunar resources, told Congress in May. "The discovery of water on the moon

Getty Images/Bloomberg/Matthew Staver

Amazon CEO Jeff Bezos, founder of the Blue Origin aerospace firm, unveils the company's reusable New Shepard launch system at the 33rd annual Space Symposium, in Colorado Springs, Colo., on April 5. Blue Origin plans to offer space tourism flights by the end of 2018. Bezos circulated a white paper to NASA leaders in March indicating his interest in developing a lunar lander and establishing a base on the moon.

is a game changer, not just for the economic viability of lunar resources, but for the economics of reaching Mars and other deep-space destinations."[40]

William Gerstenmaier, NASA's chief of human exploration, said in 2015 that large amounts of ice at the lunar poles could provide the oxygen and hydrogen needed to fuel a spacecraft for a journey from the moon to Mars.

"If propellant was available from the moon, this could dramatically lower the [amount of fuel] needed from the Earth for a NASA Mars mission," he said.[41]

Other experts warn that a moon mission could set back the Mars program.

"The moon could be a useful test bed for human exploration of Mars, part of a staged campaign of exploration," says Lewis of the Center for Strategic and International Studies. "But there is a concern that lunar missions would divert resources away from the Mars programs."

According to NASA scientists, establishing a moon base would cost $10 billion, a little more than half the agency's current annual budget.[42]

Tom Young, former director of NASA's Goddard Space Flight Center, says the United States lacks the wherewithal to build a base on the moon and also plan a manned

mission to Mars. "There is a need to focus our attention, capability and resources on one option," he said.[43]

The moon-or-Mars debate has also revived discussion about whether NASA should focus on human or robotic missions.

Cambridge University astrophysicist Martin Rees famously predicted in 2010 that manned missions to space would soon be a thing of the past.

"The moon landings were an important impetus to technology, but you have to ask the question, what is the case for sending people back into space?" he said. "The practical case gets weaker and weaker with every advance in robotics and miniaturization. It's hard to see any particular reason or purpose in going back to the moon or indeed sending people into space at all."[44]

Sending humans into space is also dangerous. Accidents involving the space shuttles *Challenger* (1986) and *Columbia* (2003) killed 14 astronauts, and three *Apollo 1* astronauts were killed in 1967 during a preflight test when their capsule caught on fire.[45]

Former shuttle astronaut Rick Hauck noted that about 4 percent of humans who made it into space were killed during their missions. "Would I have flown if I had known there was a 4 percent chance of death?" Hauck said in 2003. "No, I don't think I would have flown."[46]

NASA's robotic exploration program, meanwhile, has scored impressive successes, landing three rovers — *Spirit*, *Opportunity* and *Curiosity* — on Mars. *Spirit* and *Opportunity* landed in 2004. Each was expected to last about three months, but *Spirit* worked for six years and *Opportunity* is still active.[47] The two-year mission for *Curiosity*, which landed in 2012, has been extended.[48]

Lewis called NASA's robotics work "the coolest space program in the world." Still, he favors sending astronauts back to the moon "and creating some sort of semipermanent presence, just because I think it's easy." Giving up on manned spaceflight would be "a hard blow" for NASA, he says.

Other experts argue that manned missions help boost public support for space exploration. "Human exploration gets people excited about space, and the private sector can increase how much exploration the government gets for its money," says Tumlinson. "The more you can provide of that excitement, the more public support you're going to get, the more taxpayer dollars you're going to get."

BACKGROUND

First Space Race

Most historians mark Oct. 4, 1957 — the date the Soviet Union launched *Sputnik*, the first satellite, into Earth orbit — as the beginning of the first space race. The next day, President Dwight D. Eisenhower's press secretary called the Russian launch "no surprise" and said the United States was "not in a race with the Soviets."

"Both of the statements were naïve at best," wrote space historian Ted Spitzmiller.[49]

The Soviets' success in making it into space first stunned the American public, but the nation's policy-makers also focused on *Sputnik*'s weight, Spitzmiller wrote in *The History of Human Spaceflight*. At 184 pounds, the satellite offered "convincing evidence that the Russians did have the power, the guidance, and the ability to launch ICBMs," or intercontinental ballistic missiles, he wrote. "This was seen as a threat to the very existence of the free world."[50]

The Eisenhower administration and Congress moved quickly to expand U.S. space programs. In signing the 1958 National Aeronautics and Space Act, Eisenhower commended Congress for acting quickly to approve the legislation, which he said equipped the United States "for leadership in the space age."[51]

Besides creating NASA, the act specified that the Defense Department would manage U.S. military activities in space. Eisenhower initially wanted the Pentagon to direct all U.S. space efforts, according to John Logsdon, a historian at the Smithsonian Institution's Air and Space Museum.

But his science adviser, James Killian, and Vice President Richard M. Nixon convinced him that it made more sense to create a separate civilian space agency "to carry out an open program of scientific activities and to engage in international cooperation," wrote Logsdon. "This would provide a contrast to the closed and secretive Soviet space effort."[52]

NASA did not have to start from scratch. It absorbed the earlier National Advisory Committee for Aeronautics, with its 8,000 employees, an annual budget of $100 million and three major research laboratories — the Langley Aeronautical Laboratory in Virginia, the Ames Aeronautical Laboratory in California and the Lewis Flight Propulsion Laboratory in Ohio.[53]

Apollo 11 astronaut Edwin E. "Buzz" Aldrin Jr. walks on the moon on July 20, 1969. When the Trump administration said in June it would resurrect the National Space Council to oversee all U.S. activities and policies in space, Aldrin said the council would be "absolutely critical in ensuring that the president's space priorities are clearly articulated and effectively executed." Trump has said he wants NASA to send astronauts back to the moon by 2019.

The new space agency immediately undertook its first manned space program — Project Mercury, with the goal of putting a U.S. astronaut into Earth orbit and returning him safely to Earth. But a month before Project Mercury's first launch in 1961, Soviet cosmonaut Yuri Gagarin became the first human to orbit the Earth. The next year, on Feb. 20, 1962, U.S. astronaut John Glenn circled the planet three times before splashing down in the Atlantic Ocean near Bermuda.[54]

Eisenhower's proposed fiscal 1961 budget called for reducing NASA's budget. He warned John F. Kennedy's incoming administration that "further tests and experiments will be necessary to establish if there are any valid scientific reasons for extending manned spaceflight beyond the Mercury program."[55]

But in 1961, while Project Mercury was still active, NASA started Project Gemini. The new program involved 10 launches of two-man crews performing the first spacewalks and other tasks, and testing technologies for the upcoming Apollo Program, which aimed to land astronauts on the moon.[56]

According to Logsdon, Kennedy began his presidency with a "complex" attitude toward space. He initially viewed space exploration as a way to ease relations with

CHRONOLOGY

1957–1969 *United States, Soviet Union compete for space firsts.*

1957 Soviet Union launches unmanned *Sputnik* satellite into orbit, fueling urgency of U.S. space program development.

1958 National Aeronautics and Space Act creates NASA and directs the Pentagon to manage military space activities.

1961 President John F. Kennedy announces plan to send astronauts to the moon before the end of the decade and increases NASA's budget request by 89 percent.

1962 U.S. launches its first astronaut, Marine Lt. Col. John Glenn, into orbit.

1967 U.N. Outer Space Treaty bans weapons of mass destruction in space and limits use of the moon and other celestial bodies to peaceful purposes.

1969 U.S. astronaut Neil Armstrong walks on the moon.

1970–1980 *U.S. pares space budgets.*

1970 President Richard M. Nixon sharply reduces NASA's budget.

1972 Nixon announces development of a new reusable space vehicle, the space shuttle, to deliver astronauts and satellites into orbit for less money.

1972 U.S. launches the Apollo program's final human mission to the moon.

1973 First crewmembers arrive at *SkyLab*, America's first space station.

1981–2010 *The space shuttle era brings successes, tragedies.*

1981 U.S. launches *Columbia*, the first space shuttle, into orbit.

1984 The Commercial Space Launch Act aims to increase the private sector's role in space programs.

1986 Space shuttle *Challenger* explodes shortly after liftoff, killing all seven crewmembers.

1988 Commercial Space Launch Amendments Act requires companies to buy commercial insurance for launches.

1998 Congress requires NASA to take steps to commercialize space activities. . . . First pieces of International Space Station are launched into orbit.

2003 Space shuttle *Columbia* disintegrates during re-entry, killing all seven crew members.

2004 President George W. Bush unveils Constellation Program — to take humans back to the moon and to Mars.

2007 China destroys one of its own weather satellites to test an antisatellite weapon.

2008–Present *Private sector's role in space grows.*

2008 On its fourth try, SpaceX launches a rocket into orbit. The company's first successful launch of a commercial payload follows in July 2009.

2010 President Barack Obama cancels the Constellation Program and directs NASA to plan for sending astronauts to an asteroid by 2015 and into Mars orbit by the mid-2030s. . . . NASA awards almost $50 million to five U.S. companies working with the agency to develop a replacement for the space shuttle as part of the Commercial Crew Program.

2015 Aerospace companies book $2.6 billion in revenues, launching 83 payloads into orbit.

2016 NASA's *Juno* probe reaches Jupiter. . . . SpaceX's reusable *Falcon 9* rocket lands upright on a drone ship in the Atlantic Ocean.

2017 President Trump proposes reducing NASA's budget 3 percent, with the largest cuts coming from programs that study the Earth's surface and climate.

the Soviet Union, but before the end of 1961 he would commit to sending U.S. astronauts to the moon by the end of the decade.[57]

Eight days after the Soviet Union sent Gagarin into orbit on April 12, 1961, Kennedy called on his administration to identify a "space program which promises dramatic results in which we could win." On May 25, he told a joint session of Congress of his plan to send astronauts to the moon and backed up that commitment by increasing NASA's budget 89 percent.[58]

On July 20, 1969, *Apollo 11* astronaut Neil Armstrong became the first human to walk on the lunar surface. By the time the Apollo program ended in 1972, 12 astronauts — all Americans — had set foot on the moon. No humans have been there since.[59]

As the United States and Soviet Union expanded their investments in the space race, they also began developing anti-satellite weapons. As early as 1959, the United States attempted to hit one of its own aging satellites with a missile. The Soviets began developing anti-satellite capabilities as early as 1960 and in 1967 successfully used a satellite to intercept another in the same orbit. In the late 1950s and early '60s, the United States and the Soviet Union even tested nuclear bombs in space.[60]

In 1967, the two space superpowers signed the Outer Space Treaty, which bans weapons of mass destruction in space, limits use of the moon and other celestial bodies to peaceful purposes and prohibits countries from claiming sovereignty over space or celestial bodies.[61]

Détente in Space

The tremendous feeling of national triumph following the first moon landings was fleeting," wrote Logsdon. He said Nixon, who began his first term as president six months before the 1969 moon landing, rejected NASA's ambitious post-*Apollo* plans. Those plans included a series of large space stations, continued missions to the moon and a mission to Mars in the 1980s.[62]

"We must think of [space activities] as part of a continuing process and not as a series of separate leaps, each requiring a massive concentration of energy," Nixon said in announcing a new U.S. space policy on March 7, 1970. "Space expenditures must take their proper place within a rigorous system of national priorities."[63]

NASA's resources dropped sharply during the Nixon administration. The agency's budget, which peaked in 1966 at 4.4 percent of federal spending, had fallen to less than 1 percent by the time Nixon left office in 1974, when the agency received $3.3 billion.[64]

Public support for lunar missions declined after *Apollo 14*, the third mission to land astronauts on the moon, in part due to a sense that the United States had won the space race, according to Spitzmiller.[65]

NASA would send three more Apollo missions to the moon, the last one launching on Dec. 7, 1972.[66] Earlier that year, despite cutting NASA's budget, Nixon had approved development of a reusable space vehicle — the space shuttle.

"The new system will differ radically from all existing booster systems, in that most of this new system will be recovered and used again and again — up to 100 times," he said in announcing the project on Jan. 5. "The resulting economies may bring operating costs down as low as one-tenth of those present launch vehicles."[67]

However, it took nine years before NASA sent the first shuttle into space. During that time, the agency also turned its attention to building the first space station, called *Skylab*. Working with constrained budgets, NASA engineers designed the station using the third stage of a Saturn heavy-lift rocket designed to reach the moon, adding adapters that allowed two Apollo spacecraft to dock at the station.[68]

Skylab's first crew arrived at the station on May 25, 1973. Over the next six years, it would be occupied for only 171 days, with the last crew logging the longest stay, 84 days.[69] *Skylab* delivered valuable information about the long-term effects of space on the human body of living without gravity, according to Spitzmiller. "It was obvious that a flight to Mars was feasible except for the possible problem with bone loss, which continued to plague the crews," he wrote.[70]

Space Shuttle Era

NASA's space shuttle program flew 135 missions — delivering and repairing satellites and performing scientific experiments — before ending in 2011 because of ongoing safety concerns.[71] It sent the first American woman into space — Sally Ride — helped build the International Space Station and deployed the Hubble

China Challenges U.S. Dominance in Space

"China arguably has become a space superpower."

When the Chinese blew up one of their own weather satellites a decade ago to test an anti-satellite missile, sending thousands of pieces of debris potentially into the path of other countries' spacecraft, U.S. scientists and officials reacted with shock and alarm.

Harvard astrophysicist Jonathan McDowell accused the Chinese of escalating the "weaponization of space," and a White House official derided them for violating a "spirit of cooperation" between the United States and China in the use of space.[1]

Since then, China has made rapid advances in its space program. Western observers say Beijing's top goal in space is national security, followed by international prestige, projection of power and competition for space-related business.

"Chinese military writings emphasize the importance of establishing space dominance . . . as the key to winning future local wars," says Dean Cheng, a senior research fellow at the Heritage Foundation, a conservative think tank in Washington. He says the People's Liberation Army "pretty much" runs China's space program.

Adds Peter Singer, a national security analyst at New America, a nonpartisan think tank in Washington, "China arguably has become a space superpower."

China did not send its first astronaut into space until 2003. Five years later, a Chinese astronaut took the country's first spacewalk, and in 2011 China launched a small space station. The country has conducted multiple unmanned lunar exploration missions and, according to one report, has studied the feasibility of sending a manned mission to the moon.[2]

In November 2016, representatives of China and the European Space Agency discussed collaborating on establishing a human outpost on the moon.[3] And last year for the first time, China surpassed Russia in successful space launches and matched the 22 by NASA and U.S. aerospace companies.[4]

China spent about $6.1 billion on all space-related programs in 2013, the most recent year for which figures are available. The United States spent about $39.3 billion (including about $18 billion at NASA), and Russia spent about $5.3 billion.[5]

However, figures for China's spending on space are misleading, said James A. Lewis, senior vice president at the Center for Strategic and International Studies, a think tank in Washington.

"Chinese budget figures are opaque, disguise some sources of funding, and do not reflect differences in purchasing power," Lewis told a congressional hearing last September.[6]

Telescope high above the atmosphere to study the universe beyond our solar system.[72]

"It was the first launch vehicle to lift off like a rocket, orbit the Earth as a spacecraft and then land as a glider," space historian Robert Pearlman said of the shuttle.[73]

As the first reusable spacecraft, the shuttles were supposed to provide reliable access to space at a lower cost. However, significant cost reductions did not materialize, according to Steven Dick, a former NASA chief historian.[74]

As the first shuttle flights transfixed the nation during the early 1980s, President Ronald Reagan's administration worked to give private companies a greater role in space beyond that of traditional contractors.

"One of the important objectives of my administration has been, and will continue to be, the encouragement of the private sector in commercial space endeavors," Reagan said in signing the 1984 Commercial Space Launch Act. The law required the government to "encourage private-sector launches, reentries and associated services."[75] That same year, NASA created an Office of Commercial Programs to encourage private-sector involvement in space activities — such as making launch vehicles and satellites — and help commercialize NASA-developed technologies.[76]

However, progress in the shuttle program stalled after Jan. 28, 1986, when leaks in the rocket boosters attached to the space shuttle *Challenger* caused it to explode about

Some Chinese officials reportedly are pushing the government to triple spending on the country's space programs.[7]

Rep. Brian Babin, R-Texas, chairman of the House Science, Space and Technology Subcommittee on Space, said the United States isn't taking China seriously enough as a potential threat in space.

"The strategic choices we make clearly impact China's space capabilities — something that we should all pay attention to given that China's civil space activities are inseparable from their military," he said at the same congressional hearing where Lewis testified.[8]

China's expanding space program also may mean increasing competition for U.S. aerospace companies such as SpaceX, Blue Origin and Sierra Nevada. "They're looking for business around the world," Singer says of the Chinese. "There is going to be competition even in the private space realm."

China has built and launched satellites for Nigeria, Venezuela, Pakistan and Bolivia, signed contracts for satellites with Belarus, Laos and Sri Lanka and agreed to build and launch a satellite for Venezuela, according to a U.S.-China Economic and Security Review Commission report. The report says Chinese satellites are cheaper than those sold by other countries, and "China offers a competitive package that includes launch services, training for local operators and low-cost loans through its export-import bank."[9]

Lewis says the United States, which has relied on Russia for access to the International Space Station since the retirement of the space shuttle program in 2011, is falling behind in what some experts say is a "new space race."

"We are sitting on our laurels," he says. "We are the rabbit and China is the tortoise."

— *Patrick Marshall*

---

[1] Marc Kaufman and Dafna Linzer, "China Criticized for Anti-Satellite Missile Test," *The Washington Post*, Jan. 19, 2007, https://tinyurl.com/33w2dr; William J. Broad and David E. Sanger, "China Tests Anti-Satellite Weapon, Unnerving U.S.," *The New York Times*, Jan. 18, 2007, https://tinyurl.com/y9lf3hjb.

[2] Kevin Pollpeter, Eric Anderson, Jordan Wilson, Fan Yang, "China Dream, Space Dream: China's Progress in Space Technologies and Implications for the United States," report prepared for the U.S.-China Economic and Security Review Commission, March 2, 2015, https://tinyurl.com/yb8nsoej.

[3] Matthew Brown, "China talking with European Space Agency about moon outpost," Phys.org, April 26, 2016, https://tinyurl.com/k7hqmy2.

[4] Clay Dillow, "China's secret plan to crush SpaceX and the US space program," CNBC.com, March 28, 2017, https://tinyurl.com/lhupsrr.

[5] Joe Myers, "The rise and rise of China's space programme — in numbers," World Economic Forum, Oct. 24, 2016, https://tinyurl.com/yaa5voa5.

[6] Testimony of James Lewis before the House Science, Space and Technology Subcommittee on Space, Sept. 27, 2016, https://tinyurl.com/yaqdpndh.pdf.

[7] Dillow, op. cit.

[8] Statement of Rep. Brian Babin before the House Science, Space and Technology Subcommittee on Space, Sept. 27, 2016, https://tinyurl.com/yc3mof4f.

[9] Ibid.

---

one minute after launch, killing all seven astronauts, including New Hampshire school teacher Christa McAuliffe. The other shuttles remained grounded until September 1988.

"As a result, many questioned the role of NASA as the primary satellite delivery route to space," the space agency said in a report.[77]

In addition to the *Challenger* disaster, Titan rocket launch failures in 1993 caused military satellite launches to be suspended for a year.[78]

"The period spanning the late 1980s to the early 1990s was a particularly difficult era for spaceflight in the United States," according to a report by CSIS' Aerospace Security Project. "The United States needed a new launch vehicle that could provide assured access to space . . . and stay cost competitive over time."[79]

In 1988, Congress required companies involved in space launch activities to buy commercial insurance or demonstrate the ability to cover any third-party losses.[80]

Congress followed up in 1998 with the Commercial Space Act, which required NASA to encourage commercialization of space services.[81]

That same year, Russia launched the first module of the International Space Station into orbit. The $100 billion station took more than 10 years and 30 missions to build and was the joint project of five space agencies representing 15 countries, with the United States, Russia, the European Union, Canada and Japan having the

Orbiting Debris Poses a Growing Threat

Experts say global cooperation is needed to avoid spacecraft damage.

An estimated 150 million pieces of space debris whiz constantly around the Earth. Moving at about 5 miles per second, this "space junk" — ranging from tiny flecks of paint to bulky stages of discarded launch vehicles — poses a growing threat to satellites.[1]

"In orbit, these objects . . . [are] faster than a bullet and can damage or destroy functioning space infrastructure, like economically vital telecom, weather, navigation, broadcast and climate-monitoring satellites," Holger Krag, head of the European Space Agency's (ESA) debris office, told a conference on space debris in April.[2]

About 5,000 pieces of space debris are more than three feet long, according to one expert. And about 20,000 measure more than four inches.[3]

So far, the debris has caused only minor damage, including a 16-inch gash that a piece of orbiting junk punched in the solar panel of an ESA satellite last August.[4]

But scientists say more-serious strikes are inevitable. As early as 1978, NASA astrophysicists warned that as space debris accumulates, more collisions will occur, spawning still more collisions in a cascading effect that will be impossible to halt.[5]

Two agencies — NASA and the Defense Department's Space Command — track satellites and space debris using ground-based radar and telescopes on land and in space.

But that equipment only tracks objects at least four inches long, and scientists say fragments as small as 0.04 of an inch can cause significant damage.[6]

The problem became more severe after Jan. 11, 2007, when China tested an anti-satellite weapon by firing an unarmed missile at one of its own defunct weather satellites

orbiting at an altitude of 534 miles. The collision created more than 3,000 pieces of debris that still threaten other objects in orbit. One analyst called the test "the most prolific and severe fragmentation in the course of five decades of space operations."[7]

By 1987, U.S. and European space agencies had begun work on what would eventually become the Interagency Space Debris Coordination Committee. The committee is made up of government officials from 13 countries, including the United States, Russia and China. The countries are responsible not only for their own governments' satellites but also for satellites owned by private companies within their borders.

The committee issued space debris mitigation guidelines in 2007, but member countries are not implementing them, according to Krag and other experts. Krag says only 60 percent of satellites are disposed of as the committee recommends.[8]

The committee's guidelines say satellites nearing the end of their useful life should be parked out of orbit or burned up in Earth's atmosphere to keep them from colliding with other satellites and creating debris, says Michael Krepon, co-founder of the Stimson Center, a think tank in Washington focused on security issues. But he says satellite operators prefer to keep dying satellites in service until they use up every last bit of their expensive fuel.

"If you put a satellite up and that satellite is a revenue generator, you want to extract the most money from that investment," Krepon says. He warns that unless countries agree to enforce the guidelines, "we will lose space like we're losing fisheries in the ocean."

greatest involvement.[82] Those five agencies — NASA, Russia's Roscosmos State Corporation for Space Activities, the European Space Agency, the Canadian Space Agency and the Japan Aerospace Exploration Agency — continue to operate the station today.[83]

By the early 1980s, the U.S. military was becoming increasingly dependent on its satellites for reconnaissance, communications and navigation, and more and

more concerned about keeping them safe as the Soviet Union worked to improve its anti-satellite weapons.[84]

The United States conducted its first anti-satellite test in 1985, when an Air Force F-15 fighter flying at 38,000 feet launched a missile that destroyed a failing U.S. satellite.[85]

Another space shuttle tragedy occurred on Feb. 1, 2003, when the space shuttle *Columbia* disintegrated during re-entry, killing all seven astronauts aboard.

Rolf Densing, the ESA's director of operations, told a recent conference, "This problem can only be solved globally."[9]

Some economists suggest imposing a user fee on space launches to pay for debris mitigation.[10] A British company has proposed a system — called Necropolis — that would collect defunct satellites and move them into an orbit that active satellites don't use. And researchers at the University of Colorado at Boulder have proposed pushing pieces of space junk into higher orbit by firing beams of electrons at them.[11]

The ESA plans a RemoveDEBRIS mission this year to test a net that could be used to drag pieces of space junk into the atmosphere to burn up. It also will test a "dragsail" — like the sail on a boat but pushed by photons of light from the sun instead of wind — to accomplish the same objective.[12]

James A. Lewis, senior vice president at the Center for Strategic and International Studies, a think tank in Washington, says dealing with space debris is the most obvious starting point for international cooperation in space. He calls it one of the few issues where "we can possibly get some utility out of a new agreement."

— *Patrick Marshall*

An illustration of Earth created by the National Aeronautics and Space Administration (NASA) in 1989 graphically shows space debris in low-Earth orbit.

Getty Images/NASA

[1] "Frequently Asked Questions: Orbital Debris," NASA, undated, https://tinyurl.com/yag6tr7w. Richard Ingham, "Space debris problem getting worse, say scientists," Phys.org, April 18, 2017, https://tinyurl.com/y8xnajhz.

[2] Sarah Knapton, "750,000 pieces of debris orbiting Earth threaten future of spaceflight, warn experts," *The Telegraph*, April 21, 2017, https://tinyurl.com/y9x9cftl.

[3] Ingham, op. cit.

[4] Tereza Pultarova, "Experts Call for Legislation and Improved Tracking to Deal with Orbital Debris," *Space News*, April 25, 2017, https://tinyurl.com/y9rral7q.

[5] Brad Plumer, "Space trash is a big problem. These economists have a solution," *The Washington Post*, Oct. 24, 2013, https://tinyurl.com/ycvhs5jf.

[6] Pultarova, op. cit.

[7] Brian Weeden, "2007 Chinese Anti-Satellite Test Fact Sheet," Secure World Foundation, updated Nov. 23, 2010, https://tinyurl.com/ya63f4fa.

[8] Ibid.

[9] Ingham, op. cit.

[10] Plumer, op. cit.

[11] Pultarova, op. cit.

[12] Tereza Pultarova, "Meet the Space Custodians: Debris Cleanup Plans Emerge," Space.com, April 26, 2017, https://tinyurl.com/ybrvypu2.

Investigators determined that a piece of insulating foam from the shuttle's external fuel tank had come loose during launch, striking the spacecraft's wing and damaging its heat shield.[86]

In January 2004, President George W. Bush called for returning astronauts to the moon by 2020 and sending a manned mission to Mars. The result was NASA's Constellation Program.[87]

New Competition

Two years after taking office in 2008, President Obama canceled the Constellation Program, calling it "over budget, behind schedule and lacking in innovation due to a failure to invest in critical new technologies."[88]

His decision effectively eliminated any chance the United States would send astronauts to the moon during his administration. Instead, Obama called for NASA to send astronauts to an asteroid by 2025 and into orbit around Mars by the mid-2030s. But Congress had other ideas and funded NASA to proceed with a program essentially equivalent to the Constellation Program.[89]

Meanwhile, private-sector spaceflight companies were working to develop their own launch capabilities. SpaceX's first three launches failed, but its fourth, in 2008, was a success, as was a 2009 launch that sent the company's first commercial payload, a Malaysian satellite, into orbit.[90]

Zimmerman said SpaceX's fortunes improved from that point on. "SpaceX quickly signed up a large number of customers, even though the company was barely half a decade old," he wrote. "By 2012 . . . the company possessed launch contracts with private satellite companies valued at more than $1 billion. SpaceX's biggest new customer, however, was not a private company; it was NASA."[91]

Private companies' role in space also got a boost from NASA's Commercial Crew Program, created to help the space agency build a replacement for the space shuttle.

Previously, NASA had provided private contractors with detailed specifications for the equipment it wanted them to build, and once it was built, NASA owned it. The plan under the Commercial Crew Program was for contractors to develop the spacecraft and other equipment themselves, with full ownership of the final product.[92]

Congress also acted to boost private-sector activities in space with the U.S. Commercial Space Launch Competitiveness Act of 2015.

Although the 1967 Outer Space Treaty prohibits countries from claiming sovereignty over space or celestial bodies, the act grants rights to resources extracted by companies from asteroids, the moon and other celestial bodies.[93]

CURRENT SITUATION

Regulatory Debate

The United States is the only country where private aerospace companies play a significant role in space, and that role is expanding rapidly. Perhaps not surprisingly, a vigorous debate is unfolding about how much the government should regulate these companies' activities in space.

Article 6 of the 1967 Outer Space Treaty requires that participating countries provide "continuing supervision" of private space-related activities.[94] Some experts say the U.S. government regulates those activities so weakly that it may be violating the treaty.

"The United States has clear rules controlling the export of sensitive space technologies on Earth, but lacks clear rules for private-sector operations in space," wrote Pace, of the Space Policy Institute. "This has caused some countries, such as Russia, to question whether private U.S. space companies are being supervised properly as required by international law. The United States can and should create a supportive regulatory regime for commercial space activities, but at present there is no clear, central authority for doing so."[95]

Matthew P. Schaefer, co-director of the Space, Cyber and Telecommunications Law Program at the University of Nebraska, warned a Senate subcommittee in May that unless the United States takes "minimal steps" to comply with Article 6, U.S. aerospace companies "may face foreign retaliation in the form of denying access to customers or partners, and investors from abroad may shy away as well."[96]

In addition, he said, the United States could not then insist that foreign governments "not harmfully interfere with U.S. commercial activities" in space.[97]

Other experts, however, say the treaty leaves it up to each country to define "continuing supervision."

"How a country chooses to assure that its citizens do not violate these provisions is completely up to that country," James E. Dunstan, a senior adjunct fellow at TechFreedom, a technology policy think tank in Washington, and Berin Szoka, TechFreedom's president, told the same Senate panel where Schaefer testified.[98]

While the Outer Space Treaty does not specify the type or degree of oversight countries should exercise over private-sector activities, industry leaders say uncertainty about the regulatory environment is bad for business. "Internal and external investors, as well as insurers, need to know what, if any, regulatory risks a particular project will face before financing an initiative," Michael Gold, vice president of Space Systems Loral, a Palo Alto, Calif., company that designs and builds satellite and spacecraft systems, said at the hearing.[99]

U.S. regulatory responsibilities are clearly defined. The Federal Aviation Administration oversees launches and re-entries of spacecraft, the Commerce Department licenses commercial satellites, and the Commerce, State and Defense departments oversee export controls and licensing of strategic technologies.[100]

Some industry advocates call that arrangement complex and unpredictable. "The problem . . . is not a 'regulatory gap' for current space activities, but rather a patchwork regulatory system that is complex, nontransparent and extremely expensive to navigate," Dunstan and Szoka told Congress. "Before we start overlaying a whole new 'Mission Authorization' regulatory regime on innovative space activities, we must first streamline the existing regime to reduce cost, redundancy and most of all, opaqueness, where bureaucrats can still pick winners and losers with impunity."[101]

Several free-market advocates want "permissionless approval" for commercial space activities.

"I urge the Congress to consider blanket authorization for all nongovernmental operations in space that do not cause tangible harm to other parties, whether foreign or domestic, in their peaceful exploration and use of outer space," Eli Dourado, director of the Technology Policy Program at George Mason University, said at a House committee hearing in March. "Such an approach would meet our treaty obligations while maximizing the scope for innovation and experimentation in space."[102]

But aerospace firms are not equipped to know whether their space activities might cause harm, other experts say.

"Few if any individual operators have the ability to either assess the risk their activities may pose to other space flight missions, especially U.S. or other government missions, nor the resources or ability to ameliorate the damages their actions might have on those missions," Douglas L. Loverro, former deputy assistant secretary of Defense for space policy, said at the House hearing. "And to ask them to try to develop those capabilities would be a greater constraint to their entrepreneurial activities than some well-designed government-sponsored measures."[103]

Some policymakers have called for amending the Outer Space Treaty to clarify regulatory responsibilities in space and better support the activities of private companies. Sen. Ted Cruz, R-Texas, said in April that 1967 was "a different time and era" and called on Congress to evaluate how a treaty enacted 50 years ago "will impact new and innovative activity within space."[104]

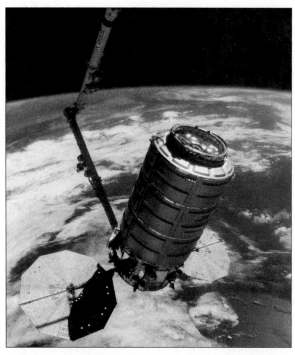

NASA/Mark Garcia

A resupply ship operated by Orbital ATK, an aerospace firm in Virginia, prepares to dock with the International Space Station on April 22. Some analysts and industry leaders say the nation's growing number of private-sector companies — rather than NASA — should handle deep-space exploration.

Most experts, however, see little chance the treaty will be modified or replaced. Even if U.S. policymakers agreed to amend the treaty, other space powers would be suspicious of their motives, said CSIS' Lewis. "People always think that it is the United States in some way trying to create opportunity for itself," he says.

Muncy of PoliSpace says the pact does not need to be changed. Instead, he says, the State Department needs to ensure the treaty's provisions are implemented in ways that benefit the United States.

National Space Council

The Trump administration's announcement in June that it will resurrect the National Space Council — with Vice President Mike Pence in charge — to oversee all U.S. activities and policies in space has also stirred controversy. The original council, established in 1958, was disbanded in 1973, revived in 1989 and disbanded again in 1993.[105]

AT ISSUE

Should the private sector take over the management and design of U.S. space exploration from NASA?

YES
Rick Tumlinson
Chairman, Deep Space Industries, and Founder, New Worlds Institute

Written for *CQ Researcher*, August 2017

Exploring and opening space should no longer be something exclusive to the government — that it does for the people — rather it should answer the needs of government, and support those who want to go there themselves, to explore and create new homes.

To put the issue in context, let us separate science from exploration, settlement and development. In the first, the customer is the scientist. In the others, the customer is the people. A scientist wants data and information. If the private sector can provide the data cheaper, better and faster, it should get the job — and in most cases it can.

In exploration, the payoff can be science, strategic power, prestige or information that supports the nation or its people's ability to utilize or live in the places explored. Explorers on Earth have always been funded through a mix of sources. In the past, many were employed by government, as were Lewis and Clark. Today, some explorers are government employees, but many operate on grants from the government or private sources.

Settlement and development in space must be initiated by citizens but should be supported by the government. By being so, every other aspect of national interest is satisfied. To the extent that NASA funds can be allocated in ways that enhance human development and settlement of areas of space where people want to go, the agency should be allowed and encouraged to play a role. Yet it need not lead, and it definitely should not plan or control the pace of these activities.

In areas where the interest is purely scientific or at a stage where scientific return is the primary driver, NASA and other science-oriented elements of the government, working with academia, should continue to lead the way. However, funds spent on science and exploration should leverage citizen activities, especially activities that enable government-funded scientists and explorers to do more, and more cheaply.

The private sector will quickly become more efficient than government agencies in gathering data and building infrastructure in space as it already is here on Earth. The government can lease or purchase from businesses, stimulating the economy and lowering taxpayer costs.

NASA should carefully pick science and exploration missions that are not best accomplished by and for the private sector itself, and when possible invest taxpayer funds back into the people, support institutional exploration and help solve the technical challenges we all face as we begin to settle the frontier.

NO
Scott Pace
Director, Space Policy Institute, George Washington University

Written for *CQ Researcher*, June 2017

This is a simple question that obscures a deeper public policy question about how governments and markets create public goods, such as scientific knowledge, in the course of space exploration. To answer the question simply: no. Rather, the question should be how to use government to provide appropriate structures and incentives for the private sector, so as to obtain the greatest national good from space explorations.

Governments are responsible for providing public goods — among them national security, basic scientific research and exploration — for which no commercial market exists or is likely to exist.

There are fundamental differences between a publicly funded and directed enterprise chartered to define, explore and exploit a new frontier, and enterprises founded and directed for the purpose of creating wealth and providing shareholder returns. Private philanthropy can and does support science and exploration, but these are, in general, noncommercial, nonmarket activities even if they use private goods, services and capital.

In using the private sector in missions of exploration, the question is, who reports to whom? Is the goal the creation of public goods or the private success of companies? If a private actor who is providing a public good or service fails, changes priorities or slips schedule, the loss cannot always be made whole merely by paying monetary damages. Money is not a substitute for public-good failures in the way it is for commercial failures. Not everything which matters to our society will necessarily look good on a corporate balance sheet.

NASA is responsible for determining when and how it explores space using public funds. It cannot and should not be merely a passive buyer of just those exploration-related goods and services that contractors find it profitable to sell at a particular time. This means that NASA must be a "smart customer" — a role that would be undermined if it outsourced its design and management capabilities to a private contractor.

We do not really know what the human future in space will be. That is a question that exploration is intended to answer. In exploring space, we necessarily employ imperfect options, markets and governments in our portfolio of tools. The most effective exploration strategy will be a mixed one of government initiative and private innovation, not one entirely driven by NASA or left to the uncertainty of dynamic markets. There is room and need for both.

Muncy of PoliSpace says the new council will give President Trump the information he needs to tell individual agencies overseeing space-related activities "whether or not they are actually holding up their end of the bargain to serve the national interest beyond their institutional interest."

When the idea of reviving the council was floated in December, *Apollo 11* astronaut Edwin E. "Buzz" Aldrin Jr. told a reporter it would be "absolutely critical in ensuring that the president's space priorities are clearly articulated and effectively executed."[106]

James Reuter, deputy associate administrator at NASA's Space Technology Mission Directorate, said in May that a new National Space Council might improve communication between the White House and Congress. "There's a lot of congressional guidance on the programs [that members of Congress] fund, and they don't always align with the administration's viewpoints," he said. "Perhaps a space council could help us."[107]

Air and Space Museum historian Logsdon said earlier versions of the council failed to prove "its superiority as an organizational approach to developing a space strategy or coordinating the space activities of executive agencies." After it was revived in 1989, he wrote, the council "managed to alienate most executive agencies."[108]

Aaron Oesterle, project manager at the Space Frontier Foundation, which supports rapid action to colonize other planets, also is skeptical. "Taking all of the various space stuff and putting it under a single regulatory authority is not viable in the long term, and in the short term it is so disruptive," he says.

OUTLOOK
New Challenges

Policymakers and analysts fear that failing to fund U.S. space programs at sufficient levels could have serious implications for U.S. national security. U.S. satellites must be better protected soon or the country could lose strategic advantages in communication, guidance, intelligence gathering and other areas important to the military, they say.

"The era of unchallenged U.S. dominance of space is over," said Colby at the Center for a New American Security. The United States, he said, must "induce, convince, coerce, deter, dissuade, coax, incentivize or

otherwise persuade" other countries not to exploit the vulnerabilities of U.S. satellites or the country's other space assets.[109]

Military officials are working to make U.S. satellites more maneuverable and resistant to jamming, but it is unclear whether Trump administration members understand why such steps are necessary, says Singer, of the New America think tank.

He also says competing interests in space among countries such as the United States, China and Russia make war on Earth more likely. "For most of the 20th century, the idea of great state powers going to war against each other was thinkable," he says. "It is thinkable once more."

Some policymakers say the United States must do more to assert its leadership over activities in Earth's orbit. Otherwise, they say, U.S. officials will treat China's progress in space as a potential military threat and will not want aerospace companies involved in space after all.

"China already has demonstrated a strong disregard for interests of other countries in outer space through its anti-satellite tests," Rep. Smith said at a hearing before his House committee in September. "Here on Earth, illegal incursions into the South China Sea represent a blatant disregard for the international rule of law. Will their disregard of international law continue to extend into outer space?"[110]

Some experts warn of potential trouble in space from rogue organizations or even individuals.

"Given the revolution in [private space flight], it's possible to imagine other nonstate actors having a go at space as well," wrote Baiocchi and Welser. "Nongovernmental organizations may start pursuing missions that undermine governments' objectives. An activist billionaire wanting to promote transparency could deploy a constellation of satellites to monitor and then tweet the movements of troops worldwide. Criminal syndicates could use satellites to monitor the patterns of law enforcement in order [to] elude capture, or a junta could use them to track rivals after a coup."[111]

Pace of the Space Policy Institute recommends that the United States work not only with private companies but with other countries as well in planning and conducting space programs.

"In the Cold War, space leadership was about, 'Look what I can do by myself that nobody else can do? I can land on the moon and nobody else can,'" Pace says. "Today, when there are many more state and nonstate actors in space — a lot more players — leadership is about, 'What can I get others to do with me?'"

NOTES

1. Ben Evans, "Soyuz TMA-12M Crew Ready for Six-Hour Fast Ride to Space Station," *America Space*, undated, https://tinyurl.com/ycuxmtek; The Soyuz Experience in Photos," Canadian Space Agency, undated, https://tinyurl.com/q8ykklx; "NASA Astronaut Randy Bresnik Available for Interviews Before Space Station Mission," media advisory, NASA, July 17, 2017, https://tinyurl.com/y99o9lwn.

2. Sean O'Kane, "NASA buys two more seats to the International Space Station on Russia's Soyuz rocket," *The Verge*, Feb. 28, 2017, https://tinyurl.com/y7ox8uh9.

3. Doug Lamborn, "Time to get serious about space threats," *The Hill*, May 14, 2015, https://tinyurl.com/ya5osknh.

4. Dave Baiocchi and William Welser IV, "The Democratization of Space New Actors Need New Rules," *Foreign Affairs*, May/June 2015, p. 98, https://tinyurl.com/ycspycls.

5. Bill Canis, "Commercial Space Industry Launches a New Phase," Congressional Research Service, Dec. 12, 2016, p. 1, https://tinyurl.com/y7kw5lxa.

6. Elbridge Colby, "From Sanctuary to Battlefield: A Framework for a U.S. Defense and Deterrence Strategy for Space," Center for a New American Security, January 2017, https://tinyurl.com/ya6wx3a2.

7. Testimony of Lt. Gen. John W. Raymond before the House Armed Services Subcommittee on Strategic Forces, March 25, 2015, https://tinyurl.com/yd8sv7nh.

8. "U.S. Should Stop Relying on Russian Rockets," editorial board, *Observer*, May 17, 2016, https://tinyurl.com/ybmw93nr; O'Kane, op. cit.

9. Anthony Cave, "John McCain on target about American reliance on Russian rocket engines," *PolitiFact Arizona*, Jan. 29, 2016, https://tinyurl.com/y733n7z2.

10. Testimony of James A. Lewis before the House Science, Space, and Technology Subcommittee on Space, "Are We Losing the Space Race to China?" Sept. 27, 2016, https://tinyurl.com/yb3q6hs4.

11. "China's Secretive Space Program Threatens NASA's dominance," Bloomberg News, Nov. 28, 2016, https://tinyurl.com/hlf6wnl.

12. Steven Jiang, "China: We will be on Mars by the end of 2020," CNN, Jan. 5, 2017, https://tinyurl.com/z7czqwm.

13. Leonard David, "China's Anti-Satellite Test: Worrisome Debris Cloud Circles Earth," Space.com, Feb. 2, 2007, https://tinyurl.com/yasn5o5w; "China's President Urges Militarization of Space," Fox News, April 15, 2014, https://tinyurl.com/yde5q75p.

14. "National Security Space Defense and Protection," National Academies Press, 2016, https://tinyurl.com/y8hpetr7; "UCS Satellite Database," Union of Concerned Scientists, April 11, 2017, https://tinyurl.com/y9pjvegd.

15. John Logsdon, "Ten Presidents and NASA," *50th Magazine*, NASA, undated, https://tinyurl.com/y8jao7rw.

16. Kerry Sheridan, "NASA delays deep-space Orion test to 2019 due to costs," Phys.org, May 12, 2017, https://tinyurl.com/y7yruzft; Loren Grush, "Trump's NASA budget cancels Europa lander and Asteroid Redirect Mission," *The Verge*, March 16, 2017, https://tinyurl.com/ybq3gluk.

17. Statement of Chairman Lamar Smith, R-Texas, "Next Steps to Mars: Deep Space Habitats," House Science, Space and Technology Committee, May 18, 2016, https://tinyurl.com/yckrl2dw.

18. "SpaceX blasts off cargo using recycled spaceship," Phys.org, June 3, 2017, https://tinyurl.com/y7qs7lzk; "Completed Missions," SpaceX, https://tinyurl.com/mngp9rq; "SpaceX To Send Privately Crewed Dragon Spacecraft Beyond The Moon Next Year," *SpaceX News*, Feb. 27, 2017, https://tinyurl.com/hbrjw2b.

19. Rolfe Winkler and Andy Pasztor, "Exclusive Peek at SpaceX Data Shows Loss in 2015, Heavy Expectations for Nascent Internet Service," *The*

Wall Street Journal, Jan. 13, 2017, https://tinyurl .com/zskb2ua.

20. Canis, op. cit., pp. 4, 10; "The Commercial Space Industry and Launch Market," everyCRS Report. com, April 20, 2012, https://tinyurl.com/y7dls4e8.

21. Robin McKie, "Astronauts lift our spirits. But can we afford to send humans into space?" *The Guardian*, Dec. 6, 2014, https://tinyurl.com/y9qc5xzp; Andrew Follett, "NASA Vetoes Trump's Plan To Return Astronauts To Moon In 2019," *The Daily Caller*, May 14, 2017, https://tinyurl.com/lrvlw9z.

22. Colby, op. cit., p. 10.

23. "Treaty on Principles Governing the Activities of States in the Exploration and Use of Outer Space, Including the Moon and Other Celestial Bodies," U.S. Department of State, undated, https://tinyurl .com/yanl9blx.

24. Jonathan Broder, "Why the Next Pearl Harbor Could Happen in Space," *Newsweek*, May 4, 2016, https://tinyurl.com/ybex9noe.

25. Ibid.

26. James R. Clapper, "Statement for the Record: Worldwide Threat Assessment of the US Intelligence Community," Senate Armed Services Committee, Feb. 9, 2016, https://tinyurl.com/y8hhynfe.

27. Calla Cofield, "What President Trump Means for NASA," Space.com, Nov. 10, 2016, https://tinyurl .com/hxb8hlh.

28. "NASA Space Station Cargo Launches aboard Orbital ATK Resupply Mission," news release, NASA, April 18, 2017, https://tinyurl.com/ y73w77dq; Jeff Foust, "Blue Origin still planning commercial suborbital flights in 2018," *Space News*, April 5, 2017, https://tinyurl.com/yccqr6vd.

29. "Commercial Crew Program — The Essentials," NASA, undated, https://tinyurl.com/ybvr96oj.

30. Robert Zimmerman, "Capitalism in Space: Private Enterprise and Competition Reshape the Global Aerospace Launch Industry," Center for a New American Security, January 2017, p. 27, https:// tinyurl.com/ycrgydsu.

31. Loren Thompson, "Capitalism In Space: The Beguiling Myth Market Forces Can Fix Everything,"

Forbes, March 16, 2017, https://tinyurl.com/ y7rc7umm.

32. Canis, op. cit., p. 8.

33. Scott Pace, "Wishful thinking collides with policy, economic realities in 'Capitalism in Space,'" *Space News*, April 4, 2017, https://tinyurl.com/y8t3tt2r.

34. Ben Guarino, "Stephen Hawking calls for a return to the moon as Earth's clock runs out," *The Washington Post*, June 21, 2017, https://tinyurl .com/y7cjukcr.

35. Darlene Superville, "Trump Wants to Send Humans to Mars," The Associated Press, *U.S. News & World Report*, March 21, 2017, https://tinyurl.com/ y9m7yjy4; S.A. Miller, "Trump renews NASA mission for human space travel, deep space exploration," *The Washington Times*, March 21, 2017, https://tinyurl.com/y927gglo.

36. Marina Koren, "Trump's Advisers Want to Return Humans to the Moon in Three Years," *The Atlantic*, Feb. 9, 2017, https://tinyurl.com/y9aq3zch.

37. Christian Davenport, "An exclusive look at Jeff Bezos's plan to set up Amazon-like delivery for 'future human settlement' of the moon," *The Washington Post*, March 2, 2017, https://tinyurl .com/y779sb6r.

38. Text of H.R.870 — REAL Space Act, Congress.gov, undated, https://tinyurl.com/yc2dp3au; Damien Sharkov, "Russia Plans New Rocket For Future Moon Base," *Newsweek*, Nov. 11, 2016, https:// tinyurl.com/hjbwyz5; and Andrew Griffin, "China and Europe to build a base on the moon and launch other projects into space," *The Independent*, April 26, 2017, https://tinyurl.com/y8lwng2p.

39. Shannon Stirone, "Meet the Republican Congressman Obsessed With Sending America Back to the Moon," *Motherboard*, Feb. 27, 2017, https://tinyurl.com/zm9c2j5.

40. Testimony of Robert Richards before the Senate Commerce, Science, and Transportation Sub-committee on Science, Space, and Competitiveness, May 23, 2017, https://tinyurl.com/yb34ad9d.

41. Eric Berger, "Quietly, NASA is reconsidering the moon as a destination," *The Houston Chronicle*, April 3, 2015, https://tinyurl.com/qbzk2zf.

42. Richard Gray, " 'We could be living on the moon by 2022': Nasa claims a 'cheap' $10 billion lunar base will be ready for humans in just six years," *The Daily Mail*, March 24, 2016, https://tinyurl.com/h9hhc6v.

43. Calla Cofield, "The Moon or Mars? NASA Must Pick 1 Goal for Astronauts, Experts Tell Congress," Space.com, Feb. 4, 2016, https://tinyurl.com/y9hdrheu.

44. Cian O'Luanaigh, "No need for manned spaceflight, says astronomer royal Martin Rees," *The Guardian*, July 26, 2010, https://tinyurl.com/y8cc9h8t.

45. Hanneke Weitering, "50th Anniversary of Apollo 1 Fire: What NASA Learned from the Tragic Accident," Space.com, Jan. 27, 2017, https://tinyurl.com/ycsaaqzn.

46. Jeff Foust, "Weighing the risks of human spaceflight," *The Space Review*, July 21, 2003, https://tinyurl.com/29o7o6r.

47. "Spirit and Opportunity," NASA, undated, https://tinyurl.com/y9w87lc6.

48. Davod Szondy, "NASA works to wake up Curiosity as mission gets two-year extension," *New Atlas*, July 7, 2016, https://tinyurl.com/y74j3ou8.

49. Ted Spitzmiller, *The History Of Human Space Flight* (2017), p. 128.

50. Ibid., p. 129.

51. Statement by the President Upon Signing the National Aeronautics and Space Act of 1958, July 29, 1958, The American Presidency Project, University of California, Santa Barbara, http://tinyurl.com/y7oyql3d.

52. Logsdon, op. cit.

53. Steven J. Dick, "50 Years of NASA History," *50th Magazine*, NASA, undated, http://tinyurl.com/yc4g5p4t.

54. "Glenn Orbits the Earth," NASA, Feb. 16, 2012, http://tinyurl.com/pb399qr.

55. Spitzmiller, op. cit., p. 226.

56. "What Was the Gemini Program?" NASA, March 16, 2011, http://tinyurl.com/y9azc8t9.

57. Logsdon, op. cit.

58. Ibid.; William Harwood, "JFK legacy: Setting America on course for the moon," CBS News, Nov. 21, 2013, http://tinyurl.com/y99qk98e.

59. "What Was the Apollo Program?" NASA, July 19, 2017, http://tinyurl.com/y98jr8m2; Rochelle Oliver and Amisha Padnani, "They Walked on the Moon," *The New York Times*, Jan. 17, 2017, http://tinyurl.com/ycwdvx7w.

60. "National Security Space Defense and Protection," Committee on National Security Space Defense and Protection, Division on Engineering and Physical Sciences, National Academy of Sciences, 2016, p. 9, http://tinyurl.com/y8hpetr7; Lee Billings, "War in Space May Be Closer Than Ever," *Scientific American*, Aug. 10, 2015, http://tinyurl.com/ycrzxj4f.

61. "Treaty on Principles Governing the Activities of States in the Exploration and Use of Outer Space, including the Moon and Other Celestial Bodies," Office for Outer Space Affairs, United Nations, undated, http://tinyurl.com/oxpq3qp.

62. Logsdon, op. cit.

63. Ibid.

64. "Nasa budgets: US spending on space travel since 1958," DataBlog, *The Guardian*, undated, http://tinyurl.com/m72mnb8.

65. Spitzmiller, op. cit., p. 429.

66. "What Was the Apollo Program?" op. cit.

67. "President Nixon's 1972 Announcement on the Space Shuttle," NASA, undated, http://tinyurl.com/yc6e95uj.

68. Spitzmiller, op. cit., p. 460.

69. "The Skylab Crewed Missions," NASA, May 6, 2013, http://tinyurl.com/y74m8n5q.

70. Spitzmiller, op. cit., p. 464.

71. "Why Did NASA End the Space Shuttle Program?" *Forbes*, Feb. 2, 2017, http://tinyurl.com/y8c6539k.

72. "Space Shuttle Era," NASA, undated, https://www.nasa.gov/mission_pages/shuttle/flyout/index.html; "First American Woman in Space," NASA, updated July 31, 2015, http://tinyurl.com/y8vh27ux; Clara Moskowitz, "Space Shuttle's Lasting Legacy:

30 Years of Historic Feats," Space.com, April 6, 2011, http://tinyurl.com/ybjowc7m.

73. Moskowitz, op. cit.

74. Dick, op. cit.

75. Canis, op. cit., p. 1; President Ronald Reagan, "Statement on Signing the Commercial Space Launch Act," The American Presidency Project, University of California, Santa Barbara, Oct. 30, 1984, http://tinyurl.com/kjf6q2a.

76. "Commercial Orbital Transportation Service: A New Era in Space," NASA, February 2014, p. 10, http://tinyurl.com/ybdg2mcj.

77. Ibid., p. 3.

78. Tim Weiner, "Titan Lost Payload: Spy-Satellite System Worth $800 Million," *The New York Times*, Aug. 4, 1993, http://tinyurl.com/y8nvnwrf.

79. Todd Harrison et al., "Beyond the RD-180," Center for Strategic and International Studies, March 2017, p. 1, http://tinyurl.com/y8gmtdng.

80. "H.R. 4399 (100th): Commercial Space Launch Act Amendments of 1988," govtrack, Nov. 15, 1988, http://tinyurl.com/y9lktncd.

81. "Commercial Space Act of 1998, Title II — P.L. 105-303," Office of the General Counsel, NASA, undated, http://tinyurl.com/y9dqnmgz.

82. "History and Timeline of the ISS," Center for the Advancement of Science in Space, undated, http://tinyurl.com/y78e8xvr; Tim Sharp, "International Space Station: Facts, History & Tracking," Space.com, April 5, 2016, http://tinyurl.com/y73suodm.

83. "International Space Station Legal Framework," European Space Agency, undated, http://tinyurl.com/y92k46pt.

84. Anatoly Zak, "The Hidden History of the Soviet Satellite-Killer," *Popular Mechanics*, Nov. 1, 2013, http://tinyurl.com/ycbs8xqa.

85. Broder, op. cit.

86. Karl Tate, "Columbia Space Shuttle Disaster Explained (Infographic)," Space.com, Feb. 1, 2013, http://tinyurl.com/y9a77qkg.

87. "President Bush Offers New Vision For NASA," NASA, Jan. 14, 2004, http://tinyurl.com/yd3ra2mz.

88. Ker Than, "Obama Scrubs NASA's Manned Moon Missions," *National Geographic News*, Feb. 1, 2010, http://tinyurl.com/y72woscm; Clara Moskowitz, "NASA Stuck in Limbo as New Congress Takes Over," Space.com, Jan. 7, 2011, http://tinyurl.com/ydcmwysj; Zimmerman, op. cit., p. 10.

89. Zimmerman, op. cit., p. 6.

90. Ibid.

91. Ibid., p. 15.

92. "Commercial Crew Program — The Essentials," op. cit.

93. "H.R.2262 — U.S. Commercial Space Launch Competitiveness Act," Congress.gov, undated, http://tinyurl.com/o7j7grl.

94. "Treaty on Principles Governing the Activities of States in the Exploration and Use of Outer Space, Including the Moon and Other Celestial Bodies," op. cit.

95. Scott Pace, "Regulating Outer Space: Making Space Commerce a Priority," *Foreign Affairs*, May 12, 2016, http://tinyurl.com/yd75n9dp.

96. Testimony of Matthew P. Schaefer before the Senate Commerce, Science, and Transportation Subcommittee on Space, Science, and Competitiveness, May 23, 2017, http://tinyurl.com/yb34ad9d.

97. Ibid.

98. Testimony of James E. Dunstan and Berin Szoka before the Senate Commerce, Science, and Transportation Subcommittee on Space, Science, and Competitiveness, May 23, 2017, http://tinyurl.com/yb34ad9d.

99. Testimony of Michael Gold before the Senate Commerce, Science and Transportation Subcommittee on Space, Science and Competitiveness, May 23, 2017, http://tinyurl.com/yb34ad9d.

100. Canis, op. cit., p. 14.

101. Testimony of James E. Dunstan and Berin Szoka, op. cit.

102. Testimony of Eli Dourado before the House Science, Space, and Technology Subcommittee on Space, "Creating an Environment of Permissionless

Innovation in Outer Space," March 8, 2017, http://tinyurl.com/y7rdmp7q.

103. Testimony of Douglas L. Loverro before the House Science, Space, and Technology Subcommittee on Space, March 8, 2017, http://tinyurl.com/yc4abc59.

104. Jeff Foust, "Cruz interested in updating Outer Space Treaty to support commercial space activities," *Space News*, April 26, 2017, http://tinyurl.com/ybmu33ag.

105. Sarah Schlieder, "Trump Is Bringing Back The National Space Council . . . What's That?" abc2news.com, June 7, 2017, http://tinyurl.com/ycsufh5k; "NASA Statement on National Space Council," news release, NASA, June 30, 2017, http://tinyurl.com/yb2w8hqv.

106. Leonard David, "Playing the Space Trump Card: Relaunching a National Space Council," Space.com, Dec. 29, 2016, http://tinyurl.com/y9p2h3dq.

107. Jeff Foust, "Executive order creating National Space Council expected soon," *Space News*, May 2, 2017, http://tinyurl.com/n7bz6dh.

108. John Logsdon, "Is creating a National Space Council the best choice?" *The Space Review*, Jan. 3, 2017, http://tinyurl.com/jc5odex.

109. Colby, op. cit., p. 17.

110. Statement of Rep. Lamar Smith, House Science, Space, and Technology Committee, Sept. 27, 2016, http://tinyurl.com/y7h5un67.

111. Baiocchi and Welser, op. cit., p. 100.

BIBLIOGRAPHY

Selected Sources

Books

Spitzmiller, Ted, *The History of Human Spaceflight,* **University Press of Florida, 2017.**
An aviation historian and pilot delivers a colorful history of human space flight, beginning in 1783 with balloonists and ending with the debate over returning humans to the moon and colonizing other planets.

MacDonald, Alexander, *The Long Space Age: The Economic Origins of Space Exploration from Colonial America to the Cold War,* **Yale University Press, 2017.**
An economist with NASA's Jet Propulsion Laboratory says philanthropists and private companies historically have provided crucial financing for space programs.

Sivolella, Davide, *The Space Shuttle Program: Technologies and Accomplishments,* **Springer Praxis Books, 2017.**
An aerospace engineer offers a detailed history of the space shuttle program.

Articles

Baiocchi, Dave, and William Welser IV, "The Democratization of Space: New Actors Need New Rules," *Foreign Affairs,* **May/June 2015, https://tinyurl.com/ycspycls.**
Two engineers with the RAND Corp. think tank argue that governments need to develop a new legal framework to accommodate the growing role of private companies in space.

Chow, Brian G., "Stalkers in Space: Defeating the Threat," *Strategic Studies Quarterly,* **Summer 2017, https://tinyurl.com/y8mk5ntk.**
An adjunct physical scientist at the RAND Corp. says the best way to defend U.S. satellite systems against anti-satellite weapons is to announce a policy of pre-emptive strikes against potential adversaries who behave suspiciously.

Pace, Scott, "Regulating Outer Space: Making Space Commerce a Priority," *Foreign Affairs,* **May 12, 2016, https://tinyurl.com/yd75n9dp.**
The director of the Space Policy Institute at George Washington University says the Outer Space Treaty of 1967 does not adequately cover the activities of private aerospace companies and that the United States needs to take the lead in setting international norms for using space.

Thompson, Loren, "Capitalism In Space: The Beguiling Myth Market Forces Can Fix Everything," *Forbes,* **March 16, 2017, https://tinyurl.com/y7rc7umm.**
A public-policy analyst challenges the argument that the private sector is better suited than NASA to manage space programs, saying private efforts have regularly run behind schedule, and concern for profits may cause companies to skimp on safety.

Reports and Studies

"National Security Space Defense and Protection: Public Report," Committee on National Security Space Defense and Protection; Division on Engineering and Physical Sciences, National Academies of Sciences, Engineering, and Medicine, National Academies Press, 2016.

A panel of military, academic and private-sector experts assesses the risks to U.S. national security presented by other countries' space capabilities as well as potential measures for countering those risks.

Canis, Bill, "Commercial Space Industry Launches a New Phase," Congressional Research Service, Dec. 12, 2016, https://tinyurl.com/y7kw5lxa.

An analyst for the research arm of Congress describes the growing role of private companies in space, their relationship with NASA and federal regulation of private-sector activities in space.

Colby, Elbridge, "From Sanctuary to Battlefield: A Framework for a U.S. Defense and Deterrence Strategy for Space," Center for a New American Security, January 2017, https://tinyurl.com/ya6wx3a2.

A senior fellow at a national security think tank assesses the vulnerability of U.S. satellite systems and other space-related technology, details the limited steps taken to mitigate those vulnerabilities and explores potential ways to deter attacks by other countries.

Harrison, Todd, Andrew Hunter, Kaitlyn Johnson, Evan Linck and Thomas Roberts, "Beyond the RD-180," Center for Strategic and International Studies, March 2017, https://tinyurl.com/ydgcdwjm.

Analysts at a centrist think tank explore how the U.S. government came to depend on Russian rockets for trips to the International Space Station and options for ending that dependence.

Pollpeter, Kevin, Eric Anderson, Jordan Wilson and Fan Yang, "China Dream, Space Dream: China's Progress in Space Technologies and Implications for the United States," prepared for the U.S.-China Economic and Security Review Commission, March 2, 2015, https://tinyurl.com/yb8nsoej.

Scholars from the University of California's Institute on Global Conflict and Cooperation say China's space program poses challenges for the United States but also may present opportunities for scientific collaboration.

Zimmerman, Robert, "Capitalism in Space: Private Enterprise and Competition Reshape the Global Aerospace Launch Industry," Center for a New American Security, January 2017, https://tinyurl.com/ycrgydsu.

In a report that prompted heated debate among space analysts, a space historian argues that private-sector companies are more efficient than NASA at designing and managing space programs.

For More Information

Center for a New American Security, 1152 15th St., N.W., Suite 950, Washington, DC 20005; 202-457-9400; www.cnas.org. Nonpartisan think tank that analyzes and proposes national security and defense policies.

Center for Strategic and International Studies, 1800 K St., N.W., Washington, DC 20006; 202-887-0200; www.csis.org. Centrist think tank that has analyzed space-related national security concerns for the United States, including the risks involved in depending on Russia for launches to the International Space Station.

The Heritage Foundation, 214 Massachusetts Ave., N.E., Washington, DC 20002; 202-546-4400; www.heritage.org. Conservative public policy think tank that reports on space-related security issues and other topics.

National Aeronautics and Space Administration, 300 E St., S.W., Suite 5R30, Washington, DC 20546; 202-358-0001; www.nasa.gov. The primary federal agency responsible for civilian space programs.

(Continued)

(Continued)

New America, 740 15th St., N.W., Suite 900, Washington, DC 20005; 202-986-2700; www.newamerica.org. Centrist think tank focused primarily on technology and public policy.

Space Frontier Foundation, 4539 Seminary Road, Alexandria, VA 22304; info@spacefrontier.org; www .spacefrontier.org. Nonprofit group that advocates for settling other planets.

Space Policy Institute, Elliott School of International Affairs, George Washington University, 1957 E St., N.W., Suite 403, Washington, DC 20052; 202-994-1592; https://spi.elliott .gwu.edu/. Conducts research and organizes conferences on domestic and international space policy.

Stimson Center, 1211 Connecticut Ave., N.W., 8th Floor, Washington, DC 20036; 202-223-5956; www.stimson.org. Think tank focused on issues that include space-related global security and prosperity.

11

Stolen Antiquities

Sarah Glazer

The Rosetta Stone — an ancient Egyptian stone inscribed with text that later provided the key to unlocking hieroglyphics — undergoes conservation at The British Museum in London. The British have owned the stone since 1801, when it was ceded to them by the French. Egypt repeatedly has demanded the relic's return, reflecting the ongoing debate about whether artifacts should be returned to their country of origin.

From *CQ Researcher,*
November 10, 2017

In packages labeled "ceramic tiles," thousands of ancient Babylonian tablets and cylinder seals from Iraq were smuggled into the United States in 2011, headed for their U.S. buyer — the American arts and crafts chain Hobby Lobby.[1]

In July, the company agreed to forfeit the 5,500 artifacts along with $3 million in a civil settlement with federal prosecutors in Brooklyn, N.Y.[2]

Since 2009, Hobby Lobby's evangelical Christian owners have been collecting ancient objects from the Fertile Crescent — an area of biblical holy lands stretching from the Tigris and Euphrates rivers in the Middle East to the Nile Delta in Egypt — while building a Museum of the Bible in Washington, D.C.[3]

Some experts say the case is illustrative of the worldwide market in ancient artifacts trafficked illegally through smuggling and private transactions outside of the limelight of public auctions. Often, experts say, such items have been looted from archaeological excavations but have phony ownership papers disguising that fact.

Despite a 1970 international treaty ratified by 134 nations aimed at preventing such looting and trafficking, critics say the international antiquities market remains largely self-regulated.[4]

Most countries do not require sellers to reveal details about such sales or provide proof of ownership to buyers. Smugglers exploit weak export-import laws and lax border controls and create false paper trails. And the antiquities market has a long tradition of not asking too many questions about an item's previous owners.[5]

Key Antiquities Legislation

Law	Country	Year	Description
American Antiquities Act	U.S.	1906	Barred digging on public land without a permit; aimed at controlling Pueblo artifacts trade.
National Stolen Property Act	U.S.	1934	Prohibited movement of stolen or fraudulently acquired goods worth at least $5,000 across state or national borders.
Convention for the Protection of Cultural Property in the Event of Armed Conflict*	129 countries	1954	First international treaty devoted to protecting cultural property during war. Countries agreed to refrain from damaging cultural property within their borders and in other signatory nations.
Convention on the Means of Prohibiting and Preventing the Illicit Import, Export and Transfer of Ownership of Cultural Property*	134 countries	1970	Signatories agreed to require export certificates for artifacts and their return to the source country upon request. Enforcement depended on the strength of each country's implementing law.
Antiquities Law of the State of Israel	Israel	1978	First law in Israel establishing a legal antiquities market through state-licensed dealers. Required dealers to inventory all pre-1700 objects and obtain a license to export an antiquity.
Archaeological Resources Protection Act	U.S.	1979	Imposed fines of up to $20,000 and a year in jail for looting artifacts on Indian or federal land; up to 5 years and $100,000 for second offense.
Convention on Cultural Property Implementation Act	U.S.	1983	Implemented the 1970 treaty in the United States; scope limited by requirement that countries have a bilateral agreement with the U.S. before they can request the U.S. ban imports of imperiled artifacts. Sixteen countries have such agreements.
Egyptian Law on the Protection of Antiquities	Egypt	1983	Declared antiquities discovered after 1983 the property of the Egyptian government and barred export.
Native American Graves Protection and Repatriation Act	U.S.	1990	Required museums and federal agencies to return human remains and funerary objects requested by culturally affiliated Native American tribes for reburial.
Iraq Sanctions Act	U.S.	1990	Banned import of Iraqi antiquities.
Act on the Protection of Cultural Property	Germany	2016	Required documentation that an imported antiquity was legally exported from source country.
Protect and Preserve International Cultural Property Act	U.S.	2016	Restricted importation of Syrian "archeological or ethnological material."
EU Regulation on the Import of Cultural Goods (proposed)	European Union	2016	Would ban the import of goods at least 250 years old without proof of legal export from source country.

* Administered by U.N. Educational, Scientific and Cultural Organization (UNESCO)

The laws passed by nations to implement the 1970 treaty vary widely, as does enforcement. Whether an object is "illicit" depends on what country it comes from, whether that nation has prohibited such exports and whether the item left the country before or after the ban was imposed. Finally, criminal prosecutions for violating such laws are rare. For most dealers the more common penalty of forfeiture of trafficked antiquities — the approach used by authorities in the Hobby Lobby case — becomes a cost of doing business, so it is not an effective deterrent, says Patty Gerstenblith, a professor of law at DePaul University in Chicago and an expert on cultural property law.

Although it is unclear how or when the Hobby Lobby purchases left Iraq, prosecutors said the dealers provided conflicting explanations of the items' ownership history.

In addition, a cultural property expert advised Hobby Lobby before the sale that certain objects could have been looted from Iraqi sites, which have been pillaged repeatedly since the 1990s. And, under a 1936 Iraqi law, all antiquities — objects at least 200 years old — found in Iraq belong to the state and cannot be exported.[6]

The issue has received renewed attention lately because of United Nations (U.N.) and law enforcement reports that the Islamic State (ISIS) and other terrorist groups have looted and trafficked antiquities, possibly funding terrorism. In response, the international community and the United States have banned the importation of ancient cultural objects from Iraq and Syria, two conflict zones where such looting has been rampant.

The Hobby Lobby case is "a really good example" of how the illicit antiquities market is operating for high-priced artifacts or collections, says Neil Brodie, an archaeologist at the University of Oxford in England, who studies the market. "We don't expect to see them come up for public auction or to be stuck in a gallery's window on Madison Avenue. We expect them to be changing hands in secret transactions in Dubai."

The court filings in the case present a rare snapshot of one route by which illicit archaeological artifacts may be reaching collectors in the United States. According to federal prosecutors, Hobby Lobby agreed to purchase the artifacts for $1.6 million in December 2010 after company president Steve Green traveled to the United Arab Emirates to inspect them. However, prosecutors say the company ignored several warnings and "red flags" signaling illegal activity.

A cultural property law expert had warned the company that U.S. Customs officials would likely seize any package from Iraq because of a 1990 U.S. ban on antiquities imports from Iraqi.[7] The packages had falsely listed Turkey or Israel as the country of origin, and one of the dealers involved in the sale instructed Green to wire the money to seven different personal bank accounts.[8]

Green said the company was "new to the world of acquiring these items, and did not fully appreciate the complexities of the acquisitions process." He added that "regrettable mistakes" were made and that he should have "exercised more oversight."[9] He also said

the company never purchased "items from dealers in Iraq or from anyone who indicated that they acquired items from that country." He said the company has now "implemented acquisition policies and procedures based on the industry's highest standards."[10]

Experts disagree on the size of the illegal antiquities trade, by its nature an invisible one. That is partly because the definition of antiquities, broadly understood as man-made objects from the ancient past, differs depending on the country, law or organization monitoring or regulating the trade. Estimates of the market value of trafficked artifacts range as high as $7 billion worldwide, according to a widely quoted figure from a U.N. Educational, Scientific and Cultural Organization (UNESCO) official.[11]

But some antiquities dealers and archaeologists, including Oxford's Brodie, consider such figures unrealistically high. The International Association of Dealers in Ancient Art (IADAA) estimates that the legal antiquities market is only $200 million to $250 million a year.[12]

"If the legitimate market is not more than $200 million, how can the illicit market be 40 times as big?" asks Vincent Geerling, chairman of the Zurich-based IADAA, referring to estimates cited in the press. While Brodie thinks Geerling's estimate for the legal market is low, he agrees it would be hard to move billions of dollars' worth of artifacts in the "invisible" or illicit market without being detected.

Some archaeologists say any trade in archeological objects is essentially a "gray" market: While an ancient piece of art may appear legal by the time it shows up in a Madison Avenue gallery, there is usually an illegal link somewhere along the object's journey — whether an illegal export, faked ownership history papers or illegal excavation, according to Donna Yates, an American archaeologist at the University of Glasgow in Scotland, who specializes in antiquities crime.

"There's no way to distinguish" between legal and illicit ancient objects for sale, she says, because "there's no requirement to prove anything sold is legal."

More important than the dollar value of the trade, say many archaeologists, is the damage caused by looters to ancient monuments and archaeological sites — many of which are registered by UNESCO as World Heritage Site[13] — containing important links to understanding

Archaeologists: Looting Is a Global Problem

The vast majority of the 2,358 field archaeologists surveyed in 2013 said antiquities looting exists in nearly every country, and nearly 80 percent said they had personally encountered it.

What Field Archaeologists Say About Antiquities Looting

It exists	97.9%
It exists in all countries	89.6%
Have personally encountered looting	78.5%

Source: Blythe Bowman Proulx, "Archeological Site Looting in 'Glocal' Perspective: Nature, Scope, and Frequency," *American Journal of Archaeology*, 2013, https://tinyurl.com/yazvt76a

the past. Since ISIS' rise, excavation sites in Syria have been bulldozed, "strip-mined and even tunneled" by looters, destroying 2,000 to 3,000 years of buried civilization, according to Michael Danti, academic director of a project to document the damage, the Cultural Heritage Initiatives of the American Schools of Oriental Research.

"That's a cultural loss that's inestimable, says Colgate University archaeologist Danti, whose excavation storerooms in Syria were looted while ISIS controlled the territory.

A survey of archaeologists conducted in 2013 by Blythe Bowman Proulx, an associate professor of criminal justice at Virginia Commonwealth University, found that looting was reported in 103 of the 118 countries with primary archaeological fieldwork locations. "[T]he global looting phenomenon is not an exaggerated problem," Proulx wrote.[14]

Geerling contends that major artworks from Syria such as Roman mosaics are not showing up on the international market, but Brodie says he sees heavy traffic in smaller, portable objects such as coins advertised on eBay and other websites. Such objects are "very difficult for customs and law enforcement to detect," he says.

At least 100,000 antiquities and ancient coins are offered for sale online on any given day, with an estimated value of over $10 million, according to Brodie.[15] He says digging for low-value objects is just as damaging to the historical record contained in archaeological sites as looting for pricier statues or mosaics.

Archaeologists, who often say the existence of an antiquities market incentivizes looters, tend to support tougher legal restrictions, better documentation of provenance (previous ownership) and criminal prosecutions of violators. Dealers and collectors, however, say good ownership documentation has rarely existed.

Radically different views about whether the international trade is inherently criminal comes down to a fundamental difference of opinion over the best home for antiquities. "[T]o participate in the antiquities market is to some extent to participate in, or at least benefit from, criminal enterprise," write Simon Mackenzie and Yates, two experts on antiquities trafficking at the University of Glasgow.[16] Archaeologists like Yates often favor keeping ancient objects in their home countries to retain the historical context of an excavation.

But dealers say objects have independent value as works of art and are often safer with collectors and museums than in the chaotic countries or conflict zones where the objects originate.

Moreover, dealers say, strengthening requirements that antiquities are legally imported from their country of origin, as Germany did last year, will drive the trade elsewhere or underground. But supporters of such rules say the days of "don't ask, don't tell" in the antiquities trade are numbered.

The debate has played out in disputes between nations over important pieces of ancient art, such as the long-running struggle between Britain and Greece over the Elgin Marbles, sculptures taken from the Parthenon by British diplomat Lord Thomas Elgin in the 19th century.

Within the United States, the debate about preserving a people's culture has focused on thousands of Native American skeletons and sacred funerary objects in U.S. museums, many plundered from American Indian lands. A 1990 law, the Native American Graves Protection and Repatriation Act (NAGPRA), requires museums and federal agencies to return those remains and objects to culturally affiliated tribes who request them for reburial.

However, some archaeologists say ancient bones not clearly linked to a particular tribe should be available for scientific study.

As archeologists, antiquities dealers and regulators try to deal with the widespread looting of cultural objects, here are some of the questions being debated:

Should anti-trafficking regulations be strengthened?

The United States and more than 100 other countries have signed a landmark treaty — the Convention on the Means of Prohibiting and Preventing the Illicit Import, Export and Transfer of Ownership of Cultural Property — that aimed to restrict the importation of illicit cultural objects.

Brokered by UNESCO in 1970, the treaty established the general principle that any antiquity being sold today must have documents showing it was either found before that year or was legally exported from its home country.[17] The treaty said nations rich in archaeological artifacts should require dealers, purchasers or museums to obtain certificates before exporting such items from the country. So-called market countries — those that mainly buy such artifacts — were to ban their import (without proper papers) and penalize violators. In response, many museums changed their policies to ensure that acquisitions have documented provenance going back at least to 1970.

Nevertheless, well into the 1980s "curators didn't demand a bill of sale," says Maxwell Anderson, formerly an assistant curator of Greek and Roman art at the Metropolitan Museum of Art in New York City and now a consulting scholar at the University of Pennsylvania Museum of Archaeology and Anthropology. He says he saw works looted from their country of origin that "ended up in an attractive gallery in a major European city."

In the 1990s, however, some spectacular prosecutions of antiquities traffickers made museums more scrupulous about the need to check an object's history, says Anderson. But other experts say antiquities remains a largely undocumented market, where many objects lack a paper trail of ownership and origin.

Some archaeologists seeking to protect archaeological sites want this to change. To sell a house, one must provide a deed proving ownership, notes Glasgow's Yates. "Some antiquities cost more than a house," she points out, but

"when it comes to dealers and auction houses, there's absolutely no requirement to disclose previous owners; and they don't have to share that information with buyers." She adds: "A lot of the market is self-regulated. As we know from banking and finance, self-regulation doesn't work when a lot of money is involved."

When it comes to initial onsite looting and trafficking, the 1970 treaty is only as good as a source country's laws and ability to enforce it, Yates says. Under the U.S. law implementing the treaty — which was not adopted until 1983 — a source country can ask the United States to restrict antiquities imports from that country that are at least 250 years old if the objects are in danger of being pillaged.[18] However, the legislation reduced the treaty's scope by restricting its application to countries that negotiate a bilateral agreement with the United States. Currently, only 16 nations have such agreements because they are cumbersome and expensive to negotiate, Yates says.

Museums and dealers traditionally have relied on self-regulation through trade association codes of ethics. But that has not deterred looting or trafficking. For example, the Association of Art Museum Directors (AAMD), which represents more than 200 directors of leading North American museums, says museums should not acquire an archaeological work unless there is proof the object had been removed from its probable source country before 1970 or was legally exported from the source country after 1970.[19] However, museums can acquire a piece if it is important enough or fills a gap in their collection, according to Gerstenblith, at DePaul University.

Citing concerns that looted artworks are being used to fund terrorism, Germany has gone further than most countries to require expanded documentation to prove an antiquity was exported legally from its source country. A 2016 law shifts the burden of proof to the owner or importer.[20] "It makes the market account for itself," says Yates, who supports the law.

Dealers continue to protest the new German law, saying it is rare that ancient artifacts have the kind of paper trail required. Last year, German antiques and antiquities dealers started moving their businesses abroad in anticipation of the new law, according to the trade press.[21]

In July, European Union (EU) officials announced a similar proposal, calling it a step in fighting terrorism.[22] The proposed rule would ban the import into the EU of goods 250 years old or older without proof of legal export.

How Looting May Help Terror Groups

Terror groups, such as the Islamic State, sometimes called ISIS, ISIL or Daesh, may use profits from selling looted Syrian or Iraqi artifacts on the black market to fund their activities, says the Antiquities Coalition, an international group that fights cultural racketeering. It says terrorist groups can make up to $1 million by selling one "masterpiece," enough to finance sizable arsenals.

What $1 Million Can Buy

11,667 AK47s
and

1,250 rocket launchers
and

2.5 million bullets

5,000 mortars

Source: "Culture in Conflict: Where Can Daesh Get $1 Million?" Antiquities Coalition, undated, https://tinyurl.com/yablnn3k

"The problem . . . is that antique and ancient objects in circulation for decades have never before required documentation — so none exists," protested a blog posted on the website of the Committee for Cultural Policy, a think tank in Sante Fe, N.M., critical of such restrictions. "Almost no ancient objects have any permit or evidence showing when they were exported from source countries."[23]

In an email response to *CQ Researcher*, an EU spokesperson said, "It is extremely doubtful that items of such high value are never accompanied by evidence documenting their provenance. It's also important for genuine buyers to know that goods [are] not fakes, stolen from museums" or known to the authorities.

Most archaeologically rich nations have patrimony laws, which make antiquities from within their borders the property of the state, prohibit their export and usually make their trade illegal. But such restrictions just ensure "an active, profitable and corrupting black market," the late Stanford law professor John Henry Merryman wrote in a famous 1986 article.[24]

Dealers and the AAMD say if more countries created legal markets it would make the trade more transparent. Israel is the only Middle Eastern country that permits state-licensed dealers to sell antiquities legally for export. Under a 1978 law, dealers must keep an inventory of objects dating from before 1700, and Israel's Antiquities Authority must approve the removal of an antiquity from the country.[25]

But even Israel has run into difficulties. "The dealers that we gave permission to deal antiquities are using our law to deal in looted artifacts," Eitan Klein, deputy director of the Antiquities Authority's Unit for the Prevention of Antiquities Looting, told the *Times of Israel.*[26]

"The legal market in Israel doesn't mean looting stopped in the area," says De Paul University archaeologist Morag Kersel, who has traced pots looted from Jordanian archaeological sites. Looted material still shows up in Israel's market, she says.

Should archaeological artifacts be returned to their country of origin?

Visitors to the Elgin Marbles in London's British Museum have long been greeted with signs and pamphlets defending the museum's continued ownership of this famous frieze from Athens' Parthenon. The fifth-century B.C. sculptures of a religious procession were hacked from the Parthenon in the 19th century by the British ambassador to the Ottoman empire, Lord Elgin, with the permission of the ruling Ottoman government, according to the museum. By staying in the museum, the frieze has been rescued from military destruction and Athenian air pollution and has given millions of people the opportunity to appreciate Hellenic culture, the British Museum argues.[27]

Since the 1980s, however, Greek governments have demanded the sculptures back. "Greece is determined to break the deadlock caused by the continuous refusal of the British government to return the Parthenon sculptures to their country of origin," Lydia Koniordou, the Greek minister of culture, told *The Times* of London in September, saying Greece was not ruling out legal action.[28]

The dispute epitomizes the ongoing debate about where antiquities should reside. Many archaeologists say ancient objects should be exhibited in their proper historical context — in this case at Athens' anthropological museum with views of the sculptures' original home on the Acropolis. Similar debates have swirled around Egypt's effort to repatriate a bust of Queen Nefertiti from a Berlin museum, China's demand for thousands of items in the British museum plundered in war and Nigeria's demand that museums in Boston and London return bronzes looted from southern Nigeria's Benin kingdom 120 years ago.[29]

"It's time to shed our imperialistic cloak," says Marlen Godwin, a spokesperson for the British Committee for the Reunification of the Parthenon Marbles. By letting the broken marble frieze rejoin its other half in the Acropolis museum, she says, "we can put it right."

The Elgin Marbles "are the DNA, in art, of the people of Greece," argued the late Nobel Prize-winning South African writer Nadine Gordimer in a book of essays by prominent intellectuals arguing for their return. "[W]here else should they be but where they were created?"[30]

However, in his landmark 1986 essay, Stanford's Merryman condemned this view as a narrow "nationalist" perspective. He favored a culturally "internationalist" view, which sees historical artifacts as part of the "cultural heritage of all mankind" — not just the heritage of one country. If smog is eating away at the Parthenon, "all of mankind loses something irreplaceable," he wrote.[31]

When a country like Peru has failed to protect its archaeological sites from looting, the artifacts would be better preserved in a rich country like the United States, with museums and collectors "knowledgeable about and respectful of such works," he argued.[32] In a book published last year, *Keeping Their Marbles*, British cultural commentator Tiffany Jenkins sided with Merryman, arguing that a visitor to the British Museum's encyclopedic exhibits of art from every era and region of the world can better learn how ancient Greek artworks influenced the art, architecture and society of Europe and London itself. The Parthenon marbles' London story "is a major part of that history," she wrote.[33]

The debate continues to divide archaeologists and collectors, with museums taking different sides depending on the artifact in question. However, since the adoption of the 1970 UNESCO convention, law and opinion have been moving closer to the nationalist perspective that antiquities — at least those recently discovered — should go back to their countries of origin. In support of this idea, archaeologically rich countries since the 1900s have enacted patrimony laws, which make all antiquities found within their borders the property of the state and typically outlaw their export.[34]

William Pearlstein, a New York lawyer who has represented antiquities collectors, including the owners of Hobby Lobby, condemns this trend as "rampant nationalism" and says it represents the "collapse of any sense of international exchange" and undermines "the concept of private ownership."

"Our museums would be empty if we were to enforce all these laws," says Kate Fitz Gibbon, executive director of the Committee for Cultural Policy, referring to the national patrimony laws and a U.S. law that makes such objects crossing into the United States stolen property.[35]

Exhibitions of art from other countries "help us to understand our neighbors next door and the cultures they come from," Fitz Gibbon says. "When you see an official policy that encourages blanket nationalization of the entire heritage of a geographic region, that's a dangerous situation."

DePaul's Gerstenblith counters that cultural exchange can occur just as well through long-term loans between countries and their museums — something both the UNESCO convention and the U.S. implementing legislation encouraged.

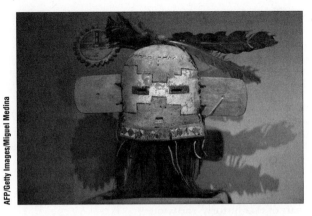

A sacred Hopi Indian mask known as the "Hilili" was offered for auction in Paris in 2013 — over the tribe's objections — along with other Hopi relics. In the United States, the ongoing debate over repatriation of relics has focused on the tens of thousands of Native American skeletons and sacred funerary objects in U.S. museums, many plundered from American Indian lands.

Peter Der Manuelian, a Harvard University professor of Egyptology and director of the university's Semitic Museum, says the decision about whether to return an artifact to its country of origin should depend on the object's history. While some objects such as the Rosetta Stone were removed as war booty from Egypt, many artifacts left Egypt in the early 1900s under the official "partage" system, which split an expedition's finds between the foreign excavation team and the Cairo museum, he notes.[36]

These objects can be "wonderful cultural ambassadors" educating people around the world about Egypt, Der Manuelian observes. "I think there are great encyclopedic collections around the world that have done a great service," he says. "I would probably not be one to argue that all the Egyptian antiquities at the Louvre should be sent back to Egypt immediately."

Has the 1990 law on Native American skeletal remains and other relics fulfilled its goals?

While international tussles over the Parthenon marbles and Nefertiti's bust grab the world's attention, they are dwarfed in sheer scale by a repatriation debate in the United States involving Native Americans' patrimony. Hundreds of tribes have challenged 1,500 museums in recent years over the fate of some 200,000 Native

American skeletons and 1 million funerary items and sacred objects from graves on Indian lands.[37]

Those confrontations — which in some cases have involved legal challenges and in others negotiations — result from long-standing claims of Native Americans, whose rights were codified in the 1990 Native American Graves Protection and Repatriation Act. It requires federal agencies and museums to return human remains and burial objects to lineal descendants and culturally affiliated tribes. NAGPRA was intended to give Native Americans equal rights with other Americans when it comes to reburying ancestors as well as to redress historic wrongs against Indian tribes.

Yet, more than 25 years after NAGPRA's passage, debate continues over the law's original goals and whether they have been met, especially when it comes to early human remains not clearly linked to a particular tribe.

The Society for American Archaeology (SAA) contends the law originally was intended as a compromise between the interests of science in studying the skeletons and that of tribes in reburying their ancestors, says its president, Susan Chandler. Some archaeologists say the law, as implemented, has moved too far in the direction of satisfying tribal claims at the expense of science.

Some groups representing Native Americans, on the other hand, say museums and federal agencies have dragged their feet in returning their ancestors' skeletal remains for proper reburial.[38]

Of the more than 200,000 skeletal remains believed to have been taken from Native American graves, 182,112 ended up in museums or are being held by federal agencies. Only 26 percent of those held in agencies or museums — or about 57,847 — have been returned to tribes or identified as ready to be claimed, according to the National Park Service's National NAGPRA program, which administers the law.[39] About 123,000 are still culturally unidentifiable, according to NAGPRA.

The debate came to a head recently when scientists lost a suit over two skeletons found in 1976 by an archaeology class digging on land in La Jolla, Calif., owned by the University of California, San Diego. The 9,500-year-old skeletons are among the oldest found in the United States.

In 2006, a group of local tribes claimed the skeletons, and the university initiated the process of handing them over. But several archaeologists sued to block the move, arguing that scientists should have a chance to study the skeletons.[40]

Last year, the U.S. Supreme Court declined to hear the case, and the Kumeyaay tribes in San Diego County — the closest geographical tribe — reburied the bones on May 20, 2016.[41]

Archaeologist Robert Bettinger, a plaintiff in the suit and professor emeritus at the University of California, Davis, calls the resolution "a loss for science." If the bones had been made available for DNA analysis, he says, scientists could have learned a great deal about humanity, including how the earliest people arrived on the North American continent.

"This case was about some of the oldest human remains in the New World; the older they are the rarer they get," says Bettinger. "If it's decided you can't study those, that changes the course of science."

But D. Bambi Kraus, president of the National Association of Tribal Historical Preservation Officers, an organization in Washington, D.C., of tribal leaders who implement federal and tribal preservation laws, says Native Americans already have creation stories to explain how they got here. Native Americans are "not looking to Western science to explain their existence. That's just a clash of values, and it's patronizing for a non-Native scientist to think we want to be part of that," she says.

To Elizabeth Weiss, a professor of anthropology at San Jose State University, the law's accommodation to Native American religious beliefs is an "attack on scientific freedom" and violates the Constitution's separation of church and state. The law gives equal weight to Native origin myths and to scientific evidence in deciding whether a tribe is culturally linked to remains, she has written.[42]

Today, the federally appointed committee that resolves disputes over remains operates in an "environment hostile to science," opening its meetings with a Native American prayer, says Weiss, who is writing a book on the law. Only a handful of studies on Native American bones appear in journals these days, says Weiss, who attributes the small number to NAGPRA's rules. The law's attempt to balance the interests of science and religion is "like mixing oil and water," she says, and was always doomed to fail.

Some archaeologists argue for delaying reburials — particularly remains not yet linked to any tribe — to allow for future technological advances that may enable scientists to discover even more about ancient bones

An American service member views looted art treasures at a former Luftwaffe barracks near Königssee, Germany, in May 1945. During World War II, the Nazis seized thousands of paintings and other art objects worth billions of dollars. The widespread theft and destruction of cultural monuments during the war resulted in an international treaty to protect cultural heritage in wartime.

Getty Images/Keystone/Horace Abrahams

than today's DNA tools, says Keith Kintigh, a professor of archaeology at Arizona State University, Tempe, and a past president of the SAA.

Choctaw tribe member Joe Watkins, the National Park Service's American Indian liaison officer and an anthropologist at the University of Maryland, College Park, acknowledges that "advances in biological anthropology can be made and derived from information on human remains. But as an American Indian, I recognize [that] the spiritual benefits of being able to rebury" the human remains override the scientific benefits.

Chip Colwell, senior curator at the Denver Museum of Nature and Science, and author of a new book on the debate, *Plundered Skulls and Stolen Spirits*, says the decision about whether to hand over skeletons and sacred objects to the tribes comes down to a question of human rights and religious freedom. "At the end of the day it's not about what science can do but about ethical obligations to fellow humans that also have a stake in these cultural items," he says.

BACKGROUND
Age of Plunder

During the 18th and 19th centuries, as England, France and other European countries were expanding their empires, "there was a relatively uncontested free and open dealing in looted cultural objects . . . supported by imperialist values," writes Simon Mackenzie, a professor of criminology, law and society at the University of Glasgow in Scotland.[43]

In one of the most famous finds, following Napoleon's conquest of Egypt, French troops in 1799 stumbled upon the Rosetta Stone, which would provide the key to unlocking Egyptian hieroglyphics. When the British defeated the French at Alexandria in 1801, the stone was ceded to the British by treaty. Upon its arrival in Britain, the stone was hailed as a symbol of triumph over the French. Today, it sits in the British Museum, despite repeated demands by Egyptian governments to send it back.[44]

After Napoleon's defeat, Europeans increasingly were interested in acquiring collections from Egypt. And after any British military victory, the British Museum became the "first port of call" for British diplomats with collections to donate, writes British cultural commentator Jenkins.[45]

Throughout the period, adventurers, political leaders and antiquarians raided Italy, Greece and the Middle East, digging deep in the ground or chopping off chunks of monuments in an era when there were few restrictions on carting such materials away.[46]

Other objects were seized under more violent circumstances. In 1897, British troops massacred the inhabitants of the capital of the Benin kingdom in southern Nigeria and hauled off hundreds of bronze sculptures and plaques from the burning palace, selling them off to museums and collectors. In an emotional plea, a Nigerian official in 2012 urged the Boston Museum of Fine Arts, unsuccessfully, to return a collection of Benin bronzes and ivory sculptures that had been donated by New York banker Robert Lehman.[47]

China has appealed to Britain to return 23,000 objects it says were plundered when British troops put down the Boxer Rebellion, a Chinese uprising in 1900 against Western influence.[48]

Many antiquities from the age of plunder ended up in America's first great museums modeled after those in Europe — the Smithsonian Institution, which opened in 1846, and the Metropolitan Museum of Art in New York City, founded in 1870.[49]

The widespread destruction wreaked by both the Axis and Allied powers during World War II on great cultural monuments and the Nazis' plunder of art in German-occupied areas eventually resulted in an international treaty to protect cultural heritage during wartime. The Nazis seized hundreds of thousands of paintings and art objects worth billions of dollars. After the war, many of the artworks were returned to their country of origin. However, thousands of pieces did not go to their rightful owner or were never relocated.[50] Some are still being discovered in private collections today.

In the wake of the war's massive destruction of cultural heritage, nations signed the Convention for the Protection of Cultural Property in the Event of Armed Conflict in 1954, administered by UNESCO, the first international treaty devoted solely to protecting cultural property in wartime. It has since been ratified by more than 100 countries, including Syria and Iraq.[51]

Preventing Looting

Following growing concerns in the 1960s about archaeological looting, nations adopted the 1970 UNESCO-brokered treaty to prevent the illicit export of cultural artifacts. It mandated that countries take preventive actions, such as requiring export certificates for culturally significant objects leaving archaeologically rich nations. Most relevant to the United States — one of the world's largest markets for the purchase of antiquities — signatories agreed to limit the import of such objects and to facilitate their return to the country of origin.[52]

"The Age of Piracy is over," declared Thomas Hoving, then director of the Metropolitan Museum of Art, one of many museums that publicly supported the UNESCO treaty. Yet, since then museum officials have "routinely violated the spirit" of the treaty, buying "ancient art they knew had been illegally excavated," write Jason Felch and Ralph Frammolino, investigative reporters and authors of *Chasing Aphrodite*, which documents some of the more spectacular thefts that ended up at museums.[53]

The treaty covered any cultural property designated by a nation as important for archaeological, historical, artistic, literary or scientific reasons and antiquities more than 100 years old.[54]

American dealers, collectors and some museums feared the treaty would redefine whole categories of traded antiquities as illicit; they sought to limit the government's ability to agree to newly restrictive policies being imposed by other nations on what the United

CHRONOLOGY

1700s–1800s *European countries seize artifacts in conquered lands.*

1799 The Rosetta Stone, an ancient Egyptian bilingual text used to decipher hieroglyphics, is discovered by the French, who cede it to the victorious British after the Battle of Alexandria in 1801.

1870 Metropolitan Museum of Art, an "encyclopedic" museum covering global art throughout history, is founded in New York.

1901–1954 *Countries begin to protect cultural heritage. Nazi Germany loots art owned by Jews.*

1906 U.S. Antiquities Act bans digging on federal land without permit.

1932 Greece declares ownership of all cultural property discovered in the country.

1954 International treaty protects cultural property during war.

1970s–1990s *Antiquities trade and looting boom.*

1970 UNESCO treaty gives countries the right to recover stolen cultural property from other nations, including the United States.

1979 Archaeological Resources Protection Act toughens penalties for looting Native American sites on federal lands in the United States.

1983 United States adopts law implementing UNESCO treaty, after limiting its scope in response to objections from art dealers and collectors.

1990 Native American Graves Protection and Repatriation Act allows tribes to reclaim looted skeletons and funerary artifacts.

1995 Raid on Italian dealer Giacomo Medici yields thousands of looted antiquities and photos of many already in U.S. museums.

2000–Present *Trafficking trials lead to changes in museum practices.*

2002 Raid on Italian dealer Gianfranco Becchina nets thousands of relics.

2003 Appeals court upholds conviction of U.S. dealer Frederick Schultz for conspiracy to receive stolen Egyptian artifacts. . . . More than 13,000 items are stolen from Baghdad Museum after the fall of Iraqi dictator Saddam Hussein following invasion by a U.S.-led coalition.

2005 Italy indicts Marion True, curator of antiquities at the J. Paul Getty Museum in Los Angeles, on charges of conspiring to traffic in illicit antiquities; her trial ends in 2010 with no verdict after statute of limitations expires. . . . Medici is convicted of conspiring to traffic in illegal exports.

2008 Association of Art Museum Directors says museum acquisitions should have documentation back to at least 1970.

2010 Controversial federal regulations enable Indian tribes to claim unidentifiable human remains and funerary objects; archaeologists say the rules impede scientific study.

2015 Islamic State, which controls large swaths of Syria, seizes ancient city of Palmyra, destroys ancient monuments and beheads a longtime antiquities curator.

2016 President Obama blocks imports of archaeological artifacts from Syria; he later agrees to turn over prehistoric Kennewick Man to tribes for reburial. . . . Germany bans importation of artworks that lack export licenses from source countries.

2017 Nine nations sign treaty criminalizing unlawful excavation and trafficking (May). . . . Metropolitan Museum surrenders ancient Greek vase to Italy (July). . . . U.S. collectors surrender bull's head sculpture to Lebanon (October). . . . Proposed STOP Act would prohibit export of Native American artifacts. . . . European Union considers requiring antiquities imports to have valid export licenses (July).

2018 U.S. has until September to return to Iraq a trove of Jewish objects stolen by Saddam Hussein, strongly opposed by U.S. Jewish groups.

Iraqi Jews Want Stolen Documents to Stay in U.S.

The archive "should not be given back to the thief that stole it."

Just days after coalition forces captured Baghdad during the U.S.-led invasion of Iraq in May 2003, several Americans heard about a hidden Jewish archive in President Saddam Hussein's bombed-out intelligence headquarters.[1]

In the facility's flooded basement, U.S. soldiers found 2,700 books and thousands of documents relating to Iraq's Jewish community. The cache included a 16th-century Bible, Torah scrolls, other religious objects, community records and a Jewish calendar from 1971-72 in Hebrew and Arabic, one of the last examples of Hebrew printing in Iraq.[2]

Under an agreement with the Iraqis, U.S. forces sent the waterlogged trove to the United States, where they were dried out, restored and exhibited by the National Archives and Records Administration in Washington. A National Archives exhibit of the recovered documents is on display until Jan. 15 at the Jewish Museum of Maryland in Baltimore. But under the agreement, the archive must be returned to the Iraqi government next September.

Several American Jewish groups oppose the archive's planned return, noting that a succession of Iraqi governments persecuted and expelled their Jewish populations.

"The Jewish community of Iraq was mistreated and forced to flee. Their patrimony — which includes all the religious artifacts, Torahs and personal and communal property — was stolen from them," says Gina Waldman, co-founder and president of the San Francisco-based

Jews Indigenous to the Middle East and North Africa. Thus, the archive "should not be given back to the thief that stole it."

Sen. Charles Schumer, D-N.Y., agrees. "This collection . . . belongs to the ancient and proud Iraqi Jewish community," he said. He wrote to Secretary of State Rex Tillerson on Oct. 3, urging him to work with the Iraqi Jewish community in the United States and abroad to find a permanent home for the collection of Judaica.[3]

The State Department did not respond to *CQ Researcher's* request for comment. However, in October a department spokesman said the archive would be returned next September under the agreement with the Iraqis. "Maintaining the archive outside of Iraq is possible," State Department spokesman Pablo Rodriguez told the Jewish Telegraphic Agency, "but would require a new agreement between the government of Iraq and a temporary host institution or government."[4]

Patty Gerstenblith, a law professor at DePaul University in Chicago and an expert on cultural property law, says if the United States does not return the trove to Iraq it would breach the agreement and violate international law.

The Iraqi Jews, one of the oldest Jewish communities in the world, are believed to have arrived in Babylonia, site of present-day Iraq, in the sixth century B.C.[5] Although 130,000 Jews made up a third of Baghdad's population at the beginning of the 20th century, today only five Jews remain in Iraq, according to Waldman.

Jewish life in Iraq was all but obliterated after the rise of pro-Nazi leaders in the 1930s, the development of the

States could import. That debate is partly why it took more than 10 years for the United States to pass implementing legislation — the Convention on Cultural Property Implementation Act — finally signed in 1983 by President Ronald Reagan.[55]

That act said only nations with a bilateral agreement with the United States — currently only 16 countries — can request an import ban. Under the law, the bans

cover only items of "archaeological interest" that are at least 250 years old and of ethnological interest, such as tribal objects.[56] The law also allows the U.S. president to impose emergency import bans on artifacts in danger of pillage from a country that does not have a bilateral agreement in times of crisis such as civil war.[57] For instance, the United States imposed emergency bans on items coming from Iraq in 1990 and Syria last year.[58]

modern Iraqi state and its growing hostility toward Israel. When Nazi sympathizer Rashid Ali became prime minister in 1933, Jews faced discrimination and employment quotas. He invited Nazi propagandists to Baghdad, which became the early base for the Nazis' Middle East intelligence operations during World War II. On April 3, 1941, Ali staged a pro-Nazi coup, but his regime was toppled by the British a month later, and Ali fled to Berlin. In June 1941, hundreds of Jews were killed and thousands injured in an anti-Jewish riot known as the Farhood.[6]

The persecution increased in 1948 when Iraq entered the war against the new state of Israel. From 1949 to '51, Jews could leave if they renounced their citizenship and gave up their assets. More than 100,000 Jews left Iraq, most ending up in Israel, the United States or England.[7]

Harold Rhode, an Arabic- and Hebrew-speaking policy analyst on assignment in Baghdad for the secretary of Defense, was part of the group that rescued the documents in 2003. He learned that Iraqi Jews had stored most of their remaining community records and holy books in the women's balcony of the last functioning synagogue, but Hussein's armed henchmen arrived one night in 1984 and carted them away.[8]

Kate Fitz Gibbon, executive director of the Committee for Cultural Policy, a think tank in New Mexico, says the State Department has been too eager to turn over cultural property to its country of origin in the Middle East.[9]

"Despite the egregious abuse of human rights by governments or government-supported militias in Syria, Libya, Egypt and Iraq, the State Department has encouraged making cultural property agreements with these nations," which often means returning historic objects belonging to oppressed communities, she wrote. As recently as 2010, she noted, any person associated with Zionist principles or organizations was subject to punishment by death under Iraq's criminal code.[10]

But Gerstenblith says returning the Jewish artifacts to Baghdad could show Iraqis that "their history is diverse and would be a good thing for Iraqis to learn."

Rhode said he is appalled at the prospect of returning to Iraq the archive he helped to save. "It would be as if Germany demanded material looted from German Jewish communities under the Nazis [be placed] in German government hands," he wrote in 2013.[11]

— *Sarah Glazer*

[1] Harold Rhode, "Outrage: U.S. Returning Artifacts Looted from Iraqi Jews to Iraq, Instead of Lawful Owners," PJ Media, Aug. 26, 2013, https://tinyurl.com/y8y2rltn.

[2] "Discovery and Recovery: Preserving Iraqi Jewish Heritage," Jewish Museum of Maryland, Oct. 15, 2017, https://tinyurl.com/yar4qll2.

[3] "Schumer: State Department Once Again Unwisely Plans to Return Confiscated Judaica Collection to Iraq," press release, Office of Sen. Charles Schumer, U.S. Senate, Oct. 3, 2017, https://tinyurl.com/yc8mev5j.

[4] Josefin Dolstein, "Schumer: Don't Return Trove of Jewish Artifacts to Iraq," Jewish Telegraphic Agency, Oct. 3, 2017, https://tinyurl.com/y8jv7m9f.

[5] "Jewish History," Jews Indigenous to the Middle East and North Africa, 2017, https://tinyurl.com/y78594ex.

[6] "Rashid-Ali-al-Gaylani," *Encyclopedia Britannica*, https://tinyurl.com/ya4mvzce. Also See Bernard Lewis, *The Crisis of Islam: Holy War and Unholy Terror* (2003).

[7] "Jewish History," op. cit.

[8] Rhode, op. cit. Also see video interview at Iraqi Jewish Archives, https://tinyurl.com/yc4gs3xg.

[9] Under the Convention on Cultural Property Implementation Act of 1983, a country with a bilateral agreement with the United States can seek a U.S. ban on imports of cultural property in danger of being pillaged and demand that any property imported after the date of the agreement be returned to the source country.

[10] Kate Fitz Gibbon, "Iraq, Syria, Libya and Egypt: Beyond Rescuing the Iraqi Jewish Archives," Committee for Culture Policy, Oct. 2, 2017, https://tinyurl.com/y7xuzxtr.

[11] Rhode, op. cit.

Many dealers say the treaty changed the rules of the game midstream for a market where artifacts have never been well documented. But Gerstenblith counters that dealers have had notice since 1970.

"It's a choice the market has made not to document over the past 40 to 45 years," she says. "Having made that choice, I don't think they should get away with the excuse [that] it's undocumented."

Indian Grave Robbers

In the United States, there is a long history of looting Native American graves and pillaging Indian villages.

One of the worst such incidents, called the Sand Creek Massacre, occurred in 1864, when American troops slaughtered an entire Native American village in their sleep. The army took scalps and other objects; some of the remains were sent to the Smithsonian Institution in Washington, D.C.[59]

ISIS "Systematized" Looting, Ex-Official Says

"The control and sale of looted antiquities is extremely lucrative."

Looting archaeological sites has long been a common practice among impoverished Syrians. During the ongoing Syrian civil war that began in 2011, rebel forces, regime troops and neighboring Kurdish groups have joined local residents in widespread looting, according to experts.

However, the Islamic State, also known as ISIS, ISIL or Daesh, "industrialized and systematized it," says Amr Al-Azm, a former Syrian antiquities official who is an associate professor of Middle East history and anthropology at Shawnee State University in Portsmouth, Ohio.

After the terrorist group began to occupy large stretches of territory in Syria in 2013 and 2014, it imposed a 20 percent tax on the sale of looted items, Al-Azm says. It also issued digging permits, he says, and joined in the looting, using a network of dealers and routinely using bulldozers and crews of up to 60 people.

"This indicates that the control and sale of looted antiquities is extremely lucrative, well worth the time and financial investment by ISIS," Al-Azm writes in a forthcoming book.[1]

When reports emerged that ISIS was using the antiquities trade to fund its activities, the U.N. Security Council passed resolutions in 2015 and this year urging countries to limit the trade from ISIS-controlled areas and to make involvement in terrorism-related antiquities trading a punishable offense.[2]

Tess Davis, executive director of the Antiquities Coalition, an advocacy group in Washington fighting the illicit antiquities trade, says, "This is an attractive source of terrorist financing." The coalition cites estimates that looters in Syria have removed more than $2 billion worth of antiquities.[3]

But some dealers and experts doubt that ISIS has earned billions from antiquities. Fiona Greenland, a University of Virginia sociologist trained in archaeology, has been studying the likely market value of objects from Dura-Europos, a historic site in Syria dating to 300 B.C. that was heavily looted before and during the Islamic State occupation.

"There's the question of how many objects are worth enough money to generate millions or billions in profit," she says. "The Near Eastern archaeologists with whom I've worked say the majority of objects out of their excavation sites are humble objects — broken pottery, coins, tools, sometimes pieces of mosaic or sculpture. But few are masterpieces" that would fetch hundreds of thousands of dollars, let alone millions, she says.

According to the U.S. government, "ISIL has probably earned several million dollars from antiquities sales since mid-2014, but the precise amount is unknown," said Andrew Keller, the State Department's deputy assistant secretary for counter-threat finance and sanctions. He was speaking at a September 2015 presentation at the Metropolitan Museum of Art in New York City in which he showed photographs from a May 2015 raid on the quarters of Abu Sayyaf, an ISIS leader in charge of uncovering antiquities in Syria.[4]

Under the Theodore Roosevelt administration, Congress passed one of the earliest efforts to halt looting on Native American lands — the American Antiquities Act of 1906 — which made digging on public lands illegal without a permit. The law aimed to control the enormous trade in artifacts from ancestral Pueblo sites in the Southwest.[60]

However, difficulties in enforcing the law led to the passage in 1979 of the Archaeological Resources Protection Act (ARPA), which imposed fines of up to $20,000 and a year in jail for looting artifacts from archaeological sites on Indian and federal land, and up to five years and $100,000 for a second offense.[61] The largest ARPA case unfolded in 2009, when 24 people were charged with digging up Native American artifacts from federal lands in Utah.[62]

But ARPA did not address an inequity towards Native Americans in U.S. law. While state laws have long required states to bury paupers and unidentified bodies,

But Randall Hixenbaugh, a New York City antiquities dealer and appraiser who attended that event, called the ISIS collection displayed in the photos "laughable." The artifacts included fakes, "low-grade" antiquities, tourist items such as a miniature head of Egyptian Queen Nefertiti, and Roman and Islamic coins that are so plentiful they fetch only about $50 each.

"The market isn't that voracious; it doesn't need more of the same," Hixenbaugh says, putting the total value of the artifacts in the photos at $10,000.[5]

But Al-Azm says some items are more valuable than that. "I have seen looted mosaics ripped out of the ground from Syria and offered to me for sale in Turkey," he says, "and these mosaics fetch tens of thousands of dollars."

Hans-Jakob Schindler, coordinator of the U.N. Security Council's ISIL, Al-Qaeda and Taliban Monitoring Team, says his team has never published a figure for ISIL's looting profits. But "terrorism isn't an expensive business; a couple of thousand will get you very far," he says.

For instance, he says, it cost only about $10,000 for terrorists to carry out the 2015 Paris attack in which several ISIS members with bombs and guns killed 130 people. More importantly, he adds, ISIS is demonstrating to other groups that antiquities are "a viable income source."

Al-Azm says ISIS in Syria probably copied tactics from Tunisian Salafists, or ultraconservative Sunni Muslims, who in 2013 destroyed shrines built by Muslim mystics — the Sufis. The Salafists, who consider Sufis infidels, also looted antiquities and helped turn Tunisia into a trafficking highway.

Tunisian fighters who joined ISIS in Syria will be returning home soon, following recent territorial losses there, Al-Azm says. "If you see a spike in cultural heritage looting [in Tunisia], that means someone is trying to fund

AFP/Getty Images/Joseph Eid

In the ancient Syrian city of Palmyra, the Temple of Bel was blown up by the Islamic State in August 2015.

themselves," he says, "a potential indicator that ISIS is active again."

— *Sarah Glazer*

[1] Amr al-Azm, "The Importance of Cultural Heritage in Enhancing a Syrian National Identity and the Role of Local Non-State Actors in Preserving It," in Paul Newsome and Ruth Young, eds., *Post-Conflict Archaeology and Cultural Heritage* (forthcoming, 2018), p. 98.

[2] Resolution 2253, U.N. Security Council, 2015, https://tinyurl.com/yd74yhgl. Resolution 2347, UN Security Council, March 24, 2017, https://tinyurl.com/y7qgpdd3. This resolution urged countries to introduce legislative and other measures to prevent trafficking in cultural property and to make such trafficking that may benefit terrorists a serious crime.

[3] Deborah M. Lehr and Katie A. Paul, "Rocking the Cradle of Civilization," *The Huffington Post*, Sept. 1 2014, https://tinyurl.com/yb3ctr7m.

[4] "Remarks, Andrew Keller," U.S. Department of State, Sept. 29, 2015, https://tinyurl.com/ybrdkznv.

[5] "Rethinking Antiquities," transcript of conference, Cardozo School of Law, New York, March 2016, https://tinyurl.com/y7xkg44s.

such laws did not apply to American Indians. For example, in 1971 a highway construction project in Glenwood, Iowa, uncovered a historic cemetery. The 26 bodies deemed to be white were reburied in the local cemetery, but the remains of a woman and child identified as Native American were sent in a box to the state archaeologist.[63]

To give Indians equal burial rights, Congress in 1990 passed the Native American Graves Protection and Repatriation Act, which said federal agencies and museums must return human remains to Indian descendants or culturally affiliated tribes.

However, more than 100,000 Native American human remains now in the hands of museums and federal agencies cannot be clearly linked to a specific tribe. A controversial 2010 regulation directed museums to return such "culturally unidentifiable" skeletons to the tribe that is closest geographically or on whose aboriginal lands the remains were found (if the tribe makes such a claim).[64]

Marion True, former curator of antiquities at the J. Paul Getty Museum in Los Angeles, was indicted by the Italian government in 2005 on charges of conspiring to traffic in illicit antiquities. Her trial ended in 2010 without a conviction after the statute of limitations expired, but the case had a chilling effect on other museums and potential buyers of antiquities that lack proper documentation.

The issue came to the fore in 1996, when two hikers in Kennewick, Wash., found an 8,500-year-old skeleton while wading in the Columbia River. Five tribes, including the local Colvilles, immediately laid claim to the skeleton, which became known as Kennewick Man. But a group of scientists sued to stop the transfer, saying the skeleton was not clearly linked to any tribe and could yield valuable information about early American inhabitants.[65]

After eight years of legal battles, a federal judge, convinced by an analysis of the skull that the skeleton was not Native American, allowed the scientists to study the bones and prevented a reburial.[66] However, a subsequent DNA analysis determined the skeleton was a closer match to the local Colville tribe than to any other modern peoples.[67]

In December 2016, President Obama signed legislation turning the Kennewick Man over to a coalition of tribes that included the Colvilles, who laid the remains to rest in a ritual ceremony last February.[68]

Antiquities Boom

The 1990s and early 2000s saw a boom in the antiquities market coinciding with the rise of extremely wealthy American collectors. In addition, large-scale operations to dig up and sell antiquities illegally were uncovered in several countries. And archaeological source countries, led by Italy, increasingly agitated for the return of their cultural property.[69]

In 1995, Italian and Swiss authorities raided a Geneva warehouse of the antiquities dealer Giacomo Medici, discovering 3,800 looted antiquities and photos of thousands more antiquities, some broken and dirty from recent excavation. From photos found in the warehouse, authorities were able to trace looted artifacts to museums across the United States, Europe and Asia.[70] In another high-profile discovery, Italian and Swiss authorities in May 2002 raided the warehouses of Swiss antiquities dealer Gianfranco Becchina, recovering 5,200 looted antiquities and more than 8,500 photos of artifacts, some pictured with soil still on them that showed they had been dug up recently.[71]

The photos from the raids became known as the Medici and Becchina "archives," because they led to hundreds of repatriations around the world and continue to provide evidence that some objects found in museums and private hands had been looted. Medici was convicted in 2005 of receiving stolen goods, illegally exporting artifacts and conspiring to traffic thousands of illegal artifacts. He was sentenced to 10 years in prison and received a 10 million euro fine.[72]

In the 2000s, several spectacular trials led to the return of antiquities from museums to source countries. Frederick Schultz, the former president of the National Association of Dealers in Ancient, Oriental and Primitive Art, was convicted in 2002 under the 1934 National Stolen Property Act (NSPA) of conspiracy to receive antiquities stolen from Egypt. The court found that the NSPA, which prohibits dealing in stolen or fraudulently acquired goods valued at $5,000 or more across state or national borders, applied to "property stolen from a foreign government" — in this case Egypt, which asserted ownership under its patrimony law.[73]

U.S. courts have upheld foreign patrimony laws in cases testing whether imported antiquities from countries with such laws were "stolen" under the NSPA. In a landmark 2003 case, *U.S. v. Schultz*, the Second U.S. Circuit Court of Appeals upheld Schultz's conviction, saying Egypt's patrimony law — designating all antiquities discovered after 1983 as property of the state — had standing in the United States; therefore the property had been stolen.

Should the antiquities trade be legalized in more countries?

YES Kate Fitz Gibbon
Executive Director, Commitee for Cultural Policy

Written for *CQ Researcher*, November 2017

Legal markets guided by sensible rules and positive values are often the fastest way to put illegal markets out of business. A regulated trade in ancient art would deincentivize looting. Transparency would earn trust. Collectors would have good title. Source countries could track objects internationally. Worldwide, an inventory of art already in circulation would facilitate legitimate claims for return and allow free trade in other objects, curtail local corruption, eliminate profits from looting and enable global academic access.

Documentation is key. If properly documented, any stolen object can be claimed, and no stolen object can be sold.

In the past, documentation (or provenance) was not considered important. It wasn't required to legally import artworks or for museum acquisition. Most important, it wasn't required because art-source countries never set up systems to enable lawful trade. Many nations simply made everything more than 100 years old illegal to export, from postage stamps to ancient statues, and then ignored or unofficially facilitated the outward flow.

All that has changed. Source nations now argue for universal restitution (even if it means that each country would possess only its own art). U.S. museums cooperate in returns, although they worry about core collections and how best to serve a multicultural population. Digital documentation of collections nowadays sometimes triggers source-country claims.

Museums also are frustrated by acquisition guidelines that require a paper trail back to 1970. Lack of documentation has turned hundreds of thousands of objects into "orphans," unable to be donated to public institutions.

Digital technology can solve the orphan problem and the fate of unprovenanced antiquities. It is feasible to catalog millions of objects, using a descriptive standard such as Object ID and a photograph.

Objects and their provenance could be inventoried on a universally accessible database. After a reasonable period to allow claims, title would be deemed free and clear, unless new information became available. The system could be fee-based, similar to paying for title insurance for one's home. If that fee helps to build museums, secure archaeological sites or foster academic research, so much the better.

The easy part is the technology. The hard part is building trust among foreign governments, museums and collectors. All should see the sense of a global permitting system, fair opportunities to reclaim heritage and secure title. A legal trade in antiquities can serve both our museums and the public.

NO Morag Kersel
Associate Professor of Anthropology, DePaul University

Written for *CQ Researcher*, November 2017

While researching my dissertation on the topic of legalizing the antiquities trade, I collected data from archival documents, archaeological surveys and excavations and interviewed those with a vested interest in the topic — archaeologists, collectors, dealers, government employees, looters, museum professionals and tourists. After three years of research, I arrived at some insights concerning the efficacy of the legal trade to stem looting.

Israel's Antiquities Law of 1978 — which establishes a legal antiquities market in that country — provides a lens to study this issue. Israel's antiquities market, it turns out, encouraged, rather than deterred, looting in Israel and surrounding areas such as Jordan and Palestine. The ready market for material, which looters and middlemen exploited through a loophole in the 1978 law, allowed illegally excavated material to enter the legal market through a laundering process involving an exchange of inventory registry numbers.

Here's how the system worked: Unless buyers (predominantly tourists or pilgrims to the Holy Land) knew to ask for an export license for their purchase, dealers did not need to offer one. As a result, the sale often was not registered with the Israel Antiquities Authority, which oversees antiquities sales. Without an official record of the sale, the inventory number for the artifact could be reused for a similar artifact: One buff-colored Middle Bronze pot looks like the next.

I do not have the temerity to suggest that my early research affected policy or regulations related to the Israeli trade, but it did increase awareness of problems in the antiquities market. In the 10 years since the completion of my dissertation, the Israel Antiquities Authority has enacted a series of measures to tighten loopholes in the system.

The real question is not whether a legal market prevents archaeological looting. The concept of a legal market presents a misleading binary of legal and illegal. In fact, they are often the same thing. There are corrupt actors, illegal elements and loopholes in these markets that make it impossible to consider them "legal."

Given the unequal power balance between First World buyers and Third World suppliers, the focus should be on *demand* for antiquities without provenance, or what Colgate University associate professor of art and history Elizabeth Marlowe, in her 2013 book *Shaky Ground*, calls "ungrounded" archaeological material. As long as demand for ungrounded antiquities exists, looting will occur.

"If an American conspired to steal the Liberty Bell" and send it to a foreign collector, he would be prosecuted, said U.S. District Judge Jed S. Rakoff. "The same is true" when a U.S. resident conspires to steal Egyptian antiquities, he said.[74]

The judge also criticized the "no questions asked" approach employed for decades by collectors and museums, telling the jury that "to purposefully remain ignorant" of Egypt's patrimony law, as Schultz had claimed, was no excuse.[75]

Schultz served 33 months in federal prison for conspiring to smuggle antiquities out of Egypt by disguising them as cheap souvenirs dipped in plastic and preparing false provenances.[76]

In 2005, Marion True, curator of antiquities at the J. Paul Getty Museum in Los Angeles was indicted by the Italian government on charges of conspiring to traffic in illicit antiquities, many of which had been found in Medici's photos.

Her trial ended in 2010 without a conviction after the statute of limitations expired, but the case had a chilling effect on both potential buyers of antiquities without well-documented provenance and on other museums, according to Anderson, the former Metropolitan Museum of Art assistant curator. U.S. museums returned more than 100 antiquities to Italy during True's five-year trial.[77]

Conflict Antiquities

The Middle East, an area rich in ancient archaeological sites, has been hard hit by wars, uprisings and terrorism. In 2003, following the fall of Saddam Hussein, more than 13,000 items were stolen from the Iraq Museum. Many were recovered by law enforcement officials, but some are still missing.[78]

Looted items can still be seen for sale on eBay, according to George Washington University archaeologist Eric H. Cline.[79]

Satellite images indicate that looting in Egypt's Nile Valley and delta escalated sharply during the global economic crisis in 2009 and intensified following the so-called Arab Spring political upheavals in 2011, according to research published by University of Alabama researchers last year.[80]

Some of the destruction of cultural icons in that region has been driven by religious intolerance. For instance, in 2001, Muslim extremists in Afghanistan dynamited two colossal sixth-century Buddhist statues in the Bamiyan Valley — a World Heritage Site — after declaring them idolatrous. And in May 2015, in an effort to demonstrate its power and condemn pre-Islamic idol-worshipping, ISIS demolished the 17 A.D. temple dedicated to the Canaanite sky god Baalshamin in Palmyra, Syria.[81]

On March 9, 2016, then-President Obama signed the Protect and Preserve International Cultural Property Act, which blocked the importation of archaeological artifacts from Syria, bringing U.S. policy in line with a U.N. Security Council resolution calling on nations to deny funding to ISIS by preventing antiquities trafficking from Syria and Iraq.[82]

CURRENT SITUATION

New International Laws

The European Parliament is expected to consider new rules aimed at blocking terrorists from funding themselves by trafficking antiquities into Europe. European Union regulations, proposed in July, would require antiquities importers to show that an archaeological object was exported legally from the source country if from outside the EU, and to obtain an import license from the EU country where the object is arriving, European Commission spokesperson Vanessa Mock said in an email interview.[83]

EU officials have described the proposed rules as an effort to prevent trade in looted antiquities from the Middle East from being used to finance ISIS' terrorist activities.

However, dealers say the kind of documentation the EU is requiring is not typically available for antiquities and argue that fears about ISIS profiting from trafficking in Syrian antiquities are unfounded. "Against general expectations, no objects of any importance from Syria have surfaced in Europe or the USA recently," says IADAA Chairman Geerling.

Antiquities dealers blame a new German law passed last year that cracks down on art imports for killing their trade in Germany and forcing them to move their businesses abroad. The German law puts the burden on dealers to prove an antiquity was exported legally from its country of origin and requires a license to export it from Germany.[84]

Court challenges are expected on the grounds that the new German rules violate the German constitution, and a coalition of dealers has filed a complaint with the EU charging its proposed rules violate the EU guarantee of free trade, according to Geerling.

Meanwhile, nine nations, including Greece and Mexico, have signed a new treaty criminalizing unlawful excavation and trafficking in cultural property. The treaty was promulgated in May by the Council of Europe, a human rights organization with 47 member states, including the United States.[85]

Experts say "market" countries such as the United States, with a strong commitment to free enterprise, are unlikely to sign on to the Council of Europe treaty.

Repatriation Issues

In July, the Metropolitan Museum of Art surrendered a 2,300-year-old Greek vase after Manhattan prosecutors served the museum with a warrant for its seizure, citing evidence it had been looted from an ancient Greek site in an area of modern-day Italy that was once part of the ancient Greek empire.[86] Christos Tsirogiannis, a forensic archaeologist who published his suspicions about the vase, said his evidence included photos seized from Medici storehouses in 1995 that showed the vase still encrusted with dirt.[87]

In another case, a 2,300-year-old sculpture of a bull's head that had been on loan to the Met also came under suspicion and will be repatriated to Lebanon. The Colorado couple that owned it, Lynda and William Beierwaltes, originally said they had bought the sculpture in good faith from a dealer for $1 million in 1996. They filed suit to prevent the Manhattan district attorney from returning it to the Lebanese government.

But in early October, their attorney said they were dropping their suit in the face of "incontrovertible evidence" the sculpture was stolen. According to prosecutors, a state-sponsored excavation in Lebanon uncovered the work in 1967. It was stored and then stolen in 1981 during Lebanon's civil war.[88]

In a new twist, the Manhattan district attorney announced in October he would pursue the return to Lebanon of a second work, an ancient sculpture of a person carrying a calf, seen in a photo accompanying a *House and Garden* magazine profile of the Beierwaltes in June 1998. The sculpture had been sold to another private collector.

Native American Relics

A bipartisan bill introduced in both chambers of Congress aims to stop the export of Native American grave relics and artifacts. The Safeguard Tribal Objects of Patrimony Act of 2017 (STOP Act) was introduced by Sen. Martin Heinrich, D-N.M., in response to a high-profile Paris auction in the summer of 2016, according to a press release from his office.[89]

The Eve auction house in Paris offered for sale a shield from the Acoma Pueblo tribe of New Mexico, over the tribe's protests. Kurt Riley, governor of the tribe, said the shield is a "sacred item which no individual can own." Last year U.S. District Judge Martha Vasquez approved a warrant to repatriate the shield to the Acoma Pueblo.[90]

The French government has said the lack of an explicit U.S. law prohibiting the export of such items prevents the French from enforcing American laws protecting Native American objects in France, according to Heinrich's office. Heinrich's bill would explicitly prohibit the export of items obtained in violation of NAGPRA, which bars trafficking in Native American remains and cultural objects, and other U.S. laws. It also would increase penalties for NAGPRA violations and offer a two-year amnesty for anyone who returns illegally possessed cultural items to Indian tribes.[91]

Native American groups and the Society for American Archaeology support the legislation. Society president Chandler says with federal and state agencies suffering budget cuts, "it's difficult to catch someone looting Indian sites" across the millions of federal acres and called the extent of looting and trafficking "heartbreaking." (Besides the federal law banning digging on federal land, numerous state and local laws prohibit the taking of Native American goods on private land.[92])

However, the bill is opposed by the Antique Tribal Art Dealers Association, an association of collectors and dealers in Rio Rancho, N.M. "Collectors may be pressured to give up objects" that they lawfully own "to tribes that do not want them," the association said.[93]

OUTLOOK
Attitude Adjustment

Continued concern about the looting of archaeological artifacts and the ineffectiveness of existing laws has led some archaeologists to stress the need for a societal change in attitude.

Critics of the trade have taken to referring to looted artifacts as "blood antiquities" — taking a lead from the condemnation of luxury items such as "blood diamonds," fur coats or ivory for their exploitative impact on source communities.[94]

"If you have a big ivory object at the dinner table, your friends are thinking 'dead elephants,'" says Glasgow's Yates. Similarly, she says she would like to "change hearts and minds" of potential buyers through public education about the destructive impact of illegal digging, something she seeks to do with her free online course "Antiquities Trafficking and Art Crime."[95]

The University of Chicago recently held several workshops with experts from academia, the legal profession and the antiquities trade to investigate new approaches to stemming archaeological looting.[96] While no final consensus was achieved among these traditionally warring forces, participants proposed several novel ideas, including taxing antiquities without provenance to help fund more security at archaeological sites.[97]

Other ideas included encouraging museums to take artifacts on long-term loan in lieu of ownership and requiring solid documentation of provenance on donated items before the donor can claim a charitable tax deduction. And more looted items might be seized at the border if international customs rules required more detailed declarations on antiquities, says DePaul's Gerstenblith.

Some archaeologists and collectors also favor the creation of a comprehensive database of artifacts — archaeologists want it for detecting looted items and collectors for assurance that their artifacts are legal. Fitz Gibbon of the Committee for Cultural Policy has proposed such a database.

"After a reasonable period to allow claims, title would be deemed free and clear, unless new information became available," she says.

However, the deep divide between dealers and archaeologists, at least for the present, remains a chasm for some. "If a buyer acquires an object that has been looted, its cultural and scientific value has been destroyed," part of the cultural and historical record of humanity, says Gerstenblith. "If you put that against the delight a private collector has for something on their mantelpiece, for me, there's no question which one is more important."

NOTES

1. A cylinder seal is a small round tube, typically about one inch in length, engraved with characters and/or figurative scenes, used in ancient times to roll an impression onto a surface, generally wet clay.

2. "United States Files Civil Action to Forfeit Thousands of Ancient Iraqi Artifacts Imported by Hobby Lobby," press release, U.S. Attorney's Office, Eastern District of New York, U.S. Department of Justice, July 5, 2017, https://tinyurl.com/y73a4h9d.

3. Ibid. Also see David Smith, "Inside the sprawling controversial $500m Museum of the Bible," *The Guardian*, Oct. 16, 2017, https://tinyurl.com/y8uqegwh.

4. "Illicit Trafficking of Cultural Property," U.N. Educational, Scientific and Cultural Organization, https://tinyurl.com/ydx5pdxf.

5. Simon Mackenzie and Donna Yates, "What is Grey about the "Grey Market" in Antiquities?" in Jens Beckert and Matías Dewey, eds., *The Architecture of Illegal Markets* (2016), https://tinyurl.com/yc9knvdr.

6. "U.S. v. Approximately 450 Ancient Cuneiform Tablets and Approximately 3,000 Ancient Clay Bullae," complaint in rem, U.S. District Court, Eastern District of New York, July 5, 2017, p. 10, https://tinyurl.com/ya2q4d2m.

7. Ibid.

8. Ibid.

9. Alan Fever, "Hobby Lobby Agrees to Forfeit 5,500 Artifacts Smuggled out of Iraq," *The New York Times*, July 5, 2017, https://tinyurl.com/yb427cs7.

10. "Hobby Lobby to forfeit ancient Iraqi artifacts in settlement with D.O.J.," Reuters, July 5, 2017, https://tinyurl.com/y8amzyko.

11. "How Terrorists Tap a Black Market Fueled by Stolen Antiquities," NBC News, June 23, 2014, https://tinyurl.com/y99ynj4e. Deborah M. Lehr and Katie A. Paul, "Rocking the Cradle of Civilization," *The Huffington Post*, Sept. 1, 2014, https://tinyurl.com/yb3ctr7m.

12. The estimate includes Greek, Roman and Near Eastern objects from about 8,000 B.C. to 500 A.D., but not objects from South America, Asia or Africa.

13. More than 1,000 locations in over 160 countries have been designated for protection as World Heritage Sites for their cultural, historical, scientific, natural or other significance. Of those, 832 have cultural significance.

14. Blythe Bowman Proulx, "Archeological Site Looting in 'Glocal' Perspective: Nature, Scope, and Frequency," *American Journal of Archaeology*, 2013, p. 117, https://tinyurl.com/yazvt76a.

15. Georgi Kantchev, "Buyer Beware: Looted Antiquities Flood Online Sites like Amazon, Facebook," *The Wall Street Journal*, Nov. 1, 2017, http://tinyurl.com/yddrsyd8.

16. Mackenzie and Yates, op. cit.

17. Eric Cline, *Three Stones Make a Wall* (2017), p. 330.

18. See Convention on Cultural Policy Implementation Act, pp. 1-2, https://tinyurl.com/y8ev79se.

19. "2013 Guidelines on the Acquisition of Archaeological Material and Ancient Art," Association of Art Museum Directors, Jan. 29, 2013, https://tinyurl.com/y7bfhpjh.

20. "Key Aspects of the New Act on the Protection of Cultural Property," Federal Government Commissioner for Culture and Media, Government of Germany, September 2016, https://tinyurl.com/yc9vrwze.

21. Roland Arkell, "Sales move out of Germany as controversial culture bill becomes law," *Antiques Trade Gazette*, July 18, 2016, https://tinyurl.com/y98hu6ds.

22. "Security Union: Cracking down on the illegal import of cultural goods used to finance terrorism," press release, European Commission, July 13, 2017, https://tinyurl.com/y8mu62ay. Also see accompanying Fact Sheet, July 13, 2017, https://tinyurl.com/y7ksmxld.

23. "New EU Regulations on Art Trade," Committee for Cultural Policy, Aug. 29, 2017, https://tinyurl.com/yaqdp88l.

24. John Henry Merryman, "Two Ways of Thinking about Cultural Property," *The American Journal of International Law*, October 1986, pp. 831-853, https://tinyurl.com/y9thxdgr.

25. Michele Chabin, "After the Hobby Lobby Scandal," *Deseret News*, Aug. 17. 2017, https://tinyurl.com/ycs43g97.

26. Ibid.

27. "The Parthenon Sculptures, Facts and Figures," British Museum, https://tinyurl.com/7uvzs26.

28. Anthee Carassava," Greece threatens legal action to win back 'stolen' Elgin Marbles," *The Times* (London), Sept. 18, 2017, https://tinyurl.com/yd5jbmu3.

29. Khanya Mtshali, "British Museum is in talks to return bronze artifacts looted from Benin Kingdom 120 years ago," *Quartz Africa*, Aug. 16, 2017, https://tinyurl.com/yc9addnv.

30. "Remembering Nadine Gordimer," British Committee for the Reunification of the British Marbles, July 15, 2014, https://tinyurl.com/yam8nktv. Also See Christopher Hitchens, *The Parthenon Marbles: The Case for Reunification* (2008), p. viii.

31. Merryman, op. cit.

32. Ibid., p. 846.

33. Tiffany Jenkins, *Keeping their Marbles* (2016), pp. 245-246.

34. Merryman, op. cit.

35. The National Stolen Property Act (1934) prohibits movement of stolen goods valued at $5,000 or more across state or national borders. U.S. courts have upheld foreign patrimony laws in cases testing whether antiquities imported from those countries were stolen under the U.S. law. *See U.S. v McClain* (1977) 5th Circuit Court of Appeals and *U.S. v. Schultz* (2003) 2nd Circuit Court of Appeals.

36. "1799 Rosetta Stone Found," This Day in History, https://tinyurl.com/22wwq9r. Napoleon's troops discovered the Rosetta stone in 1799 in Egypt. When the British defeated the French in 1801 they were ceded the stone by treaty.

37. Chip Colwell, *Plundered Skulls and Stolen Spirits: Inside the Fight to Reclaim Native America's Culture* (2017), pp. 3-4.

38. Dylan Brown, "The Spoils of Wars and Massacres: NAGPRA 25 Years Later," *Indian Country Today*, June 9, 2015, https://tinyurl.com/y9y7orwb.

39. According to an Oct. 17, 2017 email from Melanie O'Brien, Program Manager, National NAGPRA Program.

40. Carl Zimmer, "Tribes' Win in Fight for La Jolla Bones Clouds Hope for DNA Studies," *The New York Times*, Jan. 29, 2016, https://tinyurl.com/ybun3mca.

41. Dorothy Alther, *White* et al. *v. California Board of Regents* et al., Summary from NATHPO program, August 2017, https://tinyurl.com/ycp9r6fh.

42. Elizabeth Weiss, "The bone battle: The attack on scientific freedom," *Liberty*, December 2009, available at: https://tinyurl.com/yatzodtk. Also See "Determining Cultural Affiliation within NAGPRA," National Park Service, Sept. 1, 2013, https://tinyurl.com/y7u2ff37.

43. Simon Mackenzie, "While Elgin Marbles debate rages, there is still a market for looted antiquities" *The Conversation*, Feb. 14, 2014, https://tinyurl.com/yda4pjkk.

44. Jenkins, op. cit., pp. 76-80.

45. Ibid.

46. Ibid., p. 67.

47. "Boston's Museum of Fine Arts urged to Return Looted Artifacts to Nigeria," *The Huffington Post*, July 20, 2012, https://tinyurl.com/yb9ccjd3.

48. "Return the treasures Britain looted, Chinese tell Cameron," Agence France-Press, *Express Tribune*, Dec. 4, 2013, https://tinyurl.com/y9cx96te.

49. Jenkins, op. cit., pp. 63-65.

50. "Holocaust Restitution: Recovering Stolen Art," Jewish Virtual Library, updated March 2017, https://tinyurl.com/yaqn4bpc.

51. "Convention for the Protection of Cultural Property," UNESCO, https://tinyurl.com/y79tm9md.

52. Ibid.

53. Jason Felch and Ralph Frammolino, *Chasing Aphrodite* (2011), p. 5.

54. "Convention on the Means of Prohibiting and Preventing the Illicit Import, Export and Transfer of Ownership of Cultural Property," UNESCO, 1970, https://tinyurl.com/ybtely9q.

55. Merryman, op. cit.

56. "Convention on Cultural Property Implementation Act," https://tinyurl.com/y8ev79se.

57. "Emergency Implementation of Import Restrictions," https://tinyurl.com/yaeuvvg3.

58. See PL 114-151, https://tinyurl.com/y9jnub56.

59. Colwell, op. cit., pp. 84-85.

60. Cline, op. cit., p. 331.

61. "The Archaeological Resources Protection Act of 1979," National Park Service, updated March 15, 2016, https://tinyurl.com/y7chazqd.

62. Cline, *op cit*. Also see, Kirk Johnson, "23 people are arrested or sought in the Looting of Indian Artifacts," *The New York Times*, June 10, 2009, https://tinyurl.com/kjpkug.

63. Colwell, op. cit., pp. 213, 225–226.

64. Ibid., p. 253. Native American Graves Protection and Repatriation Act Regulations, Federal Register, March 15, 2010, https://tinyurl.com/ycrh9hlw.

65. Ibid., Carl Zimmer, "New DNA Results Show Kennewick Man Was Native American," *The New York Times*, June 18, 2015, https://tinyurl.com/y9brvvh9.

66. Carl Zimmer, "Tribes' Win in Fight for La Jolla Bones Clouds Hope for DNA Studies," *The New York Times*, Jan. 29, 2016, https://tinyurl.com/ybun3mca.

67. Morten Rasmussen et al., "The Ancestry and Affiliations of Kennewick Man," *Nature*, July 23, 2015, https://tinyurl.com/y8y7gtbv.

68. "Tribes Lay Remains of Kennewick Man to Rest," The Associated Press, Feb. 23, 2017, https://tinyurl.com/yd3taa42.

69. Felch and Frammolino, op. cit.

70. Application for Turnover Order, filed by Matthew Bogdanos, New York Country District Attorney, Supreme Court of the State of New York, County of New York, p. 33, https://tinyurl.com/y8gu6th5.

71. Ibid., p. 34.

72. Ibid., p. 36.

73. "Egyptian Archaeological Objects," Arthemis Art-Law Centre, University of Geneva, https://tinyurl.com/yc2cfr2y.

74. *Chasing Aphrodite* (2011), op. cit., p. 228. For Appeals Court decision, see: *United States v. Frederick Schultz*, 333 F.3d 393 (2nd Cir. (N.Y.)

June 25, 2003) (No. 02-1357), https://tinyurl.com/yakydd2c.

75. Ibid., *Chasing Aphrodite*.

76. Application for Turnover Order, op. cit., p. 43.

77. "Charges Dismissed Against ex-Getty curator Marion True by Italian Judge," *Los Angeles Times*, Oct. 13, 2010, https://tinyurl.com/2ebmwqu.

78. David Randall, "Revealed," *The Independent*, Nov. 13, 2005, https://tinyurl.com/pjk3ugb.

79. Cline, op. cit., p. 328.

80. Tiffany Westry, "UAB Archaeologists Sarah Parcak, Gregory Mumford awarded Antiquity Prize," Alabama News Center, April 27, 2017, https://tinyurl.com/ydyxne2q. For background, see Kenneth Jost, "Financial Crisis," *CQ Researcher*, May 9, 2008, pp. 409-432, and Kenneth Jost, "Unrest in the Arab world," *CQ Researcher*, Feb. 1, 2013, pp. 105-132.

81. Ammar Cheikh Omar, Richard Engel and Aggelos Petropoulos, "Smuggler of stolen artifacts from Palmyra speaks out about ISIS' illicit operation," NBC, April 6, 2016, https://tinyurl.com/ycfusw6c.

82. "President Signs Engel Bill to Stop ISIS from Looting Antiquities," U.S. Committee of the Blue Shield, May 9, 2016, https://tinyurl.com/ydggpdza.

83. Also see "Security Union," press release, European Commission, July 13, 2017, https://tinyurl.com/y8mu62ay.

84. "Key Aspects of the New Act on the Protection of Cultural Property in Germany," op. cit.

85. "Combatting illicit trafficking and destruction of cultural property," Council of Europe, May 3, 2017, https://tinyurl.com/ydd6bk6a. Also see Chart of Signatures and Ratifications of Treaty 221, as of Nov. 6, 2017, https://tinyurl.com/ya78st8l.

86. The vase was seized under a New York state law against criminal possession of stolen property.

87. Tom Mashberg, "Ancient Vase Seized from Met Museum on Suspicion It Was Looted," *The New York Times*, July 31, 2017, https://tinyurl.com/ybf75988.

88. Colin Moynihan, "Looted Antiquity, once at Met Museum, to Return to Lebanon," *The New York Times*, Oct. 11, 2017, https://tinyurl.com/yc2ob65j.

89. Sen. Martin Heinrich, "Heinrich introduces bill to prohibit exporting sacred Native American items," U.S. Senate, July 6, 2016, https://tinyurl.com/yb3t7ndp.

90. Lillia McEnaney, "The STOP Act," SAFE, Sept. 9, 2016, https://tinyurl.com/yaqckszt.

91. Heinrich, op. cit.

92. Dennis Gaffney, "Indian Artifacts: Understanding the Law," PBS, April 7, 2014, https://tinyurl.com/yd84xf3s.

93. "Update on the Safeguard Tribal Objects of Patrimony Act (STOP Act)," Antique Tribal Art Dealers Association, Nov. 28, 2016, https://tinyurl.com/y9wyp48w. Also see John Molloy, President, "Written Testimony submitted to U.S. Senate Committee on Indian Affairs," Antique Tribal Art Dealers Association, Oct. 24, 2016, https://tinyurl.com/y9j4j88c.

94. Deborah Lehr, "Blood Antiquities," Antiquities Coalition, Feb. 1, 2016, https://tinyurl.com/y9qg9lo6.

95. "Antiquities Trafficking and Art Crime," Future Learn online course, University of Glasgow, https://tinyurl.com/ybd5jv7p.

96. Laura Demanski, "Heritage in Peril," *University of Chicago Magazine*, Summer 2017, https://tinyurl.com/y8whqdon. Also see "The Past for Sale," University of Chicago, https://tinyurl.com/y9luagxp.

97. Lawrence Rothfield, "How Can We Fund the Fight Against Antiquities Looting and Trafficking? A 'Pollution' Tax on the Antiquities Trade," *Antiquities Coalition*, December 2016, https://tinyurl.com/yd8f6a38.

BIBLIOGRAPHY
Selected Sources
Books

Anderson, Maxwell L., *Antiquities: What Everyone Needs to Know*, Oxford University Press, 2017.
In this primer on antiquities, a consulting scholar at the University of Pennsylvania Museum of Archaeology and Anthropology frames the key debates over the legal and illicit trade.

Cline, Eric H., *Three Stones Make a Wall: The Story of Archaeology,* **Princeton University Press, 2017.**
A professor of classics and anthropology at George Washington University traces the history of archaeology from an amateur pursuit to today's scientific approaches.

Colwell, Chip, *Plundered Skulls and Stolen Spirits: Inside the Fight to Reclaim Native America's Culture,* **University of Chicago Press, 2017.**
A senior curator of anthropology at the Denver Museum of Nature & Science describes the debate between scientists and tribes over who gets to keep American Indian bones and sacred objects and how his museum resolved such dilemmas.

Felch, Jason, and Ralph Frammolino, *Chasing Aphrodite: The Hunt for Looted Antiquities at the World's Richest Museum,* **Houghton Mifflin Harcourt, 2011.**
Two investigative journalists expose the role the J. Paul Getty Museum and other U.S. museums played in the black market for looted antiquities.

Jenkins, Tiffany, *Keeping Their Marbles: How the Treasures of the Past Ended Up in Museums . . . and Why They Should Stay There,* **Oxford University Press, 2016.**
The Parthenon's Elgin marbles should stay in Britain, says a cultural commentator and sociologist, adding that arguments for repatriating antiquities like the marbles pose a threat to museums and our understanding of past civilizations.

Articles

Demanski, Laura, "Heritage in Peril," *University of Chicago Magazine,* **Summer 2017, https://tinyurl .com/y8wh qdon.**
Experts in archaeology, law and culture convened by the *University of Chicago Magazine* discuss approaches to stopping the illicit trade in archaeological artifacts.

Dolstein, Josefin, "Schumer: Don't return Jewish trove of artifacts to Iraq," **Jewish Telegraphic Agency, Oct. 3, 2017, https://tinyurl.com/y8jv7m9f.**
Sen. Charles Schumer, D-N.Y., joined Jewish groups in protesting the U.S. government's plan to return to the Iraqi government a trove of Jewish books, documents and sacred objects that the Iraqi government stole from Iraqi Jews.

Felch, Jason, "The Sidon Bull's Head: Court Documents a Journey through the Illicit Antiquities Trade," *Chasing Aphrodite,* **Sept. 24, 2017, https:// tinyurl.com/ya36ovl8.**
An investigative reporter and coauthor of the book *Chasing Aphrodite* traces the journey of an ancient bull's head sculpture from its theft during the Lebanon civil war through the antiquities black market to the Metropolitan Museum of Art.

Kantchev, Georgi, "Buyer Beware: Looted Antiquities Flood Online Sites like Amazon, Facebook," *The Wall Street Journal,* **Nov. 1, 2017, https://tinyurl .com/yddrsyd8.**
A flood of possibly stolen antiquities is for sale on eBay and WhatsApp at the same time that the Islamic State has been exploiting social media to cut out the middleman in antiquities sales, the business newspaper reports.

Merryman, John Henry, "Two Ways of Thinking about Cultural Property," *The American Journal of International Law,* **October 1986, https://tinyurl .com/y8uaqr3v.**
In this landmark article, the late Stanford law professor promoted an "internationalist" perspective, treating cultural objects, such as the Elgin marbles in the British Museum, as part of all humans' heritage, rather than the property of Greece.

Moynihan, Colin, "Looted Antiquity, Once at Met Museum, to Return to Lebanon," *The New York Times,* **Oct. 11, 2017, https://tinyurl.com/yc2ob65j.**
An ancient sculpture of a bull's head, loaned to the Metropolitan Museum of Art in New York City by a Colorado couple, will be returned to Lebanon after the owners accepted proof it was looted during Lebanon's civil war.

Reports and Studies

Brodie, Neal, "How to Control the Internet Market in Antiquities? The Need for Regulation and Monitoring," **Antiquities Coalition, July 2017, https://tinyurl.com/ycqewrss.**
A University of Oxford archaeologist reports that looted antiquities increasingly are being sold online and says the United States needs stricter oversight of websites such as eBay.

Mackenzie, Simon, and Donna Yates, "What Is Grey about the 'Grey Market' in Antiquities?" in Jens Beckert and Matias Dewey, eds., *The Architecture of Illegal Markets*, 2016, https://tinyurl.com/yc9knvdr. Two researchers with the Scottish Centre for Crime and Justice Research at the University of Glasgow report that the legitimate antiquities market is "a mix of legality and illegality."

Parcak, Sarah, et al., "Satellite evidence of archaeological site looting in Egypt: 2002-2013," *Antiquity*, February 2016, https://tinyurl.com/ydhwuymk. This widely cited study based on satellite photos by a University of Alabama, Birmingham, anthropologist found that looting at Egyptian archaeological sites rose in 2009-11, mirrored by increased sales of Egyptian antiquities at Sotheby's auctions.

For More Information

Anonymous Swiss Collector, www.anonymousswisscollector.com. A weekly compilation of news articles on antiquities thefts and art crime.

Antiquities Coalition, 1875 Connecticut Ave., N.W., Washington, DC 20009; 202-798-5245; https://theantiquitiescoalition.org. Nonprofit advocacy group fighting illicit trade in ancient art.

Committee for Cultural Policy, Box 4881, Santa Fe, NM 87502; 917-546-6724; https://committeeforculturalpolicy.org. Think tank supporting art and antiquities collecting and a legal market in antiquities.

International Association of Dealers in Ancient Art, Seestrasse 92; 8803, Rüschlikon, Zurich, Switzerland; www.iadaa.org. International association of leading dealers in works of ancient art.

Jews Indigenous to the Middle East and North Africa, 415-626-5062; www.jimena.org/. Advocacy group that seeks recognition for Jews displaced from the Middle East and North Africa in the 20th century and seeks to preserve their culture.

National Association of Tribal Historic Preservation Leaders, PO Box 19189, Washington, DC 20036-9189; 202-258-2101; http://nathpo.org. National group of tribal leaders who implement federal and tribal preservation laws.

National NAGPRA Program, National Park Service, 1849 C St., N.W., Mail Stop 7360, Washington, DC 20240; 202-354-2201; https://www.nps.gov/nagpra. Federal program that administers the Native American Graves Protection and Repatriation Act.

Trafficking Culture, SCCJR, University of Glasgow, Ivy Lodge, 63 Gibson St., Glasgow G12 8LR; trafficking culture.org. Research consortium that produces research on the contemporary global trade in looted cultural objects.

12

Reforming the U.N.

Reed Karaim

Food and other emergency supplies are unloaded after a U.N. aid convoy entered the rebel-held Syrian town of Douma, near the capital of Damascus, on June 10. Critics say corruption, bureaucracy and other problems have slowed the U.N. response to recent international crises, including the flood of Middle Eastern refugees trying to enter Europe.

From *CQ Researcher,*
June 24, 2016

To many observers, it was the United Nations at its finest — and its most controversial. A 2015 U.N. report catalogued the many ways in which war had harmed children that year and which countries were to blame, an account that one activist described as "a list of shame." Near the top was Saudi Arabia.[1]

The Saudis and a coalition of Arab partners are supporting the Yemeni government in its ongoing civil war by bombing insurgents' military targets. But the aerial campaign also has struck schools and hospitals, leading the U.N. report to blame Saudi Arabia and its partners for 60 percent of the nearly 2,000 children killed and injured in the conflict in 2015.[2]

But in June 2016, then-U.N. Secretary-General Ban Ki-moon removed Saudi Arabia and its coalition partners from an annex to the report that listed countries violating children's rights. Ban acknowledged he made the decision in response to threats by unnamed countries that the report could cost the U.N. crucial funding, saying he had to consider "the very real prospect that millions of other children would suffer grievously if, as was suggested to me, countries would defund many U.N. programs."[3]

Saudi Arabia denied that it had tried to intimidate the secretary-general, but observers said it was clear Ban had come under pressure from the Saudis and other coalition members.[4]

The episode highlights the crosswinds buffeting the United Nations as it enters its eighth decade of existence — trying to do right, but facing blowback nearly every step of the way. To its critics, the United Nations is an ineffectual colossus, hamstrung by bickering membership, ineffective leadership and a slow-moving bureaucracy. More fundamentally, many question whether the 193-member organization, founded in 1945 to foster global peace and promote human rights, remains relevant in today's world.

But to its supporters, the U.N. is still essential and effective, especially in its promotion of economic development and social justice. The organization has more than 30 specialized agencies and funds, staffed by 44,000 people worldwide, dealing with everything from peacekeeping and vaccinations to maritime regulations and international refugees. The agencies are involved in a wide range of development, health, education and social welfare activities across the globe. And the organization remains central to negotiations on many of the world's most pressing issues, from global climate change to violent regional conflicts, supporters say.[5]

But critics say the U.N.'s management has become so inept and its bureaucracy so inefficient that it cannot react swiftly enough to today's challenges. "If you locked a team of evil geniuses in a laboratory, they could not design a bureaucracy so maddeningly complex," Anthony Banbury, a former U.N. assistant secretary-general, wrote recently, explaining his resignation from the organization.[6]

New U.N. Secretary-General António Guterres, who replaced Ban this October, acknowledged that the international organization's rules and regulations have hindered efficient operation in his acceptance speech upon taking office last December.

"We need to create a consensus around simplification, decentralization and flexibility," Guterres said. "It benefits no one if it takes nine months to deploy a staff member to the field."[7]

Still, some analysts say inefficiencies in the U.N.'s operations reflect the complicated structure of the organization. Under the 1945 charter, member nations meet in a General Assembly where they debate issues and pass resolutions calling for action in areas of concern. But the real authority is largely reserved to the 15-member Security Council, which can make binding decisions that the U.N. charter requires member countries to follow.

Ten seats on the council are held for two-year terms by nations representing different regions. Five countries — the United States, Russia, China, France and Great Britain — have permanent seats on the council and have

veto power over U.N. resolutions, enabling any one of them to block action.[8]

The secretary-general — the chief administrative officer of the U.N. — is appointed by the General Assembly to renewable five-year terms, but the Security Council nominates the candidates, so the five veto-wielding permanent members of the council effectively select the secretary-general. The secretary-general supervises all U.N. staff at the organization's New York City headquarters and in offices and missions around the world. The General Assembly annually elects a president who oversees that body.[9]

But critics note that many U.N. agencies operate as autonomous fiefdoms and fill senior positions based on patronage rather than competency. And many agencies or other entities operating within the U.N. duplicate effort, they say, wasting money and diluting the organization's focus.[10]

This flawed governing structure, critics say, means the United Nations has struggled to respond to recent international crises, such as Africa's Ebola outbreak and the flood of Middle Eastern refugees now trying to enter Europe.

Scandals are another serious problem: U.N. peacekeepers from France and the Democratic Republic of the Congo have been accused of sexually exploiting and abusing women and children during the ongoing peacekeeping mission in the Central African Republic.[11] And charges of corruption among senior U.N. officials have led to calls for the organization to become more transparent and democratic.

Conservative critics in the United States, meanwhile, have raised concerns that U.N. treaties and initiatives could supersede U.S. national authority, although the organization's supporters dismiss the possibility as exaggerated.

Others who have worked closely with the U.N. say it operates more effectively and accomplishes more than it's given credit for. "The U.N. isn't a perfect organization, but it still provides enormous net benefits to the world and the United States," says Esther Brimmer, a former U.S. assistant secretary of State for international organization affairs and a professor of international affairs at George Washington University in Washington.

Among the U.N.'s most important work, she says, is economic and social development. In 2000, the U.N.

U.N. Oversees 15 Peacekeeping Operations

The 15 ongoing United Nations peacekeeping operations, primarily in Africa and the Middle East, involve about 103,000 uniformed personnel from 123 countries. Nearly 1,700 peacekeepers have died in those operations, with more than half of the deaths occurring in Lebanon, Darfur (Sudan), Cyprus and Haiti (not shown). That death toll represents about half of the nearly 3,500 peacekeepers killed during all of the 71 peacekeeping missions begun by the U.N. since 1948.

Locations of Current Peacekeeping Operations

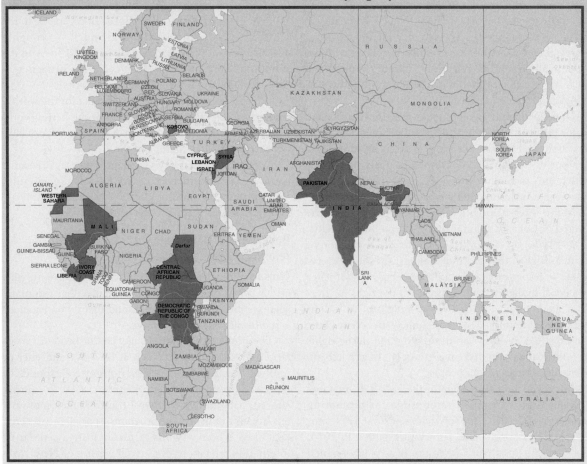

Sources: "Current peacekeeping operations," http://tinyurl.com/44cgkku, and "Peacekeeping Fact Sheet," http://tinyurl.com/5tzmet7, United Nations Peacekeeping.

committed itself to an ambitious agenda — the so-called Millennium Development Goals — which aimed by 2015 to eliminate extreme poverty and hunger, achieve universal primary education, reduce child mortality, promote gender equality, improve maternal health, combat diseases, promote environmental sustainability and boost aid donations to developing countries.[12]

A 2015 U.N. assessment found that impressive gains had been made in all key areas, including lifting more than 1 billion people out of extreme poverty, increasing from 83 percent to 91 percent the percentage of primary-school-age children in developing countries who are attending school and cutting under-5 child mortality by more than half. The report also noted that global HIV/AIDS cases have fallen by about 40 percent and malaria by more than a third. Malaria is being conquered in part due to a massive U.N.-coordinated effort to deliver more than 900 million insecticide-treated mosquito nets to African countries between 2004 and 2014.[13]

Nongovernmental organizations (NGOs) and national aid agencies, such as the U.S. Agency for International Development (USAID), have worked in concert with the U.N. in all these areas. But the organization's supporters say it has played a central role by establishing global priorities and helping to coordinate activities.

"It helped create a single conversation among the major players in development," says Brimmer. The U.N. has continued leading that conversation by adopting a new set of "sustainable development goals" for 2030, which aim to further promote peace, prosperity and responsible environmental stewardship.[14]

Many international affairs experts also credit the United Nations for shining a spotlight on human rights. In 1948, the U.N. adopted a "Universal Declaration of Human Rights" that called on nations and people everywhere to recognize that "all human beings are born free and equal in dignity and rights," with the right to "freedom of thought, conscience and religion," as well as "freedom of opinion and expression."[15] In recent years, the U.N. has devoted significant attention to the rights of women and promoted equal treatment of gay, lesbian, bisexual and transgender people.[16]

But critics say the makeup of the U.N.'s 47-member Human Rights Council, responsible for promoting human rights, reflects the subversion of some U.N. programs by including several autocratic regimes. In 2015, the council chose Saudi Arabia to head a key council panel. "Saudi Arabia has arguably the worst record in the world when it comes to religious freedom and women's rights," said Hillel Neuer, executive director of U.N. Watch, an independent watchdog organization based in Geneva.[17] A conservative strain of Islam, Wahhabism is the state religion in Saudi Arabia, which bans the public practice of any other religion, and strictly limits women's rights. Saudi Arabia insists it is an active defender of human rights.[18]

Critics further complain that, even accounting for inflation, U.N. program costs are 40 times higher than in the early 1950s. The organization's core budget has more than doubled in the last two decades to $5.4 billion biannually.[19] Yet some of the organization's humanitarian programs are on the verge of bankruptcy as they struggle to deal with the refugee crisis stemming from conflicts in Syria and other parts of the Middle East.[20]

U.N. supporters say the budget remains relatively modest, given the scope of its efforts. In comparison, the United States spent 10 times as much — roughly $40 billion — on international affairs in 2015.[21] And the European Union and United States are also struggling to find solutions to the refugee crisis, they note.

"It's easy to make the U.N. a scapegoat for the world's challenges," says Peter Yeo, president of the Better World Campaign, which works to foster a strong relationship between the United States and the U.N.

As new U.N. Secretary-General Guterres takes charge and the U.N.'s members consider how the organization can continue promoting global peace and prosperity, here are some of the questions being debated:

Does the U.N. need major reforms to remain relevant?

Calls to reform the United Nations are a constant, with critics complaining that the organization has too many agencies pursuing similar goals and that its bureaucracy is too insular and unresponsive.

The problem of multiple agencies tasked with overlapping responsibilities, such as in water and energy, resulted because the United Nations often responds to perceived needs by adding initiatives similar to existing efforts, analysts say. "We have 70 years' accretion of various organizations, funds, programs, special entities etc., etc.," says Thomas Weiss, a distinguished scholar of international relations at City University of New York. "More and more of them are doing the same things."

Because each initiative develops its own constituency within the U.N., it becomes almost impossible to get rid of them once they've been established, Weiss explains, leading to a maze of competing, largely independent bureaucracies. While the core U.N. budget is supported through assessed contributions from each member nation based on its wealth, many programs are supported by voluntary, direct contributions from countries or NGOs, he continues, which means agencies are competing for the same resources.

The bureaucratic overlap, Weiss says, combined with what he characterizes as weak leadership at the top, particularly under former Secretary-General Ban, has created a U.N. often at odds with itself. "There used to be something that might be characterized as a [U.N.] 'system'" when the organization was new and smaller, he says, "but now I use the word *family* – because like most of our families, this one is terribly dysfunctional."

If the United Nations continues on its present path, he says, "it's not going to disappear, but it is going to become a kind of relic and diminished presence on the world stage."

Weiss, the author of *What's Wrong With the United Nations and How to Fix It*, says greater centralization, including greater authority over spending, would help end the problem of overlapping missions and competition for resources. This would also require member nations to be focused more on the greater global good, rather than on protecting pet programs, he adds.

But Erin Graham, an assistant professor of politics specializing in international relations at Drexel University in Philadelphia, said the United Nations already has made changes in response to criticism that its agencies operate too independently. "There are new funding mechanisms designed to reward U.N. agencies if they coordinate," she said.

In 2003 the U.N. established the Multi-Partner Trust Fund Office, which was "designed to distribute money across multiple agencies and facilitate coordination between them," she said. The U.N. also has made the budgetary process more transparent, she said, allowing donors to better track how money is spent.[22]

Moreover, member nations support a system whereby various U.N. agencies compete for financial resources from individual countries, because it increases the countries' leverage over U.N. activities, Graham said. While reformers want increased centralization to make the U.N. more efficient, the current approach makes agencies accountable to the countries and NGOs that are paying for much of their work, she said. "U.N. agencies know that donors can give more or less," she said, "depending on how happy they are with performance."[23]

But Banbury, the former U.N. official, said the organization's administrative bureaucracy remains unresponsive

Former Slovenian President Danilo Türk is interviewed by video by U.N. officials on April 13. He was among the 10 candidates being considered to replace Former Secretary-General Ban Ki-moon, whose term expired in December 2016.

AFP/Getty Images/Jewel Samad

in key ways, most notably in staffing up quickly to respond to rapidly unfolding crises such as pandemics or natural disasters. "The United Nations needs to be able to attract and quickly deploy the world's best talent. And yet, it takes on average 213 days to recruit someone," he said, adding that recent changes in hiring policies by the U.N.'s Department of Management increased the delay even further.[24]

In addition, Weiss notes, U.N. staff appointments often are made to satisfy different countries or constituents. "The leadership at the top, . . . the senior and junior posts, are often very politicized appointments," he says, so competency and expertise are not top priorities.

Making matters worse, Banbury said, operational leaders on the ground cannot hire their own staff or reassign incompetent personnel. "Short of a serious crime, it is virtually impossible to fire someone in the United Nations," Banbury said. While he acknowledges the U.N. is still doing valuable work in some areas, thanks to "colossal mismanagement, the United Nations is failing," he said.[25]

But Stanley Meisler, author of *United Nations: A History*, who has covered the organization over a 30-year career as a foreign-policy journalist, says calls for an operational overhaul are overstated. The U.N. bureaucracy must deal with people from many different nations and cultures, and the process of learning how to work together can sometimes be cumbersome and slow, Meisler says. But the slow pace doesn't strike him as significantly worse than other governmental entities, he says.

"In my experience, I found [the U.N.] was just as efficient as the U.S. State Department," he says. "I think reform is a phony issue."

Other experts believe improvements in hiring procedures and accountability could be helpful, but in most cases the problems haven't kept the U.N. from getting the job done. "You have some dead wood there, no question, and it can be slow and cumbersome as all bureaucracies are, but I would say that the secretary-general has learned to work around it," says David Forsythe, an emeritus professor of political science at the University of Nebraska, Lincoln, and co-author of *The United Nations and Changing World Politics.* "It's a problem, but it's not the major problem at the U.N."

Yeo, of the Better World Campaign, says the United Nations is streamlining operations. The campaign reports that the U.N.'s 2016–2017 budget was down slightly and eliminated 150 redundant staff posts, while reducing equipment and travel expenses by 5 percent.[26] "The U.N. is reforming, but it needs to reform much more deeply and quickly," Yeo says. "Number one is finding a way to sunset programs that no longer serve a purpose. There's a real opportunity for the new secretary-general to insist that programs that aren't working be shuttered."

But other analysts say the United Nations has proven largely impervious to reform. Kelly-Kate Pease, an international relations professor at Webster University in St. Louis, an expert on international organizations, says the complexity of the U.N.'s operations and the fact that its member nations have different priorities make it extremely difficult to impose real reform.

"It's like punching a featherbed," Pease says. "You can punch it all day long, and at the end, it's going to look pretty much the same."

Can U.N. peacekeepers be effective in today's armed conflicts?

For more than half a century, the blue helmets and berets worn by U.N. peacekeepers have been a highly visible sign the United Nations was on the ground in the world's trouble-spots. Former Secretary-General Ban called peacekeeping "the flagship of the United Nations enterprise."

The U.N. currently has 15 missions underway in countries as different as Haiti and Cyprus. Twelve missions are in the Middle East or Sub-Saharan Africa.[27]

But peacekeeping has only become "more and more dangerous," Ban acknowledged in 2016. "In some areas, . . . our blue flag has gone from being a shield to a target."[28] A stark illustration of the threat occurred December 7, 2017, in the Democratic Republic of the Congo when 14 U.N. peacekeepers from Tanzania were killed by rebels, described by the U.N. as the worst attack on peacekeeping forces in recent history.[29]

Radical Islamic groups such as the Islamic State (also known as ISIS and ISIL) and al Qaeda reject the underlying notions that give the U.N. authority, says Michael Boyle, an associate professor of political science at La Salle University in Philadelphia whose research focuses on international relations and terrorism.

"If you reject nation states and groups that represent nation states, then the U.N. means nothing to you," Boyle says. "They see the U.N. as an institution representing the West. They see it as representing the United States," a secular, Western democracy they consider contrary to the wishes of God.

In Mali, where drug smugglers, arms dealers and jihadists have created a chaotic and violent situation, the U.N says 146 peacekeepers have died since the U.N. mission began there in 2013, currently making it the U.N.'s deadliest peacekeeping mission. Other missions have resulted in more deaths, but over longer periods of time.[30]

Throughout the organization's history, U.N. troops most often were not sent to fight but to help preserve a tentative peace between warring parties and to shield vulnerable civilian populations. Analysts note the effectiveness of such missions largely depended on a willingness by combatants to see an end to conflict and a respect for the United Nations as a neutral arbiter. It also depended on an acceptance of the U.N.'s legitimacy as a representative of world order.

Elizabeth Cousens, deputy chief executive officer of the United Nations Foundation, a nonprofit advocacy group for the U.N. based in Washington, D.C., that works to build partnerships between the organization and groups around the world, says U.N. personnel, both peacekeeping forces and other staff, still play a unique role that allows them to step into many conflicts in a way others cannot. "The U.N. is still understood to have a degree of impartiality, and that's not to be underestimated," she says. "The U.N. mediator in Syria, he's still seen as trying to broker a peace between all parties, and that's a huge advantage."

In Syria, however, several of the principal actors, including ISIS and the local affiliate of al Qaeda, are transnational terrorist groups. Battling these groups presents a challenge to the United Nations, which was set up to deal with member states, says Sue Eckert, adjunct senior fellow at the Center for a New American Security, a nonpartisan think tank in Washington, D.C.

"These nonstate actors are entirely different, and how you deal with them is different," Eckert says. "It's hard because the U.N. was not set up to deal with these threats, but I think [the U.N.] is evolving and has taken some innovative approaches."

Those approaches include non-military options, such as imposing targeted economic sanctions against terrorist groups to cripple their financing capabilities and helping member nations increase security along their borders.[31]

But U.N. peacekeeping forces increasingly have pursued "coercive action," abandoning neutrality and taking offensive military action against local militias or insurgent forces in an effort to protect civilians or restore order.

"You get into 'second-generation' peacekeeping, which tends toward combat. You have these military operations which are not neutral operations at all," says the University of Nebraska's Forsythe. "They are really efforts to coerce militias and other groups into not attacking civilians . . . and you've got to have some real capability to carry these out."

Some analysts doubt the United Nations can carry out more aggressive missions, given that its annual peacekeeping budget is $7.87 billion.[32] Moreover, the U.N. does not have its own military. It borrows troops and

Significant Progress Made on Development Goals

The United Nations has made impressive strides toward reaching the eight Millennium Development Goals it adopted in 2000, such as eliminating extreme poverty and cutting child mortality, according to a 2015 U.N. assessment. The report found that both extreme poverty and under-5 child mortality have fallen by more than half, while the number of primary-school-age children not attending school has dropped by almost half. Foreign aid, meanwhile, rose by 66 percent between 2000 and 2014.

Progress in Reaching Millennium Development Goals

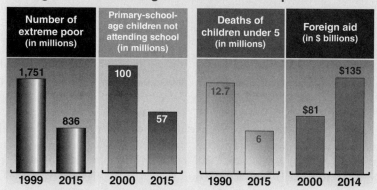

Source: "The Millennium Development Goals Report 2015," United Nations, pp. 4-5, http://tinyurl.com/p92xdd3

equipment from member nations for each mission. Many troops come from developing countries and are not considered as well trained as more professional armies.

"Even though these international security deployments have been around since 1956, they're still put together with duct tape and chewing gum," Forsythe says. "The secretary-general has to go around and ask for countries to volunteer forces and equipment, and sometimes the equipment sent is cast-off stuff that doesn't work, so it's very hard for international forces to prove themselves against these very nasty guys."

In September 2015, President Obama chaired a U.N. summit of more than 50 world leaders to discuss bolstering the U.N.'s peacekeeping capacity. Countries pledged 40,000 new troops and more equipment, including 10 field hospitals. China made the biggest pledge, promising up to 8,000 soldiers.[33] The United States, which provides only a handful of troops but pays a quarter of the peacekeeping budget, has been pushing for a more aggressive use of peacekeeping forces.

U.N. peacekeepers carry the coffins of seven Guinean soldiers killed on Feb. 12, 2016 during a jihadist attack against their camp in Mali, where 86 peacekeepers have died since the U.N. mission began there in 2013. The U.N. currently has 16 missions underway, including 12 in the Middle East or Sub-Saharan Africa.

Some experts believe that's a mistake. "We may be stumbling into an enormous strategic trap because, if we have learned over the last decade that very highly capable NATO forces, U.S. forces, actually can't suppress Islamic extremist groups, why on Earth do we think slightly strengthening U.N. missions is going to give us a tool that allows us to fight terrorists?" said Richard Gowan, a non-resident fellow at the Center on International Cooperation at New York University.[34]

But Yeo, of the Better World Campaign, says U.N. peacekeepers, with the proper support and training, can effectively share some of the burden the United States has shouldered to maintain world order. The United Nations, he says, "allows us to avoid going it alone." Peacekeeping operations are also less expensive than comparable U.S. military operations, which cost eight times as much, according to a study by the U.S. Government Accountability Office.[35]

Should the U.N. Security Council be enlarged to expand participation?

The United Nations may have 193 members in the General Assembly, but the 15-member Security Council has most of the institution's power. The council can block any resolution by a majority vote, and any one of the council's five permanent members can veto any resolution.

The 10 nonpermanent council members serve two-year terms. The seats are parceled out by region: five for Africa and Asia, one for Eastern Europe, two for Latin America and the Caribbean, and two for Western Europe and other states.

The Security Council has expanded once since 1945, going from 11 members to 15 in 1965. But the five permanent members — the United States, Russia, China, France and Great Britain — have essentially remained the same since the end of World War II, with Communist China's government replacing Taiwan in 1971 and Russia taking the former Soviet Union's seat after it dissolved in 1991.

Critics say the choice of the permanent members is a relic of the immediate postwar era, favoring nations that defeated the Axis powers. With three European nations and the United States as four of the five members, they note, it also reflects the dominant Western power when many of today's developing nations were still European colonies.

Members of the General Assembly repeatedly have called for expanding the number of permanent council seats to make it more reflective of the global community. But while the United States, Russia and China have publicly expressed openness to adding new members, they have quietly worked behind the scenes to prevent expansion, analysts say.[36]

Calls for expansion grew stronger during the U.N.'s 70th anniversary in 2015.[37] Several proposals were put forward. One would add Germany and Japan, the former Axis powers that now have two of the world's largest economies and are among the biggest financial contributors to the U.N., along with Brazil and India, two emerging powers. Another proposal would add a representative from Africa, with South Africa and Nigeria considered the strongest possibilities. Other ideas include adding up to eight new seats.[38]

The Elders, a group of former world leaders that includes former Secretary-General Kofi Annan, have proposed a compromise that would add a new class of members to the Security Council that would serve for longer than two-years and could be re-elected, giving them de facto permanent status. The Elders' plan would leave veto power with the five original permanent members but ask those nations to pledge not to use it to block U.N. action in certain crises, especially threats of mass genocide or atrocity.[39]

Some analysts believe change makes sense. "There's a case for expanding the Security Council — I think in the five- to six-[nation] category," says former assistant secretary of state Brimmer. "There are gaps in the council. One of those gaps is that there's no permanent member from Africa.

"But you have to get it right," she adds. "We've expanded the Security Council once since 1945, so this is not something to be taken lightly." She adds that "a modest increase into the low 20s would be possible — too large, and it won't function."

But other experts say disagreements between members with veto power, particularly the United States and Russia, often deadlock the Security Council already. "In terms of the big important issues, the Security Council has rarely been able to act, and I don't see that expanding it and allowing more participation is going to help matters," says Webster University's Pease. "Part of the problem with the Security Council as an effective governing institution is that nations have real disagreements about what is causing specific problems, and because you have a disagreement about what's causing the problem, your solution is going to be different."

Other observers say the challenge in expanding the council is not just the concerns of the five permanent members but the divisions between other nations. "Everybody agrees the Security Council needs to be reformed. This isn't 1945. You've got very important states that are not permanently on the council, such as India, Brazil or South Africa or Nigeria," says the University of Nebraska's Forsythe. "The problem is, nobody can agree on the specifics. How do you add India without Pakistan jumping ship? Which African state do you add — South Africa or Nigeria? When it comes to Latin America, should it be Mexico or Brazil? The regional caucuses can't agree. So nothing happens."

Brimmer, however, says the objections can probably be overcome. "I think it will take several more years to work this out, but I think enough member states want it that it could happen," she says "I think it could be good for the institution if done well with serious intent."

She says India, the world's most populous democracy, seems to have the most support for being added as a permanent member, an idea President Obama endorsed during a visit to New Delhi in 2010.[40]

But Yeo, of the Better World Campaign, doubts expansion will happen anytime soon. "It would require the [five permanent] members of the council to give up

A Syrian war refugee is sheltered in a camp near Aleppo, Syria, run by the U.N. High Commissioner for Refugees and Turkish humanitarian organizations. At the start of the year, the agency and other aid groups called for an additional $550 million to help deal with the immigrants fleeing the Middle East.

some of their powers, and they don't want to do that," he says. "I think Security Council reform is long overdue and highly unlikely in the foreseeable future."

BACKGROUND
Postwar Idealism

On June 25, 1945, delegates from 50 nations met in the San Francisco Opera House. It was the final session of a two-month conference to work out the basic structure of a new international body that organizers hoped could create lasting global peace out of the ashes of World War II.[41]

Lord Halifax, the British ambassador to the United States, presided. As he placed the final draft of the organization's charter before the delegates, he said, "The issue upon which we are about to vote is as important as any we shall ever vote in our lifetime."[42]

One by one, the delegates from each nation stood to signify their support. The crowd gathered to witness the historic moment broke into applause as the U.N. charter was adopted unanimously.[43]

The vote and signing ceremony the next day did not immediately bring the U.N. into existence. It took until Oct. 24, four more months, before enough signatories had ratified the agreement and the United Nations was officially created. But the international attention given

CHRONOLOGY

1945–1950 *The United Nations is founded.*

1945 Delegates from 50 nations gather in San Francisco to draw up the U.N. charter, which becomes effective in October.

1946 The first General Assembly meets in London; U.N. moves to New York City later in year.

1950 North Korea invades South Korea. With the Soviet Union boycotting the Security Council, the council's other members authorize an armed intervention by U.N. states to defend South Korea in the first significant conflict of the Cold War.

1956–1968 *U.N. peacekeepers begin operating, but hopes the world's great powers could work in concert are dashed by the Cold War.*

1956 First armed U.N. peacekeeping force replaces British, French and Israeli troops who invaded Egypt after it nationalized the Suez Canal.

1960 A record 17 newly independent states join U.N. as colonialism winds down in Africa.

1964 U.N. dispatches peacekeepers to Cyprus to prevent a recurrence of fighting between Greek and Turkish communities. The mission, still ongoing, is U.N.'s longest peacekeeping effort.

1967 Security Council adopts Resolution 242, which calls for Israel to return territory seized in the Six-Day War in return for recognition and peace from its Arab neighbors.

1968 General Assembly approves first treaty on nuclear weapons.

1972–1987 *U.N. treaties and agencies extend the organization's global influence.*

1972 First U.N. environmental conference meets in Stockholm.

1975 U.N. holds its first world conference on the status of women in Mexico City.

1987 Forty-six nations sign landmark U.N. global environmental agreement.

1990–2000 *Cold War's end brings hope that a more unified and influential United Nations can emerge.*

1990 U.N. approves U.S.-led intervention to drive Iraqi troops out of Kuwait.

1992 U.N. sends peacekeepers to the Balkan republics, beginning an involvement in the ethnic conflict that will lead to U.N.-authorized airstrikes.

1997 U.N. ban on chemical weapons takes effect.

2000 U.N. adopts the Global Millennium Development Goals, to reduce poverty over the next 15 years.

2001–Present *Terrorist attacks on U.S. mark a new era of conflict that tests U.N. capabilities.*

2001 In the wake of al Qaeda's Sept. 11 attacks that killed nearly 3,000 in the United States, U.N. declares right of member states to defend themselves against terrorism.

2005 U.N. adopts the Responsibility to Protect (R2P) doctrine, which declares that the U.N. has the responsibility to intervene if a nation fails to protect its population from crimes against humanity.

2010 U.N. creates UN Women to support gender equality and the empowerment of women.

2013 First U.N. Youth Assembly is held. Malala Yousafzai, a Pakistani schoolgirl shot by the Taliban for attending classes, urges the delegates to use education as a weapon against extremism.

2015 U.N. turns 70 and establishes a new global development goals. . . . UN-led effort culminates in historic international accord to fight climate change.

2016 Ten candidates vie to replace Ban Ki-moon, whose term as secretary-general expires in December.

the San Francisco conference signified the great hopes for the new organization.

Author and journalist Meisler says the hope was that, through the United Nations, the United States, Great Britain and Russia — who had spearheaded the Allied victory in World War II — along with China and France, could work together as "policemen" who would keep global peace.

Even before the war had ended, President Franklin D. Roosevelt had forcefully pressed the concept of creating an international organization where countries could resolve their differences, hoping to extend the cooperation of the Allied nations once Germany, Italy and Japan were defeated. "It was a vision of Franklin Roosevelt that the powers that were going to the win the Second World War would unite and prevent any further aggression by future Hitlers," Meisler says.

The power and authority Roosevelt envisioned for the United Nations was to stand in contrast to the League of Nations, an earlier attempt following World War I to create an international body of nations to keep the peace. The League, which was headquartered in Geneva, was hampered by the refusal of the U.S. Senate to ratify American membership and by an unwillingness of members to take action to stop aggression by powerful nations.[44]

Roosevelt hoped for different results for the United Nations. A series of meetings during and immediately after World War II fleshed out his idealistic concept. But it quickly ran into difficulties. Behind-the-scenes negotiations between the Soviet Union and the United States over several issues were intense.[45]

The main sticking point was the veto power of the Security Council's five permanent members. The Soviet Union wanted the permanent members to have the authority to veto even the discussion of a dispute. The United States wanted the veto restricted to decisions, not debate. The disagreement was serious enough that Harry S. Truman, who had become president when Roosevelt died in April 1945, sent a special envoy to Soviet leader Joseph Stalin to plead the U.S. position, to which Stalin finally agreed.[46]

That disagreement, although patched up, foreshadowed the split that would soon emerge between the Americans and the Soviets. As the Cold War began, pitting the U.S.-led alliance of Western democracies against the communist bloc led by the Soviet Union, the idea that the world's great powers would work in concert to police the globe evaporated.

"With the onslaught of the Cold War, it all got thrown out the window," says City University's Weiss. "It totally disappears in a matter of months."

Cold War Era

The Korean War, which began on June 25, 1950, when North Korea invaded South Korea, marked the first time the United Nations authorized member states to use military force to defend a country. A coalition of 16 U.N. countries led by the United States fought on behalf of South Korea.[47]

Ironically, the first conflict of the Cold War was one of the few times the United Nations was able to react to aggression in a manner close to its founding vision. The Security Council decision to authorize force was possible because the Soviet Union was boycotting the council in protest over the U.N.'s decision to seat the government of the Republic of China in Taiwan instead of the communist government led by Mao Zedong that had taken control of mainland China.[48]

The Soviet Union soon ended its boycott, however, and would use its veto frequently in the years ahead. In 1956, after the Soviet army invaded Hungary to topple an anti-communist government that had taken power, the Soviet Union vetoed a U.S. resolution calling for Soviet forces to withdraw.[49] During the height of the Cold War, from the mid-1950s through the mid-1980s, vetoes by Andrei Gromyko, Soviet foreign minister, were so familiar that he became known as "Mr. Nyet" (Mr. No).[50]

While the United States or the Soviet Union blocked U.N. action in many Cold War disputes, the organization still provided a forum for the two sides to air their disagreements, says Cousens, the United Nations Foundation official. "Through the long period of the Cold War, the U.N.'s biggest security job was to take the edge off the tensions between the big powers — in the U.S.-Soviet rivalry," she says.

The United Nations, Cousens says, also helped manage the decolonization of Africa and Asia, providing technical assistance to new governments as they assumed power in countries previously controlled by Western powers. In 1960, 17 newly independent nations, a record number, would join the United Nations.[51]

The U.N.'s first armed peacekeeping mission came in 1956 when the United Nations objected to a military

Americans Remain Wary of U.N.

They generally support it — with qualms.

Americans long have had a love-hate relationship with the United Nations. The international organization was founded under U.S. leadership, and the United States remains its most powerful member and biggest financial contributor, providing 22 percent of its core budget.[1] The United States works within the U.N. framework on many international issues, including climate change and the fight against terrorism.

But polling indicates the American public has mixed feelings about the United Nations. Since the 1950s, Gallup has regularly asked Americans whether they thought the U.N. was doing a good or bad job. In most years, less than half have chosen good job, and in the last 10 years, a majority annually said they thought the U.N. was doing a bad job.[2]

Yet at the same time, Gallup polling shows very little support for a U.S. withdrawal from the U.N.[3] And other polling finds that Americans consistently have had an overall favorable opinion of the United Nations.[4]

The United Nations also has been a target of harsh criticism, particularly within conservative circles. "For those on the right side of the political spectrum, there is a strong belief in unilateralism, and there is part of the Republican Party that disdains the U.N. and multilateralism," says David Forsythe, emeritus political science professor at the University of Nebraska, Lincoln, and co-author of *The United Nations and Changing World Politics*.

John Bolton, former U.S. ambassador to the U.N. under Republican President George W. Bush and one of its more vocal critics, has proposed that the United States should only pay for U.N. programs it supports.[5]

The far-right John Birch Society has been campaigning to get the United States out of the United Nations for more than half a century, arguing the U.N. is an effort to create a "socialist global government" that would strip the United States of its sovereignty.[6]

In the last 25 years, suspicions that the U.N. is superseding national authority have moved from fringe views into more mainstream discourse.

Conservative distrust of the United Nations — inflamed by false rumors that U.N. "black helicopters" were scouting America's national parks for a possible takeover — grew strong enough in the 1990s that the Clinton administration vetoed a traditional second term for Secretary-General Boutros Boutros-Ghali in an effort to appease Republican critics.[7]

During the recent presidential campaign, several Republican candidates criticized the United Nations and voiced fears it was being used to undermine U.S. independence. President Donald Trump, a former real estate developer and reality TV star, has dismissed the U.N. as "a political game" and indicated he will dramatically cut support for the organization."[8]

The United Nations has not been an issue on the Democratic side of the presidential race, and nominee Hillary Clinton and her opponent, Sen. Bernie Sanders of Vermont, support multinational approaches to solving global problems.

Still, liberal politicians and groups also have been frustrated with the United Nations, most recently in the area of human rights. The U.N. Human Rights Council has been criticized for passing resolutions viewed as limiting free speech. The rights of gay and lesbian people also have been a point of contention, with Russia and several Islamic countries recently uniting to pass a council resolution that critics felt favored traditional marriage and family structures.[9]

Both Democrats and Republicans have been sharply critical over the years of several U.N. resolutions concerning Israel, most particularly a 1975 statement equating Zionism

incursion by British, French and Israeli troops in Egypt. The three countries had sent troops into Egypt after it nationalized the Suez Canal Company, which operated the key Middle Eastern waterway.[52]

The three nations had acted without U.N. authority, and the backlash was swift, with both the Soviet Union and the United States demanding the troops withdraw. The three countries finally agreed to allow a U.N. force to replace their soldiers. Secretary-General Dag Hammarskjöld hastily assembled a U.N. peacekeeping force from troops volunteered by 10 nations. The peacekeepers supervised the gradual withdrawal of with racism — a statement that the U.N. General Assembly repealed in 1991.[10]

Yet despite all these concerns, the United States has remained a central player in the United Nations, with no administration seriously suggesting leaving. Despite the frequently stark divide in rhetoric between the two parties, Peter Yeo, president of the Better World Campaign, a non-profit effort to strengthen U.S.-U.N. ties, points out that Republicans and Democrats both have supported the U.N. on Capitol Hill.

"Seven years running, the U.S. Congress, led by Republicans in both the House and Senate, has fully paid our dues to the U.N.," he says. "And that's significant."

— Reed Karaim

[1] "Assessment of Member States' advances to the Working Capital Fund for the biennium 2016-2017 and contributions to the United Nations regular budget for 2016," United Nations Secretariat, Dec. 28, 2015, http://tinyurl.com/h66vp77.

[2] "United Nations," Gallup, April 18, 2016, http://tinyurl.com/7m95wrw.

[3] Ibid.

[4] "The U.S and the U.N. in 2016, Congressional Briefing Book," Better World Campaign and United Nations Association of USA, p. 14, http://tinyurl.com/h99dvlv.

[5] John Bolton, "The U.N. doesn't work. Here's a fix," American Enterprise Institute, Oct. 15, 2015, http://tinyurl.com/hg6hukp.

[6] "Get Us Out! of the United Nations," The John Birch Society, http://tinyurl.com/m9nrwxf.

[7] John Goshko, "U.N. becomes lightning rod for rightist fears," *The Washington Post*, Sept. 23, 1996, http://tinyurl.com/j7qwjee.

[8] Ashley Parker, "Donald Trump Says NATO is 'Obsolete,' UN is 'Political Game,'" *The New York Times*, April 2, 2016, http://tinyurl.com/j5hdu2d.

[9] "A new global force is fighting liberal social mores," Erasmus blog, *The Economist*, July 11, 2015, http://tinyurl.com/gn86sku.

[10] Paul Lewis, "U.N. Repeals Its '75 Resolution Equating Zionism With Racism," *The New York Times*, Dec. 17, 1991, http://tinyurl.com/gw2wluu.

Americans Have Mixed Views on the U.N.

In 2015, more than six in 10 voters had a favorable opinion of the United Nations, the highest since 2009, according to bipartisan polling sponsored by the pro-U.N. Better World Campaign (top). But an annual Gallup poll has found sharply fluctuating opinions since 1990 on whether the U.N. has done a good job at solving problems (bottom).

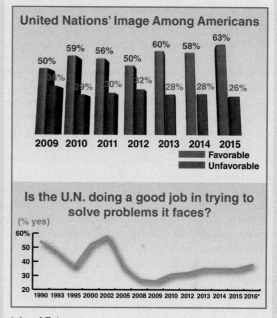

United Nations' Image Among Americans

* As of February

Sources: "Executive Summary," Fall poll, Better World Campaign, http://tinyurl.com/zd7jfgb; "United Nations," Gallup, April 18, 2016, http://tinyurl.com/7m95wrw

Israeli forces and monitored the border between Egypt and Israel, setting a template for future missions.[53]

The U.N's actions and the subsequent retreat by Britain and France were widely seen as signaling the passing of the colonial era.[54] Since that first operation in Egypt, the United Nations has operated 70 other peacekeeping missions, and U.N. Peacekeeping Forces won the 1988 Nobel Peace Prize in recognition of their work.[55]

Economic Development

The dissolution of the Soviet Union in 1991 following reforms implemented by Soviet President Mikhail

Peacekeepers Accused of Sexual Assault

"It's a real problem that stems from the fact that the U.N. does not have its own troops."

The distinctive blue helmets worn by United Nations peacekeeping forces are supposed to herald the arrival of an outside force that will protect civilians and restore order. But in Central Africa over the last couple of years, they have been connected to reports of the horrific sexual exploitation of women and children.

The claims involve some French troops, but most commonly peacekeeping forces from the Democratic Republic of Congo. The troops have been accused of paying girls and women in refugee camps as little as 50 cents for sexual acts and of sexually assaulting under-age girls. A *Washington Post* report included interviews with several girls who had born "peacekeeper babies."[1]

The case is one of several over the past 20 years in which U.N. peacekeepers have been accused of exploiting and mistreating the people they were supposed to be protecting. Charges of rape, sexual abuse and even collaboration with local human traffickers have been made against U.N. forces operating in Eastern Europe, Haiti and several African nations. Some incidents have involved children as young as 6.[2]

"It's a serious problem," says David Forsythe, emeritus professor of political science at the University of Nebraska, Lincoln, who has co-authored a book on the U.N. "It's a real problem that stems from the fact that the U.N. does not have its own troops."

When the United Nations puts together a peacekeeping force, it essentially has to beg for troops and equipment from member nations who agree to participate. "Some of these national forces, not only in Africa but elsewhere, are not very well trained," says Forsythe. "They're not well versed in the laws of war and the Geneva Conventions [rules of wartime conduct]. They have abused civilians."

A study by Transparency International, an anti-corruption monitoring group based in Berlin, found that the militaries of the 30 countries that provide the most personnel to U.N. peacekeeping are among those that have the biggest problems with corruption within the ranks. Three countries — Bangladesh, Ethiopia and India — contribute almost one-quarter of the troops used in U.N. peacekeeping, and all scored poorly in the study.[3]

Former U.N. Secretary-General Ban Ki-moon acknowledged the severity of the problem, calling sexual abuse by peacekeepers "a cancer in our system."[4] The United Nations has removed nearly 1,000 troops connected to the abuse from Central Africa, including an entire battalion — about 800 soldiers — from the Democratic Republic of Congo.[5]

But punishment of U.N. peacekeepers is left to the military command of the individual nations providing troops, and observers say penalties are often insufficient. In countries with less professional militaries, it means soldiers know they have a good chance of escaping punishment when on peacekeeping missions.

The problem, however, has included peacekeeping forces from Western nations with highly trained personnel. In the 1990s, U.N. peacekeepers and aid workers, including police and staff from several European nations, were accused of collaborating with Bosnian prostitution rings in the trafficking of young women into sexual slavery, even helping to bribe officials and forge documents as part of the criminal operations. The scandal attracted so much attention that it later served as the basis for a 2010 movie "The Whistleblower," starring Rachel Weisz.[6]

Yet the number of peacekeepers accused of abuse are only a small portion of the more than 121,000 U.N.

Gorbachev and the emergence of a more democratic Russia marked the end of the Cold War.[56]

The conclusion of decades-long tensions between the United States and Russia sparked a burst of optimism that the United Nations would be able to play a larger role in maintaining the new order. In 1992 the leaders of the 15 nations on the Security Council met

to adopt "an agenda for peace," later adopted by the Security Council.

The new secretary-general, Boutros Boutros Ghali, who laid out the U.N.'s renewed ambitions, started by acknowledging that "the adversarial decades of the Cold War made the original promise of the [U.N.] impossible to fulfill." But with the end of tensions, he said, "an opportunity has peacekeeping personnel currently serving in 16 different operations around the world.[7]

Still, the U.N. Security Council was concerned enough about the sexual abuse cases that it passed a resolution in March 2016 authorizing the secretary-general to replace all troops or other peacekeeping forces sent from a particular country if that nation fails to properly investigate or hold its forces accountable. The council also emphasized its concern over the "continuing and serious allegations" of sexual exploitation by U.N. peacekeepers in the Central African Republic.[8]

Forsythe says that until the U.N. gains more direct control over peacekeeping forces, including the ability to punish those who commit crimes while serving, the problem is likely to continue. "The whole thing stems from the weakness and lack of authority of the personnel who are supposedly in charge," he says.

But other observers say the U.N. already has the authority to act more forcefully. Anders Kompass, a senior U.N. aid official in Africa, was suspended and placed under investigation by the United Nations after he brought French peacekeepers' alleged abuse to the attention of French officials.[9] U.N. administrators said he had not followed official channels, but Miranda Brown, Kompass's former assistant, says he only spoke out after U.N. officials failed to act despite repeated reports about the abuse. "His sole reason for taking action was to stop this abuse," she says.

Brown, who also spoke out, was reassigned to Fiji and dismissed when she refused the transfer. She is seeking reinstatement. She says the United Nations needs to reform its procedures to respond more aggressively to reports of wrongdoing. "Unless you have recognition that you are responsible . . . you're not going to fix the problem," she says. "And from what I can see at this point, there isn't recognition that the U.N. has to fix its own mess."

— *Reed Karaim*

Hervé Ladsous, former U.N. undersecretary general for peacekeeping operations, briefs reporters at U.N. headquarters on his trip to the Central African Republic to investigate possible rapes by peacekeepers from France and the Democratic Republic of the Congo.

Getty Images/LightRocket/Luiz Rampelotto

[1] Kevin Sieff, " 'Sometimes when I'm alone with my baby, I think about killing him. He reminds me of the man who raped me,'" *The Washington Post*, Feb. 27, 2016, http://tinyurl.com/jrv4vzy.

[2] Elsa Buchanan, "UN Peacekeeping: Allegations of sexual exploitation and abuse — a 20 year history of shame," *International Business Times*, March 7, 2016, http://tinyurl.com/z3bwr8q.

[3] Rick Gladstone, "Armies used by U.N. Fail Watchdog Group's Test," *The New York Times*, April 3, 2016, http://tinyurl.com/hsj7nvw.

[4] Sieff, op. cit.

[5] Ibid.

[6] Ed Vulliamy, "Has the UN learned lessons of Bosnian sex slavery revealed in Rachel Weisz film?" *The Guardian*, Jan. 14, 2012, http://tinyurl.com/h5la9fm.

[7] "Peacekeeping Fact Sheet," United Nations, March 31, 2016, http://tinyurl.com/5tzmet7.

[8] "Security Council endorses steps to combat sexual exploitation by UN peacekeepers," UN News Centre, April 30, 2016, http://tinyurl.com/h89ruzm.

[9] "UN whistleblower resigns over French peacekeeper 'child abuse,'" BBC News, June 8, 2016, http://tinyurl.com/jmggf65.

been regained to achieve the great objectives of the Charter — a United Nations capable of maintaining international peace and security, of securing justice and human rights and of promoting, in the words of the Charter, 'social progress and better standards of life in larger freedom.'"[57]

The U.N.'s new confidence showed in both the number and size of peacekeeping missions in the 1990s. "In the first four decades, the Security Council authorized only 13 peacekeeping missions. In the fifth decade, another 20 were launched," wrote Meisler in his history, *The United Nations: The First Fifty Years*.[58] Three of the missions deployed more than 20,000 troops each, significantly larger than most prior peacekeeping forces.[59]

But in Somalia and Bosnia, U.N. forces found themselves in the middle of complicated and violent conflicts in which the peacekeepers struggled to assert their authority. In Bosnia in the early 1990s, peacekeepers were accused of standing by while Serbian soldiers killed Muslims. And in Somalia in 1993, U.S.-led U.N. forces withdrew after 18 Americans were killed in a failed mission that became the basis for the book and movie *Black Hawk Down*.[60]

The following year, the U.N. faced intense criticism after peacekeepers stood by while Hutu militia slaughtered about 800,000 Tutsis in Rwanda.[61] Kofi Annan, who was in charge of U.N. peacekeeping at the time, later expressed personal regret at the U.N.'s failure to take stronger action. "I realized after the genocide that there was more that I could and should have done to sound the alarm and rally support," he said.[62]

"There were a lot of what looked like failures," says Meisler, "so the U.N. became skittish about these kinds of missions."[63]

But others say the U.N.'s effort yielded meaningful results. "From the 1990s to the 2000s, we saw a dramatic decline in the number of wars, the lethality of wars and the number of deaths," says Cousens. "It's a tremendous success story that's rarely told . . . and a huge contribution to that came from the United Nations."

Peacekeeping was only part of the U.N.'s ambitious program. In 1994, the United Nations also adopted an agenda for development, which sought to boost sustainable economic development around the world and called on U.N. member states to embrace the effort.[64]

The agenda stressed the need for coordinating the efforts of nations, NGOs and other international donors, a role Webster University's Pease says the U.N. increasingly plays in the developing world. "I liken it to a cop directing traffic, trying to get the aid to where it needs to be. Without the cop, people would still sort it out, but it wouldn't operate as smoothly."

The U.N.'s emphasis on helping nations develop their own capabilities is key to sustainable development, she adds. "Where the U.N. is really valuable is in its education function, its training function," says Pease. "They're helping states to build the capacity to do these things for themselves, and I think that's really important."

Taken together, the agenda for peace and the agenda for development were an attempt to refocus the U.N. on its historic missions in the post–Cold War era. But as the 20th century ended, the global picture was about to be redrawn by the emergence of a new threat: radical Islamic terrorism.

Post-9/11 Era

The terrorist attacks on Sept. 11, 2001, that killed 2,977 people in New York City, at the Pentagon and outside Shanksville, Pa., when al Qaeda terrorists hijacked four jetliners marked a new era of international conflict.[65]

"Terrorism is a global menace. It calls for a united global response," Secretary-General Annan said after the attack. "To defeat it, all nations must take counsel together and act in unison. That is why we have the United Nations."[66]

In the past, the United Nations had struggled to define terrorism, with some nations believing that violent, nongovernmental resistance could be legitimate if it was against an occupying foreign force or a dominating power.[67]

But after 9/11, the Security Council moved to support the United States, unanimously approving a resolution declaring that a "terrorist attack on one country was an attack on all humanity" and recognizing the right of nations to defend themselves against terrorist groups.[68] The council also passed a wide-ranging measure targeting terrorist financing and calling on members to share intelligence to combat terrorism.[69]

U.N. support for U.S. actions, however, would founder as the United States went to war against Iraq, which wasn't involved in the 9/11 attacks. In 2003, then-Secretary of State Colin Powell infamously told the Security Council that Iraq was hiding weapons of mass destruction, but U.N. inspectors found no such weapons, and the Security Council opposed the U.S. invasion.[70] Annan would later call the war "illegal" because it did not conform to the U.N. charter.[71]

Despite the discord over Iraq, the United Nations has taken a more aggressive stance on terrorism since 9/11, analysts say, and has been essential in imposing international sanctions on terrorist groups and their supporters.

"The U.N., in a way that isn't well noticed, provides technical assistance to over 60 countries to help them comply with these international sanctions," says the Better World Campaign's Yeo. "That's an important contribution because it's one thing for the Security Council

Is the U.N. still an effective agency for international change?

YES
Peter Yeo
President, Better World Campaign

Written for *CQ Researcher*, June 2016

NO
U.S. Rep. Mike Rogers, R-Ala.
Sponsor, Restore American Sovereignty Act

Written for *CQ Researcher*, June 2016

Seventy years after its creation, the United Nations is more relevant and needed than at any time in its history to advance U.S. national security priorities while fostering burden-sharing among nations.

Peace and stability remain at the core of the institution's efforts as they did when President Harry S. Truman signed its charter, with peacekeepers constituting the world's largest deployed military force. However, the kinds of conflict they take on are much different than the brutality the world feared after World War II.

Today's peacekeepers operate in terrorist hotbeds like Mali and in nations wracked by civil war like South Sudan. Their presence often means the difference between life and death. A 2013 study found that deploying large numbers of U.N. peacekeepers "dramatically reduces civilian killings." A Columbia University study found that, in the post-Cold War era, deploying U.N. peacekeepers reduces by half the hazard that a country will slide back into all-out war. As former Joint Chiefs of Staff Chairman Mike Mullen noted, peacekeepers "help promote stability. . . . Therefore, the success of these operations is very much in our national interest."

Yet some of the U.N.'s value is hidden in the stories that don't make the front pages — or perhaps the stories it prevents from happening. Take its delivery of vaccines: They are one of the most cost-effective ways to save the lives of children, improve health and ensure long-term prosperity in developing countries.

Immunizations have saved more children than any other medical intervention in the last 50 years. The U.N. is a leader in this field, vaccinating 58 percent of the world's children. As a result, polio is close to being eradicated, and vaccines for measles, diphtheria, tetanus and pertussis save some 2.5 million lives each year.

Similarly, as the Zika virus affects thousands of pregnant women throughout the Americas, the U.N. is on the front lines: The World Health Organization is coordinating the international response; the U.N. Population Fund is providing voluntary contraception and family planning; UNICEF is helping affected families.

The U.N. is not a perfect institution, and U.S. involvement will remain essential to continue reforms and ensure improvement. Yet, as global crises become more complex, so too do the work and reach of the U.N. Today more than ever, no single country can resolve the world's most pressing challenges. By working with the U.N., we don't have to go it alone.

According to its charter, the United Nations can take action on a wide range of issues confronting humanity in the 21st century, from peace and security, climate change, sustainable development, human rights, disarmament and terrorism to gender equality and food production. As noble as its mission sounds, the U.N. has lost its way and become an ineffective and bloated international organization.

The United States funds 22 percent of the U.N.'s operations, significantly more than any other member state. Despite relying on American taxpayer dollars, recent U.N. actions go directly against the interests and values of our nation. The proposed U.N. Arms Treaty is a threat to our Second Amendment rights, and the Law of the Sea Treaty directly infringes upon American sovereignty. Recently, the U.N. Human Rights Council condemned Israel with five resolutions, but human rights abusers like China were never mentioned. The United Nations cannot balance its broad mission with so many member nations.

Another aspect the U.N. fails in is as an international peacekeeper. The world is more dangerous than ever. With North Korea, China and Iran provoking America and its allies, national security is at the forefront of my mind. We need a deliberative body that acts quickly and forcefully to neutralize threats across the world.

However, the United Nations Security Council, tasked with this exact job, remains gridlocked. Its sanctions against North Korea after that country's most recent provocations amount to nothing more than a slap on the wrist.

When Syrian President Bashar al-Assad began using chemical weapons against his owns citizens, the Security Council was inactive in a response. Russia, led by President Vladmir Putin, continues to ignore internationally recognized nuclear treaties. Yet, as one of the five permanent council members, Russia remains unpunished.

Many people have tried to prescribe a fix for the U.N. I won't do that. Former U.N. Ambassador Jeane Kirkpatrick was once asked why the United States didn't leave the U.N. She responded that it's not worth the trouble.

I disagree. I have introduced H.R. 1205, the Restore American Sovereignty Act, that would remove the United States from the United Nations. When American taxpayers pay for an organization that actively works against them, I think it's time we step up and move on.

In Paris in December 2016, U.N. and French officials — including former U.N. Secretary General Ban Ki-moon, center, and former French President François Hollande, far right — raise their arms in celebration of the adoption of the pact committing 195 nations to fight climate change. Unlike previous agreements, the pact requires all nations to act regardless of their economic status.

to say, 'We're going to freeze the assets of al Qaeda affiliates,' but if you're a nation without the technical skills to do that, you can ask the U.N. for help, and the U.N says here's what you do."

In 2005, a U.N.-sponsored summit of world leaders for the first time condemned terrorism and approved a doctrine called "the responsibility to protect," or R2P. Under the doctrine, nations were obligated to protect their population from war crimes, genocide and other harms.[72]

The U.N. helps countries improve their ability to battle terrorism in other ways, Cousens says, including through improved border controls and counterterrorism skills. Terrorists find harbor in politically unstable or economically ravaged countries, Cousens adds, and the U.N.'s experience with economic and political development are important parts of the "U.N. toolkit" in the battle against terrorism.

CURRENT SITUATION
Leadership Battle

In keeping with tradition, the U.N. General Assembly appointed António Guterres, a former prime minister of Portugal, as the new secretary-general by acclimation in

October 2016, acting on the recommendation of the Security Council.[73]

The Security Council had recommended Guterres a week earlier. The announcement he had emerged as the favorite was made jointly by Vitaly Churckin, then the Russian ambassador to the U.N., and Samantha Power, then U.S. ambassador to the U.N., a rare moment of public cooperation between two nations whose relationship had grown increasingly confrontational during the Obama administration.[74]

"In the end there was a candidate whose experience, vision and versatility across a range of areas proved compelling, and it was remarkably uncontentious, controversial," Power said. In an indirect reference to the tensions that have plagued the Security Council, she added, "Every day we go into Security Council, we aspire for the kind of unity we saw today."[75]

Despite the public show of unanimity, the content to replace Secretary-General Ban had been spirited. Thirteen men and women vied for the job, although the field narrowed as favorites emerged.[76]

Pressure had mounted for the council to select the first female secretary-general in the U.N's history. A group of prominent women formed "The Campaign to Elect a Woman U.N. Secretary General," an independent lobbying effort that listed qualified candidates from different global regions on its website.[77]

At the United Nations, at least 44 nations signed on to an initiative, organized by Colombia, to promote women for the job. "Gender equality is one of the world's most serious challenges, an unfulfilled goal that remains critical to advance towards an inclusive and sustainable future," María Emma Mejía, the Colombian ambassador to the U.N., wrote in a letter promoting the idea of a female secretary-general.[78]

Among the prominent female candidates were Helen Clark, a former prime minister of New Zealand who was then the head of the U.N. Development Programme, and Susana Malcora, then Argentina's foreign minister.

The Security Council has followed a loose tradition of appointing people from different regions, and Eastern Europe had been considered next in line. Vuk Jeremic, a former Serbian foreign minister, and Miroslav Lajcak, foreign minister of the Slovak Republic and the current president of the U.N. General Assembly, were the candidates closest to Guterres in straw polls taken by the Security Council before the decision.[79]

But Guterres is an experienced international diplomat. He served as the United Nations High Commissioner for Refugees from 2005 to 2015 and is credited with cutting costs and improving that agency's performance during his tenure.[80]

In his acceptance speech before the General Assembly, Guterres pledged to continue reforming the U.N. bureaucracy. He said promoting "gender equity" would be a primary focus of his administration and reemphasized the organization's commitment to dealing with refugees, improving life in the developing world and seeking an end to violent conflict. "Humanitarian response, sustainable development and sustaining peace are three sides of the same triangle," Guterres told the assembled delegations.[81]

A key to the United Nations success under Guterres will be his relationship with the United States and President Trump, who has been critical of the international organization in the past.[82] In a personal meeting between the two leaders at the White House in October, Trump described Guterres as doing a "spectacular job" and described him as his "friend."

But Trump added, "The United Nations has tremendous potential. It hasn't been used over the years nearly as it should be . . . We'll see what happens. I'll report back to you in about seven years."[83]

Climate Change

President Trump's announcement in June that the United States would withdraw from the Paris climate change accord dealt a blow to the United Nation's ongoing effort to battle global warming.[84]

Trump's proclamation does not immediately remove the United States from the accord signed by 195 nations in April 2016. The formal process could take up to three years. But with the decisions this fall by Syria and Nicaragua to join the pact, the United States, the second largest emitter of global warming gases after China, is now the only nation in the world saying no to the agreement.[85]

Battling climate change has been on the U.N. agenda since at least 1988, when the General Assembly created the Intergovernmental Panel on Climate Change. Two years later, the panel released its first scientific assessment on climate change, saying human activity was warming the planet.[86]

U.N. diplomats worked on the latest accord for nine years.[87] Previous climate change pacts required developed countries such as the United States and European nations to cut greenhouse gas emissions, while largely exempting developing countries such as China and India. The agreement reached in Paris in late December 2015 requires countries to act regardless of economic status.[88]

The United States took a leading role in crafting the Paris accord under President Barack Obama, but following Trump's announcement, the United Nations and leaders of the world's major powers vowed to press on without the United States. China said it would continue to abide by the accord, and the leaders of France, Germany and Italy issued a joint statement reaffirming "our strongest commitment to swiftly implement the Paris agreement."[89]

Trump, who has called climate change a "hoax," said the agreement leaves the United States at a competitive economic disadvantage. He suggested he was open to renegotiating the deal, although other nations noted the agreement is multinational and cannot be reopened by a single party.[90]

Even if the plan is fully implemented, scientists caution that it will only slow, not reverse, global warming. Following Trump's decision, U.S. Secretary General Guterres issued a similar alarm.[91] If the emissions targets in the Paris accord are met, Guterres said, "We would still have an increasing temperature above 3 degrees and that would be catastrophic for the world."[92]

Further action will be required by the international community to trim emissions by an additional 25 percent by 2020, he said, but in the interim, "it is crucial for all countries to follow through on their Paris commitments."[93]

Corruption and Reform

Corruption among senior officials remains an embarrassment to the United Nations. The most recent scandal involved bribery charges against John Ashe, a diplomat from Antigua and Barbuda, who served as General Assembly president from September 2013 to September 2014.

A task force appointed by Secretary-General Ban to look at reforms in the wake of Ashe's bribery scandal recommended greater transparency in the financial operations of the president's office. The task force also recommended that future General Assembly presidents make annual financial disclosures.[94]

In October 2015, the U.S. Attorney's Office in Manhattan indicted Ashe on charges he accepted more than $1 million in payments from Ng Lap Seng, a Chinese businessman. In return, according to the indictment, Ashe helped Ng obtain "potentially lucrative investments in Antiqua."[95]

Authorities said Ashe spent some of the money on luxury goods, including $59,000 worth of hand-tailored suits and two Rolex watches worth $54,000. Ashe has denied the charges.[96] Francis Lorenzo, deputy permanent representative to the U.N. from the Dominican Republic, was also charged in the case. Lorenzo is accused of serving as Ng's agent, helping to transmit more than $500,000 in bribes to Ashe.[97]

The limited nature of the task force's recommendations highlights the difficulty of achieving reform in the complicated U.N. structure. The General Assembly president does not report to the secretary-general. Presidents receive a $326,000 annual budget but are free to raise money from outside sources, including private companies. In its report, the task force noted this creates "significant loopholes and blindspots" when it comes to tracking the office's finances.[98]

Another case highlights a further challenge to U.N. reforms: Those who expose corruption can face retaliation. A senior U.N. aid official, Anders Kompass, was suspended and faced possible dismissal after he reported sexual abuse of children by peacekeepers from France and the Democratic Republic of Congo, serving in the Central African Republic (CAR). The U.N. has removed nearly 1,000 troops connected to the abuse from the CAR.

Kompass was later cleared of charges that he went outside established channels to leak a U.N. report on the abuse to French officials. Still, he resigned in June 2016, saying he did not feel senior U.N. officials had been held accountable for their failure.[99] Miranda Brown, a former assistant to Kompass, says the case illustrates the need for greater protection for whistleblowers who speak out about U.N. abuses. Brown backed him publicly and was transferred to Fiji, a move she contested, leading to her dismissal. A Freedom of Information Act that allows the media to request internal U.N. documents would be an important step toward greater accountability, she says.

Without those changes, Brown says, corruption and cover-ups will continue at the United Nations "and people will suffer, and those that will suffer the most are the people the United Nations is supposed to protect, such as children suffering from sexual abuse."

OUTLOOK
Relevance Debated

For all the challenges facing the United Nations, no one expects it to disappear anytime soon. After all, the 72-year-old organization has survived the Cold War; the birth of dozens of new nations following the collapse of colonialism and communism; the emergence of new economic powers in China, India and Brazil; the transformation of the global economy through free trade; and the rise of the Internet age.

But opinions differ sharply on how significant the U.N. will remain in the changing world.

As global prosperity grows and developing nations gain confidence and security, former assistant secretary of State Brimmer predicts a U.N. no longer as dominated by the traditional powers. "We might find some countries that have not been as active beginning to play a larger role — Indonesia and Mexico, for example — which would be good for all of us," she says. "I think you'll see more countries with candidates for leading offices or running for the Security Council."

Brimmer says Canada, which has been active in peacekeeping, is an example of how a middle-power country can play a critical role at the U.N. "The role these middle or emerging powers can play is really important. They can help with mediation. They can take areas of specialty and drill down and become specialists, and that's really helpful for the globe as a whole."

City University's Weiss sees a bleaker outlook for the U.N., believing it must make fundamental changes in how it operates — by centralizing power and reining in the bureaucracy — if it hopes to remain an effective player on the world stage. Absent significant changes, Weiss says, "it's going to become more and more marginal. And at least the way I read the conversations . . . there's a kind of complacency that there's really no urgency to change."

Other U.N. observers say big-power conflicts — as occurred during the Cold War — once again define and limit the U.N.'s ability to act. Author Meisler notes that the re-emergence of fundamental disagreements between the United States and Russia over how the international community should react to trouble spots in the Middle East and elsewhere, along with increased tension between the United States and China over several issues, have put three of the five permanent members of the Security Council at odds.

"The only evolution that can occur is if Russia and the United States" stop opposing each other again, Meisler says. "And then you have the question of how China and the U.S. get along. Otherwise, I see the [U.N's role in the world] being pretty much as it is right now."

Webster University's Pease also believes that the U.N. is probably going to "continue business as usual." But even with its flaws, she says, the United Nations provides an essential platform for global discussion and action that helps to avert some global crises and prevents others from getting worse.

"There's an old saying from [the second U.N. Secretary-General] Dag Hammarskjöld: The purpose of the U.N. is not to get us into heaven, but to save us from hell," Pease says. "I think what it's designed to do is provide a forum for states and other actors to be heard. It provides that forum and tries to address collective problems, and it's always going to be messy, and people aren't going to agree. But it's the only game in town. There is no other place to go."

NOTES

1. Michele Kelemen, "Saudi Arabia Dropped From List of Those Harming Children; U.N. Cites Pressure," National Public Radio, June 9, 2016, http://tinyurl.com/jht2jyc.

2. Ibid.

3. Ibid.

4. Ibid.

5. "Funds, Programmes, Specialized Agencies and Others," The United Nations, 2016, http://tinyurl.com/nffg4jd; "Where We Are," United Nations Careers, 2016, http://tinyurl.com/hrzobke.

6. Anthony Banbury, "I Love the U.N., But It Is Failing," *The New York Times,* March 18, 2016, http://tinyurl.com/z57x2ev.

7. "Secretary-General-Designate António Guterres' Remarks to the General Assembly on Taking the Oath of Office," United Nations Secretary-General, Dec. 12, 2016, https://www.un.org/sg/en/content/sg/speeches/2016-12-12/secretary-general-designate-antónio-guterres-oath-office-speech.

8. "About the UN," The United Nations, http://tinyurl.com/jnug35l.

9. Ibid.

10. Chris McGreal, "70 Years and Half a Trillion Dollars Later: What Has the UN Achieved?" *The Guardian,* Sept. 15, 2015, http://tinyurl.com/nc8nsd6.

11. Kevin Sief, "'Sometimes When I'm Alone With My Baby, I Think About Killing Him. He Reminds Me of the Man Who Raped Me,'" *The Washington Post,* Feb. 27, 2016, http://tinyurl.com/jrv4vzy.

12. "The Millennium Goals Report 2015," The United Nations, 2015, http://tinyurl.com/p92xdd3.

13. Ibid.

14. "Transforming Our World: The 2030 Agenda for Sustainable Development," The United Nations, Sept. 25, 2015, http://tinyurl.com/q9k2rk9.

15. "The Universal Declaration of Human Rights," The United Nations, http://tinyurl.com/pnjck5h.

16. "UN Women," The United Nations, http://tinyurl.com/hvhnc5q; "Free and Equal," The United Nations, http://tinyurl.com/ow2umgm.

17. Christopher Ingraham, "Why one of the world's worst human rights offenders is leading a U.N. human rights panel," The Washington Post, Sept. 28, 2015, http://tinyurl.com/jo9tzu2.

18. Alexandra Sims, "Saudi Arabia Issues Extraordinary Defence of Human Rights Record in Speech to UN Council," *The Independent,* March 9, 2016, http://tinyurl.com/hrbrfeu.

19. Ibid.

20. Harriet Grant, "UN Agencies 'Broke and Failing' in Face of Ever-Growing Refugee Crisis," *The Guardian,* Sept. 6, 2015, http://tinyurl.com/paoaa6s.

21. "Federal Spending: Where Does the Money Go," National Priorities Project, http://tinyurl.com/kakej6h.

22. Erin Graham, "Ignore the Old Complaints About U.N. Funding. Here Are Some New Ones," *The Washington Post,* Sept. 30, 2015, http://tinyurl .com/zhnfuyr.

23. Ibid.

24. Banbury, op. cit.

25. Ibid.

26. "The U.S. and the U.N. in 2016, Congressional Briefing Book," Better World Campaign and United Nations Association of USA, p. 35, http://tinyurl .com/h99dvlv.

27. "Peacekeeping Fact Sheet," https://peacekeeping .un.org/en; "Peacekeeping 'Flagship of the UN Enterprise,' Ban Says Ahead of Day Honouring 'Blue Helmets,'" U.N. News Centre, May 19, 2016, http://tinyurl.com/j5xu8jz.

28. "Peacekeeping 'Flagship of the UN Enterprise,' Ban Says Ahead of Day Honouring 'Blue Helmets,'" op. cit.

29. "UN honours 14 peacekeepers killed in eastern DR Congo," United Nations Peacekeeping, Dec. 11, 2017, http://peacekeeping.un.org/en/un-honours-14-peacekeepers-killed-eastern-dr-congo.

30. Kevin Sieff, "The World's Most Dangerous Peacekeeping Mission," *The Washington Post,* Feb. 17, 2017, http://www.washingtonpost.com/sf/world/2017/02/17/the-worlds-deadliest-u-n-peace keeping-mission/?utm_term=.0c738e13ca3c; "MINUSMA Fact Sheet," United Nations Peacekeeping, November 16, 2017, https://peace keeping.un.org/en/mission/minusma.

31. "Themes and Priorities," United Nations Counter-terrorism Center, 2016, http://tinyurl.com/h4engh8.

32. "Peacekeeping Fact Sheet," The United Nations, March 31, 2017, https://peacekeeping.un.org/sites/default/files/pk_factsheet_03_17_e.pdf.

33. Michelle Nichols, "Countries Pledge 40,000 U.N. Peacekeepers at U.N. Summit," Reuters, Sept. 28, 2015, http://tinyurl.com/jdglglp.

34. Chris McGreal, "What's the Point of Peacekeepers When They Don't Keep the Peace?" *The Guardian,* Sept. 17, 2015, http://tinyurl.com/nchbqeu.

35. "The U.S. and the U.N. in 2016, Congressional Briefing Book," op. cit., p. 17.

36. Lydia Swart and Cile Pace, "Changing the Composition of the Security Council: Is There a Viable Solution?" Center for U.N. Reform Education, March 1, 2015, http://tinyurl.com/zujx2m8.

37. "General Assembly Adopts, Without Vote, 'Landmark' Decision on Advancing Efforts to Reform, Increase Membership of Security Council," The United Nations, Sept. 14, 2015, http://tinyurl .com/zq6ty9a.

38. "Membership Including Expansion and Representation," Global Policy Forum, 2016, http://tinyurl.com/jxf9xvp.

39. "Strengthening the United Nations," The Elders, Feb. 7, 2015, http://tinyurl.com/zm48lrv.

40. Sheryl Gay Stolberg and Jim Yardley, "Countering China, Obama Backs India for U.N. Council," *The New York Times,* Nov. 8, 2010, http://tinyurl .com/3867ru4.

41. "1945: The San Francisco Conference," The United Nations, http://tinyurl.com/zm76eq8.

42. Ibid.

43. Ibid.

44. Charles Townshend, "The League of Nations and the United Nations," BBC History, Feb. 17, 2011, http://tinyurl.com/avzb896.

45. Stanley Meisler, "United Nations: The First 50 years," *Atlantic Monthly Press,* 1995, pp. 16–18.

46. Ibid.

47. C. N. Trueman, "The United Nations and the Korean War," History Learning Site, March 3, 2016, http://tinyurl.com/hfspa7t.

48. Ibid.

49. "Hungary, 1956," U.S. Department of State Archive, http://tinyurl.com/zvhgppv.

50. Tarik Kafala, "The Veto and How to Use It," BBC News, Sept. 17, 2003, http://tinyurl.com/6lhnnp.

51. "Milestones, 1951–1960," History of the United Nations, 2016, http://tinyurl.com/guwbjad.

52. Meisler, op. cit., pp. 94–114.

53. Ibid.

54. Derek Brown, "1956: Suez and the End of Empire," *The Guardian,* March 14, 2001, http://tinyurl.com/h9tcr6v.

55. "The Nobel Peace Prize 1988," Nobelprize.org, May 23, 2016, http://tinyurl.com/jaemshl.

56. "The Collapse of the Soviet Union," Office of the Historian, U.S. Department of State, http://tinyurl.com/hyj94f2.

57. Boutras Boutras Ghali, "An Agenda for Peace, Preventative Diplomacy, Peacemaking and Peacekeeping, Report of the Secretary General pursuant to the statement adopted by the Summit Meeting of the Security Council on 31 January 1002," The United Nations, http://tinyurl.com/zlrjosq.

58. Meisler, op. cit., p. 287.

59. Ibid., p. 288.

60. Paul Alexander, "Fallout From Somalia Still Haunts US Policy 20 Years Later," *Stars and Stripes,* Oct. 2, 2013, http://tinyurl.com/z5rocmn.

61. McGreal, op. cit.

62. "UN Chief's Rwanda Genocide Regret," BBC News, March 26, 2004, http://tinyurl.com/d783pfo.

63. Paul Alexander, "Fallout From Somalia Still Haunts US Policy 20 Years Later," *Stars and Stripes,* Oct. 2, 2013, http://tinyurl.com/z5rocmn.

64. "Boutras Boutras Ghali, Development and International Economic Development, An Agenda for Development, Report of the Secretary General," The United Nations, May 6, 1994, http://tinyurl.com/h6d6u2p.

65. "September 11th Fast Facts," CNN, Sept. 7, 2015, http://tinyurl.com/pvhfoh9.

66. Thomas Weiss et al., "The United Nations and Changing World Politics" (2007), p. 95.

67. Ibid., p. 96.

68. "Security Council Condemns, 'In Strongest Terms', Terrorist Attacks on United States," The United Nations, Sept. 12, 2001, http://tinyurl.com/k6t4jy7.

69. "Security Council Unanimously Adopts Wide-Ranging Anti-Terrorism Resolution; Calls for Suppressing Financing, Improving International Cooperation," The United Nations, Sept. 28, 2001, http://tinyurl.com/pkmqp4c.

70. Elaine Sciolino, "France to Veto Resolution on Iraq War, Chirac Says," *The New York Times,* March 11, 2003, http://tinyurl.com/hkzb3ff.

71. Ewen MacAskill and Julian Borger, "Iraq War Was Illegal and Breached UN Charter, Says Annan," *The Guardian,* Sept. 15, 2004, http://tinyurl.com/l3vv2vh.

72. For background, see Tom Price, "Assessing the United Nations," *CQ Global Researcher,* March 20, 2012, pp. 129–152.

73. "António Guterres Appointed Next UN Secretary-General by Acclamation," UN News Centre, Oct. 13, 2016, http://www.un.org/apps/news/story.asp?NewsID=55285#.Wg8WvRRUalI.

74. Somini Sengupta, "Security Council Backs António Guterres to Be Next U.N. Secretary General," *The New York Times,* Oct. 5, 2016, https://www.nytimes.com/2016/10/06/world/americas/antonio-guterres-un-secretary-general-united-nations.html?_r=0.

75. Ibid.

76. Tim Hume, "Portugal's Antonio Guterres Poised to Become Next UN Secretary-General," CNN, Oct. 5, 2016, http://www.cnn.com/2016/10/05/world/un-secretary-general-antonio-guterres/index.html.

77. Campaign to Elect a Women Secretary General, 2016, https://www.womansg.org.

78. "The Push for a Women to Run the U.N.," *The New York Times,* Aug. 22, 2015, http://tinyurl.com/noybaok.

79. Hume, op. cit.

80. Hume.

81. "Secretary-General-Designate António Guterres' Remarks to the General Assembly on Taking the Oath of Office," op. cit.

82. Maya Rhodan, "Here Are All the Times Donald Trump Bashed the United Nations Before Speaking There," *Time,* Sept. 18, 2017, http://time.com/4946276/donald-trump-united-nations-general-assembly/.

83. "Trump Full Meeting With U.N. Secretary General," *Politico,* Oct. 20, 2017, https://www.politico.com/video/2017/10/20/trump-full-meeting-with-un-secretary-general-antonio-guterres-064200.

84. Michael Shear, "Trump Will Withdraw U.S. From Paris Climate Agreement," *The New York Times,* June 1, 2017, https://www.nytimes.com/2017/06/01/climate/trump-paris-climate-agreement.html.

85. Brady Dennis, "As Syria Embraces Paris Climate Deal, It's the United States Against the World," *The Washington Post,* Nov. 7, 2017, https://www.washingtonpost.com/news/energy-environment/wp/2017/11/07/as-syria-embraces-paris-climate-deal-its-the-united-states-against-the-world/?utm_term=.96c32a56f6bc.

86. Karl Ritter, "Timeline of Key Events in International Effort to Combat Climate Change," *U.S. News & World Report,* Nov. 30, 2015, http://tinyurl.com/h7nn3o2.

87. Davenport, op. cit.

88. Davenport, op. cit.

89. Somini Sengupta, et al., "As Trump Exits Paris Agreement, Other Nations Are Defiant," *The New York Times,* June 1, 2017, https://www.nytimes.com/2017/06/01/world/europe/climate-paris-agreement-trump-china.html.

90. Ibid.

91. Justin Gillis and Coral Davenport, "Leaders Roll Up Sleeves on Climate, But Experts Say Plans Don't Pack a Wallop," *The New York Times,* April 21, 2016, http://tinyurl.com/hdps9hg.

92. António Guterres, "Opening Statement to the Press at COP23," Nov. 15, 2017, https://www.un.org/sg/en/content/sg/speeches/2017-11-15/opening-statement-press-cop23.

93. António Guterres, "Remarks at the High-Level Event at COP23," Nov. 15, 2017, https://www.un.org/sg/en/content/sg/speeches/2017-11-15/secretary-general-cop23-remarks.

94. Somini Sengupta, "U.N. Panel's Call for Transparency Highlights Limits of Oversight," *The New York Times,* March 29, 2016, http://tinyurl.com/z5nwcjx.

95. Marc Santora, Somini Sengupta and Benjamin Weiser, "Former U.N. President and Chinese Billionaire Are Accused in Graft Scheme," *The New York Times,* http://tinyurl.com/hoe2egc.

96. Ibid.

97. Rebecca Davis O'Brien, Christopher Matthews and Farnaz Fassihi, "Former United Nations General Assembly President Charged in Bribery Scheme," *The Wall Street Journal,* Oct. 6, 2015, http://tinyurl.com/nf36xyp.

98. Sengupta, op. cit.

99. "UN whistleblower resigns over French peacekeeper 'child abuse'," BBC News, June 8, 2016, http://www.bbc.com/news/world-africa-36481372.

BIBLIOGRAPHY
Selected Sources
Books

Fasulo, Linda, *An Insider's Guide to the UN: Third Edition,* **Yale University Press, 2015.**
An NBC News correspondent who covers the United Nations provides a guide to the U.N.'s different bodies and programs, along with a review of how the organization addresses terrorism, climate change and other key issues.

Meisler, Stanley, *United Nations: A History,* **Grove Press, 2011.**
A veteran foreign affairs journalist who wrote about the U.N. looks at its origins in World War II, including the hopes the founders had for the organization, and how it has evolved in the years since.

Weiss, Thomas, *What's Wrong With the United Nations and How to Fix It,* **2nd ed., Polity, 2012.**
The director of the Ralph Bunche Institute for International Studies at City University of New York examines the institutional ills he believes leave the U.N. poorly equipped to deal with today's problems, and suggests ways to reform it.

Weiss, Thomas, et al., *The United Nations and Changing World Politics,* **Westview Press, 2013.**
Four foreign policy scholars examine the U.N.'s role in three areas: building international peace and security; human rights and humanitarian relief; and promoting peace through sustainable economic development.

Articles

Banbury, Anthony, "I Love the U.N., but It Is Failing," *The New York Times*, March 18, 2016, http://tinyurl.com/z57x2ev.
A longtime U.N. official says the international organization's "colossal mismanagement" leaves it unable to achieve its mission in key areas, including protecting world health and keeping the peace.

Brady, Dennis, "Why outgoing U.N. chief Ban Ki-moon was willing to bet big on a climate change deal," *The Washington Post*, May 6, 2016, http://tinyurl.com/jo2nklg.
U.N. Secretary-General Ban Ki-moon explains why he felt the United Nations could play an important role in bringing the nations of the world together to limit global climate change.

Buchanan, Elsa, "UN Peacekeeping: Allegations of sexual exploitation and abuse — a 20 year history of shame," *International Business Times*, March 7, 2016, http://tinyurl.com/z3bwr8q.
A review of sexual abuse charges against U.N. peacekeeping forces finds that accusations have reoccurred repeatedly for 20 years.

Charbonneau, Louis, Nate Raymond and Michelle Nichols, "Exclusive: U.N. audit identifies serious lapses linked to alleged bribery," Reuters, April 3, 2016, http://tinyurl.com/glxh6q7.
An internal U.N. investigation faults officials' lack of oversight in a bribery case involving a former president of the U.N. General Assembly.

McGreal, Chris, "70 years and half a trillion dollars later: what has the UN achieved?" *The Guardian*, Sept. 7, 2015, http://tinyurl.com/nc8nsd6.
On the 70th anniversary of the U.N.'s founding, a review of the organization's history finds real accomplishments — saving lives and boosting health and education in much of the world — but also a bloated and undemocratic structure.

Sengupta, Somini, "At U.N., Ambassadors Hold Auditions for Next Secretary General," *The New York Times*, April 15, 2016, http://tinyurl.com/hk2hjwz.
Nine candidates vying to become the next U.N. secretary-general face the ambassadors of various nations to answer questions about the future of the international organization.

Reports and Studies

"Confronting the Crisis of Global Governance: The Report of the Commission on Global Security, Justice & Governance," The Hague Institute for Global Justice and the Stimson Center, June 2015, http://tinyurl.com/hg36mmd.
A commission of former senior diplomats concludes that a range of global challenges — from international terrorism to climate change — calls for a strengthening of international organizations, including the United Nations.

"The Millennium Development Goals Report 2015," United Nations, 2015, http://tinyurl.com/p92xdd3.
A U.N. report assesses the progress made toward reducing world poverty and hunger, improving health and education and other goals set by nations of the United Nations and at least 23 other international organizations at the start of the new millennium.

"Uniting Our Strengths for Peace — Politics, Partnership and People," Report of the High-Level Independent Panel on United Nations Peace Operations, United Nations, June 2015, http://tinyurl.com/jot68lo.
A panel appointed by U.N. Secretary-General Ban Ki-moon to assess the relevance and effectiveness of U.N. peacekeeping operations calls for greater clarity in the use of force and a greater emphasis on conflict prevention and mediation.

Troszczynska-van Genderen, Wanda, "Reforming the United Nations: State of Play, Ways Forward," European Parliament, Directorate-General for External Policies, Policy Department, March 2015, http://tinyurl.com/o28ycsb.
A study sponsored by the European Union's Parliament looks at proposed U.N. reforms in a variety of areas, including budgeting and management, and assesses where the proposals stand.

For More Information

American Enterprise Institute, 1150 17th St., N.W., Washington, DC 20036; 202-862-5800; https://www.aei .org. Conservative think tank that seeks to make the United Nations more responsive to Western interests.

Brookings Institution, 1775 Massachusetts Ave., N.W., Washington, DC 20036; 202-797-6000; www.brookings .edu. Liberal think tank that conducts studies and analysis of global development, foreign aid and world health issues.

Council on Foreign Relations, The Harold Pratt House, 58 E. 68th St., New York, NY 10065; 212-434-9400; www .cfr.org. Nonpartisan think tank that promotes debate on major foreign policy issues.

The Elders Foundation, PO Box 67772, London W14 4EH, United Kingdom; +44-0-207-013-4646; http://theelders .org. Organization of retired world leaders that promotes peace and human rights and has proposed several U.N. reforms.

United Nations, 405 E. 42nd St., New York, NY 10017; 212-963-9999; www.un.org/en/index.html. Organization of 193 member nations that works on issues of international importance, including peace, disarmament, climate change, sustainable development, terrorism, global health and humanitarian aid.

United Nations Foundation, 1750 Pennsylvania Ave., N.W., Suite 300, Washington, DC 20006; 202-887-9040; www.unfoundation.org. Philanthropy begun in 1988 with a $1 billion gift from media mogul Ted Turner to support the U.N.

United Nations Watch, Case Postale 191, 1211 Geneva 20, Switzerland; +41-22-734-1472; www.unwatch.org/en/. Nongovernmental organization that monitors the performance of the United Nations.

13

Rethinking Foreign Aid

Patrick Marshall

President Trump has proposed cutting U.S. foreign aid by about a third, saying he wants to spend more money on infrastructure projects at home and to bolster the military. Foreign aid advocates say aid to countries that support the U.S. fight against terrorism is vital to U.S. national security. Critics say aid is often wasted on inefficient programs or stolen by corrupt foreign dictators and officials.

Getty Images/Bloomberg/Aude Guerrucci

From *CQ Researcher,*
April 14, 2017

In announcing his candidacy for president, Donald Trump said the United States should stop spending so much money helping other nations and instead use the funds at home. "It is necessary," he declared, "that we . . . stop sending foreign aid to countries that hate us and use that money to rebuild our tunnels, roads, bridges and schools."[1]

As president, Trump followed through on that idea, proposing a budget in February that would slash funds for the U.S. Agency for International Development (USAID) — the primary conduit for foreign aid — by nearly a third, with the biggest cuts in economic development assistance.[2]

Aid specialists reject the proposal, as do some members of Trump's own Republican Party. "Foreign aid is not charity" but is crucial to national security, Florida Sen. Marco Rubio tweeted. "A disaster," South Carolina Sen. Lindsey Graham said of the plan, which he predicted would be "dead on arrival" in the Senate.[3]

Foreign aid "helps build stable, democratic partners who share our interests and values," says Shannon Green, a senior analyst at the Center for Strategic and International Studies, a think tank in Washington.

While foreign aid may play a central role in national security and U.S. relations abroad, Trump's skepticism about its importance has helped revive several longstanding questions: How effectively is aid dispensed to struggling nations? What are the strategic goals of aid? Does aid to despotic regimes have positive or negative effects?

Where the Money Goes

The U.S. government spent $26.2 billion on anti-poverty and humanitarian programs in other countries in fiscal 2015, slightly more than half of the $48.1 billion appropriated for foreign aid, according to the latest available data. Military and security-related aid accounted for the rest — $21.9 billion, or 46 percent.

U.S. Foreign Aid, Fiscal 2015

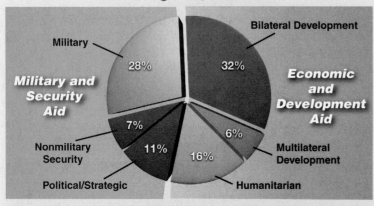

Aid Programs and Amount Allocated in Fiscal 2015

Bilateral development: $15.8 billion. Funds programs promoting poverty reduction, sustainable agriculture, anti-HIV/AIDS efforts, private-sector development and good governance; funds the Peace Corps, Millennium Challenge Corp. and USAID operations.

Multilateral development: $2.8 billion. Funds U.S. share of UNICEF, U.N. Development Fund, World Bank and other multilateral development banks.

Humanitarian assistance: $7.6 billion. Provides disaster assistance and food aid; supports U.N. High Commissioner for Refugees and International Red Cross.

Political/Strategic: $5.4 billion. Promotes economic, political and security interests, particularly in countries important to U.S. counter-terrorism strategy. A significant portion — 27 percent — supports Egypt, the West Bank and Jordan as part of the 1979 Middle East peace agreement known as the Camp David Accords.

Nonmilitary security: $3 billion. Supports efforts to counter illicit drugs, crime and weapons proliferation and to detect and dismantle terrorist financial networks.

Military: $13.5 billion. Provides military equipment, training and weapons to U.S. allies, primarily Israel, Egypt, Jordan, Pakistan and Iraq.

Source: Curt Tarnoff and Marian L. Lawson, "Foreign Aid: An Introduction to U.S. Programs and Policy," Congressional Research Service, June 17, 2016, p. 6, http://tinyurl.com/nymlqwz

"Foreign aid has long been notorious for breeding kleptocracies — governments of thieves," libertarian commentator James Bovard wrote in 2016.[4]

Foreign assistance has always stirred controversy far greater than its share of the federal budget. Americans typically think aid consumes "somewhere between one-fourth and one-third" of the budget, says Lindsay Koshgarian, research director at the National Priorities Project, a nonpartisan research group in Northampton, Mass., that focuses on the federal budget. In fact, the $48.1 billion spent on aid in fiscal 2015 amounted to about 1.3 percent of the $3.7 trillion federal budget, according to the latest available data.[5]

Just over half of that aid went to anti-poverty and humanitarian programs, and nearly half was in the form of military and security-related assistance, much of it going to countries cooperating in the fight against terrorism.[6]

Despite the minuscule portion of the federal budget consumed by foreign aid, fiscal hawks question whether it is wasted on inefficient programs. Meanwhile, some humanitarian-aid advocates worry about aid falling into the hands of dictators who use it to suppress their own people. And "America First" proponents such as Trump argue that domestic needs should take priority over causes in remote corners of the globe.

Sen. Rand Paul, R-Ky., is on the side of cuts. In 2015 he called for taking a "meat ax to foreign aid, because I think we ought to quit sending it to countries that hate us," Paul said in 2015.[7]

Development aid "for the most part is a waste," echoes Doug Bandow, a senior fellow at the Cato Institute, a libertarian think tank in Washington. "I don't think that economic development aid produces economic growth in poor countries."

However, aid proponents say bipartisan reforms enacted by Congress in the Foreign Aid Transparency and Accountability Act of 2016 have improved how aid projects are evaluated. "There's a great deal of confidence in USAID on the Republican side of the aisle as well as the Democratic side now," says J. Brian Atwood, administrator of USAID during the Clinton administration and now professor emeritus at the Humphrey School of Public Affairs at the University of Minnesota.

Nevertheless, even some aid advocates agree a certain amount of assistance is wasted because of inefficiencies or corruption. "In some severe cases of systemic corruption, we have seen substantial portions of country budgets lost to waste, fraud and abuse, stalling and, in some cases, halting development progress altogether," USAID Administrator Gayle E. Smith told the Senate Foreign Relations Committee last June.[8] The solution, she said, is to support local watchdog groups that can hold governments, businesses and citizens accountable by monitoring public spending.

Indeed, according to a 2016 report by the Special Inspector General for Afghanistan Reconstruction, an independent office created by Congress, much of the more than $100 billion in aid provided to Afghanistan after the U.S. invasion of that country in 2001 was "subverted by systemic corruption [which] cut across all aspects of the reconstruction effort, jeopardizing progress made in security, rule of law, governance, and economic growth."[9]

John Sopko, the new agency's inspector general, blamed the flood of foreign assistance since 2001, inadequate oversight and "unsavory" partners for creating "endemic corruption" that posed an "existential threat" to the country.[10]

Both critics and advocates of foreign assistance also say the U.S. aid bureaucracy — with programs scattered across two dozen agencies — could be more efficient, with some suggesting consolidating all aid programs into fewer agencies, and others wanting to see more aid programs privatized.

"You want to have a unified approach to a country or region and not have the sorts of stove-piping and Balkanization that you might have with these independent power bases within the U.S. government," says James M. Roberts, a research fellow at the Heritage Foundation, a conservative think tank in Washington.

In an earlier effort to fight corruption and make foreign aid more efficient, Republican President George W. Bush in 2004 created an independent agency — the Millennium Challenge Corp. (MCC) — to deliver development aid only to countries that meet stringent economic, political and social standards. That agency has produced mixed results.

Other recent attempts to modernize and reform U.S. aid programs have been insufficient, says Roberts. "We are urging a complete top-down review of all forms of U.S. development assistance," as well as "a frank conversation" about priorities, he says.

Historically, national security has been a major objective of U.S. foreign aid. By supporting economic development in poor countries that might become targets — or breeding grounds — of terrorists, aid agencies "are critical to preventing conflict and reducing the need to put our men and women in uniform in harm's way," according to 121 retired three- and four-star flag and general officers who wrote to Congress protesting Trump's proposed foreign aid cuts.[11]

U.S. military aid since the Sept. 11, 2001, terrorist attacks has gone mostly to allies in the fight against Islamic extremism, such as Jordan, Pakistan and Afghanistan. Israel received the most military assistance in fiscal 2014 ($3.1 billion) and Egypt the second-largest amount ($1.3 billion), but those countries historically have received the bulk of U.S. military aid as a result of the Middle East peace settlement of 1978 known as the Camp David Accords.[12]

Providing aid to countries accused of suppressing human rights, such as Egypt, presents a moral dilemma for donors. Indeed, human rights advocates were dismayed when Trump welcomed Egyptian President Abdel Fattah el-Sissi to the White House on April 3 and reportedly promised to "maintain a strong and sufficient level of support to Egypt."[13] In 2013, the Obama administration suspended its $1.3 billion aid package after the Egyptian military ousted democratically elected

Top Aid Recipients: Israel, Egypt, Afghanistan

Israel received the most U.S. foreign aid, all of it in the form of weapons and military training, in fiscal 2015, according to the latest available data. Egypt, the second-largest aid recipient, received mostly military assistance. Afghanistan received the most economic and development aid.

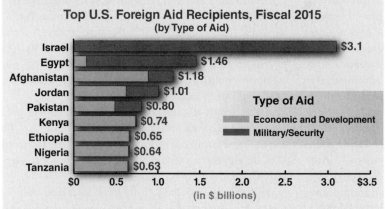

Top U.S. Foreign Aid Recipients, Fiscal 2015
(by Type of Aid)

Israel	$3.1
Egypt	$1.46
Afghanistan	$1.18
Jordan	$1.01
Pakistan	$0.80
Kenya	$0.74
Ethiopia	$0.65
Nigeria	$0.64
Tanzania	$0.63

Type of Aid
■ Economic and Development
■ Military/Security

(in $ billions)

Source: "Congressional Budget Justification: Foreign Assistance," U.S. Department of State, Fiscal Year 2017, pp. 7-10, http://tinyurl.com/knrn6a2

President Mohamed Morsi and the Sissi-led government cracked down on domestic opponents and jailed dozens of Americans who were working at charities in Egypt.[14]

"Inviting [Sissi] for an official visit to Washington as tens of thousands of Egyptians rot in jail and when torture is again the order of the day is a strange way to build a stable strategic relationship," said Sarah Margon, Washington director at Human Rights Watch.[15]

To gain support for foreign aid, proponents have long argued that aid helps expand markets for U.S. exports by improving receiving countries' economies so they can eventually buy U.S. products. In addition, some American aid is required to be in the form of U.S. products and services.

Trump's proposed budget cuts have given new urgency to a longstanding debate about whether attaching such conditions to U.S. aid is wise. For instance, while a requirement that 50 percent of U.S. food aid be shipped on U.S.-flagged vessels supports the maritime industry, aid advocates say using such vessels is often costly and inefficient.

Others warn that tightening restrictions on aid may push recipients into closer relations with less-demanding donors, including economic rivals such as China. The Chinese, who generally do not require aid recipients to respect human rights or adopt free-market policies, have increased aid to Africa in recent years.

The renewed debate about the appropriate size and nature of U.S. foreign aid is playing out as more than 20 million people in Yemen and three other countries in Africa — South Sudan, Somalia and Nigeria — face starvation and famine. "We are facing the largest humanitarian crisis since the creation of the United Nations," Stephen O'Brien, the U.N.'s top official for humanitarian affairs, said in early March.[16] Others warn that in coming decades, as climate change begins to cause drought, floods and other damaging conditions, struggling countries' needs will increase even more.

As policy makers and politicians consider U.S. foreign aid policies, here are some of the questions they are asking:

Should the United States increase its economic aid to other countries?

The more than $30 billion in nonmilitary, or economic, aid contributed by the United States in 2015 was far more in total dollars than any other country donated.[17] But when viewed as a percentage of overall national wealth — or gross national income (GNI) — the United States ranks 24th among the world's industrialized countries.

By donating less than 0.2 percent of its GNI in economic aid in 2015, the United States ranked far below the 0.7 percent goal set for wealthy countries by the United Nations in 1970.[18] In 2005, 15 of the 28 European Union countries committed to reaching that goal by 2015, and six succeeded: Luxembourg, Denmark, Norway, the Netherlands, the United Kingdom and Sweden, which donated the highest percentage (1.4 percent).[19] The United States never agreed to the 0.7 percent target but has said that while it did not subscribe to specific targets or timetables, it supported the general aims of the U.N. goal.[20]

"The U.S. does not invest enough in foreign assistance programs that help people living in extreme poverty around the world become self-sufficient," Inter-Action, an alliance of U.S.-based nongovernmental development organizations, said. "This approach is short-sighted and does not reflect American values."[21]

However, some critics of foreign aid argue that the United States should actually reduce — or even eliminate — its government-to-government development aid, which they say often does not generate economic growth and can hinder local development. "The best solution that I can offer is to move away from the government-to-government transfer model," says Ryan Young, a fellow at the Competitive Enterprise Institute, a free-market think tank in Washington. Young argues that free markets are better at generating economic growth than government-run programs.

Subsidizing governments may discourage them from adopting needed economic reforms, says the Cato Institute's Bandow. Instead of aid, "They need good policies, they need open markets."

Nobel Prize-winning British economist Angus Deaton argued in a 2013 book that development aid

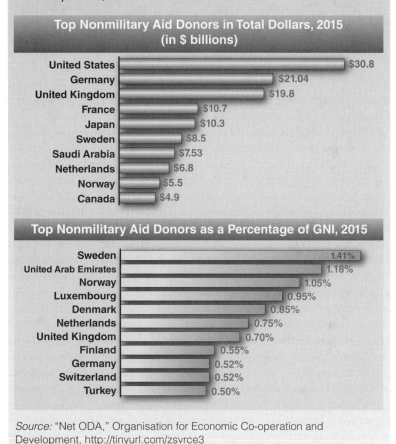

U.S. Ranks 24th in Aid as Share of Wealth

The United States provided $30.8 billion in nonmilitary foreign aid in 2015, more than any other country. But it ranked 24th in the percentage of national wealth, or gross national income (GNI), allocated for such aid. Top-ranked Sweden donated 1.4 percent of its GNI and was among seven industrialized countries that reached the U.N. goal of donating at least 0.7 percent of GNI. The U.S. spent less than 0.2 percent, its lowest level since 2007.

Top Nonmilitary Aid Donors in Total Dollars, 2015 (in $ billions)

Country	$ billions
United States	$30.8
Germany	$21.04
United Kingdom	$19.8
France	$10.7
Japan	$10.3
Sweden	$8.5
Saudi Arabia	$7.53
Netherlands	$6.8
Norway	$5.5
Canada	$4.9

Top Nonmilitary Aid Donors as a Percentage of GNI, 2015

Country	Percentage
Sweden	1.41%
United Arab Emirates	1.18%
Norway	1.05%
Luxembourg	0.95%
Denmark	0.85%
Netherlands	0.75%
United Kingdom	0.70%
Finland	0.55%
Germany	0.52%
Switzerland	0.52%
Turkey	0.50%

Source: "Net ODA," Organisation for Economic Co-operation and Development, http://tinyurl.com/zsvrce3

works only where it isn't needed. If a country already has the elements needed for development to occur, such as basic infrastructure, financial institutions and effective government, then aid isn't needed because capital will be available from taxes or investors, he wrote. But when poverty is the result of "poor institutions, poor government and toxic politics, giving money to poor countries — particularly giving money to the governments of

poor countries — is likely to perpetuate [poverty], not eliminate it," wrote Deaton.[22]

He cited studies showing that when foreign aid to Africa reached its highest point during the Cold War, the economies of recipient countries grew more slowly than before or after the Cold War, when aid dropped. "Growth decreased steadily while aid increased steadily," Deaton wrote. "When aid fell off after the end of the Cold War, growth picked up."[23] The Cold War competition between the United States and the Soviet Union for global influence resulted in massive injections of foreign aid in some regions, especially in Africa and Latin America.

Others, however, say Deaton's arguments are outdated. According to Alex Thier, executive director of the Overseas Development Institute, an anti-poverty think tank in London, aid agencies have invested heavily in recent years in monitoring and evaluating development programs so that now "we actually see what works." Those new tools, he says, are "helping all of us to make sure that we are spending all of these resources better and more effectively."

Green, who worked at USAID for 11 years before joining CSIS, says Deaton's argument is "decades-old and doesn't reflect the sophistication in the science and the norms in the development community these days." While some development projects occasionally may be ineffective or even cause harm, she says, they are not the norm. "USAID and the other major bilateral donors are much more sophisticated, and [perform] an array of analyses to make sure that the project they're going to do will be beneficial in that environment," she says.

A 2016 report by the Congressional Research Service (CRS), the nonpartisan research arm of Congress, found that aid agencies have taken steps in recent years "to improve both the quantity and quality of aid evaluations, and to make better use of the information gleaned from those efforts." However, CRS said, determining the success or failure of previous aid programs "is not entirely clear," in part, because most aid programs in the past were not "evaluated for the purpose of determining their actual impact."[24]

USAID's Smith told Congress that instead of cutting or eliminating aid, the United States could better fight corruption by holding "governments, corporations, organizations and individuals to account through enforcement measures and by other means."[25]

Reducing foreign aid, some contend, also reduces America's economic influence in emerging markets, where other countries, such as China, are investing heavily in infrastructure and other development projects, especially in Africa.

According to Junyi Zhang, a U.S.-China policy exchange fellow at the Brookings Institution think tank in Washington, since launching a "Go Global" strategy of aid to developing countries in 2005, especially those with natural resources critical to China's economy, "China has deepened its financial engagement with the world, and its foreign aid totals have grown at an average rate of 21.8 percent annually."[26]

Does the United States attach too many conditions to its foreign aid?

Three days after his inauguration, President Trump reinstated a prohibition, instituted in 1984 during the administration of Republican Ronald Reagan, on U.S. foreign aid to groups that provide abortions or even discuss them as an option in family planning.[27]

U.S. foreign aid comes with many such conditions. Some ban aid to countries that violate human rights or require recipient countries to enact specific financial or business regulatory reforms. Other conditions, particularly in bilateral aid programs, require that food or other aid be provided by American companies or shipped on U.S.-flag vessels.

The anti-abortion condition is among the most controversial. It has been repeatedly rescinded by Democratic presidents and then reinstated by Republican presidents.

Human rights conditions, first imposed on U.S. aid by the 1961 Foreign Assistance Act, prohibit foreign aid to "the government of any country which engages in a consistent pattern of gross violations of internationally recognized human rights."[28]

But the law allows exceptions for "emergency conditions" and when compliance "would be seriously detrimental to the foreign policy interests of the United States."[29] Some critics have argued that since the Sept. 11, 2001, terrorist attacks on New York City and the Pentagon, the U.S. government has often exempted authoritarian countries, such as Egypt, from the human rights requirement because they cooperate in the U.S. fight against terrorism.

Some experts see little evidence that human rights conditions accomplish anything and argue that aid should be given where it is needed regardless of a government's human rights record. CSIS's Green, for instance, does not think humanitarian or "lifesaving health assistance should be conditioned," but that the United States "should do a better job leveraging assistance" to get recipient governments to honor human rights.

University of Chicago law professor Eric Posner has argued that Western human rights norms are the exception rather than the rule in many developing countries.

He wrote that there is no reason to believe "institutionally enforced human rights . . . [are] appropriate for poor countries with different traditions and facing a range of challenges that belong, in the view of Western countries, to the distant past." Developed countries should provide aid, he wrote, "with the understanding that helping other countries is not the same as forcing them to adopt Western institutions, modes of governance, dispute-resolution systems and rights."[30]

Others warn that taking too strong a stance on human rights could make countries more inclined to seek aid from China, which generally does not impose human rights requirements on aid. However, China does tie its aid to the use of Chinese products and services, experts say, even to a much greater extent than the United States does.

"Chinese [aid] projects create access to Africa's natural resources and local markets, business opportunities for Chinese companies and employment for Chinese laborers," wrote Yun Sun, a fellow at the Brookings Institution.[31]

Ironically, when countries turn to China for aid to avoid U.S. demands on human rights, it can worsen conditions for citizens in those countries, because of "China's tendency to facilitate authoritarianism and corruption," according to Zhang, at Brookings.[32]

Also controversial are the requirements that some U.S. aid be tied to the use of U.S. food and other products and services. Such conditions are designed to boost domestic support for foreign aid, experts say. They usually involve food aid and include requirements that:

- All agricultural commodities come from the United States.
- At least 75 percent of nonemergency in-kind food aid be in processed, fortified or bagged form.
- At least 50 percent of food aid be shipped on U.S.-flag vessels.[33]

The Heritage Foundation's Roberts opposes requiring aid to be shipped on U.S. vessels. "If that sort of conditionality were eliminated, you could deliver a lot more food because you wouldn't waste so much money on logistics," he says.

But the U.S. maritime industry defends the so-called cargo preference requirement. "The government has said that cargo preference is key to maintaining and supporting

Protesters in Washington denounce Egyptian President Abdel Fattah el-Sissi during his meeting with President Trump at the White House on April 3, 2017. Human-rights advocates criticized Trump's decision to continue providing more than $1 billion in mostly military aid to Egypt, which has been accused of suppressing human rights and is the second-largest recipient of U.S. aid. In 2013, the Obama administration temporarily suspended Egypt's aid package after the military ousted democratically elected President Mohamed Morsi and the Sissi-led government cracked down on domestic opponents.

the U.S. Merchant Marine," which provides sealift capability to the government during wartime and other emergencies, says Bryant Gardner, spokesman and counsel for Liberty Maritime Corp., a U.S. shipping company. Previous cuts in cargo preference requirements have led to a dangerous 26 percent decline in the merchant fleet since 2012, according to Gardner.

According to a 2010 study commissioned by USA Maritime, a coalition of cargo carriers, requirements that food aid be grown in the United States and that half must be shipped on U.S. carriers add approximately $2 billion a year to the U.S. economy. Dropping those requirements, according to the study, would cost between 16,000 and 33,000 U.S. jobs in agriculture and shipping.[34]

But two analysts at the American Enterprise Institute (AEI) think tank say vessels used to ship most food aid are too old and slow to be considered critical to the Defense Department. "Over the past five years," AEI researcher Ryan Nabil and visiting scholar Vincent H. Smith, wrote in 2016, "more than 80 percent of U.S. food aid carried under cargo preference has been shipped on vessels that the Department of Defense considers inappropriate for military purposes."[35]

Others say such preference conditions should be eliminated, or at least reduced, in favor of sending money to buy commodities locally, which USAID Administrator Smith says saves time and lives.[36]

"New research suggests that cash grants to the poor are as good as or better than many traditional forms of aid when it comes to reducing poverty," wrote Christopher Blattman, an assistant professor of international affairs at Columbia University, and Paul Niehaus, assistant professor of economics at the University of California, San Diego. Given the growing ease of transferring cash via cellphones, they wrote, donors should view cash payments as "one of the most sensible tools of poverty alleviation."[37]

The tradeoff, some say, is between efficient delivery of aid and maintaining political support at home for foreign aid.

"It's really tricky, because those domestic requirements are the things that garner bipartisan support," says Green. "If you drop them, there's a real possibility that there would be less and less support domestically for international development, and it's already pretty low, to be honest. It's just one of those political trade-offs to maintain bipartisan domestic support."

Are public-private aid partnerships more effective than government-run projects?

U.S. aid agencies increasingly have been partnering with for-profit companies.

"In the late 1990s, we began to more proactively engage the private sector as true partners," Eric G. Postel, associate administrator at USAID, told senators at a hearing in July 2016. "This was an important shift."[38]

Under the Global Development Alliances program, established in 2001 to promote public-private partnerships, he said, the agency began to rely less on traditional client-vendor arrangements, with USAID consultants and contractors designing and implementing projects. Today, private companies increasingly design, manage and fund development projects.

"Today, as we partner more, we are focusing on those instances where business interests and development objectives align," Postel said. "When they don't align, we should not and do not pursue partnerships. And, as

always, all of our partnerships adhere to all of the safeguards we have in place to protect against misuse of funds and other challenges."[39]

Over the past 15 years, USAID has created more than 1,500 partnership projects involving more than 3,500 private-sector partners, according to Postel. The projects have ranged from the ongoing Advanced Maize Seed Adoption Program in Ethiopia, with a division of DuPont as the partner, to a garment-worker safety program in which two Bangladeshi banks are partnering with the Alliance for Bangladesh Worker Safety, an advocacy group.[40]

Another example, he said: USAID's Power Africa program, aimed at doubling access to electricity in sub-Saharan Africa, has received $7 billion in funds from the U.S. government and $31 billion from private-sector partners.[41]

Some experts agree public-private aid partnerships, which represent a growing part of U.S. foreign assistance, can effectively leverage funding and expertise for development projects. Public-private partnerships, however, give some analysts pause. Thier, of the Overseas Development Institute, sees the advantages of public-private partnerships, but he worries they may sometimes result in the realignment of aid programs in ways that benefit the partnering companies more than the recipients. Such partnerships may pull agencies toward projects that are "the cream of the crop," where the companies see the potential for profits. "What you really need to do is to make sure that your program is targeted toward the people that our aid dollars are intended to help, the poorest of the poor," Thier says. The goal of development, he adds, "is not just to get deals done and to bring in the private sector."

So far, he says, USAID partnerships have appeared to be crafted to minimize such concerns.

According to the Congressional Research Service, the public-private partnership model pioneered by USAID and adopted by the State Department and the Millennium Challenge Corp., the independent aid agency created at the behest of President Bush, involves other risks. Most partnerships require more time and effort to design and implement than traditional contract-based programs and it is "difficult to judge whether this effort is justified by development impact," CRS said.[42]

In addition, it said, U.S. agencies could be damaged if they partner with disreputable private-sector entities. "Some development professionals are uneasy, for example, about USAID partnering with mining and oil companies in Angola, the Democratic Republic of the Congo and Ghana because of the corruption and exploitation often associated with these industries," according to CRS. It also warned that some public-private partnerships could support the outsourcing of American jobs to developing countries.[43]

However, others say partnerships could help steer aid to needy countries that are not particularly important in the fight against terrorism. Official development aid "tends to be skewed towards big strategic partners, . . . who aren't necessarily among the least developed countries, and [to] basket-case countries on the other," says CSIS's Green. Other countries get left out, she says. "That's where I think the private sector can help fill the gap."

But like Thier, Green warns that using public-private partnerships requires tight oversight. "So long as there really is a shared goal and there is a commitment to advancing that shared goal, they can be terrific," she says. "But you have to be careful."

BACKGROUND

Ancient Aid

Nations have employed foreign aid — in the form of economic subsidies, technical assistance and humanitarian aid — as a tool of diplomacy for more than 2,000 years.

As early as 336 B.C., Alexander the Great offered Egypt technical advisers to help build the port city of Alexandria. And the earliest recorded instance of humanitarian assistance took place when nations around the Mediterranean Sea in 226 B.C. sent food and other aid to the earthquake-devastated island of Rhodes.[44]

It wasn't until the mid-19th century, however, during the age of European imperialism, that some nations began systematically offering development aid to encourage economic growth in other countries, typically colonies of the donor countries. Colonial powers such as Britain, France, Belgium, Holland and Germany provided grants and discounted loans to their colonies, protectorates and dependencies to expand infrastructure,

Greek children receive food made from flour distributed after World War II. Postwar concerns about the political stability of war-devastated countries in Europe, along with the threat of an increasingly aggressive Soviet Union, led the United States in 1947 to create the European Recovery Program. Better known as the Marshall Plan, it pumped $12.5 billion into Western Europe and helped put the continent on the road to recovery.

develop health services and fund education, according to Louis A. Picard, a professor of public and international affairs at the University of Pittsburgh, and Terry F. Buss, a professor of public policy at Carnegie Mellon University in Pittsburgh.

In the late 1800s, the United States and other Western countries competed to provide technical advisers to developing countries, especially in Asia. The technical advisers were sent abroad, Picard and Buss wrote, "as much to promote the donor country's products and equipment or its strategic interests as it was to provide assistance."[45]

Apart from technical support, U.S. aid efforts before the 1930s primarily were focused on humanitarian relief. During World War I, the United States contributed $387 million to the Commission for Relief in Belgium, founded by future President Herbert Hoover.[46] In 1917, as the United States entered the war, Hoover was appointed director of the U.S. Food Administration, an agency tasked with providing food for the U.S. Army and allies in Europe. In 1919, Congress created the American Relief Administration, also directed by Hoover, to coordinate the delivery of relief supplies to war-torn Europe.[47]

Federal humanitarian aid efforts in this period were supplemented — and in some cases dwarfed — by aid from private foundations, notably the Ford, Rockefeller and Carnegie foundations, and from religious organizations, such as the American Friends Service Committee.

Partly to deter growing Nazi influence in the Western Hemisphere, the United States began to offer development aid in the 1930s, primarily to Latin American countries.[48]

Marshall Plan

Foreign aid became a consistent, ongoing element of U.S. foreign policy beginning with the Lend-Lease Act of 1941, which provided military and other aid to cash-strapped Britain as it struggled to fend off German aggression at the start of World War II. With the British unable to pay for ships and supplies, the United States "lent" them the matériel under the Lend-Lease Act.

It was understood, according to a State Department historian, that eventual repayment would not be in dollars but "would primarily take the form of a 'consideration' granted by Britain to the United States." After many months of negotiation, the two countries agreed that this consideration "would primarily consist of joint action directed towards the creation of a liberalized international economic order in the postwar world."[49] Eventually, Lend-Lease was extended to other allies, including Free France, China and the Soviet Union.

After the war, concerns about the political stability of war-devastated countries in Europe, along with the threat of an increasingly aggressive Soviet Union, led the United States in 1947 to create the European Recovery Program, also known as the Marshall Plan. Named after Secretary of State and former chairman of the Joint Chiefs Gen. George C. Marshall, the plan pumped $12.5 billion into Western Europe to help rebuild the economy and was at that time by far the largest development aid package ever undertaken by the United States.[50]

As the Cold War got underway between the communist Soviet Union and the democracies of the West, the administration of Democratic President Harry S. Truman saw foreign assistance as a tool. "It must be the policy of the United States to support free people who are resisting attempted subjugation by armed minorities or by outside pressures," Truman told Congress on March 12, 1947, when he announced a policy of Soviet "containment" that came to be known as the Truman Doctrine. "I believe that our help should be primarily through economic and financial aid, which is essential to economic stability and orderly political processes."[51]

Meanwhile, at Truman's request Congress provided $400 million in aid for Greece and Turkey, countries with significant domestic unrest attributed in part to communist political parties.

During the Cold War, wrote Picard and Buss, foreign aid was "at least nominally premised on the thesis that economic and social development, and democratic government, [were] essential to national security."[52]

On Nov. 3, 1961, at the height of the Cold War, Democratic President John F. Kennedy signed the Foreign Assistance Act, which created an array of programs and long-term goals aimed at the economic, political and social development of underdeveloped countries. "The Congress declares that the individual liberties, economic prosperity, and security of the people of the United States are best sustained and enhanced in a community of nations which respect individual civil and economic rights and freedoms," the legislation said.[53]

The law also created the U.S. Agency for International Development to oversee most of the country's bilateral development and humanitarian aid programs.

However, during the Vietnam War, some policymakers grew concerned that military priorities were skewing aid priorities.[54] In 1965, approximately 90 percent of USAID's aid budget went to military forces and intelligence services in Vietnam and only a fraction went to Vietnam's industrial or agricultural development.[55]

In December 1962, Kennedy appointed Gen. Lucius D. Clay to lead a committee to assess the effectiveness of U.S. foreign aid programs. The so-called Clay report raised crucial questions about the effectiveness of foreign aid, leading to increased focus on market economics, wrote Picard and Buss. To some observers, the report also created frustration about foreign aid that would later be dubbed "donor fatigue," they added.[56]

Frustrations with aid programs and concerns over the mounting costs of the Vietnam War made Congress increasingly reluctant to fund aid programs. In 1971, U.S. development aid dropped below $3 billion for the first time since passage of the Foreign Assistance Act in 1961.

CHRONOLOGY

1850–1930s *Foreign aid takes root in the West.*

1850 European colonial powers, including Britain, France, Belgium, Holland and Germany, begin to provide financial assistance to their colonies, protectorates and dependencies.

1914-1919 The United States contributes $387 million to the Commission for Relief in Belgium, an aid organization founded by future U.S. president Herbert Hoover to help Belgium and northern France during World War I. After America enters the war, Hoover directs the U.S. Food Administration, which provides food to the U.S. Army and allies in Europe. . . . After the war, Congress creates American Relief Administration, also directed by Hoover, to coordinate the delivery of aid to war-torn Europe.

1930 U.S. begins offering development aid, primarily to Latin American countries, to deter growing Nazi influence in the Western Hemisphere.

1941–1960s *United States uses aid to counter Nazi and, later, Soviet influence.*

1941 Under the Lend-Lease Act, a still-neutral United States "lends" military and other supplies to the British during World War II, a program later extended to Free France, China and the Soviet Union.

1947 Concerned about postwar stability in Europe, the United States pumps $12.5 billion into the Western European economy under the Marshall Plan. . . . As part of the Truman Doctrine — an effort to curtail Soviet geopolitical expansion — Congress approves $400 million in aid for Greece and Turkey.

1961 President John F. Kennedy signs the Foreign Assistance Act, which aims to help further economic, political and social development in underdeveloped countries and creates the U.S. Agency for International Development (USAID) to disburse most U.S. aid.

1980s–1990s *U.S. aid focuses on helping developing countries restructure their economies to be more market-oriented.*

1981 President Ronald Reagan announces the Private Enterprise Initiative, an aid program that aims to boost private enterprise in developing countries.

1984 Reagan administration halts aid to overseas health providers who discuss or provide abortions as an option in family planning, a controversial condition that will be attached to U.S. aid — or rescinded — by successive administrations.

1993 President Bill Clinton rescinds Reagan ban on aid for abortion providers and counselors.

1997 The Clinton administration responds to congressional calls to restructure or abolish USAID by requiring the agency's director to report to the secretary of State.

2001–Present *Foreign aid after 9/11 focuses on countries helping to fight the war on terrorism.*

2001 President George W. Bush reverses Clinton aid abortion policy. . . . U.S. government increases foreign aid in the aftermath of the Sept. 11 terrorist attacks. Aid to Afghanistan and Pakistan, in particular, soars from $70 million and $45.7 million annually, respectively, to $4.7 billion and $1.9 billion by 2010.

2004 Congress creates the Millennium Challenge Corp., an independent aid agency that awards grants to developing countries that meet economic and political criteria.

2005 The Bush administration begins a series of foreign aid reforms; USAID is required to improve staff training and institute annual evaluations for aid programs.

2006 Secretary of State Condoleezza Rice creates Office of Foreign Assistance Resources within the State Department.

2016 Congress passes the Foreign Aid Transparency and Accountability Act of 2016, which requires stronger monitoring and reporting of foreign aid effectiveness.

2017 President Trump's administration announces plans to cut USAID's budget by nearly 30 percent.

Millennium Challenge Corp. Pushes Countries to Reform

Agency "only works in a fairly narrow range of countries," critics say.

Its admirers call it "the MCC effect" — how the Millennium Challenge Corp. (MCC), a federal agency that distributes anti-poverty aid, pushes recipient countries to govern themselves responsibly and transparently.

On its first bid for aid, Cote d'Ivoire passed only three of 20 MCC "scorecard indicators," or political, economic and social benchmarks showing that a country is committed to "just and democratic governance, investments in its people and economic freedom."[1] But five years later, the West African nation received an MCC grant after meeting 13 indicators.

"MCC's scorecard and global brand have created a powerful incentive for countries to undertake reforms to achieve eligibility," Dana J. Hyde, then MCC's chief executive officer, told Congress in March 2016.[2]

But critics say the agency is underfunded and limited in scope. "MCC only works in a fairly narrow range of countries," says Steven Koltai, former State Department entrepreneurship director, and most of those are not, from a foreign policy standpoint, where U.S. aid can have the most impact.

The MCC has signed 33 compacts with 27 countries, most of them in Africa, worth more than $11 billion, according to Laura M. Allen, press secretary for the MCC Office of Congressional and Public Affairs. Recipient countries must be classified as low income or lower middle income by the World Bank. In fiscal 2017, a country's per capita gross national income must be below $4,035, according to Allen.

Created by Congress in 2004 at the urging of President George W. Bush, the MCC emerged from post-9/11 concerns about terrorist groups forming in Africa. In 2002, Bush announced he wanted to increase U.S. foreign aid by 15 percent a year, with much of the increase directed to Africa. Republican lawmakers, however, worried that corrupt African governments would swallow up much of the money.[3]

Bush responded by creating the MCC, an independent entity operating separate from the traditional foreign aid community, which established a set of "good governance" criteria that countries would have to meet before they would get any grants. "Money will now be given to countries that have shown a willingness to establish an environment where foreign aid will be most effective," Joshua Bolten, director of the Office of Management and Budget under Bush, said at the time.[4]

Governed by a board that includes the secretaries of State and Treasury, the U.S. Trade Representative and the administrator of the U.S. Agency for International Development (USAID), the MCC offers two types of grants: large, five-year grants, called compacts, for countries that meet the MCC's eligibility benchmarks; and smaller grants for countries on the threshold of meeting those criteria.

Besides meeting MCC's eligibility requirements, countries must establish priorities for achieving sustainable economic growth and poverty reduction.[5] Moreover, recipients must demonstrate "rigorous and transparent" monitoring of funds. "Many countries view their ability to perform well on MCC's scorecard as a seal of approval, signaling to their citizens and to the private sector that the country is well-governed and open for business," says Allen.

Still, the MCC has struggled with lower-than-expected funding and questions about its effectiveness.

At its founding, the MCC was expected within a few years to be funded at $5 billion annually, according to the Congressional Research Service (CRS), the nonpartisan research arm of Congress. "For a variety of reasons, not least of which is the limitation on available funding for foreign aid more broadly, the MCC never achieved anywhere near that level of funding," the CRS said. "In fact, in most years since the MCC was established, its enacted appropriation has been below the president's request."

Only $901 million was appropriated in 2016; $1 billion was requested for 2017.[6]

CRS said questions had been raised about the sustainability of some MCC projects. In the West African island nation of Cape Verde, a road project reportedly met only half of its requirements for maintenance funds, and Honduras did not increase its national road maintenance funds sufficiently, CRS said.

The lure of MCC funding apparently was not enough to bring Sierra Leone and Benin in conformance with the agency's anti-corruption requirements. The MCC dropped both countries from consideration for grants in 2013 for failing to satisfy the "control of corruption" indicator.[7]

James Roberts, research fellow at the conservative Heritage Foundation think tank, originally supported the MCC, arguing in 2009 that the federal government should shift aid funds from USAID to the agency.[8] "We were enthusiastic in the beginning," he says, especially because of its anti-corruption standards. "It forced country ownership, country accountability."

But as the MCC has evolved, "it kind of went the way of all flesh," he says. "You ended up with a lot of bureaucrats running it and . . . during the Obama years it kind of morphed into a mini-USAID. That was not what conservative thinkers behind it had in mind."

Alicia Phillips Mandaville, vice president for global development policy and learning at InterAction, an association of U.S.-based nongovernmental aid organizations, disagrees with Roberts' assessment. The MCC model has been and continues to be very effective, she says.

"Countries come in and look at that scorecard and talk with MCC about whether they've met those criteria or not," says Mandaville, a former MCC chief strategy officer. "A number of countries really put in serious policy reforms in an effort to become eligible to work with MCC." In fact, Benin, one of the countries turned away by the MCC in 2013, did subsequently institute reforms that resulted in the MCC awarding a compact to Benin in 2015 with the signing of a $375 million grant to develop its energy sector.

— *Patrick Marshall*

AFP/Getty Images/Saul Loeb

Jordanian Foreign Minister Nasser Judeh meets with then Secretary of State Hillary Clinton during a signing ceremony for an agreement to fund an anti-poverty program in Jordan through a Millennium Development Corp. grant.

[1] "Who We Fund," Millennium Challenge Corp., http://tinyurl.com/ly9vd4w.

[2] "Testimony of Dana J. Hyde before the House Committee on Foreign Affairs," U.S. House of Representatives, March 15, 2016, http://tinyurl.com/mtp946g.

[3] Elizabeth Becker, "With Record Rise in Foreign Aid Comes Change in How It Is Monitored," *The New York Times*, Dec. 7, 2003, http://tinyurl.com/n2jjchj.

[4] Ibid.

[5] "About MCC," Millennium Challenge Corp., http://tinyurl.com/khrkdzs.

[6] Curt Tarnoff, "Millennium Challenge Corporation," Congressional Research Service, Jan. 11, 2017, p. 19, http://tinyurl.com/lfesl39; http://tinyurl.com/k4qxl53.

[7] "MCC Board Selects Countries Eligible for Compacts and Threshold Programs," press release, Millennium Challenge Corp., Dec. 10, 2013, http://tinyurl.com/myu5dog.

[8] James Roberts, "Foreign Aid: Congress Should Shift USAID Funds to the Millennium Challenge Account," The Heritage Foundation, Aug. 4, 2009, http://tinyurl.com/k3oad45.

Corrupt Governments Pose Donor Dilemma

"Cuts to aid disproportionately hurt people living in poverty."

From Nigeria to Syria and beyond, aid donors face an excruciating question: Is their aid helping or hurting people living under corrupt or repressive regimes?

One side argues foreign aid props up corrupt governments and ultimately harms those it is intended to help. Others say cutting off assistance disproportionately hurts those in need.

For instance, in the Syrian civil war, some observers say, the regime of strongman Bashar al Assad has forced aid agencies to choose the lesser of two evils: Don't give any aid, or give it to President Assad, who distributes it to civilians in "friendly" areas rather than to those in besieged rebel areas.

Between Jan. 1 and Aug. 31, 2015, U.N. humanitarian health assistance reached only about 4 percent of Syrian civilians in embattled areas each month, wrote physician and health activist Annie Sparrow, an assistant professor at the Icahn School of Medicine in New York City. The agencies were even less successful in getting food and other items — such as tents, blankets and soap — to those in need, she said. Because the Syrian government controls most aid coming into the country, she wrote, "the main effect is to relieve the government of responsibility for caring for its own citizens, freeing up resources for it to pursue its military strategy of targeting civilians in politically unsympathetic areas."[1]

Sparrow said aid agencies' rationale that any aid delivered through the Assad regime is better than none "has not been weighed against the human and financial cost of bolstering a regime that is deliberately increasing the hardship of people in opposition-held areas."[2]

David Saldivar, a policy and advocacy manager at Oxfam America, an international anti-poverty organization, says it is "a real challenge" to find a proper balance, but his organization comes down on the side of getting aid to those who are suffering. "You can make a morally defensible assessment that [this] is, on balance, doing good for those people versus harming them by propping up a government that's hostile to people's rights," he says.

Like Syria, Nigeria, a nation of about 190 million on Africa's west-central coast, poses great challenges for donors. "Corruption in Nigeria is endemic — from parents bribing teachers to get hold of exam papers for their children through clerks handed 'dash' money to get round the country's stifling bureaucracy to policemen taking money for turning a blind eye," wrote British historian Michael Burleigh. Since gaining independence in 1960, he said, Nigeria has received $400 billion in aid — "six times what the U.S. pumped into reconstructing the whole of Western Europe after World War II."[3]

Meanwhile, nearly the same amount — $380 billion — has been diverted by corruption, according to Burleigh.

The steadily dropping American aid in the 1960s and early '70s troubled many. Unless the United States substantially increased its contribution, its global aid efforts could fail, "triggering a confrontation with poor nations that could make the Cold War pale in comparison," *New York Times* reporter Felix Belair Jr. wrote in 1971.[57]

But the warning went unheeded, and U.S. development and humanitarian aid dropped further in the 1970s and '80s. USAID funding would not reach its 1965 level of $12.8 billion (in 2015 dollars) again until 2002.[58]

"Structural Adjustment"

In the 1980s, U.S.-led multilateral institutions such as the World Bank and International Monetary Fund pushed policies of "structural adjustment," or requiring aid recipients to adopt market-based economic reforms to enhance the role of private enterprise over that of local governments. The Reagan administration pursued similar policies in American bilateral aid.

The Private Enterprise Initiative, begun under Reagan in 1981, focused on improving the policy environment for private enterprise in developing countries. Beginning in 1989, the initiative established several enterprise funds, which invested USAID money in small and medium-sized private businesses, initially in Central and Eastern Europe. The goal, according to a CRS report, was to spur "private-sector development in countries transitioning toward market-based economies."[59]

"Given the appalling levels of corruption in that nation, this largesse is utterly sickening," he concluded. "Frankly, we might as well flush our cash away or burn it for all the good it's doing for ordinary Nigerians."[4]

Some analysts say critics are vastly exaggerating the amount of aid lost to corruption. According to a United Nations study, only 0.006 percent to 0.16 percent of six donors' aid money (given collectively) was lost to fraud or corruption in 2011.[5]

A 2015 Oxfam report said aid organizations can do several things to reduce losses to corruption, including "nurturing a country's domestic accountability system" and support local approaches that affect "the root causes of corruption."[6] The report also advised donors against automatically cutting off aid in response to corruption.

"There is no evidence that cutting off aid to a country with deteriorating governance conditions has any long-term effect on reducing corruption or increasing accountability," the report said. "Cuts to aid disproportionately hurt people living in poverty, who are already experiencing the brunt of the effects of corruption, while having little impact on the power or comfort of corrupt elites."[7]

— *Patrick Marshall*

A Syrian child wounded during an air strike is comforted at a Damascus-area hospital on April 4, 2017. The Syrian civil war has forced aid agencies to choose between not giving any aid or giving it to President Bashar al Assad, who distributes it in "friendly" areas rather than in besieged rebel areas.

[1] Annie Sparrow, "Aiding Disaster: How the United Nations' OCHA Helped Assad and Hurt Syrians in Need," *Foreign Affairs*, Feb. 1, 2016, http://tinyurl.com/lgssous.

[2] Ibid.

[3] Michael Burleigh, "A country so corrupt is would be better to burn our aid money," *The Daily Mail*, Aug. 8, 2013, http://tinyurl.com/nxfgz8v.

[4] Ibid.

[5] Paul Farmer, "Rethinking Foreign Aid: Five Ways to Improve Development Assistance," *Foreign Affairs*, Dec. 12, 2013, http://tinyurl.com/m6wuh4x. The six donors were Australia, Belgium, Denmark, the European Commission, the United Kingdom and the United States.

[6] Jennifer Lentfer, "4 new ways to think about foreign aid's role in fighting corruption around the world," Oxfam America, March 25, 2015, http://tinyurl.com/lfgpm2a.

[7] Ibid.

The kind of single-minded reliance on structural adjustment popular under the Reagan administration would be abandoned in the 1990s as an increasing number of studies showed that free-market policies were not effective under the conditions present in most developing countries.

Besides pursuing market-based economic reforms, the Reagan administration sought to enforce the values of its conservative and religious supporters. In 1984, the administration announced it would no longer provide aid to overseas groups that performed abortions or that counseled abortion as a method of birth control. The policy became a political football: Democratic President Bill Clinton reversed the policy in 1993;

Republican George W. Bush reinstated it in 2001; Democrat Barack Obama reversed it in 2009; and Republican Trump reinstated it in 2017 as one of the first acts of his presidency.[60]

In the 1990s, policymakers increasingly worried that aid was being poorly coordinated and lacked sufficient monitoring. "Many U.S. departments and agencies had adopted their own assistance programs, funded out of their own budgets and commonly in the form of professional exchanges with counterpart agencies abroad — the Environmental Protection Agency, for example, providing water quality expertise to other governments," wrote Congressional Research Service analysts Curt Tarnoff and Marian Lawson.[61]

USAID came under the most scrutiny. "Many observers believe that, for more than a decade, USAID neglected its evaluation processes and capacities," wrote Tarnoff. In 1995, in an attempt to better focus its monitoring and evaluation resources, the agency decided to permit senior managers to determine which programs needed more oversight, rather than requiring evaluations of all programs. According to Tarnoff, "While the intention was to eliminate pro-forma evaluations, it apparently did not have this effect."[62]

In April 1997 the Clinton administration responded to congressional calls to restructure or abolish USAID by requiring the agency director to report to the secretary of State, even though USAID would continue to remain an independent agency with its own appropriations.[63]

The terrorist attacks on the World Trade Center and the Pentagon on Sept. 11, 2001, were a turning point for U.S. foreign aid.[64] The United States immediately boosted aid to two countries considered hotspots in what the Bush administration was calling a war on terrorism: Afghanistan and Pakistan.

Economic aid to Pakistan soared from $45.7 million in 2001 to $1.9 billion in 2010.[65] Afghanistan's economic aid jumped from $70 million in 2000 to $4.7 billion in 2010.[66]

With such huge increases, the Bush administration undertook a series of foreign aid reforms, particularly at USAID. In 2005, the agency began an Initiative to Revitalize Evaluation, which included expanded staff training and requirements for annual evaluations.[67] A year later, Secretary of State Condoleezza Rice brought the agency more firmly under State Department control and made the director of USAID the director of foreign assistance within the State Department.

"The moves eased fears at USAID that the agency, set up in 1961 under President John F. Kennedy, would be merged into the State Department," wrote *The Washington Post*. "But it prompted other worries, . . . that USAID's strategic planning role might end up diminished and that the agency's corps of experienced foreign aid specialists might be superseded by Foreign Service officers."[68]

The Bush administration also undertook two programs that would have a lasting impact on foreign aid. In his 2003 State of the Union address, President Bush called for a five-year, $15 billion program to combat AIDS in 15 countries, 12 of which were in Africa. Called the President's Emergency Plan for AIDS Relief, or PEPFAR, the project remains the largest-ever global health initiative dedicated to a single disease.[69]

Also at Bush's request, Congress in 2004 created the Millennium Challenge Corp., an independent agency that provides aid only to countries that meet specified economic, political and social conditions. President Obama continued support for PEPFAR and the MCC.

Questions about the massive amounts of aid that went to Afghanistan after 9/11 were raised in 2014, when the Office of the Special Inspector General for Afghanistan Reconstruction charged that USAID had "covered up information" that some aid funds delivered to the Afghan government couldn't be accounted for and may have gone to terrorist groups. USAID denied the charge.[70]

Obama sponsored two major aid efforts. He signed into law the Electrify Africa Act of 2015, a partnership with African governments, multilateral development organizations and private-sector companies that aims to deliver electricity to at least 50 million people by 2020.[71] And in 2016, Obama signed the Global Food Security Act, which allocated more than $7 billion to promote agriculture, small-scale food producers and nutrition for women and children worldwide.[72]

Congress produced a significant piece of bipartisanship foreign aid legislation in 2016. The Foreign Aid Transparency and Accountability Act, sponsored by two Republicans and two Democrats, requires agencies to closely monitor and evaluate the effectiveness of all aid programs and to make that data public.[73]

CURRENT SITUATION
Hunger Crisis

On March 7, while visiting Somalia, U.N. Secretary General António Guterres appealed to the global donor community for $825 million in immediate aid to the East Africa nation, which is on the brink of famine because of drought and an insurgency by Islamic extremists. Guterres said half of Somalia's population of 11 million may not survive six months without the aid.[74]

In addition to Somalia, two other African countries and Yemen are suffering from food shortages stemming from drought and conflict, putting some 20 million

Should USAID be the primary manager of U.S. development aid?

YES
Alex Thier
*Executive Director, Overseas
Development Institute*

NO
Retired Adm. James G. Stavridis
Dean, Fletcher School, Tufts University; and
Steven R. Koltai
*Former Senior Adviser for Entrepreneurship,
U.S. Department of State*

Written for CQ Researcher, April 2017

Written for CQ Researcher, April 2017

The U.S. government has 24 departments and agencies that manage foreign assistance. USAID, the largest, with a 54-year track record, has a deep bench of expertise, tools and evidence to guide what it does.

However, other agencies have unique mandates and perspectives that can make them a critical part of the development portfolio. The Overseas Private Investment Corp. for example, provides access to credit and financial analysis for potential investors. The Millennium Challenge Corp. has flexibility to deliver funds for infrastructure and other needs.

When these agencies are aligned around a common agenda and working together, the impact can be powerful. This was true for former President Barack Obama's Power Africa initiative, which brought together many agencies and private-sector partners into a tight circle to get things done.

The various streams of assistance, however, are often not well coordinated. When agencies have separate authorities and budgets, they tend to use them separately. Their leaders have different objectives, and the effort to bring those objectives, timing and systems together in Washington or on the ground can be very challenging.

So how can things be done better? In the last few years, USAID has invested heavily in people, innovation and evidence. Today, it has some of the most creative, rigorous tools to leverage outside resources and deliver results of any aid agency in the world. We know this because USAID subjects its work to intensive evaluation and publishes all the evidence — good, bad and otherwise. This transparency pushes accountability and performance in a virtuous cycle.

We also know this because recent independent assessments from places such as the Organisation for Economic Co-operation and Development and Results for America gave very high ratings to USAID for its evidence-based decision-making. Finally — and most important — we know this because millions of people have demonstrably benefited from the increased access to food, health, education and electricity that USAID programs have supported.

Given this record of success and the level of investment it took to get there, U.S. taxpayers would get even more bang for their buck if more of the foreign assistance and creative financing tools were housed within USAID.

This is especially true since foreign aid work increasingly is taking place in fragile states, where an in-country presence, understanding of political dynamics and long-term relationships can be key to getting things done.

USAID and its contractor-centric development projects are not delivering the local jobs needed to deter violent extremism and grow economies. With America's foreign policy — and especially foreign aid as expressed through USAID — seemingly about to go through a "redo," there is an opportunity to reconfigure USAID, the Department of State and some related agencies.

Coincidentally, America has a new "Entrepreneur-in-Chief," President Trump, so this is a doubly auspicious moment to leverage that know-how against the single biggest driver of international instability — joblessness. Nothing creates more jobs than entrepreneurship. We can make entrepreneurship promotion a pillar of U.S. foreign development policy and make America safer.

Supporting entrepreneurship not only uses America's soft power in today's world but also generates economic opportunities for U.S. businesses and investors. Creating consumers for U.S. products and investment opportunities for America's companies are important additional benefits to an entrepreneurship-focused foreign development policy.

The Overseas Private Investment Corp. (OPIC) — the perfect place to house this effort — would not require new federal funding. Here are the key elements of the plan:

- Consolidate people and dollars from the 20-plus offices involved in international entrepreneurship development.
- Coordinate funding for multilateral development agencies, such as the World Bank, to get them to pursue more entrepreneurship development.
- Put OPIC on equal footing with other Western development finance agencies (i.e., trading competitors) and authorize it to take minority, direct equity stakes in equity funds.
- Lastly, create a Peace Corps for Entrepreneurship that attracts experienced American entrepreneurs and early-stage investors, a great many of whom are from some of the very countries in which we need to spur entrepreneurship. This program would be administered by private-sector development organizations but staffed with experienced people working on short-term contracts (six months to two years).

The president sees himself as an "entrepreneur par excellence." As Trump takes the helm, it may be the best chance yet to put entrepreneurship in the service of foreign policy.

people at risk of famine. Those are Nigeria, where the Islamic extremist group Boko Haram has been attacking villages and killing residents for years; South Sudan, struggling with both a drought and civil war; and Yemen, which has been riven by civil war since 2011.[75]

The U.N. requested a total of $4.4 billion in aid for the four countries.[76] Last year, the United States provided approximately 28 percent of that aid. "Nobody can replace the U.S. in terms of funding," Yves Daccord, the director general of the International Committee of the Red Cross (ICRC), told *The Washington Post*.[77]

The Trump administration thus far has not responded publicly to the U.N. request for emergency aid.[78]

Congress also has said little about the hunger crisis, but Sens. Rubio and Graham have criticized Trump's proposal to cut foreign aid, with Graham giving it little chance of passage in the Senate.[79]

"U.S. foreign assistance priorities have been remarkably bipartisan for the last decade, with investments for reducing HIV/AIDS and malaria, increasing food security, energizing Africa and stabilizing Afghanistan getting consistent support on both sides of the aisle," according to the Overseas Development Institute's Thier. "Foreign aid is also something conservatives frequently decry when they don't control it, and see as a vital tool when they do."[80]

Only two foreign aid bills — both of which focus on delivering specific types of aid — passed either chamber of Congress last session. The Digital Gap Act, introduced by Rep. Edward Royce, R-Calif., aims to promote Internet access in developing countries. It passed the House on Sept. 7, 2016, but died in the Senate. It was reintroduced and passed again in January and is pending in the Senate Foreign Relations Committee.

The Reinforcing Education Accountability in Development Act, which passed the House on Jan. 24, is also pending before the Senate Foreign Relations Committee. Sponsored by Rep. Nita Lowey, D-N.Y., it would improve the transparency and reach of basic education programs managed by U.S. aid agencies. No hearings have been scheduled for either bill.

Another bill, the Criminal Alien Deportation Enforcement Act introduced by Rep. Brian Babin, R-Texas, would require the United States to suspend foreign aid and travel visa privileges for countries that refuse to accept their citizens when the United States tries to deport them.

"The problem is hundreds of Americans are being robbed, assaulted, raped or murdered every year by criminal aliens who are then released back onto the streets because their countries of origins refuse to take them back," Babin claimed. "I have personally met with a number of these victims, or if the victim is deceased, I have met with their families. It is heart-wrenching."[81]

However, the bill, which is being reviewed by the House Judiciary Committee, is given only a 4 percent chance of being enacted by GovTrack, an independent company that monitors federal legislation.[82]

Reform Recommendations

Talk of budget cuts and inefficiencies in foreign aid has highlighted proposals for reorganizing how American aid is administered.

Currently, foreign aid is administered through USAID and more than 20 other agencies and departments, including Defense, Energy, Health and Human Services, Interior, State and Treasury.[83]

Thier, of the Overseas Development Institute, says the problem goes beyond the mere number of agencies. "In trying to do a lot of different things we spread ourselves too thinly," he says. "I think that having a focused and strategic program that does fewer things well in a lot of our partner countries is going to yield better outcomes than having a lot of different parts of the government working on a lot of different things."

The Heritage Foundation's Roberts says the scattered nature of the aid bureaucracy has been problematic for years. To "focus and prioritize scarce resources," Roberts favors fully integrating USAID into the State Department, "desk officer by desk officer, really ending the agency's independent role."

USAID was created as fully independent, but in 2006 the Bush administration, seeking to align aid more directly with U.S. foreign policy, brought the agency more firmly under State Department control by having the USAID director report to the secretary of State.

While the idea Roberts favors would consolidate most development and humanitarian aid programs into one agency, other aid programs, such as those administered by the Department of Defense, would remain separate.

Others, such as former State Department entrepreneurship director Steven Koltai and Retired Adm. James G. Stavridis, dean of the Fletcher School of Law and

Diplomacy at Tufts University, would like to see development aid coordinated by the Overseas Private Investment Corporation (OPIC), an independent agency that mobilizes private capital for development projects, including promoting entrepreneurship. "There are 60 offices and 12 different departments that are involved in one way or another with international entrepreneurship development," one type of foreign aid, Koltai says. "You can't do this successfully if it's this disaggregated."

But others say charges of poor coordination and inefficiencies are overblown. "I would argue that there has been more progress on that front than perhaps is appreciated during the time of the Obama administration," says Scott Morris, a senior fellow at the Center for Global Development, a pro-aid think tank in Washington. "There was more effective coordination going on, particularly around the big initiatives, such as Power Africa," which aims to bring electricity to much of the continent.

Still, he says, "there probably are some elements of consolidation that make sense. But I don't think it's realistic, or ultimately effective, to collapse everything together in a supersized agency."

Alicia Phillips Mandaville, vice president of global development policy and learning at InterAction, the alliance of U.S.-based nongovernmental aid organizations, echoes that view. "Consolidating all U.S. foreign assistance through a single point would be counterproductive," she says. Different aid agencies manage different kinds of projects and have different skill sets, she says. For instance, the kind of work OPIC does in encouraging private enterprise requires different skills than the work performed by USAID in delivering health care or education, she says.

Even those who argue for consolidation do not argue for combining all economic aid programs into a single entity. Nonmilitary economic aid managed by the Defense Department, says Roberts, should not be moved to another agency. "One of the things that DoD does well, and we would want them to continue to do well, is to respond to humanitarian crises — tsunamis, earthquakes."

With all the consolidation talk, Mandaville says that without clear policy proposals from the Trump administration, "People are nervous about a merger of things that shouldn't be merged."

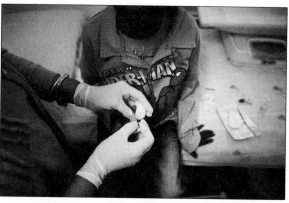

A youngster receives an HIV test at a U.S.-funded AIDS clinic in Johannesburg, South Africa. President George W. Bush's President's Emergency Plan for AIDS Relief, or PEPFAR, called for a $15 billion program to combat AIDS in 15 countries. The project remains the largest-ever global health initiative dedicated to a single disease.

Gallo Images/Foto24

Others worry that proposed cuts to foreign aid may leave too much of the development efforts up to the Defense Department, whose funding Trump wants to increase significantly. "If major budget cuts to foreign assistance go through at the same time DoD's budget is increased, the imbalance between DoD and its sister agencies — State and USAID — will continue to grow with devastating effects on our diplomacy and foreign assistance capabilities," says CSIS's Green. Cutting foreign assistance, "especially of the magnitude proposed, will exacerbate the tendency to militarize U.S. foreign policy and to see every problem as a nail."

Morris, of the Center for Global Development, agrees. The proposed budget cuts would "put more pressure on the Defense Department to engage in these activities if . . . they can no longer lean on a USAID to do it," he says. But, he warns, there is "less transparency" at the Defense Department.

Former USAID Administrator Atwood sees another problem in consolidating economic aid under either the State Department or the DoD. "When the State Department or DoD take over an aid program, as in Afghanistan, they are likely to have 15 short-term projects, whereas they should have one 15-year, effective, sustainable project," Atwood says.

Some experts have recommended encouraging a greater role for the private sector as a way to make foreign aid programs more efficient.

"Step one is to consolidate. Step two is to put it in an agency that is closer to working with the private sector than USAID or the State Department," says Koltai. He advocates creation of an Office of Private Sector Development at OPIC that would make investments in developing countries as a seed investor in projects that are minority-government, majority-private enterprises.

OPIC provides loans and guaranties, political risk insurance and support for American businesses expanding into emerging markets, especially where risks of economic losses through political turmoil or nationalization of industries are high.

"The only reason I hesitate about privatizing OPIC completely is that in many of the places where this work has to happen, the private sector is not going to invest," says Koltai, noting the risks of political and economic uncertainty in many developing countries.

Others, however, have called for full privatization of OPIC, arguing that its involvement in high-risk areas only encourages bad behavior on the part of governments. Countries with favorable investment climates will attract foreign investors without government help, wrote Heritage Foundation analysts Brett Schaefer and Bryan Riley in 2014. But, they argued, "When OPIC guarantees investments in risky foreign environments, those countries have less reason to adopt policies that are friendly to foreign investors."[84]

Young, of the Competitive Enterprise Institute, argues for privatizing OPIC and all aid agencies. Moving all government aid through nongovernmental organizations (NGOs) would be a better model, he says, "although once they have that kind of guaranteed revenue source, NGOs can become their own special interest. That's something we need to look out for."

OUTLOOK
Coming Crisis

Oxfam International, an independent association of antipoverty organizations, predicts that the current aid crisis in eastern Africa and Yemen is only the beginning. When the full impact of climate change kicks in, the group says, conditions will get much worse unless industrialized nations act quickly to limit and remediate the damage.

"Developing countries' economies face being crushed under the double burden of climate change adaptation costs of almost $800 billion and more than twice that in economic losses every year by 2050 if pledges to cut [carbon] emissions are not improved," the organization warned in 2015. "World leaders need to step up. We need further cuts to emissions and more climate funding so vulnerable communities — who are already facing unpredictable floods, droughts and hunger — can adapt to survive."[85]

On March 28, Trump signed an executive order that would unwind most of President Obama's efforts to battle climate change, and he has said he intends to withdraw from a 2015 international agreement to curb carbon emissions.[86] Factions within the administration reportedly are in heated debate over whether to withdraw from the accord.[87]

In addition, most experts expect U.S. foreign aid to decline. "The aid budget is going to shrink," says the Heritage Foundation's Roberts, and it will be "prioritized to match up with the most immediate and crucial U.S. national security objectives."

But other experts say expanding foreign aid will be essential to protect U.S. national security interests. The administration's proposed budget cuts would signal "U.S. withdrawal from the world, rather than continued leadership and engagement," says Travis Adkins, senior director for public policy and government relations at InterAction.

"Slashing foreign assistance would provide no significant debt relief but would have dire impacts for people in the world's poorest places, as well as U.S. national interests," he says. Global crises today "demand U.S. global engagement, because we as Americans feel the consequences of these global challenges."

Supporting foreign aid is a good way to put "America first," according to Adkins, because it ensures "that our people are safe and secure and that there is stability in the world so that our security interests aren't threatened."

Former USAID administrator Atwood agrees and adds, "I don't know whether I'm terribly confident that the Trump administration is going to think in those terms." Furthermore, he warns, U.S. foreign aid cutbacks could snowball across the globe. "The way the United States goes, the rest of the world goes."

Since Trump released his proposal in late February to slash foreign aid by nearly one-third, the aid community has been anxiously awaiting further details, and some experts say they still hope the administration will recognize the importance of aid to national security.

"With any new administration, and potentially with this one, there's a desire to show that there are things being improved," says InterAction's Mandaville. "That is always a good instinct."

NOTES

1. Michael Gerson and Raj Shah, " 'America first' shouldn't mean cutting foreign aid," *The Washington Post*, Feb. 24, 2017, http://tinyurl.com/mgqha7d.

2. The Associated Press, "Trump's budget entails steep cuts for diplomacy, foreign aid," CNBC, Feb. 28, 2017, http://tinyurl.com/zy9ox8r.

3. Sylvan Lane and Rebecca Kheel, "Trump's cuts to foreign aid face resistance in Congress," *The Hill*, Feb. 28, 2017, http://tinyurl.com/hnggcjg.

4. James Bovard, "Obama's global anti-corruption cops should call Internal Affairs," *USA Today*, May 19, 2016, http://tinyurl.com/l2drnfa.

5. "Final Monthly Treasury Statement of Receipts and Outlays of the United States Government For Fiscal Year 2015 Through September 30, 2015, and Other Periods," U.S. Department of the Treasury, September 2015, http://tinyurl.com/mxr3hfr.

6. Curt Tarnoff and Marian L. Lawson, "Foreign Aid: An Introduction to U.S. Programs and Policy," Congressional Research Service, June 17, 2016, p. 6, http://tinyurl.com/nymlqwz

7. "On the Issues," Fox News, http://tinyurl.com/kj6tu7w.

8. "Testimony of Gayle E. Smith before the Senate Foreign Relations Committee," USAID, June 30, 2016, http://tinyurl.com/mjsp6vc.

9. "Corruption in Conflict: Lessons from the U.S. Experience in Afghanistan," Special Inspector General for Afghanistan Reconstruction, September 2016, http://tinyurl.com/lpcjdc9.

10. Geoff Dyer, "US aid fuelled corruption in Afghanistan, watchdog says," *Financial Times*, Sept. 14, 2016, http://tinyurl.com/hz84sma.

11. Sidney Traynham, "Over 120 Retired Generals, Admirals on State and USAID Budget: 'Now is not the time to retreat,'" U.S. Global Leadership Coalition, Feb. 27, 2017, http://tinyurl.com/k423vg3.

12. Nick Thompson, "Seventy-five percent of U.S. foreign military financing goes to two countries," CNN, Nov. 11, 2015, http://tinyurl.com/ja3kvse.

13. Tracy Wilkinson and Noah Bierman, "Egypt's authoritarian-minded president gets a warm White House welcome," *The Chicago Tribune*, April 3, 2017, http://tinyurl.com/krqgqtv.

14. See "Detained Americans Fast Facts," CNN Library, March 29, 2017, http://tinyurl.com/mgard3k.

15. Ibid.

16. "Statement of Stephen O'Brien to the United Nations Security Council," United Nations, March 10, 2017, http://tinyurl.com/mcobh7z.

17. "Net ODA," Organisation for Economic Co-operation and Development, http://tinyurl.com/zsvrce3. This $30 billion figure is for calendar 2015. It differs from the $26.2 billion figure cited elsewhere, which is for fiscal 2015.

18. Ibid.

19. Naomi Larsson, "Foreign aid: which countries are the most generous?" *The Guardian*, Sept. 9, 2015, http://tinyurl.com/kusonku.

20. "The 0.7% ODA/GNI target — a history," Organisation for Economic Co-operation and Development, http://tinyurl.com/jo9zl6s.

21. "Policy Brief: U.S. International Development Funding," InterAction, January 2013, http://tinyurl.com/mgeqn28.

22. Angus Deaton, *The Great Escape: Health, Wealth, and the Origins of Inequality* (2013), p. 273.

23. Ibid., p. 285.

24. Marian L. Lawson, "Does Foreign Aid Work? Efforts to Evaluate U.S. Foreign Assistance," Congressional Research Service, June 23, 2016, p. 4, http://tinyurl.com/lv7lj84.

25. "Testimony of Gayle E. Smith before the Senate Foreign Relations Committee," op. cit.

26. Junyi Zhang, "Order from Chaos: Chinese foreign assistance, explained," Brookings Institution, July 19, 2016, http://tinyurl.com/kr33vo3.

27. Somini Sengupta, "Trump Revives Ban on Foreign Aid to Groups That Give Abortion Counseling," *The New York Times*, Jan. 23, 2017, http://tinyurl.com/hr4qkts.

28. The Foreign Assistance Act of 1961, Section 116, 22 U.S.C. 2151n, http://tinyurl.com/k29bw4y.

29. Ibid.

30. Eric Posner, "The Case Against Human Rights," *The Guardian*, Dec. 4, 2014, http://tinyurl.com/l8agpzd.

31. Yun Sun, "China's Aid to Africa: Monster or Messiah?" Brookings Institution, Feb. 7, 2014, http://tinyurl.com/lj6juxg.

32. Zhang, op. cit.

33. Randy Schnepf, "U.S. International Food Aid Programs: Background and Issues," Congressional Research Service, Sept. 14, 2016, p. 2, http://tinyurl.com/k4wlvw3.

34. Olga Khazan, "Here Are the U.S. States That Benefit Most From America's Wacky International Food-Aid Program," *The Atlantic*, April 5, 2013, http://tinyurl.com/kurxoxa.

35. Ryan Nabil and Vincent H. Smith, "U.S. food aid's costly problem," *Foreign Affairs*, Nov. 1, 2016, http://tinyurl.com/hqkf9v5.

36. "Testimony of Gayle Smith before the House Committee on Foreign Affairs," op. cit.

37. Christopher Blattman and Paul Niehaus, "Show Them the Money: Why Giving Cash Helps Alleviate Poverty," *Foreign Affairs*, May/June 2014, http://tinyurl.com/lobd9lc.

38. "Testimony of Eric G. Postel before the Senate Foreign Relations Committee Subcommittee on State Department and USAID Management," U.S. Senate, July 12, 2016, http://tinyurl.com/kffr7cf.

39. Ibid.

40. Ibid.

41. Ibid.

42. Marian L. Lawson, "Foreign Assistance: Public-Private Partnerships," Congressional Research Service, Oct. 28, 2013, p. 14, http://tinyurl.com/kj34mfs.

43. Ibid., p. 14.

44. Louis A. Picard and Terry F. Buss, *A Fragile Balance: Re-examining the History of Foreign Aid, Security, and Diplomacy* (2013), p. 14.

45. Ibid., p. 46.

46. George I. Gay, "Public Relations of the Commission for the Relief in Belgium, Documents," Stanford University Press, 1929, http://tinyurl.com/kl9w7mw.

47. C. E. Noyes, "American relief of famine in Europe," *Editorial Research Reports*, (Vol. II), (1940), http://tinyurl.com/m5jye3f.

48. Picard and Buss, op. cit., p. 21.

49. "Lend-Lease and Military Aid to the Allies in the Early Years of World War II," Office of the Historian, U.S. Department of State, http://tinyurl.com/ln4d573.

50. "The Plan: As the Marshall Plan Becomes the Test Between the U.S. and the U.S.S.R, the Main Needs of Europe According to the President," *The New York Times*, Dec. 21, 1947, http://tinyurl.com/kwndcml.

51. Felix Belair Jr., "President Blunt in Plea to Combat Coercion as World Peril," *The New York Times*, March 13, 1947, http://tinyurl.com/l9rko73.

52. Picard, op. cit., p. 76.

53. "Legislation on Foreign Relations Through 2002," House and Senate Committees on International Relations and Committees on Foreign Relations, July 2003, http://tinyurl.com/mawldqj.

54. Charles Mohr, "U.S. Opens Study of Aid in Vietnam," *The New York Times*, Sept. 5, 1966, http://tinyurl.com/k7c2utb.

55. Picard, op. cit., p. 110.

56. Ibid., p. 97.

57. Felix Belair Jr., "Foreign Aid Off as Need Rises," *The New York Times*, Jan. 10, 1971, http://tinyurl.com/k8t8qaa.

58. "Trends," Foreign Aid Explorer, USAID, undated, http://tinyurl.com/zokmdh9.

59. Lawson, "Foreign Assistance: Public-Private Partnerships," op. cit.

60. Amanda Terkel and Laura Bassett, "Donald Trump Reinstates Ronald Reagan's Abortion 'Global Gag Rule,' " *The Huffington Post*, Jan. 23, 2017, http://tinyurl.com/z273q3s.

61. Tarnoff and Lawson, op. cit., p. 2, http://tinyurl.com/nymlqwz.

62. Curt Tarnoff, "U.S. Agency for International Development (USAID): Background, Operations, and Issues," Congressional Research Service, July 21, 2015, p. 35, http://tinyurl.com/mhbdvxh.

63. Ibid., p. 53.

64. Tarnoff and Lawson, op. cit., p. 1.

65. "Sixty years of US aid to Pakistan: Get the data," *The Guardian*, http://tinyurl.com/k7nqzyg.

66. Kiran Dhillon, "Afghanistan Is The Big Winner In U.S. Foreign Aid," *Time*, March 31, 2014, http://tinyurl.com/nbamrve.

67. Tarnoff, op. cit., p. 36.

68. Bradley Graham and Glenn Kessler, "Rice Explains Aid Restructuring to USAID Employees," *The Washington Post*, Jan. 20, 2006, http://tinyurl.com/l4are3w.

69. Myra Sessions, "Overview of the President's Emergency Plan for AIDS Relief (PEPFAR)," Center for Global Development, undated, http://tinyurl.com/kgsaaxr.

70. Tom Vanden Brook, "Aid agency accused of coverup in Afghanistan," *USA Today*, April 2, 2014, http://tinyurl.com/kfovoph.

71. "Electrify Africa Act of 2015 — Report to Congress," USAID, Aug. 10, 2016, http://tinyurl.com/gn5kqb6.

72. Fernanda Crescente, "Obama signs Global Food Security Act to end hunger," *USA Today*, July 21, 2016, http://tinyurl.com/jvfjmjm.

73. Adva Saldinger, "US Congress approves long-sought Foreign Aid Transparency and Accountability Act," Devex, July 7, 2016, http://tinyurl.com/jwjuukp.

74. Hussein Mohamed and Sewell Chan, "U.N. Chief, Visiting Somalia, Pleads for Aid to Avert Famine," *The New York Times*, March 7, 2017, http://tinyurl.com/lsxg9u7.

75. For background, see Brian Beary, "Terrorism in Africa," *CQ Researcher*, July 10, 2015, pp. 577-600.

76. Kevin Sieff, "Trump's plan to slash foreign aid comes as famine threat is surging," *The Washington Post*, March 1, 2017, http://tinyurl.com/n773swb.

77. Ibid.

78. Ibid.

79. Sylvan Lane, "GOP senator: Trump budget 'dead on arrival,' " *The Hill*, Feb. 28, 2017, http://tinyurl.com/jyx2h79.

80. Alex Thier, "Foreign aid under Trump's 'America-first' doctrine," Devex, Nov. 11, 2016, http://tinyurl.com/ls2n83q.

81. Malia Zimmerman, "Law would cut off aid to countries that refuse to accept illegal immigrant criminals," Fox News, Jan. 16, 2017, http://tinyurl.com/jybu3bc.

82. "H.R. 82: Criminal Alien Deportation Enforcement Act of 2017," Gov.track, http://tinyurl.com/lz2xk3f.

83. "Total Obligations," Foreign Aid Explorer, USAID, undated, http://tinyurl.com/n6fqfqx.

84. Brett Schaefer and Bryan Riley, "Time to Privatize OPIC," The Heritage Foundation, May 19, 2014, http://tinyurl.com/k9nnmnn.

85. "Delays in cutting emissions set to cost developing countries hundreds of billions of dollars more," press release, Oxfam International, Nov. 25, 2015, http://tinyurl.com/lsnybbg.

86. Coral Davenport and Alissa J. Rubin, "Trump Signs Executive Order Unwinding Obama Climate Policies," *The New York Times*, March 28, 2017, http://tinyurl.com/k7vyjr6. See also Jill U. Adams, "Energy and Climate Change," *CQ Researcher*, June 15, 2016.

87. Coral Davenport, "Top Trump Advisers Are Split on Paris Agreement on Climate Change," *The New York Times*, March 2, 2017, http://tinyurl.com/jccavzh.

BIBLIOGRAPHY

Selected Sources

Books

Deaton, Angus, *The Great Escape: Health, Wealth, and the Origins of Inequality,* **Princeton University Press, 2013.**
A professor of economics and international affairs at Princeton University and winner of the 2015 Nobel Prize in economics argues that development aid works only where it isn't needed and that it can hinder the conditions that encourage economic growth.

Koltai, Steven R., and Matthew Muspratt, *Peace Through Entrepreneurship: Investing in a Startup Culture for Security and Development,* **Brookings Institution Press, 2016.**
A former director of the State Department's Global Entrepreneurship Program (Koltai) and a development consultant (Muspratt) say joblessness is the main cause of violent unrest in developing countries and that encouraging entrepreneurship is more effective than traditional development programs at delivering jobs.

Picard, Louis A., and Terry F. Buss, *A Fragile Balance: Re-examining the History of Foreign Aid, Security, and Diplomacy,* **Kumarian Press, 2013.**
A professor of public and international affairs at the University of Pittsburgh (Picard) and a professor of public policy at Carnegie Mellon University (Buss) present a history of foreign development and humanitarian aid policies.

Articles

De Luce, Dan, David Francis and John Hudson, "Will Foreign Aid Get Cut on Trump's Chopping Block?" *Foreign Policy,* **Nov. 23, 2016, http://tinyurl .com/lqelqmd.**
Journalists say President Trump brings uncertainty to the foreign-aid community, and they explore the level of Republican support in Congress for aid programs.

Greenberg, Jon, "Most U.S. foreign aid flows through U.S. organizations," *PolitiFact,* **March 8, 2017, http://tinyurl.com/l3km9t7.**
The Congressional Research Service reported that only about 4 percent of U.S. foreign aid in 2014 went directly to foreign governments; most of the funds were funneled through U.S. private partners.

Miliband, David, and Ravi Gurumurthy, "Improving Humanitarian Aid: How to Make Relief More Efficient and Effective," *Foreign Affairs,* **July/August 2015, http://tinyurl.com/nqxsltv.**
The president (Miliband) and a vice president (Gurumurthy) of the International Rescue Committee, a global relief organization, say humanitarian aid can be improved through better analysis of program effectiveness.

Posner, Eric, "The Case Against Human Rights," *The Guardian,* **Dec. 4, 2014, http://tinyurl.com/l8agpzd.**
A University of Chicago law professor says it is misguided to expect developing countries to improve their human rights records in return for foreign aid.

Smith, Vincent H., and Ryan Nabil, "U.S. Food Aid's Costly Problem," *Foreign Affairs,* **Nov. 1, 2016, http://tinyurl.com/hqkf9v5.**
A visiting scholar at the conservative American Enterprise Institute (AEI) think tank and Montana State University economics professor (Smith) and an AEI researcher (Nabil) say it is time to eliminate requirements that American-flagged ships carry U.S. food aid.

Reports and Studies

"Foreign Assistance Briefing Book 2016: Critical problems, recommendations, and actions for the new administration and the 115th Congress," InterAction, **2016, http://tinyurl.com/l4w4w4e.**
An alliance of U.S.-based nongovernmental organizations lists the most critical issues facing the aid community in its attempt to boost economic development and fight poverty and disease in developing countries.

Lawson, Marian L., "Does Foreign Aid Work? Efforts to Evaluate U.S. Foreign Assistance," Congressional Research Service, **June 23, 2016, http://tinyurl.com/lv7lj84.**
A foreign-assistance analyst for Congress' research arm describes U.S. aid agencies' efforts to evaluate program effectiveness and obstacles faced in making assessments.

Lawson, Marian L., "Foreign Assistance: Public-Private Partnerships (PPPs)," Congressional Research Service, **Oct. 28, 2013, http://tinyurl.com/mu9pjw6.**

A foreign-assistance analyst traces the evolution of private sector involvement in U.S. foreign assistance programs over recent decades.

Tarnoff, Curt, "Millennium Challenge Corporation," Congressional Research Service, Jan. 11, 2017, http://tinyurl.com/lfesl39.
A specialist in foreign affairs recounts the history of the Millennium Challenge Corp., a U.S. foreign aid agency, and the challenges it faces.

Tarnoff, Curt, and Marian L. Lawson, "Foreign Aid: An Introduction to U.S. Programs and Policy," Congressional Research Service, June 17, 2016, http://tinyurl.com/nymlqwz.
Analysts provide an overview of U.S. foreign-aid policies and programs, discuss recent priorities and trends in the field and explore the growing role of the private sector in aid programs.

For More Information

Cato Institute, 1000 Massachusetts Ave., N.W., Washington, DC 20001-5403; 202-842-0200; www.cato.org. Libertarian think tank that opposes most foreign aid spending.

Center for Global Development, 2055 L St., N.W., Fifth Floor, Washington, DC 20036; 202-416-4000; www.cgdev.org. Research and advocacy organization focused on global poverty and inequality.

Center for Strategic and International Studies, 1800 K St., N.W., Washington, DC 20006; 202-887-0200; www.csis.org. Centrist think tank that researches U.S. security issues.

Heritage Foundation, 214 Massachusetts Ave., N.E., Washington, DC 20002; 202-546-4400; www.heritage.org. Conservative think tank that focuses on foreign aid as one of its areas of policy concerns.

InterAction, 1400 16th St., N.W., Suite 210, Washington, DC 20036; 202-667-8227; www.interaction.org. Association of U.S.-based nongovernmental aid organizations.

Millennium Challenge Corp., 1099 14th St., N.W., Suite 700, Washington, DC 20005-3550; 202-521-3600; www.mcc.gov. A federal foreign aid agency.

Overseas Development Institute, 203 Blackfriars Road, London SE1 8NJ, United Kingdom; +44 (0)20 7922 0300; www.odi.org. Independent think tank on international development and humanitarian issues.

Oxfam America, 1101 17th St., N.W., Suite 1300, Washington, DC 20036-4710; 800-862-5800; www.oxfamamerica.org. Nonpartisan advocacy group working to end poverty.

U.S. Agency for International Development, Ronald Reagan Building and International Trade Center, Washington, DC 20523-1000; 202-712-0000; www.usaid.gov. Primary federal agency managing foreign development and humanitarian aid programs.

14

Anti-Semitism

Sarah Glazer

AFP/Getty Images/Jack Guez

Michael Ron David Kadar, 18, is escorted on March 23 from a courtroom in Israel, where he was charged in connection with hundreds of bomb threats. In April, the U.S. Justice Department charged the Jewish Israeli-American teen in connection with dozens of fake bomb threats in the United States between January and March of this year, many of them targeting Jewish community centers.

From *CQ Researcher,*
May 12, 2017

"Heil Trump," said an email threatening Jews and African-Americans, received by hundreds of University of Michigan students in February from a forged, or "spoofed," faculty address. The messages, being investigated by the FBI, followed the appearance of racist fliers on campus last fall.[1]

"We've been riding this wave of Donald Trump's election — definitely," said a member of Identity Evropa, a white supremacist group that says it has distributed fliers on more than two dozen campuses. "He's the closest to us we've ever had in recent memory, although we would like to see him go a lot further."[2]

White nationalists "feel emboldened in this current political climate" and are engaged in an "unprecedented" campaign to target college campuses, said Jonathan A. Greenblatt, CEO of the Anti-Defamation League (ADL), a Jewish civil rights group. Extremist anti-Semitic and white supremacist fliers and messages have popped up on more than 100 campuses in 33 states, according to the league, in at least 145 instances since the beginning of the school year.[3] In 2016, the group counted 108 campus incidents specifically targeting Jewish students.[4]

The Southern Poverty Law Center (SPLC), a liberal hate-watch group based in Montgomery, Ala., has blamed a nationwide "wave of hate speech and harassment" against Jews and others on Trump's election.[5] SPLC senior fellow Mark Potok said such groups were "electrified" by Trump's presidential campaign.[6]

Jewish groups both here and in Europe say anti-Semitic incidents are on the rise, and not just on college campuses. Anti-Jewish incidents jumped 34 percent last year to 1,266 — up from

942 in 2015 — and continued to rise in the first quarter of this year, the ADL said. This year saw disturbing incidents of harassment or vandalism, including more than 100 bomb threats called in to Jewish schools and community centers and the desecration in February of dozens of Jewish graves at cemeteries in Philadelphia and near St. Louis, Mo.[7]

"Over the past six months we've seen a surge of bias incidents and hate crimes we haven't seen before," says Greenblatt. The Trump campaign, he says, legitimized so-called alt-right groups who "brought with them a kind of intolerance that has never before been in the center of the public debate — not just about Jews but about Mexicans, Muslims and other minorities."

The alt-right, short for "alternative right," refers to a loose amalgam of far-right groups and individuals associated with implicit or explicit racism, anti-Semitism and white supremacy.[8] President Trump's chief strategist Steve Bannon has called the Breitbart News website he headed before joining the Trump campaign "a platform for the alt-right." Rob Eshman, editor-in-chief of the *Jewish Journal*, said the website fomented "a deep antagonism towards Jews," especially in its comments section.[9]

However, some Jewish observers doubt anti-Semitism is any worse under Trump; it just gets more media attention, they say. Others, such as Rep. Chris Smith, R-N.J., who has written legislation to combat anti-Semitism, strongly disagree with the accusation that Trump has inspired anti-Semitism.

"I think it's a very serious diversionary tactic by some," Smith says. "When people make those comments I think it does a disservice to the genuine and systemic causes [of anti-Semitism] we're trying to combat."

Others point out that, historically speaking, anti-Semitic incidents in both the United States and worldwide are substantially lower than they were in the mid-2000s, when Israeli-Arab conflicts were in the news, including the 2006 Israel-Lebanon war — events that experts say helped trigger waves of anti-Semitic sentiment.[10]

Criticism of Trump reached a new peak on April 11, when White House Press Secretary Sean Spicer said Nazi leader Adolf Hitler "didn't even sink to using chemical weapons" like Syrian President Bashar Assad did when he killed dozens of people with deadly sarin gas in April. Spicer seemed to have forgotten that the Nazis used poison gas to systematically kill millions of Jews.[11] Although Spicer later apologized, Jewish groups and historians said the administration was either phenomenally insensitive about Jews or verging on the anti-Semitic.

Journalists, Jewish groups and liberal bloggers cited previous occasions when the administration had "sent a clear dog-whistle of approval to anti-Semites," as a blogger from the liberal Center for American Progress in Washington described Spicer's April 11 words. For instance, the administration failed to mention Jews in its International Holocaust Remembrance Day statement and had been slow to denounce the rise in anti-Semitic incidents across the country. Earlier, Trump's campaign had tweeted a white supremacist image showing his opponent Hillary Clinton's face atop $100 bills with a Star of David.[12]

Perhaps to deflect the criticism, Trump recently has condemned anti-Semitism and explicitly mentioned the 6 million Jews killed by Nazis during an April 25 speech at the U.S. Holocaust Memorial Museum. "We will confront anti-Semitism; we will stamp out prejudice, we will condemn hatred and we will act," he told the museum audience, which included Holocaust survivors.[13]

Meanwhile, experts have attributed a rise in anti-Semitism in some parts of Europe to increasingly popular right-wing parties as well as anti-Israel sentiment among Muslims and the political left. Anti-Jewish feeling is linked to hostility toward immigrants and any ethnic group seen as the "other," experts say, such as in the rhetoric of right-wing parties opposed to the influx of more than 2 million immigrants, mostly Muslim, from the Middle East and Africa.

"It's going to be harder and harder for visible Jews to live in France," especially those who wear religious garb such as a *kippah* (skullcap worn by Orthodox male Jews), says Bruno Chaouat, a professor of French at the University of Minnesota who studies French attitudes towards Jews. "Jews are caught in a vise between the far-right wing and anti-Semitism from Muslim youth and the left."

Hate crimes and anti-Semitic incidents spiked in Britain after the U.K. voted last June to leave the European Union (EU), according to the Community Security Trust, a London-based group that tracks anti-Semitism. Limiting immigration was a central issue in that vote.

In addition, says Mark Gardner, the trust's communications director, Jews have been "the target of jihadi terrorists" in recent years, often exacerbated by the internet. A "widespread increase" in anti-Semitism online has made the internet the main platform for "bigotry and hate," according to Tel Aviv University's Kantor Center, a watchdog group that publishes an annual report on anti-Semitic incidents globally.[14] The increase has stimulated a vigorous debate in Europe about whether to ratchet up penalties against hate speech online.

As for anti-Semitism among young Muslims, Günther Jikeli, a visiting associate professor in Jewish studies at Indiana University in Bloomington, had discovered startling sentiments among young Muslim men in London, Paris and Berlin when he interviewed them in 2007 for a book. They often said they wanted to "kill Jews before they died," Jikeli says.[15] At the time, that was not seen as a realistic possibility. "Now it is," he says, adding, "There are very explicit, detailed instructions on social media by ISIS and others calling for violence against Jews."

Jews are painfully aware of that in cities where deadly Islamist terrorist attacks have occurred at Jewish gathering places in recent years: a Paris kosher grocery and a Copenhagen synagogue in 2015, the Jewish Museum in Brussels in 2014 and a Jewish school in Toulouse in 2012.

The attack on the Paris grocery led to expressions of solidarity with Jews. "France without Jews is not France," said then-French Prime Minister Manuel Valls, promising to protect places of worship.[16] Officials beefed up security at Jewish institutions in Europe, and the number of violent anti-Semitic incidents worldwide fell by 12 percent — from 410 in 2015 to 361 last year.[17] But the brutality of individual events has intensified in recent years, according to the Kantor Center, such as the Paris grocery attack, which left four people dead.

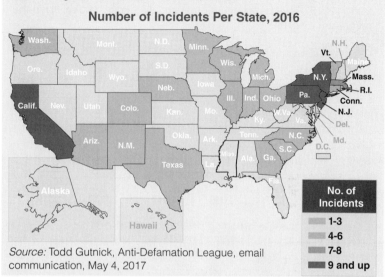

U.S. Colleges Targeted by Anti-Semitism

College campuses in 24 states experienced 108 incidents of anti-Semitism last year, according to data compiled by the Anti-Defamation League. The incidents ranged from threats and slurs to distribution of hate propaganda. California and New Jersey had the highest number of incidents, 19 each.

Number of Incidents Per State, 2016

Source: Todd Gutnick, Anti-Defamation League, email communication, May 4, 2017

No. of Incidents
- 1-3
- 4-6
- 7-8
- 9 and up

Europe's refugee influx has shifted right-wing animosity more toward Muslims than Jews, according to the center. Still, many of the Muslim refugees come from Syria and Iraq, where anti-Semitic views are widespread, Jikeli points out, adding to nervousness in Europe's Jewish communities.

Some right-wing politicians in Europe have tried to capitalize on that Jewish anxiety. Marine Le Pen, who represents the anti-immigrant National Front, has tried to soften her party's historic anti-Semitism, saying French Jews have more to fear from jihadists than from organizations like hers. However, she recently declared that France was not culpable in rounding up Jews for concentration camps during World War II, which Emory University holocaust historian Deborah Lipstadt calls "soft-core Holocaust denial."[18] (Le Pen was soundly defeated by Emmanuel Macron in the May 7 election to select France's next president.)

Paradoxically, some extreme right-wing groups in Germany blame Europe's refugee influx on an international Jewish conspiracy. Once hatred turns against

Anti-Semitic Incidents Surged in Early 2017

The number of anti-Semitic incidents in the United States — including vandalism and harassment — jumped to 541 in the first quarter of this year — up from 291 in the same period in 2016. However, many of the 2017 incidents were fake bomb threats allegedly made by two individuals. On an annual basis, assaults declined — from 56 in 2015 to 36 in 2016 — but harassment and vandalism rose, especially in the last quarter of 2016.

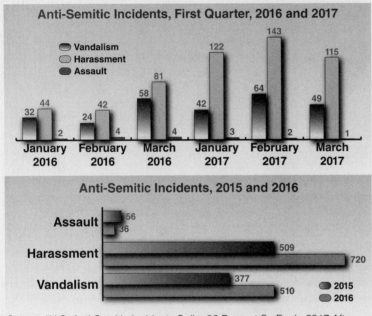

Anti-Semitic Incidents, First Quarter, 2016 and 2017

Vandalism
Harassment
Assault

January 2016: 32, 44, 2
February 2016: 24, 42, 4
March 2016: 58, 81, 4
January 2017: 42, 122, 3
February 2017: 64, 143, 2
March 2017: 49, 115, 1

Anti-Semitic Incidents, 2015 and 2016

Assault: 56, 36
Harassment: 509, 720
Vandalism: 377, 510

2015
2016

Source: "U.S. Anti-Semitic Incidents Spike 86 Percent So Far in 2017 After Surging Last Year, ADL Finds," Anti-Defamation League, April 24, 2017, http://tinyurl.com/lk2zj2d

people seen as alien, experts say, the fallout has historically been bad news for Jews, who have been the target of what some historians call humanity's "longest hatred."[19]

As U.S. and European civil rights groups monitor anti-Semitism, here are some questions being debated in academia, national and state legislatures and the public arena:

Is anti-Semitism on the rise?

Civil rights groups say the United States has experienced an unprecedented number of hate crimes directed at Jews since the Trump presidential campaign. According to the ADL, nearly a third of the 1,266 anti-Semitic

incidents last year occurred during the last two months after Trump's election.

As an example of the role the election played, the ADL cited graffiti in Denver last year that said: "Kill the Jews, Vote Trump."[20]

The surge in incidents continued into the first three months of this year, the league said, spiking 86 percent compared to last year's first quarter. By late March, however, most of that spike was attributed to bomb hoaxes allegedly perpetrated by two disturbed individuals.[21] Israeli authorities charged an Israeli-American teenager, Michael Ron David Kadar, 18, with making hundreds of bomb threats around the world, and a man in St. Louis was charged with making a handful of them.[22]

Nevertheless, says the ADL's Greenblatt, the total number of anti-Semitic incidents spiked, even discounting the fake bomb threats, and the two individuals were not responsible for the cemetery desecrations.

Ryan Lenz, a spokesman for the SPLC, agrees with the charge that Trump's campaign contributed to the rise in anti-Semitism, citing the use of an age-old anti-Semitic stereotype in what he calls Trump's "horrifying final campaign ad, where a series of Jewish financial figures were identified by name as part of a global secret banking cabal."

Lenz adds, "While we're not saying Donald Trump caused this, he is part of a giant mix of racist expression that somehow has been legitimized."

Oren Segal, director of the ADL Center on Extremism, says such incidents "need to be seen in the context of a general resurgence of white supremacist activity in the United States."[23] In the month after the election, more than 1,000 bias crimes were reported, mostly anti-immigrant, anti-black and anti-Muslim in nature.[24]

But U.S. anti-Semitism "may have deeper roots" than Trump-inspired hate, according to Seth Frantzman, a fellow at the Jerusalem Institute for Market Studies and the op-ed editor at *The Jerusalem Post*, both based in Israel. More than 7,000 anti-Semitic incidents occurred during President Obama's eight years in office, he pointed out.[25]

"Every six days, a Jewish person in America was being attacked in 2015, and it went largely ignored," Frantzman wrote in the Jewish newspaper *The Algemeiner* in March, at the height of the bomb scares. "On average, there were threats every day against Jews and Jewish institutions over the last eight years, and most of them did not receive headlines."[26]

Mark Oppenheimer, host of *Tablet* magazine's podcast "Unorthodox," contended that the media have focused more attention on such attacks since Trump's victory. "My best guess is that we are facing a continued march of the low-level, but ineradicable, Jew hatred that we always live with," he wrote in February.[27]

The arrest of Kadar led George Mason University law professor David Bernstein to repeat an earlier claim that the ADL "chose to hype" the numbers; he said that would worsen racism and anti-Semitism.[28]

"There's no evidence whatsoever that there's a general increase in anti-Semitic attitudes, given the Pew survey that just came out showing Jews are the most popular religious group in the United States," says Bernstein. According to the survey, half of U.S. adults expressed warm feelings towards Jews, rating them at 67 degrees on a 0-to-100 scale, ahead of Catholics and mainline Protestants.[29]

The impact of the 2016 election aside, accurately counting anti-Semitic incidents is a challenge, partly because many police departments do not report hate crimes separately. The latest FBI statistics show that Jews were the targets in more than half of religiously motivated hate crimes in 2014 and 2015.[30]

The SPLC, which monitors hate groups, has never counted hate crimes before, so it has no previous annual statistics to compare them with, according to spokesman Lenz.

Further, methods of gathering statistics on anti-Semitic hate crimes differ around the world, with some countries and organizations showing a decline while others show an uptick.

For instance, the Kantor Center in Tel Aviv, which collects data on anti-Semitism from 40 countries, found violent anti-Semitic incidents worldwide falling 12 percent in 2016 to 361, a 10-year low. And the French government reported a 61 percent plunge in all forms of anti-Semitism last year, which the center largely attributed to increased security after recent terrorist attacks.

However, contrary to claims from right-wing groups, newly arrived Muslim immigrants have not been responsible for rising anti-Semitic incidents, such as a 16 percent uptick in Berlin, said the center. "The perpetrators continue to be the radical circles of the previous Muslim immigrants" including European-born children of Muslim immigrants, and the extreme right, the center said. New immigrants, it said, are "busy surviving," looking for work and learning a new language.[31]

Anti-Semitic hate crimes rose in some countries, including in Austria and Britain, where they reached a record last year, according to London's Community Security Trust.[32]

In addition, the Kantor Center reported "a widespread increase" in anti-Semitism on the web that "cannot be quantified."[33]

In 2016, an anti-Semitic message was posted every 83 seconds in cyberspace, mostly on Twitter, according to the World Jewish Congress.[34]

"Hate against Jews is not really dropping; it has just moved" onto the internet, where enforcement is "less well developed," said European Jewish Congress President Moshe Kantor, after whom the Kantor Center is named. As hate has migrated online, he said, the sense of security in Jewish communities "remains fragile."[35]

Is opposition to Israel a form of anti-Semitism?

Scholars and activists have debated for more than a decade whether opposition to the state of Israel is a new form of anti-Semitism. Bernard Lewis, a professor emeritus of Near Eastern Studies at Princeton University, used the term "the new antisemitism" in a 2004 paper.[36]

Since then, the concept has been adopted by the State Department and some prominent scholars, but it remains highly controversial. Natan Sharansky, a Soviet dissident who became an Israeli politician, said the new anti-Semitism could be recognized by using his "three Ds" test: Demonization (comparing the Israelis to Nazis); a double standard (singling Israel out for its

Messages of sympathy, "We are all Jews," hang outside a kosher grocery store in Paris where four people were killed in a terrorist attack in 2015. Muslim extremists have been implicated in several deadly terrorist attacks in recent years on Jewish gathering places in Europe, including a Copenhagen synagogue, the Jewish Museum in Brussels and a Jewish school in Toulouse, France.

alleged human-rights violations when other countries are far worse); and delegitimization (denying Israel's right to exist).[37]

Since then Sharansky's three Ds have been incorporated into the State Department's "working definition" of anti-Semitism.[38] The formulation also was adopted last year as a non-legally binding definition by Britain and by the International Holocaust Remembrance Alliance — 31 nations committed to Holocaust education.[39]

The question of when criticism of Israel becomes anti-Semitism has been at the heart of two recent controversies: proposals to include the State Department definition in federal and state legislation and claims that the Boycott, Divestment and Sanctions (BDS) movement is anti-Semitic.

The movement is a worldwide campaign to get governments, universities and individuals to boycott Israeli products and divest themselves of investments in Israeli holdings as a way to protest Israel's 50-year occupation of the West Bank and Gaza territories. The debate over the boycott centers on whether the movement is just aimed against Israel's treatment of Palestinians living in the territories or is also a protest against Israel's existence.

Last year the Senate passed a bill to require the federal government to use the State Department definition of anti-Semitism when investigating discrimination

complaints on college campuses. Known as the Anti-Semitism Awareness Act, the measure died without reaching the House floor but is expected to be reintroduced. Several prominent Jewish groups strongly support it, but the American Civil Liberties Union (ACLU) says it infringes on free speech.[40] Several state legislatures also have considered similar bills.

Kenneth Marcus, president of the Washington-based Louis D. Brandeis Center, which fights anti-Semitism, says the bill is needed because harassment of Jewish students on college campuses has been rising and is often associated with BDS demonstrations.

AMCHA, a college watchdog group named after the Hebrew word for "your people" or "grassroots," reported a 45 percent increase in anti-Semitic incidents on campuses in the first half of 2016, to 287, over the same period the previous year.[41]

But according to Mitchell Bard, executive director of the American-Israeli Cooperative Enterprise, a nonprofit that aims to strengthen relations between the two countries, more than a third of the events were lectures, "echo chambers attended by the like-minded," and some were peaceful protests against Israeli policies. "[W]hile some guerrilla theater meant to highlight Israel's alleged abuses is disturbing, it is not de facto anti-Semitic," he wrote.[42]

Marcus says the legislation is needed to deal with "campuses where there's a large amount of severe pervasive hostility to Jews, not just in protest activities but threats, vandalism and physical assaults — where the perpetrators often hide behind the notion that they're merely anti-Zionist." (Historically Zionism referred to the movement to establish a Jewish homeland in Israel; in modern times, it usually refers to support for the modern state of Israel.)

However, Kenneth S. Stern, who helped draft the original definition of anti-Semitism for a European monitoring group, strongly opposes the congressional legislation. The three Ds were intended to help countries collect data on anti-Semitic acts by using a uniform definition, says Stern, who is now executive director of the Justus and Karin Rosenberg Foundation, which combats anti-Semitism. "That's quite different from using it as a way to chill discussion on college campuses," he says.

Some Jewish groups have used the definition to try to stop protests against Israel's treatment of Palestinians, he says, such as the annual "Apartheid Week" held on many campuses or debates over the BDS movement. If the bill becomes law, university administrators would likely shut down such protests and debate to avoid losing federal funding or being sued for discrimination, he says.

Doing so would shut down a chance to develop a deeper understanding of what actually constitutes anti-Semitism, Stern says.

Yet some who are troubled by the "new anti-Semitism" say they do not oppose criticism of Israeli policies but draw a line when it evolves into opposition to Israel's existence. In a recent essay entitled "Why present-day 'anti-Zionism' is anti-Semitic," Bernard Harrison, emeritus professor of philosophy at the University of Utah, defined anti-Zionism as "political anti-Semitism," because it aims to bring about the destruction of Israel.[43]

The ADL's Greenblatt echoes that view. The BDS movement is "a global effort designed to isolate and punish Israel and end the Jewish state," he says, "denying solely to the Jewish people a universal right of self-determination."

However, Liz Jackson, a staff attorney at Palestine Legal, a group that litigates on behalf of Americans advocating for Palestinian rights, says she does not see opposition to Israel's existence as anti-Semitic. She does not believe in a separate state for Jews, she says, even though she is Jewish.

"Jews have to be safe everywhere in the world; not in just one country," she says. "You can't have a democratic society which privileges one religious group above another; anti-Jewish hatred has nothing to do with that."

In England, a similar debate is raging over the Conservative government's adoption of the State Department definition of anti-Semitism. Jewish groups supporting Palestinian rights say it could chill speech.[44]

The question of whether Israel should exist is a legitimate political argument, says Naomi Wayne, an Executive Committee member of the London-based Jews for Justice for Palestinians. "Was Israel founded

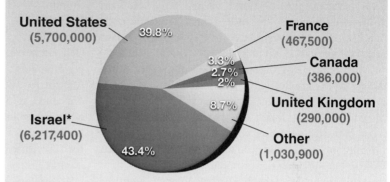

Israel, U.S. Have Biggest Jewish Populations

More than 90 percent of the global Jewish population lives in just five countries, with Israel and the United States home to the largest numbers by far.

Countries With Largest Jewish Populations and Their Percentage of World Jewish Population, 2015

United States (5,700,000) — 39.8%
France (467,500) — 3.3%
Canada (386,000) — 2.7%
United Kingdom (290,000) — 2%
Other (1,030,900) — 8.7%
Israel* (6,217,400) — 43.4%

* Includes Jewish residents in East Jerusalem, the West Bank and the Golan Heights.

Source: "Antisemitism Worldwide 2015," Tel Aviv University Kantor Center, p.66, http://tinyurl.com/keubxwk

in compliance with international law? People have different . . . views. What is wrong with having those debates?" she asks.

Should online anti-Semitic speech be further restricted?

In a YouTube video entitled "Jews Admit Organizing White Genocide," former Ku Klux Klan Imperial Wizard David Duke says "Zionists" are "ethnically cleansing" Israel of Palestinians and planning "to do the same thing" in Europe and America by promoting the immigration of non-whites.[45]

That video triggered controversy in Britain after a Parliamentary committee investigating hate crimes recently flagged it to Google, which owns YouTube. However, Google vice president Peter Barron told the committee his company had not removed the video because it did not meet the company's standards for speech so objectionable it should be blocked.[46]

The committee's chair, Yvette Cooper, was incredulous. "You allow David Duke to upload an entire video which is all about malicious and hateful comments about

Jewish people. How on Earth is that not a breach of your own guidelines?"[47]

Cooper's frustration is shared by groups fighting anti-Semitism in Europe and the United States, where online anti-Semitism is becoming increasingly hard to monitor or control. In fact, the Duke video was just one of more than 200 anti-Semitic YouTube videos discovered by a *Times of London* investigation.[48] In the United States, an ADL investigation found more than 2.6 million anti-Semitic tweets between August 2015 and July 2016, many directed at Jewish journalists.[49]

Most of the 28 EU countries ban hate speech, but debate rages over how to apply those laws to the fast-changing world of online interactions. The major hosting companies — Google, Facebook and Twitter — are based in the United States, where hate speech is constitutionally protected except when used to incite imminent violence and in other narrow circumstances.[50]

Thus, regulating the borderless internet requires negotiation between American companies and the European Union or its members.[51] Under a voluntary agreement with the EU, Google and other major media companies have agreed to review and remove illegal hate speech within 24 hours after it has been identified by an internet user.[52]

Critics say Twitter and Facebook have been even less responsive. In Germany, a recent survey by the Justice Ministry found that Twitter deletes only 1 percent of offensive content, and Facebook, about half.[53]

In response, and due to politicians' concerns that "fake news" and hate speech could sway upcoming elections, Germany became the first EU country to impose clear guidelines for penalizing online hate speech in April, when the cabinet approved controversial new fines for such speech. The law imposes fines of up to 50 million euros ($53 million) for social media companies that do not remove hate speech within 24 hours for clearly illegal content, as defined by German law, and within seven days in more ambiguous cases.[54]

The tech industry and civil liberties groups oppose the measure. Human Rights First has called it "a dangerous abridgement of free speech rights" that would embolden authoritarian governments to suppress legitimate speech. Such a broad attempt "tends to drive those sympathetic to such ideas underground, likely reinforcing their ideology," said Erika Asgeirsson, a fellow at Human Rights First. And clamping down on social media "will just change the means of dissemination."[55]

"We don't need more restrictions," says Barbora Bukovská, senior director for law and policy at Article 19, a London-based international group that advocates for free speech. Restricting speech of figures like Duke elevates them "to a pedestal as a hero and gives them exposure they don't deserve," she says.

Bitkom, an association representing digital companies, said the short deadlines and high penalties in the German law would seriously curtail free speech by forcing providers to delete doubtful content as a precaution. And the law would make "private companies rather than the courts . . . the judges of what is illegal in Germany," said a Facebook spokesman.[56]

In Britain, it is unclear whether the government will try to penalize Google under existing law or propose legislation similar to Germany's.[57] Either step would likely raise similar objections. Stephen Pollard, the editor of the London-based *Jewish Chronicle*, has said Duke's video should remain online so his assertions can be debated. Exposure of anti-Semites' lies is what "actually defeats them," he wrote.[58]

In the United States, banning online hate speech would run afoul of the First Amendment and Section 230 of the Communications Decency Act, which immunizes internet service providers (ISPs) from prosecution for content created by others.[59]

However, Rep. Smith, a senior member of the House Foreign Relations Committee, says he wants such immunity eliminated so ISPs that host speech inciting people to violence can be penalized. "I love the First Amendment, but it is not absolute," Smith says. Some websites, he says, are getting people "ginned up to commit horrific violence."[60]

Groups such as the ADL and Human Rights First say they will continue working with Google and other media companies on a voluntary basis to help improve their ability to identify hate speech.

But the "haters have honed their skills to skirt the websites' terms of service in a skillful way," says Jonathan Vick, the ADL's associate director for investigative technology and cyber-hate response. Once a Duke video is taken down, supporters repeatedly repost it under different titles, reducing the exercise to a game of "whack-a-mole," he says.

BACKGROUND

'Blood Libel'

Anti-Semitism has endured for centuries and been almost universal — causing Jews to be repeatedly expelled from their home countries and to become the target of unparalleled levels of violence. Anti-Semitism has long been rooted in Christian teachings that Jews killed Jesus Christ, although many Christian leaders, including recent popes, have disavowed that view.[61]

One of the oldest slanders about Jews — that they killed Christian children as part of a ritual murder — originated in 12th-century Europe. The fabricated story that a young Christian boy in Norwich, England, had been killed by Jews for a religious ritual would become one of the most common incitements to anti-Jewish riots and killings during the Middle Ages.

Partly as a result of this "blood libel," Christians increasingly saw Jews as evil; in many countries Jews were forced to live apart and wear special clothing or badges to alert strangers to the dangers they supposedly posed, such as starting plagues or poisoning wells.[62]

In Europe riots against Jews erupted even as they were denied equal rights with Christians. Jews were barred from owning land and from craft guilds, forcing them to depend on money-lending or commerce, leading to the stereotype of the Jew as a greedy money-lender.

In the first large-scale deportation of Jews from a European country, King Edward expelled all Jews from England in 1290, ending their presence there for 400 years. In 1306 and 1394 Jews were expelled from France and over the next 150 years from Hungary, Austria, Lithuania and various German localities. Jews were expelled from Spain in 1492. Jews escaping Catholic persecution in Brazil in 1654 became the first Jewish settlers in North America.[63]

During the French Revolution in 1791, Jews were granted full equal rights based on the radical idea that citizenship should be granted without regard to religion or ethnicity.

"In the 19th century, France was the one country where Jews faced no legal obstacles to social and economic integration," says Maurice Samuels, director of the Yale Program for the Study of Antisemitism and author of *The Right to Difference: French Universalism and the Jews* (2016). By contrast, he notes, some American states

Members of Jewish groups and their supporters protest in Beverly Hills, Calif., on Dec. 4, 2016, against President-elect Donald Trump for what they saw as his failure to condemn a spate of anti-Semitic incidents and his hiring of Stephen Bannon as his chief strategist. Bannon, the former head of Breitbart News, has called the website "a platform for the alt-right," referring to the alternative right, which includes anti-Semitic and white nationalist groups.

Getty Images/NurPhoto/Ronen Tivony

such as New Hampshire, until 1877, still barred Jews from holding public office, even though the Constitution granted them equal rights at the federal level.

Compared to France, he says, "there was prevailing anti-Semitism in American life that lasted to the 1960s — quotas at universities, de facto exclusion from law firms and corporations, and housing covenants," which barred Jews from buying or renting in certain neighborhoods. They were also excluded from private schools and clubs and hotels.

By the late 19th century, most of continental Europe had enacted full Jewish emancipation, but that roused resentment — most famously in a German journalist and Jew-hater, Wilhelm Marr. In 1879, he coined the term "anti-Semitism" declaring himself a proud "anti-Semite." Like the Nazis later, Marr saw the Jews as a threatening race that had seized control of the German economy and society, and he argued that the only solution was their forced removal from Germany. He used the term "Semite" for Jews, according to historians, because it sounded scientifically neutral and modern.[64]

Some Jewish intellectuals began to wonder if they were welcome in Europe. Theodor Herzl, an Austro-Hungarian Jewish journalist for a Viennese newspaper, covered the notorious 1894 trial of Capt. Alfred Dreyfus, a French Jew falsely accused of spying for the Germans. During the trial Herzl witnessed anti-Jewish demonstrations in Paris, during which cries of "death to the Jews" were common; Jewish businesses, synagogues and homes were attacked and anti-Jewish riots erupted in about 70 cities. The so-called Dreyfus Affair became a watershed event for French Jews, who felt increasingly vulnerable. Dreyfus' innocence was not officially recognized until 1906.

Herzl, a secular Jew, decided that if anti-Semitism was so entrenched in the capital of the European Enlightenment, Jews could never assimilate in Europe. In 1907 he organized the First Zionist Congress in Basel, Switzerland, which voted to establish a "publicly and legally secured home" for the Jews in the geographic region between the Mediterranean Sea and the Jordan River known as Palestine.[65]

In Herzl's utopian vision of a Jewish homeland, he imagined that Arabs in Palestine would welcome the gifts of science brought by the Jews. But Arab opposition to the influx of Jews only hardened over time, leading to the development of the Palestine national liberation movement.

Fabricated Charge

The elaborate forgery known as the "Protocols of the Learned Elders of Zion" is the most infamous document to libel the Jews. It purportedly comprised the minutes from a conference of Jewish groups plotting a takeover of the world. It first appeared in Russia between 1903 and 1905, concocted by the Russian secret police as part of a campaign against the Jews. In 1921, the *Times of London* exposed the tract as a fraud, showing how the author had copied fictional works to create it.[66]

However, "The Nazis saw its value immediately," as evidence of an alleged Jewish conspiracy theory, wrote Stephen Eric Bronner, a professor of political science at Rutgers University. "The Jew is not simply a capitalist or a communist revolutionary, but the Jew is now any enemy required by the anti-Semite," Bronner wrote.[67]

In the United States, automobile manufacturer Henry Ford was the strongest booster of the "Protocols." In 1920, he began serializing them in his newspaper, *The Dearborn Independent*. American Jews tried to persuade him it was a forgery, and in 1921 President Woodrow Wilson signed a letter denouncing *The Independent* for its anti-Semitic campaign.[68]

But the "Protocols" continued to be popular, contributing to a rise in anti-Semitism in the United States. In May 1924, President Calvin Coolidge signed the National Origins Act, effectively closing the United States to most Jewish immigrants, particularly those from eastern and southern Europe.[69]

The term Holocaust did not come into use until several years after World War II ended. In 1943, Jews were barely mentioned in Allied propaganda.[70]

Soon after the war's end, it was widely known that the Germans had killed 6 million Jews during World War II, and 21 Nazi Party leaders were tried for war crimes in Nuremberg, Germany, in 1945 and 1946. But European Jewry's fate under the Nazis did not enter European public consciousness until the 1960s, when Israel tried Nazi official Adolf Eichmann and Germany tried former Auschwitz guards, said historian Tony Judt in his book *Postwar*.[71]

Then in 1979, the acclaimed 1978 American TV miniseries "Holocaust," starring Meryl Streep, was shown in Germany and watched by half of the German population. During discussion forums following each of the four episodes, some 10,000 phone calls poured in from viewers. For many Germans, the series was "an emotional introduction, the first encounter with the almost incomprehensible horrors of the Nazi regime," according to Jewish historian Julius H. Schoeps.[72]

Afterward, the word "Holocaust" entered common usage in Germany, and Germans became "among the best-informed Europeans on the subject of the Shoah [Hebrew for Holocaust] and at the forefront of all efforts to maintain public awareness of their country's singular crime," according to Judt.[73]

Meanwhile, the French did not acknowledge their wartime guilt in sending Jews to their death until 1995, when President Jacques Chirac admitted that the French helped to round up nearly 13,000 Jews — more than 4,000 of them children — for deportation to Auschwitz in July 1942.

Resurging Hostility

Much of the anti-Semitism that emerged in the 1990s and 2000s can be traced to the proclamation establishing the state of Israel by the Jewish community in Palestine

CHRONOLOGY

Middle Ages–19th Century *Ritual-murder rumors incite pogroms; Jews are persecuted during Spanish inquisition.*

1144 "Blood libel" claim that Jews murder Christian children for religious ritual emerges in England.

1290 Jews expelled from England.

1492–1498 Jews expelled from Spain, then Portugal and France.

1654 Jewish families arrive in New Amsterdam (later called New York), after fleeing Portuguese persecution in Brazil.

1791 During French Revolution France gives Jews equal rights.

1879 German journalist Wilhelm Marr coins term "anti-Semitism."

1894–99 Capt. Alfred Dreyfus, a French Jew, is falsely accused of treason. Affair radicalizes journalist Theodor Herzl, who later leads Zionist movement.

1900s–1960s *Immigration laws aim to keep Jews out of the United States; Nazis kill 6 million Jews. Holocaust enters public consciousness.*

1903 "Protocols of the Learned Elders of Zion," a hoax claiming a Jewish plot for world domination, published in Russia.

1907 First Zionist Congress in Basel, Switzerland, votes to establish Jewish homeland in Palestine, which later becomes Israel.

1920 Industrialist Henry Ford serializes "Protocols of Zion."

1924 National Origins Law closes United States to most Jewish immigrants.

1942 Mass gassings begin at Nazis' Auschwitz-Birkenau camp. Vichy government deports 15,000 French Jews to Auschwitz.

1945 World War II ends. Allied troops liberate German concentration camps. An estimated 6 million Jews have died at Nazi hands. Nuremberg war crimes trials begin.

1948 Jewish community in Palestine proclaims state of Israel.

1962 Israelis find former Nazi official Adolf Eichmann guilty of crimes against the Jewish people; he is hanged.

2000–Present *Jews become targets of terrorist attacks in Europe and rising anti-Semitism in the United States and Britain.*

2000 Second Palestinian uprising ("intifada") spurs anti-Semitic crimes in Europe. . . . European Union begins tracking anti-Jewish incidents.

Sept. 11, 2001 Islamist terrorists fly hijacked passenger planes into the World Trade Center in New York and the Pentagon, sparking rumors that Jews knew about it in advance.

2002 Pakistani Islamist terrorists kill *Wall Street Journal* reporter Daniel Pearl.

2012 French Muslim attacks Jewish school in Toulouse, France, killing four.

2014 Four people killed at Jewish Museum of Brussels in Belgium.

2015 Islamist gunman kills four people in kosher grocery in Paris after attack on *Charlie Hebdo* magazine (Jan. 9). . . . Gunman opens fire on Copenhagen synagogue, killing one (Feb. 14).

2016 Record number of anti-Semitic attacks reported in Britain; U.S. Senate passes Anti-Semitism Awareness Act, defining anti- Semitism as including "demonization" of Israel; it dies in House.

2017 More than 100 bomb threats at U.S. Jewish institutions raise fear of growing anti-Semitism; Jewish Israeli-American man arrested, alleged to have made most of the threats. . . . Anti-Defamation League reports spikes in anti-Semitic incidents in United States in 2016 and 2017, citing increases in white supremacist activity by groups following presidential election campaign. . . . Violent attacks on Jews decline worldwide, Tel Aviv University reports, citing beefed-up security.

Anti-Semitism Persists in an Unsettled Poland

"We didn't resolve the problem of what Poles did to Jews."

The image of an ultra-orthodox Jew being burned in effigy at an anti-refugee rally in Poland in 2015 outraged many people around the world — and puzzled them as well. Why were Jews being blamed for the influx of refugees — most of them Muslims — arriving in Europe from Syria and elsewhere?

During his trial last November for inciting hatred by burning the effigy, Polish businessman Piotr Rybak, one of the rally's organizers, explained that his straw man represented billionaire Jewish-American financier George Soros.[1]

Poles with anti-Muslim views "generally blame Jews for being liberals, and there are a lot of conspiracy theories about liberals such as George Soros bringing Muslims to Europe," explains Michal Bilewicz, director of the Center for Research on Prejudice at the University of Warsaw. A survey released by the center in January, he says, showed anti-Semitism rising between 2014 and 2016 "fueled by the anti-Muslim panic that spread towards other religious and ethnic groups — for example Jewish people."

The survey also found that fewer Poles today consider anti-Semitic statements offensive. For example, a media reference to Jews as "scumbags" was offensive to only 43 percent of young people in 2016 — down from 66 percent in 2014.[2]

Bilewicz attributes the rise in anti-Semitism to an increase in anti-Semitic and right-wing rhetoric online. More than 90 percent of young people have daily contact on the internet with hate speech — against Roma (gypsies), Muslims and Jews, he says. And in a survey of 18- to 35-year-olds a week before Poland's October 2015 parliamentary elections, he found that most young voters were supporting "extremely conservative, anti-immigrant and xenophobic" political parties.

It has long been a mystery why anti-Jewish attitudes persist in a country where few Jews remained after World War II. Most of Poland's 3 million Jews were murdered in the Holocaust.[3] About 300,000 Jews survived, but the majority of them left the country after the war or never returned to their homes as word spread of Poles killing returning Jews. Most emigrated to Central Europe, the United States or Israel.[4] According to the last census, only about 10,000 Jews live in Poland, out of a population of 38 million, but there could be up to 20-30,000, says Bilewicz, because "it's a society where not a lot of people are open about their Jewish identity."

Poles have struggled to come to terms with the Holocaust and their role in it. A flare-up arose recently after a 2015 article by Polish-born Princeton historian Jan T. Gross, who wrote that Poles killed more Jews than Germans during the war.[5] The Polish public prosecutor has been investigating whether to charge Gross with "insulting the Polish nation," a crime punishable by up to three years in prison.[6]

In addition, a proposed law would make it a crime, also with a maximum three-year prison sentence, to say Poles were complicit in the murder of Jews during the Holocaust.[7] In his 2001 book *Neighbors*, Gross described how Polish citizens of the town Jedwabne killed their Jewish neighbors in 1941 by corralling up to 1,600 men, women and children into a barn and setting it on fire. And Gross' 2006 book *Fear* described the 1946 massacre by Poles of Jews returning to their homes in the city of Kielce after the war.[8]

Gross told the *Haaretz* newspaper that he would welcome the chance to defend his research in court, but blamed the push to prosecute him on the right-wing conservative government elected in Poland in 2015. "This strange regime works very hard on falsification of history," he said.[9]

These days, Poles are mainly interested in hearing about Polish heroes who risked their lives to save Jews, not those who killed them, says Anna Bikont, a journalist for Poland's largest paper, *Gazeta Wyborcza*. "It's all about the pride of Poland," she says. "You use Jews only to say how we [Poles] saved them . . . , how we were brave and fantastic. We have

on May 14, 1948. The U.N. General Assembly had tried to partition the territory into Jewish and Arab states in 1947, but the Arab League and Palestinian institutions rejected the plan.[74]

Israel's Arab neighbors immediately declared war, resulting in hundreds of thousands of Palestinian refugees fleeing to neighboring Jordan, Lebanon and Syria. An equal number of Jews were driven from their ancestral homes in the region.[75]

The Six-Day War in 1967 led to Israel's occupation of Gaza and the West Bank, where more than a million Palestinians still live under Israeli occupation today. In 1987 such a bad attitude towards immigrants because we didn't resolve the problem of what Poles did to Jews."

The proposed law is aimed at Gross and writers like herself, says Bikont, whose forthcoming book about Irena Sendler, a Pole who saved 2,500 Jewish children from the Warsaw Ghetto, describes those efforts as a lonely struggle amidst Poles who wanted to denounce or kill Jews.[10] "For my new book, I could theoretically be sentenced," Bikont says.

Scholars around the world protested the news that Gross was under prosecutorial investigation.[11] And the proposed legislation, widely condemned as historical censorship, is unlikely to pass, according to Maciej Kozlowski, a former Polish ambassador to Israel who teaches Holocaust history at Collegium Civitas university in Warsaw. But it could discourage writers and scholars from publishing on the controversial topic, Bikont says.

Although Bilewicz's survey has found growing anti-Semitic attitudes, Michael Schudrich, the American-born Chief Rabbi of Poland, says he hasn't sensed any recent upsurge in overt anti-Jewish behavior. Thousands of Jewish visitors come to Poland every year, he says, but "there are almost no acts of anti-Semitism."

Schudrich presides over a small but growing community of about 700 Jewish families in Warsaw, many of them converts from Catholicism. "I have people still coming to me saying, 'I discovered three months ago my grandfather is Jewish. What do I do?' "

Poland's Jewish community has a future, Schudrich maintains, "and that couldn't be said 20 years ago."

— Sarah Glazer

Getty Images/NurPhoto/Artur Widak

Edward Mosberg, a Holocaust survivor from New Jersey, and his granddaughter participate on April 24 in the annual March of the Living between Auschwitz and Birkenau, the sites of two former Nazi death camps in Poland. The Polish people in recent years have struggled to come to terms with their role in the Holocaust.

---

[1] "Polish man jailed for burning effigy of ultra-Orthodox Jew," *The Times of Israel*, Nov. 21, 2016, http://tinyurl.com/m77zmd6. The effigy-burning occurred in Wroclaw, Poland, in November 2015. The sentence was reduced from 10 months to three months by a district court in April. See "There is a verdict for burning a Jewish puppet on a Wroclaw Market," *Newsweek*, April 13, 2017, http://tinyurl.com/kewgqf4.

[2] Don Snyder, "Anti-Semitism Spikes in Poland — Stoked by Populist Surge against Refugees," Reuters, Jan. 24, 2017, http://tinyurl.com/ml9ygtt.

[3] "Polish Victims," *Holocaust Encyclopedia*, U.S. Holocaust Memorial Museum, http://tinyurl.com/n5dycy8.

[4] Yad Vashem, "Frequently Asked Questions: In what condition were the Jews in Germany and Poland after the liberation?" http://tinyurl.com/l3xnd3x.

[5] Jan T. Gross, "Eastern Europe's Crisis of Shame," Project Syndicate, Sept. 13, 2015, http://tinyurl.com/n55ayro.

[6] Ofer Aderet, "Historian May Face Charges in Poland for Writing that Poles Killed Jews in World War II," *Haaretz*, Oct. 30, 2016, http://tinyurl.com/h7wx5s2.

[7] "Testimony of Mark Weitzman," Simon Wiesenthal Center, Subcommittee on Africa, Global Health, Global Human Rights, and International Organizations, House Committee on Foreign Affairs, March 22, 2017, p. 3, http://tinyurl.com/l4362ut.

[8] Alex Duval Smith, "Polish move to strip Holocaust expert of award sparks protests," *The Observer*, Feb. 14, 2016, http://tinyurl.com/lv6wd6z.

[9] "Historians May Face Charges," op. cit.

[10] Anna Bikont, *Sendlerowa: In Hiding* (forthcoming).

[11] "Historian May Face Charges in Poland for Writing that Poles Killed Jews in World War II," op. cit.

---

and 2000, Palestinian resentment erupted into violent so-called *intifadas* ("shaking off" in Arabic).[76] Anti-Semitic incidents surged in Europe after the Second Intifada.

Muslim terrorists' hatred of Jews surfaced in a spectacular way on Sept. 11, 2001, when 19 Islamist radicals flew hijacked planes into the World Trade Center in New York City and into the Pentagon, killing approximately 3,000 people. A former member of the al-Qaeda cell that planned the attack testified that New York City was targeted because it was the "center of world Jewry." A Lebanese TV station falsely claimed the Israeli secret police knew of the impending attack and warned Jews

Anti-Semitism Charges Roil Britain's Left

Labour Party suspends a prominent member for controversial remarks.

For the past year, Britain's opposition Labour Party, representing the country's liberal left, has been convulsed by charges of endemic anti-Semitism.

The issue came to a head in April as Labour considered whether to expel former London Mayor Ken Livingstone permanently for bringing disrepute to the party in connection with remarks he made linking Nazi leader Adolf Hitler with Zionism.

On April 4, after an 11-month inquiry, Labour's constitutional committee recommended a one-year suspension, during which Livingstone may not run for office.[1] The sanction followed a one-year suspension already imposed on him.

Livingstone's remarks came last year while defending a Labour member of Parliament, Naz Shah, against charges of anti-Semitism. In 2014 she had shared a post on Facebook proposing to "relocate" Israel to America as a "solution" to the Middle East crisis.[2]

Livingstone called the criticism against Shah "a very well-orchestrated campaign by the Israel lobby to smear anybody who criticizes Israeli policy as anti-Semitic." He told a BBC interviewer that Hitler supported Zionism "before he went mad and ended up killing 6 million Jews."[3] Zionism is the national movement to re-establish a Jewish homeland in the territory now known as Israel; since establishment of Israel in 1948, Zionism has referred to the development and protection of the Jewish nation in Israel.[4]

Livingstone apparently was referring to an agreement Hitler made in 1933 with several German Zionists to allow some Jews to emigrate to Palestine. Nazi regulations prohibited German Jews from taking their savings out of Germany. But under the agreement, the Palestinian Jewish community was allowed to buy German agricultural equipment with some of the funds blocked by the Nazis.

Jews who came to Palestine from Israel were able to "claw back a portion of their funds upon arrival," explains Emory University Holocaust historian Deborah Lipstadt.[5]

But historians dispute the idea that Hitler favored a Jewish homeland.[6] The Nazis' primary motive, it seems, was to break an economic boycott initiated by American Jews a few months' earlier.[7]

David Baddiel, a British Jewish comedian, observed that Livingstone's interpretation showed "no compassion" for this moment when the Nazis were "taking advantage of the terror and despair of fleeing refugees to get more of them to leave the country." That reflects a feeling on the left, Baddiel said, that "Jews don't quite fit into the category of The Oppressed, and so therefore don't deserve the same protections and sympathy as other minorities."[8]

"Livingstone's comments about Zionist-Nazi so-called collaboration are part of a longstanding undercurrent on the British far left of accusing Zionists of being party to the Holocaust," says Paul Bogdanor, a British writer and co-editor of the 2006 book *The Jewish Divide over Israel.*

It's not surprising, he says, that the 2015 election of leftist Jeremy Corbyn as Labour's leader coincided with "a vast outpouring of anti-Semitism among Labour's far left forces," including thousands of anti-Semitic tweets and social-media messages received by Jewish members of Parliament. Corbyn has described Hamas and Hezbollah — labeled as terrorist groups by the United States — as "friends" and argues that Palestinian refugees who left Israel in 1948 and their descendants have the right to return to Israel and reclaim their property.[9]

Last April, Labour suspended Shah for the social-media remarks she made about Israel, for which she apologized. But the media publicity about her suspension was followed by a spike of anti-Semitic incidents in May, reaching a record high for a single month, according to the Community Security Trust (CST), a London-based group that tracks such incidents.[10]

Overall the organization counted a record 1,309 anti-Semitic incidents in 2016, up 36 percent from 2015, including a record 106 violent assaults.[11]

Anti-Semitism has been growing on the right as well. The CST attributed the increase partly to an uptick in xenophobia and racist hate crimes following Brexit — Britain's vote on June 23, 2016, to leave the European Union.

"The debate at the time turned ugly, and it was a debate about who is British and who is not and who belongs . . . ," says Mark Gardner, the group's communications director. "When you have that sort of language, Jews don't benefit." Hate crimes rose 41 percent in the first month after the Brexit vote, but they weren't all against Jews. News reports also cited the killing of a Polish man, anti-Polish graffiti and anti-Muslim demonstrations.[12]

"The discourse is being allowed to fester in far right, far left and Islamist circles," says Gideon Falter, chairman of the Campaign Against Antisemitism, a British charity that organizes volunteers to counter anti-Semitism through education and alerting law enforcement. "If you allow this kind of hate to fester it becomes acts of hate."

Some pro-Palestinian advocates have called the recent turmoil in the Labour Party a "witch hunt" against party members for their criticism of Israel.[13]

While Livingstone's interpretation that Hitler supported Zionism was wrong, that doesn't make Livingstone anti-Semitic, said Donald Sassoon, emeritus professor of comparative history at Queen Mary University of London, one of 32 Jewish academics and Labour Party members who signed a letter condemning the disciplinary charges. "To be anti-Semitic you have to hate Jews, believe they control the world and so on," he said. "Nothing in [Livingstone's] statement suggests that."[14]

But others say the party has not gone far enough to discipline Livingstone. Nearly half of Labour's 229 members of Parliament signed an open letter protesting the decision not to expel Livingstone from the party. "[W]e will not allow our party to be a home for anti-Semitism and Holocaust revisionism," said the letter.[15]

The controversy seems unlikely to go away. Within hours of the April 4 announcement that he was being suspended, Livingstone was repeating his assertions about Nazi-Zionist collaboration in media interviews in which he appeared far from contrite.[16]

Party leader Corbyn responded by calling for Labour's ruling executive committee to consider further action based on Livingstone's new "offensive" remarks.[17]

— *Sarah Glazer*

Getty Images/Chris Ratcliffe

Former London Mayor Ken Livingstone received a one-year suspension from the Labour Party in Britain in connection with remarks — considered anti-Semitic — linking Adolf Hitler with Zionism.

[1] Rowena Mason and Jessica Elgot, "Labour suspends Livingstone for another year over Hitler comments," *The Guardian*, April 5, 2017, http://tinyurl.com/kythu9l.

[2] Heather Stewart, "Naz Shah suspended by Labour Party amid anti-Semitism row," *The Guardian*, April 27, 2016, http://tinyurl.com/m9pxrue.

[3] "UK Rabbi: Nothing more offensive than Livingstone's equation of Zionism and Nazism," *Times of Israel*, April 28, 2016, http://tinyurl.com/zy3dxtt.

[4] "Zionism," Jewish Virtual Library, http://tinyurl.com/m8d84qe.

[5] Deborah Lipstadt, "End the Misuse of Holocaust History," *The Atlantic*, April 14, 2017, http://tinyurl.com/krfzvs4.

[6] This was known as the Ha'avara ("transfer") agreement. See Edwin Black, "The Holocaust," Jewish Virtual Library, http://tinyurl.com/kfenpn7.

Also see, Paul Bogdanor, "Ken Livingstone's claims are an insult to the truth," *Jewish Chronicle*, March 31, 2017, http://tinyurl.com/lr7l34c.

[7] Black, op. cit.

[8] David Baddiel, "Why Ken Livingstone has it so wrong over Hitler and Zionism," *The Guardian*, April 6, 2017, http://tinyurl.com/khdldo3.

[9] Paul Bogdanor, "Jeremy Corbyn is placing himself at the head of Britain's 'Palestine Solidarity' Lynch Mobs," *The Algemeiner*, Sept. 17, 2015, http://tinyurl.com/lpmbp3k.

[10] Kate McCann, "Labour Party linked to increase in anti-Semitic incidents, according to charity report," *The Telegraph*, Feb. 2, 2017, http://tinyurl.com/j2q6nvc.

[11] Community Security Trust, "Antisemitic Incidents Report 2016," p. 6, http://tinyurl.com/mzvoz3b.

[12] Community Security Trust, op. cit., p. 13.

Also see, Katie Forster, "Hate Crimes Soared by 41 percent after Brexit vote," *The Independent*, Oct. 13, 2016, http://tinyurl.com/hs5wnb7.

Also see, "Brexit: Increase in Racist attacks after EU referendum," Aljazeera, June 28, 2016, http://tinyurl.com/gvxbvbf.

[13] Jonathan Cook, "Labour's witch hunt against Ken Livingstone," Free Speech on Israel, April 2, 2017, http://tinyurl.com/mcg3c9l.

[14] Koos Couve, "Ken Livingstone's comments were not anti-semitic, leading Jewish academics say," *Islington Tribune*, April 14, 2017, http://tinyurl.com/k6zv55a.

[15] Ben Kentish, "Almost half of Labour's MPs sign letter criticizing decision to allow Ken Livingstone to remain in party," *The Independent*, April 5, 2017, http://tinyurl.com/l7o9apv.

[16] See video of Ken Livingstone's remarks here: http://tinyurl.com/khdldo3.

[17] Joe Watts and Jon Stone, "Jeremy Corbyn calls meeting of Labour executive to probe fresh Ken Livingstone Nazi-Zionist comments," *The Independent*, April 5, 2017, http://tinyurl.com/mrkzkoc.

not to go to work at the trade center that day, even though 400 Jews died there.[77]

In 2002, radical Islam's anti-Semitism resurfaced when Pakistani terrorists slit the throat of American *Wall Street Journal* reporter Daniel Pearl on camera, and later decapitated him, after forcing him to say "I am a Jew."[78]

Other deadly attacks on Jews by Muslims include the 2012 attack on a Jewish school in Toulouse, France, killing a rabbi and three children, two of them his own.[79] A French Muslim, Mehdi Nemmouche, who had reportedly returned from a stint with ISIS in Syria before killing four people at the Jewish Museum in Brussels in 2014, is awaiting trial in that case.[80]

After the 2015 attack on the Paris office of the satirical magazine *Charlie Hebdo*, a gunman who had pledged his allegiance to the Islamic State killed four people in a kosher grocery in Paris before being killed by police.[81] A month later, a gunman killed a Jewish security guard at a Copenhagen synagogue during a bat mitzvah celebration. The suspected shooter, who grew up in Denmark and Jordan of Palestinian parentage, was killed during a shootout with police.[82]

The rise of right-wing parties in Europe has driven some of the growth of anti-Semitic crime in Europe, as politicians capitalize on xenophobic fear of new immigrants. When German hate crimes doubled in 2015, right-wing extremists were responsible for 91 percent of the anti-Jewish incidents, according to the Ministry of the Interior.[83]

In April, the U.S. Justice Department filed 36 charges against David Kadar, 18, the Israeli-American arrested in connection with the recent fake bomb threats, detailing 245 threatening calls, many targeting Jewish community centers, between January and March. Kadar appears to be linked to more than 240 hoax threats in the United States and Canada between August and December 2015.[84]

A few days later, the Israeli government indicted the teenager, whose name is under a gag order in Israel, for some 2,000 bomb threats over the past two to three years in the United States, Canada and other countries. His lawyer has said he has a brain tumor and suffers from autism.[85]

CURRENT SITUATION
Criticizing Trump

President Trump has been criticized by Jewish groups for being slow to condemn the rise in anti-Semitic incidents, but he recently made two statements sharply denouncing anti-Jewish hatred.

In a video address on April 21, Israel's Holocaust Remembrance Day, Trump called the murder of 6 million Jews by the Nazis the "darkest chapter in human history," adding: "The mind cannot fathom the pain, the horror and the loss" of the Holocaust.[86] Four days later he made his comments during the U.S. Holocaust Memorial Museum's annual days of remembrance.

But those comments followed at least two missteps by his administration — the failure to mention Jews in the International Holocaust Remembrance Day statement and his press secretary Sean Spicer's inaccurate claim that Hitler had never used poison gas on his own people.[87]

More worrying, however, says Susan Corke, director of countering anti-Semitism at Human Rights First, an international human-rights organization based in New York and Washington, are reports that Trump's counter-terrorism adviser, Sebastian Gorka, was a sworn member of the anti-Semitic, quasi-Nazi Hungarian nationalist group, Vitezi Rend. Gorka has denied the charge.[88]

Human Rights First has asked Trump to fire him.[89] His status remained unclear at press time.[90]

In April, the State Department announced that it would appoint a special envoy to monitor and counter anti-Semitism, a position created by Congress in 2004 but that has been vacant since January. Several watchdog groups have expressed concern that Trump's proposed budget cuts and a hiring freeze could cripple the office.[91] GOP Rep. Smith, who wrote the 2004 legislation, has introduced a bill to elevate the position to that of ambassador, saying the office must be "adequately staffed and resourced."[92]

In other legislation, opposing sides are gearing up to debate the Anti-Semitism Awareness Act, expected to be re-introduced. It would require the Education Department's Office of Civil Rights (OCR) to use the State Department's definition of anti-Semitism when investigating claims of discrimination and harassment on college campuses. The controversy centers on the State Department explanation of when anti-Israel criticism crosses the line into anti-Semitism — such as "demonizing" Israel by comparing it to Nazi Germany.

Under Title VI of the Civil Rights Act of 1964, the Education Department can withhold federal funding from a university found to have discriminated on the basis of race, color, or national origin. In 2004, the office said Jewish, Sikh and Muslim students also were protected from discrimination under Title VI.[93]

Yet the Brandeis Center's Marcus, who drafted the policy while serving as an official at the OCR, says the department has not found any civil rights violation in any anti-Semitism case it has investigated. "That system just isn't working. And Congress really needs to take action," he says. The proposed law "is the best solution because it gets to the root of OCR's and the universities' problems [about how to define anti-Semitism], while fully protecting freedom of speech and academic freedom."

Opponents of the measure say the department never found discrimination in any of these cases because there wasn't any. "Exposure to such discordant and robust expressions, even when offensive and hurtful, is a circumstance that a reasonable student in higher education may experience," the OCR said in dismissing a 2012 harassment complaint at the University of California about two anti-Israel speakers.[94]

The ACLU likely will oppose the bill, as it did last year, saying it could infringe on freedom of expression. "You don't want government making decisions about whether people have access to federal programs simply based upon their expression of political beliefs," says Michael W. Macleod-Ball, chief of staff and First Amendment counsel at the ACLU's Washington office. The organization and other opponents have complained the bill was passed without hearings or floor debate under the Senate's expedited unanimous consent procedure.

However, several prominent Jewish groups, including the ADL, strongly support the measure. Jewish students frequently say they feel uncomfortable or ostracized by demonstrations favoring boycotts of Israel or during Apartheid Week, especially if demonstrators use Nazi images or call Israelis "baby-killers" — reminiscent of the historic blood libel against Jews. "The effect is to isolate and to alienate Jews," says the ADL's Greenblatt.

Jackson of Palestine Legal, which opposes the bill, agrees that "criticism of Israeli policy often is vigorous, emotional, passionate, upsetting and uncomfortable for Jewish students; I experienced it as a Jewish student myself." But the goal of a university is "to have your ideas and world views challenged; that discomfort is not something universities should protect students from."

Legislatures in Tennessee, South Carolina and Virginia have been considering bills to require public universities or state agencies to use the State Department definition of anti-Semitism when investigating allegations of discrimination, but states do not have the power to threaten the ultimate penalty — to withdraw federal funding. The South Carolina bill passed the House.[95] A similar measure died in Virginia's short legislative session this spring.[96] Another is pending in Tennessee.[97]

International Action

Britain is one of the first countries to declare sweeping condemnation of Israel a form of anti-Semitism. The Conservative government announced the decision last December after it was agreed upon by the International Holocaust Remembrance Alliance in May 2016.

While the U.S. State Department has a similar definition, it is employed only in diplomatic efforts. The British government has said the new definition should apply to anti-Israel activities at home and was needed to "ensure that culprits will not be able to get away with being anti-Semitic because the term is ill-defined or because different organizations or bodies have different interpretations of it."[98]

Jewish groups in Britain who advocate for Palestinian rights oppose widespread adoption of the definition, citing two universities' decision to cancel their Israel Apartheid Week events in February 2017 as examples of the potential "chilling" effect of the measure.[99] The cancellations followed a letter to universities from government minister Jo Johnson just ahead of Apartheid Week saying they should have "zero tolerance" for anti-Semitism following recent anti-Semitic incidents on British campuses.[100]

While pro-Palestinian groups and some professors condemned the cancellations as suppression of free speech, the British watchdog group Campaign Against Anti-Semitism hailed them as successfully preventing expressions of anti-Jewish hatred.[101]

In April, the Austrian government joined Britain and Israel in defining anti-Semitism as including assaults on Israel's legitimacy, following reports that anti-Jewish incidents had reached a record high last year.[102]

BDS Movement

Local and national governments worldwide are writing legislation and Jewish groups are filing lawsuits aimed at

Has President Trump spurred anti-Semitism in the U.S.?

YES
Rob Eshman
Publisher and Editor-in-Chief, jewishjournal .com and Tribe Media Corp.

Written for *CQ Researcher*, May 2017

There has been an increase in anti-Semitic acts since Donald Trump's presidential campaign got underway. Nonprofit groups have documented an increase, as have government agencies such as the Los Angeles and New York City police departments. The only institution yet to weigh in is the FBI, which won't release its 2016 hate-crime statistics until year-end. Maybe the FBI will give a different picture, but as of now, anti-Semitism is worse.

To argue that Trump bears some responsibility for this is not to accuse him of being anti-Semitic. In fact, the Trump White House may be the most "Jewish" in American history. His two top advisers, daughter Ivanka and son-in-law Jared Kushner, are Jewish, as are senior officials such as Treasury Secretary Steven Mnuchin, National Economic Council Director Gary Cohn, senior adviser Steven Miller and Jason Greenblatt, special representative for international negotiations. If Trump is an anti-Semite, he's really bad at it.

But one doesn't have to be anti-Semitic to give cover to anti-Semites, and here is where Trump's campaign and administration are guilty.

During the campaign Trump refused to reject an endorsement from white supremacist David Duke. He retweeted an image of Hillary Clinton under the influence of stacks of $100 bills and a Star of David. By retweeting several posts from white supremacists, he garnered what the Southern Poverty Law Center called "unprecedented support" from this radical fringe. That support grew when Trump brought on Steve Bannon as a senior adviser. Bannon took over the website Breitbart.com and — in his words — recreated it as a "platform for the alt-right."

And these alt-right trolls unleashed their bile on Trump's Jewish critics. There has been truly unprecedented online harassment of Jewish journalists who dare criticize Trump.

"I've experienced more pure, unadulterated anti-Semitism since coming out against Trump's candidacy than at any other time in my political career," the conservative columnist Ben Shapiro wrote in the *National Review*.

Long after the campaign was over, Trump finally took a stand against this hate in his address to Congress. But he never explained why his administration left the mention of Jews out of its Holocaust Memorial Day announcement. De-Judaizing the Holocaust is a long-term goal of the radical right.

Trump an anti-Semite? No. Trump as someone who out of ignorance, instinct or connivance has used and given cover to anti-Semites? The evidence for that is strong, and unforgiveable.

NO
David E. Bernstein
Professor, George Mason University School of Law

Written for *CQ Researcher*, May 2017

Donald Trump has not inspired a new wave of American anti-Semitism. A Pew survey early in 2017 showed that Jews are the most admired religious group in the United States. A March Anti-Defamation League (ADL) survey shows a slight uptick in the percentage of Americans deemed anti-Semitic, but it was still near a historic low at 14 percent.

Nevertheless, some American Jews, especially among those who lean liberal politically, have been in something of an unwarranted panic over a purported surge in American anti-Semitism they attribute to Trump.

Part of this is Trump's fault. Trump has a Jewish daughter and grandchildren and a record of friendship with the Jewish community and has been an outspoken supporter of Israel, but his behavior during the campaign raised concerns that he is at best indifferent to anti-Semitism and at worst was purposely stoking it for political gain. Trump seemed to hesitate to renounce David Duke's support, failed to condemn anti-Semitic Twitter attacks on Jewish reporters and opponents, and retweeted memes with anti-Semitic origins. More generally, Trump's Euro-right style of nationalistic populism and insulting remarks about Muslims and Mexicans have raised concerns about rising intolerance against minorities, from which Jews are unlikely to be immune.

Much of the panic over anti-Semitism, however, ranged from overreaction to outright fantasy. Trump adviser Steve Bannon, for example, was widely but unfairly depicted as an anti-Semitic white nationalist. A few acts of vandalism at Jewish cemeteries, common during the Obama administration, were treated as an unprecedented outgrowth of Trumpism. A handful of alt-right provocateurs meeting in a hotel ballroom near Washington received wildly outsized media attention.

The hysteria reached a fever pitch in early 2017 when a wave of bomb threats against Jewish institutions was widely but prematurely attributed to white supremacists emboldened by the anti-Semitic environment purportedly created by Trump. In fact, the threats were the product of a psychologically disturbed Jewish Israeli and a copycat left-wing journalist angry at his girlfriend.

Unfortunately, the ADL, America's leading anti-Semitism watchdog, has fanned the flames. Leader Jonathan Greenblatt made the absurd claim that anti-Semitic discourse in the United States was at its worst level since the 1930s. Such overheated rhetoric may be good for fundraising, but it stoked unwarranted panic.

Americans, and especially American Jews, should always be vigilant about anti-Semitism. But anti-Semitism didn't disappear during the Obama years, and it hasn't suddenly become a crisis under Trump.

blocking the Boycott, Divestment and Sanctions (BDS) movement to boycott Israeli products and academic institutions. Proponents describe the movement, launched by pro-Palestinian groups in 2005, as a protest against Israel's occupation of Palestinian territories. Opponents call it an effort to bring about the end of Israel as a Jewish state.

In the United States, 17 states have passed laws either barring government contracts with groups that support the boycott or requiring state pension funds to divest themselves of companies that support it. Several states — including Texas, Washington, Nevada and New York — are considering anti-BDS legislation, as are some local governments.[103]

The Palestine Legal group says such laws are unconstitutional, citing legal opinions that boycotts are a form of protected speech.[104] In any case, says Palestine Legal attorney Jackson, the movement is growing in popularity. "People's interest in BDS is growing," especially as the peace process between Israel and Palestine seems perpetually stalled, she says. "There is no alternative to a peaceful solution; this is the only thing out there," Jackson says.

Numerous efforts are underway on campuses to persuade universities to join the boycott, but so far no American university has agreed to divest of its Israeli investments. Since 2012, however, 51 campuses have voted on resolutions urging divestment, mostly by student governments. Slightly fewer than half have passed.[105]

Last December Fordham University in New York City denied a student group's application to form a chapter of Students for Justice in Palestine, which supports the BDS movement. Dean of Students Keith Eldredge said in rejecting the application that the movement "presents a barrier to open dialogue and mutual learning and understanding" and creates the potential for campus "polarization."[106]

Four students, represented by Palestine Legal and the Center for Constitutional Rights, sued Fordham on April 26, saying the rejection represents discrimination based on students' political viewpoint and violates the university's free-speech policies.[107]

In Britain, the government has prohibited local governments from boycotting Israeli products.[108] The Palestine Solidarity Campaign, a British organization that supports Palestinian human rights, is taking the government to court over the prohibition, calling it a threat to freedom of expression.

Campaign Director Ben Jamal says boycotts are "used across the world to oppose human rights violations and in situations where diplomatic routes have failed." He adds, "The line that it's anti-Semitic doesn't hold and is a very dangerous line, because it conflates criticism of Israel with hatred of the Jewish people and by doing so undermines the fight against racism."

U.S. associations representing professors in academic specialties, such as the American Anthropological Association, have been bitterly divided over BDS resolutions, which some critics have said would prevent Israeli scholars from participating in conferences in the United States or other two-country exchanges. Both sides have raised concerns about academic freedom.[109]

After the American Studies Association voted for an academic boycott in 2013, eight academic organizations followed suit, according to Jackson. Four professors have sued the association, saying the boycott violated the association's own rules on how votes should be conducted.[110]

However, several larger academic organizations, including the American Anthropological Association and the Modern Language Association, have rejected the boycott, and numerous university presidents have condemned it.

OUTLOOK
'New Era'

The recent wave of bomb threats and cemetery desecrations created an unusual sense of uncertainty among American Jews, who until now have felt mostly comfortable in their home country compared to Jews in Europe. American Jews have rarely had to ask — as French Jews did after the 2012 attack on a Jewish school in Toulouse — whether they have a future in their own country. Nearly 7,000 Jews left France and immigrated to Israel in 2014.[111]

Perhaps the greatest fear in Europe remains the threat of another terrorist attack by radical Islamists animated by anti-Jewish hatred.

In Germany, young Muslim male refugees often hold "conspiratorial notions of Jewish power," according to Alvin H. Rosenfeld, director of the Institute for the Study of Contemporary Antisemitism at Indiana University in Bloomington, who is interviewing the refugees for a book.

Those underlying views, combined with a conservative religious upbringing, "don't mesh with liberal societies in the democratic West. It will take a generation or two to resolve," Rosenfeld says. "The last thing Germany wants, given its history, is a return of anti-Semitism. But whether Germany is successful remains to be seen."

With anti-Jewish screeds migrating to the internet, some experts fear the impact of thousands of widely shared toxic messages could be enormous. "One person who was sitting in a basement 10 years ago using a printer to print Nazi leaflets can now reach tens of thousands with a single click," says Paul Goldenberg, national director of the Secure Community Network in New York, which works with law enforcement officials and Jewish communities to provide security against attacks.

Yet French anti-Semitism expert Chaouat predicts that a government clampdown on anti-Semitic expression, online or off, could be "counterproductive." When the French government has banned the shows of anti-Semitic comedian Dieudonné M'Bala M'Bala, it only boosts his popularity, he says.[112] "The more Dieudonné is sued, the more people go to his shows," he says.

Today's anti-Semitism is fundamentally different from that of centuries past, when it was driven by Christian teachings that Jews killed Christ, says Rosenfeld. Instead, he says, Jews now must be aware of threats from all directions — rising populist nationalist movements hostile to minorities, radicalized Muslims, far-left politicians and hate-filled cyberspace.

That increased uncertainty can give Jews an ominous feeling about the future, even in America. Rosenfeld says he was taken aback upon seeing armed security guards inside and outside of a synagogue in Boca Raton, Fla., where he recently attended services. Another worshipper told him it was now normal.

"I wasn't used to that in America," Rosenfeld says. "It told me we've entered a new era."

NOTES

1. Amy Crawford, "White nationalists are targeting college campuses," Southern Poverty Law Center, May 2, 2017, http://tinyurl.com/lu4cc4c.

2. "Reports of Hate Crimes on the Rise at American Universities," CBS News, May 3, 2017, http://tinyurl.com/m7o2bys.

3. "ADL: White Supremacists Making Unprecedented Effort on U.S. College Campuses to Spread their Message, Recruit," Anti-Defamation League, April 24, 2017, http://tinyurl.com/jljmr5u.

4. Todd Gutnick, email communication, Anti-Defamation League, May 4, 2017.

5. Crawford, op. cit.

6. Mark Potok, "The Year in Hate and Extremism," *Intelligence Report*, Spring 2015, Southern Poverty Law Center, http://tinyurl.com/hhfvcwj.

7. Daniel Victor, "Muslims Give Money to Jewish Institutions that are Attacked," *The New York Times*, Feb. 27, 2017, http://tinyurl.com/zr5vzrp.

8. Marcia Clemmitt, "'Alt-Right' Movement," *CQ Researcher*, March 17, 2017, pp. 241–264.

9. Rachael Revesz, "Steve Bannon connects network of white nationalists at the White House," *The Independent*, Feb. 7, 2017, http://tinyurl.com/zwof6m2.

10. "Study: Anti-Semitic Incidents Worldwide Doubled in 2006," *Haaretz*, April 15, 2007, http://tinyurl.com/n4ydxca.

11. "Gassing Operations," *Holocaust Encyclopedia*, U.S. Holocaust Memorial Museum, http://tinyurl.com/n32az25.

12. Laurel Raymond, "The Trump Team's history of flirting with Holocaust deniers," Think Progress, April 11, 2017, http://tinyurl.com/ll5cw4w.

13. "Watch: Trump Remarks at the U.S. Holocaust Memorial Museum's National Days of Remembrance," *USA Today*, April 25, 2017, http://tinyurl.com/lyobqcx.

14. "Antisemitism Worldwide 2016," Tel Aviv University Kantor Center for the Study of Contemporary Antisemitism and Racism, April 23, 2017, p. 5, http://tinyurl.com/mhwg98n.

15. The book was: *European Muslim Antisemitism: Why Young Urban Males Say They Don't Like Jews* (2015).

16. " 'France without Jews is not France,' " *The New York Times*, Jan. 13, 2015, http://tinyurl.com/l78yu4o.

17. "Antisemitism Worldwide 2016," op. cit. Also see "Antisemitism Worldwide 2015," Kantor Center, May 4, 2016, http://tinyurl.com/keubxwk.

18. Deborah Lipstadt, "End the Misuse of Holocaust History," *The Atlantic*, April 14, 2017, http://tinyurl.com/krfzvs4.

19. Robert S. Wistrich, *Antisemitism: The Longest Hatred* (1991).

20. "U.S. Anti-Semitic Incidents Spike 86 Percent So Far in 2017 After Surging Last Year, ADL Finds," Anti-Defamation League, April 24, 2017, http://tinyurl.com/lk2zj2d.

21. Ibid.

22. In early March, Juan Thompson, a former reporter was arrested and charged with fewer than a dozen of the bomb threats. See Benjamin Weiser, "Ex-reporter Charged with Making Bomb Threats against Jewish Sites," *The New York Times*, March 3, 2017, http://tinyurl.com/hcvz7ao.

23. "U.S. Anti-Semitic Incidents Spike 86 Percent So Far in 2017 After Surging Last Year, ADL Finds," op. cit.

24. "Hatewatch, Update," Southern Poverty Law Center, Dec. 16, 2016, http://tinyurl.com/j8asg8e.

25. Seth Frantzman, "Why were the 7,000 Incidents under Obama Largely Ignored?" *The Algemeiner*, March 1, 2017, http://tinyurl.com/k69uexw.

26. Ibid.

27. Mark Oppenheimer, "Is anti-semitism truly on the rise in the U.S.? It's not so clear," *The Washington Post*, Feb. 17, 2017, http://tinyurl.com/kvs4jmj.

28. David Bernstein, "19-year-old American-Israeli Jew arrested in JCC bomb threats," *The Washington Post*, March 23, 2017, http://tinyurl.com/mgh6dvm.

29. "Americans Express Increasingly Warm Feelings Toward Religious Groups," Pew Research Center, Feb. 15, 2017, http://tinyurl.com/grkmch5.

30. "2015 Hate Crime Statistics," FBI, http://tinyurl.com/kl854ot.

31. "Antisemitism Worldwide 2016," op. cit., pp. 5–8.

32. Community Security Trust, "Antisemitic Incidents Report 2016," p. 6, http://tinyurl.com/mzvoz3b.

33. "Antisemitism Worldwide 2016," op. cit., p. 5.

34. Ibid., p. 8.

35. See video at "Antisemitism Worldwide 2016," op. cit.

36. Bernard Lewis, "The New Anti-Semitism," *The American Scholar*, Dec. 1, 2005, http://tinyurl.com/mgbx5qf.

37. Natan Sharansky, "3D Test of Anti-Semitism: Demonization, Double Standards, Delegitimization," *Jewish Political Studies Review*, Fall 2004, http://tinyurl.com/lbep7tk.

38. "What is Anti-Semitism Relative to Israel?" U.S. Department of State, http://tinyurl.com/ljysro7.

39. "Working Definition of Anti-Semitism," International Holocaust Remembrance Alliance, Dec. 12, 2016, http://tinyurl.com/lhjxokq.

40. Tana Ganeva, "How legitimate fear over bias-motivated crimes is generating potentially unconstitutional policies," *The Washington Post*, Dec. 7, 2016, http://tinyurl.com/ltmm98g.

41. "Study: 45 percent spike in anti-Semitic campus incidents," *The Jewish News of Northern California*, June 29, 2016, http://tinyurl.com/lapeg63.

42. Mitchell Bard, "Facts vs. Hysteria," *The Times of Israel*, Dec. 1, 2016, http://tinyurl.com/ny7dtnv.

43. Bernard Harrison, "Why present-day 'anti-Zionism' is anti-Semitic," paper presented at University of Bristol-Sheffield Hallam Colloquium on Contemporary Antisemitism, Sept. 13–15, 2016.

44. "QC's opinion: major faults with government IHRA anti-Semitism definition," Jews for Justice for Palestinians, March 27, 2017, http://tinyurl.com/kn3fxyy.

45. "Jews admit organizing white genocide," YouTube, http://tinyurl.com/n5jndln.

46. "Oral Evidence: Hate Crime and its Violent Consequences," House of Commons Home Affairs Committee, March 21, 2017, http://tinyurl.com/gnflr5w.

47. Rob Merrick, "Google condemned by MPs after refusing to ban anti-Semitic YouTube video by ex KKK Leader," *The Independent*, March 14, 2017, http://tinyurl.com/mhalv5l.

48. Mark Bridge, "Google lets anti-Semitic videos stay on YouTube," *The Times* (London), March 18, 2017, http://tinyurl.com/luyb27n.

49. "ADL Task Force Issues Report Detailing Widespread Anti-Semitic Harassment of Journalists

on Twitter during 2016 Campaign," Anti-Defamation League, Oct. 19, 2016, http://tinyurl.com/mssooan.

50. Eugene Volokh, "No, there's no 'hate speech' exception to the First Amendment," *The Washington Post*, May 7, 2015, http://tinyurl.com/mxoblkt.

51. "Antisemitism Worldwide 2016," op. cit.

52. "European Commission and IT companies announce code of conduct on illegal online hate speech," press release, European Commission, May 31, 2016, http://tinyurl.com/jlhbcqp.

53. "Antisemitism Worldwide 2016," op. cit.

54. "German Justice minister calls for hefty fines to combat online hate speech," *DW*, April 6, 2017, http://tinyurl.com/lxe2tef.

55. Erika Asgeirsson, "German Social Media Law Threatens Free Speech," Human Rights First, April 10, 2017, http://tinyurl.com/ljr7tbd.

56. Emma Thomasson, "German Cabinet agrees to fine social media over hate speech," Reuters, April 5, 2017, http://tinyurl.com/mevkwy7.

57. "Seedier Media," *The Times* (London), March 16, 2017, http://tinyurl.com/kv35ctr. Also see, "Clean up YouTube or Face Fines, Bosses Told," *The Times*, March 18, 2017, http://tinyurl.com/l3bfaap.

58. Stephen Pollard, "Why I, editor of the Jewish Chronicle, think anti-Semites should be allowed on YouTube," *The Telegraph*, March 15, 2017, http://tinyurl.com/homrwyk.

59. "CDA 230," Electronic Frontier Foundation, http://tinyurl.com/klr7ohb.

60. Rep. Chris Smith is chairman of the House Foreign Affairs Committee Subcommittee on Africa, Global Health, Global Human Rights, and International Organizations. His subcommittee held a hearing, "Anti-Semitism Across Borders," on March 22, 2017, http://tinyurl.com/n7vocq4.

61. Dennis Prager and Joseph Telushkin, *Why the Jews?* (2016), p. 3. Also see "Declaration on the Relation of the Church to Non-Christian Religions, Nostra Aetate, Proclaimed by His Holiness Pope Paul VI, on October 28, 1965," Vatican, http://tinyurl.com/k4dj.

62. Phyllis Goldstein, *A Convenient Hatred* (2012), pp. 75–91.

63. Prager and Telushkin, op. cit., p. 4. Also see, Nathan Glazer, *American Judaism* (1957), p. 45.

64. Robert Fine and Philip Spencer, *Antisemitism and the Left* (2017), pp. 3–4. Also see Sarah Glazer, "Anti-Semitism in Europe," *CQ Researcher*, June 1, 2008, pp. 149-181.

65. Ibid., Glazer, p. 169.

66. Goldstein, op cit., p. 250.

67. Sarah Glazer, op. cit., p. 168.

68. Goldstein, op. cit., p. 252.

69. Ibid., p. 256.

70. See Sarah Glazer, op. cit., p. 170.

71. Tony Judt, *Postwar* (2007), p. 811.

72. "The Emotional Impact of the Airing of 'Holocaust,' an American TV Miniseries, in the Federal Republic," Two Germanies, 1961–1989 (1979), http://tinyurl.com/kl3qh7y.

73. Judt, op. cit., p. 811.

74. "UN Partition Plan," BBC News, http://tinyurl.com/2igr.

75. Goldstein, op cit., p. 311. Also see "The Six-Day War," Jewish Virtual Library, http://tinyurl.com/m8aqca7. Also see "Six-Day War," *Encyclopedia Britannica*, http://tinyurl.com/lt68lqg.

76. For background, see David Masci, "Middle East Conflict," *CQ Researcher*, April 6, 2001, pp. 273–296.

77. Goldstein, op cit., p. 343, and p. 3 of Foreword.

78. "Philosopher on the trail of Daniel Pearl's Killer," *The New York Times*, Aug. 30, 2003, http://tinyurl.com/l5gl54n.

79. Joseph Strich, "On Two-Year Anniversary of Toulouse shooting, Europe's Jews Still Wary of Terrorism," *The Jerusalem Post*, March 19, 2014, http://tinyurl.com/l57qcbd. Also see Jeffrey Goldberg, "Is it time for the Jews to leave Europe?" *The Atlantic*, April 2015, http://tinyurl.com/ksu3c6s.

80. Alan Hope, "Jewish Museum shooting investigation complete," *Flanders Today*, April 17, 2017, http://tinyurl.com/kcrudfa.

81. Julian Borger, "Paris gunman Amedy Coulibaly declared allegiance to Isis," *The Guardian*, Jan. 12, 2015, http://tinyurl.com/kbd5pvm.

82 "Four charged with helping gunman attack Copenhagen synagogue," The Associated Press, *Times of Israel*, Feb. 3, 2016, http://tinyurl.com/jt3o2og.

83. "Germany Conflicted," Human Rights First, Feb. 6, 2017, http://tinyurl.com/l8jljcr.

84. Joseph Ax, "U.S. identifies, charges Israeli teen accused of Jewish threats," Reuters, April 21, 2017, http://tinyurl.com/kq8tm6g.

85. "Teen accused of JCC bomb threats," *Times of Israel*, April 24, 2017, http://tinyurl.com/ka4kdk8.

86. "Trump Condemns Anti-Semitism on Israel's Holocaust Remembrance Day," Reuters, April 23, 2017, http://tinyurl.com/mquacfc.

87. Ibid.

88. David A. Graham, "Sebastian Gorka and the White House's Questionable Vetting," *The Atlantic*, March 16, 2017, http://tinyurl.com/k8lsxfj.

89. Dora Illei, "Sebastian Gorka's Shady Ties to Racist Groups," Human Rights First, April 11, 2017, http://tinyurl.com/kp7saar.

90. Vivian Salama, "Trump advisor to leave White House," The Associated Press, *The Washington Post*, April 30, 2017, http://tinyurl.com/kshk7hz.

91. "Anti-Semitism Envoy Post to be Filled, State Dept. Says," *New York Jewish Week*, April 16, 2017, http://tinyurl.com/m52n5gm.

92. Rep. Chris Smith, press release: "Smith Introduces Legislation to Help Combat Anti-Semitism," U.S. House of Representatives, April 5, 2017, http://tinyurl.com/myjpx4o.

93. Kenneth Marcus, "How the Government Can Crack Down on anti-Semitism on college campuses," *Politico*, Jan. 11, 2017, http://tinyurl.com/j3co77f.

94. "Anti-Semitism complaints against two California universities are dismissed," Jewish Telegraphic Agency, Aug. 28, 2013, http://tinyurl.com/ma2r69j.

95. Avery G. Wilks, "Anti-Semitism bill passes SC House," *The State*, March 9, 2017, http://tinyurl.com/mnype28.

96. "Update: Victory!" *Palestine Legal*, Feb. 8, 2017, http://tinyurl.com/kaw87jv. Also see, "Controversial Anti-Semitism Bill dies in House," Jewish Telegraphic Agency, Dec. 10, 2016, http://tinyurl.com/m8hhs8r.

97. See "Brandeis Center Calls on Tennessee Lawmakers to Combat Rising Anti-Semitism," press release, Louis B. Brandeis Center for Human Rights Under Law, March 29, 2017, http://tinyurl.com/k7vb36h.

98. Peter Walker, "UK adopts antisemitism definition to combat hate crime against Jews," *The Guardian*, Dec. 12, 2016, http://tinyurl.com/jpdocvb.

99. "QC's Opinion," Free Speech on Israel, March 27, 2017, http://tinyurl.com/kn3fxyy.

100. Jasmin Gray, "Universities urged to adopt 'Zero Tolerance' Policy to Anti-Semitism Ahead of Israel Apartheid Week," *The Huffington Post*, Feb. 27, 2017, http://tinyurl.com/mrhe5wa.

101. "Universities spark free-speech row after halting pro-Palestinian events," *The Guardian*, Feb. 27, 2017, http://tinyurl.com/ztdmn3b.

102. Tamara Zieve, "Jewish Officials Hail Austria's Decision to Adopt Anti-Semitism Definition," *The Jerusalem Post*, April 28, 2017, http://tinyurl.com/l6xz675.

103. "What to Know about anti-BDS legislation," Palestine Legal, April 4, 2017, http://tinyurl.com/krgqnfg.

104. Ibid.

105. "Antisemitic Divestment from Israel Initiatives Scorecard on U.S. Campuses 2012–2016," AMCHA, April 4, 2017, http://tinyurl.com/k8uk3a4.

106. Elizabeth Redden, "Pro-Palestinian Group Banned on Political Grounds," *Inside Higher Ed*, Jan. 18, 2017, http://tinyurl.com/kdjf3cd.

107. *Ahmad Awad v. Fordham University*, http://tinyurl.com/mhqxu6q.

108. "Javid to place Israeli boycott restrictions on legal footing," *Public Finance*, Feb. 15, 2017, http://tinyurl.com/k8uk3a4.

109. See Sarah Glazer, "Free Speech on Campus," *CQ Researcher*, May 8, 2015, pp. 409-432.

110. "Federal Judge Advances Lawsuit Challenging Academia Boycotting Israel," Brandeis Center, April 4, 2017, http://tinyurl.com/kedsvun.

111. "France without Jews is not France," op. cit.

112. See Laurence Dodds, "Who is Dieudonne," *The Telegraph*, Nov. 25, 2015, http://tinyurl.com/lsmj8o5.

BIBLIOGRAPHY

Selected Sources

Books

Beller, Steven, *Antisemitism: A Very Short Introduction,* **Oxford University Press, 2015.**
An independent scholar in Washington, D.C., discusses the history of anti-Semitism from antiquity to today, focusing on schools of philosophical thought, including nationalism and romanticism, that have been marshaled to support it.

Fine, Robert, and Philip Spencer, *Antisemitism and the Left,* **Manchester University Press, 2017.**
An emeritus professor of sociology at the University of Warwick, England, (Fine) and an emeritus professor in holocaust studies at the University of London (Spencer) analyze anti-Semitism on the left historically from Marxism to today's anti-Zionism.

Goldstein, Phyllis, *A Convenient Hatred: The History of Antisemitism,* **Facing History and Ourselves, 2012.**
Facing History and Ourselves, an educational organization in Brookline, Mass., that helps students study the Holocaust in order to put today's moral choices in perspective, produced this history from ancient times to the post-Cold War era in Europe, the Middle East and the United States.

Jewish Voice for Peace, ed., *On Anti-Semitism: Solidarity and the Struggle for Justice,* **Haymarket Books, 2017.**
In a collection of essays edited by a national advocacy group for Palestinian rights, academics and activists argue that criticism of Israel, including the boycott movement, does not constitute anti-Semitism.

Julius, Anthony, *Trials of the Diaspora: A History of Anti-Semitism in England,* **Oxford University Press, 2010.**
A British lawyer who famously headed the legal team defending historian Deborah Lipstadt against a libel suit brought by Holocaust-denier David Irving provides a comprehensive history of anti-Semitism in England.

Articles

Bikont, Anna, "Jan Gross' Order of Merit," *Tablet,* **March 15, 2016, http://tinyurl.com/mnz2ajh.**
A Polish journalist describes the controversy over historian Jan Gross' accounts of Poles who killed Jews during World War II.

Hankes, Keegan, "Eye of the Stormer," *Intelligence Report,* **Feb. 9, 2017, http://tinyurl.com/mdnzuod.**
The magazine of the Southern Poverty Law Center describes how "The Daily Stormer" became the top hate site in America.

Lipstadt, Deborah, "End the Misuse of Holocaust History," *The Atlantic,* **April 14, 2017, http://tinyurl.com/krfzvs4.**
A professor of modern Jewish history and Holocaust studies at Emory University and author of *Denying the Holocaust* says politicians who manipulate Nazi history for their own ends are guilty of "soft-core" Holocaust denial — a form of anti-Semitism.

Oppenheimer, Mark, "Is anti-semitism truly on the rise in the U.S.? It's not so clear," *The Washington Post,* **Feb. 17, 2017, http://tinyurl.com/kvs4jmj.**
The host of *Tablet Magazine*'s podcast "Unorthodox" raises questions about whether hate crimes and anti-Semitic incidents in the United States have been rising, noting the data are often faulty.

Raymond, Laurel, "The Trump Team's history of flirting with Holocaust deniers," Think Progress, April 11, 2017, http://tinyurl.com/mbkwqck.
A blogger for Think Progress, part of the liberal Center for American Progress think tank in Washington, asserts that President Trump and his White House team have a long history of thinly veiled anti-Semitism.

Reports and Studies

"ADL Audit: U.S. Anti-Semitic Incidents Surged in 2016–2017," Anti-Defamation League, April 24, 2017, http://tinyurl.com/mro6ds7.

In its annual report, the Jewish civil rights group finds that anti-Semitic incidents in the United States surged by one-third in 2016 compared to 2015. The report also says anti-Semitic incidents spiked 86 percent in the first three months of 2017, compared to the same period last year, but about two-thirds of that was due to bomb threats attributed to two individuals. "The 2016 presidential election and the heightened political atmosphere played a role in the increase," the report says.

"Antisemitism: Overview of Data Available in the European Union, 2005–2015," European Union Agency for Fundamental Rights, November 2016, http://tinyurl.com/lsl46m9.
The European Union agency that tracks anti-Semitic incidents in each of its 28 member countries reported increased security measures and closed schools in Jewish communities in the wake of terrorist attacks in Europe in 2012, 2014 and 2015.

"Antisemitism Worldwide 2016," Kantor Center for the Study of Contemporary European Jewry, 2017, http://tinyurl.com/mv6x947.
A Tel Aviv University center issues an annual report on the level of anti-Semitism worldwide.

"Special Status Report," Center for the Study of Hate and Extremism, 2017, http://tinyurl.com/lb6dq4u.
A research center at California State University San Bernardino found that hate crimes in New York City doubled in the first four months of this year compared to the same period in 2016, led by a surge in anti-Semitic incidents.

For More Information

AMCHA (Hebrew for "Your People" or "grassroots") Initiative, P.O. Box 408, Santa Cruz, CA 95061; www.amchainitiative.org. Investigates, documents and combats anti-Semitism on college campuses.

American Jewish Committee, 212-751-4000; www.ajc.org. Global Jewish advocacy organization.

Anti-Defamation League, www.adl.org. International organization fighting anti-Semitism, headquartered in New York City.

Community Security Trust, https://cst.org.uk/about-cst. British charity that seeks to protect British Jews from anti-Semitism; issues annual report on anti-Semitism in Britain.

Human Rights First, 75 Broad St., 31st Floor, New York, NY 10004; 202-370-3323; www.humanrightsfirst.org. International advocacy organization that monitors hate crimes in Germany and France and government policies affecting anti-Semitism.

Jewish Voice for Peace, 1611 Telegraph Ave., Suite 1020, Oakland, CA 94612; 510-465-1777; https://jewishvoiceforpeace.org. Supports Palestinian rights and the boycott against Israel.

Kantor Center for the Study of Contemporary European Jewry, Gilman Building, Room 454 C [454 Gimmel] Tel Aviv University, P.O.B. 39040, Ramat Aviv, Tel Aviv, 6139001, Israel; 972-3-6406073; http://kantorcenter.tau.ac.il. Research center that issues annual report on anti-Semitism worldwide.

Palestine Legal, 637 S. Dearborn St., 3rd Floor, Chicago, IL 60605; 312-212-0448; http://palestinelegal.org. Provides legal advice, advocacy and litigation support to those advocating justice in Palestine.

Southern Poverty Law Center, 400 Washington Ave., Montgomery, AL 36104; 888-414-7752; www.splcenter.org. Litigation and education group aimed at fighting bigotry; tracks hate crimes; has filed landmark suits against racism, anti-Semitism.

15

Climate Change and National Security

William Wanlund

Fourteen-year-old Achwaq and her family fled warfare in western Yemen to seek shelter in Khamir in May. The civil uprisings that began in 2011 in Yemen and other countries in the Middle East, known as the Arab Spring, can be blamed in part on drought and heavy rains caused by climate change, many analysts say.

From *CQ Researcher,*
September 22, 2017

The deadly six-year civil war in Syria has many causes, including brutal government repression, economic mismanagement and ethnic and religious tensions. But a less obvious force may have helped fuel what has become one of the most violent conflagrations in recent history: climate change.

Environmental scientists, military officials and others say an unprecedented drought in Syria from 2006 to 2009 and torrid temperatures led to soaring food prices and mass migration, which in turn sparked civil unrest, a government crackdown and, finally, a war that has killed nearly a half-million people, displaced millions more and unleashed new waves of terrorism.[1]

"First, brutally hot temperatures and drought in western Russia fed fires which reduced the wheat crop," causing Russia — a major supplier of wheat to Syria — to stop exporting the grain, says retired U.S. Marine Brig. Gen. Stephen Cheney. "Then, a four-year drought in Syria caused crop failures there, leading to massive internal migration and social unrest." The chaos and instability that followed made Syria fertile ground for terrorists, he says.

Cheney, now head of the American Security Project (ASP), a defense policy think tank in Washington, says the Syrian crisis arose out of a series of 2011 civil uprisings in the Middle East known as the Arab Spring. Nonetheless, he says, "climate change was a contributor. . . . Syria's civil war is a poster child for climate change as a national security threat."

Many other analysts trace some of the impetus for other Arab Spring uprisings — in Egypt, Tunisia, Yemen and Libya — to soaring global food prices resulting from drought in some

Coastal Bases Vulnerable to Climate Change

A three-foot sea level rise could damage 128 U.S. coastal military installations, nearly half of them naval bases, according to the Union of Concerned Scientists. Eighteen installations along the East and Gulf coasts are at highest risk of flooding that could damage roads and other infrastructure. Even under conservative climate change estimates, nine installations would lose at least one-fourth of their land area by the end of the century.

Key Military Bases on East and Gulf Coasts

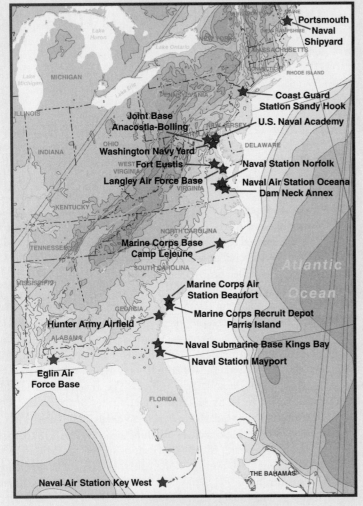

Source: "The US Military on the Front Lines of Rising Seas," Union of Concerned Scientists, July 2016, https://tinyurl.com/hq9u2zd

agricultural exporting regions and to ruinously heavy rains in others.[2]

"No one would say that climate change caused the Arab Spring or the conflicts in those countries," says Francesco Femia, president of the Center for Climate and Security, a Washington think tank. "You can't distinguish it in isolation from other threats and risks." Still, Femia says, climate change "exacerbated conditions in those countries and helped precipitate those conflicts."

Not everyone is ready to accept the link between climate change and the Syrian conflict. In September, a multi-disciplinary group of researchers led by Jan Selby, an international relations professor at the University of Sussex in England, cast doubt on the theory that Syria's drought caused large-scale internal migration and that the migrants were a major cause of the unrest that sparked the civil war.[3]

But researchers and military officials generally agree that climate change represents an international security concern. The U.S. Department of Defense (DOD) considers climate change a "threat multiplier" — a factor that can aggravate other conditions, such as poverty and political or social instability, and create security or geopolitical risks for the United States or its allies.[4]

"By increasing the intensity, frequency and severity of extreme weather events, climate change can make states more unstable, which can lead to increased power of terrorist organizations," Femia says. "It can affect the geostrategic environment in areas that are important to the United States, like the Arctic, Asia and the Middle East."

Drought is not the only potential manifestation of climate change that concerns Pentagon leaders. Another is sea-level rise, stemming largely from the melting of glaciers in Greenland and Antarctica.

In addition, melting Arctic sea ice has unlocked ice-bound areas, opening them to shipping, oil and gas drilling, mining and even tourism and leading to intensified economic competition for access rights. Russia has increased its military presence in the region, a buildup that Russian officials say is intended to strengthen homeland defense and protect commercial interests. Some U.S. military observers, however, worry that Russia's actions may signal future aggression, such as efforts to take control of shipping lanes at the top of the globe.

Military planners also fear that rising coastal waters could harm the readiness of U.S. forces. A report by the Union of Concerned Scientists said a "roughly three-foot increase in sea level would threaten 128 coastal DOD installations in the United States."[5]

Global warming is expected to raise sea levels between 0.3 meters (1 foot) and 2.5 meters (8.2 feet) by 2100, according to a January report from the National Oceanic and Atmospheric Administration.[6] The report identifies a rise of 1 meter as an "intermediate" projected increase. That, say Navy veterans, could result in troop-deployment delays and reduced access to docking and repair facilities.

Naval Station Norfolk in Virginia, the world's largest naval base and the headquarters of the Navy's Atlantic Fleet, is among the threatened facilities. Parts of the base already flood 10 times a year during extreme high tides.[7] "If you can't get ships underway with a crew intact out of Norfolk, you're going to delay the application of military force or humanitarian assistance somewhere else where they are called upon to go," says retired Navy Vice Adm. Dennis McGinn, president of the American Council on Renewable Energy.

But Dakota Wood, a former Marine officer who is a senior research fellow for defense programs at the Heritage Foundation, a conservative think tank in Washington, says the military's options are limited. "If you accept that sea levels are rising and you expect more localized flooding of coastal areas with major naval bases like San Diego or Norfolk, what is the military supposed to do?" he asks. "Preemptively move a major naval base 50 miles upriver? Where's the funding for that?"

The Navy is already taking steps to fortify its facilities against the effects of climate change, for example by strengthening piers and erecting structures on higher ground, according to Todd Lyman, a spokesman for the Navy Facilities Engineering Command for the mid-Atlantic region.[8]

Former President Barack Obama believed climate change constituted an economic and security threat to the nation. In 2015 he signed the Paris climate agreement, which pledged its nearly 200 participants to work to stem global warming. Without such a worldwide effort, Obama said, "we are going to have to devote more and more and more of our economic and military resources not to growing opportunity for our people, but to adapting to the various consequences of a changing planet."[9]

On Sept. 21, 2016, he instructed federal agencies to consider climate change when drawing up their national security plans.[10] The same day, the National Intelligence Council (NIC), which performs analytical work for the 16 U.S. intelligence agencies, backed Obama with a report saying climate change is "almost certain to have significant direct and indirect social, economic, political, and security implications [and] pose significant national security challenges for the United States over the next two decades."[11]

But President Trump, who succeeded Obama in January, once tweeted that climate change was "a total, and very expensive, hoax."[12] He later said he was keeping an "open mind" on the subject.[13] Nevertheless, on March 28, he declared the costs of complying with government regulations designed to limit climate change pose a greater threat to national security than do the changes themselves, and he rescinded Obama's 2016 national security memorandum and many of Obama's other climate-related directives. Trump said his aim was to end "regulatory burdens that unnecessarily encumber energy production, constrain economic growth and prevent job creation."[14] On June 1, he made similar comments in announcing the United States would withdraw from the Paris agreement.[15]

James Taylor, a senior fellow for environment and energy policy at the Heartland Institute, a libertarian

Natural Disasters Force Millions from Homes

From 2008 to 2016, 227.6 million people were displaced worldwide, most of them within their own country's borders, by weather-related or geophysical disasters, such as earthquakes. Weather-related disasters were responsible for 86 percent of the displacements. In the first half of 2017, disasters in 76 countries and territories uprooted another 4.5 million people.

Displacements by Weather or Geophysical Disasters, 2008-16

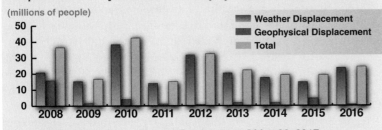

Sources: "Global Report on Internal Displacement," May 22, 2017, https://tinyurl.com/y8dvj789; "Provisional Mid-year Figures, Internal Displacement in 2017," Aug. 16, 2017, https://tinyurl.com/ybhc676k, Norwegian Refugee Council and Internal Displacement Monitoring Centre

and requiring the Pentagon to report on how climate change affects military operations and readiness. (The legislation has not yet reached the Senate floor.)[17]

In late summer, back-to-back hurricanes caused devastating flooding in Texas and Louisiana and widespread destruction in Florida and other Southeastern states, raising new worries about potential links between climate change and extreme weather. Scientists did not attribute the hurricanes to climate change, but a number said warming ocean temperatures increase the intensity and frequency of such storms. At the same time, the hurricanes tested the military's ability to both protect its assets and contribute to relief efforts.

As Americans debate possible effects of global climate change on national security, here are some key questions they are asking:

Does a weakened commitment to slowing climate change make the United States less secure?

President Trump's announcement on June 1 that the United States would withdraw from the Paris agreement on climate change pleased some members of his administration and GOP lawmakers but dismayed many world leaders who had counted on participation by the planet's second-largest polluter.[18]

The agreement, adopted in 2015 and signed by 196 nations, aims to limit global temperature increases and encourages adoption of renewable-energy resources.[19] British Prime Minister Theresa May called it "the right global framework for protecting the prosperity and security of future generations."[20]

Trump's critics say withdrawing from the accord will isolate the United States and diminish its global influence. But others say the decision will help the country negotiate better trade and other international deals.

"Both the diplomatic costs of leaving and the benefits of staying have been exaggerated," said Nicolas Loris, an economist with the Heritage Foundation.[21] Withdrawing

think tank in Arlington Heights, Ill., agrees with Trump. "Climate change certainly isn't a national security threat the way the Obama administration said it was, whereby global warming is causing catastrophes and migrations of people and scarce resources and food and water shortages, which they said would be threat multipliers," Taylor says. "You're not seeing any of these. The greater threat to national security would be forcing our economy onto an expensive renewable-power trajectory."

However, Trump's Defense secretary, James Mattis, said in written responses to questions at his Senate confirmation hearing in January that "climate change is impacting stability in areas of the world where our troops are operating today. It is appropriate for [military commanders] to incorporate drivers of instability that impact the security environment in their areas into their planning."[16]

Some observers see signs that the political split over climate change may be narrowing. The House of Representatives has established a bipartisan Climate Solutions Caucus to explore approaches to dealing with a changing climate. The caucus was instrumental in the House's July passage of legislation declaring climate change to be "a direct threat" to U.S. national security from the accord could help the United States negotiate future agreements by showing other governments "the U.S. is willing and able to resist diplomatic pressure in order to protect American interests," he said.[22]

Peter Engelke, a senior fellow with the Strategic Foresight Initiative at the Atlantic Council think tank in Washington, says Trump's decision will have the opposite effect and will make it "a real challenge . . . to craft complex international agreements in the future."

"There's a real risk that we could have harmed our position as the world's foremost power," says Engelke, whose group works to help international decision-makers by identifying global trends.

In addition to withdrawing from the Paris agreement, Trump appointed a climate change skeptic, former Oklahoma Attorney General Scott Pruitt, to head the Environmental Protection Agency (EPA). Trump has reversed Obama administration policies aimed at addressing climate change and recently disbanded the federal advisory panel for the National Climate Assessment, which helps policymakers and private-sector officials incorporate the government's climate analysis into long-term planning.[23]

Nigel Purvis, who participated in climate change negotiations as a State Department official in the Clinton and George W. Bush administrations, says most other countries view climate change as their biggest threat. The U.S. withdrawal from the Paris agreement means "foreign leaders will think twice about whether to cooperate with President Trump in trade, security and other foreign policy areas," says Purvis, now president of Climate Advisers, a Washington consulting firm that advocates for a low-carbon economy.

Roger Pielke, a political scientist and environmental studies professor at the University of Colorado, says withdrawing from the agreement made little sense, because its goals are voluntary. Trump's decision, he says, "is not a meaningful action unless you want to stick your finger in someone's eye."

Opponents of the Paris agreement say the United States plays too important a role in the world for Trump's decision to jeopardize national security.

"Other countries have a multitude of security, economic, and diplomatic reasons to work with America to address issues of mutual concern," Loris wrote. "Withdrawal from the agreement will not change that."

Under the terms of the Paris agreement, no country can withdraw from it before Nov. 4, 2020 — by chance, the day after the next U.S. presidential election.[24]

Much of the debate over U.S. security and action on climate change focuses on China, the world's biggest polluter, and whether Beijing wants to use the Trump administration's skepticism of climate change to gain political and economic leverage.

"China is stepping up to say, 'We are going to be a leader' in green technology innovation and development while the U.S. is appearing to retreat," Engelke says. "This is an important geopolitical question, because it speaks to who can develop the technology and be a step ahead of the other in seizing the commercial high ground for trade, for seizing military advantages, for having the best technology, etc."

Five of the world's top six solar panel manufacturers and five of the top 10 wind turbine makers are in China. The country invested $88 billion in renewable energy in 2016, more than any other country.[25] In January, China's National Energy Administration announced plans to invest another $360 billion in renewable-power generation by 2020.[26]

Kelly Sims Gallagher, a China specialist and energy and environmental policy professor at the Fletcher School of Law and Diplomacy at Tufts University in Medford, Mass., says Chinese officials see green-energy investments as "key to their own economic development during the 21st century" — and a chance to gain a competitive advantage over the United States. "That's what's at risk: technological leadership and the socioeconomic consequences of ceding this market to the Chinese," she says.

Yale University researchers Angel Hsu and Carlin Rosengarten doubt China will assume the climate change leadership mantle. "Despite China's massive investments in renewable energy, the country is still investing in coal and exporting it," they wrote. China cannot develop as quickly as it wants to "while simultaneously filling a climate leadership vacuum," they said.[27]

But even if that is true, China still stands to gain diplomatically from Trump's decision to leave the Paris climate deal, says David Livingston, an associate fellow in the Energy and Climate Program at the Carnegie Endowment for International Peace. "Headlines like, 'China steps in to help climate adaptation in Africa because the U.S. will no longer fund the Green Climate

Russia has established a military base on Alexandra Land island in the Arctic. Russia says it has increased its military presence in the region to strengthen homeland defense and protect commercial interests. Some U.S. military observers, however, worry that Russia's actions may signal future aggression.

fund' — this is partially reality, partially rhetoric, but it's a powerful source of leverage for China," he says.

Does climate change affect U.S. military preparedness?

Naval Station Norfolk occupies about 3,400 acres on the Atlantic Coast of southeastern Virginia. The base is home to 75 ships, 134 aircraft and about 70,000 military and civilian employees.[28]

It also is highly vulnerable to the effects of climate change. Ocean levels around Norfolk could rise 4.5 to 6.9 feet by the end of the century, largely because of melting polar ice, according to the Union of Concerned Scientists, a research and advocacy group in Cambridge, Mass. The group says that at the upper end of its estimate, about 20 percent of the base would flood every day by the year 2100, with storm surges creating even more severe problems.[29]

Flooding already is disrupting operations at the base. At least 10 times a year, personnel cut power to the piers that service ships because strong winds or unusually high tides threaten to submerge electrical cables. "It's more than an inconvenience," said retired Navy Capt. Joseph Bouchard, the base's former commander and an expert on the national security aspects of climate change policy. "A ship is on a tight timeline to do all the training and maintenance that's required to be combat ready for

deployment. If you interrupt that . . . they have a hard time being ready for deployment."[30]

Climate change raises the possibility that U.S. military assets may not always be available when needed, says retired Vice Adm. McGinn, of the American Council on Renewable Energy. "If you can't get ships underway with a crew intact out of [Norfolk], you're going to delay the application of military force or humanitarian assistance somewhere else," he says.

Fifty-six naval installations around the country could be affected by a sea-level rise of at least 3.3 feet. Such a rise would damage piers and repair facilities, electrical and communications equipment and sewage treatment facilities, according to a 2011 book published by the National Academy of Sciences.[31]

U.S. military bases overseas also are facing climate change challenges, according to a report by the American Security Project. It rated the naval facility on the Indian Ocean island of Diego Garcia as the military's most climate change-vulnerable installation — the island, with a mean elevation of four feet above sea level, is at risk from coastal erosion and flooding, the report said, noting "A sea-level rise of . . . several feet would force the U.S. military to undertake a costly and difficult military relocation process."[32]

Another American Security Project study noted that the U.S. base on the Pacific island of Guam, while not unusually threatened by rising sea levels, could suffer diminished combat readiness. "Because of a changing climate, the joint military base on Guam could lose access to essentials like food and water and will be increasingly threated by extreme weather events" such as extreme storms and erosion, senior fellow for energy and climate Andrew Holland wrote in August.[33]

Michael Werz, a senior fellow at the Center for American Progress, a liberal think tank in Washington, says that in times of global emergency, the U.S. Navy "becomes the 911 number."

Adds Werz, whose work focuses on the intersection of climate change, migration and security, "If friendly neighbors or partners have a climate-related crisis and need a tent city and medical supplies for 40,000 refugees, only the Navy has the capacity to provide it quickly. It would be impossible just to say, 'Sorry, you're on your own.'"

Langley Air Force Base, about 21 miles from Norfolk, is home to nearly 12,000 military and civilian personnel.

Retired Gen. Ronald Keys, former commander of the Air Force's Air Combat Command, headquartered at Langley, said the base is only 7 feet above sea level. In about 15 years, he said, the base could experience 100 days of tidal flooding a year due to climate change, meaning "we [would] lose access to certain parts of our base" at high tide.[34]

Sea-level rise is not the military's only climate concern. Prolonged droughts have disrupted artillery practice because of wildfire risks, and flash flooding in the Southwestern desert forced the closure of an emergency runway for training and testing aircraft for about eight months, according to the Government Accountability Office (GAO), the investigative arm of Congress. The GAO also said rising temperatures at one Army installation halted training for three weeks because the thawed ground was too soft to traverse and made airborne training areas unsafe.[35]

But a 2015 report by the libertarian Heartland Institute challenged the GAO's findings, concluding that reports of climate change's negative effects on military infrastructure are overblown and unsupported by scientific evidence. "Requiring DOD to invest in mitigation or adaptation to address phantom risks could divert resources from other more urgent needs, reducing military preparedness," the think tank said.[36]

In 2014, the Pentagon said climate change will create conditions that make terrorist activity and humanitarian crises more likely — for example by causing or exacerbating food and water shortages and degrading the environment. Such stressors aggravate social tensions and political and social instability — while making U.S. military intervention more difficult.[37]

But the Heritage Foundation's Wood says typhoons and other major storms are nothing new and occur every year. "Are we proposing then that the U.S. Navy or Marine Corps should push more forces into the Western Pacific, and be poised in the event that some major series of storms comes through the region?" he asks. "That's deploy time, it's increased manpower costs, you're tying your ships up on a 'be prepared to' mission rather than being off doing other sorts of things."

Femia of the Center for Climate and Security says the U.S. military already understands the challenge posed by climate change. "It's part of the culture of security institutions, the U.S. military in particular, to plan for long-term risks," he says. "It has to take into account a lot of scenarios, and in a lot of cases plan for the worst."

Does climate change pose a global economic threat?

The World Bank says climate change threatens its "core mission" of supporting economic growth and reducing poverty around the globe.

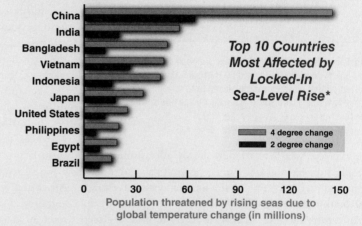

Asia at Highest Risk of Rising Seas

If the planet warms by 4 degrees Celsius, which scientists expect to happen unless nations act aggressively to stem greenhouse gas emissions, seas would eventually submerge land that currently is home to 145 million Chinese, 55 million Indians and millions of others worldwide, according to Climate Central. If warming rises a less drastic 2 degrees Celsius, the current goal of the Paris climate agreement, the number of people threatened in China and India by rising seas would drop by more than half.

*Top 10 Countries Most Affected by Locked-In Sea-Level Rise**

☐ 4 degree change
■ 2 degree change

Population threatened by rising seas due to global temperature change (in millions)

* Figures based on 2015 projections of 2010 population data.

Source: "Mapping Choices, Carbon Climate, and Rising Seas, Our Global Legacy," Climate Central, November 2015, https://tinyurl.com/yd9u7p2p

The Texas National Guard helps rescue people in Orange, Texas, on Aug. 31 from floods caused by Hurricane Harvey. The havoc caused by that disaster and Hurricane Irma raised new concerns about potential links between climate change and extreme weather.

"Current weather extremes already affect millions of people, putting food and water security at risk and threatening agricultural supply chains and many coastal cities," the bank reported in 2016. "Without further action to reduce extreme poverty, provide access to basic services and strengthen resilience, climate impacts could push an additional 100 million people into poverty by 2030."[38]

Many parts of the business world also see climate change as a compelling danger. Mars, the U.S. candy company, remains committed to achieving "the carbon reduction targets the planet needs," said CEO Grant Reid. Mars is among dozens of firms that recently announced they will submit a plan to the United Nations for meeting U.S. emissions targets under the Paris agreement, even though Trump has pulled the country out of the accord.[39]

The World Economic Forum (WEF) — a Swiss nonprofit that promotes business involvement in global economic, political and social issues — ranks climate change along with cultural polarization and wealth and income disparities as "one of the truly existential risks to our world."[40]

Others who have studied climate change, however, say accurately predicting its economic effects is virtually impossible. Such forecasts fall into a range, and at the low end of that range "are some fairly benign outcomes with which we could probably muddle along without

terrible consequence," says the University of Colorado's Pielke. "It's a risk-management problem, like buying insurance," he says. "How much do you need to be covered, and how much is too much?"

Scientists at Stanford University and the University of California, Berkeley, said in 2015 that if climate change is not mitigated, the global economy could be more than 20 percent smaller by 2100.[41] That does not mean the world will be poorer in 2100 than it is today, however, because other factors will cause economies to grow, said the study's lead author, Marshall Burke, an assistant professor in Stanford's Department of Earth System Science.

"Instead, it means that the world will be substantially less rich than it would have been had temperatures not warmed," Burke said.[42]

The study also concluded that not all countries will suffer equally from global warming. About 20 percent — including countries in cooler climates such as Northern Europe and much of Russia — may benefit from rising temperatures, thanks largely to a longer growing season. Warmer countries, including those in Africa and South America, will suffer lower crop yields and drops in labor productivity, the study said. This will result in "a huge redistribution of wealth from the global poor to the wealthy," said study co-author Solomon Hsiang, a professor in the Goldman School of Public Policy at UC-Berkeley.[43]

Poor people also will suffer if countries curtail the use of fossil fuels in response to global warming, said Iain Murray, vice president for strategy at the libertarian Competitive Enterprise Institute, a think tank in Washington.[44]

Pielke says that while climate change threatens the economy over the long term, "there's an ignorance factor, too. We just don't know how things are going to turn out. We're not good at predicting the future 100 years from now."

William Nordhaus, an economics professor at Yale University, agrees, saying human ingenuity and advances in technology add to the uncertainty surrounding the economic impact of climate change. "We don't actually have a good handle on when the impacts will become dangerous," he said. "We're taking something that might happen 50 years from now and addressing aspects of economy and human life that will change in unknown ways."[45]

Some believe a warming climate can, at least in the near term, be beneficial. Matthew Ridley, a Conservative Party member in the British House of Lords, cites a study that indicates adding carbon dioxide, a primary culprit in global warming, to the atmosphere has actually contributed to a greener planet. In the last three decades, he wrote, data showed that worldwide plant growth has increased dramatically thanks to the increasing presence of atmospheric carbon dioxide. Another study noted by Ridley found that global economic output has been rising, thanks to climate change, and will continue to do so until around 2080.

Ridley said the real problem stems from government policies designed to fight climate change. These, he said, "have had negligible effects on carbon dioxide emissions" but they have caused food and fuel prices to go up, made industries uncompetitive, hastened destruction of forestland, killed rare birds of prey and divided communities. Strategies to mitigate climate change, he said, are [impeding] "a change that will produce net benefits for 70 years."[46]

BACKGROUND
Weaponizing the Weather

In 1824, French physicist Joseph Fourier theorized that gases in the Earth's atmosphere keep the planet warm by trapping heat from the sun — a phenomenon now known as the greenhouse effect.[47]

Swedish scientist Svante Arrhenius advanced the theory in 1896 by demonstrating that the heat trapped by carbon dioxide (CO_2) increases as concentrations of the gas increase in the atmosphere. Eight years later, he concluded that human use of fossil fuels was causing carbon dioxide to build up in the atmosphere, but he considered this a benefit, reasoning that a warming atmosphere would help the world grow crops and feed its growing population.[48]

Most scientists dismissed or ignored Arrhenius' work, but in 1938 British engineer Guy S. Callendar confirmed that historically, higher concentrations of CO_2 in the atmosphere raised global temperatures.[49]

Beginning in the late 1940s, scientists started studying the possibility of changing the weather to gain a military advantage, by creating a drought that would ruin an enemy's agricultural harvest, or producing other catastrophic weather events.

By the 1950s, Pentagon planners were investigating whether "seeding" clouds with silver iodide crystals would produce rain. That led to Operation Popeye, a 1967 project (motto: "Make mud, not war") designed to create heavy rainfall over enemy communication lines during the Vietnam War "to interdict or at least interfere with truck traffic between North and South Vietnam."[50]

Public opinion turned against Operation Popeye after *The New York Times* disclosed details of the program in July 1972. It was quickly shut down — after 2,602 cloud-seeding flights over North and South Vietnam, Laos and Cambodia — without its having achieved evidence of success.[51]

The following year, the Senate approved a resolution calling for an international treaty to ban "environmental or geophysical modification activity as a weapon of war," and in 1976 the U.N. General Assembly approved a treaty banning environmental modification techniques for hostile purposes.[52]

CIA officials had begun studying climate change by 1974, when the agency's Office of Political Research said that climate change's potential effect on global food supplies "could have an enormous impact, not only on the food-population balance, but also on the world balance of power."[53]

The 1974 CIA report said wealthier countries, including the United States, probably would escape the worst effects of a cooling climate, while U.S. foes such as the Soviet Union and China likely would suffer. It also said, however, that if climate change caused severe food shortages, potential risks to the United States would rise as other, militarily powerful nations made "increasingly desperate attempts" to get food. "Massive migration backed by force would become a very live issue," the report said. "Nuclear blackmail is not inconceivable."[54]

Fears Gain Momentum

Public awareness of climate change's dangers began increasing in the 1980s. The topic first made the front page of *The New York Times* on Aug. 22, 1981, in a story about a NASA report tracing evidence of a global warming trend back to 1880 and predicting global warming of "almost unprecedented magnitude" in the next century.[55]

In 1989, Al Gore, then a Democratic senator from Tennessee, said in a *Washington Post* op-ed that "America's future is inextricably tied to the fate of the globe."

"In effect, the environment is becoming a matter of national security — an issue that directly and imminently menaces the interests of the state or the welfare of the people," wrote Gore, who became President Bill Clinton's vice president in 1993 and shared the 2007 Nobel Peace Prize with the Intergovernmental Panel on Climate Change (IPCC) for his efforts to raise awareness of global warming.[56]

Meanwhile, scientists were becoming increasingly convinced that human activity was causing climate change. In 1990, the IPCC, established by the United Nations to study climate change and develop strategies to counter it, asserted in its first report that the greenhouse effect was real, human activity contributed to it, and global temperatures and sea levels would continue to rise.[57]

Republican President George H.W. Bush acknowledged in a 1990 speech that "human activities are changing the atmosphere in unexpected and in unprecedented ways," but stopped short of committing the United States to strong measures to curb greenhouse gas emissions.[58]

His secretary of State, James Baker, however, told an IPCC conference the world needed to address climate change immediately rather than waiting "until all the uncertainties have been resolved."[59] In 1990, Baker linked environmental protection to national security, saying, "Traditional concepts of what constitutes a threat to national and global security need to be updated and extended to such divergent concerns as environmental degradation, narcotics trafficking, and terrorism."[60]

In 1997, President Bill Clinton signed the Kyoto Protocol, a U.N. treaty requiring developed countries to reduce greenhouse gas emissions to below-1990 levels by 2012. However, U.S. auto and steel manufacturers, oil and gas companies and other industries lobbied against the treaty, saying it would drive up fuel prices and destroy jobs.[61] In addition, the Senate unanimously passed a resolution saying no climate treaty was acceptable that did not require developing countries to reduce their emissions as well. Clinton never submitted the Kyoto Protocol to the Senate for ratification.[62]

Many experts regard the Kyoto debate as the point when U.S. attitudes regarding climate change began to form along partisan lines. Edward Maibach, director of the Center for Climate Change Communication at George Mason University in Virginia, notes that congressional Republicans deeply disliked Clinton, "and when he asked Congress to ratify the Kyoto Protocol . . . they essentially said, 'Screw you,' and that really started the differential trajectory of public understanding of climate change."

In a 1997 Gallup Poll, 46 percent of Democrats and 47 percent of Republicans said they believed "the effects of global warming have already begun." Ten years later, 76 percent of Democrats told Gallup they held that view, but only 41 percent of Republicans said the same.[63]

In 2001, Republican President George W. Bush announced the United States would not adhere to the Kyoto Protocol, saying the treaty's emission reduction targets "were arbitrary and not based upon science." He also noted that China and India, the world's No. 2 and No. 3 polluters, were exempt from Kyoto's mandates.[64]

Security Concerns

After the Sept. 11, 2001, terrorist attacks on the United States, U.S. defense officials began paying more attention to the effects of climate change on military operations. In 2003, a report prepared for the Pentagon predicted that abrupt climate change could "destabilize the geopolitical environment, leading to skirmishes, battles, and even war" due to food and water shortages and disrupted access to energy. The report recommended elevating the possibility of abrupt climate change "beyond a scientific debate to a U.S. national security concern."[65]

In 2008, the Pentagon said in its "National Defense Strategy" report that climate change would affect "existing security concerns such as international terrorism and weapons proliferation," marking defense officials' first major public statement that they would factor climate change into planning.[66]

Two years later, the Pentagon warned that "climate change will shape the operating environment, roles and missions that we undertake." It noted that rising sea levels would threaten coastal military bases, saying defense officials "will need to adjust to the impacts of climate change on our facilities and military capabilities."[67]

Climate change gained new attention during Obama's second term. "We will respond to the threat of climate change," Obama said in his 2013 inaugural address. "Some may still deny the overwhelming judgment of

CHRONOLOGY

1940s–1970s *Climate becomes a tool of war.*

1946 American scientist Bernard Vonnegut discovers that seeding clouds with silver iodide crystals can produce rain.

1967 U.S. military's Operation Popeye seeds clouds over Southeast Asia to interfere with enemy logistics during the Vietnam War. . . . National Oceanic and Atmospheric Administration scientists Syukuro Manabe and Richard T. Wetherald publish a paper widely considered the first to accurately model climate change.

1972 In response to public pressure, U.S. military officials end Operation Popeye without evidence of success. . . . U.N. Environmental Program is founded to promote sound global environmental practices.

1974 CIA report warns that climate change could alter "the world balance of power" by affecting food supplies.

1980s–1990s *World confronts climate change.*

1981 NASA scientists predict global warming "of almost unprecedented magnitude" over the next century.

1988 United Nations Intergovernmental Panel on Climate Change (IPCC) is formed to monitor the effects of climate change and develop strategies to cope with them.

1990 IPCC says human activity contributes to climate change and the resulting rise in global temperatures.

1992 U.N.'s Framework Convention on Climate Change is signed by the U.S. and 191 other nations seeking to stabilize greenhouse gas emissions.

1997 Kyoto Protocol commits participating countries to establishing targets for reducing greenhouse gas emissions; Democratic President Bill Clinton signs the agreement, but opposition from industry groups and Republican senators keeps it from being ratified.

1998 Gallup Poll finds Republicans and Democrats share similar views on the effects of climate change, with roughly half of respondents saying those effects are already evident.

2000s *Climate change becomes a security issue.*

2003 Defense Department report says abrupt climate change could "destabilize the geopolitical environment" and recommends elevating the issue "beyond a scientific debate to a U.S. national security concern."

2006 Former Democratic Vice President Al Gore releases "An Inconvenient Truth," a documentary about the dangers of global warming.

2007 Gore and the IPCC share the Nobel Peace Prize for their efforts to educate the public about human-caused climate change.

2008 Pentagon calls climate change a "national security challenge." . . . Gallup Poll shows partisan divide on climate change, with 76 percent of Democrats saying the effects "have already begun" and 41 percent of Republicans agreeing.

2011 Climate change-related drought from 2006 to 2009 is cited as one cause of Syria's civil war.

2014 Defense Department says the effects of climate change could "enable terrorist activity and other forms of violence." . . . United States and China agree to reduce greenhouse gas emissions.

2015 Obama administration calls climate change a national security priority. . . . President Obama signs Paris climate change agreement, a global pact signed by more than 190 countries to reduce carbon emissions.

2016 Obama directs federal agencies to take climate change into account in national security plans.

2017 President Trump signs executive order reversing Obama administration actions on climate change, including the directive on climate change and national security. . . . Trump announces United States will withdraw from Paris climate change agreement. . . . Hurricane Harvey slams Houston with record-breaking rainfall and flooding, and Hurricane Irma causes widespread devastation in the Caribbean and Florida, raising new concerns about potential links between climate change and extreme weather.

Climate Change Stoking Fear of Migration, Conflict

Weather events could result in up to 1 billion refugees.

It's only a tiny island amid the vast Louisiana bayous, but it could foreshadow what is ahead for tens of millions of people living in small island countries and coastal communities around the world.

Isle de Jean Charles, located in the Gulf of Mexico about 80 miles from New Orleans, has lost 98 percent of its land since 1955 to coastal erosion and rising sea levels attributed to climate change. The Department of Housing and Urban Development (HUD) and the Rockefeller Foundation, a private philanthropy, have provided $48 million in grant money to relocate people living on the island's remaining 320 acres, making them the country's first official climate refugees.[1] By some estimates, the island will disappear completely by 2055.[2]

Around the world, rising sea levels, droughts, intense storms, floods and other extreme conditions caused by climate change could lead to mass migrations to higher ground, competition for scarce resources, political instability and conflict, experts say. "The impacts of climate change combine to make it a clear threat to collective security and global order in the first half of the 21st Century," the International Institute for Strategic Studies, a London security policy think tank, said in a 2011 report.[3]

The report said that "in areas with weak or brittle states, climate change will increase the risks of resource shortages, mass migrations, and civil conflict. These could lead to failed states, which threaten global stability and security."[4]

As climate change worsens, seas could rise one meter — 3.3 feet — by 2100, displacing up to 2 billion people.[5] According to regional studies, 5 million to 10 million people in the Philippines and 10 million in Vietnam would be displaced. Seventy percent of the Nigerian coast would be swamped, displacing 4 million people, and 5 million people would be forced to leave areas in the South Pacific. In the

United States, a sea level rise of 2.95 feet could inundate the homes of 4.2 million people.[6]

By 2050, between 25 million and 1 billion "environmental migrants" will move within their own countries or across borders, with 200 million being the most widely cited estimate, according to the International Organization for Migration in Switzerland, which works for international cooperation on migration issues. "It is evident that gradual and sudden environmental changes are already resulting in substantial population movements," the group said.[7]

Koko Warner at the United Nations University in Bonn, Germany, wrote in a blog post that people displaced by climate change will move to areas "they hope will provide safe and sustainable livelihoods."

"All countries and governments will be affected by people on the move whether those countries are areas of origin, transit or destination," wrote Warner, who runs the university's Environmental Migration, Social Vulnerability and Adaptation section."[8]

Environmental migration on such a large scale is frequently cited as a major security threat. The Pentagon's 2014 "Climate Change Adaptation Roadmap" said it could affect the deployment of U.S forces and test the Defense Department's "capability to provide logistical material and security assistance on a massive scale or in rapid fashion."[9]

Some experts say climate-driven migration is a factor behind the vicious ethnic conflict that has been underway in Darfur in western Sudan since 2003. "[A] decade of drought in the 1970s and 1980s . . . prompted large movements of people within the region of Darfur as well as into it from neighboring areas seeking more fertile land," said a report by the Woodrow Wilson International Center for Scholars, a think tank in Washington. "The new arrivals' need for land — both for agriculture and grazing — caused tension, which slowly escalated into outright hostility and eventually the explosive violence."[10] The conflict had killed as many as 300,000 people as of 2008, when the U.N. released its last estimate of casualty figures.[11]

Some experts attribute the Darfur migration mainly to forces other than climate change. Most migrants into Darfur's pastoral areas were "Arab nomadic groups who had been squeezed out of Chad" by a civil war there and competed with "pastoral groups whose animals were dying and needed land to cultivate," says Alex de Waal, executive director of the World Peace Foundation at the Fletcher School of Law and Diplomacy at Tufts University. "You can see a little climatic factor in there, but it wasn't a big one," he says.

Experts acknowledge that it is difficult to gauge the effects of climate change, migration and other factors in causing conflict or instability, but they say climate change is an increasingly important factor to consider.

"Climate change and large movements of people clearly present major societal and governance challenges," the Woodrow Wilson center report said. "Governments, international organizations and civil society are being asked to respond, whether they are prepared or not."[12]

In a 2016 report, the National Intelligence Council, composed of intelligence experts from government, academia, and the private sector who aid the U.S. director of national intelligence, said that "even if climate-induced environmental stresses do not lead to conflict, they are likely to contribute to migrations that exacerbate social and political tensions, some of which could overwhelm host governments and populations."

— *William Wanlund*

Isle De Jean Charles, an island off the Louisiana coast, has lost 98 percent of its land to coastal erosion and rising sea levels attributed to climate change.

[4] Ibid.

[5] Ariel Scotti, "Two billion people may become refugees from climate change by the end of the century," *New York Daily News*, June 27, 2017, https://tinyurl.com/yauqr3fx.

[6] "Living with the oceans. — A report on the state of the world's oceans," *World Ocean Review*, undated, https://tinyurl.com/jgogzjr; Don Hinrichsen, "The Oceans Are Coming Ashore," *World Watch*, November/December 2000, https://tinyurl.com/ya2uckmf; and Matthew E. Hauer, Jason M. Evans and Deepak R. Mishra, "Millions projected to be at risk from sea-level rise in the continental United States," *Nature Climate Change*, March 14, 2016, https://tinyurl.com/ya8xcfr7.

[7] "Migration, Climate Change and the Environment," International Organization for Migration, undated, https://tinyurl.com/y88vzstl.

[8] Koko Warner, "Climate Change and Migration: The World Must Be Prepared," *The Huffington Post*, Dec. 1, 2015, https://tinyurl.com/y7bospoo; updated Nov. 20, 2016.

[9] "2014 Climate Change Adaptation Roadmap," U.S. Department of Defense, June 2014, https://tinyurl.com/y9kxrm9o.

[10] Schuyler Null and Heather Herzer Risi, "Navigating Complexity: Climate, Migration, and Conflict in a Changing World," Woodrow Wilson International Center for Scholars, Nov. 22, 2016, https://tinyurl.com/yd8arm5q.

[11] "Darfur death toll could be as high as 300,000: UN official," CBC News, April 22, 2008, https://tinyurl.com/yah2tjao.

[12] Null and Risi, op. cit.

[1] Laura Small, "Government Awards $48 Million to Help Climate Change-Impacted Tribe Relocate," Environmental and Energy Study Institute, Feb. 24, 2016, https://tinyurl.com/yacvvezr.

[2] Katy Reckdahl, "Losing Louisiana," Weather.com, undated, https://tinyurl.com/moufhny.

[3] "The IISS Transatlantic Dialogue on Climate Change and Security," International Institute for Strategic Studies, January 2011, https://tinyurl.com/y9j3wu3f.

Rising Sea Levels Threaten a Nation's Future

Climate change could displace millions of Bangladeshis.

Countries around the world view climate change as a national security threat, but for some, the threat is potentially existential.

Bangladesh, an impoverished nation of 158 million on the Bay of Bengal, is among them.

Global warming is expected to raise sea levels between 0.3 meters (1 foot) and 2.5 meters (8.2 feet) by 2100, according to a January report from the National Oceanic and Atmospheric Administration.[1] An "intermediate" increase of 1 meter (3.3 feet) could cost Bangladesh 20 percent of its land mass and force 30 million people to move elsewhere inside the country, says ANM Muniruzzaman, founder and president of the Bangladesh Institute of Peace and Security Studies, a research group focused on South and Southeast Asia.

"My country is on the front lines of the climate change crisis," says Muniruzzaman, who is a retired major general in the Bangladeshi army. "In Bangladesh, climate change is not a theory or a concept — it is a way of life."

Bangladesh is emblematic of nations with limited resources confronting potentially catastrophic climate change challenges. Rising sea levels also threaten to permanently inundate low-lying island states in the Pacific Ocean (the Marshall Islands, Kiribati, Tuvalu, Tonga, the Federated States of Micronesia and the Cook Islands), the Caribbean Sea (Antigua and Nevis) and the Indian Ocean (the Maldives).[2]

Worldwide, rising ocean water will increase the potential for violent conflict by wiping out supplies of fresh water and creating "economic turmoil, migration, and social instability," said Aubrey Paris, a senior fellow at the Institute on Science for Global Policy, a science and technology think tank in Tucson, Ariz.[3]

"The impact of rising seas . . . is severe enough to threaten the national security of the United States and nearly all other countries, Paris said.[4]

In 2010, the United Nations established the Green Climate Fund, financed by industrialized nations, to help poorer countries limit their greenhouse gas emissions and take other steps to mitigate and adapt to climate change. The fund aims to raise $100 billion a year by 2020. So far, it has collected $10.3 billion in pledges.[5]

In Bangladesh, the fund has approved $40 million — to be matched by contributions from Bangladesh and Germany — for a six-year project to build cyclone shelters, protect access to critical roads and make urban infrastructure more climate-resistant.[6]

"Bangladesh is one of the worst victims of climate change," Prime Minister Sheikh Hasina said. "We need the developed countries to keep their promise and help us."[7]

Other South Asian countries also face severe climate-change threats, with potentially serious consequences for security, according to the Global Military Advisory Council on Climate Change, a network of active and retired military officers concerned about the potential security implications of climate change. The council describes the region as "already politically unstable and particularly vulnerable to further impacts."[8]

Pakistan, for example, has a weak government, terrorist groups operating inside its borders and a black market in nuclear weapons, says Francesco Femia, co-founder and president of the Center for Climate and Security, a policy group in Washington. Global warming is melting Pakistan's glaciers, leading to flooding and shrinking water supplies for drinking and farming.[9] "Climate change can exacerbate

science, but none can avoid the devastating impact of raging fires and crippling drought and more powerful storms."[68]

In 2014, defense officials described the effects of climate change as potential "threat multipliers that will aggravate stressors abroad such as poverty, environmental degradation, political instability, and social tensions — conditions that can enable terrorist activity and other forms of violence."[69] Later that year, the Defense Department released a "Climate Change Adaptation Roadmap" outlining the steps it would take to confront such conditions, such as upgrading construction standards to provide better protection from severe storms and reviewing weapons systems to ensure they can operate under extreme weather conditions such as excessive heat or rainfall.[70]

In November 2014, Obama and Chinese President Xi Jinping agreed to cooperate on climate change

Pakistan's political instability, with global repercussions," Femia says.

In Bangladesh, people displaced by rising sea levels will have few options to leave the country. The country is bordered by India on three sides (except for a 169-mile border with Myanmar), and India protects that border with fencing and armed guards, Muniruzzaman says. "If large numbers of climate migrants try to cross over into India, it will certainly result in a human catastrophe of unknown proportion," he says.

Bangladesh has developed a climate change action plan that addresses food security, public health, national infrastructure and other issues.[10] Muniruzzaman says the plan includes "technical" steps such as planting grains that can tolerate higher salinity, raising the foundations of houses and building cyclone shelters. "Beyond that, I don't think there's much that can be done," he says. "The government hasn't been able to implement the adaptation strategies for lack of funds."

Benjamin Strauss, a vice president at Climate Central, a New Jersey organization composed of scientists who study climate change, said Bangladesh's future beyond 2100 depends on whether global greenhouse gas emissions drop. "It is very plausible that the amount of carbon we put in the atmosphere between today and 2050 will determine whether Bangladesh can even exist in the far future," he said."[11]

— William Wanlund

A monitoring station measures melting at the Passu glacier in Pakistan's Gojal Valley. Global warming is melting Pakistan's glaciers, leading to flooding and shrinking water supplies.

[4] Ibid.

[5] "Resource Mobilization," Green Climate Fund, undated, https://tinyurl.com/yd5fecrp.

[6] "Project FP004 — Climate-Resilient Infrastructure Mainstreaming in Bangladesh," Green Climate Fund, June 14, 2017, https://tinyurl.com/ybju8j9f.

[7] Anup Kaphle, "An interview with Bangladeshi Prime Minister Sheikh Hasina," *The Washington Post*, Oct. 11, 2011, https://tinyurl.com/yaoxxycx.

[8] Tariq Waseem Ghazi, A.N.M. Muniruzzaman and A.K. Singh," Climate Change and Security in South Asia," Global Military Advisory Council on Climate Change, May 2016, https://tinyurl.com/z856o2s.

[9] "Pakistan seeks to track flood risk from melting glaciers," Climate Himalaya, Sept. 20, 2011, https://tinyurl.com/yd9gnwvj.

[10] "Bangladesh Climate Change Strategy and Action Plan 2009," Bangladesh Ministry of Environment and Forests, September 2009, https://tinyurl.com/ybl5pfhy.

[11] Megan Darby, "What will become of Bangladesh's climate migrants?" *Climate Change News*, Aug. 14, 2017, https://tinyurl.com/yb8vddpa.

[1] "Global And Regional Sea Level Rise Scenarios For The United States," National Oceanic and Atmospheric Administration, January 2017, p. 23, https://tinyurl.com/zvn25ua.

[2] "Working Group II: Impacts, Adaptation and Vulnerability," Intergovernmental Panel on Climate Change, undated, https://tinyurl.com/yd8h7n47.

[3] Aubrey Paris, "Sea Level Rise: Sink or Swim," War Room, U.S. Army War College, July 21, 2017, https://tinyurl.com/y7tkrda5.

abatement and reduce their countries' greenhouse gas emissions, which account for an estimated 38 percent of emissions worldwide. They also said they would work to persuade other countries to limit their emissions.[71]

The United States and 195 other countries on Dec. 12, 2015, signed the Paris Agreement on climate change, which aims to limit global temperature increases through use of renewable energy resources. It also calls on developed countries to contribute $100 billion a year to a fund created to help developing countries switch to renewable energy sources.[72]

The Obama administration's 2015 National Security Strategy identified climate change as a major national security priority, drawing ridicule from some Republicans. Then-GOP presidential candidate Jeb Bush told Fox News that "perhaps the most ludicrous comment I've ever heard [is] that climate change is a bigger threat to our country than radical Islamic terrorism. It's baffling to me that the leader of the free world, the commander-in-chief of the greatest armed forces ever created, would state that."[73]

Obama was undeterred. In a 2016 interview with *The Atlantic*, he said climate change represented a more serious threat than the jihadist Islamic State.

"Climate change is a potential existential threat to the entire world if we don't do something about it," he said. "It involves every single country, and it is a comparatively slow-moving emergency, so there is always something seemingly more urgent on the agenda."[74]

On Sept 21 last year, Obama directed federal agencies to identify climate change-related risks that affect national security objectives and develop plans to address them.[75]

Trump issued an executive order in March rescinding the Sept. 21 directive and other Obama administration energy-and climate-related regulatory actions, including the recommendations for action in the military's 2014 "Climate Change Adaptation Roadmap."[76] Trump's order said the move was "in the national interest, to promote clean and safe development of our Nation's vast energy resources, while . . . avoiding regulatory burdens that unnecessarily encumber energy production, constrain economic growth, and prevent job creation."[77]

The White House later announced the United States would withdraw from the Paris Agreement, saying the accord worked against U.S. economic interests.[78] He added, however, that the country would continue to participate in international climate change negotiations and meetings "to protect U.S. interests and ensure all future policy options remain open to the administration."[79]

A Pew Research Center survey conducted in 37 countries before Trump announced his decision on the Paris accord found 71 percent disapproval for withdrawal, with 19 percent voicing approval.[80] In a U.S. poll taken the week after Trump's announcement by The Associated Press and University of Chicago, 46 percent of those surveyed said they opposed the withdrawal, with 29 percent saying they supported it. In that poll, 51 percent of Republicans supported the withdrawal and 69 percent of Democrats opposed it.[81]

CURRENT SITUATION
Military Leaders See Risks

Although President Trump has made clear he wants to roll back many Obama-era environmental initiatives, Pentagon leaders apparently plan to continue factoring climate change into their strategic and operational planning.[82]

Air Force Gen. Paul Selva, vice chairman of the Joint Chiefs of Staff, told the Senate Armed Services Committee on July 18 that "the dynamics that are happening in our climate will drive uncertainty and will drive conflict."

"If we see tidal rises, if we see increasing weather patterns of drought and flood and forest fires and other natural events . . . then we're gonna have to be prepared for what that means in terms of the potential for instability," Selva said.[83]

Geoffrey Dabelko, director of environmental studies at the George V. Voinovich School of Leadership and Public Affairs at Ohio University, believes the military needs to stay above the partisan fray over climate change.

"The military is rightly agnostic in terms of threats and opportunities," he says. "They can't afford to ignore any of them just because they may be out of fashion with whoever's in power. Environment and climate change are among the appropriate issues to track."

Other experts are skeptical that the military needs to deal with climate change now. "There's a temporal component here — how urgent is the issue?" says Wood of the Heritage Foundation. "If it's urgent, then funding should go along with that — so where's the funding? If it's not going to happen for 40 or 50 years, well, the nation has problems we need to deal with today."

A Worrisome Arctic

"Arctic amplification" is the top climate-related concern for David Titley, director of the Center for Solutions to Weather and Climate Risk at Pennsylvania State University. The term refers to the process that causes temperatures to increase faster at the poles than elsewhere. That causes the Arctic ice cap to melt, warming the surrounding water and leading to still more melting.

Diminished sea ice enables more human activity, including "energy and mineral exploitation, fishing, tourism, even celebrity cruises," says Titley, a retired rear admiral who established the Navy's climate change task force in 2009.

That means a bigger job for the Navy, he says. "One of the duties of the Navy is to protect the sea lines of communication" — the maritime routes between ports, which are becoming more extensive as Arctic sea ice melts. "We want to be able to do that, especially when the U.S. has sovereign territory — Alaska — in that Arctic region," Titley says.

Fran Ulmer, chair of the U.S. Arctic Research Commission, an independent federal agency that advises the president and Congress on Arctic policy, says Arctic temperatures are increasing two to three times faster than temperatures around the world. Since the 1970s, she says, the volume of sea ice has declined 75 percent and the area it covers has declined 50 percent.

"That is a very dramatic change for a place that has been covered with ice for a very, very long time," Ulmer says.

This year, the area covered by Arctic winter ice reached a record low, continuing a decades-long trend toward diminished ice coverage.[84] The melting polar ice cap, along with rising ocean temperatures and thawing glaciers, has contributed to an average sea-level rise of 3 inches since 1992, according to satellite data. Seas could rise between 1 and 3 feet by the end of the century, NASA has reported.[85]

The Arctic warming trend has made Russian officials "particularly enthusiastic about their northern sea routes that connect eastern Russia and Europe across the Arctic," Ulmer says. "Russia has a lot of oil and gas resources, and they are developing them in the Yamal region [in northern Siberia]," she says. "Less ice means easier access in and out of their northern ports."

In late August, the *Christophe de Margerie*, a modified 984-foot Russian tanker, became the first merchant vessel without an icebreaker escort to pass through the Northern Sea Route, which runs through the Arctic waters connecting the Atlantic and Pacific oceans along the Siberian coast. The ship, carrying liquefied natural gas from Norway to South Korea, made the trip via the Arctic Ocean in 19 days, about 30 percent faster than the conventional route through the Suez Canal,

The Chinese aircraft carrier Liaoning steams past a wind turbine as it approaches Hong Kong on July 7, 2017. Much of the debate over U.S. security and action on climate change focuses on China, and whether Beijing wants to use the Trump administration's skepticism of climate change to gain political and economic leverage, in part by embracing green technology.

according to the ship's owner, Sovcomflot. The ship, which is designed to break through ice 7 feet thick, is the first of a reported 15 ships constructed by Russia to take advantage of diminishing Arctic sea ice and allow faster and cheaper shipment of goods between European and Asian ports.[86]

Sherri Goodman, a public policy fellow at the Woodrow Wilson International Center for Scholars, says the United States should not underestimate the economic significance of climate change's effects on the Arctic. "With economic opportunity comes political influence," she says. "That's why U.S. global leadership in [the Arctic] is so important, and we ignore the Arctic at our peril. We'd wake up to find this great land mass right off Canada that isn't too far from the U.S., [and] is no longer under friendly leadership."

The melting ice also has military implications. Reuters has reported that Russia also plans to open or reopen six Arctic military facilities "as it pushes ahead with a claim to almost half a million square miles" there. Some of the facilities are equipped with air defense and anti-ship missiles, and possibly military fighters and bombers, the news agency said.[87]

A 2015 Russian military exercise involved 45,000 personnel, 15 submarines and 41 warships, and "practiced full combat readiness," according to a report by the Center for Strategic and International Studies, a Washington think tank.[88] Russian military incursions into other countries' airspace also have picked up, according to the Henry Jackson Society, a conservative British think tank, which said that in 2016, the Norwegian air force intercepted 74 Russian warplanes patrolling its coast, up from 58 in 2015.

Nikolay Lakhonin, press secretary at the Russian Embassy in Washington, says Russia's Arctic policy is "very transparent and predictable." He cites a Russian policy document that says the country's Arctic interests include tapping oil, gas and other strategic raw materials, maintaining a military force to protect Russia's borders and conducting environmental and scientific research.[89]

But Penn State's Titley says Russia's intentions in the Arctic aren't clear. "They talk about having search-and-rescue bases, but these bases have missiles on them," he says. "It's more than search-and-rescue, it's more than constabulary — it's real military capability."

U.S. military officials have taken notice. "What concerns me about Russia is . . . the offensive military capability that they are adding to their force that's Arctic-capable," said Air Force Lt. Gen. Kenneth Wilsbach, the senior U.S. military officer in Alaska. "If you really want to keep the Arctic a peaceful place . . . then why are you building offensive capabilities?"[90]

The two massive storms that struck the United States in late summer — Hurricane Harvey wreaking havoc mainly in Texas and Louisiana, and Hurricane Irma in Florida — showed how weather can affect military operations, causing some military bases to curtail or suspend operations.

The military moved aircraft, ships and thousands of civilian and military workers ahead of the storms from Army, Navy and Air Force bases in Texas and Florida.[91] "Local training and work schedules were affected by the storms, but it did not impact military readiness," DOD spokesperson Heather Babb told *CQ Researcher* in an email.

The storms also highlighted the military's humanitarian responsibilities: Thousands of state and U.S. military personnel were deployed to help with law enforcement and rescue efforts. Republican Texas Gov. Greg Abbott mobilized all 12,000 members of the Texas National Guard, and Republican Florida Gov. Rick Scott called up nearly 8,000 of his state's Guard to help with law enforcement and search and rescue efforts. Guard units from other states also contributed equipment and personnel.[92]

Some climate scientists believe climate change affected the severity of the storm. Michael Mann, a professor of atmospheric science at Pennsylvania State University, said rising sea levels caused by global warming made Hurricane Harvey's storm surge — the sea water driven inland by the hurricane's winds — considerably higher than would have occurred a few decades ago, causing "far more flooding and destruction."[93]

Mann also said warmer water temperatures brought on by global warming put more moisture into the atmosphere, causing greater rainfalls and coastal flooding. Over six days, Harvey dumped an estimated 27 trillion gallons of rain over Texas and Louisiana, according to meteorologist Ryan Maue of WeatherBELL, a meteorology consulting firm.[94]

But Clifford Mass, a University of Washington professor of atmospheric sciences, said climate change can't be blamed for the enormity of Harvey. "You really can't pin global warming on something this extreme. It has to be natural variability. It may juice it up slightly but not create this phenomenal anomaly."[95]

A 2014 government national climate assessment said North Atlantic hurricanes have all increased in intensity, frequency and duration since the 1980s. "Hurricane-associated storm intensity and rainfall rates are projected to increase as the climate continues to warm," it said.[96]

Emerging Bipartisanship?

In July, the House approved an amendment to the fiscal 2018 defense authorization bill calling climate change "a direct threat to the national security of the United States." The amendment, sponsored by Rep. Jim Langevin, D-R.I., would require the secretary of Defense to submit to Congress within one year "a report on vulnerabilities to military installations and combatant commander requirements resulting from climate change over the next 20 years."[97] Forty-six Republicans joined 188 Democrats in voting for the amendment. All 185 "no" votes came from Republicans.

Femia, of the Center for Climate Change and Security, calls the vote "the most significant climate security action in many years."

Should climate change be a national security priority?

YES — Rep. Jim Langevin, D-R.I.
Member, House Committee on Armed Services

Written for *CQ Researcher*, September 2017

There is widespread consensus that the effects of climate change threaten not only our environment and our economy, but also our national security. In fact, the Pentagon's top military and civilian officials have repeatedly stated that climate change poses a direct threat to the national security of the United States, an assessment echoed and amplified by leaders in the intelligence community. Defense Secretary James Mattis understands the risks, as evidenced by testimony given at his confirmation hearing: "The effects of a changing climate — such as increased maritime access to the Arctic, rising sea levels, desertification, among others — will impact our security situation."

We are already feeling those effects. Mission-critical assets like Naval Station Norfolk, home of the Atlantic Fleet, are experiencing "nuisance flooding," and the storm surges are only expected to get worse. Warmer temperatures and more volatile weather could affect training operations at inland bases, reducing readiness capabilities. Moreover, the changing global climate is expected to lead to increased instability due to migration, competition over resources and possibly more failed states, which we know to be breeding grounds for extremism and terrorism.

Policymakers cannot turn a blind eye to the changing environment, because doing so places our troops at risk. Unfortunately, President Trump and his administration seem to be doing just that, withdrawing the United States from the Paris climate accord and rescinding executive actions supporting climate research.

Congress must support our servicemen and women and address the concerns raised by our military leaders about global warming, which is why I amended the fiscal 2018 National Defense Authorization Act to ensure that climate change is properly incorporated into our national security strategy. Specifically, the provision acknowledges that climate change is a direct threat to the national security of the United States and requires the secretary of Defense to provide an assessment of — and recommendations to mitigate vulnerabilities to — the top 10 most threatened military installations in each service branch. It also requires the Department of Defense to address how combatant commander requirements will change as a result of this threat.

Climate change is real, and the threat it poses to our national security is imminent. Congress is listening to the warnings of our military and intelligence leaders. It's time the president does the same.

NO — Marlo Lewis
Senior Fellow, Competitive Enterprise Institute

Written for *CQ Researcher*, September 2017

Climate change should not be a national security priority. Directing the Pentagon to focus on it will actually make America less secure. Generals know how to fight and win wars. They know little about nation building and even less about "sustainable development." Compelling the Department of Defense (DOD) to incorporate climate assessments and strategies in scores of programs, as the Obama administration did, can only promote groupthink, wasteful mission creep and inattention to bona fide security threats.

Climate change would indeed be a security issue if, as is often claimed, it were an existential threat. However, the latest U.N. climate report poured cold water on global warming doomsday scenarios. In the 21st century, Atlantic Ocean circulation collapse is "very unlikely," ice sheet crackup is "exceptionally unlikely" and catastrophic release of methane from melting permafrost is "very unlikely."

The Obama DOD defined climate change as a "threat multiplier," exacerbating conditions like poverty and political stability that "enable" terrorism and violence. However, the research linking climate change to conflict is highly dubious. For example, warming will supposedly exacerbate drought, leading to "water wars." However, studies repeatedly find that water scarcity promotes cooperation rather than conflict.

Climate campaigners have long sought military leaders as spokespersons, hoping to split conservatives on energy policy. But preaching climate peril and carbon taxes would ill-serve both DOD and U.S. national security.

President Trump seeks to secure an era of U.S. "energy dominance" as part of a strategy to achieve 3 percent annual GDP growth. A return to carbon-suppression policies would chill growth, forcing painful tradeoffs between guns and butter.

As an analysis by the Institute for 21st Century Energy shows, if we assume the validity of "consensus" climatology, the world cannot achieve the Paris agreement's goal of limiting global warming to 2 degrees Celsius unless developing countries dramatically reduce their current consumption of fossil fuels. Yet more than 1 billion people in those countries have no access to electricity, and billions more have too little to support development.

Putting energy-poor people on an energy diet would be a cure worse than the alleged disease. It would not promote stability or peace.

"Most of those 46 Republicans belong to the Climate Solutions Caucus, and a lot of them are in coastal districts and/or in districts that have been affected by climate and/or have military bases that are vulnerable," he says.

As of mid-September, the Senate had not acted on the defense authorization legislation.

The Climate Solutions Caucus was set up in 2016 by two House members from Florida "to educate members on economically viable options to reduce climate risk and protect our nation's economy, security, infrastructure, agriculture, water supply and public safety." Caucus membership is equally divided between the parties, currently with 28 Republicans and 28 Democrats.[98]

Mark Reynolds, executive director of the Citizens' Climate Lobby, a nonprofit in California that advocates for national policies to address climate change, said it is only a matter of time before caucus members take steps to produce "meaningful legislation to combat climate change."

"At a time when the Trump administration has turned its back on the Paris agreement and partisanship plagues Washington, a bipartisan effort of this size shows the tide is turning on the climate issue," he said.[99]

Some climate change experts say the vote on Langevin's amendment could signal that partisanship on climate change is moderating.

"We have to wait and see, but it's certainly a positive step," says Dabelko of Ohio University. "The true test of whether a reemerging bipartisan approach to climate change is actually taking hold in Congress will be when it comes to budgets and allocating money."

OUTLOOK

More People, Higher Temperatures

In January, the National Intelligence Council predicted that "more extreme weather, water and soil stress, and food insecurity will disrupt societies. Sea-level rise, ocean acidification, glacial melt and pollution will change living patterns." The threat "will require collective action to address — even as cooperation becomes harder," the council said.[100]

But whether climate change is accepted by Americans as a national security concern that must be addressed is another question.

Some experts believe that evidence that the climate is changing is too distant in time and space for many Americans to fully absorb its significance.

Veteran environmental journalist Andrew Revkin of the nonprofit investigative news organization ProPublica says environmental policies implemented today won't show any effect for many years. "Our vulnerability to floods and wildfire and agricultural destruction will get worse, and nothing we do right now will have any effect for decades to come," he says. "Global population is heading for 9 billion by 2050 or 2060, and that vulnerability is built in until at least then."

Engelke of the Atlantic Council says there is no question climate change is a national security concern but that more Americans need to understand "it's not just happening to people living in low-lying island states or in the Sahel [in Africa]. And not only is it going to happen to us, it already is."

In June, 13 federal agencies released a report saying average annual temperatures in the United States have risen 1.5 degrees Fahrenheit since 1901 and will increase another 5 to 7.5 degrees by the end of the century. It is "extremely likely" that human activity has caused most of the global temperature increase since 1951, it said.[101]

Engelke believes such evidence will help end the rancorous partisan debate over climate change within 20 years. "There will no longer be a debate about whether climate change is occurring, but rather about how to mitigate it and how to adapt to its effects," he says.

Femia at the Center for Climate and Security says dealing with climate change as a national security issue "will take more than just technical solutions like putting more money into drought-resistant crops or building a seawall — it's going to take a large-scale national and international approach."

He also says technology will allow researchers to be increasingly accurate in predicting the effects of a warming climate. "Climate change is an unprecedented security risk," Femia says. "But we also have unprecedented foresight."

NOTES

1. "Syrian war monitor says 465,000 killed in six years of fighting," Reuters, March 13, 2017, https://tinyurl.com/y7qktus3.

2. Caitlin E. Werrell and Francesco Femia, eds., "The Arab Spring and Climate Change," Center for American Progress, February 2013, https://tinyurl.com/ovlsq4j.

3. Jan Selby et al., "Climate change and the Syrian civil war revisited," *Political Geography*, September 2017, https://tinyurl.com/ybr3ppe6.

4. "Quadrennial Defense Review 2014," U.S. Department of Defense, March 4, 2014, https://tinyurl.com/j9yf7l3.

5. Spanger-Siegfried et al., "The US Military on the Front Lines of Rising Seas," Union of Concerned Scientists, 2016, https://tinyurl.com/hq9u2zd.

6. "Global And Regional Sea Level Rise Scenarios For The United States," National Oceanic and Atmospheric Administration, January 2017, p. 23, https://tinyurl.com/zvn25ua.

7. Laura Parker, "Who's Still Fighting Climate Change? The U.S. Military," *National Geographic*, Feb. 7, 2017, https://tinyurl.com/jppz85j.

8. Tara Copp, "Pentagon is still preparing for global warming even though Trump said to stop," *Military Times*, Sept. 12, 2017, https://tinyurl.com/y7dz6mrz.

9. "Press Conference by President Obama," The White House, Dec. 1, 2015, https://tinyurl.com/yd3l6fc9.

10. "Presidential Memorandum — Climate Change and National Security," The White House, Sept. 21, 2016, https://tinyurl.com/ychwqf36.

11. "Implications for US National Security of Anticipated Climate Change," National Intelligence Council, Sept. 21, 2016, https://tinyurl.com/hp9arwj.

12. Donald J. Trump, Twitter post, Dec. 6, 2013, https://tinyurl.com/jaelpj7.

13. Transcript, Donald J. Trump interview with *The New York Times*, Nov. 23, 2016, https://tinyurl.com/juymes5.

14. "Presidential Executive Order on Promoting Energy Independence and Economic Growth," The White House, March 28, 2017, https://tinyurl.com/ny2k4wt.

15. "Statement by President Trump on the Paris Climate Accord," The White House, June 1, 2017, https://tinyurl.com/ydaz28yb.

16. "Secretary of Defense James Mattis's Views on Climate, Energy and More," document obtained by *Pro Publica* journalist Andrew Revkin, March 14, 2017, https://tinyurl.com/yd9obggm.

17. Mark Hand, "46 Republicans buck party to help Democrats take down anti-climate action amendment," *Think Progress Blog*, July 14, 2017, https://tinyurl.com/yc8bynvp.

18. Michael D. Shear, "Trump Will Withdraw U.S. From Paris Climate Agreement," *The New York Times*, June 1, 2017, https://tinyurl.com/y7hj9x7k.

19. "Paris Agreement," United Nations, 2015, https://tinyurl.com/y75g5pqb.

20. Anushka Asthana, "No 10 defends May not signing letter opposing US on Paris climate deal," *The Guardian*, June 2, 2017, https://tinyurl.com/ya47xdp4.

21. Nicolas Loris, "Trump's Decision to Ditch the Climate Agreement Will Help America Negotiate Better Deals," Heritage Foundation, June 7, 2017, https://tinyurl.com/yahurm5w.

22. Loris, op. cit.

23. Juliet Eilperin, "The Trump administration just disbanded a federal advisory committee on climate change," *The Washington Post*, Aug. 20, 2017, https://tinyurl.com/ydbtvup4.

24. Brad Plumer, "The U.S. Won't Actually Leave the Paris Deal Anytime Soon," *The New York Times*, June 7, 2017, https://tinyurl.com/yb4bcagv.

25. Nicholas Stern, "China is shaping up to be a world leader on climate change," *Financial Times*, Jan. 20, 2017, https://tinyurl.com/y8amfz24.

26. "Here's How Much Money China Is Throwing at Renewable Energy," *Fortune*, Jan. 5, 2017, https://tinyurl.com/jxcne9q.

27. Angel Hsu and Carlin Rosengarten, "The leadership void on climate change," *China Dialogue*, April 21, 2017, https://tinyurl.com/y8jfqumn.

28. "Naval Station Norfolk: Welcome to the World's Largest Naval Station," Military.com, https://tinyurl.com/y9hgn8cq.

29. "On the Front Lines of Rising Seas: Naval Station Norfolk, Virginia," Union of Concerned Scientists, July 27, 2016, https://tinyurl.com/y9fspcnv.

30. Evan Lehmann, "Inside one naval base's battle with sea-level rise," *E&E News*, Oct. 27, 2016, https://tinyurl.com/je482eq.

31. *National Security Implications of Climate Change for U.S. Naval Forces* (2011), National Academies Press, https://tinyurl.com/y9c3wezn.

32. Catherine Foley, "Military Basing and Climate Change," American Security Project, November 2012, https://tinyurl.com/y99p5p5y.

33. Andrew Holland, "North Korea Threatens Guam Today; Climate Change Threatens it in the Long Term," American Security Project, Aug. 10, 2017, https://tinyurl.com/y8ndq4x5.

34. Caitlin Werrell and Francesco Femia, "General Keys: The military thinks climate change is serious," Center for Climate and Security, June 2016, https://tinyurl.com/y8na8dgy.

35. "Climate Change Adaptation: DOD Can Improve Infrastructure Planning and Processes to Better Account for Potential Impacts," U.S. Government Accountability Office, May 2014, https://tinyurl.com/ya6x8obk.

36. Taylor Smith, "Critique of 'Climate Change Adaptation: DOD Can Improve Infrastructure Planning and Processes to Better Account for Potential Impacts,'" Heartland Institute, Feb. 5, 2015, https://tinyurl.com/ya97c3u8.

37. "Quadrennial Defense Review 2014," U.S. Department of Defense, March 4, 2014, https://tinyurl.com/j9yf7l3.

38. "Climate Change Action Plan 2016–2020," World Bank Group, 2016, https://tinyurl.com/yc7kveo3.

39. Hiroko Tabuchi and Henry Fountain, "Bucking Trump, These Cities, States and Companies Commit to Paris Accord," *The New York Times*, June 1, 2017, https://tinyurl.com/y9wkrawd.

40. Cecilia Reyes, "Four key areas for global risks in 2017," World Economic Forum, Jan. 11, 2017, http://tinyurl.com/y889qp8r.

41. Marshall Burke, Solomon M. Hsiang and Edward Miguel, "Global non-linear effect of temperature on economic production," stanford.edu, Oct. 21, 2015, https://tinyurl.com/y9n3ytqk. Originally published in *Nature*, Nov. 12, 2013, pp. 235–239.

42. Marshall Burke, "The global economic costs from climate change may be worse than expected," Brookings Institution, Dec. 9, 2015, https://tinyurl.com/ycg7phd5.

43. David Rotman, "Hotter Days Will Drive Global Inequality," *MIT Technology Review*, Dec. 20, 2016, https://tinyurl.com/jxshnb5.

44. Iain Murray, "An Issue of Science and Economics," Competitive Enterprise Institute, 2008, https://tinyurl.com/y73hrwts.

45. "The Economics of Climate Change: Cocktails and Conversation with William Nordhaus," Becker Friedman Institute for Research in Economics, University of Chicago, April 16, 2014, https://tinyurl.com/yby4eham.

46. Matt Ridley, "Why climate change is good for the world," *The Spectator*, Oct. 19, 2013, https://tinyurl.com/yanh9vvm.

47. David Wogan, "Why we know about the greenhouse gas effect," *Scientific American*, May 16, 2013, https://tinyurl.com/y8fehazt.

48. Steve Graham, "Svante Arrhenius (1859–1927)," NASA, Jan. 18, 2000, https://tinyurl.com/y9vhbo6d.

49. "The Carbon Dioxide Greenhouse Effect," American Institute of Physics, January 2017, https://tinyurl.com/yaqnh5l9.

50. Edward C. Keefer, ed., "Foreign Relations of the United States, 1964–1968, Vol. XXVIII, Laos," Office of the Historian, U.S. State Department, https://tinyurl.com/y7laoxa7.

51. "Memorandum From the Deputy Under Secretary of State for Political Affairs (Kohler) to Secretary of State Rusk," Office of the Historian, U.S. Department of State, http://tinyurl.com/yccsgu49.

52. "Convention on the Prohibition of Military or Any Other Hostile Use of Environmental Modification Techniques," U.S. State Department, undated, https://tinyurl.com/ydxoqsnt.

53. "Potential Implications of Trends in World Population, Food Production, and Climate," CIA, made available through The Black Vault, August 1974, https://tinyurl.com/yc36rosb.

54. "Potential Implications of Trends in World Population, Food Production, and Climate," op. cit.

55. Walter Sullivan, "Study Finds Warming Trend That Could Raise Sea Levels," *The New York Times*, Aug. 22, 1981, https://tinyurl.com/ycc88cp2.

56. Al Gore, "Earth's Fate Is the No. 1 National Security Issue," *The Washington Post*, Oct. 12, 2007, https://tinyurl.com/y6vqzou8.

57. J.T. Houghton, G.J. Jenkins and J.J. Ephraums, eds., "Climate Change: The IPCC Scientific Assessment," U.N. International Panel on Climate Change, Cambridge University Press, 1990, https://tinyurl.com/n7r4lyj.

58. President George H.W. Bush, "Remarks to the Intergovernmental Panel on Climate Change," American Presidency Project, Feb. 5, 1990, https://tinyurl.com/yakl8acu.

59. John H. Goshko, "Baker Urges Steps on Global Warming," *The Washington Post*, Jan. 31, 1989, https://tinyurl.com/yd5ewl3n.

60. "U.S. Foreign Policy Priorities and FY 1991 Budget Request," Secretary of State James Baker's statement to the Senate Foreign Relations Committee, Feb. 1, 1990, https://tinyurl.com/y8k2uo6l.

61. John H. Cushman Jr., "Intense Lobbying Against Global Warming Treaty," *The New York Times*, Dec. 7, 1997, https://tinyurl.com/ybbkjpoy.

62. Amy Royden, "U.S. Climate Change Policy Under President Clinton: A Look Back," *Golden Gate University Law Review*, January 2002, https://tinyurl.com/yapzyucf.

63. Riley E. Dunlap, "Partisan Gap on Global Warming Grows," Gallup, May 29, 2008, https://tinyurl.com/y7toqhw8.

64. "President Bush Discusses Global Climate Change," The White House, June 11, 2001, https://tinyurl.com/y6tvzksb.

65. Peter Schwartz and Doug Randall, "An Abrupt Climate Change Scenario and Its Implications for United States National Security," report for the Department of Defense, October 2003, https://tinyurl.com/ybd2bzss.

66. "National Defense Strategy," Department of Defense, June 2008, https://tinyurl.com/jcvrjnk.

67. "Quadrennial Defense Review Report," Department of Defense, February 2010, https://tinyurl.com/yd5enopn.

68. "Inaugural Address by President Barack Obama," The White House, Jan. 21, 2013, https://tinyurl.com/y9lhewr7.

69. "Quadrennial Defense Review 2014," op. cit.

70. "2014 Climate Change Adaptation Roadmap," op. cit.

71. "U.S.-China Joint Announcement on Climate Change," The White House, Nov. 11, 2014, https://tinyurl.com/yd6kxfj6.

72. "Paris Agreement," United Nations, 2015, https://tinyurl.com/y75g5pqb.

73. "National Security Strategy," The White House, February 2015, https://tinyurl.com/y9nj6jx3; Colin Campbell, "Jeb Bush is spitting fire at Obama for touting climate-change efforts after Paris attacks," *Business Insider*, Nov. 25, 2015, https://tinyurl.com/y7l6oswp.

74. Jeffrey Goldberg, "The Obama Doctrine," *The Atlantic*, April 2016, https://tinyurl.com/zfzlg5g.

75. "Presidential Memorandum — Climate Change and National Security," The White House, Sept. 21, 2016, https://tinyurl.com/hj6c6fw.

76. Copp, op. cit.

77. "Presidential Executive Order on Promoting Energy Independence and Economic Growth," The White House, March 28, 2017, https://tinyurl.com/ny2k4wt.

78. "Statement by President Trump on the Paris Climate Accord," The White House, June 1, 2017, https://tinyurl.com/ydaz28yb.

79. "Communication Regarding Intent To Withdraw From Paris Agreement," Office of the Spokesperson, State Department, Aug. 4, 2017, https://tinyurl.com/ybyk5ury.

80. Richard Wike et al., "U.S. Image Suffers as Publics Around World Question Trump's Leadership," Pew Research Center, June 26, 2017, https://tinyurl.com/ya65l6js.

81. "Views on the Paris Climate Agreement," AP-NORC poll, June 2017, https://tinyurl.com/y9os6hqy.

82. "Secretary of Defense James Mattis's Views on Climate, Energy and More," op. cit.

83. "Vice Chairman of the Joint Chiefs on Climate Instability and Political Instability," Center for Climate and Security, July 25, 2017, https://tinyurl.com/y7x63jsg.

84. "Sea Ice Extent Sinks to Record Lows at Both Poles," NASA, March 22, 2017, https://tinyurl.com/k96bsdo.

85. "NASA Science Zeros in on Ocean Rise: How Much? How Soon?" press release, NASA, Aug. 26, 2015, https://tinyurl.com/yd87goqh.

86. Patrick Barkham, "Russian tanker sails through Arctic without icebreaker for first time," The Guardian, Aug. 24, 2017, https://tinyurl.com/ybqgo9ru; "Sovcomflot's unique LNG carrier sets new record with Northern Sea Route transit of just 6.5 days," press release, Sovcomflot, Aug. 23, 2017, https://tinyurl.com/ybyfyrh7.

87. Andrew Osborn, "Putin's Russia in biggest Arctic military push since Soviet fall," Reuters, Jan. 30, 2017, https://tinyurl.com/jpheshv.

88. Heather A. Conley and Caroline Rohloff, "The New Ice Curtain," Center for Strategic & International Studies, August 2015, https://tinyurl.com/ycuyqevt.

89. "Russian Federation Policy for the Arctic to 2020," Arctis Knowledge Hub, undated, https://tinyurl.com/y7wcxjct.

90. "U.S. General Concerned About Russia's Arctic Military Buildup," Radio Free Europe/Radio Liberty, May 26, 2017, https://tinyurl.com/ya6zkbom.

91. Ellen Mitchell, "Governor activates entire Texas National Guard in response to Harvey," The Hill, Aug. 28, 2017, https://tinyurl.com/yaac5llw;

Melissa Nelson Gabriel, "Military bases in Hurricane Irma's path assess storm damage," Pensacola News Journal, Sept. 11, 2017, https://tinyurl.com/y7f8tu4z.

92. Ibid.

93. Michael E. Mann, "It's a fact: climate change made Hurricane Harvey more deadly," The Guardian, Aug. 28, 2017, https://tinyurl.com/ycamv4bl.

94. Ibid., Ellen Mitchell, http://tinyurl.com/yaac5llw.

95. Seth Borenstein, "Is there a connection between Harvey and global warming?" The Associated Press, Aug. 28, 2017, https://tinyurl.com/y7x2bjkk.

96. "Climate Change Impacts in the United States," U.S. Global Change Research Program, October 2014, https://tinyurl.com/jfruuux.

97. "Amendment to H.R. 2810 Offered by Mr. Langevin of Rhode Island," House.gov, June 21, 2017, https://tinyurl.com/ybrjqedy.

98. "What is the Climate Solutions Caucus?" Citizens' Climate Lobby, https://tinyurl.com/yd26bc4v.

99. Steve Valk, "25 Republicans And 25 Democrats Now Belong To The Climate Solutions Caucus," Ecosystem Marketplace, July 29, 2017, https://tinyurl.com/ycnd9w2k.

100. "Paradox of Progress: Trends Transforming the Global Landscape," National Intelligence Council, Jan. 9, 2017, https://tinyurl.com/yagksyqa.

101. "U.S. Global Change Research Program Climate Science Special Report (CSSR)," DocumentCloud.org, June 28, 2017, https://tinyurl.com/y9fvnjs2.

BIBLIOGRAPHY
Selected Sources
Books

Campbell, Kurt M., ed., *Climatic Cataclysm: The Foreign Policy and National Security Implications of Climate Change*, Brookings Institution Press, 2008.
Experts discuss climate-change scenarios and their effects on science, politics, foreign policy and national security.

Miller, Todd, *Storming the Wall: Climate Change, Migration, and Homeland Security*, City Lights Books, 2017.

A journalist predicts border battles as more climate change-displaced migrants seek refuge in developed countries; he chronicles examples of recent climate-induced struggles and forecasts where future clashes might occur.

Moran, Daniel, ed., *Climate Change and National Security: A Country-Level Analysis*, Georgetown University Press, 2011.
An international collection of scholars analyzes the security risks posed by climate change in 19 countries and regions.

Articles

Bromund, Theodore R., "Climate change is not a national security threat," Heritage Foundation Commentary, June 4, 2015, https://tinyurl.com/y7rdm3jk.
A senior research fellow at a conservative think tank argues that ideology, not climate, endangers national security.

Busby, Joshua W., "Climate and Security," *Duck of Minerva* (blog), Oct. 17, 2014, https://tinyurl.com/y8gcn6vf.
An associate professor of public affairs wonders if the climate change-security link might be "a finding in need of a theory" and questions framing the climate change debate in national security terms.

Epstein, Richard A., "Containing Climate Change Hysteria," Hoover Institution, June 5, 2017, https://tinyurl.com/y7sotxj4.
A law professor says American withdrawal from the Paris climate agreement isn't the threat to U.S. security and economic prosperity that President Trump's critics claim.

Lehmann, Evan, "Inside one naval base's battle with sea-level rise," Climatewire, E&E News, Oct. 27, 2016, https://tinyurl.com/je482eq.
A journalist examines the threat that rising sea levels pose to Naval Station Norfolk in Virginia.

Werrell, Caitlin, and Francesco Femia, "Climate Change and Security," *Crisis-Response*, April 2017, https://tinyurl.com/ycwwdbqh.
The co-presidents of the Center for Climate Change and Security, a Washington think tank, discuss how and why the U.S. military views climate change as a "threat multiplier."

Reports and Studies

"Implications for US National Security of Anticipated Climate Change," National Intelligence Council, Sept. 21, 2016, https://tinyurl.com/hp9arwj.
The 16 agencies of the National Intelligence Community look at how climate change could affect global social, economic, political and security conditions in the next 20 years.

"National Security Implications of Climate-Related Risks and a Changing Climate," U.S. Department of Defense, July 23, 2015, https://tinyurl.com/p5qlyz9.
A Pentagon report to the Senate Appropriations Committee outlines the climate-related security risks for each geographic military command and how the commands intend to mitigate those risks.

"Quarterly Defense Review 2014," U.S. Department of Defense, March 14, 2014, https://tinyurl.com/j9yf7l3.
The most recent edition of the Defense Department's quadrennial outline of security issues and strategies identifies climate change as a "threat multiplier" and a "significant challenge for the U.S. and the world at large."

Dellink, Rob and Elisa Lanzi, "TheEconomic Consequences of Climate Change," Organisation for Economic Co-operation and Development, Nov. 3, 2015, https://tinyurl.com/y7dwmrse.
An intergovernmental organization predicts the possible geographic and sectoral consequences of climate change.

Idso, Craig D., Robert M. Carter and S. Fred Singer, "Why Scientists Disagree About Global Warming: The NIPCC Report on Scientific Consensus, (Second Ed.)" The Heartland Institute, 2016, https://tinyurl.com/y8jhjcaa.
The Nongovernmental International Panel on Climate Change argues against the claim that scientists are virtually unanimous in acknowledging the dangers of climate change.

Pezard, Stephanie, et al., "Maintaining Arctic Cooperation With Russia: Planning for Regional Change in the Far North," RAND Corp., March 7, 2017, https://tinyurl.com/ybpnqgmk.

Researchers consider the effects of climate change, along with a host of geopolitical issues, in analyzing Russian-U.S. tensions in the Arctic.

Selby, Jan, et al., "Climate Change and the Syrian civil war revisited," *Political Geography*, **September 2017, https://tinyurl.com/ybr3ppe6.**

Researchers from the United Kingdom, United States and Germany conclude that, so far, there is "no convincing evidence" linking climate change to the Syrian civil war, and further investigation is required.

For More Information

American Security Project, 1100 New York Ave., N.W., Suite 710W, Washington, DC 20005; 202-347-4267; www.americansecurityproject.org. Public policy organization focused on national security issues, including climate change.

Center for American Progress, 1333 H St., N.W., Washington, DC 20005; 202-682-1611; www.americanprogress.org. Progressive think tank that addresses a range of social, economic and political issues, including climate change and security.

Center for Climate and Security, 1025 Connecticut Ave., N.W., Suite 1000, Washington, DC 20036; 202-246–8612; climateandsecurity.org. Organization that researches and disseminates information about the impact of climate.

Competitive Enterprise Institute, 1310 L St., N.W., 7th Floor, Washington, DC 20005; 202-331-1010; https://cei.org/. Libertarian think tank that questions concerns about global warming and advocates access to affordable energy.

Heritage Foundation, 214 Massachusetts Ave., N.E., Washington DC 20002-4999; 202-546-4400; www.heritage.org. Conservative think tank that researches and disseminates information about climate change, national security and other issues.

Intergovernmental Panel on Climate Change, c/o World Meteorological Organization, 7bis Avenue de la Paix, C.P. 2300, CH- 1211 Geneva 2, Switzerland; +41-22-730-8208/54/84; www.ipcc.ch. Group set up under the United Nations that regularly updates policymakers on the scientific evidence of climate change.

NASA Global Climate Change, 300 E St., S.W., Washington, DC 20546; 202-358-0000; climate.nasa.gov. Provides information on the effects of global warming.

16

Pandemic Threat

Bara Vaida

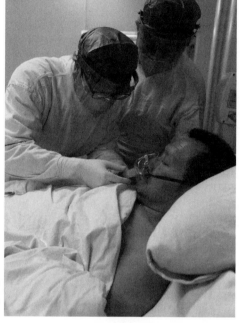

A man in Sichuan province, China, is treated on Feb. 3 after he was infected by the H7N9 virus, or avian flu. Public health experts warn the virus has the potential to become a lethal, fast-moving pandemic on the scale of the 1918 Spanish flu that killed an estimated 50 million people worldwide.

From *CQ Researcher*, June 2, 2017

The killer is small, hidden and elusive. Known by the mundane name of H7N9, the influenza virus has taken hold in China, lurking inside the guts of chickens and other fowl.[1] It is sickening a growing number of humans, including street-market poultry workers.[2]

The virus causes severe pneumonia in most victims and kills one-third of them, according to public health officials. And it is wily, like other flu viruses. H7N9 mixes with other viruses, swapping genes and circulating among birds. Every 10 to 50 years, influenza viruses mutate so drastically that large numbers of healthy people are vulnerable to contracting the flu.[3]

If H7N9 gains the ability to move more easily between humans, public health experts warn, it could cause a pandemic — a lethal, fast-moving and global infectious disease outbreak. A century ago, an influenza virus caused the 1918 Spanish flu pandemic that killed an estimated 20-50 million people worldwide.[4] Some experts say H7N9 could be equally deadly.

"I think this virus poses the greatest threat to humanity than any other in the past 100 years," said Guan Yi, director of the State Key Laboratory of Emerging Infectious Diseases and the Center of Influenza Research at the University of Hong Kong.[5]

Equally alarming, public health officials say, vaccines exist for just a fraction of the 300 or so known infectious viruses.[6]

Microsoft co-founder Bill Gates, a billionaire philanthropist who is working to eradicate infectious diseases, warns that the global health community must do more to prepare for a pandemic.

Predicting the Next Pandemic

The U.S. Agency for International Development (USAID) is monitoring disease outbreaks in 20 countries for their potential to become the next pandemic. Nearly 75 percent of infectious diseases that have afflicted humans this century originated in animals. Disease outbreaks have included severe acute respiratory syndrome (SARS), H7N9 avian influenza and the 2009 pandemic known as swine flu.

USAID Monitors Disease Outbreaks in 20 African, Asian Nations

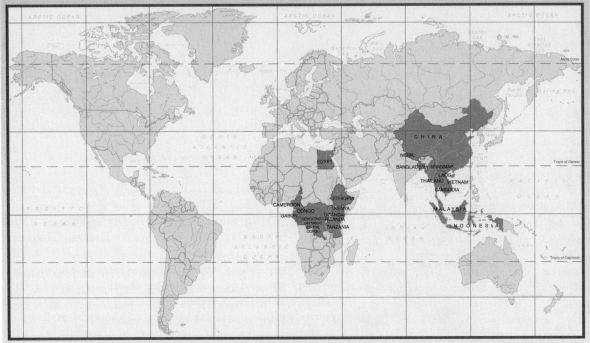

Sources: "Emerging Pandemic Threats Program," U.S. Agency for International Development, Jan. 11, 2016, https://tinyurl.com/ktbf35c; "The Road To EPT-2," U.S. Agency for International Development, undated, p. 5, https://tinyurl.com/k65okjy; and "Emerging Pandemic Threats 2 Program (EPT- 2)," U.S. Agency for International Development, Aug. 1, 2016, https://tinyurl.com/k9rntro

"Epidemiologists say a fast-moving airborne pathogen could kill more than 30 million people in less than a year," he told an international security conference in Munich in February. "And they say there is a reasonable probability the world will experience such an outbreak in the next 10 to 15 years."[7]

The global health community was slow to respond to two recent disease outbreaks — Ebola in West Africa in 2014 and Zika in Brazil and elsewhere in 2015 and 2016. If officials had responded sooner, the death toll likely would have been lower, experts say. Now they are questioning whether the world will be ready if H7N9 or another infectious disease becomes a pandemic. They attributed the world's poor response to the Ebola and Zika crises to several factors: bureaucratic infighting and insufficient resources at the World Health Organization (WHO); weak public health systems in poor countries; gaps in international and local cooperation; scarcity of vaccines for fast-spreading diseases; and inattention by some in power.[8]

Some experts, however, say health agencies and governments are getting ahead of the pandemic threat.

"I'm optimistic that we are pre-pared for a pandemic," says Dr. Steven Gordon, chair of the Department of Infectious Disease at the Cleveland Clinic in Ohio. "We have learned so much from past out-breaks [that fell short of a pandemic]. There has been lots of preparation, there have been tremendous advances in the development of vaccines, and the U.S. has [established] lots of sur-veillance and information-sharing measures."

WHO, the arm of the United Nations charged with coordinating responses to world health emergen-cies, has a global surveillance network watching for potential pandemics and an emergency fund if a one should arise.[9]

In recent years the United States has made substantial investments of time and money to prepare for a pandemic, and it has shared its expertise worldwide. In 2014, Washington expanded the Global Health Security Agenda, which is helping poor and middle-income countries build stronger public health systems capable of fighting a pandemic. In addition, a public-private consortium of govern-ments, nonprofits and pharmaceutical companies is aiming to raise $2 billion to create vaccines for infec-tious diseases.[10]

Further, technological advances have enabled scien-tists to hasten development of new vaccines, including one for Zika that entered the testing phase within a year of the outbreak in Brazil.

But even the most optimistic observers say crucial gaps remain, ranging from financial to organizational. WHO faces a difficult leadership transition, and President Trump is proposing deep cuts in foreign aid and domestic programs that could halt or diminish U.S. preparedness, they say.[11]

Further, key leadership posts in U.S. health agencies remain unfilled by the Trump administration. Most poor governments still don't have a functioning public health system, and nationalistic movements in Europe and the

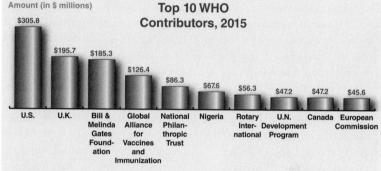

U.S. Is Biggest Donor to WHO

The World Health Organization (WHO) relies on donors for 70 percent of its budget. The two largest contributors are the United States and the United Kingdom. WHO's $4.7 billion budget has been flat for decades and is far smaller than the $7 billion budget for the U.S. Centers for Disease Control and Prevention.

Amount (in $ millions) — **Top 10 WHO Contributors, 2015**

Contributor	Amount
U.S.	$305.8
U.K.	$195.7
Bill & Melinda Gates Foundation	$185.3
Global Alliance for Vaccines and Immunization	$126.4
National Philanthropic Trust	$86.3
Nigeria	$67.6
Rotary International	$56.3
U.N. Development Program	$47.2
Canada	$47.2
European Commission	$45.6

* A public charity in Pennsylvania.

Sources: "Voluntary contributions by fund and by contributor, 2015," World Health Organization, May 13, 2016, https://tinyurl.com/mekl5a3; Donald G. McNeil Jr., "The Campaign to Lead the World Health Organization," *The New York Times*, April 3, 2017, http://tinyurl.com/kylbmmu

United States are threatening the international coopera-tion necessary to make global health systems work.[12]

"We aren't prepared [for a pandemic]," says Michael Osterholm, director of the Center for Infectious Disease Research and Policy (CIDRAP) at the University of Minnesota.

Today's planet is a perfect incubator for pandemics, scientists say, due to an expanding global population of 7.3 billion, industrialized farming, destruction of wildlife habitats, easy access to foreign travel that can speed the spread of viruses, unstable governments and climate-change-induced proliferation of disease-carrying mosquitos.

Between January 2016 and May 23, 2017, dozens of disease outbreaks occurred in 55 countries, according to WHO, and a new outbreak of Ebola struck the Democratic Republic of the Congo. The last pandemic was in 2009, when the swine flu, originating in Mexico, killed up to 575,000 people worldwide.[13]

Localized disease outbreaks, which affect fewer peo-ple than pandemics, are costly. In 2003, an outbreak of severe acute respiratory syndrome (SARS) cost the global economy $54 billion in lost trade and transportation and health care costs. A flu pandemic, on the other hand, could cost the global economy $4 trillion, according to the World Bank.[14]

Gates advises the world community to treat the pandemic threat as an urgent matter of national security and not just a health issue. "What we need to do is prepare for epidemics the way the military prepares for war," he said. "This includes germ games and other preparedness exercises so we can better understand how diseases will spread, how people will respond in a panic, and how to deal with things like overloaded highways and communications systems."[15]

The threat, public health experts say, is even greater than in 1918 because of the ease of international travel today. A person in China with a flu virus can get on a plane, cough and sneeze on fellow passengers and be in the United States in 13 hours.

Public health officials also worry about the growing antibiotic resistance of microbes. Since the 1940s, when antibiotics came into wide use to treat people and animals, many strains of bacteria, fungi and parasites have evolved into antibiotic-resistant "superbugs."

Currently, 2 million Americans contract antibiotic-resistant bacteria annually, and 23,000 die as a result. In one dramatic example that garnered national headlines, a woman died in Nevada in 2016 because the microbe she contracted was resistant to antibiotics.[16]

If superbugs become more common, it could be the end of much of modern medicine, experts say. Without certainty that antibiotics would work to control infection, any surgery, joint replacement, or cancer chemotherapy would become so dangerous that most hospitals would refuse to perform them, according to Dr. Ali Khan, former director of the Office of Public Health Preparedness and Response at the Centers for Disease Control and Prevention (CDC).

"If this trend continues, eventually we'll reach a new post-antibiotic age in which we slip back a century or more in terms of health care programs" because doctors won't be able to perform surgery, Khan said.[17]

Experts also worry that terrorists could use pathogens as weapons. When someone in 2001 sent weaponized spores of the anthrax bacterium through the mail — the FBI said it was a rogue scientist, but the culprit remains unknown — the United States spent billions to create anti-bioterrorism programs, including a detection system to flag airborne toxins in major U.S. cities. But funding has fallen, and the aging bioterrorist detection system has "outlived its usefulness," according to former Homeland Security Secretary Tom Ridge.[18]

Meanwhile, technological advances have enabled scientists worldwide to create deadly viruses and bacteria to study how they evolve and to develop potential treatments. Security experts worry that a rogue scientist could launch a bioterrorism attack or share the expertise with terrorists.[19]

"All the know-how needed to create a bioterrorism tool is publicly available," says Tara O'Toole, executive vice president at In-Q-Tel, a nonprofit venture capital firm that invests in security companies. "A bioterrorism attack would be like a flu epidemic on steroids."

As scientists and health agencies prepare for the next pandemic, here are some of the questions being debated:

Are the World Health Organization and other groups prepared to stop the next pandemic?

Three years after the Ebola outbreak, WHO, the United States and other wealthy nations have made progress toward improving global responses to pandemics, many experts say.

The United States, in partnership with WHO, funded the expansion of the Global Health Security Agenda to work with poor and middle-income countries, particularly in Africa, on preventing, detecting and responding to outbreaks before they become pandemics.[20]

Before the Ebola crisis, all 194 member countries of WHO were supposed to adhere to the organization's international health regulations that specify how to report outbreaks and prevent their proliferation. However, most poor and middle-income countries, such as Liberia and Sierra Leone, were not complying with the regulations. They feared reporting on a disease would harm their economies and lacked the resources to bolster their public health systems, according to a report in the journal *Globalization and Health*.[21]

Ebola galvanized the G-7 countries — Canada, France, Germany, Italy, Japan, the United Kingdom and the United States — to make sure poorer nations had the resources needed to adopt the WHO regulations.[22]

The health agenda has served as a roadmap to help nations prevent or mitigate infectious diseases, detect and report outbreaks when they occur and employ a global network that can respond effectively to an outbreak. The United States also has partnered with the African Union Commission, the administrative branch of the African Union, to create the African Centers for Disease Control and Prevention, which is modeled after the U.S. CDC.[23]

And the U.S. Agency for International Development (USAID) expanded its Emerging Pandemic Threats program, in coordination with WHO, to boost surveillance of potential emerging infections in 20 African and Asian countries. Because about 60 to 75 percent of emerging and re-emerging diseases originate in animals, USAID is training local health workers to detect and respond to pathogens that may be jumping from animals to people.[24]

"Outbreaks are like fires," said Eddy Rubin, chief science officer at Metabiota, a San Francisco startup that developed software to predict and prevent outbreaks. "If you're able to understand where there is a greater likelihood of their occurring and detect them early on, you can shift the impact."[25]

Cameroon has developed an emergency operations center able to respond within 24 hours to an avian flu outbreak. Last year the West African country quickly killed 67,000 birds that could have spread the virus to humans. A year before that, Cameroon took two months to respond to a cholera outbreak.[26]

"I feel quite heartened by what is going on," says John Lange, senior fellow of global health diplomacy at the U.N. Foundation and former U.S. ambassador to Botswana in southern Africa. "The world has woken up to the need to improve capabilities to prepare for infectious disease outbreaks. I think the global community is prepared to fight a pandemic."

Still, global health experts say far more needs to be done. The Commission on a Global Health Risk Framework for the Future — an international panel that gathered the input of 250 global health experts — declared in 2016 that the world needs to invest at least $3.4 billion annually to strengthen national health systems and spend another $1 billion to speed development of new drugs and to stockpile vaccines. WHO and the World Bank should invest up to $155 million in pandemic preparedness funding, it said.[27]

But WHO is underfunded, say global health experts. Its budget of about $2.2 billion is much smaller than the CDC's budget which was over $7 billion in fiscal 2016.[28]

In addition, WHO's operational structure stymies its ability to respond quickly to outbreaks, health experts say. The organization must contend with the competing priorities of the 194 countries who make up its governing body and the priorities of six regional offices. WHO infighting over the economic impact of declaring an emergency was blamed in part for the organization's failure to respond quickly to Ebola, according to a report in *The Lancet* medical journal in November 2015.[29] It also was slow to respond to the Zika outbreak, experts say.

"While WHO should serve as a global front-line defense against pandemics and bioterror attacks, at the moment, it does not look like it's up to the job," wrote Annie Sparrow, assistant professor of global health at Mount Sinai Hospital in New York City.[30]

On May 23, WHO members elected Dr. Tedros Adhanom Ghebreyesus to be director-general, replacing Margaret Chan of China, who has run the organization since 2007. Many experts say Tedros' leadership will be critical to WHO's ability to respond to a pandemic.[31]

In addition, few vaccines are available for the dozens of viruses posing the greatest global health risks. Yet, pharmaceutical companies in recent decades have devoted less than 1 percent of their research and development budgets to vaccines for emerging diseases, judging the profit margin to be too small.[32]

To counteract that trend, an effort to bolster vaccine research was begun in January by the Bill & Melinda Gates Foundation, the European Commission, six vaccine makers and others. Called the Coalition for Epidemic Preparedness Innovations (CEPI), the group is pledging to develop a vaccine for at least three of the 11 viruses identified by WHO as the most contagious and dangerous: Lassa fever, the Nipah virus and Middle East Respiratory Syndrome (MERS).*

CEPI also is supporting the development of technologies to speed up vaccine development.[33]

"The work that CEPI is doing is really important and could be a game changer," says Dr. Rebecca Katz, co-director of the Center for Global Health Science and Security at Georgetown University. "If we had vaccines for these emerging diseases, then we'd have something in our toolkit to confront these threats."

Is the United States spending enough on pandemic preparedness?

The federal government is spending about $13 billion in fiscal 2017 on programs to improve medical and health infrastructure in the United States, address bioterrorism and prevent pandemic influenza.[34]

While that figure may seem large, it is a tiny fraction of the $3.6 trillion federal budget and is spread among at least 10 federal departments, including Commerce, Health and Human Services and Homeland Security. Related programs are in the Environmental Protection Agency, USAID and the National Science Foundation.[35]

The United States is the largest contributor to WHO, providing about $341 million in 2016.[36]

The effectiveness of U.S. anti-bioterrorism programs is hampered by poor interagency coordination, according to the Center for Health Security at Johns Hopkins University in Baltimore. "Currently, there is no systematic accounting by the federal government of those programs that are essential for building health security," said center senior associate Crystal Watson and senior analyst Matthew Watson in a January memo to President Trump on biosecurity.[37]

Many health experts want the Trump administration to appoint a leader to coordinate all the federal health security programs. The Blue Ribbon Study Panel on Biodefense, a bipartisan nonprofit created in 2014 to assess U.S. biodefense readiness, said that person should be in the White House — preferably the vice president.[38]

"We have questions about who is overseeing the $6 [billion] or $7 billion [for biosecurity] in multiple agencies which seemed to be siloed from one another," said panel co-chair Ridge. "Who is coordinating it? We want it to be the vice president."[39]

Health security experts also worry that spending on U.S. preparedness and response has declined. A frugally minded Congress worried about wasteful spending has cut the CDC's budget about 20 percent since 2008 — to $7.3 billion in fiscal 2017. Meanwhile, public health emergency preparedness spending has dropped from a high of $940 million in 2002 (the year after the Sept. 11 terror attacks on the United States) to $660 million in 2017.[40]

"The threat environment isn't dwindling," says James Blumenstock, chief of health security at the Association of State and Territorial Health Officials, representing various public health agencies. "It's getting more intense, more difficult and more challenging, but resources are leveling off or [have] declined. That isn't a healthy situation."

Despite the cuts, Blumenstock and a number of other experts say U.S. pandemic preparedness has improved dramatically since the 2001 anthrax and terrorist attacks. The U.S. government created national strategies to prevent or respond to an infectious disease outbreak or a bioterrorist event. And this year, the National Health Security Preparedness Index, a collaboration of the nation's health security experts, including the Association of State and Territorial Health Officials and the Robert Wood Johnson Foundation, said the U.S. government has made progress in "health security surveillance" and information-sharing systems.[41]

But the index also said work remains to be done, which is why many health security experts worry about the huge budget cuts Trump has proposed for fiscal 2018 to agencies involved in preparedness. They include an 18 percent cut at the Health and Human Services Department, which would mean a $1.2 billion reduction in funds to the CDC; the latter provides grants to hospitals and international infectious disease programs.

Trump also proposed reducing the National Institutes of Health (NIH) budget by $5.8 billion, including $838 million from the NIH's National Institute of Allergy and Infectious Diseases, which oversees flu and Zika vaccine programs.[42]

The "proposed CDC budget [is] unsafe at any level of enactment," said former CDC Director Tom Friedan. "It would increase illness, death, risks to Americans, and health care costs."[43]

Trump has also proposed a 33 percent cut in the State Department budget, which could reduce U.S. funding for WHO and USAID health-related programs. And he has proposed a 21 percent cut in the Agriculture

---

* Lassa, spread by rodents, is a hemorrhagic illness that kills about 1 percent to 15 percent who contract it and is endemic in parts of Africa. Nipah, spread by fruit bats, can cause severe brain inflammation. It can be found in parts of Asia and Australia and has a fatality rate of 40 to 75 percent. MERS, spread through contact with camels, causes severe respiratory disease and has a mortality rate of about 36 percent.

Department's budget, even though the Government Accountability Office (GAO) said in a report in April that the department faces "ongoing challenges" getting poultry farmers to control viruses in birds with pandemic potential.[44] Controlling bird viruses is especially important because eggs are used to produce flu vaccines.

As funding for health security preparedness has declined, Congress has funded the U.S. response to outbreaks disease by disease, after a disease reaches crisis level, health officials say. With the Ebola and Zika outbreaks, the Obama administration had to ask for supplemental money to fight both. "We literally had to rob Peter to pay Paul," said Ron Klain, President Obama's Ebola czar.[45]

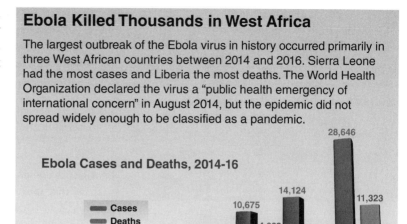

Ebola Killed Thousands in West Africa

The largest outbreak of the Ebola virus in history occurred primarily in three West African countries between 2014 and 2016. Sierra Leone had the most cases and Liberia the most deaths. The World Health Organization declared the virus a "public health emergency of international concern" in August 2014, but the epidemic did not spread widely enough to be classified as a pandemic.

Ebola Cases and Deaths, 2014-16

Cases
Deaths

Guinea: 3,811 cases, 2,543 deaths
Liberia: 10,675 cases, 4,809 deaths
Sierra Leone: 14,124 cases, 3,956 deaths
Worldwide Total: 28,646 cases, 11,323 deaths

Source: "Ebola Situation Reports," World Health Organization, March 27, 2016, http://tinyurl.com/q4j88p7

Health experts prefer a permanent emergency-response fund for public health threats, similar to that earmarked for natural disasters at the Federal Emergency Management Agency (FEMA). When a hurricane or flood strikes, FEMA can tap the fund to help local communities.

"It would be an example of good government if we were able to put something in place to ensure that [health emergency] responses can get dealt with quickly," said Matthew Watson, former managing senior analyst of the Center for Health Security at the University of Pittsburgh Medical Center. Watson is now a senior managing analyst at Johns Hopkins Center for Health Security.[46]

Should governments mandate quarantines and vaccinations to prevent pandemics?

The U.S. government has the authority to restrict the movement of Americans and can block sick people from entering the country. But many public health officials say quarantines can spark panic and worsen an outbreak.[47]

Quarantines involve sequestering individuals who may have been exposed to an infection and monitoring them during the contagious period.

In extreme cases when an epidemic has no known medical treatment, a nation can close its borders to all travelers from a country experiencing an outbreak — something Trump as a private citizen recommended in 2014 during the Ebola outbreak.[48]

With Ebola spreading that year, Liberia deployed riot police to shut off neighborhoods in the capital after people raided an Ebola center and stole medical equipment. When people tried to flee the quarantine, the government cracked down. Violence followed, and the country had to end the quarantine. In neighboring Sierra Leone, the government imposed a three-day national quarantine, but some people fled instead.[49]

"If you tell people that a deadly disease is afoot and you can't leave, people will always try to leave," says In-Q-Tel's O'Toole.

A WHO task force in 2014 said traveler quarantines are ineffective and recommended nations not impose them during the Ebola crisis. Quarantines on trade and travel bans "can create a false impression of control," it said. "Such measures may also adversely reduce essential trade, including shipments of food, fuel and medical equipment to the affected countries, contributing to their humanitarian and economic hardship."[50]

Quarantines can work if a person with an incubating disease is identified and complies with the quarantine, said Richard Schabas, former chief of staff at Canada's York Central Hospital in Richmond Hill, Ontario.[51]

Workers prepare to bury an Ebola victim in Monrovia, Liberia, on Jan. 5, 2015. The largest outbreak of the Ebola virus, spread by bats, monkeys and other animals, occurred primarily in West Africa between 2014 and 2016. More than 11,000 people died. Experts say the toll would have been lower if the global health community had responded more quickly to the crisis.

To get people to comply, authorities must engage communities and seek their cooperation, says Khan, former director of the CDC's Office of Public Health Preparedness and Response. "Making an effort to understand what people are going through, what they believe, what they fear and then trying to come up with a solution that doesn't push people to hide or flee can solve an outbreak of a magnitude like Ebola," he said.

The 2014 Ebola crisis in Sierra Leone and Guinea was contained after health care workers learned to track patients with potential exposure and got them to agree to limit their exposure to others for 21 days.[52]

In the United States, the CDC has authority to impose a quarantine on people with cholera, diphtheria, tuberculosis plague, smallpox, yellow fever, hemorrhagic illnesses such as Ebola or severe respiratory syndromes like a flu that can cause a pandemic.[53]

The CDC in January issued new guidelines giving it broad authority to quarantine individuals for 72 hours if officials suspect someone poses a risk.[54] The new rules were necessary because the agency "has been operating its infectious disease powers under really antiquated regulations," said Lawrence Gostin, a professor of global health law at Georgetown University.[55]

However, the new powers raise concerns that Americans' civil liberties could be threatened, said Northeastern University health policy law professor Wendy Parmet.[56]

When American nurse Kaci Hickox returned from volunteering in Sierra Leone during the Ebola outbreak, she landed at Newark Liberty International Airport in New Jersey and was flagged for extra screening. Although she had no symptoms, Republican Gov. Chris Christie ordered her quarantined in a tent at the airport; she was released three days later. Hickox sued the state, saying "my liberty, my interests and consequently my civil rights were ignored because some ambitious governors saw an opportunity to use an age-old political tactic: fear." Christie defended his actions, and New Jersey is contesting the suit.[57]

As for mandating vaccinations, public health experts say vaccines are the most effective way to stem the spread of infectious diseases, such as diphtheria and measles. Each year, vaccines for infectious diseases save 3 million lives, and 3 million more children around the world could be saved if they were vaccinated, according to the Children's Hospital of Philadelphia.[58]

"Immunizations are the safest, longest-lasting and most effective way to prevent communicable diseases," said Dr. Ian Gemmill, past chair of the Canadian Coalition for Immunization Awareness and Promotion, a nongovernmental advocacy organization.[59]

In the United States, in the event of a spreading contagion overseas, the federal government could ask immigrants at the border to show proof of vaccination. But inside the country, only the states have the authority to mandate vaccinations.

All 50 states and the District of Columbia require children to be vaccinated — typically for diphtheria, measles, rubella and polio — before they can attend public school, but some states allow exemptions for medical, religious or philosophical reasons.[60]

Since 1998, a small but growing number of parents have been refusing vaccinations for their children due to fears that vaccines cause autism. The fears stem from a now discredited study that a British scientist said demonstrated an association between autism and vaccination.[61]

Countless studies have shown the safety of vaccinations. Nevertheless, childhood vaccination rates have fallen. The decline has caused measles outbreaks to flare, most recently in Minnesota, where 44 unvaccinated children in a Somali community contracted the disease.[62]

Parental fears have been supported by some celebrities and prominent politicians such as Christie; Housing and Urban Development Secretary Ben Carson, a neurosurgeon; and Sen. Rand Paul, a physician and Kentucky Republican, who say vaccination decisions should be left to parents.

"I think the parent should have input," Paul said. "The state doesn't own your children. You own your children, and it is an issue of freedom."[63]

Trump invigorated the anti-vaccine movement when he said — contradicting the numerous studies — during a 2015 Republican presidential debate: "You take this little beautiful baby, and you pump — I mean, it looks like just it's meant for a horse and not for a child," he said. "We had so many instances . . . a beautiful child, went to have the vaccine and came back and a week later got a tremendous fever, got very, very sick. Now is autistic." He is considering creating a commission to look into vaccine safety.[64]

At least 19 states have passed legislation since 2001 allowing mandated vaccinations during a health emergency, but experts say ongoing doubts about vaccines' safety could make people resistant to such requirements. Opponents, on the other hand, say the measures "could allow governments to abuse their power," said the American Civil Liberties Union.[65]

BACKGROUND

First Pandemics

Humans have been threatened by pandemics for most of history.

Scientists believe widespread infections began when humans domesticated animals about 10,000 to 15,000 years ago, coming in contact with an army of bacteria, viruses and fungi that could pass to humans. Most of these microbes were harmless, but some evolved to become pathogenic. Throughout history, 60 to 75 percent of emerging infectious diseases can be traced to furred or winged animals.[66]

The animal microbes that became harmful to humans spread by direct person-to-person contact, such as through coughing, sneezing, sweating or sexual interaction. Fleas, mosquitos and other carriers (known as vectors) can spread disease when they bit animals and then humans. From cows came measles and tuberculosis;

from pigs and birds, influenza; from primates and mosquitos, malaria; and from bats, Ebola. Rats have been particularly lethal to humans as the source, through fleas, of the bubonic plague of the Middle Ages, which killed an estimated 20-25 million in Europe over five years.

At first, dangerous diseases spread slowly because people lived in small, isolated groups. But as agriculture took hold in about 9,000 B.C., populations grew and humans ventured farther from their homes to trade and wage war.[67]

"Global transportation networks, exploration, conquest and trade" enabled diseases endemic in one region to spread, blossoming into epidemics elsewhere as new populations without immunity were exposed to them, said Peter Daszak, a scientist who is president of the EcoHealth Alliance, a global health research group.[68]

For centuries, people were virtually helpless to stop the spread of disease. People thought diseases were caused by imbalances in the body, evil spirits or the will of God. Living conditions, meanwhile, contributed to the spread of contagions. Many humans lived in houses along with their livestock. Human excrement and garbage were dumped onto streets. One of the few tools societies had to prevent disease was to separate sick people from the healthy.[69]

Plague and Quarantines

Bubonic plague prompted one of the first society-wide responses to a pandemic.

In October 1347, a dozen Genoese trading ships docked in Sicily after journeying to ports along the Black Sea. The ships likely contained rats that harbored *Yersinia pestis*, the bacterium causing bubonic plague. The bacterium lived inside the fleas that fed off the rats. When the rats died, the fleas jumped to the nearest warm mammal, usually humans. Eventually the pathogen became known as "the Black Death" because people would develop skin boils that turned black before they died.[70]

The plague spread throughout Italy, wiping out entire towns. In 1348, Venetian leaders cut off access to outsiders. Boats from areas suspected of having a plague outbreak were kept away. Travelers coming from areas beyond Venice were told to wait up to 40 days before they could enter. "Quarantine" is derived from the Italian words *quarante giorni*, or 40 days.[71]

The containment was effective because symptoms became visible within 40 days and after that people could be considered "medically harmless." Some historians credit the use of quarantines with Europe's ultimate control of the plague, which largely disappeared by the mid-19th century.[72]

Quarantines also were used during the worst pandemic in modern history — the Spanish flu outbreak in 1918. Governments in the United States and Europe closed schools, churches and theaters and banned most public gatherings. However, the CDC said the quarantines and closures were ineffective because "the measures were implemented too late and in an uncoordinated manner."[73]

Modern quarantines face new challenges, as the 2003 SARS outbreak showed. SARS is a respiratory coronavirus that scientists had never seen before. It originated in Guangdong province in China and became a global threat because it spread rapidly along air-travel routes. The illness went from Hong Kong to Southeast Asia, to Canada and then Europe. It sickened more than 8,000 worldwide and killed 774.[74]

China's government quickly imposed quarantines, closing off buildings inhabited by infected individuals and imposing checkpoints. Violators were punished.

SARS died out at the end of 2003. Some public health officials believe the quarantines worked because SARS had an incubation period of two to 10 days, which gave governments time to limit people's interactions.[75]

Vaccines and Antibiotics

As far back as A.D. 1000, the Chinese used an inoculation technique, called variolation, against smallpox, a virus that causes fever and disfiguring pustules. Physicians would take ground smallpox scab and insert it in the noses of healthy people, inducing a mild form of the disease and thus creating immunity against smallpox.[76]

Vaccination began in 1796 with English doctor Edward Jenner. He had long heard stories of how milkmaids were immune from smallpox, which according to one estimate was killing 400,000 Europeans a year during the 18th century. Jenner found a milkmaid with fresh lesions from cowpox, a mild virus related to smallpox, and he inserted pus from her cowpox into a cut on an 8-year-old boy's arm. The boy became immune to smallpox, proving a person could be protected from smallpox without being directly exposed to it.[77]

By the end of the 19th century, governments in Egypt, Germany began mandating vaccination against smallpox. Great Britain in 1853 required children to be vaccinated, while in the United States, Massachusetts in 1809 became the first state to mandate smallpox vaccination. In 1813, President James Madison created the National Vaccine Agency to encourage vaccinations.[78]

In the late 1880s, microscopes had improved enough that scientists could see bacteria and viruses, paving the way for medical treatments, the understanding of how disease spreads from animals to humans and the connection between sanitary conditions and health.

Physicians now understood that contaminated water was making people sick with cholera and that bacterium carried by fleas had caused the bubonic plague. Breakthroughs followed. Researchers developed vaccines for plague (1897), typhoid (1899), cholera (1911), diphtheria (1914) and tuberculosis (1921). Vaccines for polio (1955), measles (1963), mumps (1967) and rubella (1969) came next.[79]

In 1928, Alexander Fleming discovered antibiotics, which came to be widely used to treat soldiers during World War II. Antibiotics changed the course of medicine because they could kill most bacteria that plagued humans at the time.[80]

After World War II, the world community expanded efforts to work together to prevent pandemics. In 1948, the newly founded United Nations created the World Health Organization to coordinate global efforts on health issues, and WHO became the leading global institution on epidemic control.

"The bottom line is, readiness for a pandemic is connected to our world solidarity," Laurie Garrett, a senior fellow at the Council on Foreign Relations think tank, says of WHO's importance.

Scientists, meanwhile, continued reducing the death toll from infectious diseases. With dozens of vaccines and antibiotics to use, average life expectancy in the United States rose to 78.8 by 2015, up from 48.3 for women and 46.3 for men in 1900.[81]

But nature had some surprises. Flu viruses can't be contained. Although flu virus was discovered in 1933 and the first vaccine produced in 1942, scientists learned that flu viruses constantly mutate. Frequent vaccinations are

CHRONOLOGY

1300s–1800s *Medical breakthroughs give hope for preventing pandemics.*

1347 "The Black Death" — a bubonic plague — travels from Crimea to Europe; 20 to 25 million die over the next five years.

1348 Venice responds to the plague by imposing the world's first quarantine, isolating incoming ships for 40 days.

1796 English physician Edward Jenner inoculates a boy with cowpox, immunizing him against smallpox, ushering in vaccination.

1817 Cholera spreads worldwide from Calcutta, India.

1851 Sanitary conference focusing on cholera meets in Paris, marking the first gathering of international health leaders.

1854 Physician John Snow recognizes dirty water as the source of a cholera outbreak. He hastens end of the outbreak by shutting off a London water pump.

1894 Alexandre Yersin, a French bacteriologist, discovers the bacillus responsible for bubonic plague.

1900s–1940s *Health cooperation expands.*

1918 "Spanish flu," the first pandemic involving the H1N1 influenza, kills 20-50 million.

1928 Scottish biologist Alexander Fleming discovers penicillin at a London hospital.

1940 Japan spreads plague-infested fleas over China during World War II; it also is accused of encasing disease-causing microbes in bombs.

1948 United Nations creates the World Health Organization (WHO).

1950s–1970s *As global cooperation ends many diseases, others emerge.*

1953 U.S. researcher Jonas Salk creates the polio vaccine.

1967 WHO begins immunization campaign to eliminate smallpox, declaring it eradicated in 1980.

1972 Biological Weapons Convention, the first multilateral disarmament treaty banning development, production and stockpiling of biological weapons, is signed.

1974 WHO launches vaccine campaign to eliminate six diseases — diphtheria, pertussis, tetanus, measles, polio and tuberculosis.

2000s–Present *Antibiotic-resistant microbes fuel pandemic fears.*

2001 An American scientist is accused of sending anonymous letters containing anthrax spores to news organizations in two states and to the Washington offices of two Democratic senators, killing five people and infecting 17 others. The attacks spur heavy investment in bioterrorism prevention.

2003 Severe acute respiratory syndrome (SARS), a type of pneumonia, spreads rapidly from China.

2005 U.S. creates the National Strategy for Pandemic Influenza, outlining how the nation would respond to a flu pandemic.

2009 "Swine flu" pandemic spreads worldwide; up to 575,000 die.

2013 The Centers for Disease Control and Prevention issues first-ever report on the threat the U.S. faces from antibiotic-resistant organisms, or "superbugs."

2014 Ebola emerges in three West African countries, killing more than 11,000. . . . U.S. expands the Global Health Security Agenda, an international partnership aimed at bolstering safeguards against infectious disease.

2016 WHO declares Zika a global health emergency as the mosquito-borne virus hits the southern U.S. . . . A Nevada woman dies from an infection resistant to all 26 antibiotics approved for use in the U.S.

2016–2017 China experiences its fifth epidemic of H7N9 influenza, a bird flu virus.

Waging War on Superbugs

"In China and India, there are bacteria resistant to all antibiotics."

Inside the sprawling Walter Reed Army Institute of Research in Silver Spring, Md., microbiologist Patrick McGann spends much of his time growing "superbugs" — antibiotic-resistant strains of bacteria.

A year ago, McGann and his team learned of a Pennsylvania woman infected with a strain of *E. coli* bacteria resistant to colistin, an antibiotic used when all others fail. Other antibiotics were effective against the bug, but public health officials were still alarmed. If the woman's strain combined with other antibiotic-resistant bugs, the world could be on the brink of an unstoppable outbreak.[1]

"In some ways, I think we aren't on the cusp of a post-antibiotic world; we are already there," says McGann, chief of molecular research and diagnostics at Walter Reed's Multidrug Resistant Organism Repository and Surveillance Network (MRSN). "In China and India, there are now bacteria resistant to all antibiotics."

McGann points to a 70-year-old woman who died in September 2016 in Nevada from a bacterium resistant to all approved antibiotics in the United States. The woman had traveled to India and been hospitalized there for a broken leg.[2]

At least 2 million people in the United States contract an antibiotic-resistant bacterium each year and 23,000 die as a result, according to estimates from the Centers for Disease Control and Prevention (CDC). Antibiotic-resistant bugs may kill 700,000 people worldwide annually.[3]

Microbes have mutated to resist human attempts to kill them ever since antibiotics became widely used in the 1940s. Antibiotics have all but eliminated the threat of sepsis, tuberculosis, plague, cholera and other diseases that once killed millions. But antibiotics' overuse on humans and animals has spawned a growing number of resistant superbugs.

The Army created the MRSN in 2009 to monitor potential outbreaks of dangerous pathogens inside the military. Part of McGann's work is to quickly identify superbugs and then seek to keep them from spreading. His lab houses genome-sequencing machines that categorize bacteria and search for pathogens that may have mutated to resist antibiotics.

Such work allowed McGann to discover the Pennsylvania woman's superbug, which carried a colistin-resistant gene called mcr-1. Researchers first found the gene in 2015 in pigs and people in China, where farmers had regularly used colistin in animal feed to promote growth.[4]

The colistin-resistant bacteria has since spread and been found in more than 30 additional countries, including the

necessary to prevent flu. Because flu changes so quickly, drug companies don't always make a vaccine that is an exact match for a virus.

Since 1500, 14 or more flu pandemics have been recorded, with six occurring in the past 140 years — in 1889, 1918, 1957, 1968, 1977 and 2009, according to a 2010 report in the journal *Public Health*.[82]

The 2009 outbreak of H1N1, or swine flu, moved from birds to pigs and then to humans. It was first reported as a cluster of cases in Mexico. Initially, death rates were said to be 8 percent, making it almost as deadly as the 2003 SARS outbreak. The CDC then began receiving reports of swine flu spreading in the United States and five other countries.[83]

Hospitals, at the beginning, were overwhelmed with patients. It took more than six months for drug companies to create an H1N1 vaccine. Fortunately, the flu proved not to be as lethal as the first reports from Mexico. Within the year, about 24 percent of the world was infected with the swine flu, showing how quickly a flu can spread, but the death rate was just 0.02 percent. Approximately 24,000 Americans die annually from the flu, but only about 17,000 Americans died from the swine flu.[84]

"With H1N1, we got lucky," says Dr. Stacey Schultz-Cherry, deputy director of St. Jude Children's Research Hospital's Center of Excellence in Influenza Research and Surveillance.

Bioterror Threats

On many occasions during the past 2,000 years, military leaders have used biological agents in the form of disease, human cadavers and animals. In preparing for a naval

United States. In response, China has banned the use of colistin in animal feed.

McGann found a second U.S. patient, a former military officer living in Bahrain, with bacteria carrying the mcr-1. His body fought the bacteria on its own and he recovered, says McGann. The woman who died in Nevada didn't have a bacterium with the mcr-1 gene, and scientists are still working on understanding how her bacteria became resistant.

McGann's lab is part of the CDC's National Action Plan for Combating Antibiotic Resistant Bacteria, which coordinates efforts across federal agencies and sets goals for reducing the spread of antibiotic-resistant bugs and inappropriate use of antibiotics in medicine and agriculture.[5]

In April, the CDC tapped state health department laboratories in Maryland, Minnesota, New York, Tennessee, Texas and Washington to help with testing for antibiotic-resistant bugs, according to McGann. The CDC chose these labs for strategic regional reasons. Before this, state and local labs weren't equipped to perform such tests, so it is unclear how many superbugs may be circulating in the United States.

"The more we watch for these bugs, the faster we will pick up on this," McGann says of the fight to prevent a pandemic of antibiotic-resistant disease.

— *Bara Vaida*

Microbiologist Patrick McGann, with research scientist Rosslyn Maybank, studies "superbugs" at the Walter Reed Army Institute of Research in Silver Spring, Md.

[1] Lena H. Sun and Brady Dennis, "The superbug that doctors have been dreading just reached the U.S.," *The Washington Post*, May 27, 2016, http://tinyurl.com/mmsqnhl.

[2] Lei Chan et al., "Notes from the Field: Pan-Resistant New Delhi Metallo-Beta-Lactamase-Producing Klebsiella Pneumonia — Washoe County, Nevada, 2016," Centers for Disease Control and Prevention, Jan. 13, 2017, http://tinyurl.com/zklmrwb.

[3] "Antibiotic/Antimicrobial Resistance," Centers for Disease Control and Prevention, http://tinyurl.com/la3tgtj; Maryn McKenna, "The Coming Cost of Superbugs: 10 Million Deaths per Year," *Wired*, Dec. 15, 2014, http://tinyurl.com/m7prunp.

[4] Sun and Dennis, op. cit.; Chris Dall, "Studies show spread of MCR-1 gene in China," Center for Infectious Disease Research and Policy, Jan. 27, 2017, http://tinyurl.com/mkw2t8e.

[5] "National Action Plan for Combating Antibiotic-Resistant Bacteria," The White House, March 2015, http://tinyurl.com/nylq9ey.

battle against King Eumenes of Pergamum (modern-day Turkey) in 184 B.C., Hannibal, the leader of Carthage (Tunisia), directed his sailors to fill earthen pots filled with "serpents of every kind" and launch them at enemy ships.

During the French and Indian War (1754–63), Sir Jeffrey Amherst, commander of the British forces in North America, devised a plan to send blankets infected with smallpox to Indians hostile to the British. The move triggered an epidemic among tribes in the Ohio River Valley.

Biological warfare efforts accelerated during the two world wars. In World War I, vials of anthrax were found in the luggage of a captured German spy, intended to infect animals used by the Allies. During World War II, Japan unleashed plague-infested fleas and contaminated rice in China, causing 10,000 casualties.

By the 1960s, the U.S. military had developed a biological arsenal that included numerous weaponized pathogens. Canada, France, Britain and the Soviet Union also had germ-warfare research programs.[85]

During the late 1960s, international concerns arose about the risks such programs posed to society. In 1972 a U.N. convention prohibited the development, production and stockpiling of infectious diseases. The agreement was signed by 103 countries, and since then the United States and most other countries have engaged only in biodefense research. The Soviet Union, however, continued its biological weapons program, called Biopreparat. During the late 1990s, the United States learned that before its demise, the Soviet Union had been developing dangerous pathogens, including anthrax, plague, smallpox and toxic bugs. All were ready to be deployed via a missile.[86]

Experts Warn of Growing Bioterrorism Threat

"The risk of bioterrorism goes up every day."

In 2014, a laptop belonging to an Islamic State fighter fell into the hands of Syrian rebels. Its contents raised fresh alarms about the jihadist group's plans. The ISIS fighter, a chemist and physicist identified as Muhammad S., had been teaching himself to develop biological weapons and, most alarmingly, to weaponize the bubonic plague.

"The advantage of biological weapons is that they do not cost a lot of money, while the human casualties can be huge," said a document found on the laptop.[1]

Just how close ISIS and other jihadist groups are to developing such a weapon is unknown, but U.S. intelligence sources believe "there are a lot of terrorists that keep working on it," says Jeff Schlegelmilch, deputy director of the National Center for Disaster Preparedness at Columbia University's Earth Institute.

Under the 1972 Biological Weapons Convention, all United Nations member countries pledged not to develop or stockpile weaponized biological and toxic agents.[2] But the convention had no enforcement mechanism, and states like North Korea, China, Iran and Israel are believed to have developed weapons. Syria violated the accord by using chemical weapons on at least four occasions since December 2016, including one in April on a rebel-held town, which prompted the Trump administration to order a U.S. missile attack on a Syrian air base in April.[3]

The Soviet Union developed a program called Biopreparat that produced tons of anthrax and smallpox virus, some for use in intercontinental ballistic missiles. After the Soviet Union collapsed in 1991, the United States worked with the Russians to dismantle the Biopreparat lab.[4]

Accessing pathogens and turning them into a biological weapon doesn't require the backing of a nation-state, experts say. Only determination and access to medical supplies or a laboratory are required, as the Oregon town of The Dalles discovered in 1984. A religious sect called the Rajneeshees obtained a bacterial strain of salmonella from a commercial medical supply company and spread it on salad bars to try to disrupt a local election. More than 750 in the town of 10,000 were sickened. At the time, this was the largest bioterrorist attack in the country.

Then in 2001, someone created a blend of anthrax spores and weaponized them. According to investigators, Army scientist Bruce Ivins sent the spores to the media and members of Congress in the mail, killing five people in what remains the nation's worst bioterrorist attack. Some scientists, however, questioned the investigation's findings and doubts remain whether Ivins was the culprit. He killed himself before he was charged in the case.[5]

Many security experts today remain worried that another rogue scientist or an individual with some laboratory skills could wreak havoc. New technology can alter viruses and bacteria and make them more infectious or impervious to current treatments. These tools are widely available on the internet.

"Technology gets simpler and easier every day, and the risk of bioterrorism goes up every day," says Dr. Ali Khan, former director of the CDC's Office of Public Health Preparedness and Response.

Tara O'Toole, executive vice president at In-Q-Tel, a venture capital firm in Arlington, Va., specializing in security technology, says even nonscientists could use

In 2001, just weeks after the Sept. 11 terrorist attacks on New York City and the Pentagon, letters filled with anthrax were sent to some news media and members of Congress. A massive investigation concluded that a mentally ill biodefense researcher was the source of the letters, which infected 22 people and killed five. The suspect killed himself before he was charged, and some experts doubt he was the culprit.[87]

The government by some estimates spent as much as $1 billion testing and cleaning up the contaminated

government buildings and the mail-sorting centers that handled the letters. The incident awoke many Americans to the possibility that the country was vulnerable to bioterrorism attack, not only from a terrorist organization but also from a deranged scientist.[88]

With advances in genetic engineering, a skilled scientist could alter a virus or bacterium in a lab and design it to be impervious to vaccines and antibiotics. "We no longer can concern ourselves just with highly funded national and international defense labs," wrote Michael Osterholm gene-editing tools available on the internet to develop dangerous biological agents and devise ways to disperse them.

In the bioterror version of a suicide bombing, a terrorist group also could infect people with a contagious respiratory disease and send them on multiple airline flights to spread the virus worldwide, along the lines of the 1995 movie "12 Monkeys."

"Bioterrorism remains one of the top two threats to the country, the other one being a nuclear attack," says O'Toole.

After the anthrax attacks in 2001, the United States spent more than $30 billion on programs to respond to a potential biological attack. For example, Project BioShield directs the federal government to stockpile medical countermeasures in case of a chemical, biological or nuclear attack.[6] Another program, BioWatch, is designed to detect airborne disease in major U.S. cities.[7]

"Those systems proved to be extremely valuable for the whole of the U.S. health system," says Schlegelmilch.

But Congress has cut spending on bioterrorism response by hundreds of millions of dollars in recent years. Further, BioWatch's systems for detecting airborne pathogens are old and unreliable, former Homeland Security Secretary Tom Ridge told a National Association of County and City Health Officials (NACCHO) conference on April 25.[8]

"We need a better disease and surveillance system to replace BioWatch," he said. Ridge, the nation's first Homeland Security secretary, co-chairs the Blue Ribbon Study Panel on Biodefense, created in 2014 to address gaps in the nation's biodefenses. The organization has made 33 recommendations to Congress including designating the vice president to be the lead federal coordinator in the event of a bio emergency.

"We have a lot in place to respond to and prevent biological and pandemics and biological terrorist attack, but the programs have atrophied," former Sen. Joseph Lieberman, an independent from Connecticut who is co-chair of the Blue Ribbon panel, said at the April NACCHO conference. "You get less focused on a problem that hasn't occurred lately. That makes you unprepared for when it does happen. So God forbid there should be another bioterrorism attack or infectious disease outbreak."[9]

— *Bara Vaida*

[1] Harald Doornbos and Jenan Moussa, "Found: The Islamic State's Terror Laptop of Doom," *ForeignPolicy.com*, Aug. 28, 2014, http://tinyurl.com/kqjkxes.

[2] "Convention on the Prohibition of the Development, Production and Stockpiling of Bacteriological (Biological) and Toxin Weapons and on their Destruction (BWC)," U.S. Department of State, March 26, 1975, http://tinyurl.com/m9ywuje.

[3] "North Korea's Biological Weapon Program," *Biological Warfare Blog*, April 2, 2014, http://tinyurl.com/kcel9jw; Missy Ryan, "Chemical attack in Syria that drew U.S. response was just one in a series, rights group alleges," *The Washington Post*, May 1, 2017, http://tinyurl.com/mh63voo.

[4] Michael T. Osterholm and Mark Olshaker, *Deadliest Enemy: Our War Against Killer Germs* (2017).

[5] Mara Bovsun, "750 sickened in Oregon restaurants as cult known as the Rajneeshees spread salmonella in town of The Dalles," *N.Y. Daily News*, June 15, 2013, http://tinyurl.com/karkvvk; Joby Warrick, "FBI investigation of 2001 anthrax attacks concluded; U.S. releases details," *The Washington Post*, Feb. 20, 2010, http://tinyurl.com/ybgtvr2.

[6] Milton Leitenberg, "Assessing the Biological Weapons and Bioterrorism Threat," Strategic Studies Institute, December 2005, http://tinyurl.com/k34nbv3.

[7] Frank Gottron, "Science and Technology Issues in the 115th Congress," Congressional Research Service, March 14, 2017, http://tinyurl.com/k6fzook.

[8] Tom Ridge remarks via webcast of Preparedness Summit, National Association of County and City Health Officials conference, April 25–28, 2017, http://tinyurl.com/lbhfd5d. For more on the conference, see Preparedness Summit, http://tinyurl.com/ozfwfb5, and "Biodefense advocates take on U.S. preparedness funding fight," *Homeland Preparedness News*, April 25, 2017, http://tinyurl.com/lkk637z.

[9] Ibid., webcast of the April 25-28 conference.

and Mark Olshaker in their 2017 book, *Deadliest Enemy: Our War Against Killer Germs*. "Information on how to gin up a potential killer microbe with new lab technology tools is readily available on the Internet."[89]

CURRENT SITUATION
Emerging Threats

Hundreds of infections are constantly emerging around the world and spreading among and between animals and humans.

During one week at the beginning of May, there were 847 alerts about a patient or group of patients with potentially dangerous infectious diseases ranging from Zika, Ebola and measles to yellow fever. Poultry, swine and cow illnesses were reported, too, according to HealthMap, a website that tracks infectious disease outbreaks worldwide.[90]

"Are we sitting on the edge of the next pandemic? I hope not," says Osterholm of the Center for Infectious Disease Research and Policy. "But could it happen tomorrow? Yes."

One-year-old twins Heloisa and Heloa Barbosa of Areia, Brazil, were born with microcephaly after their mother was bitten by a mosquito with the Zika virus. Although technological advances have enabled scientists to develop new vaccines faster, including one for Zika, vaccines exist for only a fraction of the 300 or so known infectious diseases.

WHO is tracking these outbreaks through its Global Outbreak Alert and Response Network, which links local, regional, national and international networks of laboratories and medical centers. The organization also monitors flu outbreaks through its Global Influenza Surveillance and Response System, which is connected to hundreds of laboratories around the world.[91]

The most worrisome potential outbreak could be in China. A growing market for poultry in that nation has led to an explosion in chicken farming. In Shanghai alone, farmers hatch 100 million chickens a month, increasing the opportunity for novel influenza viruses to thrive.

One of those, the H7N9 virus, has been circulating among birds for years but has mutated to become more dangerous for both birds and humans handling the birds. The virus' changes are raising worries that it might lead to a pandemic, according to *Eurosurveillance*, Europe's journal of infectious disease epidemiology.[92]

China has reported more than 700 cases of H7N9 in humans and 203 deaths since October 2016. Nearly every victim was exposed to poultry, although a few cases may have been transmitted between individuals.[93]

Other outbreaks at the end of April included measles in Italy and Romania and yellow fever in Brazil. There also were outbreaks of MERS and three viruses — Lassa fever, Nipah and Crimean-Congo hemorrhagic fever. In early May, WHO reported an outbreak of Ebola in the Democratic Republic of Congo; by mid-May, four people had died and the number of cases had risen to 37.[94]

Experts say climate change increases the pandemic risk because certain diseases, such as Zika, thrive in hot and humid regions. Warming temperatures also increase the populations of disease carriers — mosquitos and parasites — making disease transmission easier.[95]

Leadership Vacuum

During this time of global risk, health policy experts are particularly worried about leadership gaps in the health community.[96]

Within the White House, the Trump administration's National Security Council (NSC) doesn't have a point person on global health security, although the White House told *The Washington Post* that Trump's homeland security adviser at the NSC, Thomas Bossert, has global health in his overall portfolio. Both Presidents George W. Bush and Obama dedicated one person solely to global health security.

At the Health and Human Services Department, Trump has yet to nominate anyone to serve as assistant secretary for preparedness and response.[97]

The president also has not named a permanent director at the CDC. Dr. Anne Schuchat, a respected CDC veteran, is running the agency, but because she's only acting director, her ability to mobilize resources during an emergency could be stymied, experts say.[98]

At the Defense Department, the administration has not nominated an assistant secretary for nuclear, chemical and biological defense, who would oversee the global emerging infectious disease surveillance and response programs, as well as the National Center for Medical Intelligence.[99]

"No one is in charge" of bioterrorism strategy, says In-Q-Tel's O'Toole, which is worrisome because "this is a national security issue. As Bill Gates says, the only thing that can kill millions of people is a bioterrorist attack or a pandemic."

Many health security experts were pleased when the Trump administration in early May nominated former Rep. Mark Green, R-Wis., to run USAID. Green was an ambassador to Tanzania under President George W. Bush and worked on his global AIDS initiative. Many health experts see him as an advocate for international aid programs.

Should governments mandate quarantines?

YES — Centers for Disease Control and Prevention (CDC)

Excerpted from CDC Website

Isolation and quarantine help protect the public by preventing exposure to people who have or may have a contagious disease. Isolation involves separating sick people with a contagious disease from people who are not sick. . . .

The duration and scope of quarantine measures would vary, depending on their purpose and what is known about the incubation period (how long it takes for symptoms to develop after exposure) of the disease-causing agent.

If people in a certain area were potentially exposed to a contagious disease, this is what would happen: State and local health authorities would let people know that they may have been exposed and would direct them to get medical attention, undergo diagnostic tests, and stay at home, limiting their contact with people who have not been exposed to the disease. Only rarely would federal, state, or local health authorities issue an "order" for quarantine and isolation.

However, both quarantine and isolation may be compelled on a mandatory basis through legal authority as well as conducted on a voluntary basis. States have the authority to declare and enforce quarantine and isolation within their borders. This authority varies widely, depending on state laws. It derives from the authority of state governments granted by the U.S. Constitution to enact laws and promote regulations to safeguard the health and welfare of people within state borders.

Further, at the national level, the CDC may detain, medically examine or conditionally release persons suspected of having certain contagious diseases. This authority applies to individuals arriving from foreign countries, including Canada and Mexico, on airplanes, trains, automobiles, boats or by foot. It also applies to individuals traveling from one state to another or in the event of "inadequate local control."

The CDC regularly uses its authority to monitor passengers arriving in the United States for contagious diseases. In modern times, most quarantine measures have been imposed on a small scale, typically involving small numbers of travelers (airline or cruise ship passengers) who have curable diseases, such as infectious tuberculosis or cholera. No instances of large-scale quarantine have occurred in the U.S. since the "Spanish Flu" pandemic of 1918–1919.

Based on years of experience working with state and local partners, the CDC anticipates that the need to use its federal authority to involuntarily quarantine a person would occur only in rare situations — for example, if a person posed a threat to public health and refused to cooperate with a voluntary request.

NO — Jeffrey A. Tucker

Director of Content, Foundation for Economic Education; Policy Adviser, Heartland Institute

Excerpted from Foundation for Economic Education Website

The government already has the power to create sick camps, kidnap and intern people upon suspicion that they are diseased, and keep people in camps for an undetermined amount of time. Anyone concerned about human freedom should be uncomfortable with this policy, especially given the hysteria that surrounds the issue of communicable diseases. It is easy to imagine a scenario in which such powers end up exposing undiseased people rather than protecting people from the disease.

Quarantine powers have been around since the ancient world and have been invoked through U.S. history since colonial times. But government can use those powers any way it wants. In World War I, prostitutes were routinely arrested and quarantined in the name of preventing the spread of diseases.

In the 1892 typhus outbreak, it became common to arrest and quarantine any immigrant from Russia, Italy or Ireland, even without any evidence of disease. In 1900, the San Francisco Board of Health quarantined 25,000 Chinese residents and gave them a dangerous injection to prevent the spread of bubonic plague (it turned out later to have been entirely pointless). In more recent times, fears of AIDS have led to calls for arresting Mexican immigrants. And it's not just about disease. The quarantine power has been used by despotic governments worldwide to round up political enemies.

Does the government really need quarantine power? Let's think rationally and normally about this. Government power is not necessary, nor is it likely to be effective. And when it is not effective, the tendency is to overreact, clamping down and abusing, as we've seen with the war on terror. People assume government is doing its job, but government fails and then government gets more power and does awful things with it.

Remember, it is not government that discovers the disease, treats it, keeps diseased patients from wandering around or otherwise compels sick people to stay in their sick beds. Institutions do this, institutions that are part of the social order and not exogenous to it.

Individuals don't like to get others sick. People don't like to get sick. Given this, we have a mechanism that actually works. Society has an ability and power of its own to bring about quarantine-like results without introducing the risk that the state's quarantine power will be used and abused for political purposes.

"Mark Green is a really strong choice to head USAID," Jeremy Konyndyk, former head of the agency's Office of U.S. Foreign Disaster Assistance, told NPR.[100]

The U.N. Foundation's Lange says he is not too worried about the lack of nominees. Most of the positions are filled by experienced acting caretakers such as Schuchat at the CDC, he says. "The people that are there are of very high caliber and in a real emergency, their expertise [would] prevail," Lange says.

Health and Human Services Secretary Tom Price assured Congress in March that health security is a top priority for the administration and that it would provide resources to fund preparedness.

"This is an absolute priority," Price testified at a March 29 hearing of the House Appropriations Subcommittee on Labor, Health and Human Services, Education and Related Agencies. When asked if HHS would have the money it needs to fund public health emergency preparedness, he said: "The American people expect us to be prepared and to be able to respond in the event of a challenge, especially in a bioterror area."[101]

WHO, too, is in the middle of a leadership transition as Tedros readies to become director-general. His election came as the organization struggles with financial challenges and an ongoing restructuring to better respond to emergency health outbreaks like Ebola. In May, The Associated Press published a scathing report criticizing WHO's $200 million travel budget, which is more than the agency devotes to AIDS, malaria and tuberculosis combined.[102]

Although WHO began a capital drive in 2015 for an emergency contingency fund for pandemics, some experts say that without decisive leadership the organization has been unable to reach its goal of $100 million. Tedros is a malaria expert who will have his work cut out for him. He is best known for drastically reducing deaths from malaria, AIDS, tuberculosis and neonatal problems when he was Ethiopia's health minister.[103]

Meanwhile, the Global Fund to Fight AIDS, Tuberculosis and Malaria also is seeking a new leader. The organization gets one-third of its money from the United States and estimates that it saves 2 million lives a year worldwide. It is unclear whether the United States will continue providing money under Trump and whether a new leader can fulfill the organization's goals without U.S. aid.[104]

Global Collaboration

The uncertainty surrounding the Trump administration's commitment to international health funding has created anxiety among global researchers who have been working together on vaccines and other medical countermeasures for a potential pandemic.

The first successful Ebola vaccine, which is awaiting regulatory approval in the United States, demonstrates the importance of global collaboration, experts say. The vaccine was developed in conjunction with WHO and companies, governments and universities from the United States, Canada, Europe and West Africa. Brazilian and European researchers collaborated with U.S. researchers to produce a Zika vaccine.[105]

But Trump's proposed temporary ban on travel from six Muslim countries alarmed researchers, who say the ban, although on hold, has slowed collaboration on tropical-disease vaccines and other emerging infectious-disease treatments. It also leaves international researchers wary of working with Americans and could place the United States at risk over the long term, said infectious disease expert Peter Hotez at the Baylor College of Medicine in Houston.

"Scientific communities across the world need collaborators in these countries who can combat epidemics before they arrive in the U.S.," said Hotez.[106]

The United States also needs to continue working with international researchers on influenza vaccines, because the flu spreads so quickly between borders, global health experts say. WHO maintains centers in Australia, the United States, China, Japan and the United Kingdom for collaborating on influenza vaccine research. The CDC developed three vaccines for H7N9 and stockpiled 12 million doses. Officials say, however, that virus has mutated, making the stockpiled vaccine less effective against the current H7N9 strain.[107]

To create another vaccine to match the version of H7N9 that is circulating now, the United States needs to keep working with China and other international colleagues, says Richard Webby, director of WHO's Collaborating Center for Studies on the Ecology of Influenza in Animals in Memphis, Tenn.

Further, the United States needs international partners when it comes to manufacturing vaccines. Companies produce a flu vaccine by growing it in fertilized eggs. The

United States relies on four pharmaceutical companies for flu vaccines, but only one has a manufacturing facility in the U.S. If a flu pandemic struck and killed the chickens needed to produce eggs, the United States might have trouble getting enough vaccine produced, because the three non-U.S. companies may decide to withhold the vaccines for their own populations, the Government Accountability Office said.[108]

If the United States can develop technologies that do not use eggs to produce vaccines, it would be less vulnerable, said Osterholm of the Center for Infectious Disease Research and Policy. "It would be the single most important thing we can do in public health today," he said.[109]

Researchers are making progress toward that goal. University of Georgia scientists are working to create a vaccine with genetic sequences of flu strains that have circulated over the past century. At Mount Sinai Hospital researchers are using genome sequencing to help the immune system better target a flu virus.[110]

OUTLOOK
Preventing Pandemics

Public health leaders agree that, statistically, the world is overdue for a lethal pandemic. They don't know whether it would begin with a rapidly evolving regional outbreak such as occurred with Ebola and Zika or a flu virus that has mutated to a point that no vaccine is effective; or a bioterrorist attack.

Preventing massive loss of life will require the world to continue working together to help poor and middle-income countries bolster their health systems, public health officials say, adding that the United States must maintain its investments in vaccine research and emergency preparedness.

"We should always have a good, high guard and never be complacent," said David Nabarro, an international health expert from Great Britain who was a candidate to lead WHO.[111]

Global health experts are optimistic that the Ebola and Zika crises have awakened leaders to the potential threats and that countries are on guard. They say the Global Health Security Agenda, the G-20 countries and individual nations are laying the groundwork to fight a pandemic. Further, advances in computing power and genetic engineering could bolster scientists' efforts to develop vaccines to fight the flu and other diseases.

Possibly as soon as the end of 2017, a total of 68 countries are expected to be evaluated by a multilateral body associated with WHO. The G-20 and World Bank have pledged funding to help them close preparedness gaps. The efforts involve wide swaths of governments — from the health ministries to environmental agencies to agriculture departments. The private sector also is stepping up.

"I am encouraged about the future," says Georgetown's Katz. "There are some smart people who have awakened to this threat."

Efforts by vaccine researchers and the Coalition for Epidemic Preparedness Innovations are expected to bear fruit within the decade, says John-Arne Rottingen, chief executive of the Research Council of Norway.

"We will probably have developed six to 10 vaccines for what we believe will be the most likely threats," he says of the next 10 years. "Hopefully we will have a couple of technology platforms based on [genetic engineering] techniques, so we can fast-track new vaccines for new, emerging pathogens, and that will increase our capacities to prevent and stop a new epidemic."

Microsoft's Gates and former Harvard University President Lawrence Summers are among the private-sector leaders whom Katz says are aggressively pushing leaders worldwide to see pandemic preparedness as a matter of national security and economics — and not just of health. Ebola cost the world economy about $32 billion, and Zika could cost North and South America and the Caribbean up to $18 billion by the end of 2017.[112]

"This is a big deal," Katz says. "Public health experts can bang the drums all day about pandemic threats, but ministers of health tend not to be politically important. Gates, Sands and Summers, however, are able to make strong arguments to ministers of finance to encourage their governments that investing in this [affects business]," she says, "and they are changing the framework of this discussion."

NOTES

1. Researchers name influenza viruses by their particular strains, with the "H" and "N" designating the kind of proteins covering the flu virus.

2. "Human infection with avian influenza A(H7N9) virus — China," World Health Organization, April 20, 2017, http://tinyurl.com/mrwycej.

3. Lisa Schnirring, "China reports 23 more H7N9 cases, 7 fatal," Center for Infectious Disease Research and Policy, May 12, 2017, http://tinyurl.com/kutlvk8; Jeffrey K. Taubenberger and David M. Morens, "Influenza: The Once and Future Pandemic," *Public Health Reports*, U.S. National Library of Medicine, 2010, http://tinyurl.com/ldh4rfu.

4. Dan Vergano, "Mystery of 1918 Flu That Killed 50 Million Solved?" *National Geographic*, April 29 2014, http://tinyurl.com/moxx767.

5. Rob Schmitz, "Why Chinese Scientists Are More Worried Than Ever About Bird Flu," *Goats and Soda blog*, NPR, April 11, 2017, http://tinyurl.com/mjnk6yk.

6. James Joyce, "Why the nation must prepare for future pandemic threats," *San Diego Union-Tribune*, Nov. 24, 2016, http://tinyurl.com/morjhhy.

7. Bill Gates, "A new kind of terrorism could wipe out 30 million people in less than a year and we are not prepared," *Business Insider*, Feb. 18, 2017, http://tinyurl.com/z5pc9rn.

8. Annie Sparrow, "Who isn't equipped for a pandemic or a bioterror attack? The WHO," *Bulletin of the Atomic Scientists*, June 20, 2016, http://tinyurl.com/msrpmy2; Sheri Fink, "Cuts at W.H.O. Hurt Response to Ebola Crises," *The New York Times*, Sept. 3, 2014, http://tinyurl.com/m4ppmys.

9. "The WHO Contingency Fund for Emergencies," World Health Organization, November 2015, http://tinyurl.com/k7xdkbo.

10. "Fact Sheet: The Global Health Security Agenda," Office of the Press Secretary, The White House, July 28, 2015, http://tinyurl.com/m6ybyd9; "The Global Health Security Agenda," http://tinyurl.com/m8wjl5k; "Coalition for Epidemic Preparedness Innovations (CEPI) Presentation to the WHO," World Health Organization, July 21, 2017, http://tinyurl.com/l3msobz.

11. Donald G. McNeil Jr., "The Campaign to Lead the World Health Organization," *The New York Times*, April 3, 2017, http://tinyurl.com/kylbmmu; Julia Belluz, "Trump has set the US up to botch a global health crises," *Vox.com*, April 3, 2017, http://tinyurl.com/ksvb83q.

12. Lena H. Sun, "The Trump administration is ill-prepared for a global pandemic," *The Washington Post*, April 18, 2017, http://tinyurl.com/n3ocur8; Lawrence Gostin and Eric Friedman, "Global Health: A Pivotal Moment of Opportunity and Peril," *Health Affairs*, Feb. 28, 2017, http://tinyurl.com/mf6gmht.

13. "Emergency Preparedness and Response 2016," World Health Organization, http://tinyurl.com/l25xwpa; "First Global Estimates of 2009 H1N1 Pandemic Mortality Released by CDC-Led Collaboration," Centers for Disease Control and Prevention, June 25, 2012, http://tinyurl.com/lunzuhk; Denise Grady, "Suspected Cases of Ebola Rise to 29 in Democratic Republic of Congo," *The New York Times*, May 18, 2017, http://tinyurl.com/l4kw7ya.

14. Anmar Frangoul, "Counting the costs of a global epidemic," CNBC.com, Feb. 5, 2014, http://tinyurl.com/kkh8nep; "World Bank Group Launches Groundbreaking Financing Facility to Protect Poorest Countries Against Pandemics," World Bank, May 21, 2016, http://tinyurl.com/mwtgsjd.

15. Gates, op. cit.

16. "Antibiotic/Antimicrobial Resistance," Centers for Disease Control and Prevention, April 27, 2017, http://tinyurl.com/la3tgtj; Helen Branswell, "A Nevada woman dies of a superbug resistant to every available antibiotic in the US," *STAT*, Jan. 12, 2017, http://tinyurl.com/hdxdcmq.

17. Ali S. Khan with William Patrick, "The Next Pandemic: On the Front Lines Against Humankind's Gravest Dangers," *PublicAffairs*, 2016, p. 250, http://tinyurl.com/mk8gneo.

18. Tom Ridge remarks via webcast of Preparedness Summit, National Association of County and City Health Officials conference, April 25–28, 2017, http://tinyurl.com/lbhfd5d.

19. Michael Osterholm and Mark Olshaker, *Deadlist Enemy: Our War Against Killer Germs* (2017), chap. 11, http://tinyurl.com/myacoga.

20. "Fact Sheet: The Global Health Security Agenda," op. cit.

21. "International Health Regulations," World Health Organization, 2005, http://tinyurl.com/n5lv3qz;

Haitham Shoman, "The link between the West African Ebola outbreak and health systems in Guinea, Liberia, and Sierra Leone: A systematic review," *Globalization and Health*, Oct. 17, 2016, http://tinyurl.com/mqqmphl.

22. "U.S. Launches Global Health Security Agenda, Partners With 26 Countries," Henry J. Kaiser Family Foundation, Feb. 14, 2014, http://tinyurl.com/lkfn745.

23. "African Union launches Africa CDC, a continent-wide public health agency," *ReliefWeb*, Feb. 2, 2017, http://tinyurl.com/mpbv5yx.

24. "USAID announces second phase of Predict project with global partners," EcoHealth Alliance, Nov. 21, 2014, http://tinyurl.com/lyt2zk4; "Factsheet: Emerging Pandemic Threats," USAID, http://tinyurl.com/n86geuu.

25. Bryan Walsh, "The World Is Not Ready for the Next Pandemic," *Time*, May 3, 2017, http://tinyurl.com/mopxrys.

26. Sun, op. cit.

27. Peter Sands et al., "The Neglected Dimension of Global Security — A Framework for Countering Infectious-Disease Crises," *The New England Journal of Medicine*, March 31, 2016, http://tinyurl.com/lfqkub4.

28. McNeil Jr., op. cit.; "Budget Fact Sheets," Centers for Disease Control and Prevention, http://tinyurl.com/mw9ox53.

29. Suerie Moon et al., "Will Ebola Change the Game? Ten Essential Reforms Before the Next Pandemic," *The Lancet*, Nov. 22, 2015, http://tinyurl.com/lyq6o89.

30. Sparrow, op. cit.

31. "World Health Assembly elects Dr. Tedros Adhanom Ghebreyesus as new WHO Director-General," World Health Organization, May 23, 2017, http://tinyurl.com/lhj7yn7; McNeil Jr., op. cit.

32. Helen Branswell, "Finding the World's Unknown Viruses — Before They Find Us," *STAT*, Dec. 13, 2016, http://tinyurl.com/keruja7.

33. "What is CEPI?" Center for Epidemic Preparedness Innovations, http://tinyurl.com/m29tyam.

34. Crystal Watson and Matthew Watson, "Funding and Organization of US Federal Biosecurity Security Programs," Johns Hopkins Bloomberg School of Public Health Center for Health Security, January/February 2017, http://tinyurl.com/mu3lwf4.

35. "2017 United States Budget Estimate," *Inside Gov*, http://tinyurl.com/mtc2fc3.

36. "The U.S. Government and the World Health Organization," Henry J. Kaiser Family Foundation, March 16, 2017, http://tinyurl.com/mcoswva.

37. Watson and Watson, op. cit.

38. "Biodefense Indicators: One Year Later, Events Outpacing Federal Efforts to Defend the Nation," Blue Ribbon Study Panel on Defense, December 2016, http://tinyurl.com/y97jvw3q.

39. Ridge, op. cit.

40. "FY2010 Budget Overview," CDC Coalition, http://tinyurl.com/k64o4v6; "Division H — Departments of Labor, Health and Human Services, and Education and Related Agencies Appropriations Act 2017," House of Representatives, May 2017, http://tinyurl.com/lao845n.

41. "Prepared, National Health Security Preparedness Index," Robert Wood Johnson Foundation, http://tinyurl.com/ltj8wyh.

42. Ilene MacDonald, "Trump budget proposal cuts billions and would 'devastate' healthcare programs," *FierceHealthcare*, May 23, 2017, http://tinyurl.com/lkeauwx.

43. Tom Friedan tweet by Friedan, May 23, 2017.

44. Donovan Slack and Gregory Korte, "Trump's first budget slashes education, health spending to make way for military buildup," *USA Today*, March 16, 2017, http://tinyurl.com/kw8c977; "Avian Influenza: USDA Has Taken Actions to Reduce Risks but Needs a Plan to Evaluate Its Efforts," U.S. Government Accountability Office, April 2017, http://tinyurl.com/mcptyjj.

45. Walsh, op. cit.

46. Zoë Carpenter, "The United States Has an Emergency Fund for Natural Disasters. Why Not for Pandemics?" *The Nation*, Aug. 25, 2016, http://tinyurl.com/k4q2lh5.

47. "Specific Laws and Regulations Governing the Control of Communicable Diseases," Centers for Disease Control and Prevention, March 21, 2017, http://tinyurl.com/mkbzxbd.

48. Lenny Bernstein, "Trump wanted to keep Americans critically ill with Ebola out of the U.S.," *The Washington Post*, Aug. 24, 2016, http://tinyurl.com/mhyzqdu.

49. Norimitsu Onishi, "Clashes Erupt as Liberia Sets an Ebola Quarantine," *The New York Times*, Aug. 20, 2014, http://tinyurl.com/k2d5ggn; Adam Nassiter, "Sierra Leone to Impose 3-Day Ebola Quarantine," *The New York Times*, Sept. 6, 2014, http://tinyurl.com/lnh7dgu.

50. "Statement from the Travel and Transport Task Force on Ebola virus disease outbreak in West Africa," World Health Organization, Nov. 7, 2014, http://tinyurl.com/lprlxaz.

51. Richard Schabas, "Severe Acute Respiratory Syndrome: Did Quarantine Help?" *Canadian Journal of Infectious Diseases and Medical Microbiology*, July/August 2004, http://tinyurl.com/krr8jbf.

52. Shoman, op. cit.

53. "Legal Authorities for Isolation and Quarantine," Centers for Disease Control and Prevention, Oct. 8, 2014, http://tinyurl.com/n8xx33a.

54. Kyle Edwards, Wendy Parmet and Scott Burris, "Why the C.D.C.'s Power to Quarantine Should Worry Us," *The New York Times*, Jan. 23, 2017, http://tinyurl.com/l3bsrhk.

55. Rob Stein, "CDC Seeks Controversial New Quarantine Powers to Stope Outbreaks," *Shots blog*, NPR, Feb. 2, 2017, http://tinyurl.com/zm6azve.

56. Ibid.

57. Matt Arco, "Ebola Nurse Lawsuit Against Christie Continues Despite Judge Tossing Federal Claims," NJ.com, Sept. 9, 2016, http://tinyurl.com/kus22dx.

58. "Global Immunization: Worldwide Disease Incidence," Children's Hospital of Philadelphia, December 2014, http://tinyurl.com/jktr3ot.

59. Erin Walkinshaw, "Mandatory Vaccinations: No Middle Ground," *Canadian Medical Association Journal*, Nov. 8, 2011, http://tinyurl.com/lfynf5f.

60. Kathleen S. Swendiman, "Mandatory Vaccinations: Precedent and Current Laws," Congressional Research Service, March 10, 2011.

61. "Background of the Issue" ProCon.org, March 22, 2016, http://tinyurl.com/zmqo9xq.

62. "Health, United States, 2015," Department of Health and Human Services, 2016, http://tinyurl.com/m8uz5gs; Lena H. Sun, "Anti-vaccine activists spark a state's worst measles outbreak in decades," *The Washington Post*, May 5, 2017, http://tinyurl.com/l9wjpto.

63. "Hardball with Chris Matthews," NBCNews. com, Feb. 3, 2015, http://tinyurl.com/ko2bwrb.

64. Lena H. Sun, "Trump energizes the anti-vaccine movement in Texas," *The Washington Post*, Feb. 20, 2017, http://tinyurl.com/n5cnzom; Dylan Scott, "Robert K. Kennedy Jr. Says He Expects Trump Vaccine Panel Will Move Forward," *STAT*, Feb. 16, 2012, http://tinyurl.com/jhor5gb.

65. "The Model State Emergency Health Powers Act," Network for Public Health Law, Aug. 1, 2011, http://tinyurl.com/l2shxah; "Q&A Model State Emergency Health Powers Act," American Civil Liberties Union, http://tinyurl.com/mzutrgh.

66. Sonia Shah, *Pandemic: Tracking Contagions, from Cholera to Ebola and Beyond* (2016), chap. 1.

67. Ibid.

68. Marcia Clemmitt, "Emerging Infectious Diseases," *CQ Researcher*, Feb. 13, 2015, pp. 145-168.

69. "Black Death," History.com, http://tinyurl.com/bk3z46l.

70. Ibid.; Eugenia Tognotti, "Lessons from the History of Quarantine, From Plague to Influenza A," Centers for Disease Control and Prevention, February 2013, http://tinyurl.com/lmd34wx.

71. Shah, op. cit.

72. Ibid.; Tognotti, op. cit.

73. Ibid., Tognotti.

74. For background see Mary H. Cooper, "Fighting SARS," *CQ Researcher*, June 20, 2003, pp. 569–592.

75. "Lessons from the History of Quarantine, From Plague to Influenza A," op. cit.

76. "Background of the Issue," op. cit.

77. "Edward Jenner," Science Museum, http://tinyurl .com/my93qbn; Max Roser, "Eradication of Diseases," *Our World in Data*, http://tinyurl.com/n42crl6.

78. "Background of the Issue," op. cit.; Cole and Swendiman, op. cit.

79. Ibid., Swendiman.

80. Rustam I. Aminov, "A Brief History of the Antibiotic Era: Lessons Learned and Challenges for the Future," *Frontiers in Microbiology*, Oct. 29, 2010, http://tinyurl.com/lv4elnd.

81. "Life Expectancy in the USA," University of California, Berkeley, http://tinyurl.com/l3qzudg; Rob Stein, "Life Expectancy in U.S. Drops For First Time In Decades, Report Finds," NPR, Dec. 6, 2016, http://tinyurl.com/grf86xv.

82. Taubenberger and Morens, op. cit.

83. James A. Wilde, "A(H1N1) 'Swine Flu' 2009/2010: Where We've Been, What We Know, Where We May Be Heading," AHC Media, March 1, 2010, http://tinyurl.com/kgoafgq.

84. Robert Roos, "Study Puts Global 2009 Pandemic H1N1 Infection Rate at 24%," Center for Infectious Disease Research and Policy, Jan. 24, 2013, http:// tinyurl.com/k2sa5r3; Joe Neel, "How Many People Die From Flu Each Year? Depends On How You Slice The Data," *Shots blog*, NPR, Aug. 26, 2010, http://tinyurl.com/jlo9wtd.

85. Osterholm and Olshaker, op. cit., chap. 11.

86. Ibid.

87. Joby Warrick, "FBI investigation of 2001 anthrax attacks concluded; U.S. releases details," *The Washington Post*, Feb. 20, 2010, http://tinyurl.com/ybgtvr2.

88. Khan and Patrick, op. cit., chap. 5.

89. Osterholm and Olshaker, op. cit.

90. "Alerts for the Week," *HealthMap*, May 14, 2017, http://tinyurl.com/24eyvvh.

91. "Global Influenza Surveillance and Response System," World Health Organization, http:// tinyurl.com/72ex3oa; "Global Outbreak Alert and Response Network," World Health Organization, http://tinyurl.com/hpblh9j.

92. "Eurosurveillance: Preliminary Epidemiology and Analysis of Jiangsu's 5th H7N9 Wave," *Avian Flu Diary*, March 30, 2017, http://tinyurl.com/ kb9sbyv.

93. Schnirring, op. cit.

94. Stephanie Soucheray, "WHO: 37Ebola cases in the DRC, 4 Deaths" Center for Infectious Disease Research and Policy, May 22, 2017, http://tinyurl .com/mwlbvkm.

95. "Climate Change and Infectious Diseases," World Health Organization, http://tinyurl.com/o9ylyme.

96. Belluz, op. cit.

97. "Political Appointee Trackers," Partnership for Public Service, May 23, 2017, http://tinyurl.com/ lxxhv6k.

98. Sun, "The Trump administration is ill-prepared for a global pandemic," op. cit.

99. "Political Appointee Tracker," op. cit.

100. Jason Beaubien, "Trump's Proposed USAID Head Knows Aid — And Politics," *Goats and Soda blog*, NPR, May 11, 2017, http://tinyurl.com/k7d8k6l.

101. Testimony of Tom Price, Budget Hearing, Department of Health and Human Services, March 29, 2017, http://tinyurl.com/mvvc85z.

102. "AP Exclusive: UN Health Agency Slammed for High Travel Costs," The Associated Press, *The New York Times*, May 22, 2017, http://tinyurl.com/n5ezobw.

103. McNeil Jr., op. cit.; Donald G. McNeil Jr. and Nick Cumming-Bruce, "WHO Elects Ethopia's Tedros as First Director General from Africa," *The New York Times*, May 23, 2017, http://tinyurl .com/lx6gw7d.

104. Jeremy Youde, "Wanted: A New Executive Director for the Global Fund," *Duck of Minerva*, March 4, 2017, http://tinyurl.com/mjmdl8m.

105. Belluz, op. cit.

106. Amy Maxmen, "Trump immigration ban upends international work on disease," *Nature*, Feb. 1, 2017, http://tinyurl.com/l7afwuc.

107. "Asian Lineage Avian Influenza A (H7N9)," Centers for Disease Control and Prevention, May 9, 2017, http://tinyurl.com/l7qd6ou.

108. "Avian Influenza: USDA Has Taken Actions to Reduce Risks but Needs a Plan to Evaluate Its Efforts," op. cit.

109. Marlene Cimons, "There may someday be a way to avoid the yearly flu shot," *The Washington Post*, Jan. 7, 2017, http://tinyurl.com/k4g3gy3.

110. Ibid.

111. Stephanie Nebehay, "World must not miss early signals of any flu pandemic: WHO," Reuters, Jan. 23, 2017, http://tinyurl.com/kkf2mb5.

112. Deb Reichmann, "World Bank: Economic impact of Ebola epidemic could top $32.6 billion by end of year," The Associated Press, *USA Today*, Oct. 8, 2014, http://tinyurl.com/lqkp5ff; "Report says cost of Zika estimated at up to $18 billion," The Associated Press, WTOP.com, April 6, 2017, http://tinyurl.com/mc5kf7e.

BIBLIOGRAPHY
Selected Sources
Books

Khan, Ali S., *The Next Pandemic: On the Front Lines Against Humankind's Gravest Dangers*, PublicAffairs, 2016.
The former head of the Office of Public Health Preparedness and Response at the Centers for Disease Control and Prevention (CDC) recalls investigating frightening disease outbreaks and offers advice on how to prevent pandemics.

Osterholm, Michael T., and Mark Olshaker, *Deadliest Enemy: Our War Against Killer Germs*, Little Brown & Company, 2017.
The founder of the University of Minnesota's Center for Infectious Disease Research and Policy recounts the history of pandemics and explains how political leaders can implement policy initiatives to prevent them.

Shah, Sonia, *Pandemic: Tracking Contagions from Cholera to Ebola and Beyond*, Picador USA, 2016.
A science journalist summarizes past pandemics and explains how dealing with cholera helped prepare the world to prevent future pandemics.

Articles

"AP Exclusive: UN Health Agency Slammed for High Travel Costs," The Associated Press, *The New York Times*, May 22, 2017, http://tinyurl.com/n5ezobw.
The World Health Organization is spending $200 million a year on travel expenses, more than what it spends fighting AIDS, malaria and tuberculosis combined, according to an Associated Press investigation.

"Lessons from the History of Quarantine, from Plague to Influenza A," Centers for Disease Control and Prevention, February 2013, http://tinyurl.com/lmd34wx.
The federal agency in charge of preventing the spread of infectious diseases reflects on lessons learned from quarantines imposed during pandemics and how quarantines can be used to safeguard public health without violating civil rights.

Boyce, Nell Greenfield, "Inside a Secret Government Warehouse Prepped for Health Catastrophes," NPR, June 27, 2016, http://tinyurl.com/jyxgply.
The CDC is stockpiling drugs, vaccines and medical equipment in preparation for potential health emergencies.

Gostin, Lawrence, and Eric Friedman, "Global Health: A Pivotal Moment of Opportunity and Peril," *Health Affairs*, January 2017, http://tinyurl.com/lyvxkac.
Two Georgetown University researchers highlight policies they say are needed to strengthen global health security.

McNeil, Donald G. Jr., "Turning the Tide Against Cholera," *The New York Times Magazine*, Feb. 6, 2017, http://tinyurl.com/hzlx7uq.
A journalist examines efforts to eliminate cholera, an infectious disease that can be contracted from contaminated water or food.

Rull, Monica, Ilona Kickbusch and Helen Lauer, "Policy Debate: International Responses to Global Epidemics: Ebola and Beyond," *International Development Policy*, February 2015, http://tinyurl.com/kuo6l6k.
Researchers look at a policy debate about the World Health Organization's response to Ebola.

Saunders-Hastings, Patrick R., and Daniel Krewski, "Reviewing the History of Pandemic Influenza: Understanding Patterns of Emergence and Transmission," *Pathogens*, Dec. 6, 2016, http://tinyurl.com/n5fqu7l.
Researchers from the University of Ottawa offer a historical primer on influenza pandemics.

Reports and Studies

"Avian Influenza: USDA Has Taken Actions to Reduce Risks but Needs a Plan to Evaluate Its Efforts," Government Accountability Office, April 2017, http://tinyurl.com/mcptyjj.
A government report outlines steps the Agriculture Department has taken to protect the country from an avian pandemic and raises questions about whether the nation is too reliant on a single U.S.-based egg producer for the manufacturing of influenza vaccines.

"Biodefense Indicators: One Year Later, Events Outpacing Federal Efforts to Defend the Nation," Blue Ribbon Study Panel on Biodefense, December 2016, http://tinyurl.com/m9lsq3z.
A bipartisan group, created in 2014 to assess the nation's biodefense readiness, updates efforts to encourage Congress to devote more attention and funding to preparing for health emergencies.

"Ready or Not? Protecting the Public's Health From Diseases, Disasters and Bioterrorism," Trust for America's Health, December 2016, http://tinyurl.com/mafd4gf.
A public health advocacy group provides a snapshot of federal and state investment in emergency health preparedness.

"Tackling Drug Resistant Infections Globally: Final Report and Recommendations," Review on Antimicrobial Resistance, Wellcome Trust, May 2016, http://tinyurl.com/zxxjmww.
A report funded by the British government focuses on the growing number of antibiotic-resistant bacterial infections and discusses policy recommendations for halting their spread.

Gottron, Frank, "The Project BioShield Act: Issues for the 113th Congress," Congressional Research Service, June 18, 2014, http://tinyurl.com/mreoqgu.
Congress' nonpartisan research arm updates the status of U.S. spending on bio-preparedness.

For More Information

Association of State and Territorial Health Officials, 2231 Crystal Drive, Suite 450, Arlington, VA 22202; 202-371-9090; www.astho.org. Represents public health agencies and professionals.

Center for Global Health Science and Security, Georgetown University Medical Center, N.W., 306, Medical-Dental Building, 3900 Reservoir Rd., N.W., Washington, DC 20007; 202-687-9823; https://ghss.georgetown.edu/. Works on global health security with policy leaders worldwide.

Center for Infectious Disease Research and Policy, University of Minnesota, Academic Health Center, 420 Delaware St., S.E., MMC 263, C315 Mayo, Minneapolis, MN 55455; 612-626-6770; www.cidrap.umn.edu/. Provides research and news on infectious-disease outbreaks and policy response.

Centers for Disease Control and Prevention, Division of Global Health Protection and Security, 1600 Clifton Rd., Atlanta, GA 30329-4027; 800-232-4636; www.cdc.gov/globalhealth/healthprotection/index.html. Federal agency that works with international partners on global health and infectious-disease surveillance and response.

HealthMap, Boston Children's Hospital, Computational Epidemiology Lab, Landmark Center, Seventh Floor, 401

(Continued)

(Continued)

Park Drive, Boston, MA 02215; 617-355-6000; www .healthmap.org/en/. Internet-based reporting system.

International Society for Infectious Disease, 9 Babcock St., Unit 3, Brookline MA 02446; 617-277-0551; www.isid .org. Membership organization for professionals specializing in infectious diseases.

Trust for America's Health, 1730 M St., N.W., Suite 900, Washington, DC 20036; 202-223-9870; http://healthy americans.org/. Public health advocacy group.

World Health Organization, Regional Office for the Americas, 525 23rd St., N.W., Washington, DC 20037; 202-974-3000; www.who.int/about/regions/amro/en/. United Nations agency that helps shape global policy and research.